Unreading Shakespeare

Unreading

Shakespeare

David P. Gontar

Published by New English Review Press
a subsidiary of World Encounter Institute
PO Box 158397
Nashville, Tennessee 37215
&
27 Old Gloucester Street
London, England, WC1N 3AX

Cover Art and Design by Kendra Mallock
Cover painting: Katherine of Aragon as Mary Magdelene
by Michael Sittow

ISBN: 978-1-943003-00-6

First Edition

NEW ENGLISH REVIEW PRESS
newenglishreview.org

"Methinks I hear him now; his plausive words
He scattered not in ears, but grafted them,
To grow there and to bear."

Horae repunt anni fugiunt.

Contents

Acknowledgments

The author wishes to thank once again his editor, Rebecca Bynum, for her tireless assistance and encouragement. Christopher Gontar's insights and suggestions have been vitally important since the inception of this project in 2011. Also deserving of thanks is Dr. Gary Livacari, who was never too busy to read the manuscript and comment. And of course, all thanks and praise to my wonderful wife for her patience and support.

March 6, 2015
Huhhot, Inner Mongolia

Introduction:
A Note on the Reading of Shakespeare

*R*eading has become problematic.

As electronic devices proliferate and books disappear, serious reading becomes less frequent, and, like any art or skill, diminishes over periods of neglect. When we find our dog-eared place again after long interval, our attention span may be shorter and we may no longer experience the same delights we once knew. Books as physical objects are increasingly uncommon. Many will access these words not via bound pages but as figures on an illuminated screen. At the same time that we are struggling with such practical difficulties, the very nature of reading is being challenged to such a degree that we are no longer sure what we are doing when we do attempt it. We are taught that in our encounters with literature the ideas or intentions of the writer are either inaccessible or irrelevant, and that the meaning of any alphabetical assemblage is essentially what we make of it. While a certain book may have been composed by this person or that, there is no "author" in the sense of an authority equipped with a special insight into the text who can serve as a check on our understanding. To make matters worse, as the status of the author recedes, we find that something called "theory" swells in importance. University students are taught a plethora of prefabricated standpoints, including, *e.g.*, Marxism, psychoanalysis, cultural materialism and feminism, and they are encouraged to approach creative literature in light of one or more of those doctrines. A barricade of preconceived ideas is thus thrown up around the text while the author at its core is erased. No wonder busy people find better things to do than engaging with literature.

Things get even worse when it comes to Shakespeare, the quintessential author. These works appear not in our own everyday language, but as poetic renditions of Elizabethan English. Though we turn to scholars and teachers for assistance, we soon find ourselves on a confusing battleground in which bi-spectacled professors archly insist that the works were produced by William of Stratford while denying in cavalier manner the very existence of the "author." We learn that while it is not permissible to treat these plays and poems in light of the biography of the poet, it is nonetheless significant that William of Stratford was a recusant Catholic and had a son with the name "Hamnet." Is it surprising that we often despair of ever gaining exegetical traction? Is reading worth the candle?

Before abandoning the library for the video arcade or the rock concert, however, we might consider what Shakespeare thought about such problems. Recall that Prospero in *The Tempest* prizes his books above his dukedom. (I, ii, 160-169) It was from them that he acquired his magical powers. What allowed Shakespeare to become our pre-eminent writer if not those musty volumes of now-forgotten lore? Yes, nowadays it isn't easy to read, but even in the 16th century it was an uphill climb. Prospero tells us that he struggled to get his learning. (I, ii, 75-78) Hamlet and Brutus are both portrayed with books in their hands, and Imogen is an habitual bookworm too. (*Cymbeline*, II, ii, 3-5) Learning can be a labor of love.

When Imogen's noble husband Posthumus suffers a breakdown and is utterly lost, he is visited by ancestral spirits who take pity on him, crying out to Jupiter for relief. The heavenly monarch hears their call and gives them a tablet which they lay on Posthumus' breast. (V, v, 205) Excited to find it beside him, but frustrated by his inability to understand its cryptic message, Posthumus is undaunted.

> 'Tis still a dream, or else such stuff as madmen
> Tongue, and brain not; either both, or nothing,
> Or senseless speaking, or a speaking such
> As sense cannot untie. Be what it is,
> The action of my life is like it, which I'll keep,
> If but for sympathy.
> (I, v, 239-244)

The retention of the text by Posthumus is symbolic. It is cherished long before it is comprehended. Though we may not understand at first, we shouldn't be discouraged. Meaning may dawdle and arrive in its own good time. In the final scene the soothsayer interprets the glad tidings to everyone's satisfaction. (V, v, 435-477) The seemingly obscure writing, Shakespeare teaches, doesn't necessarily lack significance. If we are diligent and patient we may discover more than we expected, almost in spite of ourselves. With Posthumus, we may eventually discover a connection between literature and life, and realize that to give up on the former may be to compromise the latter.

Sophisticated voices urge us to surrender, to proceed to more popular pursuits. (F. H. Bradley, *Appearance and Reality*, 1893, 1-2) Skepticism and cynicism are the order of our day. In the séance put on by the charlatan Sir John Hume for Eleanor Gloucester in *King Henry VI*, the spirit Asnath makes certain prophecies about the fate of prominent English lords, including King Henry himself. Those prognostications are scanted by the Duke of York as so much nonsense, yet we find for ourselves in the course of attentive reading that each predicted event comes to pass.

What good is education if it leads us to ignore our best instincts and intuitions?

Though Shakespeare was not a professional philosopher in his method, he remains our best teacher, for his works are churning cauldrons of ideas. In his history plays, for example, he raises the Question of political authority. The emphasis should be on the term "Question" with a capital "Q." For to look into Shakespeare is to be introduced not to "Truth" but rather to the spirit of inquiry. To wander with him is to abide with the question.

Shakespeare's King Henry VI is a weak ruler who retreats from the responsibilities of leadership into passivity and scriptural platitudes. Again and again in the trilogy bearing his name we are presented in concrete form with the question of what constitutes the basis of political authority. That issue can be traced back from the dithering King Henry VI to his father, King Henry V, himself forever linked with the character of Falstaff. *King Henry V* begins with the death of Falstaff and takes as its centerpiece Hal's doubts on the eve of Agincourt about the legitimacy of his reign. Those doubts, long suppressed, flow not only from the usurpation of Richard's throne by Bolingbroke but just as much from the influence of Falstaff. His death in *King Henry V* significantly tracks the death of Socrates in Plato's *Phaedo*. But only the closest of readings will confirm this.

Falstaff is misinterpreted when treated as a mere clown or Bacchus. He is the living embodiment of the Question. And that Question is his legacy to Hal. Just as the Athenians sought to avoid metaphysical and political inexpediencies by banishing Socrates, just so does Hal as he morphs into King Henry V seek to bury the Question by banishing Falstaff. These parallel lives lead directly to death. Socrates refuses expulsion and chooses the hemlock, while Falstaff, in shock at Hal's coarse rejection, perishes of a broken heart. But as human nature is indistinguishable from the Question, banishment of the sage and his nagging inquiries is ultimately impossible. Always the question comes back to haunt us. Just as Brutus must suffer the return of Julius Caesar at Philippi, so must Hal suffer the return of Falstaff's mocking jibes at Agincourt. Hal seeks to draw attention away from his illicit reign by following his father's cagey stratagem of "busy[ing] giddy minds with foreign quarrels." (Part Two, V, i, 215-216) The invasion of France is conceived to accomplish this end and cement his authority. But on the field of battle the stubborn Question bubbles up: Is it right that common Englishmen should be slaughtered in needless broils in order that the King might solidify his grasp on power? The doubts Falstaff raises about "honor" at Shrewsbury (Part I, V, ii, 128-139) are to be set in that context. Assume the English subject has a duty to defend his nation at the King's command. What happens when the King is an usurper and war a device used to consolidate his reign and distract attention from his plain lack of right and integrity? Hal physically banishes the person of Falstaff, but on the eve of Agincourt finds himself quarreling with his soldiers about exactly why they should die in such a king's service. His uneasy rationalizations are dissatisfying. Falstaff, in his youth page to Thomas Mowbray, Duke of Norfolk, the mortal foe of Bolingbroke, is keenly aware of Bolingbroke's sin in destroying Richard to seize the throne. That is the point of his sharp retort to Hal when the Prince refuses to participate in the robbery at Gadshill.

> PRINCE
> Who, I rob? I a thief? Not I, by my faith.

> FALSTAFF
> There's neither honesty, manhood, nor good
> fellowship in thee, nor thou cam'st not of the blood royal,
> if thou dare'st not stand for ten shillings.
> (I, ii, 18-22)

Translation: "Hal, how can you protest this insignificant hold-up when your own father Bolingbroke commandeered the English throne by gross rebellion and regicide? The son of such a royal felon should have no qualms when it comes to little escapades such as this." And Shakespeare in his genius has King Harry echo this logic in his question to the supposed traitors Cambridge, Scroop and Grey:

> If little faults, proceeding on distemper,
> Shall not be wink'd at, how shall we stretch our eye
> When capital crimes, chew'd, swallow'd, and digested,
> Appear before us?
> (*King Henry V*, II, ii, 56-57)

This is deep irony. The elephant in the room is the "capital crime" of King Henry IV's destruction of King Richard II. That high treason, which Hal himself has "chewed, swallowed and digested," lurks in the shadows and taints all his actions. Supposed "traitors" Cambridge, Scroop and Grey are, in fact, seeking to rise up against the inheritor of Bolingbroke's false title, a false title now held by the man who would appear to chastise them for their perfidy. Of this they say nothing — only because the implicit threat of torture makes them hold their tongues to lose their heads more gracefully. But Hal's soldiers in the wars in France will not be so lucky. We sense this bitter note of irony again when Hal approves the execution of Bardolph, Falstaff's aide-de-camp and Hal's own drinking companion in his greener days at the Boar's-head Tavern. Bardolph commits a trivial theft in contravention of Hal's edict. Hal is determined to make an example of this "little fault" to help everyone forget the big fault which has placed him on the throne — and all his soldiers in harm's way. The hanging of Bardolph is the final ratification of Hal's betrayal of Falstaff, his better angel.

This monitory locution of "better angel," by the way, entered current English via the practice of close reading. First used by Shakespeare in *Othello* (V, ii, 245) and Sonnet 144 (line 3), it was picked up by that bedeviled Shakespearean, Abraham Lincoln, who employed it to grandiloquent effect in his First Inaugural Address of March 4, 1861.

> The mystic chords of memory, stretching from every battlefield and patriot grave, to every heart and hearthstone, all over this broad land, will yet swell the chorus of the Union, when again touched, as they surely will be, by the better angels of our nature.

The impact of Shakespeare on Lincoln was profound. Like Prince Hal at Agincourt, Lincoln felt immense anguish and guilt over the war he initiated with the southern states. That heavy responsibility is manifest in the rhetorically inflated Gettysburg Address, in which he cites the Declaration of Independence of 1776. Well he knew that, under the principles enunciated by the Declaration, the states of the American south had an ineluctable right to withdraw from any oppressive political body. In fact, the Thirteen Colonies belonged to the British Crown and were under contractual agreements to so remain. The states united in America in 1861, on the other hand, had no such obligations and *a fortiori* deserved the liberty they claimed. Remembered as a champion of freedom, it was Lincoln who denied to the people of the south their fundamental right to secede to form their own nation. Many died as a result of Lincoln's doctrinaire intransigence, his soothing rhetoric to the contrary notwithstanding. In the process, "these united states" became a monolith, a political behemoth, in Lincoln's vaunted "Union." Lincoln wrestled with these issues when studying the Wars of the Roses in Shakespeare's Henry VI troika, yet brought on a similar conflagration in his own era, pitting father against son and brother against brother. (*King Henry VI*, Part III, II, v, 55-124) Had Lincoln learned from Shakespeare sooner and better, his countrymen might have been spared their greatest calamity. But in the end it was Lincoln's worser angels who prevailed. We can confirm this by reflecting on his revealing obsession with *Macbeth*. Plumbed to its depth, this dark preoccupation reveals the measure of Lincoln's sense of his own transgression. Like Prince Hal, Lincoln too becomes Bolingbroke. During the closing weeks of the War of Secession (1861-1865) as Old Abe regaled his Cabinet members with marathon readings from *Macbeth*, he was being stalked by his Shakespearean nemesis, prominent actor John Wilkes Boothe, who saw in him an American Caesar. Irony rises to no higher pitch than this. Acting that tragic part in exquisite somnambulism, Lincoln went dutifully forth to Ford's Theater for the rendezvous with the fate he had engineered. Shakespeare must have known that sort of thing would happen, for do not Cassius and Brutus, good soothsayers, as they bathe their hands in Caesar's blood, ask:

> How many ages hence
> Shall this our lofty scene be acted over,
> In states unborn and accents yet unknown!
> How many times shall Caesar bleed in sport,

That now on Pompey's basis lies along,
No worthier than the dust!
(III, i, 112-127)

To read *King Henry IV*, then, is more than dry homework. It is to encounter Falstaff, and through him the spirit of Socratic inquiry. This is the very essence of liberal education. Through such reading we learn not to take things at face value. We raise questions and square off against those who would presume to coerce us into adventitious expeditions. The impact of the Lincoln administration was to dramatically augment the sway and might of the central government at the expense of the states and their citizens. In our own time, the offices of the federal executive have expanded exponentially, as undeclared wars are unleashed, and costly welfare schemes devised, while citizens either cower in fear or launch hysterical and self-defeating campaigns of resistance. Meanwhile, English and philosophy departments in American schools shrivel from lack of support as books disappear to be supplanted by computer gadgetry. The result is the progressive intellectual (and mental) impoverishment of a once proud people who, having surrendered control to an all-seeing Moloch, are without the capacity to reform. That reform could be derived only from principles of classical education long ago renounced. It is the decadent who can't go home again. Today's students balk at reading "dead white males" such as Shakespeare. Instead, they prefer to play out their lives as hapless consumers of electronic toys and entertainments, *panem et circenses*. As they have their wish, so we will have our doom.

In such a setting, reading Shakespeare is for sissies. It is all frilly, old-fashioned poetry, good for nothing. That's the way Hotspur thinks of it.

I had rather be a kitten and cry mew,
Than one of these same meter ballet-mongers.
I had rather hear a brazen canstick turn'd,
Or a dry wheel grate on the axletree,
And that would set my teeth nothing on edge,
Nothing so much as mincing poetry;
'Tis like the forc'd gait of a shuffling nag.
(*King Henry IV*, Part One, III, i, 135-141)

That is Hotspur's tough-guy mindset as he falls before the implacable rage of the Prince of Wales. (Act 5, Sc. 3) Now Hotspur is dead, the cavalier American South is gone with the wind, and romantic figures like Owen Glendower are laughing stocks in the "United Kingdom." But Hamlet lives, and still whispers to us in our dreams. Falstaff thou art mighty yet. Thy question, inherited from Socrates, still lingers amongst us. We hear its resonance in Hamlet's "to be or not to be." The Question remains, beating like the heart of western consciousness.

We can now return briefly to the particular question of reading. The premature application of theory to literature functions as the suppression of the Question, especially when we are dealing with Shakespeare. As his focus at all times is the quizzical essence of life (*Measure for Measure*, IV, ii, 24-42; *Hamlet*, III, ii, 364), the genuine reader must remain open on a personal level to Shakespeare as he speaks to us directly, rather than shielding our hearts and minds with preconceived ideas and technicalities. Thus we arrive at the paradox of Paideia: the close reading we would perform must be an open one. We must have the perspicacity to find more in him than entertaining tales set in high-flown language. At all times his object is us, the audience, not quaint characters from far away and long ago. As S.T. Coleridge observed, "In the plays of Shakespeare, every man sees himself, without knowing that he does so." In fact, it becomes clear sooner or later that Shakespeare's principal concern is precisely with the blindness of human beings to themselves. We are our own blind spots, and our lives are rife with self-deception. "Tell me, good Brutus, can you see your face?" challenges Cassius. "No, Cassius," replies his friend, "for the eye sees not itself . . . ." (*Julius Caesar*, I, ii, 56-57) The Delphic imperative would seem impossible of attainment were there not sages such as Socrates and Shakespeare to serve as our looking glasses and show us what we would rather not know of our own selves. Abraham Lincoln, for example, beholden to the Railroad trust, could not permit mass secession at a time when the intercontinental railway was under construction. For that trust was busy fabricating a vast spider's web of steel threads to bind "the Union" together. Serving that scarcely acknowledged purpose, Lincoln wandered in self-imposed blindness, a blindness which short-circuited his competent reading of Shakespeare, of history, and of his own tragic nature. As a result he inevitably became preoccupied with the tragic figure of Macbeth, the notorious usurper and manipulator. Lincoln became a haunted and hunted figure trapped in a Shakespearean nightmare he could neither unravel nor escape. In ultimate terms he served the interests of the Rail trust as Macbeth served the passions of his infernal wife, the fourth witch of the

"Scottish play" whose very name is decorously avoided even today.

How is Shakespeare taught in today's universities? Those precious manuscripts, the moving images of ourselves, are reduced to a mere field of data, technique and detail about which seeming experts quibble endlessly. It is a wilderness of footnotes. "Small have continual plodders ever won, save base authority from other's books." (*Love's Labour's Lost*, I, i, 86-87) Every effort is made to direct the student's attention away from any consideration of what Shakespeare might mean to us in personal or philosophical terms. Like Lincoln, who betrayed his fellow citizens with carnage and despotism, today's academic establishment represents the traducing of Shakespeare and the betrayal of the very students it is charged with educating.

Well might we ask, then, what it is we are doing when we sit down to read Shakespeare. In this respect, we may consider the distinction often drawn between Shakespeare as theater and Shakespeare as text for reading and study. To a large extent, these are false alternatives. For what the ordinary reader does as he works through the plays is not essentially different from what the actor does as he rehearses. The goal of the actor is to become the character. The achievement of a durable impression by the actor is essential in any coherent performance. Integrating the lines, he or she aims at a sympathetic identification through which the expression of feeling is attainable. And a moment's reflection will confirm that this is what we all do, though on a more modest scale, as we absorb these remarkable texts. We become Lear, we become Cordelia, we become Prince Hamlet and Ophelia. We feel their emotions and look at life, if ever so briefly, through their eyes. This happens in spite of what we may suppose we are about. Shakespeare's creative insight embraces the totality of his characters, and we, his readers, follow him, aiming at an analogous panorama. As we continue, we find ourselves entering Shakespeare's world through his words. And as we occupy that stage, we inevitably place his world in relation to our personal lived experience, our little tragedies and comedies. The Shakespearean mystery comes to illuminate our own. Gabriel Marcel, the French philosopher, wrote:

> Being is — or should be — necessary. It is impossible that everything should be reduced to a play of successive appearances which are inconsistent with each other . . . or, in the words of Shakespeare, to "a tale told by an idiot." [*Macbeth*, V, i, 20-29] I aspire to participate in this being, in this reality — and perhaps this aspiration is already a degree of partici-

pation, however rudimentary.
(*The Philosophy of Existentialism*, Manya Harari, tr., Carol Publishing Group, 1971)

This is our hope, that traveling along the path of "words, words, words," we find something beyond all words, which lends them meaning.

The book in your hands now is the sequel to *Hamlet Made Simple and Other Essays* (2013), which sought to open a fresh path back to Shakespeare. Doing so required that we critically examine stale expositions which reflected theories and doctrines rather than authentic impressions of the text and the remarkable characters which emerge therefrom. Setting those doctrinaire programs aside freed us to probe ever more deeply into the mystery of the text. The confidence to enlist our very souls in our Shakespearean ventures may strike many as a quaint nostrum, but we have hearts as well as heads. To students seeking a prescribed method of interpretation we must report that in the case of our author none has ever been found. The openness is all: openness to the text in all its complexity and ambiguity, and openness to our own responses, a willingness to trust ourselves as we trust Shakespeare to guide us. As John Locke suggested long ago, to tread this path we must inevitably remove a great deal of rubbish. That is the task of criticism, or what we refer to as "unreading," the discarding of outworn views which operate to keep us from understanding. Unreading shields us from cheap and trendy doctrines. To be sure, no text wears a badge of truth on its breast, and every interpretation can be challenged. But when we find ourselves in the character and the character in us there is a palpable sense that alienation has abated. We have made a portion of Shakespeare our own. As we learn to quarry his immortal stanzas, so we come to fathom the incidents of our own mortality, in rueful revelation and compassion.

1

Yorick's Ghost

... and the fool shall look to the madman. — Feste

I. Introduction

*I*n the catalogue of fools and clowns who animate Shakespeare's plays, the most significant are thought to be *Twelfth Night's* Feste and Lear's fool, whose teasing jibes often bear precious insight. These are jesters of rare adroitness and sensibility, camouflaging criticism in endearing silliness, that remonstration may be sufficiently palatable to testy nobles to be assimilated. Yet before we crown this pair as Shakespeare's supreme lords of barbed banter, we might ask whether all candidates have been given a "fair shake." Not customarily included in standard lists of Shakespeare's stand-up comics is Yorick, the "joculator" belonging to old King Hamlet the Dane. (Halvorson, 2) The omission is, of course, understandable. Yorick, whose muddy skull is tossed up by a grave digger in Act V of *The Tragedy of Hamlet* — though he bore the child Prince Hamlet on his back "a thousand times" (V, i, 182) — never appears in the play, speaks no lines there, nor is he so much as quoted. What possible credentials has he? Having poured a "flagon of Rhenish" on the head of a future gravedigger? (V, i, 175) What of that? Of all his gibes, his gambols, songs and "flashes of merriment," (V, i, 185-186), not a single one survives. Is he not then but a name? Yet, if so, why mention that name? Could it be he lives on still, a revenant whose spirit pulses in textual heirs?

There is a general consensus that Shakespeare's "fools" compose a special subset of his clowns. Indeed, the gravediggers themselves are designated by the text as "two Clowns." The first of these is a wrangling sexton (V, i, 157) whose repartee gives the hyper-articulate Prince a run for his money. (V, i, 119-158) Yet the most representative clowns in Shakespeare are not wits, but rather clodpoles and simpletons whose bumbling miscomprehensions of life and language make them beguiling. We find classic instances of clowning in the malapropisms of Dogberry, Costard, and Froth. The typical Shakespearean clown delights and illuminates by way of inadvertence. The fool, on the other hand, is not hobbled by words and ideas; he is their master. Hence the first grave digger (the sexton) in *Hamlet* is actually more fool than clown, and seems to have imbibed something of the art from Yorick himself. But more of that anon.

Situated on the margins of the court, the jester often takes notice of things more acutely than preoccupied lords and ladies vying with one another for advantages and privileges. Those sharper perceptions can be used in subtle or oblique edification of lord or sovereign. Such is the "wise fool," who scatters within his badinage seeds of insight that they might reach a fertile mind and germinate. Feste, Lear's fool, and to a more sober and modest degree, Lavatch, in *All's Well That Ends Well*, exemplify this trait. As we will see, there is some reason to view Yorick retrospectively as having been a member of this rare fraternity.

II. Lear's Fool

Foolery in Shakespeare is more than cap and bells, more than chiming chorus. No daffy riddler or pointless punster, Lear's fool is a loving shadow (cp. I, iv, 213) who accompanies the King through most of his spiritual journey, a peripatetic blogger commenting on royal foibles. His passionate devotion to the retiring monarch and his youngest daughter entails a frigid season in hell and eventual death. Unlike careless courtiers, who would take their lives in their hands to directly challenge the King (as does the Earl of Kent) the fool has liberty to speak freely, serving up sanchismos on even the most sensitive of topics, *e.g.*, the succession and Lear's relationships with his miscreant elder daughters. Often fools assume the role of cryptic counselor. This goes so far that, like Feste in *Twelfth Night*, Lear's fool makes no hesitation in calling his boss a fool. (*Quarto*, 1.4, 143-145; *Folio*, iv, 137-144; See, *Twelfth Night*, I, v, 53-68) As is well known, that connection between Feste and Lear's fool is deepened by having them both sing verses of the same song: "the rain it raineth every day," pointing at the essential link between tragedy and comedy. (*Lear*, III, ii, 74-77; *Twelfth Night*, V, i, 385-404)

Somewhere on the heath we lose him. In the *Quarto* version, the fool is last on stage when he is promoted to play magistrate in the three-judge panel of the mock trial of Goneril put on by the prosecutor, King Lear. (Sc. 13, 3.5, 31-75)

LEAR

I'll see their trial first. Bring in the evidence.
[To Edgar] Thou robèd man of justice, take thy place;
[To Fool] And thou, his yokefellow of equity,
Bench by his side. [To Kent] You are o' th' commission.
Sit you too.

EDGAR

Let us deal justly.
Sleepest or wakest thou, jolly shepherd?
Thy sheep be in the corn,
And for one blast of thy minikin mouth
Thy sheep shall take no harm.
Purr, the cat is grey.

LEAR

Arraign her first. 'Tis Goneril. I here take my oath
before this honourable assembly she kicked the poor
King her father.

FOOL

Come hither, mistress. Is your name Goneril?

LEAR

She cannot deny it.

FOOL

Cry you mercy, I took you for a joint-stool.
(Sc. 13 (3.5) 31-47)

In this scene the fool has transcended his limited role of royal Jiminy Cricket and appears to enter Lear's own world of incipient madness.
Whether this is mere sympathetic patronizing on the part of the fool,
or his own derangement being brought on by recent conflicts and their
attendant stress, is not certain. We are reminded that in the Elizabethan
lexicon a so-called "natural fool" was regarded as one whose limited
mental capacity prompted him to utterances that seemed to savor of
second sight or inspiration, a view derived from Plato. The connection
between folly and madness is also touched on by Feste in *Twelfth Night*,
when he is asked about what the drunken man is like.

OLIVIA

What's a drunken man like, fool?

FESTE

Like a drowned man, a fool and a madman — one
draught above heat makes him a fool, the second mads
him, and a third drowns him.
(I, v, 126-128)

Of course, this spectrum of mental instability is reminiscent of the
observations made by Duke Theseus in *A Midsummer Night's Dream*
about the lover, lunatic and poet.

THESEUS

The lunatic, the lover and the poet
Are of imagination all compact.
One sees more devils than vast hell can hold:
That is the madman. The lover, all as frantic,
Sees Helen's beauty in a brow of Egypt.
The poet's eye, in a fine frenzy rolling,
Doth glance from heaven to earth, from earth to heaven,

And as imagination bodies forth
The forms of things unknown, the poet's pen
Turns them to shapes, and gives to airy nothing
 A local habitation and a name.
(V, i, 7-17)

These psychological taxonomies tend to suggest that to be a successful jester or court fool required an odd mental apparatus tuned to frequencies associated with aberrant behaviors, and that, given sufficient alterations in conditions, one might pass to other forms, as occurs in Hegel's *Phenomenology of Spirit*. One may start as a mere fool, suggests Feste, but it is just a single step to madness.

III. Feste

Lady Olivia in *Twelfth Night* has inherited her fool from her late father, a count. Feste gives the distinct impression of being someone who regards bourgeois consciousness as a species of quotidian madness, a proposition we associate now with the work of British analyst R. D. Laing in the 20th century. Prominent among instances of evidently "sane" people who are in Feste's view actually crazy are (i) Duke Orsino, hopelessly in love with a woman who repeatedly rejects him, (ii) static Olivia herself, and (iii) the major domo of her household, the melancholy and obsessive Malvolio, whose very name is emblematic of his conventional dysthymia. As the play opens, we learn that Olivia is in mourning for her deceased brother. She has veiled her face and intends to wear black and have no company for seven grieving years. When she seeks to dismiss "the fool" from her presence, Feste (like Lear's fool) immediately counters that it is she, the self-absorbed aristocrat, not he, who is the true fool and, to the pleasure of the audience, offers to prove it.

FESTE

Good madonna, why mournest thou?

OLIVIA

Good fool, for my brother's death.

FESTE

I think his soul is in hell, madonna.

OLIVIA

I know his soul is in heaven, fool.

FESTE

The more fool, madonna, to mourn for your
brother's soul, being in heaven. Take away the fool,
gentlemen.
(I, v, 62-68)

What seems a simple syllogistic deduction is, in fact, a telling diagnosis by Feste of socially induced neurosis. The irrationality of Olivia's protracted mourning is neatly exposed, providing her with a conceptual tool she may employ to eventually free herself from self-imposed isolation.

Throughout the play, this jester, whose ostensible job is to give mere relief of ennui to Olivia and her retinue, serves as a shaman or sage, pointing to emotionally based ideas adopted by afflicted individuals as though they were rational imperatives. Feste's psychiatric armamentarium is not restricted to logical assays such as the one above. A wide range of instruments is brought to bear by him on the self-imposed presumptions and confusions of Illyrian society, including such devices as song, poetry, epigram, paradox, argument, non-verbal communication and just plain nonsense. These darkling stratagems and tropes make him one of the most subtle and opaque of Shakespeare's characters. For where reason itself is believed tainted or corrupt, it may be necessary to have recourse to non-rational acts designed to jolt the deluded person into a more functional and salutary standpoint. An early example is found in Act Two, when Sir Toby, Sir Andrew and Feste get together.

SIR TOBY

Welcome, ass. Now let's have a catch.

SIR ANDREW

By my troth, the fool has an excellent breast.
I had rather than forty shillings I had such a leg, and
so sweet a breath to sing, as the fool has. In sooth,
thou wast in very gracious fooling last night, when
thou spokest of Pigrogromitus, of the Vapians passing
the equinoctial of Queubus. 'Twas very good, i'faith. I
sent thee sixpence for thy leman. Hadst it?

FESTE

I did impeticos thy gratility; for Malvolio's nose is
no whipstock. My lady has a white hand, and the
Myrmidons are no bottle-ale houses.

SIR ANDREW

Excellent! Why, this is the best fooling, when
all is done. Now a song.
(II, iii, 17-27)

If, dear reader, some of this colloquy seems a bit obscure, no need to worry; it's meant to be. RSC editors Jonathan Bate and Eric Rasmussen note that the line beginning "Pigrogromitus" and ending "Queubus" are "words invented by Feste as *examples of his feigned wisdom.*" So is "gratility," and the whole assemblage might be compared with the elegant nonsense of Lewis Carroll or Edward Lear. (Bate, 663, n. 12-22, emphasis added) By "feigned wisdom" is meant a satire on sententious utterances that pass for wisdom among the educated fools of society. Giving echo to the seat of such pomposity is for Feste great fun and a restorative to those fortunate enough to hear it. Putting down vain verbosity is a reversion to one of the central themes of *Love's Labour's Lost.* Feste displays the keen ear of a child who senses that adults with their swollen vocabularies make themselves ridiculous and alienated from the rudiments of life and authentic communication. Think of Mr. Darling in Barrie's *Peter Pan.* That way misery lies.

Later in the same Act, Feste sings for the obsessive lover Orsino, who hands him a coin.

ORSINO

There's for thy pains.

FESTE

No pains, sir. I take pleasure in singing, sir.

ORSINO

I'll pay thy pleasure then.

FESTE

Truly, sir, and pleasure will be paid, one time or
another.

ORSINO

Give me now leave to leave thee.

FESTE

Now the melancholy god protect thee, and the
tailor make thy doublet of changeable taffeta, for thy
mind is a very opal. I would have men of such constancy
put to sea, that their business might be everything,
and their intent everywhere, for that's it that always
makes a good voyage of nothing. Farewell.
(II, iv, 66-77)

Here we are in double-talk mode once again, as Feste the magus
addresses the narcissistic Duke, who seems to almost revel in the coils
of hopeless ardor. Though human consciousness is constantly changing,
Feste implies Orsino is the victim of fixed ideas. As his quest for one
who disdains him is nugatory, he is like a man deliberately cast on an
empty sea. Though Feste's words have the form of nonsense, they resonate, and remain with us.

This parting exchange of Feste and Orsino is reminiscent of something in *Hamlet*.

POLONIUS

How pregnant sometimes his replies are! A happiness
that often madness hits on, which reason and sanity could
not so prosperously be delivered of. I will leave him, and
suddenly contrive the means of meeting between him
and my daughter. -- My lord, I will take my leave of you.

HAMLET

You cannot, sir, take from me anything that I
will more willingly part withal -- except my life, my life,
my life.
(II, ii, 210-219)

Here the Prince appears to morph effortlessly into Harlequin, surpassing even the soaring Feste in comedic brilliance. The tedious Polonius, crawling between heaven and earth, senses that there is method
in Hamlet's "madness," and yet cannot quite grasp its purport. Hamlet's
intentions are different too; where Feste would minister to a mind diseased, Hamlet's irony is so pervasive that it cannot condescend to take
its interlocutor seriously and thus attend to his needs. As has been noted, Hamlet speaks often for his own amusement and therefore for ours.
He has no problem making others look — and feel — stupid, and that
tart tendency is part of what makes him unwelcome in the court of King
Claudius. Such persons on occasion must drink hemlock. The question
we should ask is, How did Prince Hamlet acquire this art of fiendish
foolery? Was he to this manner born? Or was he, perhaps, understudy
to some personage of infinite jest . . . ?

But let us return to Feste. Towards the end of the play, Olivia's fool
is promoted to become Malvolio's psychoanalyst. The reader will recall
how Maria dupes him into believing that haughty Lady Olivia is in love
with him. He is led by deceitful instructions he thinks are from his employer to dress "cross gartered and in yellow stockings" and appear before her as a grinning pseudo-aristocrat. He does so, and is promptly
taken for a lunatic. In those days a popular treatment of dementia was
confinement in an unlit chamber, a condition imposed forthwith at the
instigation of Sir Toby on the babbling steward. (III, iv, 133-139) With
Maria and Sir Toby in support, Feste, disguised as "Sir Topas, the cu-
rate," launches into a psychotherapeutic dialogue with his patient. This

includes a scientific test of his sanity.

MALVOLIO

I say this house is as dark as ignorance, though
ignorance were as dark as hell; and I say there was
never man thus abused. I am no more mad than you
are. Make the trial of it in any constant question.

FESTE

What is the opinion of Pythagoras concerning
wildfowl?

MALVOLIO

That the soul of our grandam might haply
inhabit a bird.

FESTE

What thinkest thou of his opinion?

MALVOLIO

I think nobly of the soul, and in no way approve
his opinion.

FESTE

Fare thee well. Remain thou still in darkness. Thou
shalt hold th' opinion of Pythagoras ere I will allow of
thy wits, and fear to kill a woodcock lest thou dispossess
the soul of thy grandam. Fare thee well.
(IV, ii, 48-60)

* * *

FESTE

Master Malvolio?

MALVOLIO

Ay, good fool.

FESTE

Alas, sir, how fell you besides your five wits?

MALVOLIO

Fool there was never man so notoriously
abused. I am as well in my wits, fool, as thou art.

FESTE

But as well? Then you are mad indeed, if you be
no better in your wits than a fool.

MALVOLIO

They have here propertied me, keep me in
darkness, send ministers to me, asses, and do all they
can to face me out of my wits.
(IV, ii, 86-95)

Feste is, of course, neither psychologist nor angel. Angered by his
treatment at the hands of the household steward, he exploits Malvolio's
captivity to torment him. No analysis of counter-transference here, just
fuel for the fire. Feeling daily the sting of a role in which he is regarded as a thing ridiculous and of small account, Feste takes advantage of
the opportunity to turn tables and subject Malvolio to the indignities
of foolery. With pen and paper received from the fool, he sends an anguished appeal to his Lady, who releases him, and the sessions with Dr.
Topas end without resolution.

IV. Yorick

The only allusions to Hamlet's childhood are his remembrances of Yorick. If anyone else made a comparable impact on him we are not told.

HAMLET

Let me see.
He takes the skull
Alas, poor Yorick. I knew him, Horatio — a fellow of
infinite jest, of most excellent fancy. He hath borne me
on his back a thousand times; and now, how abhorred
my imagination is! My gorge rises at it. Here hung
those lips that I have kissed I know not how oft. Where
be your gibes now, your gambols, your songs, your
flashes of merriment that were wont to set the table
on a roar? Not one now to mock your own grinning?
Quite chop-fallen? Now get you to my lady's chamber
and tell her, let her paint an inch thick, to this favour
she must come. Make her laugh at that.
(V, i, 179-190)

Infinite jest . . . But isn't Prince Hamlet the fellow who would be king of "infinite space," did he not have bad dreams? (II, ii, 256-258) What better equipment to face infinite space than infinite jest, *n'est-ce pas*? For what is infinite space itself but our bad dream, a wry jest of uneasy humanity?

In *Hamlet Made Simple* we found persuasive reasons to view Prince Hamlet as a court bastard whose actual identity as the biological son of his uncle Claudius is never vouchsafed to him. We confronted the possibility that the liaison of Gertrude and Claudius was of long-standing vintage. For, after all, where was Prince Claudius when King Hamlet the Dane was busy smiting the sledded Polacks on the ice? (I, i, 62) Fighting in the vaward beside his brother, or tucked neatly in incestuous sheets beside his brother's wife? Or, think historically: how do we imagine young Prince Henry felt in 1501 when he had to dance at the wedding of Prince Arthur and Katherine of Aragon? There is a tale of two brothers . . . . Hamlet's *outré* behavior, his nausea and self-hatred, are best explained as functions of his doubts about his own identity, and the unconscious feeling that he has been sired by his detested uncle. (For a full account, See Gontar, 377ff.) Let us for the sake of argument situate Yorick in that context. What kind of jester would he have been?

With hawk-like gaze, he would have seen that King Hamlet was being cuckolded by his own brother. For the fool sees more than the sober-minded.

> This fellow is wise enough to play the fool,
> And to do that well craves a kind of wit.
> He must observe their mood on whom he jests,
> The quality of persons, and the time,
> And, like the haggard, check at every feather
> That comes before his eye. This is a practice
> As full of labour as a wise man's art,
> For folly that he wisely shows is fit,
> But wise men, folly-fall'n, quite taint their wit.
> (*Twelfth Night*, III, i, 59-67)

But that information carelessly disclosed could backfire. The challenge would have been great. Without directly blurting out unpleasant facts, a faithful jester, like Lear's fool, would yet be at pains to open the King's eyes to adultery and treachery. Did he come too close to his aim and suffer liquidation? Or was he not able to employ indirection and subtlety with sufficient skill to warn King Hamlet of what was afoot? Of course, *pace* Saxo Grammaticus, *The Tragedy of Hamlet* as we have it in text today is a work of fiction; such questions are often regarded as idle speculation. We cannot know what messages Yorick, positioned as he would have been, might have sought to convey to his sovereign. But Lear's fool's behavior gives us clues.

Regardless, the text provides ample evidence that Hamlet is a schooled fool, and uses foolery to deal with his dilemma, shield himself from harm, and expose the King's guilt. In Act One, scene five, Hamlet swears Marcellus and Horatio to absolute secrecy about the appearance of the ghost and about his plan "to put an antic disposition on" to conceal his vengeful designs. (I, v, 173) And it is significant that he does not declare that he will, like Edgar, feign a state of Bedlam-like insanity, but rather put on an "antic disposition." What means this? For we have already seen abundant indications that folly and madness, though they lie cheek by jowl in relation to each other, are not identical.

Here is what our dictionary says:

Antic

1. A foolish or ludicrous act; a caper; 2. Archaic A buffoon, especially a performing clown.
(*American Heritage*, 5th. ed., 77)

That is Hamlet's stated intent. He will jest, he will sing, he will gam-
bol, and by such indirections he will find direction out.

Not one but two characters in the play reflect beyond doubt the
influence of Yorick: the bantering sexton in the graveyard scene, and
Prince Hamlet himself. Gravediggers are not commonly known for their
wit or riposte. Yet this one leads Prince Hamlet on a merry verbal chase.
How is it possible? Both Hamlet and the sexton manifest the comic influence of Yorick. Their skills mirror one another's.

HAMLET

Whose grave's this, sirrah?

FIRST CLOWN

Mine, sir.
(sings)
O, a pit of clay for to be made
For a guest is meet.

HAMLET

I think it be thine indeed, for thou liest in't.

FIRST CLOWN

You lie out on't, sir, and therefore it is not
yours. For my part, I do not lie in't, and yet it is mine.

HAMLET

Thou dost lie in't, to be in't and say 'tis thine.
'Tis for the dead, not for the quick; therefore thou liest.

FIRST CLOWN

'Tis a quick lie, sir, 'twill away again from me to you.

HAMLET

What man dost thou dig it for?

FIRST CLOWN

For no man, sir.

HAMLET

What woman, then?

FIRST CLOWN

For none, neither.

HAMLET

Who is to be buried in't?

FIRST CLOWN

One that was a woman, sir; but rest her
soul, she's dead.

HAMLET

How absolute the knave is! We must speak by
the card, or equivocation will undo us.
(V, i, 115-134)

Here is exemplary foolery, to be sure. And the sexton assures us
that Yorick was not just a wit, but "a whoreson mad fellow." (V, i, 171)
Of course, "mad" here may be nothing more than a hyperbolical way
of referring to Yorick's infinite (resourceful and unrestrained) sense of
humor.

Of one thing we may be sure: Prince Hamlet is a skilled jester. His targets are the stodgy and self-deluded, even those who preach that to our own selves we must be true. (I, iii, 78)

POLONIUS

How does my good Lord Hamlet?

HAMLET

Well, God-'a'-mercy.

POLONIUS

Do you know me, my lord?

HAMLET

Excellent, excellent well. You're a fishmonger.

POLONIUS

Not I, my lord.

HAMLET

Then I would you were so honest a man.

POLONIUS

Honest, my lord?

HAMLET

Ay, sir. To be honest, as this world goes, is to be one man picked out of ten thousand.

POLONIUS

That's very true, my lord.

HAMLET

For if the sun breed maggots in a dead dog, being
a good kissing carrion — have you a daughter?

POLONIUS

I have, my lord.

HAMLET

Let her not walk i'th' sun. Conception is a
blessing, but not as your daughter may conceive.
Friend, look to't.

POLONIUS

(aside) How say you that? Still harping on
my daughter. Yet he knew me not at first — a said I
was a fishmonger. A is far gone, far gone, and truly,
in my youth I suffered much extremity for love, very
near this. I'll speak to him again — What do you read,
my lord?

HAMLET

Words, words, words.

POLONIUS

What is the matter, my lord?

HAMLET

Between who?

POLONIUS

I mean the matter you read, my lord.

HAMLET

Slanders, sir; for the satirical slave says here that
old men have grey beards, that their faces are wrinkled,
their eyes purging thick amber, or plum-tree gum, and
that they have a plentiful lack of wit, together with
most weak hams. All which, sir, though I most
powerfully and potently believe, yet I hold it not honesty
to have it thus set down; for you yourself, sir, should
be as old as I am — if, like a crab, you could go backward.

POLONIUS

Though this be madness, yet there is method in't.
(II, ii, 173-207)

That is, Hamlet suggests that in the frankness of youth lies virtue, while age is marred by the vices of compromise. Thus Polonius could only become decent if he could reverse the course of time, and become young once more. All this sails over this courtier's grey head like the jet stream. The fool's wisdom is Greek to Polonius.

In Act Three, Sc. two, Hamlet, Claudius and Polonius discuss the expected theatrical performance.

KING CLAUDIUS

How fares our cousin Hamlet?

HAMLET

Excellent, i'faith, of the chameleon's dish. I eat
the air, promise-crammed. You cannot feed capons so.

KING CLAUDIUS

I have nothing with this answer, Hamlet.
These words are not mine.

HAMLET

No, nor mine, now. (To Polonius) My lord, you
played once i'th' university, you say.

POLONIUS

That I did, my lord, and was accounted a good
actor.

HAMLET

And what did you enact?

POLONIUS

I did enact Julius Caesar. I was killed i'th'
Capitol. Brutus killed me.

HAMLET

It was a brute part of him to kill so capital a calf
there.
(III, ii, 90-102)

It is interesting to note, by the way, that the court of King Claudius, unlike that of his late brother, has no appointed fool. None is of
record following the death of Yorick. Thus, as Nature abhors a vacuum,
so Hamlet steps into the vacancy of folly.
Two more examples will suffice.

OPHELIA

You are merry, my lord.

HAMLET

Who, I?

OPHELIA

Ay, my lord.

HAMLET

O God, your only jig-maker! What should a man
do but be merry? For look you how cheerfully my
mother looks, and my father died within's two hours.

OPHELIA

Nay, 'tis twice two months, my lord.

HAMLET

So long? Nay, then, let the devil wear black, for
I'll have a suit of sables. O, heavens, die two months
ago and not forgotten yet! Then there's hope a great
man's memory may outlive his life half a year. But
by'r Lady, a must build churches then, or else shall a
suffer not thinking on, with the hobby-horse, whose
epitaph is, 'For O, for O, the hobby-horse is forgot.
(III, ii, 119-129)

Surely Claudius would have nothing in this foolish answer too,
though Hamlet's impassioned grief and resentment bleed through easily.

Then we find this vaudeville routine, with Claudius assigned the
role of straight man.

KING CLAUDIUS

Now, Hamlet, where's Polonius?

HAMLET

At supper.

KING CLAUDIUS

At supper? Where?

HAMLET

Not where he eats but where a is eaten. A certain
convocation of politic worms are e'en at him. Your worm
is your only emperor for diet. We fat all creatures else to
fat us, and we fat ourselves for maggots. Your fat king
and your lean beggar is but variable service -- two dishes,
but to one table. That's the end.

KING CLAUDIUS

Alas, alas!

HAMLET

A man may fish with the worm that hath eat of
a king, and eat of the fish that hath fed of that worm.

KING CLAUDIUS

What dost thou mean by this?

HAMLET

Nothing but to show you how a king may go a
progress through the guts of a beggar.

KING CLAUDIUS

Where is Polonius?

HAMLET

In heaven. Send thither to see. If your messenger
find him not there, seek him i'th' other place yourself.
But indeed, if you find him not this month, you shall

nose him as you go up the stairs into the lobby.
(IV, iii, 17-36)

One is tempted to ask after all this, Was Prince Hamlet majoring in Foolish Arts in Wittenberg? What is the efficient cause of his irony, his droll style constantly slipping into the meaningful nonsense of madness?

V. Yorick's Ghost

Hamlet is Yorick's ghost. And so too is the sexton, as there is nothing to prevent an ectoplasmic juggler of words from manipulating two bodies. Any other acceptation of the text founders for lack of explanation. Both the sexton and Hamlet knew and were deeply influenced by Yorick, who seems to have sent distress signals to the aging King that he was being cuckolded by his lay-about brother, Prince Claudius. Hamlet was at an impressionable age when he came under Yorick's spell. Imagine how Yorick's sympathy must have been aroused by this brilliant boy, treated by all the world as the offspring of the infirm King, but so obviously of a different provenance. Under the King's very nose the Claudius-and-Gertrude affair continued to rage. Perhaps, as was suggested in *Hamlet Made Simple*, the King knew, but chose to turn a blind eye to his betrayal. To the question of what Yorick may have known about what the King knew, there can be no answer.

In the graveyard scene, two jesters clash, each bearing the spirit of their mentor, the "whoreson mad fellow," Yorick. The result is a verbal draw. The brave Prince will soon himself be food for worms and will, by inference, be interred by this same resilient sexton. One might say that Hamlet tumbles into the grave of Yorick, whose ghost finally expires with the death of their gravedigger.

WORKS CITED:

David P. Gontar, *Hamlet Made Simple and Other Essays*, New English Review, 2013.

Cheri Y. Halvorson, "Shakespeare's Fools: Confounding the Wise and Destabilizing Social Hierarchy," online.

William Shakespeare: The Complete Works, S. Wells, G. Taylor, eds.,

Oxford University Press, Clarendon, 2005.

William Shakespeare, Complete Works, J. Bate, E. Rasmussen, eds., The Royal Shakespeare Company, 2007.

2
Shakespeare in Black and White

I. Introduction

*S*hakespeare's plays are unique in Renaissance literature in the attention paid to race and racial relations. In scripts featuring European people in their dealings with Africans he is centuries ahead of his time. Instead of portraying blacks as poor oppressed bondsmen bereft of culture and education, in three plays he gives us well-developed black characters, Aaron in *Titus Andronicus*, the Prince of Morocco in *The Merchant of Venice*, and Othello, all models of breeding, intelligence and *savoir-faire*, full of promise but increasingly tragic. The Prince of Morocco is polite but presumptuous and aggressive, Aaron is a strange blend of destructive fury and nurture, and Othello is a hero who kills the thing he loves. Can such personages be derived and created solely on the basis of reading and imagination? One would naturally look for experiences or interactions with blacks as the foundation for such rich and evocative portrayals. Consider that two and a half centuries later, Americans were debating whether Africans should be considered human beings. What actual happenings set Shakespeare's perceptions apart from those which would follow in the New World? Placing these three figures in the context of relevant historiography might provide a foundation for approaching them more helpfully.

II. Africans in Renaissance England

In the past a formidable lack of information about the blacks in Renaissance England made such investigations nearly impossible, but recent advances by Gustav Ungere have cracked the door. Two articles of his should be required reading for students of the plays in question: "Portia and the Prince of Morocco," [PPM] *Shakespeare Studies* 31 (2003) and "The presence of Africans in Elizabethan England and the performance of *Titus Andronicus* at Burley-on-the-Hill, 1595/96," [PAEE] *Medieval and Renaissance Drama in England*, (2008). A lack of attention paid by Plantagenet historians has left most readers with a blind spot when it comes to racial demography of the era and a sense that slavery and its consequences were not domestic problems for the English people. Nothing could be further from the truth. While it is not possible to recount the vast range of Mr. Ungere's reportage and analysis, nor is agreement possible at every point, at least we have a factual context in which to set the literature we would fathom. Here is a compendium of observations culled from Mr. Ungere.

    *   England launched its slave trade as early as the 1480's. (PPM, 91)

    *   English slave traders bought captured slaves in Andalusia, and " . . . the majority of English merchants resident in Andalusia . . .were slave owners." (PPM, 91)

    *   As the slave trade expanded, English entrepreneurs came to obtain their desired commodities in Morocco. So great was the English slave trade that it resulted in a noticeable depopulation of that coastal nation.

    *   Morocco was a young Islamic state, lacking in experience dealing with English slave traders.

    *   In 1492, as a result of Spanish oppression, about 20,000 Sephardic Jews, including: "historians, physicians, merchants, goldsmiths, artisans, a printer, highly qualified military experts and gun casters took refuge in Morocco. Within a decade or two, the best qualified of them had worked their way up to the upper echelons of the civil service, had set up a nationwide network of business connections, and had marginalized the trade under the auspices of the sharifs." (PPM, 94) These sophisticated professionals became middlemen in the Moroccan slave trade.

    *   English slave traders in Andalusia and Morocco met and had first-hand dealings with black slaves, and with Muslim vendors and their Sephardic agents. Many slaves were shipped to England. English people frequented and patronized open slave markets, whose conditions of degradation are well known to those familiar with their later American equivalents. In addition, English businessmen also became acquainted with wealthy Moorish merchants of Islamic faith, and learned of their prosperity, refined culture, and various domestic arrangements (presumably confirming what had been noted during the much earlier crusades in the holy land, though Mr. Ungere does not mention this). By inference, then, the English in Morocco were exposed to both the benighted condition of blacks kidnapped in the African interior, as well as to the Moorish peoples of northern Africa, culturally associated with or descended from those who had preserved in their libraries in Arabia the writings of the ancient sages of Greece and Rome, which by 1500 had long been assiduously studied by artists and scholars in the city states of the Italian peninsula.

    *   The British Andalusian slave trade flourished from 1480 to 1532. (PAEE, pg. numbers unavailable)

    *   The next generation of English slave traders went farther south, participating in the lucrative slave markets of Guinea, which furnished slaves for the Caribbean.

    *   With the exception of an annual per capita tax, in Tudor England slavery was not regulated by law. (PAEE)

    *   The majority of the Africans in England in the early 16th century "were black domestic slaves, a few were freedmen, and some of them were Moors, mostly Berbers from North Africa." (All came under the appellation "blackamoor"). (PAEE) The reader will recall, *e.g.*, the blackamoors serving the King of Navarre in *Love's Labour's Lost* (1598). (DG)

    *   As the "blackamoor" population in England swelled in the 16th century it became a concern to the English people, their government and their Queen, who, in view of the "great numbers of Negars and Blackamoors which . . . are crept into this realm," issued three expulsion orders, two in July of 1596 and one in 1601. These had no effect, however. (PAEE)

    *   Many English slave owners were women, both noble and common. This is discussed in detail by Mr. Ungere. Though he focuses his attention on female domestics, it can hardly be supposed that there were no male slaves in their retinues. To the contrary, see below.

    *   Slave accommodations in 16th century England were spare. "Sleeping arrangements [were] mainly communal. Servants of either sex slept in the same room, and servants of the same sex often shared the bed, a fact that was well known to raise the female servants' vulnerability to rape, seduction, and, worst of all, the specter of miscegenation. The possibility that the bedrooms of early English households were immune to color discrimination cannot be ruled out. In Spain miscegenation was endemic among the servant class; in England it was certainly on the rise. The bold interracial scene in *Othello* (act 5) may have been inspired by the reality experienced in middle-class English households." (One might add that such a scene could also have occurred in households of the nobility.) (DG)

    * Many slaves were converted to Christianity. "The Anglican authorities considered slavery as reprehensible only when English [slaves] were sold to the Muslims and enticed to convert." (PAEE)

    * "[I]n early modern England, the age of consent for marriage was set at twelve for girls." (PAEE)

    * "Launcelot, the primary go-between in [*The Merchant of Venice*], who shuttles between religious communities and ethnic minorities, commits an act of interracial sex in Portia's domain at Belmont, impregnating the offstage Mooress, whose age must be put to twelve or thereabouts. His impregnation of the Mooress may have been meant to evoke a real-life incident in London." (PAEE)

    * "Among the foreign merchants residing in England, the Portuguese New Christians or *conversos*, who had been accustomed to keeping and handling slaves before they took refuge in England in the 1540's, enjoyed the privilege of keeping up their old lifestyle . . . and developing their commercial networks with their old *converso* partners in Amsterdam, Antwerp and Constantinople." (PAEE)

    * "The double-career men like the Gonsons, the Hawkinses and the Winters, who had a lifelong experience as members of the inner circle of the naval administration in charge of the royal fleet, had no scruples to take advantage of their public offices to promote their private enterprises. They became involved in slaving voyages as investors, ship owners and seafaring businessmen and did not hesitate to staff their households with colored servants." (PAEE)

    * "For his services rendered to the navy and for his private ventures [William Winter] was knighted in 1573." (PAEE)

    * The Guinea charter, signed May 3/13, 1588 by the English government and Dom Antonio, pretender to the throne of Portugal, "granted English merchants license to trade in slaves in Senegambia." (PAEE)

    * Following the Guinea charter, there were incidents in which the smuggling of a "considerable number of Guinea slaves" into England were uncovered. (PAEE)

    * Not all Senegambians were bondsmen. Some black Senegambians were sent to England to learn English and visit the country. (PAEE)

    * "The alleged influx of Guinea slaves in the early 1590's whether legal or illegal in terms of the Guinea charter of 1588, generated a sense of anxiety about the black presence in late Elizabethan London. The government, therefore, took measures to defuse the situation. In the wake of the investigations conducted by the High Court of Admiralty in 1592-94, the queen under the pretext of a threat to economic stability, was induced to issue the ineffective deportation acts of 1596, 1599, and 1601." (PAEE)

    * "Government measures alone were not sufficient to allay the fear of the citizens. By 1594 the Londoners had come to perceive the presence of Africans as an anomaly within the social body of their city . . . . *This was the moment for Shakespeare to step in to make an attempt to defuse the situation by confronting his contemporary audiences with the extraordinary figure of Aaron, a literate African, in 1594.*" (PAEE, emphasis added)

Here we must interrupt our transmission of the excellent reportage and analysis of Mr. Ungere with a question. It may be asked whether employing the figure of Aaron, arguably one of the most noxious, malevolent characters ever conjured by the human mind, was an act "defusing" the incendiary situation in London, or was rather an ignition. Those familiar with the play will recall that it is Aaron who seduces Tamora, Queen of the Goths, and leads her sons, Demetrius and Chiron, to savagely rape and dismember Titus' daughter, Lavinia. It is Aaron's perfidious scheming that leads to the beheading of two of Titus' sons, and to the amputation of Titus' hand. Aaron dispatches with his rapier his infant son's nurse, and when he is finally captured, exults over his sanguinary deeds before the stunned citizens of Rome.

> Ten thousand worse than ever yet I did
> Would I perform if I might have my will.
> If one good deed in all my life I did
> I do repent it from my very soul.
> (V, iii, 186-189)

It is not unimportant, to be sure, that Shakespeare gives us a black character who can quote poetic authors, but one must doubt that the Negrophobia sweeping through London like a contagion in the 1590's was much allayed by the presentation of a black man as the most dedicated and determined villain in the annals of literature. The combination of literacy with socio-pathological rage could not have served as a panacea or assurance of public safety, but was a reflection of Shakespear's remarkable realism.

Aaron is a seducer and a rapist, one who gratifies Tamora and plainly might have ravished Lavinia had that task not been delegated to Chiron and Demetrius. The concupiscent dimension of this black character is not plucked out of thin air by Shakespeare, but rests on the anecdotal accounts concerning blacks which stretched back from contemporary London, through the English slave trade to the crusades. The association of blacks with libido and potency inherited by Shakespeare from the sources identified by Mr. Ungere and first illustrated in the portrayal of Aaron inevitably was present when he came to write *The Merchant of Venice* and *Othello*, affecting the personalities of the Prince of Morocco and the Venetian Moor.

Thus, while few discussions of blacks in Shakespeare can rival those of Mr. Ungere, to whom we owe a large debt of gratitude, it is precisely at this critical juncture that he seems to stray.

III. Representations of Sexuality in *Titus Andronicus*

Let's lend a most careful ear to Mr. Ungere's discussion.

Besides the contemporary relevance of the play's political message, *Titus Andronicus* broke new ground in its attempt to cast doubt on the conventional perception of the African other as an inferior being. The racial discourse had not lost its immediacy in 1595-96. The foundation of the Guinea Company in 1588 had led to an increased influx of black Africans and by 1593/94, when Shakespeare was writing the play in the form it has come down to us, the black presence in Elizabethan England had reached a peak. The illicit arrival of two young African notables, the sons of the chief justice of Senegambia, and of some black students to be indoctrinated in English culture, was a conspicuous event, which alarmed the English government. Shakespeare responded to these social, legal, and ethnic tensions in staging forms of cross-cultural encounters that called in question the entrenched English position on racial hierarchies . . . . *Titus Andronicus*, besides being Shakespeare's first revenge tragedy, can claim to be the first Elizabethan play to undercut the racial discourse of positioning white over black. It challenges the ideological assumptions about the black man's racial inferiority. Aaron, the black outsider, does not correspond to the black African slaves the Londoners had come to know in increasing numbers after 1588. His most salient deviation from the real-life enslaved blackamores kept in London households is his literacy. Aaron is a literate black African well versed in the classics. He knows Ovid and Horace better than sons of Tamora, the white Queen of the Goths. Moreover, Aaron's sexual behavior does not conform to the entrenched belief and stereotyped representation of a black man's uncontrollable sexuality. Whereas Tamora herself and her two sons are figures of unrestrained sexuality, Aaron is capable of practicing sexual restraint. He thereby contradicts the current notion of the black man's boundless sexual potency. He also outdoes the Romans in setting examples of moderation and self-discipline and in acting as a vehicle of moral commentary. As a father he is pitted against Titus Andronicus, an embodiment of Roman values, who does not hesitate to resort to infanticide for political and moral considerations. Aaron, however, poses as a paragon of paternal love in his frantic attempt to save his son's life. The assumption that civilized Rome cannot be barbaric is shown to be incorrect. (PAEE)

Well, the barbarism of Rome is met immediately in the play when, over the pleas of Queen Tamora, Titus and his sons disembowel Alarbus and hack off his arms and legs, burning his entrails before his very eyes. We don't have to wait for Titus to stab his own son to know that he and his offspring are moral mongrels. Drawing a caricature of sexual vitality is not enough to relieve Aaron of the charge of sexual excess. Whatever happened in Africa, it was never reported of its male natives that their ardor was so "unrestrained" that they jumped on anything that moved. The fact that Aaron plots and schemes and chooses his victims with care shows a rapist's ability and mentality, not that he is free of nuclear libido. Aaron fairly salivates over Lavinia, but tells Tamora he is more focused on revenge than lust. (II, iii, 37-38) That is why he persuades her two sons to perform the heinous act he might have undertaken himself in other circumstances. He uses his own lurid fantasies to whet the perverse appetites of Chiron and Demetrius.

Take this of me: Lucrece was not more chaste
Than this Lavinia, Bassianus' love.
A speedier course than ling'ring languishment
Must we pursue, and I have found the path.
My lords, a solemn hunting is in hand;
There will the lovely Roman ladies troop.
The forest walks are wide and spacious,
And many unfrequented plots there are,
Fitted by kind for rape and villainy.
Single you thither then this dainty doe,
And strike her home by force, if not by words,
This way or not at all stand you in hope.
(II, i, 109-120)

Sounds Roman "restraint" thus? This is the discourse of a practiced and premeditated rapist, whose sexual dynamism is channeled by hate. Aaron is not a rutting jack rabbit, but one whose victims match his purposes. This entails precisely a massive storehouse of libido to draw on, a renewable resource not available to the louche epicures of Rome. Consider his exploitation of Tamora, who, on her honeymoon, quickly trades the etiolated attentions of husband Saturninus for the caresses of Aaron. Who exchanges dove for raven without reason? Bluntly put, Aaron gives Tamora the satisfaction Saturninus cannot afford. The name for this characteristic is virility, that for which Aaron and his forebears are renowned. Thus, in a sense we can agree with Mr. Ungere's claim that *Titus Andronicus* subverts or deconstructs the complacent bourgeois assumption current in Renaissance England of white superiority over black. It's quite the other way round. As Tamora and Aaron enjoy a liaison, it's hard to see how Tamora's id is any more prepossessing than her partner's. Aaron, the singular synthesis of classical learning, intelligence and prodigious sexual power, could well argue that he had transcended good and evil and had ascended to the rank of Nietzschean Übermensch. He loves none but self and son. Claiming that his paternal feelings are a sham would require textual evidence not furnished by Mr. Ungere. As a dangerous loose cannon, Aaron gets his comeuppance in the end, but not before Shakespeare has made his point. Never a sniveling egalitarian, our poet surprises and enlarges us by presenting whites as exponentially transcended, not "equaled." Strong and free, Aaron does what he likes. It is the envious contempt resentful whites show him that prods him to extremities. Aaron is one of Shakespeare's most compelling anti-heroes, a member of the antagonistic fraternity that includes *inter alios* Edmund, Don John, Winchester and Richard the Third. It is by now a truism that it is the villains of drama who furnish the propulsive movement carrying the plot forward. Indeed, the very word "plot" signifies both the structure of drama generally and the devious scheme of the antagonist character. Rogues act, heroes merely respond. Any Hollywood blockbuster will confirm.

Further, the Aaronian archetype understood philosophically is what is known as a permanent possibility of being. It can and does achieve instantiation in one setting after another. Consider the life and writings of abandoned American genius and civil rights activist, Eldridge Cleaver, whose personal manifesto *Soul on Ice* reprised unwittingly Shakespeare's Aaron in 1968. Unlike Aaron, Cleaver was a thinker. He brilliantly articulated the elective affinities linking the black man and the white woman, never realizing, of course, that Shakespeare, as always, had been there first. It is surely not without significance that each of Shakespeare's major black male characters is paired with a white female: The Prince of Morocco with Portia, Aaron with Tamora, Queen of the Goths, and Othello with you-know-who. Cleaver, himself a serial rapist (later reformed) and literate black man who penned a masterpiece in prison, deserves full credit for his theories, which instinctively recognize the conjunction of "supermasculine" black male and "ultrafeminine" Caucasian female. Rather than explain it, Shakespeare's approach is simpler, more elegant: he shows us. *Nicht wahr?*

Having said all this, and having been tutored by Mr. Ungere, we are now in a position to proceed to *The Merchant of Venice*.

IV. The Prince and his Portion

The lead suitor in the play, the Prince of Morocco, is of special interest for students of Shakespeare's racialism. The first words out of his mouth demonstrate that he is keenly aware of being ethnically uncleansed.

> Mislike me not for my complexion,
> The shadowed livery of the burnished sun,
> To whom I am a neighbor and near bred.
> Bring me the fairest creature northward born,
> Where Phoebus' fire scarce thaws the icicles,
> And let us make incision for your love

To prove whose blood is reddest, his or mine.
I tell thee, lady, this aspect of mine
Hath feared the valiant. By my love I swear,
The best regarded virgins of our clime
Have loved it too. I would not change this hue
Except to steal your thoughts, my gentle queen.
(II, i, 1-12)

This rings prettily, yet awkwardly, as Morocco echoes Shylock (who also sought fleshly incisions) and, of course, Aaron, who would never alter his dusky hue. Attempting to downplay his color as a perma- nent suntan, this African scion makes a cagey — yet foot-in-mouth — aspirant. Telling vain and jealous Portia that many of the "best regarded virgins of [his] clime" have loved "it" too, is vague and inept. What is "it" if not the red blood of his erotically charged flesh? Whether those "best regarded virgins" freely consented to his embraces or were compelled to do so may be one of the things that gives Portia pause. Spoiled child and habitual braggart, the Prince of Morocco is thinly disguised as a self-effacing swashbuckler before whom Portia hesitates, as visions of being locked in her own boudoir by this demon flash through her mind. The Prince of Morocco's Aaronian ravenousness shows through, as, sty- mied by the subtleties of the casket gimmick, he tries to exude love and tenderness to conceal his real identity: the Lothario-of-the-harem. His custom is to take by force.

By this scimitar,
That slew the Sophy and a Persian prince
That won three fields of Sultan Suleiman,
I would o'erstare the sternest eyes that look,
Outbrave the heart most daring on the earth,
Pluck the young sucking cubs from the she-bear,
Yea, mock the lion when a roars for prey,
To win the lady.
(II, i, 24-31)

Mr. Ungere concurs: "The 'renowned Prince' (2.1.20) has no sec- ond thoughts about advertising to his bride-to-be the sexual reputation he enjoys in Morocco, suggesting he is past master at the art of deflow- ering the virgins of the Moroccan nobility." (PPM, 112) He adds:

The body of comment by Christian authors on the aggressive sexuality and cruelty of Muslim rulers left its imprint on the stage portrait of the Prince of Morocco. The Prince conforms, in the first instance, to the paradigm of the transgressive Moor who strives for miscegenational union which is doomed to pollute his European partner. He has come from Morocco, a liminal country situated on the edge of the western world; on one of "the four corners of the earth" . . . in order to kiss the "shrine" of his "mortal breathing saint" in Belmont. On his voyage he has braved the "watery kingdom" of the Atlantic Ocean and the Mediterranean Sea, negotiating the storms and dangers as if crossing "o'er a brook to see fair Portia." However, his greatest flaw as a suitor, as I see it, is neither his bravado as a warrior under the Ottoman Sultan Suleyman the Magnificent, nor his tawny complexion, nor his cultural otherness; it is the self-indicting pose he assumes as the imperial rapist. (PPM, 112)

The reader will recall what calamity befalls Aaron when his partner in lust, Tamora, gives birth to a black baby, not easy to explain to Roman Emperor Saturninus. What, then, could be in the mind of Morocco? It's easy to see that such a birth would be the least of his concerns. Belmont would be his, to administer as he saw fit. Doors would open and close at his frown. He would decide who lives or dies. Marriage to this very independent ruler would mean manipulative Portia might find herself transported to a sultan's palace in Marrakesh, her children by the Prince sold into servitude or lodged in the sybaritic luxury of a harem. Only by the strictures of her father's will is she constrained to tolerate such a rambunctious royal suitor. Once she actually lays eyes on him, however, the impossible consequences of an actual union are plain. It's hard to know which is worse: having to submit to the clasps of this narcissistic potentate and do his bidding, or to bring a black baby into the glare of cruel public disdain. Hence no surreptitious clues are given to Morocco to solve the riddle of the caskets, as they will be later to Bassanio. (III, ii, 63-65) And so he fails. It is plainly not merely cosmetic considerations that lead Portia to mutter as the defeated Prince flees the casket room: "A gentle riddance. Draw the curtains, go. Let all of his complexion choose me so." (II, vii, 78-79)

V. What Ho, Othello

We are now prepared to tackle once more our Venetian general. As the perennial question surrounding Prince Hamlet is why he cannot kill Claudius, so the issue debated by students of this play is: Is the marriage of Desdemona and her Moor ever consummated? Of course, we can't look up the solution in the back of the textbook. We must therefore seek our edification in the inquiry itself.

What makes us doubt?

Like the Moroccan Prince, Othello stands in the textual shadow of Aaron. But unlike them, Othello is intrinsically noble, perhaps the son of a tribal chief. He is a leader by ability rather than birth and cherishes his reputation, a theme taken up expressly in the play. The narrow minded Venetians value him not for his principles so much as for his martial prowess. Venice is a racist realm which has a history in the slave trade much older than western involvement in that wretched business. Venice is always spiritually closer to exotic Byzantium than to Rome with its republican roots. It is another liminal state, a porous membrane nourished by human traffic running between Europe and the East. Othello wins Desdemona's heart by telling her of his perilous adventures, including his capture in the wars and later liberation. It's critical to appreciate that as a young man Othello was "sold to slavery." (I, iii, 137) He confesses this to Desdemona. Everyone in Venice knows. Such experiences leave scars. Think of Othello's commanding persona and demeanor. The trauma and humiliation of slavery would have been severe. Punishments would have been endured. Othello's color, calling to mind both his enslavement and the experiences of Venice in that trade, does not endear him to the Doge and his courtiers. They may respect Othello. They may fear him. But they do not love him.

Iago and Roderigo, two insecure and envious Marranos, act to destroy "the thick lips" with a plot. In what today would be identified as a hate crime, they incite Desdemona's father Brabantio against Othello by hurling crude racial epithets which challenge the humanity of one of Shakespeare's most painfully human characters.

IAGO

Awake, what ho, Brabantio, thieves, thieves, thieves!
Look to your house, your daughter, and your bags.
Thieves, thieves!

(I, i, 79-81)

'Swounds, sir, you're robbed. For shame, put on your gown.
Your heart is burst, you have lost half your soul.
Even now, now, very now, an old black ram
Is tupping your white ewe. Arise, arise!
Awake the snorting citizens with the bell,
Or else the devil will make a grandsire of you.
Arise, I say.
(I, i, 85-92)

'Swounds, sir, you are one of those
That will not serve God if the devil bid you. Because we
come to do you service and you think we are ruffians,
you'll have your daughter covered with a Barbary
horse, you'll have your nephews neigh to you,
you'll have coursers for cousins and jennets for germans.
(I, i, 112-116)

This is a frontal assault not merely on the dignity of Othello but on his status as a species member. Viewed externally, Iago's target would seem a difficult one at which to strike. Othello is deliberate yet decisive. He has more than his share of gravitas. He is naturally courageous. He is a model of Aristotelian megalopsychia (in translation, "great-souled man"). But Iago senses a crevice of weakness within, reminiscent of Hamlet's "dram of eale." This can be perceived more easily by first stepping back, rather than peering microscopically into the recesses of his mind: Othello is a black man in a white society, a society saturated with racism. Black men there must always bear the subtle taint of brutishness. Worried that they might not receive parental approval, he and Desdemona elope. But clandestine operations are not his style, and, apprehended by Brabantio, he must explain himself, putting him on the defensive. Othello is at his best in battle, conceiving bold strategies, exhorting his troops. But in the play Othello's bravery under fire is known only in retrospect. We never see it. Iago (*i.e.*, "Jacob"), most likely a converso himself and thus a kindred spirit, always vigilant in a city with its own Inquisition to detect religious backsliders, has a kind of night vision by which Othello's alienage, his hidden anguish, is perceived. Into this psychic breach Iago, like a fecundating arachnid, plants his seeds of suspicion. But as bad as it is to be a cuckold this is not Othello's worst fear. More terrible than that is the specter of collective disgust and rejection that always lies in wait for him, being exposed not as a rational being or brave soldier but as a subhuman, like Caliban, a poetic primate, the outsider *par excellence*. Doubt is an insidiously corrosive thing. For not only is there the anguish of seeing that some regard him as a beast, the more paranoid prospect is that this perception might be accurate. What is his desire for Desdemona, after all? Is it not lechery? Doesn't a small voice whisper to Othello the words we hear from Lord Angelo, the corrupt magistrate in *Measure for Measure*?

> What dost thou, or what art thou, Angelo?
> Dost thou desire her foully for those things
> That make her good?
> (II, ii, 178-180)

Lusting in his heart after this young woman, Othello must feel that transforming his love into physical intimacy can only sully this pure object of his devotion. Against his own despoiling of his love object, he recoils, losing the name of action.

We may safely presume that someone situated as Othello is in the play would have a past in which wild oats were sown. He has had conquests on and off the field of sword and shield. Now he has won the hand of Desdemona, the captain's captain. (II, i, 75) What does he want in her? Mutiny? After the unseen nuptials, is there not a moment of hesitation? Though Othello is called to the wars in Cyprus, he could have found time for gentle manifesting of his love. Isn't that why Desdemona, afraid to be left behind, a moth of peace, begs to accompany him? (I, iii, 248-259) To scour the text to try to dig up signs of consummation is not only impossible, it suggests an inability to come to terms with Othello's Ulysses Complex (the anxiety that, just as Circe transformed the companions of Odysseus into brutes, so Othello may wake up one day to find himself sporting a tail). His own anatomy seems to accuse him. On the other hand, dogged as he is with this overmastering syndrome, there is the dimly sensed possibility that he might fail to perform altogether. There is a rub indeed. (Notice Desdemona's gratuitous use of the word "impotent.") (II, i, 164) To succeed and elicit a lusty wife whose liberated sensuality mirrored his own desire might be in his estimation to transform the marriage chamber into a bordello . . . or something even more base. And as for impotence, that is the altogether unthinkable thought.

And so we come to Michael Cassio and the green-eyed monster.

The fact of the matter is that Desdemona is in love with Othello and cleaves unto him as a special, older and protective man. She is not a prude, as her sexual banter with Iago demonstrates. (II, i, 110-163) Iago goes so far to tease her with a couplet which portrays Desdemona as the libidinous negress who knows how to discover her own pleasure.

DESDEMONA

Well praised! How if she be black and witty?

IAGO

If she be black and thereto have a wit,
She'll find a white that shall her blackness fit.
(II, i, 134-136)

Had Othello made his conjugal advances she would have warmly welcomed him. But, caught in mental shackles, he cannot.

Cuckoldry is one thing, but, given the legendary sexuality of Africa, for a black man to be cuckolded by a Caucasian would be, in Othello's mind, the ultimate embarrassment, the end of the universe; hence his consuming jealousy, larger than life. And there we have it, the triple threat: (1) make love with Desdemona and turn an angel into a strumpet; (2) attempt to make love with her and be so overcome with such guilt that arousal is not achieved; or (3) by tarrying, lose her to a lesser man. Is it any wonder that such a fellow might go crazy? What is the solution? In an earlier essay we considered the possibility that cuckoldry might be a male desideratum. (Gontar, 100ff.) For by removing the husband from the theatre of action and turning him into a spectator he is absolved of all responsibility for performance and is placed in a situation of subtle control. This is the seductive lure of failure, a delicious giving in to inadequacy. Such was the behavior of many senior males in the days of the troubadours, when it was expected that a young wife would be the object of romantic attention from footloose swains.

It would not be surprising to learn that contemporary black Americans see in Othello the proverbial "Uncle Tom," the subservient, amiable negro who defers instinctively to white authority, papering over slights with a smile. It's a bit more of a stretch to see him, the invincible warrior and leader, as guilt-ridden and paralyzed, but there is a trace of this in his inextinguishable mien of propriety. He has enough resolve to break the taboo of interracial marriage, but when challenged he cannot assert himself and take what is his with confidence. Under Iago's spell he forgets that it is always within his scope to sit down with Desdemona and talk about his concerns forthrightly. He might have challenged Michael Cassio to a duel. His options were many. Doing violence to her was the least sensible of them. In harming her he punished himself under the weight of his own misgivings. A Caius Marcus or Alcibiades might have rounded up an army and invaded Venice. It would not have been impossible for the Moor to find allies. Instead, he internalizes his aggression. Othello murders his better half first, then the worse.

VI. Conclusion

Our legacies are our ghosts. We are haunted by ancestors primordial. As civilizations rise and decay, our strengths become our weaknesses. Othello inherits from Africa a sturdy reproductive drive, the envy of weaker, more inhibited peoples who content themselves with mere puzzle-solving, belittling the prerogatives of flesh and blood. Isn't it plain how jealous Iago is of his boss? In the immeasurable eons of death and survival that is Africa, a supercharged libido and ample genital capacity were appropriate and necessary tools allowing the species to endure. Virility was a source of pride. Even as late as the Roman era, the "vir" in "virtu" conveyed a respect for masculine potency and ardor. Only in the feminized, indoor, post-industrial world we inhabit now would a biologically founded virility be regarded as something to be ashamed of. This was the unheard message of Eldridge Cleaver, echoing D.H. Lawrence. In *Titus Andronicus*, Shakespeare sets the assemblage of imperial weaklings (Rome), struggling to hold the "barbarians" at bay, against the superman of *phusis*, Aaron. It is not his literacy which makes him human or "equal" to whites, but his mastery of mind and body, his *Wille zur Macht*, which renders him worthy of self-respect and hence the respect of others. That is his plain advantage. Aaron is like a giant tied down by ants and mocked. No wonder he is furious. Were he unconditionally, intrinsically evil, would he have cared so tenderly for his infant son? If it be objected that under no circumstances can such a one as Aaron ever be brought forward as an object of admiration, it may be sufficient to recall the teachings of J. J. Rousseau. The good in Aaron is the inheritance from nature and Africa; what is wicked and depraved is the residue of western slavery. There was assuredly violence and war in Africa before the advent of the slavers, but there were no Aarons.

Such revolting deeds as we see him perpetrate can hardly be winked at on grounds of his celebrated literacy. The hate within him reflects the prior hate of white racism. Whence cometh that notorious disdain of an innocent people? It was not ships flying African flags which sailed to the coasts of England to steal its people and take them back to Africa, victims of mass deportation and involuntary servitude, but vice versa. It could well be argued, too, that the dramatic purpose served by Aaron in the play is to be a foil, against which the activities of a Titus may appear tolerable. But they do not. And what is Titus but Rome writ small? What blessings did those trampling legions confer on the folk of northern Europe? Literacy? To relish that exquisite pastime were Goths and Gauls decimated? Titus appears in Shakespeare's play as a wind-up automaton who ranges over the wide world in search of "enemies" to subjugate, and though he buries most of his sizable progeny in the family crypt, not once does it occur to him to question the rationale of his missions or the viciousness of Roman customs such as led to the slaughter of Alarbus, the true cause of his tragedy.

What was the real reason that white males in the American South tended to hate the black men they brought by force to America to toil for them? Wouldn't a decorous gratitude have been more appropriate? On the pretext of ensuring health and strength, black slaves were always purchased naked in the open market. With respect to the males, there was no quibble, then, about their masculine properties, no need for conjecture. The result was white envy, which issued in vicious oppression and the consoling canard of Caucasian "superiority." Not surprisingly, this tendency is even more pronounced now, in a world in which everyone is content to sit on their behinds all day wiggling fingers over plastic keyboards. Meanwhile, our prisons have become concentration camps for millions of black men not suited to computer programming and the delusive motto of *cogito ergo sum*. One has to look no further than *Love's Labour's Lost* with its ridiculous bookmen to see what Shakespeare thought of sententious scribblers and page turners, so appropriately reviled by flesh and blood women. Aaron should therefore be regarded as the symbol of ancient wisdom, when manhood was just beginning to be a criminal offense. Shakespeare knew the value of art, but greater than art, he taught, was life.

> Why, all delights are vain, but that most vain
> Which, with pain purchased, doth inherit pain;
> As painfully to pore upon a book

To seek the light of truth while truth the while
Doth falsely blind the eyesight of his look.
Light, seeking light, doth light of light beguile;
So ere you find where light in darkness lies
Your light grows dark by losing of your eyes.
Study me how to please the eye indeed
By fixing it upon a fairer eye,
Who dazzling so, that eye shall be his heed,
And give him light that it was blinded by.
Study is like the heavens' glorious sun,
That will not be deep searched with saucy looks.
Small have continual plodders ever won
Save base authority from others' books.
These earthly godfathers of heaven's lights,
That give a name to every fixèd star,
Have no more profit of their shining nights
Than those that walk and wot not what they are.
Too much to know is to know naught but fame,
And every godfather can give a name.
(*Love's Labour's Lost*, I, i, 72-93)

The second stage of the dialectic of race is represented by the Prince of Morocco, who discreetly veils his coveting and apologizes for his earthy color. The body and its needs are matters of shame. Here shades of the prison house begin to close around us. Portia is not won, but one can't help thinking that had she thrown in her lot with Morocco she might have had a chance for a genuine happiness. This is modern apostasy, of course, but many a heretic has been right as rain. Will any say that Belmont is the citadel of happiness and joy? Him have we offended.

Finally we come to the full-blown modern neuroticism of poor Othello, a vestigial outdoorsman who has been browbeaten into accepting the white man's outlook. As a black slave, he had to learn submission, and this awful episode has left an imprint on his soul. Later, as general, towering over the profiteering Venetians with their weights and measures, he can be neither the hero he was destined to be, nor can he shrink, accommodating himself to a warren of crafty homunculi. To get where he is he has found it necessary to compromise, to absorb the creed of the white man and deny the exigencies of the body. Riven by guilt, he cannot free himself from the sense that he has purloined

Desdemona; he cannot permit himself full satisfaction with his trophy bride. Had he managed to do that, to be wholly married to her, he would have been immune to the sly insinuations of Iago. There would have been no fatal guilt associated with taking Desdemona as his spouse. Had those things been accomplished, hearing the whispered hints of Iago he would have laughed, and sent his ancient whistling down the wind, where he belonged.

WORKS CITED:

Eldridge Cleaver, *Soul on Ice*, Delta Publishing, 1999.

David P. Gontar, *Hamlet Made Simple and Other Essays*, New English Review Press, 2013.

All Shakespeare quotations from: *William Shakespeare, The Complete Works*, Second ed., S. Wells & G. Taylor, eds., Clarendon Press, Oxford, 2005.

Gustave Ungere, "Portia and the Prince of Morocco," *Shakespeare Studies,* 31 (2003).

_____, "The Presence of Africans in Elizabethan England and the Performance of *Titus Andronicus* at Burley-on-the-Hill, 1595-96," *Medieval and Renaissance Drama in England,* (2008).

3
1769-2016 and All That Jazz

They say miracles are past, and we have our
philosophical persons to make modern and familiar
things supernatural and causeless. Hence is it that we
make trifles of terrors, ensconcing ourselves into
seeming knowledge when we should submit ourselves
to an unknown fear.
                                    - Shakespeare

At the conclusion of the Seven Year's War, Britain's global empire was firmly established. North America and India were well in hand. The first of the Hanover kings to possess English as his native tongue, George III, sat amiably atop the throne. With the signing of the Treaty of Paris, February 10, 1763, the mood of security gave way to pomp and euphoria. Later that year, on September 15, 1763, trendy thespian David Garrick and his trophy bride, Viennese ballerina Eva Maria Violetta, left London for a Continental jaunt. Peter Walch observes, "Their trip was designed in part for their mutual physical relaxation and at least secondarily to give his audiences, whom he suspected of becoming weary of his dominating presence upon the English stage, a rest as well." (Walch, 523) Prof. Walch adds, "Garrick was playing the role of British gentleman on the Grand Tour with considerable relish and panache." (Walch, 523) Lionized in London, he thrived on publicity, and was so used to being the butt of criticism and satire that on occasion he even penned adverse notices of his own performances. Though he possessed a labile countenance difficult to capture with pen or brush, an

avalanche of Garrick figures and visages nonetheless inundated specta-
tors, theatre-goers and many a country seat. (See, *e.g.*, Thomas Patch's
droll caricature below) David Garrick was the "Enlightenment's" rock
star and Hollywood bombshell rolled into one; he was also the supreme
and undisputed master of Shakespearean stage repertoire.

"David Garrick in Italy" by Thomas Patch (Exeter Museum and Gallery)

The Garricks continued exploring Italy through 1764, which happened to be the bicentennial anniversary of the birth of William of Stratford-on-Avon. Though the optimal date had now passed, Garrick wasn't
fazed. As Martha Winburn England explains, by 1767 the residents of
Stratford had begun fabrication of a new town hall. (England, 11) Town
fathers approached him to request a portrait of himself and a Shakespeare bust, only to discover that their prospective donor had bigger fish
to fry. In fact, since his return from Italy Garrick had been nursing a far
more ambitious aim: a Shakespeare "Jubilee," or Brobdingnagian-pub-
licity stunt, designed to thrust Stratford and Garrick (not necessarily
in that order) up in lights forever. A drowsy sheep village nestled beside the meandering Avon would morph into a poetaster's Potemkin
Village, a theatrical extravaganza complete with ceremonies, masques,
pyrotechnics, concerts, and period balls. It was to be an Anglo-Saxon
Mardi Gras, in which art crept while pompous façades and ballyhoo

ballooned. Innocent of letters but eager for profit, the local burghers astutely grasped the plan's advantages. A verse of indigenous origin exulted:

> Come, brothers of Stratford, these flocks let us shear,
> Which bright as if washed by our Avon appear!
> The coolest are they who from fleeces are free,
> And who are such trimmers, such trimmers as we?
> Sing tantarara, shear all, shear all!
> (England, 22)

Guided by Garrick and his minions, work got under way, with an opening date projected for August 6, 1769. With the inevitable delays, the grand opening was put over to the following month.

During the interim, however, something intriguing occurred: a brilliant comet, first detected by Charles Messier (1730-1817) on August 8, 1769, swept across Europe and the British Isles. While throngs of merrymakers stared slack-jawed at the eerie display, Napoleon Bonaparte, the dread soldier who would reshape the modern world was craftily born in Corsica on August 15, 1769, the first of his many surprise attacks. In early September as the gates of the Shakespeare Jubilee burst open, this astronomical prodigy was still predominant.

Such conjunctions might be more easily dismissed had Shakespeare not deliberately brought comets into his own authorial orbit. As poet and thinker, such events seemed to him fraught with ineluctable meaning. Indeed, there are many volumes of his collected works (especially those based on *The Stratford Town Edition* of 1904) whose very first words raise the significance of a comet's arrival:

> Hung be the heavens with black! Yield day to night!
> Comets, importing change of times and states,
> Brandish your crystal tresses in the sky,
> And with them scourge the bad revolting stars
> That have consented unto Henry's death.
> (*King Henry VI*, Part One, I, i, 1-5, punctuation amended)

Similar references to portentous comets can be found in *Pericles*, *Julius Caesar* and *The Taming of the Shrew*. Naturally there are many today who wonder whether Shakespeare credits accounts of gods, omens, ghosts, and prophecies; close reading of the texts strongly suggests it.

(See, *e.g.*, Fernie, Ewan; Gontar, 161-185.) After all, this "early modern" poet had one foot planted squarely in the medieval worldview (See, *e.g.*, E.M.W. Tillyard); modern naturalism and skepticism had not yet been universally embraced. The passage above is a good example. For what force could have swept aside England's greatness under the majestic rule of the beloved King Henry the Fifth if not an hostile concatenation of stellar agencies? Unlike the fixed stars themselves, whose regular movements afforded a relative modicum of predictability, comets were adventitious and troubling invaders whose rare intrusions signaled cosmic shifts in nature. Yet in the lines quoted above, the Duke of Bedford invites comets to penetrate the sublunary realm not to subvert order directly but to "scourge" rebellious stars which have presided over the catastrophic losses of the Realm. Whether acting for good or ill, a comet was a sign of incipient ruptures in the social and political fabric. In 1769, the rebellion of the American colonies, the French Revolution and the "meteoric" rise of the Napoleonic empire all lay just beyond the horizon. Hence some of the revelers who descended on Stratford for the transmogrification of "Shakespeare" must have done so with a sense of unfolding glory. The moment was big with the Future — yet redolent of the Past. Did not the successful conclusion of the Seven Year's War hearken back to England's 1588 defeat of the Spanish Armada which launched English hegemony and the career of its bard? Fate is a two-edged sword; ahead might lie further blessings. What is known is this: under the basilisk eye of Comet Messier (1769) the name of "William Shakespeare" exploded into the firmament of public consciousness amid a frenzy of hucksterism and tawdry commercialization launched by promoter David Garrick, a turbulence that accelerates in the 21st century; and a man was born who would dazzle the world with military exploits and come to be the ruler of Europe, only to be ultimately defeated by an English officer. As the French empire emerged out of the Sphinx-like Napoleon, so from Shakespeare's mind sprang an intellectual and entertainment Hydra whose academic and popular bastions still hold sway on campuses, studios, wood stages, iPads and multiplexes around the globe.

On the other hand, by 1769 the sober naturalistic and mathematical philosophy of Sir Isaac Newton was well in the ascendant. His *Principia* was published in 1687. Telescopes were bringing into focus a cosmos controlled by laws capable of mathematical formulation. Hence for the few sophisticates in the crowd, the comet would have been nothing more than a material object in trajectory. It was the masses of common folk who lived not in thought but in feeling for whom things were more complex, more profound. Vestiges of Stonehenge, Druidism and magic flowed in Celtic blood. Behind the "seeming knowledge" advanced by natural philosophy lay the uneasy sense that there remained things in heaven and earth beyond the comforts of merely calculative explanation. Indeed, this discrepancy continues to our own time. Do we know everything? Not quite. Our age is a chiaroscuro: the rays of "science" are often felt to only heighten the dark. What, then, did the comet of 1769 betoken, destiny, doom or . . . nothing at all? Ironically, it was the groundlings of the 18th century to whom Shakespeare's spiritual cosmology spoke most keenly.

Readers interested in learning more about the Jubilee will easily find a wealth of information. Martha Winburg England's classic *Garrick's Jubilee* (Ohio State University Press, 1964) is a convenient launching pad for study. It provides a close look at the objections, criticism and satire that arose when the more refined and thoughtful sensibilities of England became apprised of the penny arcade atmosphere brewing at Garrick's "jubilee," which, for all its bardolatry, was always more about its robust impresario than its nominal subject. There is no need to catalogue the smarmy excesses which must have had our immortal poet turning in his grave. Rather than rehearse garish details (which include a giant boiled turtle), it will be sufficient to glance at Mr. Garrick's personal contribution, his "Ode to Shakespeare," the centerpiece of a cavalcade of bad taste. This Ode, modeled on William Havard's *An Ode to the Memory of Shakespeare* (1756), was spoken by Garrick as a recitative over string accompaniment (music courtesy of Thomas Arne). In his "Advertisement" Garrick presented it "to the public as an object of their good nature, — to his friends as an exercise of their partiality, — to his enemies as a lucky opportunity of venting their wit, humour, criticism, spleen or whatever else they please, should they think it worthy of their notice." In itself, of course, the "Ode" of David Garrick was plainly not worth anyone's notice. But, as a specimen of the human mind's capacity for exploitation, self-deception and *amour propre*, it has unique importance, especially in light of the projected Shakespeare hysteria about to be unleashed in 2016.

But let us pause to lend Mr. Garrick an ear.

To what blest genius of the isle,
Shall Gratitude her tribute pay.
Decree the festive day,
Erect the statue, and devote the pile?

Do not your sympathetic hearts accord,
To own the 'bosom's lord?'
'Tis he! 'Tis he! - that demi-god!
Who Avon's flow'ry margin trod,
While sportive Fancy round him flew,
Where Nature led him by the hand,
Instructed him in all she knew,
And gave him absolute command!
'Tis he! 'Tis he!
'The god of our idolatry!'
To him the song, the Edifice we raise,
He merits all our wonder, all our praise!
Yet ere impatient joy break forth,
To tell his name, and speak his worth,
And to your spell-bound minds impart
Some faint idea of his magic art;
Let awful silence still the air!

It's unlikely, of course, that there was much silence - though there should have been.

Raucous stanzas mellow not with age. Though he enacted Shakespearean personae, it has been justly doubted to what extent Garrick actually digested the corpus, for everything in this appalling sing-song palaver betrays a lack of appreciation of that 'most humorous sadness' which is Shakespeare. If ever there was anything he loathed, it was cheap doggerel and vain flattery. Yet in his effusive litany, Garrick serves up heaping helpings of both, ironically in Shakespeare's honor! This is reminiscent of Malvolio's *faux pas* in *Twelfth Night*. Duped by Maria into wooing his boss, Lady Olivia, he appears before her in cross-gartered yellow stockings, sporting a foolish grin on his face. These are things she is known to detest. (II, v, 191-199) The difference is that Malvolio is the victim of a clever plot and could urge that in his own defense, whereas Garrick (and the scribblers whose breathless dedications mar the 1623 *Folio*) have no excuses. Garrick appears as the victim not of others' schemes but of his own ambition, avarice and presumption. Readers who wish to take the measure of his blunder can review Shakespeare's firm and heartfelt repudiation of flattery in: the *Woodstock* manuscript (See, Gontar, 186); *Julius Caesar*, II, i, 202-208; III, i, 39-43; *King Henry VI, Part One* II, i, 52; *King Henry VI, Part Three*, III, ii, 143; *Twelfth Night*, I, v, 293; *King Richard II*, II, i, 88; *King Henry VI, Part Two*, I, i,

161; *Romeo and Juliet*, II, i, 181.

Did Shakespeare write for praise?

He that is proud eats up himself.
Pride is his own glass, his own trumpet, his own
chronicle — and whatever praises itself but in the deed
devours the deed in the praise.
(*Troilus and Cressida*, II, iii, 152-156)

And what is flattery but the antechamber of pride?

He does me double wrong
That wounds me with the flatteries
of his tongue.
(*King Richard II*, III, ii, 211-212)

As for quality of poetry, to understand Shakespeare's standpoint we need look no further than the sonnet sequence in *Love's Labour's Lost*, in which Biron, the King and two other lords compose love poems which descend from mediocre to downright ghastly. As Dumaine declaims his passion one can almost hear Shakespeare gritting his teeth:

On a day — alack the day —
Love, whose month is ever May,
Spied a blossom passing fair
Playing in the wanton air.
Through the velvet leaves the wind
All unseen can passage find,
That the lover, sick to death,
Wished himself the heavens' breath.
"Air", quoth he, "thy cheeks may blow;
Air, would I might triumph so.
But, alack, my hand is sworn
Ne'er to pluck thee from thy thorn —
Vow, alack, for youth unmeet,
Youth so apt to pluck a sweet.
Do not call it sin in me
That I am forsworn for thee,
Thou for whom great Jove would swear

Juno but an Ethiop were,
And deny himself for Jove,
Turning mortal for thy love."
(IV, iii, 99-118)

And let's not forget:

The raging rocks
And shivering shocks
Shall break the locks
   Of prison gates,
And Phibus' car
Shall shine from far
And make and mar
   The foolish Fates.
(*A Midsummer Night's Dream*, I, ii, 26-34)

Funny, but pretty awful. Yet David Garrick was not to be outdone in bombast. He echoes the very worst in Shakespeare.

From the dark cloud, the hidden light
Bursts tenfold bright!
Prepare! prepare! prepare!
Now swell at once the choral song,
Roll the full tide of harmony along;
Let Rapture sweep the trembling strings,
And Fame expanding all her wings,
With all her trumpet-tongues proclaim,
The lov'd, rever'd immortal name!
SHAKESPEARE! SHAKESPEARE! SHAKESPEARE!
Let th' inchanting sound,
From Avon's shores rebound;
Thro' the Air,
Let it bear,
The precious freight the envious nations round!

Well, it's the thought that counts, they say. But is this thought?

Without a clue as to how a lad from the boondocks could have so rapidly scaled the heights of Mt. Parnassus, Garrick follows Milton and other "warbling" savants in chalking up Shakespeare's preternatural abilities to the gratuitous favors of "Nature" and "Fancy." Yet philosopher John Locke had published his ground-breaking *Essay on Human Understanding* eighty years earlier, in 1689, in which he showed beyond peradventure that knowledge is based on experience. And Locke's insights were preceded by Sir Francis Bacon's "inductive" empirical method in *Novum Organum* (1620). By Garrick's time empiricism had become the epistemic English watchword. Any rational account of the writer's panoramic vistas and portrayals of courtly manners and idealized language would have been based squarely on instances of direct personal exposure. (See, Touchstone: "Wast ever in court, shepherd?", *As You Like It*, III, ii, 31-43.) It goes without saying that the stripling from Stratford had no entrée in Elizabeth's privy chamber. But an aristocratic Shakespeare lines no pockets. The Stratford tourism industry which Garrick founded relied — and still relies — on the sensational and preposterous rags-to-riches saga of the deer-poaching-Mulberry-tree planting youth who takes London by storm. That's the sterner stuff that sells tickets and souvenirs in bustling Stratford Village.

Though Shakespeare in *Romeo and Juliet* gently mocks his hyperbolical heroine by having her refer to her panting adolescent swain as "the god of my idolatry," (II, i, 156) David Garrick had no hesitation in filching this ironic trope to characterize the English people's reverence for Shakespeare. But divinity creates *ex nihilo*, without effort, without care. What human beings forge in the smithy of their souls, to the contrary, comes at the cost of anguish, blood, sweat and tears. Garrick's "Ode to Shakespeare," then, was composed not in honor of a man; it eulogizes a member of a fictive pantheon, one coarse enough to batten on trumpery as if it were nectar and ambrosia. Garrick's Shakespeare is an idol indeed, a bathetic vampire feeding on our "low-crookèd curtsies and base spaniel fawning." (*Julius Caesar*, III, i, 43)

Interspersed between Garrick's spoken lines are choral airs set in anapestic tetrameter, a metrical drone nowadays reserved for giggling babes. *'Twas The Night Before Christmas* and *Yertle the Turtle*, for example, are cast in anapestic tetrameter. ("So Yertle the Turtle King lifted his hand / And Yertle the Turtle King gave a command.") One need hardly add that Shakespeare's preferred line is iambic pentameter. Only once did he ever stoop to anything as monotonous and juvenile as anapestic tetrameter, and that was to satirize the euphuistic cadences of his era in *Love's Labour's Lost*. (See, Boyet, II, i, 234-249.) Yet Mr. Garrick was sufficiently inspired to rush in where bards fear to tread. *Attendez* — and be edified:

Thou soft-flowing Avon, by thy silver stream
Of things more than mortal, sweet Shakespeare would dream,
The fairies by moonlight dance round his green bed,
For hallow'd the turf is which pillow'd his head.

The love-stricken maiden, the soft-sighing swain,
Here rove without danger, and sigh without pain,
The sweet bud of beauty, no blight shall here dread,
For hallow'd the turf is which pillow'd his head.

Here youth shall be fam'd, for their love, and their truth
And chearful old age, feel the spirit of youth;
For the raptures of fancy here poets shall tread,
For hallow'd the turf is that pillow'd his head.

Flow on, silver Avon, in song ever flow,
Be the swans on thy bosom still whiter than snow,
Ever full be thy stream, like his fame may it spread,
And the turf ever hallow'd which pillow'd his head.

That "turf" would be truly "hallow'd" which shielded Shakespeare's ears from such twaddle. One should not, of course, condemn the poor meter, but the callow fellow who had the unmitigated chutzpah to use it in connection with the author of *Hamlet*. Evidently the lusty 18th century cultivated dozens of such dishwater ditties. Alas, each age must be accorded its Tin Pan Alley. But David Garrick was no Robbie Burns (1759-1796), who at ten years of age was too young to star at the English Jubilee. (See, "Flow Gently, Sweet Afton," 1786). On the subject of the metaphorical integrity and metrical superiority of Shakespeare's verse (as opposed to the fancy doggerel of later periods), the reader is invited to see, The Schiller Institute, online: "John Dryden's Attack on Shakespeare: The Origin of 'Sing-Song' Recitation in English Poetry," by Paul Gallagher, *Fidelio*, Vol. VI. No. 3, Fall, 1997.

* * *

Could we safely immure Mr. Garrick and his tacky confederates in the deepest bolgia of history, it would be one less headache. After all, the Russians buried their Chernobyl. The problem is, as someone once put it, past is prologue. (*The Tempest*, II, i, 258) Garrick's stentorian

Ghost still stalks the land. For you see, 2016 is the 400th anniversary of the Stratford man's death, and the Shakespeare Industry is cranking up for a rollicking good time, as we learn in the Saturday, 5 January 2013 issue of *The Observer*. According to Mr. Ewan Fernie, Chair of Shakespeare Studies at the Shakespeare Institute, University of Birmingham, the European union is being urged on this august occasion to bestow upon Shakespeare the title of "Poet Laureate of Europe" and — you guessed it — to present a spanking new version of Garrick's Ode! And why not? Has anything changed in 247 years? Part of the problem with the European Union, says Mr. Fernie, is that it has been conceived as a mere economic instrument. "What we want to do is suggest that there's a great cultural tradition to affirm and promote." Indeed, who would ever think about "economics" when there's so much damn money to be made? Never mind what Shakespeare did to the French in the Henry plays. The frogs are grown up now, and obviously in a mood to forgive and forget. Let's invite them to the party, it will be Field of Cloth of Gold all over again! Observed *The Observer* nostalgically:

> Garrick put Stratford on the international map, transforming its former image as a provincial town. The programme took Shakespeare to the streets, with fireworks, a procession of characters from the plays and a masked ball. But the highlight was Garrick's delivery of his Ode, which hailed Shakespeare as "the god of our idolatry." Set to music by Thomas Arne, it was performed by the orchestra and chorus of Drury Lane Theatre. In 2016 the performers will be the Ex Cathedra Choir and the Orchestra of the Swan.

Yes, history is poised to repeat itself (again). Curious about all this, we emailed Prof. Ewan Fernie on September 26, 2013 to learn of his progress, and were pleasantly surprised to hear back from him next day. Unfortunately, it seems the funding needed to campaign for Shakespeare as Poet Laureate of Europe was withheld. However, earnest talks with the European Union are proceeding, Prof. Fernie assures us. So, while 2016 may not see our Shakespeare crowned Europe's Poet Laureate, there is little doubt we'll be able to thrill to the fireworks, masked balls, the million chips hewn from the eternal Mulberry tree, and, best of all, a world-class broadcast of David Garrick's inimitable Ode. Jubilee: The Sequel is sure to reap megabucks for those poetry-loving merchants of County Stratford. Princess Kate and hubby Prince William will be putting in cameo appearances, as flashbulbs pop. Make your reservations early. Our own reservations are on record.

Well, there's precedent for all this. Long before 1769, Pope Leo X became famous selling "Indulgences" (that is, get-out-of-Purgatory-free cards) to obtain the cash to refurbish a drooping St. Peter's Basilica. At his installation in 1512 the brash new Pope leaned over and chortled to his brother, "Since God has given us the Papacy, let us enjoy it." And, *mutatis mutandis*, shall we not relish our bard? Let the welkin roar!

Naturally we double-checked our Almanacs to see if there's a pesky comet in the neighborhood which might spoil the fun in 2016. And — wouldn't you know it? — there is! The National Aeronautics and Space Administration had three proposals pending for 2016, one being the placement of a "Comet Hopper" on Comet 46P/Wirtaner to do whatever one does while perched on a comet. Sadly, there wasn't enough money and the "comet hopper" was scrapped. But 46P/Wirtaner must be presumed on its way and undaunted.

What, then, says our poet of things to come? Do we not whistle in the dark?

> These late eclipses in the sun and moon
> portend no good to us. Though the wisdom of nature
> Can reason it thus and thus, yet nature finds itself
> scourged by the sequent effects. Love cools, friendship
> falls off, brothers divide; in cities, mutinies; in countries,
> discord; in palaces, treason; and the bond cracked
> 'twixt son and father. This villain of mine comes under
> the prediction: there's son against father. The King
> falls from bias of nature; there's father against child.
> We have seen the best of our time. Machinations,
> hollowness, treachery, and all ruinous disorders follow
> us disquietly to our graves.
> (*King Lear*, I, ii, 101-112)

And pace cynical Edmund, goes not Shakespeare's heart with this? Old Lear is the victim of flatterers, after all. (I, i, 147-148) Mindless festivities tempt fate, like the super-elegant Titanic in its petty girth and pride, oblivious to a menacing sea. What if our giddy laughter goes not unheard, our vanities be seen? The gaze of Nemesis is pitiless and cruel.

WORKS CITED:

Martha Winburn England, *Garrick's Jubilee*, Ohio State University Press, 1964.

Spiritual Shakespeares, Ewan Fernie, ed., Routledge, 2005.

Ewan Fernie, personal correspondence, September 27, 2013.

Paul Gallagher, "John Dryden's Attack on Shakespeare: The Origin of 'Sing-Song' Recitation in English Poetry," The Schiller Institute, *Fidelio*, Vol. VI, No. 3, Fall, 1997.

David P. Gontar, *Hamlet Made Simple and Other Essays*, New English Review Press, 2013.

The Observer, January 5, 2013.

Dr. Seuss, *Yertle the Turtle*, Random House, 1958.

William Shakespeare, The Complete Works, 2d ed., S. Wells and G. Taylor, eds., Clarendon Press, Oxford, 2005.

Peter Walch, "David Garrick in Italy," *Eighteenth-Century Studies*, Vol. 3, No. 4 (Summer, 1970).

4

Unreading Lear

I. Lear

"Once upon a time, far away and long ago, there lived an old king with three daughters . . ."

$\mathcal{I}$t has been observed that in both its *Folio* and *Quarto* versions, *King Lear* bears features of a fairy tale. It has even been suggested that its archaic source is the tale of *The Goose Girl at the Well.* While the simplicity of nursery legend can render a symbolic form conceptually and emotionally accessible, there are drawbacks. The familiar folkloric theme of two wicked elder sisters taking advantage of a younger sibling lulls one into a mood of reduced scrutiny. For just an instant we occupy a world of innocent make-believe, only to have it dissolve and fade before our eyes in searing tragedy. This scenario is not without consequences. For the fairy tale aura which suspends disbelief *ab ibitio* short circuits critical judgment. Too much tends to be taken for granted.

Consider the issue of Lear's "darker purpose." (I, i, 36) Why "dark"? What is darker here? Is it not prudent to make a donation *inter vivos*? Is not a coronation of sons-in-law arranged by the reigning monarch a matter for rejoicing? ("This crownet part between you." I, i, 139) The reason we don't know what he means by that locution is because we never felt the need to investigate it. We merely accept it in our wide-eyed innocence. If audiences and readers just embrace tragedy's premises as youngsters do the implausible tenets of bedtime stories, is valid criticism even possible?

Switch on the lights.

Do we not recall the anguish of King Richard II when he and Bolingbroke clutched either side of a single crown? (IV, i, 172- 179) Were those two able to rule jointly? Theirs is the sort of government Lear proposes.

Lear's avowed purpose is to make for a smooth administrative transition at his retirement and to prevent civil strife. (I, i, 43-45) Yet there is no evidence that Britain has been afflicted in recent memory with dissension or discord. The text alludes to no uprisings or rebellions. One individual has ruled successfully. Now as he steps down he would secure the common weal and shield it from "future strife" by . . . *dividing* it into three parts, each to be ruled by a fractious son-in-law. As internal policy that is unthinkable. One doesn't take a perfectly fine fiefdom that's been functioning well under a firm and conscientious monarch and chop it into three regions each under the control of an envious satrap — certainly not as a device for securing the blessings of domestic tranquility. Remember the travails of Rome under Octavius, Lepidus and Antony. Balkanization is precisely the opposite of order and cohesion, an incomprehensible and fatal blunder. It's pathological. Contrary to the conventional wisdom, then, the story of Lear's madness begins not with the flatteries of Regan and Goneril and Cordelia's silence, but earlier, in the context of the dramatic action, with the King's big bang, his act of wanton disruption of his own realm. Instead of preventing future quarrels, this bizarre fragmentation fairly guarantees them. The sovereign has taken leave of his senses. Yet no one protests the vivisection of the nation, no one except the Fool, whose protest comes too late. (I, iv, 140-147) As in *Sleeping Beauty,* everyone is dozing. Courtiers, theater goers, readers and our most astute literary critics all snore soundly as anarchy is ignited. Seeds of destruction are already germinating as oaths of love and fidelity are sworn. From the moment he sweeps onstage with his retinue Lear is wandering in infernal darkness.

Catastrophe is born not on the heath, then, but in privy chamber. And the way we respond to opening events colors our reading of the entire play, our reception and understanding of its characters. Though the world thinks so, Lear doesn't become "mad" at the discourtesies of Regan and Goneril. He's already laboring under mental and emotional thunderheads as he utters his first syllables onstage. Bedlam is there, and all the devils loose. So long as *King Lear* is viewed as the story of a lunacy induced by cruel, ungrateful daughters it is fatally misunderstood. Instead of diagnosing the patient, we form an alliance with him and attribute his "madness" as he does to mistreatment by his daughters

(Cordelia included). Lear's insanity seems strangely infectious.

What is to be done? The defective product must be recalled, better late than never. Our reading must be scrapped. What *King Lear* demands of us is nothing less than a thorough purgation or scouring, an unreading of what we've been taught by misguided pundits and authorities, our eminent textual somnambulists and zombies. What follows are a few notes towards the demolition and reconstruction of this remarkable work of dramaturgy. Our aim is to inoculate against any interpretation which turns out to be an extension of the dream itself.

This old man is not merely retiring, nor is his action a conventional donation or setting of a trust account. He is abdicating the throne. "We will divest us of both rule, interest of territory, cares of state . . ." (I, i, 49-50) Speaking to Cornwall and Albany, he makes the performative utterance: "I do invest you jointly with my power, pre-eminence, and all the large effects that troop with majesty." (I, i, 130-132) With the disposal of Cordelia to the King of France, it is finished. Lear is no longer King of Britain. But query, having divested himself of rule and invested Cornwall and Albany with all his territories — no longer King — by what authority does he banish the Earl of Kent? It would seem the cares of state still are his. How so? Has Lear gone gently into that good night of superannuation, or does he still cling stubbornly and unaccountably to the vestments of "authority"? (I, iv, 30) This issue becomes central and runs throughout the play, a play in which the only King of Britain is Lear. Yet his legal status and the nature and character of the regime following his seeming resignation are rarely if ever taken up by commentators. He remains, curiously, more "foul" than fish.

As for the apportionment of the kingdom, there is more that deserves our attention. The heirs' speeches and their father's bequests form a comic triptych reminiscent of the rigged casket game in *The Merchant of Venice*: each daughter must pronounce a *pro forma* expression of filial devotion, the most fulsome of which will win the grand prize. In other words, the "thirds" to be bestowed are not of the same measure. The grossest flatterer will emerge the victor. The outcome, however, is predetermined by Lear, who is known to favor Cordelia, the youngest. (I, i, 82-83; 1, i, 123; 1, i, 289) There is ambiguity in Lear's locution, "our largest bounty." (I, i, 52) Goneril bursts forth with the expected rhetoric and receives a large portion of land. Regan does the same and receives: "this ample third of our fair kingdom, no less in space, validity, and pleasure than that conferred on Goneril." (I, i, 80-83) For Cordelia, however, has been set aside "a third *more opulent*" than what the elder siblings have received. (I, i, 86) Do we need to be hit over the head to apprehend this? Is this the sort of magnanimity reasonably calculated to avoid dissension and civil strife? It is pompous lunacy. For suppose that Cordelia fails to outshine her sisters in her praise and affection for the father. What then? Regan and Goneril have already been given smaller "thirds." If Cordelia's own verbiage does not outdo that of her rivals, she'll still have the largest portion and Lear will be covered in embarrassment. That is the risk he takes, a part of his "darker purpose."

There is something else, too. Lear and Cordelia are not strangers to one another. If she is his favorite he knows her well. This is his own child, after all. But her personality is quite unlike that of her sisters. Is not Cordelia Cordelia? Why then affect surprise and dismay when she responds as anyone familiar with her might expect? Is Kent surprised? Is the Fool? Not at all. What surprises them is Lear's reaction on hearing Cordelia's predictable modesty. The whole episode is a charade burdened by favoritism and short-sighted inequities. Calling disproportionate thirds "equal" was already courting disaster.

This brings us to confront directly the relationship of Lear and Cordelia, a topic gingerly sidestepped by standard literary criticism. The King is plainly a widower. Goneril and Regan live with their husbands, Albany and Cornwall. It must be presumed that as late as the first scene Cordelia still resides in the patriarchal manse, without the intercessory ministrations of a mother. Given her subdued and Spartan demeanor, is their encounter in Scene 1 the first time Cordelia's simplicity and honesty would have been experienced by Lear? Impossible. Only if received on the level of a fairy tale would his actions make the slightest sense. Transposed to real life we would need to re-think the whole matter. Additional information would help. When did Lear's wife die? How long has he been a single parent? No nurse is mentioned, as there is, say, in *Romeo and Juliet*. What's going on? Why would he expect *any* words from Cordelia out of keeping with what he has always heard from her? Moreover, it is important to ask, given her sober demeanor and Lear's importunacy, how in the world did she become his favorite? Favorite? Shouldn't that be Regan, who tells everybody within earshot that there is nothing whatsoever in life that gives her pleasure and satisfaction except her "dear highness' love"? (I, i, 69-76) Logically the truly beloved daughter should have been Regan. How would Cordelia have prevailed? What is implied in such a narrative?

As Bruno Bettelheim argued in 1976 in *The Uses of Enchantment* (Vintage, 2010), exposure to fairy tales, which treat many violent and upsetting themes, has a salutary and instructive effect on youngsters, allowing them to process in a safe way considerations that might cause distress if approached through a reality-based discourse. *Little Red Riding Hood*, for example, which involves a little girl's adventures with mother, grandparent, woodsman and a talking animal, touches in its symbolic depths the problematic motif of the good (nurturing) father versus the bad (threatening, sexually aggressive) one, allowing the infant imagination to achieve balance and integration through the resolution of the narrative. This may also be true of great works of art such as *King Lear* which are based in part on such pictorial materials. Get out the fluoroscope. Behind Lear's rage at Cordelia, then, can we not discern the outlines of an unhealthy propinquity of father and daughter? This has led to unidentified physical and emotional intimacies. As Elizabeth Archibald comments, "the great majority of literary incestuous fathers are rulers." (Archibald, 146) As Lear "crawl[s] toward death," he wishes to do so unburdened of the guilt those intimacies have occasioned. (I, i, 40-41) The mechanism for achieving this relief is two-fold: first, he will give to the child whose privacy and integrity he has invaded and whose psychic closure he has triggered an early and jumbo-sized inheritance capable of attracting the suitor of her choice, and second, her projected praise and thanks will serve as a token of the forgiveness he needs so badly. This is the rationale that lies in the "dark" recesses of the royal mind as it fashions the pageant of Lear's departure.

The theme of royal incest is familiar to Shakespeare scholars, and was discussed in some detail in *Hamlet Made Simple and Other Essays,* particularly in Chapters five, eleven and eighteen. The secondary literature on this subject is voluminous, and includes, *inter alia*, *Incest and the Literary Imagination*, Elizabeth Barnes, ed., *Partriarchy and Incest from Shakespeare to Joyce*, by Jane M. Ford, *Incest and the Medieval Imagination*, by Elizabeth Archibald, *Elizabeth's Glass,* by Marc Shell, Bruce Boehrer's *Monarchy and Incest in Renaissance England: Literature, Culture, Kinship and Kingship* (Philadelphia, 1992), and of course Otto Rank's classic, *The Incest Theme in Legend and Literature* (The Johns Hopkins University Press, 1991).

Professor Jane M. Ford draws attention to the 1954 psychoanalytic commentary of Arpad Pauncz in *American Imago* (40, 51-83):

> One critic found the father/daughter theme so central to this play that he coined the term "Lear Complex," the complex that focuses on the "neglected" adult to define the attach-

ment of the older member of the oedipal twosome. In spite of a wide variety of interpretations of Lear's initial decision to divide his kingdom, the most immediate result will be to force his periodic presence on his daughters, and Cordelia, whom "He always loved most," is the only one left unmarried." (Ford, 41)

In other words, had Cordelia succeeded in receiving her patrimony but not in obtaining a husband for some period of time, Lear's progress of roistering would have been conducted in her residence as well as those of her sisters. Looking at the denouement of the action, "Lear reaches the depths of human despair and endurance until he finds his peace in death as a smug bridegroom in blessed union with his youngest daughter as the bride." (Ford, 42) Indeed, her father says to Cordelia, "we two alone will sing like birds i' th' cage." (V, iii, 9) He then begs her forgiveness. The bitter and melancholy end uniting Lear and Cordelia in death comes to appear as the telos of an imprudent father's original intrusions. Can we not perceive the traces of the leer behind the Lear? Prof. Ford adds, "Lear's words at the height of the storm have suggested his sense of guilt" (Ford, 42):

> Tremble thou wretch,
> That hast within thee undivulgèd crimes
> Unwhipped of justice; hide thee, thou bloody hand,
> Thou perjured and thou simular of virtue
> That art incestuous . . .
> (III, ii, 50-54)

If we apprehend the rationale for viewing Lear's bond with Cordelia as incestuous, and responsible for his strange behavior in the first scene, then his "madness," that is, his emotional imbalance or dysfunction, must long antedate his rude treatment by adult daughters. In the absence of a wife, he seems to have displaced conjugal impulses from spouse to child, with disturbing consequences. Edmond speaks tellingly of "unnaturalness between the child and the parent." (Quarto, Sc. 2, 139) Cordelia's tight-lipped utterances limiting her filial affection to her duty reflect not mere modesty and a distaste for flattery, but an inability or unwillingness to give implicit sanction to her father's intrusive attentions during her childhood. Thus we also come to understand what has never been previously explained, that is, how and why Cordelia became her father's "favorite." The pieces finally fit together. Leave out incest and our play becomes a child's tale in which incomprehensible adults disport themselves in funny ways we must simply accept rather than challenge.

What is wrong with absorbing *King Lear* as myth, dream or fairy-tale, then, is that readers and viewers tend to do so unconsciously, making them unaware of contradictions, complexes and aporias whose resolution could have led to a better understanding. If the text were approached properly, we would be in a better position to address the issue of the nature and meaning of Shakespearean tragedy in general. Lear suffers. But why and how? Is that suffering fraught with religious significance? Does it serve to illustrate the self-redemptive capacities of "man," as suggested by principles of humanistic criticism? Or, as seen by such schools as "cultural materialism," is Lear's problematic best grasped in terms of social, historical and political factors, as, *e.g.*, claimed by Prof. Jonathan Dollimore and his supporters? Implicit in what we've seen above is that the bulk of contemporary criticism which purports to analyze *Lear*, whether from Christian, humanist or "radical" standpoints, is profoundly misguided. *The Tragedy of King Lear* must be approached with a clear recognition of the structure of his original desire as it is then related to the "darker purpose" declared in the first scene. Waxing emotional occlusions result in a dysfunctional plan of national dismemberment misapprehended as humble retirement from the stresses of leadership. We will find reason to conclude that, far from being illuminated by the tropes of Christianity, post-Christian humanism or cultural materialism, *King Lear* stands in a tradition of classic tragedy which descends from Ancient Greece, emphasizing the blindness of human existence to its own role in the fashioning of *Wyrd*, and the deferral of recognition until the last unavailing moment.

Progress in this venture depends most importantly on our capacity for unreading of the play and setting aside partisan analyses in the service of preconceived ideas such as Christianity and Marxism.

Having in summary form accomplished a preliminary unreading of Lear, we can advance to the figure around whom the action swirls, Edmond, and delve him, as he deserves, to the very root.

II. Edmond

Consider the following speeches.

(1)

Thou, nature, art my goddess. To the law
My services are bound. Wherefore should I
Stand in the plague of custom and permit
The curiosity of nations to deprive me
For that I am some twelve or fourteen moonshines
Lag of a brother? Why 'bastard'? Wherefore 'base',
When my dimensions are as well compact,
My mind as generous, and my shape as true
As honest madam's issue? Why brand they us
With 'base' with 'baseness, bastardy —base — base' —
Who in the lusty stealth of nature take
More composition and fierce quality
Than doth within a dull, stale, tirèd bed
Go to th' creating a whole tribe of fops
Got 'tween a sleep and wake? Well, then,
Legitimate Edgar, I must have your land.
Our father's love is to the bastard Edmond
As to th' legitimate. Fine word, 'legitimate'.
Well, my legitimate, if this letter speed
And my invention thrive, Edmond the base
Shall to th' legitimate. I grow, I prosper.
Now gods, stand up for bastards!

(2)

Hear, nature; hear, dear goddess, hear:
Suspend thy purpose if thou didst intend
To make this creature fruitful.
Into her womb convey sterility.
Dry up in her the organs of increase,
And from her derogate body never spring
A babe to honour her. If she must teem,
Create her child of spleen, that it may live

And be a thwart disnatured to torment her.
Let it stamp wrinkles in her brow of youth,
With cadent tears fret channels in her cheeks,
Turn all her mother's pains and benefits
To laughter and contempt, that she may feel —
That she may feel
How sharper than a serpent's tooth it is
To have a thankless child.

The first speech is Edmond's soliloquy from Act I, scene 2 of *The Tragedy of King Lear*. (I, ii, 1-22) A mere two scenes later we find Lear's scathing denunciation of his daughter Goneril. (I, iv, 254-269) (Importantly, versions of both speeches are also featured in the Quarto version: Sc. 2, 1-21; Sc. 4, 268-283) These passages are set so close together that it is nearly impossible to encounter the second and not be put in mind of the first—impossible, that is, as long as we're not in an hypnotic trance. Both Edmond and the king invoke the identical personified goddess, "nature," to whom they voice bitter complaints having to do with parent-child relationships. Edmond, nominally regarded as the younger and illegitimate son of the Earl of Gloucester, declares himself the votary of this goddess of nature, soliciting her approval and assistance in his plot to ruin his elder half-brother, the noble Edgar. He would induce the Earl to disinherit this legitimate son, leaving his estate to the sole remaining issue, Edmond. While Edmond feels betrayed by the customs of patrimony, legitimacy and primogeniture, Lear also, for his part, experiences betrayal in the matter of his own succession: after disinheriting his youngest, Cordelia, bequeathing the totality of his estate to his two elder daughters, he discovers neither will honor the tacitly approved stipulation in his donation *inter vivos*: that he be permitted the privilege of a monarch's "progress," a use or partial life estate burdening the demesnes of Regan and Goneril, the beneficiaries being himself (and *per accidens* his retinue of a hundred boisterous knights). Legally, on abjuration of the condition, that donation could have been nullified by the donor. But Lear hasn't sufficient rationality to retain counsel. So obdurate and condescending is Goneril that he flies into a towering rage eclipsing his anger at Cordelia's modesty. He calls on the goddess of nature to either render Goneril sterile, or mar any child of hers with ruinous malice. He too is an initiate in the cult of nature. In both cases, the "father against child" leitmotif identified by Gloucester (I, ii, 9) is featured: Edmond (the son) excoriates his putative father, while Lear rails against his daughter. The very same divinity is petitioned for favor and support. While Shakespeare often employs a subplot as a foil for the main action, here the Gloucester subplot is elevated as the plot's logical converse.

The question facing any serious reading of this play is: as it was not required by or essential to the subplot, why does Shakespeare draw this high degree of similitude in the speeches of Lear and Edmond? After all, the king is the misguided and beleaguered protagonist of the drama, Edmond its fanatical villain. Can both be friends of "Nature"? Could the goddess be sufficiently bountiful—or schizoid—to look with favor on the prayers of two such hostile supplicants? Here is the stuff of tragedy indeed. But perhaps the parallelism is meant to signal an hitherto unconsidered relationship. As these figures occupy different generations and exhibit a single remarkable trait, it would not be unexpected to raise the question of natural affinity. In this play the "unnatural" (mentioned in the text eight times) is the subtext of the theme of "nature" (mentioned 34 times). Might Edmond be regarded as Lear's son, not Gloucester's? That would seem impossible, ruled out by the *dramatis personae* we are provided: "Edmond, bastard son of Gloucester." Not once is any alternative even mentioned in the text. And yet . . . a door is left tantalizingly ajar. For all we are coyly told by Gloucester is that "this young fellow's mother . . . [conceived] him" and "had . . . a son for her cradle ere she had a husband for her bed." (I, i, 12-15) His mother was fair, "and there was good sport at his making."(I, i, 20-21) Grant that Gloucester had an extra-marital affair with Edmond's mother, does this entail that he, Gloucester, is the actual father? His sole comment is oddly oblique: "His breeding, sir, hath been at my charge. I have so often blushed to acknowledge him that now I am brazed to't." (I, i, 8-10) The facts are somewhat uncertain, and possibilities loom. For nothing is presented to rule out successive or simultaneous affairs of this unnamed woman with Gloucester and Lear. Gloucester's insinuation that he raised the child as his own ("his breeding hath been at my charge") hardly sets the matter to rest. Did Edmond's mother ascertain with absolute certainty the identity of the babe's father? Treat the issue realistically. She may have known scarce more than we do about it. Or, was she dissembling? Might a royal scandal have been avoided by placing a monarch's bastard in the Gloucester household? Shakespeare goes far out of his way to demonstrate an uncanny likeness of young man and elder. And when we check their backgrounds we find nothing to rule out an account starkly at odds with the official genealogy. Edmond is "acknowledged" by Gloucester, but obviously kept in the background, so much so that he is wholly unacquainted with the Earl of Kent. (I, i, 25) How could that be? Had Edmond resided at court or its purlieu, their paths would have crossed any number of times. Yet the claimed father confesses of his "son," "He hath been out nine years, and away he shall again." (I, i, 31-32) "Out"? He's been "out" nine years? Where? Pursuing a post-doctoral fellowship at Wittenberg? Acquiring street smarts in the alleyways of London? There is no evidence of anything in particular. Gloucester's blushing words suggest that Edmond has been kept under wraps in some undisclosed location for the better part of a decade and that Gloucester is footing the bills. If he has never met the Earl of Kent, can he be familiar with the other nobles of Lear's court? If not, he has been deliberately hidden away, and it is reasonable to think twice about the received view of his parentage. Edmond is a mystery.

If one views the play as a study of hate and anger, we might ask what the fountainhead of those emotions could be. There is nothing rancid or hostile in Gloucester. It is King Lear, rather, with his umbrageous outbursts, tantrums and rages who stands as the source of bitterness and gall. Goneril and Regan, with their seemingly inborn resentments and envies, plainly inherit their father's truculence and spite. Edmond too is a bird of that feather. In that regard it is worth noticing that Lear's experience on the stormy heath climaxes his "madness," leaving him visibly chastened and repentant. What about Edmond? He is a rogue to be sure, but unlike so many villains in Shakespeare who go to their graves with imprecations on their lips (*e.g.*, Aaron in *Titus Andronicus*), Edmond, like Lear, has a dramatic change of heart at the play's end, and not only confesses his guilt but attempts to atone with a final good deed, trying to save Lear and Cordelia from assassination. Is not this the very pattern of Lear's own life? The old King carouses in debauchery with his knights; Edmond carries on affairs with Lear's daughters. Both men swear fealty to nature, and by what appears to be a common character, each follows a trajectory of moral transgression leading them at the end to metanoia and acts of charity. In that respect it is interesting to attend to Edmond's last invocation nature, which sounds a different note:

> I pant for life. Some good I mean to do,
> *Despite of mine own nature.* Quickly send,
> Be brief on it, to th' castle; for my writ
> Is on the life of Lear and on Cordelia.
> Nay, send in time.
> (V, iii, 218-221)

Ironically the scion of "nature" here disavows the implacable goddess and in so doing recovers his deeper nature. Lear's madness culminates in comparable sentiments.

We may also observe that if Edmond is the son of Lear, he is the half brother of wicked sisters Regan and Goneril. This too prompts intriguing questions. We might accept that one of Lear's malicious daughters should become enamored of him, but when both compete for his affections one looks for some explanation. Let's assume for sake of discussion that Edmond is actually Lear's misbegotten son, and has been "out" for nine years, lately returning to the court. There is something about him that strikes their mutual fancy. What is it? His disenchantment with Gloucester, Lear and Cordelia? But that is politics, not usually a launching pad of concupiscence. There is for these ladies a certain *je ne sais quoi* about Edmond which sets him apart and piques their interest. Or, continuing with French, call it *déjà vu*. They seem to recognize him. The reader may recall in *The Winter's Tale* Leontes' excitement at seeing the long lost Perdita, his daughter, whom he believes to have been destroyed. Though she is young and in the company of Florizel, the son of Polixenes, he is instantly smitten by her. In Robert Greene's play *Pandosto*, the narrative model of *The Winter's Tale*, the King of Bohemia falls into incestuous love with daughter Fawnia. When she marries Prince Dorastus, Pandosto in his unknowingly incestuous desire commits suicide. It is clear that the aspect of consanguinity is part of daughter Fawnia's allure. Or, think of the extraordinary love shared by Posthumus Leonatus and Imogen in *Cymbeline*. They are not blood kin, but King Cymbeline has raised the orphaned Posthumus from an early age as daughter Imogen's "playfellow" (I, i, 145-146), meaning he is her *de facto* brother. As a young adult, Imogen finds she can love no man other than him. In *Pericles* the Prince of Tyre is entrapped by King Antiochus who is having a liaison with his own buxom daughter. Pericles flees Antioch after solving the Oedipal riddle, but is vengefully pursued by Antiochus, which pursuit symbolizes Pericles' own obsession with incest. He weds Thaisa, who appears to die giving birth to their daughter Marina during a storm at sea. Though Pericles comes to assume that his wife and child have both perished, Thaisa finds her way to the Temple of Diana, while Marina winds up in a brothel in Mytilene. At one point late in the action, Pericles' sad peregrinations take him to Mytilene, where his daughter, who has escaped the sex industry, has become a teacher. The implication is that only a series of fortuitous accidents prevented father and daughter from becoming intimate with one another. (See, "The

Flight from the Incestuous Father," in Archibald, 146ff., see also, 95-96)
Of course, incest figures largely in *Hamlet* as well. (Gontar, 377ff.) And
in *The Tempest* an all-powerful magician who dallied with a witch has
had, for most of Miranda's life, the craft to make her sleep instantly at
the snap of his fingers. He charts her every move and gives her almost
no information about her past and the mother she had back in Milan.
Put under the moral/psychological microscope, the Prospero/Miranda
relationship appears suspiciously incestuous. (See, Gontar, 83ff.) These
examples show that incest is central in a number of Shakespeare plays;
failing to consider its possible function in *King Lear* may be an unhelp-
ful oversight.

Furthermore, in treating issues of paternity, in at least three major plays Shakespeare seems to hint broadly that a father/son relation
obtains where superficial reading might not detect it. (Gontar, 83ff.,
139ff., 377ff.) These are *Julius Caesar*, *The Tempest* and *Hamlet*. Shakespeare based *Julius Caesar* on Plutarch, the Roman historian. Plutarch
plainly credits the account in oral history that Brutus is the illegitimate
son of Julius Caesar, a view Shakespeare does not expressly mention
but reinforces and supports through his dramaturgy, showing resemblances between these men and including a diptych of conjugal scenes
whose implications can hardly be sidestepped. In *The Tempest*, perhaps
the most cogent analysis implies that Caliban is Prospero's son through
Sycorax. Caliban inherits his father's lofty poetic syntax. (Gontar, 97-98)
And there is no denying the resemblance of Prince Hamlet to Claudius. (Gontar, 390-393) It is not surprising, then, to discover that Shakespeare builds into the structure of what is arguably his greatest tragedy
another potent but camouflaged filial relationship, that of Lear and his
illegitimate son, Edmond. Those who would respond to this argument
with skepticism are urged to go back, read the plays in question again,
followed by a study of *Hamlet Made Simple and Other Essays*. Things
will fall into place—unless popular preconceived ideas should charge
into the breach.

III. Cultural Materialism v. Shakespeare

At the very least, then, the foregoing considerations call for a thorough unreading of *King Lear*, a spring cleaning in which the staid accretions of 400 years get pared away, allowing us to face the text anew, from
the ground up. Yet that is precisely what scholarly treatments, whether conservative or revisionary, so rarely provide. This is all the more

astonishing and disappointing in the case of those movements priding themselves on their ability to shake the foundations and challenge stale renderings of Shakespeare. Let us turn to one of the most highly acclaimed of the left-of-center exegetical schools, cultural materialism, to see what it makes of this work. What we will discover is that it too is hobbled by its own intellectual (*i.e.*, Marxist) presuppositions and commitments, and is thus of limited utility when what is sought is a thorough dismantling and fresh exposition of *Lear*. Though it professes to decrypt the text and circumvent the inevitable censorship of the literary establishment, cultural materialism turns out to be yet another elitist and institutionalized recycling of clichés and truisms surrounding our greatest tragedy. Mere substitution of socialist premises for feudal ones yields nothing of significant value.

Since 1984, the leading exponent of cultural materialism has been Jonathan Dollimore. Though he has distanced himself from academe, his *Radical Tragedy* continues to exert a wide influence. It launched a broad attack on humanism, essentialism and universalism in Jacobean literary studies, relying on such renegade figures as Bertolt Brecht instead of traditional authorities such as A. C. Bradley and Harold Goddard. In the place of humanist readings exhibiting characters whose suffering leads to essentially redemptive or transcendent transformations, Dollimore sought to feature the "political" significance of the play. However, as *Radical Tragedy* passed through several editions, its own standpoint seemed to undergo something of a sea change. In a long introduction to the third edition, a strenuous effort was made to tack about and forge links to humanism, and at the same time raise fundamental questions about the very validity of literary criticism. In coming to terms with Dollimore's vision of *Lear*, then, we need ponder two distinct phases of his development, first, his campaign to discredit essentialism and humanism, and set forth the meaning of *King Lear* in political terms; and second, we must assess the effectiveness of his alliance with humanism, and his attack on criticism itself. We will find that Dollimore so compromises cultural materialism that it becomes in fact a weaker rather than a more powerful variant of the humanism it opposed; instead of exposing the dangerous and subversive element in *King Lear* (identified above), cultural materialism settles for a trite and maudlin version of Lear's development which reminds us of nothing so much as the conversion of Dickens' Ebenezer Scrooge from miserly curmudgeon to Mr. Smiley Face. Though at the end the stage floor is littered with the dead, cultural materialism's acceptation of the play gives us a diminished *Lear* and drains the play of all tragic sense.

Dollimore considers only two traditionalist options: *King Lear* is either a Christian exemplar or an illustration of later humanistic philosophy. Stiff-arming the former view, he maintains that the humanistic exegesis is just as unsatisfactory, for it too commits the unpardonable sins of metaphysics, essentialism and mystification.

> What follows is an exploration of the political dimension of *Lear*. It argues that the humanist view of that play is as inappropriate as the Christian alternative which it has generally displaced—inappropriate not least because it shares the essentialism of the latter. I do not mean to argue again the case against the Christian view since, even though it is still sometimes advanced, it has been effectively discredited . . . . The principal reason why the humanist view seems equally misguided, and not dissimilar, is this: it mystifies suffering and invests man with a quasi-transcendent identity whereas the play does neither of these things. In fact, the play repudiates the essentialism which the humanist reading of it presupposes. However, I do not intend to replace the humanist reading with one that rehearses yet again all the critical clichés about the nihilistic and chaotic 'vision' of Jacobean tragedy. In *Lear*, as in *Troilus*, man is decentered not through misanthropy but in order to make visible social processes and its forms of ideological misrecognition. (Dollimore, 190-191)

Must we be impaled on the horns of this dilemma? That would entail an absence of alternatives.

What is most significant about this sort of manifesto is that while it conceives of itself as rational discourse, it is nothing of the kind. What we have instead is a series of cavalier and unsupported claims. We are to explore the "political dimension" of *Lear*. This neatly begs the question. Is there such a thing? The only truly political aspect of the play lies in the protasis in which a demented monarch demolishes his own kingdom. This act of gross misgovernment is never once mentioned. Yet it is the fatal vivisection of Britain from which spring the fundamental conflicts of the play. In the name of "politics," Dollimore misses the signal political event in *Lear*.

Look at the rhetoric, impatient and peremptory. Instead of reasoning, we reject and "repudiate" ideas uncongenial or inexpedient. There is no need of facts and tiresome deductions. By mere wafture of an autocratic hand we sweep aside inexpedient ideas. The Christian view is already "discredited." The play "repudiates" essentialism. Nor does Dollimore "intend to replace" humanism with the "clichés" about nihilism. What are those "clichés" if not important notions we'd rather not take up? An entire hermeneutical movement is tossed aside as of no moment. Arguably, the history of "nihilism" can be traced as far back as the *Book of Job.* Why bother about that? According to the authoritative Shakespeare search engine, *Open Source Shakespeare,* "nothing" is mentioned in *King Lear* 29 times, and 590 times in the corpus. That alone would seem sufficient to induce some scholars to have a look at nihilism in Shakespeare and *King Lear,* but not the busy Mr. Dollimore, expert in "Jacobean drama." (Versions of the play date back to 1594.)

It is proposed that a humanist reading should be discarded because "it shares the essentialism" of Christianity. To say that humanism is deficient because it rests upon or entails "essentialism" has force only if it is explained what "essentialism" is and why it should not be embraced. But such tiresome exercises are left to *hoi polloi.*

This critic appears to derive his general philosophical outlook from the epigram of Jean-Paul Sartre that "existence precedes essence." (Dollimore, 195) Has that gnomic utterance now become an article of common sense and generally accepted standard of intellectual evaluation? Are we all French existentialists now? If so, it's convenient, for it relieves us of the need to rationally defend our positions. In the bibliography is listed a single book by the prolific Sartre, a collection of popular essays titled *Politics and Literature.* But those topical compositions do not reflect the ontological thinking of Sartre, merely his congenital antipathy towards the bourgeoisie. The relationship between "essence" and "existence" in Sartre's systematic philosophy is set forth in *The Transcendence of the Ego, Being and Nothingness,* and other metaphysical works, all unmentioned. If existence "precedes" essence, does that mean that essence is of no account? This is as clear as mud. Few today are willing to roll up their sleeves and tackle Sartre's major treatises. It's so much easier to drop a few philosophical slogans from the 1950's (yesterday's clichés) as the foundation for critical judgments about the meaning of *King Lear.* Does attaching the label "essentialism" to an idea mean that it is *ipso facto* disposed of? *Non sequitur.* Sartre also penned a well-known monograph called *Existentialism is a Humanism* (Yale University Press, 2007 edition). Query: If Dollimore is an existentialist of the Sartrean variety, he must be a humanist, but how can this be if "humanism" is a species of the "essentialism" he demonizes? Does reading Lear "politically" mean that we must find in Shakespeare an altruist? A Whig? An egalitarian? Before leaping to such conclusions it would be appropriate to assimilate the totality of Shakespeare, starting with the episode of the Jack Cade rebellion in *King Henry VI,* Part Two, IV, ii- ix.

Mr. Dollimore claims that humanism fails to account for *King Lear* because while it accords to "man" a "quasi-transcendent identity," the play itself doesn't do that. Its message is exclusively one of economic redistribution and social uniformity. Yet in *King Lear* "the gods" are mentioned 29 times, and always in relation to us, to human beings. When the gods "throw their incense on our sacrifices" (V, iii, 20-21) does Shakespeare refer to Magna Carta? Wouldn't it seem that in a play setting human existence in perpetual relation to divinity it might be inferred that that aspect of human life which addresses it is consistent with a quasi-transcendent humanity, that is, a characteristic not shared by tuna fish and tree toads? At wit's end with his malicious and conniving daughters, Lear cries, "You see me here, you gods, a poor old man / As full of grief as age, wretchèd in both." (II, ii, 446-447) Shall the silence of those gods be construed as the play's denial of "quasi-transcendent identity"? Why? Where poor humanity is concerned, Mts. Sinai and Olympus have never been especially loquacious, and a large part of their fascination and mystery has been their stark verbal economy. Consider again the *Book of Job.* Before the Lord speaks out of the whirlwind (Job 38) does Job renounce divinity? No. Neither does Lear. The gods are mute, but still extant is that part of the human spirit which had addressed them previously, that part of us keenly aware of death, fate and our terrible responsibility for terrible deeds. That is indeed our transcendent identity and it is this which *Lear* constantly discloses to us. Listen to Gloucester: "As flies to wanton boys are we to the gods; They kill us for their sport." (IV, i, 37-38) What sound these notes if not our oppressed and frustrated transcendence? Yet Dollimore insists that the play repudiates the "essentialism" of humanism. Sadly, no definition of essentialism is proffered, but we are assured whatever it is, it is a myth. And yet, how can we speak of "man" and "the gods" without reference to some key ontological or defining features, to nature? This, after all, is the principal focus of the play, not redistribution of the wealth in society or the weaving of social safety nets.

Few would deny that there are moments on the heath when Lear is brought face-to-face with unaccommodated man, and the ineluctable miseries of the human condition. Rude circumstances compel him to notice and reflect on injustice. And the sequent insights have importance. But those experiences and insights cannot be inflated to support the grotesque proposition that the basic meaning of the tragedy is mere rank and social inequality. Nor is Dollimore the sort of post-structural writer who would dispense altogether with the idea of inherent textual significance. For by his own admission he is in search of the essential and enduring meaning of "Jacobean" drama, and insofar as he pursues that project he tacitly accepts the essentialism he would "repudiate." Indeed, to presume that *King Lear* has "a meaning" that can be set down as the most important and valid way in which the play should be received by us is to affirm—not deny—humanism and its traditions. As our common lives possess a certain character, so do our texts have meanings. And *malgré lui*, Dollimore evinces these meta-philosophical tenets. At the end of his discourse there is a brief acknowledgement of Jacques Derrida, the French philosopher who has been understood as teaching that texts lack independent meanings. Though he cites Derrida approvingly, it isn't clear that *Radical Tragedy* is consonant with a deconstructionist approach to literary criticism.

For Derrida, the term "man" as commonly used is a vestigial leftover from religion, a relic of the onto-theological vision which progressive thinkers now so blithely surpass. (Dollimore, 257ff.) And as was observed in *Hamlet Made Simple*, there is wisdom in this project, for a moment's reflection will show that there is no such thing as "man," any more than there is such a thing as "cow" or "shark" or "polar bear." There are various species, to be sure; zoologists write properly of "Homo sapiens," the species, not "man," an onto-theological term which stood in relation to "God." For us, there are just people, cows, crabgrass, polar bears, etc. "Man" means far too much to be viewed with anything but suspicion. Yet ironically, throughout *Radical Tragedy*, with all its steadfast denial of any quasi-transcendent aspect of human existence, its author talks endlessly and earnestly about "man," the key term of art in the vocabulary of humanism. Can there be "man" and not humanism? Could anything be more obvious than the failure of *Radical Tragedy* to break free from the orbit of the very humanism it derides?

There is another curiosity. In the introduction to the second edition, it is declared that "I shall be concerned mainly (not exclusively) with feminism and gender critique . . . ." (Dollimore, xiv) It will not be thought churlish to wonder how an elite member of the male sex who constantly refers to the human race as "man" can be regarded as a sound proponent of—and advocate for—"feminism and gender critique." Why go on and on about "man" and never talk of people? It's surprising he doesn't employ the corollary term "woman," as we find, *e.g.*, in Nietzsche. We have abundant evidence in the second edition that, for all his condescending rhetoric about humanism, patriarchy and sexism, this writer is plainly unable to extricate himself spiritually and intellectually from the legacy of humanism and its various subtexts. Though fond of exposing the alleged contradictions of conventional "ideologies," he remains blind to his own ideology (a blend of retread Marxism and post-structural shibboleths) and its inconsistencies.

Nothing can be deemed "radical" which fails to acknowledge and come to terms with its own roots. That central precept of philosophy, so vital to the thinking of Socrates, Descartes and Husserl, seems to have escaped the view of cultural materialism. Mr. Dollimore remains a purveyor of mere doctrine, not dialectic, a fact of which he seems to feel inordinately proud. What would Karl Marx say? Like Brutus, Mr. Dollimore cannot perceive his own face, only the visages of his *bêtes noires*, (*Julius Caesar*, I, ii, 53); we, like Cassius, must serve as a looking glass to help him to detect his own contradictions as clearly as those he would "repudiate."

Let us return to the attempt made in the pages of *Radical Tragedy* to shore up the counterintuitive notion that Shakespeare's *Lear* is "above all, a play about power, property and inheritance." (Dollimore, 197) Think about that. "Power" here means not intensity of will and character, but legal authority. What would it take to render that suggestion persuasive? Not only would all credible rival readings need to be shown wrong-headed—which is far from accomplished—but textual evidence would need to be adduced to demonstrate that "power/property/inheritance perspective" provide greater coherence than any other theme in the play. Dollimore boasts that he reads for "discoherence," but when criticism founders in its own contradictions it fails to be helpful. For it is one thing to identify textual strands related to power/property/inheritance, but quite another to establish that such a concatenation of "political" materials is what the tragedy is "about."

Here is a compendium of textual citations offered:

1. "You houseless poverty (III, iv, 26): Oh, I have ta'en/Too little care of this!" (Dollimore, 191)

2. "What, hath your Grace no better company?" [Glouces-

ter] (III, iv, 138) (Dollimore, 192)

3. "Like Lear, Gloucester has to undergo intense suffering before he can identify with the deprived. When he does so he expresses more than compassion. He perceives, crucially, the limitation of a society that depends on empathy alone for its justice." (Dollimore, 192)

4. "[Gloucester] is led to a conception of social justice (albeit dubiously administered by the 'Heavens') whereby 'distribution should undo excess,/ And each man have enough'" (IV, i, 64-65) (Dollimore, 192)

5. "Lear experiences pity mainly as an inseparable aspect of his own grief: 'I am mightily abus'd. I should e'en die with pity/To see another thus' (IV, vi, 46-47) His compassion emerges from grief only to be obliterated by grief. He is angered, horrified, confused and, above all, dislocated." (Dollimore, 192-193)

6. "But what of Cordelia herself? She more than anyone else has been seen to embody and symbolise pity. But is it a pity which significantly alters anything? To see her death as intrinsically redemptive is simply to mystify both her life and death. Pity, like kindness, seems in Lear to be precious yet ineffectual. Far from being redemptive it is the authentic but residual expression of a scheme of values all but obliterated by a catastrophic upheaval in the power structure of society." (Dollimore, 193)

7. "Significantly, existential humanism forms the basis even of J.W. Lever's *The Tragedy of State*, one of the most astute studies of Jacobean tragedy to date. On the one hand Lever is surely right in insisting that these plays 'are not primarily treatments of characters with a so-called 'tragic flaw', whose downfall is brought about by the decree of just if inscrutable powers . . . the fundamental flaw is not in them but in the world they inhabit: in the political state, the social order it upholds, and likewise, by projection, in the cosmic state of shifting arbitrary phenomena called 'Fortune.'" (Dollimore,

194)

8. "If the Christian mystifies suffering by presenting it as intrinsic to God's redemptive and providential design for man, the humanist does likewise by representing suffering as the mysterious ground for man's self-redemption; both in effect mystify suffering by having as their common focus an essentialist conception of what it is to be human: in virtue of his spiritual essence (Christian), essential humanity (ethical humanist), or essential self (existentialist humanist), man is seen to achieve a paradoxical transcendence: in individual extinction is his apotheosis. Alternatively we might say that in mystifying closure of the historical real the categories of idealist culture are recuperated." (Dollimore, 194)

9. "Cordelia's real transgression is not unkindness as such but speaking in a way which threatens to show too clearly how the laws of human kindness operate in the service of property, contractual and power relations." (Dollimore, 198)

10. "In the act of renouncing [Cordelia], Lear brutally foregrounds the imperatives of power and property relations." (Dollimore, 199)

What in all of this—or the like—establishes cultural materialism as a force to be reckoned with in Shakespeare criticism? Has "humanism" been debunked? In what way? As we suspected, and as we will see below, Dollimore is himself a confessed humanist. We already see his mode of expression ("man") is humanist in tone and character. He is committed not to post-structuralist indeterminacy, but to a theory of interpretation which presumes that literature has a discrete meaning and that reader and critic are tasked with unfolding it. Is that radical? References in *King Lear* to the political repercussions or implications of various actions undertaken by its characters do not warrant the conclusion that the play is *über alles* "political." As most of Shakespeare's plays involve royalty and nobles one could on that basis argue that all of them are fundamentally "political." Would such a claim have any practical meaning—or leave things precisely in their *status quo ante*? If *King Lear* is essentially a "political" tragedy per Jonathan Dollimore, doesn't that commit him to the very essentialism he claims to reject? Can a play be essentially about "man" while "man" himself has no discernible being?

One of the reasons we are given for turning away from "humanism" is that it seems to find redemption in human suffering. This is set down as reprehensible mystification. If Lear achieves a state of grace or redemption, it is found in his acceptance of the responsibility he bears to those commoners whom he so often took for granted, not to his agonies on the heath. Had Lear to do things over again, he would be a kinder, gentler overlord. In that lies his redemption. In other words, as said above, cultural materialism is precisely that: material. It reduces a great tragedy to a Dickensian fable. We'll buy Poor Tom a Christmas goose to salve our conscience.

Some "humanist" scholars may have written that Shakespearean heroes are redeemed by suffering as such, but that untenable contention can be dispensed with without discarding humanism. To see suffering as such as redemptive is nonsense, unless we turn life into purgatory: the dross of callous indifference is burned away by our own trials and tribulations. Whatever we may think of that view, it isn't Shakespeare's. Dollimore is right to challenge it, but wrong to imagine that pointing to its problematic quality means humanism must be scanted. Grant that Cordelia's death is not "intrinsically redemptive;" is that the end of humanism? How so? Let's be clear about this. In Act One, Cordelia is imprisoned by the past. She can barely breathe a word. The vain recitation she is commanded to produce would replicate and sanction the abuse she has suffered at her father's hands. All she can muster at that point is silence. In Act Five we find a different Cordelia. She has witnessed her father in the latter stages of spiritual decomposition, and this has touched her heart, the heart implied in her name. Love and compassion melt away the ice within, and she is free to speak again, much as Hermione does after sixteen frozen years in the last act of *The Winter's Tale*. As she embraces her father and gives to him the forgiveness she had been unable for so long to afford, she is redeemed and so is he. And the wonder is that such evident things, the very elements of life, would need to be explained to mature adults. The play is tragic because redemption comes too late, at the cost of heroic lives.

Is the disinheritance of Cordelia best understood as the "brutal foregrounding" of "imperatives of power and property relations"? In that one pseudo-painterly trope we see everything wrong with "radical tragedy." First of all, no real attempt is made by *soi-disant* "radicals" to come to terms with or even closely examine the plainly dysfunctional relationship of father and youngest daughter, as explored above. No attention is paid to the fact that Lear's mood is "dark" well before the contre-temps triggered by Cordelia's silence. What might that "darker purpose" portend? The opportunity to get at the meaning of Lear's primal rage is waived. What generates the tragedy is not power and property, but (1) Lear's anxieties over his possessive relationship with Cordelia, for which he hopes to be absolved by her, and (2) his destructive splintering of his realm, an act not expressive of property relations but transgressive of them. Lear (like Queen Elizabeth I) declines to designate a successor to the throne and heir to his possessions, and his attempted solution, to shatter the kingdom, hastens the civil war sought to be avoided. The laws of property and inheritance are not "foregrounded" but flouted by him.

And what of the "tragic flaw"? Is Lear immune to that royal syn-drome? For Dollimore that is just another sophomoric cliché. But is it? In *Pericles*, Shakespeare finally "foregrounds" the issue of incest for the first time. But it was always there. Shall we assume that *Lear* is wholly innocent of that pathology? How then account for that vexing "darker purpose"? A strong case can be made that he has encroached on his youngest child's privacy and integrity, and conceived an imbalanced and impossible inheritance as compensation. Further, he has apparently spawned a malicious bastard driven by an unconscious urge to bring ruin to the kingdom and death to its rulers. Is this not the pith of trag-edy? We have a tragic flaw when we are undone not by our vices but by our virtues. Lear is a titanic figure, a ruler of prepossessing strength and ardor, who, in his dotage, still has enough vital energy to carouse with a hundred knights in perpetual bacchanal. In his children we see limned in diminished outlines the figure of the father. What was promethean life force in Lear reappears in Regan, Goneril and Edmond as impulsive venality. Lear rages against the gods, against Cordelia, Kent, and against his two ungrateful elder children, sure that they are the villains who are destroying Britain and himself. Only at the end, having lost his wits in the whirlwind, does the fury sufficiently abate that he can perceive that it was his own metastasizing expansiveness that undid him. Though in the introduction to the third edition Dollimore talks about Nietzsche and the diremptive agonies of the life force, in his actual reading of the play he is blind to what is actually good and what is evil in its awful protagonist.

Tragedy is a Greek invention. How does one write an entire book on "Jacobean" tragedy—or tragedy of any sort, for that matter—and never once mention the ancient Greeks? The false dilemma proffered by

Radical Tragedy is either to view *King Lear* from a Christian perspective or that of later humanism. Problem is, there were monumental tragedies long before these two outlooks ever appeared. Can we fairly discern tragedy's purport by restricting ourselves to the Christian/humanist rivalry? What happened to Sophocles, Aeschylus and Euripides? What about Aristotle? Of these four, only Aristotle is mentioned: once. The Oedipus trilogy involves a king. Is it above all "political" too? Oedipus remains an important figure in the western psyche not because of the popularized misunderstandings of a Viennese physician, but because he is emblematic of our conception of human existence, an existence that embraces both good and evil. And this is the view Dollimore begins to approximate only in the introduction to the third edition of his book.

Oedipus lives in the service of knowledge and power, and, as his answer to the riddle of the Sphinx shows, he is a symbol of human existence. It is his quest for knowledge and power which makes him great, but conduces simultaneously to his demotion. It is his destiny as the human embodiment of the life force to extend his field of dominance universally, including the celestial realm, the recognized source of mankind. He would consciously avoid that fate, but is driven to it. As Oedipus unwittingly kills his father Laius, so does mankind kill off the gods in this our modern world. Replacing them as the rulers of the earth, human kind enters into an unrestricted and exploitative relationship with maternal earth or nature which we would remake in our own image, a fundamentally incestuous act. But the incestuous aspect of that relationship must go unrecognized, and does so to this day, by everyone from Dick Cheney to Greenpeace. It is not, then, that the hero has a "tragic flaw" over and against his virtues. Rather, our human virtue (*virtu*) itself is our vice in relation to both ourselves and our world. The knowing life force bursts onto the fields of heaven and earth and scorches the cosmos. Human existence stands in a fundamentally incommensurable relation to what Karl Jaspers called "the Encompassing." To put it succinctly, we can grant that human existence bears a noble aspect, but it is a noble aspect fundamentally aggressive and dysfunctional in relation to everything else.

Jonathan Dollimore seeks to understand a profoundly Greek tragedy, *King Lear*, in terms of the very bourgeois proprieties which he finally comes to condemn in the introduction to the third edition of *Radical Tragedy*. Lear is brought down by his own evil. But that is not the evil of a 19th century London miser. Lear isn't a homunculus like Willy Loman or Ebenezer Scrooge. His evil is colossal, that of a giant, of Prometheus or Oedipus, prototypes of all humanity. Faced with imminent death, he would self-destruct and take all down with him. His death will then be *Götterdämmerung*, the wastage of an entire world. That is the destiny of *der Wille zur Macht*, the basal ontological contradiction. In spawning Edmond he gives rise to Nemesis, which is a mirror of his own expansive possessiveness. That Edmond is the double of Lear has been observed previously. Consider the comments of Doug Eskew.

> I argue . . . that Lear and Edmond are doubled through their mutual desire to rule the verge and mete out a personal justice. Moreover I argue that this doubling is reflected not simply in early modern contrariety—here, the play's hero and villain, its most legitimate character (the king) and its least (a bastard). Most important for *King Lear*, these characters are doubled chiastically both in language and in movements on the stage. With a significant exception, Lear and Edmond do not occupy the stage at the same time, but their paths cross once at the play's beginning and once at its end—times when Lear alternatively loses the verge and then, briefly, regains it. (Doug Askew, "Soldiers, Prisoners, Patrimony: King Lear and the Place of the Sovereign," *Cahiers Elisabethains* 78, Autumn, 2010, 29)

On the heath, Lear is stripped of all dissemblance. The king stands unaccommodated as other men are, yet he remains, in his own words, "every inch a king." Taking Gloucester as the mortal half of Lear, the blindness of Gloucester recalls the act of Oedipus in putting out his eyes on learning the truth about himself. It is the Sophoclean moment. That Sophoclean moment also may be seen in Lear's heath. Earl Showerman, discussing *Timon of Athens*, and citing A.D. Nutall writes:

> We have the pattern of the humiliated hero, apart from society, in a wild place. To him come, in succession, various figures to upbraid him or (more importantly) to solicit his aid. It is a pattern of great power in Sophocles, strong in Aeschylus, less strong in Euripides. In *Oedipus at Colonus* the protagonist, blind, filthy, and ragged is visited in turn by Theseus, Creon and Polynices, who wishes to raze Thebes to the earth in vengeance for the wrong he has suffered. Oedipus, for all his strange aura of sanctity, is more like Timon than

one expects. He embraces his own wickedness and curses those who have wronged him. (Earl Showerman, "Timon of Athens: Shakespeare's Sophoclean Tragedy," *The Oxfordian*, Vol. XI, 2009, 107)

King Lear and *Timon of Athens* both stand in the tragic tradition initiated by Sophocles' restatement of Greek myth, with its uncanny apprehension of the perennial overreaching of mankind. Our "nobility" in relation to the beasts prompts a lethal narcissism which reveals the actual ignobility of a species which recognizes and then traduces the gods. As they are no longer wanted by humanity, not recognized, why should they not withdraw? In the tragic moment given to us by Shakespeare, the hero lifts tear-filled eyes to heaven and implores "deaf heaven" (Sonnet 29, line 3) to hear his cries. Do the gods see our torments and remain impassive? Are they indifferent when Cassius bears his bosom to the thunderstone? (*Julius Caesar*, I, iii, 45-52) Are they blind to the ravishment and disfiguration of Lavinia? Or do they take sadistic delight in our pain? (*Titus Andronicus*, IV, i, 58-59) Can they bless Pericles with wife and child and then proceed to snatch them away, even in the very act of giving? (*Pericles*, Sc. 11, 23-26) Why are the gods silent? We have taken their place. That is the meaning of tragedy, for a man cannot usurp the powers of heaven and at the same time insist on divine succor. As long as Lear rages at the lightning, thunder and the gods, he is still laboring in delusion. Only when fully chastened on the heath, having recovered the guilelessness of childhood, only when he can smell mortality in his very palm, can he finally admit that the fault was his all along, and beg for forgiveness.

> Be your tears wet? Yes, faith. I pray, weep not.
> If you have poison for me, I will drink it.
> I know you do not love me; for your sisters
> Have, as I do remember, done me wrong.
> You have some cause; they do not.
> (IV, vi, 64-69)

> When thou dost ask me a blessing, I'll kneel down
> And ask of thee forgiveness . . . .
> (V, iii, 10-11)

But cultural materialist dogma would presume to teach us that

King Lear is "above all, a play about power, property and inheritance." (Dollimore, 197) When Lear and Cordelia meet for the last time, is there discussion of "power, property and inheritance"? No. Why not? If the play were "above all" about those things, they would be acknowledged by the principals, who strangely have nothing to say about them. When Shakespeare uses the idiom "above all," in the only tragedy sufficiently majestic to stand alongside *Lear*, it is to refer to our awareness of who and what we are ("this above all, to thine own self be true," *Hamlet*, I, iii, 78) and our fidelity to that. Lear has been false to himself and hence false to others, especially Cordelia and Kent. He listens to his "Fool" but does not heed him, and besides, the Fool's counsel comes tardily. *King Lear* is, above all, a play about age and love, and a king who loved "not wisely but too well." (*Othello*, V, ii, 353)

The ideological agenda of "cultural materialism," its preoccupation with social and political issues, could only serve to blind its proponents to the rudiments not only of literature but of life itself. Seeking to engage Cordelia in his own self-deception in Act I was a stratagem doomed to failure. Her silence implied she would not serve as an accomplice in her father's bad faith. At that point Lear was running amok, in flight from reality, well before Cordelia's excommunication. He was in flight from the truth of what he had done to her, in flight from his fatherhood of Edmond, so much his double, in flight from his inability to manage his kingdom, in flight, in the final analysis, from death itself. And it may strike thoughtful readers as rather fantastic that one could seek to comprehend *King Lear* in any context and say nothing whatsoever about an old man's thanatophobia, to which all that he does in the play is in one form or another an eloboration and a response. (I, i, 41)

Dollimore's dilemma with respect to the play in question may be summed up as follows: a so-called "political" rendering of tragic action appears to supplant a transcendent humanist reading, but in light of this critic's own recognition of promethean evil and the necessity of coming to terms with it, mere liberal sentiment falls short of the play's felt immensities. Lear is transformed from egotistical and overbearing patriarch to an elderly and infirm man who, in his traumatic fragmentation, catches a glimpse of the downtrodden subjectivities he had missed as ruler. His sore conscience is plain. Humanism's religious legacy is to "mystify" the oppressive relation in which ordinary men and women stand to the state, its grand possessors and the predominant social caste. For Dollimore, *King Lear* is Shakespeare's attempt to involve the audience in Lear's spiritual conversion and opening up to the awful plight of the Other and the oppressive inequities which keep him down.

But the problem is that *Lear* is not about inequities but iniquity. While nothing could be more apparent than his trauma and gross transformation, the so-called "political" interpretation thereof which looks to preoccupations with property and inheritance seizes a mundane theme merely eleemosynary and distal. Taking seriously the introduction to the third edition, it's hard to see how anyone could rest contented with such thin gruel as conventional leftist editorializing. For instead of one species of "humanism" we now have two, "weak" and "strong." In its attenuated form, humanism is little more than criticism's congenital revulsion over the harsh actualities of life, death, desire and malevolence. Weak humanism idealizes and so must conceal and camouflage that which is resistant to idealization. Strong humanism would represent a return to Nietzsche's recognition of the notorious intimacy of good and evil. In light of the perilous propinquity of the noble and the ignoble (*e.g.*, the curious partnership of God and Satan in the *Book of Job*) any respectable criticism of Shakespearean tragedy should foreground the tragic hero's nisus towards Mr. Hyde, the darker self, inclusive of lust, avarice and the will to power. This is not done.

The apparent shift in thinking from weak humanism to strong, is in the view of sympathetic critic Ewan Fernie, evidence of Dollimore's adroit capacity to change his mind. ("Dollimore's Challenge," *Shakespeare Studies*, 1/1/07) But what seems to be a "change of mind" turns out to be more accurately characterized as original ambiguity and contradiction. The shift to humanism in the introduction to the third edition reprises the earlier reliance on the concept of "man" and the willingness to seek a univocal exegesis of the text. It is thus no surprise that on reflection this writer would strive to retain the force of humanism while broadening the attack to target the enterprise of literary criticism itself. But in reverting to an essentially Nietzschean philosophy, which finds in human existence an inextricable jointure of good and evil, nothing is done to set aside the trivialization and reduction of *King Lear* which shrinks a sublime drama to a liberal campaign platform. Perhaps more than any other tragedy in the canon (with the possible exception of *Macbeth*), *King Lear* is an investigation into the correlations of nobility and naughtiness. Recall Sartre's maxim that "Nothingness lies coiled in the heart of Being like a worm." Having declared that the duty of criticism is at all times to fathom the good/evil connection, and have the courage to face the unruliness at work in the soul of the tragic hero, one would expect that this precept would directly if retrospectively impact the treatment of *King Lear*. Yet all is left in the *status quo ante*, as though Nietzsche had never been.

By every measure, this drama has been portrayed as an unflinching and sublime portrait of the fate of maleficence unchained, one which reports on our deepest doubts about the decency and integrity of "Homo sapiens." But though collectivism and the redistributive economic agenda may be prized, Lear's untoward demeanor and conduct cannot be reduced to mere overreaching and the acquisition of better social graces. Had the needed unreading been carried out, Lear's "darker purpose" might have been traced to its depths. One cannot call for a criticism which has the courage to recognize in literature the monstrous traits of human existence, our profound venality, yet fail to follow through by demonstrating the moral monstrosities of Lear. To call for radicalism in Shakespeare studies while declining to confront the major tragic hero in all his unappetizing glory, what is this but to "have the voice of lions and the act of hares"? (*Troilus and Cressida*, III, ii, 85)

To illustrate, here is a cross section of pertinent epigrams from the *Introduction to the Third Edition*, followed by comments.

1. "Arguably everything that distinguishes us as human—I should say everything that distinguishes us as humane—involves repression, suppression, and exclusion." (xxxii)

2. "Those who love art the most also censor it the most." (xxxii)

3. "What is censored is art in which 'what is central is a dangerous knowledge of the dissident desires which threaten rather than what confirms psychic and social equilibrium.'" (xxxiii)

4. "Time and again . . . the most compelling individual creations [characters] are the ethically confusing ones." (xxxiii)

5. "[T]he malcontents in Elizabethan . . . tragedy are charismatic anti-heroes whose deep insight into corruption derives from their willing complicity with it . . . ." (xxxiii)

6. "To comprehend something thoroughly enough is to move closer to it and to thereby risk entering its thrall . . . .

[A] knowing identification of becomes an imaginative identification with." (xxxiv)

7. "For some, this is not a matter of regret: we are most ourselves when we are in this destructive, dangerous, and suffering state of freedom, violating the restraints' very history which has produced us. This was Nietzsche's view, which he attributed to Shakespeare." (xxxv)

8. "*Macbeth* does not warn against hubris and ambition; on the contrary, it affirms their attraction." (xxxvi)

9. "Shakespeare and his guardians fall on opposite sides of Nietzsche's great divide between those who affirm the life force and those who turn away from it." (xxxvi)

10. Dollimore cites Pascal's remark "anticipating Nietzsche" that "there is a kind of evil which often passes for good because it takes as much extraordinary greatness of soul to attain such evil as to attain good." (xxxiii)

11. Sigmund Freud is then cited:

"[T]he objects to which men give most preference, their ideals, proceed from the same perceptions and experiences as the objects they most abhor, and . . . they were originally only distinguished from one another through slight modifications . . . . Indeed . . . it is possible for the original instinctual representation to be split in two, one part undergoing repression, while the remainder, precisely on account of this intimate connection undergoes idealization." (xxxxiii)

Now it should be fairly clear that to read the *Tragedy of King Lear* as a "political" object lesson is to engage in censorship, a censorship Dollimore would (or should) condemn. What is featured as Lear's "greatness" is that "noble" branch of him which can be traced back to the roots of a blindly aggressive life force. Lear is thus a classically confused ethical being, but one left unplumbed by recent criticism. Of course, the reason we are reluctant to attribute actual evil in the classical sense to Lear is that it would entail the fault of humanity as such. We are a bit squeamish about that. To revise Ingmar Bergman's *The Seventh Seal*, it is not Death against whom we play chess, but ourselves.

In the 21st century we measure out our lives with coffee spoons. From the immensity of a leviathan cosmos we hide behind mathematical doodles. Reports of genocide are sandwiched between commercials for toothpaste and dandruff shampoo. Everything about our world is shrinking, miniaturized and micro-chipped. The result is that, despite our best intentions, we cannot be great, or even take the measure of the great. Greatness is to us incommensurable and thus incomprehensible. But *Lear* is Life writ large. The 18th and 19th century philosophers got it right. The play gives out on the panorama of the sublime, in "man" and "nature." Here is some of what we have left behind in our brave new world.

> All that is literature seeks to communicate power; all that is not literature, to communicate knowledge. When in "King Lear," the height, and depth, and breadth, of human passion is revealed to us, and, for the purposes of a sublime antagonism, is revealed in the weakness of an old man's nature, and in one night two worlds of storm are brought face to face— the human world, and the world of physical nature—mirrors of each other, semi-choral antiphonies, strophe and antistrophe heaving with rival convulsions, and with the double darkness of night and madness, when I am thus startled into a feeling of the infinity of the world within me, is this power, or what may I call it? (De Quincey, 273)

If we were now to arrange the three exegetical positions we have examined, they would with respect to *King Lear* form the following hierarchy of adequacy.

    i. Strong humanism (Nietzsche, De Quincey, Hesse)

    ii. Weak humanism (traditional essentialism)

    iii. Cultural materialism ("political" exegesis)

As the least adequate of the three, cultural materialism must content itself with collecting Lear's earnest new insights about the common people: *e.g.*, "I really should have paid more attention to the living conditions of those serfs. Their cottages have such substandard drainage." Bromides like this can hardly rise to the stature of tragedy but remain at best mere sentiment and melodrama. Old TV episodes of *Lassie* functioned at that level. Only insofar as cultural materialism rises to the level of weak humanism does it attain any metaphysical backbone (essence) and recognize the possibility of redemption through self-knowledge and admission of responsibility. At the highest level we finally see the commonality of good and evil, and taste for ourselves the attractions of the will to power. Here is the realm of Nemesis and catastrophe. That is the realm of tragedy.

Platitudinous presentations of *King Lear* tend to identify Edmond as the stereotypical "bad guy," allowing us to view Lear himself with a larger and illicit measure of sympathy. This is perhaps the crux of the misreading. It is, again, melodrama. Edmond is a dramaturgical device which tends to siphon off Lear's morally repellent features, leaving a profoundly evil monarch washed clean in our crocodile tears. Questioning this way of approaching the play is thus an important aspect of "unreading." When we realize that there is still something decent about Edmond we discover at much the same time that avuncular old Lear is the real bastard, one who senses in some corner of his mixed up consciousness how dreadful he has been to his family and country and goes quite crazy. Everything we learn in the *Introduction to the Third Edition* points in the direction of a far greater depth and depravity in this demonic soul than cultural materialism could ever deliver.

Lear is Midas. He has touched his daughter and turned her into gold, still and mute, resentful of his attentions. Her heart is cold. Later he learns compassion, it is true, but Dollimore is correct that the meaning of tragedy cannot be found in this. The tragic moment arrives when we come to see the fault not in those we demonize (Cordelia, Regan, Goneril, Albany, Cornwall, *et al.*) but in ourselves. But as a being carved from the adamantine life force itself, Lear must suffer destruction to learn, and the lesson arrives too late. As Cordelia sees the flickering of compassion in the embers of her father's soul, her own compassion, long withheld, comes forth, granting him the absolution he demanded so clumsily in Act One. Today's "true minds" would present *King Lear* complacently as a cantankerous but lovable geriatric patient with advanced dementia, the victim of elder abuse wrought by his daughters. There is our modern fairy tale, how we see ourselves now, helpless consumers of Prozac, Zoloft and Wellbutrin. In designating *King Lear* as principally a drama of "power, property and inheritance," cultural materialism betrays the life force and diminishes all of us. The tragic fate of tragedy in the 21st century is that there is no tragedy.

WORKS CITED:

Elizabeth Archibald, *Incest and the Medieval Imagination*, Oxford, Clarendon Press, 2001.

Thomas De Quincey, *The Opium-Eater and Other Essays*, Ward, Locke & Co., Ltd., n.d.

Doug Askew, "Soldiers, Prisoners, Patrimony: King Lear and the Place of the Sovereign," *Cahiers Elisabethains*, 78, Autumn, 2010.

Bruno Bettelheim, *The Uses of Enchantment*, Vintage, 2010.

Jonathan Dollimore, *Radical Tragedy*, 2d ed., Duke University Press, 1993.

_____, _____, 3d ed., Palgrave Macmillan, 2010.

Ewan Fernie, "Dollimore's Challenge," *Shakespeare Studies*, January 1, 2007.

Jane Ford, *Patriarchy and Incest from Shakespeare to Joyce*, University Presses of Florida, 1998.

David P. Gontar, *Hamlet Made Simple and Other Essays*, New English Review Press, 2013.

Jean-Paul Sartre, *Existentialism is a Humanism*, Yale University Press, 2007.

William Shakespeare, The Complete Works, 2d ed., S. Wells, G. Taylor, eds., Oxford, Clarendon Press, 2005.

5

Malvolio's Defense

I. Recollections of Mr. Malvolio

*T*welfth Night has always been one of Shakespeare's most popular and beloved comedies. Our affection for this brilliant and endearing play extends to its characters, including its villain, Malvolio, the steward of Lady Olivia. This is unusual. Audiences are not drawn to bad guys, and no one goes out of his way to speak on behalf of *Much Ado About Nothing*'s Don John or Duke Frederick in *As You Like It*. What makes Malvolio different? Our response to him is reminiscent of how we felt as youngsters about Captain Hook in Barrie's *Peter Pan*, or Eeyore in Milne's *Winnie-the-Pooh* stories. These were adversaries, to be sure, but they didn't seem to unsettle. No one loves *Othello*'s Iago or Aaron in *Titus Andronicus*. Yet some of our most renowned critics have taken special pains to present Malvolio in a good light, or at least in the best light possible. And perhaps the leading question concerning *Twelfth Night* has always been about him, and how to account for his elusive charm. He is often regarded as a sort of grumpy grandfather. There's a part of us that wants to reach out to him and include him in our celebration of this lovely and touching comedy. The risk is that in seeking to rationalize Malvolio's appeal we may stray too far and gloss deficiencies which should count against him.

But how is he deficient? Let us count the ways.

1. Malvolio is hostile.

We are introduced in Act 1, Sc. 5 when Malvolio is asked by Olivia about Feste the jester, a clown who had been employed by her late father. Feste is disenchanted because his wit is not appreciated by Olivia, who is in interminable mourning for her recently deceased brother. These are the first words we hear from him.

OLIVIA

What do you think of this fool, Malvolio? Doth he not mend?

MALVOLIO

Yes, and shall do till the pangs of death shake him. Infirmity, that decays the wise, doth ever make the better fool.
(I, v, 69-73)

There is nothing in the text to account for this harshness. It sounds as though Malvolio harbors a death wish for a mere household entertainer. Notice that Olivia's inquiry is beneficent. She is suddenly pleased by Feste's humor and solicitude for her feelings about her brother, and notices that the clown's demeanor is improving. Instead of following her lead, the steward seizes the opportunity to denounce Feste, making an unpleasant scene. For one who professes dedication to her, this shows a surprisingly callous disregard for Lady Olivia. Taken aback by Malvolio's intemperance, Feste gives a witty counterpunch.

FESTE

God send you, sir, a speedy infirmity for the better increasing your folly. Sir Toby will be sworn that I am no fox, but he will not pass his word for twopence that you are no fool.

OLIVIA

How say you to that, Malvolio?
(I, v, 78)

Unfazed, Malvolio continues his unprovoked tirade.

MALVOLIO

I marvel your ladyship takes delight in such a
barren rascal. I saw him put down the other day with
an ordinary fool that has no more brain than a stone.
Look you now, he's out of his guard already. Unless
you laugh and minister occasion to him, he is gagged.
I protest I take these wise men that crow so at these
set kind of fools no better than the fools' zanies.

OLIVIA

O, you are sick of self-love, Malvolio, and taste
with a distempered appetite. To be generous, guiltless,
and of a free disposition is to take those things for
birdbolts that you deem cannon bullets. There is no
slander in an allowed fool, though he do nothing but
rail; nor no railing in a known discreet man, though
he do nothing but reprove.

FESTE

Now Mercury indue thee with leasing, for thou
speakest well of fools.
(I, v, 74-94)

Malvolio insults Feste for lack of intelligence and belittles those
who might appreciate his banter, that is, the nobility of the household
(Olivia, Sir Toby Belch, her uncle, and his good friend, Sir Andrew
Aguecheek). Of course, no one is responsible for their measure of intelligence. That is something to remember. And for a servant to deride the
houseguests in this manner is rude and impertinent. Finally, Malvolio
seems to think that on account of having been demoralized by a rival
clown, Feste is deserving of further humiliation in front of Lady Olivia.
That is logic twisted by hate.

Olivia's reaction is mild but direct. She chastens him for being so
self-centered, and points out that, after all, a jester's job is to poke fun at
dour people. Those jibes are not meant to hurt but to prompt courtiers

to lighten up. Unfortunately, Malvolio doesn't take the hint. Throughout the entire play he remains obdurate in his hostility and in fact says not one engaging or pleasant thing to anyone, except his fawning when duped into fatuous civility by Maria's prank. Confined to a dark house as a madman, he is importunate and for the moment a friend in need. Once at liberty he learns he's played the fool himself, and his rage knows no bounds. Though some find in this a tincture of humanity, it is nothing new, and merely underscores the anger we see him exhibit in Act 1.

2. Malvolio is petulant and dishonest.

Viola disguised as Cesario arrives at Olivia's house. Malvolio, never having seen this fellow before, announces him in gratuitously disparaging terms (I, v, 133-156). After hearing Orsino's message from Cesario and becoming infatuated with this youth, Olivia instructs Malvolio to catch up with him on the road and give him a ring and invitation to return.

MALVOLIO

(offering a ring)

She returns this ring to you,
sir. You might have saved me my pains to have taken
it away yourself. She adds, moreover, that you should
put your lord into a desperate assurance she will none
of him. And one thing more: that you be never so
hardy to come again in his affairs, unless it be to report
your lord's taking of this. Receive it so.

VIOLA

She took no ring of me. I'll none of it.

MALVOLIO

Come, sir, you peevishly threw it to her, and
her will is it should be so returned.

(He throws the ring down)

If it be worth stooping for, there it lies, in your eye; if
not, be it his that finds it.
(II, i, 5-16, following the Stratford Town Edition, 1904)

So what accounts for this patronizing and abrasive discourse? Viola has done no harm to him, nor has Orsino. Cesario is not a person of authority but a mere courier. What is the point of this proud man's contumely? The accusation that Cesario "peevishly threw" the ring to Olivia is a transparent fabrication, and the act of tossing it to the ground is ironic in light of Malvolio's use of the word "peevishly," which aptly describes his own disposition, not Cesario's. This ill deportment was certainly not authorized by Olivia, who, unbeknownst to Malvolio, has just fallen in love with Cesario. Out of Olivia's sight and hearing, Malvolio behaves disgracefully toward Cesario, this after being gently admonished by her for mistreating Feste.

3. Malvolio is resentful and accusatory.

In Act 2, Sc. 3, when Sir Toby, Feste and Sir Andrew sing noisy tavern ballads late at night, they are angrily chastised by Malvolio, who in the process unjustly accuses Maria of allowing or encouraging the disturbance.

MALVOLIO

Mistress Mary, if you prized my lady's favour
at anything more than contempt you would not give
means for this uncivil rule. She shall know of it, by
this hand.
(II, iii, 117-120)

What is the basis of this charge? It was Maria who first sought to make these three merrymakers keep quiet. ("What a caterwauling do you keep here!" II, iii, 69) In accusing her of complicity with this minor disturbance, Malvolio again either speaks recklessly out of ignorance or is deliberately mendacious. Not only does he lash out at Maria, he declares his intention to bear false witness as to her alleged misdeed to Olivia. It isn't hard to see that, lacking any capacity for enjoyment, relaxation or fellowship, Malvolio is envious and resentful of those who manage a modicum of happiness in life. Sir Toby hits the nail on the head.

SIR TOBY

Art any more than a steward?
Dost thou think because thou art virtuous
there shall be no more cakes and ale?
(II, iii, 109-111)

4. Malvolio is a snob and a gold digger.

This brings us to Act 2, Sc. 5.

The famous trick Maria plays on Malvolio, allowing him to find a letter apparently written by Olivia which makes him believe she is in love with him, reveals even more of his unfortunate personality. Through his monologue we are allowed to see that he regards himself as not only superior to members of the household staff, but to everyone else, including the aristocracy. Yet it is nobility he hankers after—for himself. He will take advantage of Olivia's love to marry her and become: "Count Malvolio." (II, v, 33) Olivia will be useful to him as the springboard to social advancement and at the same time to sexual indulgence. It is obvious he has no actual regard for her at all. Here Shakespeare allows Malvolio to freely indulge in fantasy.

MALVOLIO

Having been three months married to her,
sitting in my state —
Calling my officers about me, in my branched
velvet gown, having come from a day-bed where I have
left Olivia sleeping —
And then to have the humour of state and —
after a demure travel of regard, telling them I know
my place, as I would they should do theirs -- to ask for
my kinsman Toby.
Seven of my people with an obedient start
make out for him. I frown the while, and perchance
wind up my watch, or play with my —
some rich jewel. Toby approaches; curtsies there
to me.
I extend my hand to him thus, quenching my
familiar smile with an austere regard of control —

Saying, 'Cousin Toby, my fortunes, having cast
me on your niece, give me this prerogative of speech —
You must amend your drunkenness.
Besides, you waste the treasure of your time
with a foolish knight' —
(II, v, 42-75, with omissions)

In other words, Steward Malvolio dreams of being a lord not to "read politic authors" and maintain order and prosperity in his realm, but to pull rank on persons he loathes. He is the quintessential snob. Further, although in reading Maria's letter he becomes persuaded that she loves him, not once does he express any love for her. His "lady" is there strictly to provide power and sexual gratification. Hearing this, we understand why he had no trouble scanting her instructions when he thought he could get away with it. In fact, believing himself better than she, he has for Olivia not a jot of respect.

Shakespeare's genius in molding this character is to situate his vices not in a soul bent on destruction, but in a heart so consumed with the prospect of mundane advantages that it is blind to real ambition, usurpation, assassination, rape, and the other deeds we find in true villainy. To put it plainly, Malvolio desires to rise just high enough to look down on others. That is his *raison d'être*. We do not condemn him for the simple reason that there is not enough to condemn. Even his fantasies are meager. Malvolio is like a face painted on a child's balloon, which puffs with air and then bursts. In short, he is ludicrous.

When he is condemned by Olivia as a madman and locked in a dark room many in the audience cringe. After all, what harm has he done? The festive comedy reaches its crescendo, truth is unveiled, and happy marriages follow: Olivia is paired with Viola's twin, the masculine Sebastian, Viola wins Duke Orsino, and Sir Toby runs off with Maria. All is well, except for Malvolio, who emerges from his clinical confinement to discover that he has been tricked. "I'll be revenged on the whole pack of you," he cries in frustrated anguish. (V, i, 374) We have seen that although he is not dangerous, Malvolio is: petulant, vain, dishonest, vindictive, resentful, accusatory, snobbish, unloving and sexually exploitive. For all his mischief he suffers no more than a single day in darkness. When "revenge" can he expect? Will he take "revenge" on Duke Orsino and Lady Olivia? Even to make such a threat to the nobility of Illyria is impudent and imprudent.

What, then, art thou, Malvolio? Anyone can see he's a stuffed shirt, or, in Gallic terms, a *petit bourgeois* wearing his ego on his shirt sleeve. (See, Jean-Paul Sartre's discussion of "bad faith" in *Being and Nothingness*, esp. 101-102) Seeking at every moment to clamber on top of his fellows, to be by intimidation more than he is, he becomes laughable. Such a one need not slip on a banana peel to appear absurd. For that slip and fall are already implicit in his attitude and behavior. Rigid and mechanical, he is a rule-sadist who takes advantage of points of order to bully others. We encounter such pompous types every day. Children throw stones at them to see them turn purple and lose their hats. Dogs yap at their heels.

And it is just here that the ambiguity arises. For as he falls, we laugh. Malvolio is so grim he's funny. That is why Maria's postscript seeks to make him try to smile. (II, v, 169) On a face that hasn't cracked a smile in forty years, the effort to manufacture one is almost painful to behold, and in a good performance can be a *coup de théâtre* that leaves us rolling in the aisles. That comic dimension is what makes him seem vulnerable and almost likable. But it must be remembered that though we, the invisible audience, are amused, those who must suffer at the hands of such overbearing and manipulative individuals never find anything funny about it. Thus, when he finally does fall, we acknowledge that justice has been done.

The challenge, of course, is for those who have the misfortune to find themselves feelingly impersonated by Malvolio and obliquely pilloried. To recognize yourself in such a character onstage may be an uncomfortable moment. In that respect it is interesting to attend to certain critical writers and observe the lengths to which they go to obfuscate the obvious and rehabilitate a cad.

Out of fairness, let's hear the voices of those who would advocate for him.

II. Malvolio's Defense

1. Charles Lamb

Charles Lamb (1775-1834) was an English essayist and poet. In 1823 he reviewed a performance of *Twelfth Night* in which a Mr. Bensley played the part of Malvolio. Lamb wrote an article about English theatre, "On Some of the Old Actors," in which generous comments were made, not only in appreciation of Mr. Bensley, but of Mr. Malvolio as well. It was published in an issue of *London Magazine* that year, and, like all good things, it is available online. As there are no quotations from the text, it may be wondered whether Lamb actually read the play around the time he saw it onstage and composed his squib "On the Character of Malvolio" (1823). This was the era when, prompted by German scholarship and the fanfare of David Garrick, the English people were awakening to the artistic accomplishment of their native son. The failure to quote raises difficulties, as it may be that Lamb relied in his exposition largely on his impressions as a viewer rather than on close reading. His essay suffers from florid writing and special pleading. It deserves our notice, however, as it remains a staple of discourse about *Twelfth Night* and has had a significant influence (*e.g.*, H.C. Goddard).

Lamb is waist-deep in error from the very start:

(i) "Malvolio is not essentially ludicrous. He becomes comic but by accident."

Such a casual pronouncement can be salvaged thus: Malvolio is essentially ludicrous, but comic by accident. This was explained above. Applying the language of psychology, Malvolio's makeup combines a manipulative impulse with obsessive-compulsive traits. He is plainly a melancholy (depressive) personality who finds it nearly impossible to deal with others in a tolerant and relaxed manner. He is incapable of love. He is borderline paranoid. He is single at an advancing age, without friends and has no sexual relations. His demeanor is inflexible and armored against any natural feeling other than resentment and envy. He is oral aggressive and uses his authority to control and abuse subordinates while sniping at those who rank above him. As a consequence of these underlying dispositions, he is mechanical, rigid, and easily discomfited. He compensates for his inner emptiness through dreams and fantasies, which always take the same form: seeing himself above others and in a position of authority. In reality he is a servant. In his reveries he is very much a monarch, a monarch whose chief delight is in treating those beneath him with derision. The incessant contrast between what Malovolio is and what he wishes to be renders him asinine. He is absurd and incommensurable with those around him, and it is not surprising that he is found "mad" by his peers, for to a large extent he does indeed suffer from serious emotional unbalance.

However, as long as he is able to function within the circumscribed limits of the household in which he is major domo and a person of influence, he remains merely ludicrous. It is only on those occasions when he falters (that is, as the gull of Maria's scheme) that he becomes comic. That is to say, when we first meet Malvolio he is operating within his boundaries as he seeks to excoriate first Feste the jester and then Viola/Cesario. Here there is no comedy as such, but only its potential, based on the preposterous self-presentation we are offered. Maria's plot in relation to him is the "accident" (banana peel) on which this mechanical tyrant slips and falls, a comic pratfall.

Lamb continues.

(ii) "He is cold, austere, repelling, but dignified, consistent and, rather of an overstretched morality."

(iii) "But his morality and his manners are misplaced in Elyria [sic]."

Cold, austere and repellant he is, and consistently so. But dignified? Let's look in the dictionary. "Dignity: the state or quality of being worthy of honor or respect; composed or serious manner or style; a sense of pride in onself; self respect; a high or honorable rank." (*Oxford American College Dictionary*, 381) The dictionary doesn't say "imagining oneself to deserve honor" but the state of being worthy of such. Malvolio's tantrums and outbursts are the very opposite of being "composed." He loses his composure regularly. Contrast dignity with pomposity: "affectedly and irritatingly grand, solemn, or self-important: a pompous ass." (*Oxford*, 1057) That is our Malvolio, a pompous ass. Lamb is wrong.

Lamb would have us credit to Malvolio's account something called "morality." This must be confined to his distaste for drinking and partying. But teetotalism is not morality. Nor is refusal to socialize, laugh and sing in social gatherings. Morality means in this context the decent and honorable treatment of other people. Like the physician who takes the Hippocratic oath, each of us is enjoined "to do no harm." But Malvolio has a toxic constitution which prompts him to be harmful throughout the day. He publicly upbraids Feste for no apparent reason. He is rude to Olivia, insulting of Viola. In fact he's a liar and a bearer of false witness, a tattler and a snitch. Yet Lamb is willing to find "morality" in Malvolio.

Lamb is wrong.

(iv) "[H]is pride or gravity (call it what you will) is inherent, and native to the man, not mock or affected . . . . His quality is at best unlovely, but neither buffoon nor contemptible. His bearing is lofty, a little above his station, probably not much above his deserts."

Viewing Malvolio as a congenital snob as opposed to one formed by happenstance is hardly an excuse. But the main problem with Lamb's analysis is that it remains without textual support. It hangs as mere assertion, without any foundation whatsoever. He can say whatever he wishes and apparently expects that none will take exception to his revelations. Malvolio exhibits no affectations, you say? Of course, he is no more than a household domestic who believes he's the rightful count of the realm. What could be affected about that? He is "at the best unlovely" would seem to mean that his ugliness is the most exemplary thing about him, but what of that? After all, he is "neither buffoon nor contemptible." If not, why bother to mention those qualities, which someone (unnamed) must be attributing to him? The passages cited above from the text show Malvolio to be, to the contrary, both a classic buffoon and eminently repulsive.

He has his nose in the air, as though he breathed an atmosphere more refined and salubrious than that inhaled by other creatures. Remember this?

MALVOLIO

Go hang yourselves, all. You are idle shallow
things, I am not of your element. You shall know more
hereafter.
(III, iv, 121-123)

This pseudo-regal bearing is "probably not much above his deserts"? Then how foolish is Olivia not to change her dark mourning gowns for white and marry him, making him a count consonant with that lofty bearing!

(v) "His careless committal of the ring to the ground (which he was commissioned to restore to Cesario) bespeaks a generosity of birth and feeling."

It is here in the discussion that charity would bid us avert our eyes, as Charles Lamb begins to adopt some of the worst features of Malvolio. Again, did he read the play, or just hope no one did? Malvolio's gesture is not a "careless committal of the ring to the ground." It is hurled down by Malvolio in a moment of spite. The ring belongs to Malvolio's lady. He was instructed by her to give it to Cesario, the young man she loves. When Cesario indicated quite honestly that it wasn't his and he didn't want it, Malvolio was duty bound as agent of the donor (Olivia) to return it to her. By casting it in the dirt he risked damaging it or losing it altogether, which demonstrates how easily he flouts the will and prerogatives of his "lady," the woman he would wed. Worse, he states to Cesario's face that he threw it peevishly at Olivia (I, v, 13) when it should be obvious that Cesario knows full well that this utterance is a lie. Malvolio's behavior here is that of a lunatic. Are we so sure, then, that he did not belong in that dark house after all?

But hearken to Charles Lamb: Malvolio's handling of the ring "bespeaks a generosity of birth and feeling." What could this mean? Malvolio is patently dissembling when he accuses Cesario of throwing the ring at Olivia, and there appears to be a strange echo of that dissemblance in Lamb's characterization of Malvolio's deeds as "bespeaking generosity of birth and feeling." It is almost as though the base qualities of Malvolio are being mimetically absorbed and recapitulated by Charles Lamb, whose account of the scene in question is grossly misleading.

> (vi) "Even in his abused state of chains and darkness, a sort
> of greatness seems never to desert him."

Again, such a sentence could have been written by Malvolio himself had he been conducting his defense "in proper person." But query, what sort of greatness is this? For we know that 'Some are born great, some achieve greatness, and some have greatness thrust upon 'em." (II, v, 39-40) The idea of "greatness" is the bait dangled by Maria that Malvolio snatches at to transform himself into the superlative man, the *Übermensch*. The only "greatness" which never deserts him is the delusion of greatness.

> (vii) "I confess that I never saw the catastrophe of this char-
> acter, while Bensley played it, without a kind of tragic inter-
> est."

And there it is: for Charles Lamb, Malvolio, at least as portrayed by Mr. Bensley, is a tragic hero. His comic aspect is but an apparition, you see. Considering his dignity, his gravitas, his brave morality, his generosity of birth and feeling, there can be little doubt that he is a genuinely tragic figure, even though he seems quite ordinary and endured no more than a slap on the wrist by spending a day in a dark chamber whose purpose was therapeutic, not punitive. The truth is, there is a fourth category of greatness: Some lunge at greatness, grasp it for an instant, and fall on their faces.

A better adjective than "tragic" to apply Malvolio is the one used in the second Act, fourth scene by the sad Duke Orsino to characterize Feste's song of romantic lamentation ("Come away, come away, death"): "silly."

ORSINO

O fellow, come, the song we had last night.
Mark it, Cesario, it is old and plain.
The spinsters, and the knitters in the sun,
And the free maids that weave their thread with bones,
Do chant it. It is silly sooth,
And dallies with the innocence of love,
Like the old age.
(II, iii, 41-47)

"Silly" had a far richer sense in Elizabethan English than it has currently, and was related to the Germanic "Seel," or soul, as in the Shakespearean adjective "seely," which became "silly."

Crystal and Crystal in their Shakespearean glossary provide this entry.

silly (adj.)

1. helpless, defenceless, vulnerable;
2. feeble, frail, weak;
3. *foolish, stupid, ludicrous*;
4. simple, *lowly, humble*;
5. trifling, trivial, scanty.
(Crystal, 400, emphases added)

Shakespeare's use of this adjective in *Twelfth Night* may be seen to carry over to Malvolio, capturing his modest social standing and its contrast with his "silly" aspirations.

2. Harold C. Goddard

One hundred twenty-eight years after Lamb's article of 1823, in 1951, prominent Shakespearean critic Harold C. Goddard revived Lamb's interpretation of Malvolio, buttressing it with more sophisticated arguments in the 21st chapter of Volume 1 of his *The Meaning of Shakespeare*. According to Goddard, the tendency to demonize Malvolio and suppose that Shakespeare's sympathies lay with Sir Toby Belch and his roistering accomplices is based on shallow reasoning. A more patient inspection of this alleged kill-joy reveals a man of substance and ethical significance poised on the brink of sainthood, heroism or both. Of course there is nothing wrong with taking a second look at the texts of Shakespeare; we rarely do that without reaping a bountiful harvest of poetry and insight. The difficulty is that mere proximity of scrutiny is no guarantee that we will select the most suitable position. Indeed, in the foregoing discussion we ourselves gave a much more intensive analysis of Malvolio than the one proffered by Lamb, with results diametrically opposed to the views of Goddard we are about to examine. What was found above was not an heroic or tragic Malvolio, but a small-minded snob and rule-sadist who dreams of maximizing his power so as to further oppress those unfortunates under his thumb. Supporting passages were cited at length. With the previous proofs in mind, let us consider some of the arguments of Professor Goddard.

> And yet there have been critics so incapable of shaking off their theatre mood as to suggest that in this play Shakespeare is unreservedly on the side of revelry, of cakes and ale as against "virtue," of drunkenness and riot and quarreling as against sobriety and decency and some semblance of order.

* * * *

> In their dislike of Malvolio they forget that he is merely carrying out Olivia's orders, in however annoying a manner. She objects quite as much as he to having her house turned into a bedlam at any and all hours . . . . (Goddard, 296)

Pardonnez-moi? Carrying out orders? All this was scrupulously vetted above and found a palpable falsehood. Was Malvolio merely "carrying out her orders" when he upbraided Feste the Jester in Olivia's presence and found himself reprimanded by her for doing so? Hardly. Was he merely "carrying out her orders" when he threw her ring in the dirt at the feet of her beloved Cesario and berated him? Absolutely not. Was he merely "carrying out her orders" when he wrongly accused Maria of sanctioning the noisy merrymakers and threatened to report her? No, indeed. Was he merely "carrying out her orders" when he told Feste, Maria and Sir Toby to go hang themselves because they were not of his element? Surely not. Well, was he merely carrying out her orders when he planned to seduce her and use their marriage as the foundation of a power grab? Even if the letter was written by Maria, placing Malvolio under a misapprehension that it emanated from his Lady, it is clear that Malvolio is quite willing to enter into a loveless marital union in order to become "Count Malvolio," something Olivia could never countenance. In that respect, Goddard's mention of "Malvolio's love of Olivia" (Goddard, 299) is an index of his alienation from the text. Such a phenomenon appears nowhere in Shakespeare's play. At the last scene when Malvolio shouts that he would be revenged "on the whole pack of you," how are we to exclude Olivia herself from that number? Didn't she chastise him for abusing her jester? On what basis, then, does Goddard suggest that Olivia and her steward are of one mind? It is a bogus argument.

Not to be forgotten is that *Twelfth Night* is a work of dramatic fiction and as such claims of fact must be handled with circumspection and a fair regard for the recognition that none of its characters exist or ever existed in reality. As such, no investigation into the issue of whether Malvolio's actions were 100% congruent with Olivia's orders which seeks to go beyond textual evidence is conceivable. We cannot compare on an empirical basis those orders with what he has done. Yet that is what Goddard professes to accomplish in his claim that Malvolio is the alter ego of Lady Olivia. As far as the text goes, it is patently false, and who are we to stray or seek to stray beyond that text? Only if such an inference were logically implied could we stand behind it. For example, we must deny that Malvolio is blind since he finds Cesario on the road and throws a ring at his feet. Such an inference is a part of the meaning of the character. But to seek to circumvent the text which plainly shows a disparity between Olivia's personality and wishes and what Malvolio does is wholly illicit. The fact as given to us in the text is that Malvolio desires power and autonomy and flouts Olivia's wishes as often as he obeys them, depending on what he thinks he can get away with. And this textual truth is at odds with Goddard's claim that Shakespeare is not presenting the authoritarian Malvolio as less appealing than the would-be merrymakers he superintends. Goddard's argument is a strained sophism which collapses at a glance.

Other remarks made by Goddard need to be addressed. It is fairly plain that despite his alcoholism Sir Toby Belch stands as the comic opposite of Malvolio, and is in many ways the favorite of the play. He has a spirit of independence, insouciance and a sense of the tragic aspect of life which make him the very contradiction of Malvolio. Unlike the depressed Orsino and the perpetually grieving Olivia and her long-faced steward, Sir Toby has fun, and so do we watching him and Maria keep the spark of life flickering in the play. Yes, he drinks. So does Falstaff, who praises alcohol to the skies for its healthful and inspirational properties. (*King Henry IV*, Part Two, IV, i, 83-131.) Throughout both parts of *Henry IV*, Prince Hal is seen delighting in quaffing and intoxication. How then would Shakespeare elevate Falstaff as the patron saint of booze but reject his *de facto* disciple Sir Toby Belch? Here is Goddard's answer.

> Pretty nearly everybody in [the play] but Viola and Sebastian
> . . . is at the extreme point where from excess of something
> or other he is about to be converted into something else. Sir
> Toby, who is the feudal retainer at his vanishing point, is
> in the "third degree of drink," drowned in it, namely. [sic]
> (Those who liken him to Falstaff are in some still higher de-
> gree of obfuscation.) (Goddard, 297)

What could this mean? No one would argue that Sir Toby and Sir John are fungible commodities, but they are both intoxicating characters not only in themselves and their imbibing, but also in their impact on us, the audience. They are both figures of Bacchic festivity and lords of misrule, as recent scholarship has shown. How would we go about distinguishing them when their conduct renders them so similar? Goddard dismisses the inquiry with a stroke of the pen. That is a mark against him and his contentions.

Held hostage by his own logic, Goddard must pass on to condemn Maria.

> Maria's third degree is of another sort. She is a lively, alert,
> resourceful, mocking person. Her vitality and intelligence (to
> call it that) have, in her servile position, made her ambitious
> and envious, especially so of the steward whose merits her
> mistress prizes so highly. It is important to realize that it is

not just because he is Malvolio that she hates him. She would have resented anyone in his place. "I can hardly forebear hurling things at him." The remark is a giveaway. (Goddard, 298)

Non sequitur. There is zero textual evidence that Maria hates Malvolio merely in virtue of his position. Each time she ridicules him it's in the context of his abuses, and let it not be forgotten that Malvolio falsely accuses her of encouraging Sir Toby's midnight catches. The statement that "she would have resented anyone in his place" is no more than idle conjecture and flies in the face of what we see in the substance of the play.

As if to put the keystone in the arch of nonsense that Goddard produces in this vein, he goes so far as to liken Maria to Iago! (Goddard, 298) Is he not in the third degree of doctrinaire renderings and wild opinions brought in to shore up an impossible thesis? Malvolio is a hard sell, and Goddard's fallacies don't help the pitch.

As his struggle to canonize Malvolio reaches its shrill climax, Goddard tips his hand. It's all a re-run of Charles Lamb's 1823 drama review. Goddard is the prisoner of an antiquated and quixotic campaign to make Malvolio the tragic hero of the play. It just doesn't work.

Malvolio and his function in the play seem plain enough during its performance or at first reading. He is simply the antitype of the revelers, their excess drawn out equally in the opposite direction. If they are levity, he is gravity—dignity, decency, decorum, servility and severity in the cause of "good order," carried to the third degree and beyond—and as such fair game for his tormentors. No more than this is necessary to make Malvolio a success on the stage. But that more is possible even there, and much more in the imagination of a reader who reads deeper [sic], is shown in Charles Lamb's famous reminiscences of Bensley . . . . Lamb's main point, it will be remembered, is that Malvolio is not essentially ludicrous, that his pride is neither mock nor affected—and so not a fit object, as such, to excite laughter. He thinks the man had it in him to be brave, honorable, accomplished. Maria calls him a puritan, but quickly takes it back and calls him a time pleaser instead. She could not have been more mistaken. Malvolio is a man of principle rather, and being, like all "men of principle," lacking in imagination in its creative sense, is all the more prone to become a victim of it in its primitive form. (Goddard, 299)

And so the argument that was circling the drain in 1823 continues its downward spiral in 1951. There remain echoes of this bizarre and perverse view even today.

> Lamb found that he admired Malvolio's lunacy, because he understood Malvolio's desire to be Olivia's equal, and therefore didn't begrudge Malvolio his moments of delusion; in that, I think that Lamb acknowledges openly what many viewers feel in secret—an admiration for someone willing to commit themselves to attaining their inmost fantasy, no matter how misguided. (Kelly R. Fineman, "*Twelfth Night*: The Malvolio Problem," online)

III. Conclusion

The difficulty is that in order to attain their inmost fantasy many people find it necessary to trample on others. In Malvolio's case, however, things are worse, since his fantasy is exhausted in the desire to continue and consummate that trampling. There is nothing in him but delusions of grandeur that drive his demented and barbaric actions. He couldn't be further removed from principle. People of his ilk take sadistic advantage of rules to elevate themselves and make their subordinates writhe. Unfortunately, few facts of life are as common as this. Most rogues and reprobates in Shakespeare are "committed to attaining their inmost fantasy." Iago, Claudius, Aaron, Lady Macbeth, Dionyza and many more are propelled by fantasy into mayhem and misery. Malvolio and the others in this play are spared such awful consequences due to its comic form. Malvolio lacks the terrible ambition out of which so many tragic actions emerge. He is a characterological midget, eventually hoist with his own petard. And in the gullibility which arises from his fantasy he becomes comic instead of evil. Goddard says he is not a fit object to excite laughter. But laughter at Molvolio is the centerpiece of every performance of *Twelfth Night*. Professor Goddard probably would have resisted the idea that he himself was a fit object for laughter too. But it's hard to read Lamb and Goddard today without at least a smile.

WORKS CITED:

David and Ben Crystal, *Shakespeare's Words*, Penguin Books, 2002.

Kelly R. Fineman, "Twelfth Night: The Malvolio Problem," online.

Harold C. Goddard, *The Meaning of Shakespeare*, The University of Chicago Press, 1951.

Charles Lamb, "On Some of the Old Actors," *London Magazine*, 1823.

Jean-Paul Sartre, *Being and Nothingness*, Hazel Barnes, trans., Philosophical Library, 1956.

William Shakespeare, The Complete Works, 2d ed., S. Wells and G. Taylor, eds., Oxford University Press, Clarendon, 2005.

The Complete Works of William Shakespeare, Stratford Town edition, 1904, reprinted by Barnes and Noble Books, 1994.

6
Don't Kiss the Messenger: Wooing by Proxy in Shakespeare

*I*t is a commonplace that love is a paradox. Drawing us together, it is yet a third element beyond its terms, that is, an intrusion. It is in virtue of this ambiguity that it is rarely the solution we would have so much as the challenge to which we must rise. (Bradley, 21) Imperceptibly, our amorous dealings become relationships, things to which we ourselves stand in subsidiary attitudes often at odds with one another. That is perhaps why desire has so often been personified as a capricious Eros, himself quite capable of falling in love, as he does with Psyche in the old myth. He may be coveted—or resisted. Tradition has it that Cupid goes armed, and his victims experience pain and anguish rather than the popularly advertised felicity. He is a *tertium quid* insinuating himself between individuals and driving them asunder even in the very moment of conjunction. Think of the nurse and Friar Laurence in *Romeo and Juliet* or Panadrus in *Troilus and Cressida*. It is not love's blessings dramatized there so much as its proliferating complications. As Sartre says with maximum economy, "love is the desire to be loved," as such, essentially dialectical and unstable. In its intermediary role it may be hypostatized as an arrow, harbinger of desire. Shakespeare frequently illustrates the problematic of love by focusing on proxy wooing. *King Henry VI, Much Ado about Nothing, The Two Gentlemen of Verona, Twelfth Night* and *As You Like It*, all suggest that Eros has his own agenda, and willy nilly, whether we kick against the pricks or submit to his will, there is always a price to be paid.

I. William de la Pole, Duke of Suffolk in *King Henry VI*

It is therefore a small step from love to love's messenger. Arguably the earliest wooing by proxy in Shakespeare occurs in *King Henry VI*, Part Two. The agent is William de la Pole, Earl of Suffolk, deputized by young King Henry VI to go to France to win for him the hand of Lady Margaret of Anjou, daughter of René, Duke of Anjou and King of Naples and Jerusalem. We discover in Part One, however, that Suffolk has other plans.

> Thus Suffolk hath prevailed, and thus he goes
> As did the youthful Paris once to Greece,
> With hope to find the like event in love,
> But prosper better than the Trojan did.
> Margaret shall now be queen and rule the King;
> But I will rule both her, the King, and realm.
> (V, vii, 103-108)

How shall this be accomplished? By love, of course. Henry will wed Margaret by proxy, to be sure, but the relator will contrive to become beloved of the king's bride, making him not a mere bearer of royal affections but an attractive object in his own right, in fact, an impediment standing between his liege and his Queen. To put it bluntly, he will seduce her. And so he does, to the detriment of a hapless monarch still under the thumb of the Lord Protector. When poor Henry welcomes his new wife it is likely he hasn't even got a clear conception of the "facts of life," much less his deputy's scheme to control England through Margaret.

Marriage by proxy was not an unheard of way to tie the matrimonial knot in Albion at this point in history (1445 A.D.), particularly amongst the nobility. Half a century later Prince Arthur would wed Katherine of Aragon in the same fashion. But as conventional a form of merger as it might have been, it was an open door to misuse and misunderstanding, as we will see.

SUFFOLK (kneeling before King Henry)

As by your high imperial majesty
I had in charge at my depart in France,
As Procurator to your excellence.

To marry Princess Margaret for your grace,
So, in the famous ancient city of Tours,
In presence of the kings of France and Sicil,
The Dukes of Orléans, Calaber, Bretagne, and Alençon,
Seven earls, twelve barons, and twenty reverend bishops,
I have performed my task and was espoused,
And humbly now upon my bended knee,
In sight of England and her lordly peers,
Deliver up my title in the Queen
To your most gracious hands, that are the substance
Of that great shadow I did represent —
The happiest gift that ever marquis gave,
The fairest queen that ever king received.
(*King Henry VI*, Part Two, I, i, 1-16)

Under the practice of marriage by proxy, then, the procedure was not complete until "title" acquired by the agent in foreign ceremony was formally and publicly rendered up to his principal, in this case, King Henry VI. It was a delicate ambassadorial mission in which the diplomat would confer with the young lady's father and his courtiers, devise terms and sign documents. Presumably at some point there would have been personal conferences with the bride-to-be in which she would be made acquainted with her future husband by way of portraiture and the conveyance of appropriate sentiments. If consent was achieved, a full nuptial mass would follow, with the agent standing in place of the actual suitor. At that point he would be fully married to the bride, with the understanding that he would transport her to his principal untouched, transferring all right to her posthaste.

Readers of Shakespeare's *King Henry VI* know, of course, that there was an irregularity in the case of Margaret of Anjou. Somewhere along the way, Suffolk effectively alienated her affections.

QUEEN MARGARET

I tell thee, Pole, when in the city Tours
Thou rann'st a-tilt in honour of my love
And stol'st away the ladies' hearts of France,
I thought King Henry had resembled thee
In courage, courtship, and proportion.
But all his mind is bent to holiness,

To number Ave-Maries on his beads.
His champions are the prophets and apostles,
His weapons holy saws of sacred writ,
His study is his tilt-yard, and his loves
Are brazen images of canonizèd saints.
I would the college of the cardinals
Would choose him Pope, and carry him to Rome,
And set the triple crown upon his head —
That were a state fit for his holiness.
(I, iii, 3-67)

It would seem that Suffolk put on quite a show in France, giving Lady Margaret the firm impression that his Lord was cut from the same cloth as himself in all manly qualities. Obviously she was disappointed. The text strongly implies that shortly after her arrival in England she and de la Pole engaged in a torrid romance, one in which the sanctimonious King Henry starred as the willing cuckold. (Part Two, IV, vii, 20-23) Instead of requiting the love of the weak monarch who wooed her via the advances of a go-between, Margaret is captivated by the forward messenger. The principal is either reviled or barely tolerated. Such is the risk of wooing by proxy.

In appraising the consequences of this mésalliance, we must consider the nature of Shakespeare's history plays, which served as retorts from which emerged the distillates of tragedy and comedy. For example, King Richard II is plainly a tragic figure, as his play's title implies, whereas the brash and jocular Richard III tends to be received as a comedian. The entire line running from *King Henry IV* Part One through *King Henry V* is primarily comical. What then, of Shakespeare's longest play, the massive triptych *King Henry VI*? It is respectfully submitted that here we witness the emergence of tragedy from the very bowels of comedy. Part One, for example, which contains the shrewish Joan of Arc, the jocular incident involving the capture of Lord Talbot by the Countess of Auvergne and the "miracle" at St. Albans, is largely comic in form and function. But as the Wars of the Roses unfold and reach a bitter crest in Part Three, where, for example, Queen Margaret hunts down Richard and sets a paper crown on his head (I, iv, 95), we sense the seriousness of this narrative and recognize that the action has taken a distinctly tragic turn. Where does this leave Part Two? After Suffolk has assassinated the Lord Protector, the good Duke Humphrey, he is condemned and exiled by a distraught King Henry. This, of course, signals the end of the Margaret/Suffolk love affair. Their wrenching separation (III, ii, 304-417), which seems to look back to the heart-rending farewell of Richard II and his wife (Act 4, Sc. 1), is soon drained of its tragic significance. The banished Duke of Suffolk is seized by pirates in Act 4, Sc. 1, and his pseudo-heroic posturing in their hands falls flat.

SUFFOLK

Obscure and lousy swain, King Henry's blood,
The honorable blood of Lancaster,
Must not be shed by such a jady groom.
Hast thou not kissed thy hand and held my stirrup?
Bare-headed plodded by my foot-cloth mule
And thought thee happy when I shook my head?
How often hast thou waited at my cup,
Fed from my trencher, kneeled down at the board
When I have feasted with Queen Margaret?
Remember it, and let it make thee crestfall'n,
Ay, and allay this thy abortive pride,
How in our voiding lobby hast thou stood
And duly waited for my coming forth?
This hand of mine hath writ in thy behalf,
And therefore shall it charm thy riotous tongue.
(Part Two, IV, I, 51-65)

This sort of pompous palaver might have served in court, but on the deck of a pirate vessel on which all hands are sharpening their blades it is myopic and silly. Even these ruffians are fully aware of Suffolk's murder of the beloved Duke Humphrey. (IV, I, 72-103) Suffolk's high-sounding rhetoric is hollow and evokes laughter.

SUFFOLK

Suffolk's imperial tongue is stern and rough,
Used to command, untaught to plead for favour.
Far be it we should honour such as these
With humble suit. No, rather let my head
Stoop to the block than these knees bow to any
Save to the God of heaven and to my king;
And sooner dance upon a bloody pole

Than stand uncovered to the vulgar groom.
True nobility is exempt from fear;
More can I bear than you dare execute.

CAPTAIN

Hale him away, and let him talk no more.

SUFFOLK

Come, 'soldiers', show what cruelty ye can,
That this my death may never be forgot.
Great men oft die by vile Besonians;
A Roman sworder and banditto slave
Murdered sweet Tully; Brutus' bastard hand
Stabbed Julius Caesar; savage islanders
Pompey the Great; and Suffolk dies by pirates.
(IV, I, 123-140)

The last three words are often put by stage directors in the ironic mouth of the pirate captain. Suffolk is clearly hysterical as he is hauled off to the block. Any shred of dignity he might have salvaged is lost in this condescending tirade. He is revealed as supercilious and comical in his defiance. His severed head is brought onstage five lines later, and promptly delivered to Queen Margaret. (IV, i, 144-146)

We topple thence to the very bottom of bathos in Act 4, Sc. 4 when Queen Margaret appears onstage "carrying Suffolk's head."

QUEEN MARGARET

Oft have I heard that grief softens the mind,
And makes it fearful and degenerate;
Think, therefore, on revenge, and cease to weep.
But who can cease to weep and look on this?
Here may his head lie on my throbbing breast,
But where's the body that I should embrace?
(IV, iv, 1-7)

Soft indeed must be the mind that yields such utterances. For who could view this and keep from smiling tolerantly? Unless Suffolk's head were delivered to Margaret Federal Express it must be a putrefying, maggot-ridden burden she clutches to her bosom. The image is so grotesque that most directors would be sorely tempted to cut it. Margaret's own words should come back to haunt her now: "Is this the fashions in the court of England?" (Part Two, I, iii, 46) Her bizarre cry, "But where's the body I should embrace?" composed at the outset of Shakespeare's career, will reappear at its finale in *Cymbeline* in the wail of Fidele (Imogen), who awakens from her drug-induced stupor to find herself immured beside the headless trunk of Cloten.

IMOGEN

A headless man? The garments of Posthumus?
I know the shape of's leg; this is his hand,
His foot Mercurial, his Martial thigh,
The brawns of Hercules; but his Jovial face —
Murder in heaven! How? 'Tis gone.

* * *

Where is thy head? Where's that? Ay me, where's
That?
(IV, ii, 308-314; 323-324)

The passage from *Cymbeline* is another Shakespearean jab at love: Two persons could not be as different as Posthumus and Cloten, and Imogen is the former's wife. Yet she cannot distinguish her own husband's legs, hands and feet from those of the imbecile Cloten whose suit she has so often rejected. Imogen addresses the corpse she believes is Posthumus' remains, as stage instructions in *Henry VI* indicate that Margaret's words are directed "to Suffolk's head." (Part Two, IV, iv, 13) Both women seem demented in their raving to absent lovers: Suffolk sleeps with the fishes, while Posthumus Leonatus is fighting in battle, the name of saintly Imogen on his trembling lips. (*Cymbeline*, Act 5, Sc. 1)

Let it be remembered that marriage is the culmination of classical comedy. And of all marriages, none, not even that of Petruchio and his mate Kate, is more risible than that of poor Henry and his Queen of Hearts, Margaret of Anjou. Not only were these two utterly incommensurable, with Henry quivering beneath her basilisk gaze, their very inception as a couple was flawed by malicious proxy, allowing the Procurator to appropriate Henry's beauteous termagant. The tale has all the charm of a *Così fan tutte* or *Le nozze di Figaro*, and is made even more exquisite by its patina of facticity.

II. Don Pedro, Prince of Aragon in *Much Ado About Nothing*

Much Ado About Nothing is noteworthy in this context because the proxy is a disguised male, Don Pedro of Aragon. In the remaining three plays the proxies are all transvestite ladies (Julia, Viola and Rosalind). Those familiar with the text will be intrigued by the explanation of Taylor & Wells that "The action is set in Sicily, where Don Pedro, Prince of Aragon, has recently defeated his brother, the bastard Don John, in a military engagement. Apparently reconciled, they return to the capital, Messina, as guests of the Governor, Leonato." (Taylor & Wells, 569) Marjorie Garber reports, on the other hand, that "The ranking officer of the group, Don Pedro, Prince of Aragon, has a bastard brother, Don John, from whom he has been estranged for reasons the play never specifies, and with whom he has just been reconciled." (Garber, 372) Apparently, in the view of Taylor and Wells there wasn't a good deal of recreation in old Sicily, and the local militia would fight internecine wars occasionally against close relatives to stave off ennui, getting together afterwards for wine and cheese. At any rate, amongst the junior officers hosted by Leonato in this piquant romantic comedy is Claudio, enamored of Leonato's daughter, Hero. A mere girl when the squadron galloped to the front, she blossoms on its return. So enraptured is Claudio that, even without so much as a conversation, he contemplates matrimony, much to the horror of his cynical compatriots. The problem is, how to explain this sudden burst of connubial zeal to Leonato without giving the wrong impression. What is needed is a dose of avuncular gravitas. Enter Don Pedro.

DON PEDRO

Dost thou affect her, Claudio?

CLAUDIO

O my lord,
When you went onward on this ended action

I looked upon her with a soldier's eye,
That liked, but had a rougher task in hand,
Than drive liking to the name of love.
But now I am returned, and that war-thoughts
Have left their places vacant, in their rooms
Come thronging soft and delicate desires,
All prompting me how fair young Hero is,
Saying I liked her ere I went to wars.

DON PEDRO

Thou wilt be like a lover presently,
And tire the hearer with a book of words.
If thou dost love fair Hero, cherish it,
And I will break with her, and with her father,
And thou shalt have her. Was't not to this end
That thou began'st to twist so fine a story?

CLAUDIO

How sweetly you do minister to love,
That know love's grief by his complexion!
But lest my liking might too sudden seem
I would have salved it with a longer treatise.

DON PEDRO

What need the bridge much broader then the flood?
The fairest grant is the necessity.
Look what will serve is fit. 'Tis once: thou lovest,
And I will fit thee with the remedy.
I know we shall have revelling tonight.
I will assume thy part in some disguise,
And tell fair Hero I am Claudio.
And in her bosom I'll unclasp my heart
And take her hearing prisoner with the force
And strong encounter of my amorous tale.
Then after to her father will I break,
And the conclusion is, she shall be thine.
In practice let us put it presently.

(I, i, 279-311)

Now it is evening. On stage are Leonato, Antonio, his brother, Hero and Beatrice. Masked revelers enter the place of dance, including Don Pedro, Claudio and Don John.

DON PEDRO (to Hero)

Lady, will you walk about with your friend?

HERO

So you walk softly, and look sweetly, and say
Nothing, I am yours for the walk; and especially when
I walk away.

DON PEDRO

With me in your company?

HERO

I may say so when I please.

DON PEDRO

And when please you to say so?

HERO

When I like your favour; for God defend the lute
Should be like the case.

DON PEDRO

My visor is Philemon's roof. Within the house is Jove.

HERO

Why, then, your visor should be thatched.

DON PEDRO

Speak low if you speak love.
(II, I, 79-90)

(They move aside)

This is the proxy moment but it is veiled. Will Don Pedro "aggravate" his voice and plead as Claudio? To do so he must identify himself as Claudio, yet in this passage he does not, raising a sliver of doubt as to his intentions. Is it plausible he should identify himself later, after the chat is already underway? Might he admit he is Don Pedro and then woo on behalf of Claudio? Again, we do not know. In this manner Shakespeare draws attention to the vexing nature of wooing by proxy, where nearly everything can go wrong. Certainly the classical allusion to the Greek myth of Philemon and Baucis is a positive sign. They were a poor couple who gave hospitality to two of the gods in mortal form when others in their village turned these strangers away. The implication is that Hero will not be propositioned in the vulgar sense; the message is honorable and likely a proposal of marriage – but from whom?

At this delicate juncture, Claudio is espied by the malevolent Don John and his confederate Borachio. They whisper in his ear that Don Pedro is madly in love with Hero, entailing that any proposal will be made his own right. (II, I, 150-161) Claudio's fantasy comes crashing down about him as he soliloquizes:

CLAUDIO

Thus answer I in name of Benedick,
But hear these ill news with the ears of Claudio.
'Tis certain so, the Prince woos for himself.
Friendship is constant in all other things
Save in the office and affairs of love.
Therefore all hearts in love use their own tongues.
Let every eye negotiate for itself,
And trust no agent; for beauty is a witch
Against whose charms faith melteth into blood.
This is an accident of hourly proof,
Which I mistrusted not. Farewell, therefore, Hero.
(II, I, 162-172)

Thus it is that Claudio comes to believe that Don Pedro played the rogue in much the same way we saw Duke Suffolk do in the ancient city of Tours with Lady Margaret: though proxy for another, he wins her affections for himself. Notice too how credulous Claudio is, and that he attributes fault to Hero herself on account of her beauty, which gives her the powers of "a witch." Benedick, the bantering and misogynistic bachelor, has taught Claudio to distrust women and the institution of matrimony, and this corrosive spirit of doubt works to undermine Claudio's nascent idealism. Although the villain in Don John's scenario would be Don Pedro, falsely pledging to win Hero for Claudio, Claudio himself seems to almost blame Hero for succumbing to the blandishments of Don Pedro. Insofar as Hero might respond favorably to Don Pedro's wooing for himself, in Claudio's eyes she would be tainted, regardless of the fact that she would be entirely unaware of Claudio's love and Don Pedro's promise to woo on Claudio's behalf. Thus, when Claudio soon thereafter is apprised of the favorable truth, that Hero has been won for himself, his joy is muted.

DON PEDRO

I'faith, lady, I think your blazon to be true,
Though I'll be sworn, if he be so, his conceit is false.
Here, Claudio, I have wooed in thy name, and fair
Hero is won. I have broke with her father and his good
will obtained. Name the day of marriage, and God give
thee joy.

LEONATO

Count, take of me my daughter, and with her
My fortunes. His grace hath made the match, and all
Grace say amen to it.
(II, I, 277-285)

Here is the proof. Don Pedro is an honest proxy, and has wooed as Claudio himself. Leonato guarantees the match. What could be more reassuring? Yet Claudio temporizes.

BEATRICE

Speak count, 'tis your cue.

CLAUDIO

Silence is the perfectest herald of joy. I were but
Little happy if I could say how much. (To Hero) Lady,
As you are mine, I am yours. I give away myself for
You, and dote upon the exchange.

BEATRICE (To Hero)

Speak, cousin. Or, if you cannot, stop
His mouth with a kiss, and let him not speak, neither.
(II, I, 286-292)

Something is wrong here. Why must the groom need to be reminded to speak? When they come, Claudio's words are cold and reserved. There are times when silence is not golden and this is one of them. He seems to be almost pouting, as if he felt trapped. A mundane word like "exchange" feels out of place in a moment that should be excitement and pure bliss. The reason is plain: up to this very instant Claudio has been convinced that Hero has accepted the professed love of Don Pedro, leading him to dig in his heels against her. He is being asked now to perform an instant *volte-face* and hasn't the maturity or emotional agility to bring it off. His attitude remains one of distrust. Hero is therefore rightly puzzled. The man she sees before her bears no resemblance to the dashing costumed fellow who spoke to her so wittily and enchantingly last evening. Could that be a frown on his brow? In some versions, such as the Kenneth Branaugh production, Hero (Kate Beckinsale) does kiss Claudio (Keanu Reeves), but the risk is that such a kiss papers over a failure in the venture of proxy wooing. At this point the course of true love is not running smoothly. Yet in the spirit of *carpe diem*, Claudio declares the next day his wedding day. (II, i, 334-335)

A sensible thing to do to clear the air would be to question Don John. He gave palpably false information about the intentions of Don Pedro respecting Hero. (II, I, 153-160) If Leonato declares publicly that he is giving his daughter in marriage to Claudio (as he does), Don Pedro couldn't have pleaded for himself but only for Claudio. And if that is true, Don John is a manifest liar. Furthermore, the motive is plain, as it is common knowledge that Don John bears a grudge against his brother. Yet no one thinks to investigate and hold Don John accountable for bearing false witness or defamation.

On the contrary, Don John still has sufficient credit to try again. In Act 3, Sc. 3, he approaches Don Pedro and Claudio to inform them that Hero is actively unfaithful.

DON JOHN

I came hither to tell you . . . the lady is disloyal.

CLAUDIO

Who, Hero?

DON JOHN

Even she. Leonato's Hero, your Hero, every man's Hero.

CLAUDIO

Disloyal?

DON JOHN

The word is too good to paint out her
wickedness. I could say she were worse. Think you of
a worse title, and I will fit her to it. Wonder not till
further warrant. Go but with me tonight, you shall see
her chamber window entered, even the night before
her wedding day. If you love her then, tomorrow wed
her. But it would better fit your honour to change your
mind.

CLAUDIO

May this be so?

DON PEDRO

I will not think it.

DON JOHN

If you dare not trust that you see, confess not
that you know. If you will follow me I will show you
enough, and when you have seen more and heard more,
proceed accordingly.

CLAUDIO

If I see anything tonight why I should not marry
her, tomorrow, in the congregation where I should
wed, there will I shame her.

DON PEDRO

And as I wooed for thee to obtain her, I will
Join with thee to disgrace her.
(III, ii, 92-117)

Why wouldn't Don Pedro say the following to his bastard brother?

> Tarry, sir.
> Was it not but a few hours since thou whispered
> falsely in Claudio's ear that I was in love with Hero
> and wooed on my own behalf for her hand
> in marriage? Yet Leonato confirmed I
> wooed for Claudio. Why would'st thou slander
> me with your bastardly shame, tell lies of me
> to make of me a liar? Everyone can see thy
> jealousy, the ill-will thou bear'st me, how you would
> blacken my reputation. Down what path of
> folly would'st thou lead'st us now to mar us
> with your own mischief?

Yet neither Claudio nor Don Pedro challenges Don John. Instead,
they agree to gather under Hero's window to see what Don John wishes

them to see. It will be his little stage production, with the interpretation provided in advance. At this point, there is more intelligence in bumbling Dogberry and his Watch than in Don Pedro and Claudio put together. Instead of squaring off against the meretricious Don John, a proven deceiver as to this very issue, the virtue of Hero, Claudio seems to re-ignite a smoldering indignation against her, going so far as to declare that should he find ocular confirmation of her alleged infidelity he will "shame her" in the imminent nuptials. Is such an awful and irretrievable response necessary? Suppose the evidence Claudio is presented admits of more than one interpretation or construction—and leads to a revelation that Don John is again guilty of the same defamatory conduct? How will the threatened damage to Hero be undone? In his wrath, Claudio forgets he's just been down this road of error. Fooled once, he would have his folly confirmed beyond repair. And this is precisely what happens. It is arranged by Don John that in the dark of night at Hero's window Don John's associate Borachio should embrace the serving woman Margaret so as to give to Claudio and Don Pedro the false impression of Hero's promiscuous infidelity. (III, iii, 134-156) The ruse works. Hero is grossly humiliated by Claudio next morning before the priest and wedding guests, a sad scene we have no need to review. Shakespeare's concern is obviously not with the perfidious Don John but with credulous Claudio, whose love for Hero has been mishandled from the beginning. Had he been more forthright, all this harm might have been avoided. The first and most fundamental error, of course, was placing his suit in the hands of a third party, Don Pedro, who volunteered to impersonate him in disguise and win by a sort of guile Hero's love and consent to marry. Under those dubious circumstances it is not exactly clear who Hero actually consents to marry. Don Pedro does not expressly approach Hero in his own person (as Suffolk approaches Lady Margaret on behalf of Henry); rather, Don Pedro adds an additional confusion by impersonating Claudio and wooing Hero privately. This scheme plays into Don John's hands by allowing Claudio to wonder in whose name the suit to Hero proceeded. One almost wants to demand, "Why didn't you speak for yourself, Claudio?" echoing Priscilla Mullens in Longfellow's *The Courtship of Miles Standish*. It is plain that wooing by proxy has disturbing consequences in both *King Henry VI* and *Much Ado About Nothing*. Can the ladies get any better results? It's time now to turn to our cross dressing heroines. Let's not keep them waiting. (*As You Like It,* III, ii, 293-324; IV, i, 37-58)

III. Julia as Sebastian

Wooing by proxy afforded Shakespeare an opportunity in *The Two Gentlemen of Verona* and *Twelfth Night* to explore a pair of opposed features of love: eros (desire) and benevolence (caritas). Though in historical terms these forms emerged independently, the courtly love which arose in the 14th century with the Cathars and Troubadours embraced both aspects, which melded adventitiously over a period of five centuries to become our popular notion of romance. Midway in this evolutionary process, Shakespeare presented a comic dissection of modern love, exposing its heterogeneous features. Of course, so long as interests coincide no tension arises, as, for example, where the wartime nurse cares for her lover, the wounded soldier. But what happens when the beloved turns to seek his happiness in a rival admirer? Suppose the two suitors are friends? Can charity overcome jealousy for the welfare of the love object? This is the very theme Shakespeare was to return to much later in Sonnet 116, "Let me not to the marriage of true minds admit impediments," in which the narrator makes an ironic sacrifice of his own desires for the sake of his friends' happiness.

Valentine, a youth of Verona, decides to leave his friend Proteus to seek adventure in Milan. Proteus protests. He is content to pursue his love, Julia, at home in Verona, and wishes that Valentine would remain and find such bliss for himself. When Antonio sends his son Proteus to Milan shortly thereafter, his budding romance with Julia is interrupted, though the lovers exchange rings as tokens of perpetual devotion. Meanwhile, Valentine is completely captivated by Silvia, the ravishing daughter of the Duke of Milan. Outwardly vain and self-absorbed, Silvia is in fact secretly and genuinely in love with Valentine, but dallies so as to enjoy his ardent suit for her favors. No sooner does Proteus arrive than he finds himself mimetically smitten by Silvia as well, and plans to abandon Julia and steal Silvia from Valentine. His soliloquy, a string of self-serving sophisms, anatomizes unsparingly the mind of a cad.

> To leave my Julia shall I be forsworn;
> To love fair Silvia shall I be forsworn;
> To wrong my friend I shall be much forsworn.
> And e'en that power which gave me first my oath
> Provokes me to this threefold perjury.
> Love bade me swear, and bids me forswear.
> O sweet—suggesting love, if thou hast sinned

Teach me, thy tempted subject, to excuse it.
At first I did adore a twinkling star,
But now I worship a celestial sun.
Unheedful vows may heedfully be broken,
And he wants wit that wants resolvèd will
To learn his wit t'exchange the bad for better.
Fie, fie, unreverent tongue, to call her bad
Whose sovereignty so oft thou hast preferred
With twenty thousand soul-confirming oaths.
I cannot leave to love, and yet I do.
But there I leave to love where I should love.
Julia I lose, and Valentine I lose.
If I keep them I needs must lose myself.
If I lose them, thus find I by their loss
For Valentine, myself, for Julia, Silvia.
I to myself am dearer than a friend,
For love is still most precious in itself,
And Silvia—witness heaven that made her fair —
Shows Julia but a swarthy Ethiope.
I will forget that Julia is alive,
Rememb'ring that my love to her is dead,
And Valentine I'll hold an enemy,
Aiming at Silvia as a sweeter friend.
I cannot now prove constant to myself
Without some treachery used to Valentine.
This night he meaneth with a corded ladder
To climb celestial Silvia's chamber-window,
Myself in counsel his competitor.
Now presently I'll give her father notice
Of their disguising and pretended flight,
Who, all enraged, will banish Valentine;
For Thurio he intends shall wed his daughter.
But Valentine being gone, I'll quickly cross
By some sly trick blunt Thurio's dull proceeding.
Love, lend me wings to make my purpose swift,
As thou hast lent me wit to plot this drift.
(II, vi, 1-43)

After scheming to get Valentine exiled by the Duke, Proteus has eliminated his major rival, and turns his attentions to the pursuit of Silvia. Back in Verona, Julia is suffering without her swain Proteus and determines to dress as a male page, Sebastian, and travel *solus* to Milan to be reunited with him. Unfortunately, the moment she arrives, she finds her adored Proteus serenading Silvia beneath her balcony. When Silvia appears and rejects his advances, reminding him of his commitment to Julia, Proteus declares that Julia is dead—and so is Valentine! The lady is not taken in. The most she will grant this callow fellow is a portrait of herself she keeps within.

The name adopted by Julia, "Sebastian," is significant. In the only other Shakespeare comedy in which a transvestite heroine woos a woman on behalf of the man she loves, that intermediating heroine, Viola, has a twin brother called Sebastian. It is fairly plain that when Shakespeare came to compose *Twelfth Night* he did so with *The Two Gentlemen* in mind. In effect, then, Julia is Viola's spiritual sister, implying the possibility that a romantic love might spring up between Silvia and "Sebastian," as Olivia becomes hopelessly enamored of "Cesario." Of course, as Silvia is already in love with Valentine, this does not happen. And in *Twelfth Night*, Olivia, falling in love with "Cesario," later transfers this affection to Viola's doppelgänger, Sebastian.

Finding himself rebuffed in his attempted seduction, Proteus abandons hope of a frontal assault on this noble lady, and, casting about for a device, meets the page-boy "Sebastian," to whom he finds himself curiously drawn.

PROTEUS

Sebastian, I have entertainèd thee
Partly that I have need of such a youth
That can with some discretion do my business,
For 'tis no trusting to yon foolish lout,
But chiefly for thy face and thy behavior,
Which, if my augury deceive me not,
Witness good bringing up, fortune, and truth.
Therefore know thou, for this I entertain thee.
Go presently, and take this ring with thee.
Deliver it to Madam Silvia.
She loved me well delivered it to me.
(IV, iv, 61-71)

Here is the appointment of proxy captured in the instant. There is something comforting and reassuring about Sebastian's face that leads Sir Proteus to trust him. It speaks of a certain fidelity he can almost recall but not quite. In many such instances, Shakespeare toys with his characters as he teases us. It is almost as though the disguise were seen through, and yet it isn't. The observer in question knows, yet does not, in the way we fumble for a name on the tip of our tongue. If we didn't know it, how could we dredge it up? Hence the Vaishnava sages say of our sense of death: "They know, yet they know it not." Proteus sees his Julia, and yet he knows her not. That is why such scenes are successful onstage despite the audience's clear ability to recognize the disguised character: the sheer transparency of the deception illustrates the obtuseness of the misapprehending character and heightens the poignancy of the encounter.

JULIA

It seems you loved not her, to leave her token.
Is she dead belike?

PROTEUS

Not so. I think she lives.

JULIA

Alas.

PROTEUS

Why dost thou cry 'Alas'?

JULIA

I cannot choose but pity her.

PROTEUS

Wherefore should'st thou pity her?

JULIA

Because methinks that she loved you as well
As you do love your lady Silvia.
She dreams on him that has forgot her love;
You dote on her that cares not for your love.
'Tis pity love should be so contrary,
And thinking on it makes me cry 'Alas'.

PROTEUS

Well, give her that ring, and therewithal
This letter. (Pointing) That's her chamber. Tell my
Lady I claim the promise of her heavenly picture.
Your message done, hie home to my chamber,
Where thou shalt find me sad and solitary.
(IV, iv, 72-87)

He will not listen, but cuts her off with his errant errand. Then he leaves us with the central soliloquy of the play.

JULIA

How many women would do such a message?
Alas, poor Proteus, thou hast entertained
A fox to be the shepherd of thy lambs.
Alas, poor fool, why do I pity him
That with his very heart despiseth me?
Because he loves her, he despiseth me.
Because I love him, I must pity him.
This ring I gave him when he parted from me,
To bind him to remember my good will.
And now am I, unhappy messenger,
To plead for that which I would not obtain;
To carry that which I would have refused;
To praise his faith, which I would have dispraised.
I am my master's true-confirmèd love,
But cannot be true servant to my master
Unless I prove false traitor to myself.
Yet will I woo for him, but yet so coldly

As, heaven it knows, I would not have him speed.
(IV, iv, 88-105)

Things are worse, then, for Julia than they are for Viola/Cesario. The latter's dilemma is to woo as proxy for the man she loves; Julia, on the other hand, is sent to woo for him who plighted unto her his troth, and that makes a world of difference. Viola undermines herself, yet does not betray herself, as does Julia. In all of Shakespeare, it could be argued this is the most singular sacrifice. It may be done coldly, as she says, but it will be done well. How is it possible? On account of what we might call love's impurity, its divided nature: "Because I love him, I must pity him." Insofar as I need him and desire him, giving him to another is unthinkable. But insofar as I love him in the sense of caring for him, caring for his happiness, I must let him go. That is the contradiction lurking in the heart of love exposed by Shakespeare's use of suit by proxy. The problem is not imposed on love by the trope of proximate wooing, rather, the hybridized character of love, its inner tensions and inconsistencies, are revealed as in a roentgenogram in this context. Yet through it all, perhaps the reader will agree, there remains an element of hope. Who knows what lies ahead? Confrontation and quarreling would only drive a wedge between Julia and her wayward swain. After all, the ardor of Proteus is not reciprocated by Silvia. To whom might he return when steadfast Silvia passes forever out of reach and the bubble of delusion bursts, if not she who has done everything and more for him?

In their conversation, Silvia's concern for jilted Julia is most evident.

SILVIA

She is beholden to thee, gentle youth.
Alas, poor lady, desolate and left.
I weep myself to think upon thy words.
Here youth. There is my purse. I give thee this
For thy sweet mistess' sake, because thou lov'st her.
Farewell.
(IV, iv, 170-176)

And so it is. At the play's conclusion, Julia doffs her boyish garments sufficiently to show doltish Proteus the magnitude of his error.

Behold her that gave aim to all thy oaths
And entertained 'em deeply in her heart.
How oft hast thou with perjury cleft the root?
O, Proteus, let this habit make thee blush.
Be thou ashamed that I have took upon me
Such immodest raiment, if shame live
In a disguise of love.
It is the lessor blot, modesty finds,
Women to change their shapes than men their minds.
(V, iv, 100-108)

This, of course recalls such lines as:

"By all the vows that ever men have broke—
In number more than ever women spoke."
(*A Midsummer Night's Dream*, I, I, 175-176)

and the wry song in *Much Ado About Nothing*:

Sigh no more, ladies, sigh no more.
  Men were deceivers ever,
One foot in sea, and one on shore,
  To one thing constant never.
Then sigh not so, but let them go,
  And be you blithe and bonny,
Converting all your sounds of woe
  Into hey nonny, nonny.
(II, iii, 61-76).

Here the scales fall from the eyes of Proteus.

PROTEUS

Than men their minds! 'Tis true. O, heaven, were man
But constant, he were perfect. That one error
Fills him with faults, makes him run through all th' sins;
Inconstancy falls off ere it begins.
What is in Silvia's face but I may spy
More fresh in Julia's, with a constant eye?
(V, iv, 109-114)

Thus Proteus discovers that he has gained more by the failure of love by proxy than he ever could have by its supposed success.

IV. Viola as Cesario

In previous essays we have discussed Cesario's embassage unto Olivia. For our purposes, that wooing is distinguished as the finest and most brilliant proxy effort to be found in Shakespeare. No other agents rise to such heights except Rosalind, who is arguably non-mortal. But as surpassingly eloquent as Viola is, her speech is not carried aloft by her own genius alone. Rather, it is fueled by subterranean passions. She is not a mere messenger, a paid fee post who recites a script she has "conned." She is a lover who yearns for love. To understand this we should recall that Viola still feels the loss of her father, and, for most of the play, the brother Sebastian she believes has drowned in the shipwreck which cast her up into Illyria. These losses resonate with Olivia, who is in mourning for her brother and has still not recovered from her father's death. These fundamental griefs roil at the bottom of both women's souls. On top of this in Viola is her craving for Duke Orsino, for whom she woos Lady Olivia so vivaciously. Thus, when in answer to Olivia's "Why, what would you?" Viola declaims the extraordinary "Make me a willow cabin at your gate . . . ," (I, v, 257-265) her speech is inspired by the affections for a lost father, brother and potential lover, Duke Orsino. What Olivia hears in Cesario's voice, then, is far from the sort of mechanical recitation to which she has been exposed courtesy of Duke Orsino. All the throbbing emotion locked up inside her comes pouring out, not chaotically, but in the most exquisite language conceivable. And it is this passionate peroration that sweeps Olivia off her feet. Deaf to Orsino's entreaties, Olivia is won by the hunger another woman has for him, deflected to herself.

Like the proxy wooings of Suffolk, Don Pedro and Julia, that of Cesario is a failure in the sense that the intended union (Orsino and Olivia) is not achieved. Yes, it's true that Claudio and Hero eventually wed festively along with Beatrice and Benedick, but the original Hero must die first of embarrassment and be resurrected. For this Don Pedro can hardly take credit. Remember that he shared in Claudio's impulsive wish to shame her at the ill-starred wedding and in fact does so. (IV, I, 64-65; 88-94) But the excited longing Olivia feels for the impossibly gendered "Cesario" is soon transferred to sibling Sebastian, and when Orsino comes to his senses and embraces Viola, all is well as the two couples join hands.

V. Rosalind as Ganymede

What makes Ganymede stand out from the other intermediaries? To answer this question we must address another: What sets Rosalind apart? There is a kind of vibrancy in her character that intrigues us. Despite her persecution by Duke Frederick and her love for the stalwartly normal Orlando, there is about her a kind of playful autonomy, a preternatural effervescence that sets her above other lovers and proxies. We are reminded of a comment by England's poet laureate and scholar Ted Hughes: "Shakespeare seems to have difficulty in making his women real . . . One is more than a little aware that a new, much bigger, extra dimension has opened behind them. They . . . produce an uncomfortable impression . . . willfully committed to awkwardly superhuman roles. [Shakespeare] has some difficulty bringing these women down to earth. This is evident in what they say, but it is visible too in various details." Such heroines, "blushing into hectic, sexual life, are only just touching earth with their toes." (Hughes, 3-4) And it is submitted that this prescient insight of Hughes is more applicable to Rosalind than to any other female lead in Shakespeare. Rightly apprehended, then, "Ganymede" is a shadow of divinity, as his name implies.

The wooing in *As You Like It* is remarkable insofar as Rosalind serves as her own proxy in the form of Ganymede. When she and Celia (Aliena) flee to the Forest of Arden they are of course not alone. Duke Senior and his merry men are there, along with jester Touchstone and goatherd Audrey, pastorals Silvius and Phoebe, and most importantly, young Orlando, the ardent young son of Sir Rowland de Bois, who busies himself hanging his homespun verses in Rosalind's honor on the trees, or carving her name in their bark. In love with Orlando since he overthrew Charles the wrestler in Act 1, Rosalind faces a dilemma in that her identity-in-exile is Ganymede, a form she is not ready to surrender so long as she is threatened by Duke Frederick. Her male pose stands in the way of any intimacies with the love-sick Orlando.

This seeming impasse proves expedient, however, in that it provides a chance for her to test Orlando's character and love without being recognized by him. At least, that is what she supposes. In Act 3, Sc. 2 there is a piquant exchange in which Ganymede agrees to counsel Orlando to cure him of his desire for Rosalind. Once again, Shakespeare stresses the nearly pathological nature of love.

ROSALIND

Love is merely a madness, and I tell you,
deserves as well a dark house and a whip as madmen
do; and the reason why they are not so punished and
cured is that the lunacy is so ordinary that the whippers
are in love too. Yet I profess curing it by counsel.

ORLANDO

Did you ever cure any so?

ROSALIND

Yes, one; and in this manner. He was to
Imagine me his love, his mistress; and I set him every
day to woo me. At which time would I, being but a
moonish youth, grieve, be effeminate, changeable,
longing and liking, proud, fantastical, apish, shallow,
inconstant, full of tears, full of smiles; for every passion
something, and for no passion truly anything, as boys
and women are for the most part cattle of this colour –
would now like him, now loathe him; then entertain
him, then forswear him; now weep for him, then spit
at him, that I drave my suitor from his mad humour
of love to a living humour of madness, which was to
forswear the full stream of the world and to live in a
nook merely monastic. And thus I cured him, and this
way will I take upon me to wash your liver as clean
as a sound sheep's heart, that there shall not be one
spot of love in't.

ORLANDO

I would not be cured, youth.

ROSALIND

I would cure you if you would but call me
Rosalind and come every day to my cot, and woo me.

ORLANDO

Now by the faith of my love, I will. Tell me
where it is.
(III, ii, 386-413)

Here is an astonishing colloquy indeed. Ganymede, infinitely
more mature and wiser than the man 'he' adores, presumes to teach him
that love is a disease he should strive to avoid, and that "he," Ganymede,
can cure him of it by essentially driving him to distraction. And though
Orlando, festooning the forest limbs with the name of Rosalind, has no
wish to be purged of love (III, ii, 409), he nonetheless consents to submit himself to Ganymede's physic, the initial condition of which is that
he address "Ganymede" as "Rosalind." In other words, Ganymede win-
somely proposes to be a counter-proxy whose mission is to break off
Orlando's relationship with Rosalind by destroying his love for her. Why
does he consent? Again we must ask, is Rosalind's disguise effective, or
is it seen through? What does Orlando see (and hear) when he beholds
this "Ganymede"? One thing is plain: he is under her spell. As was the
case with poor Mark Antony in relation to the infinitely cunning Cleopatra, Orlando is mesmerized by the apparition of this loquacious youth
whose speech swirls around him, tying his soul in what we might call
"nots." In some way or other, he recognizes that the gentleman calling
himself "Ganymede" is not who he seems to be, but is in fact his mysterious beloved. Orlando knows and knows not. Ganymede's power over
him is thus multiplied to the nth degree.

Orlando's tutorial in love with Professor Ganymede runs in the
text from IV, i, 25 through IV, i, 190. Orlando speaks with Rosalind,
hearing her voice, seeing her movements and gestures, and addressing
her by her proper name. Is it possible he hasn't an inkling this is She?
Ganymede runs circles around this flat-footed but ardent swain, fairly
daring him to notice that the youth he is calling "Rosalind" is none other
than his Rosalind standing before him. At the apogee of this dazzling
dialogue Ganymede invites Orlando to marry him on the spot under the
name of "Rosalind." This is done with Celia officiating. It is their symbolic and therefore real wedding, the one which will follow later being a
mere rubber stamp of social recognition.

V. Conclusion

In practical terms, of course, love by proxy isn't an especially good idea. How much better would it have been, for example, had Henry wooed and won Lady Margaret directly. Had there been a positive bond between them, they might have cooperated and overcome their foes and woes. Perchance fate might have spared Henry. But knowing nothing of the opposite sex, and passively assigning responsibility for his love life to one of the wolfish earls who surrounded him, Henry effectively sealed his doom. Margaret kisses the messenger, not Henry, and this alienation of England's ruler and his Queen hastens the disintegrations we remember as the Wars of the Roses. Margaret and Henry have a son whom Henry rashly disinherits under pressure from the house of York. (Part Three, I, i, 175-273) Well may we wonder whose son he actually was. Officially married to Henry, Margaret could not maintain a viable relationship with Suffolk, lending their affair a surreal and hyperbolical cast. Filled with resentment, Henry's banishes Suffolk, in effect signing the conniving Earl's death warrant. In mourning her lover, cradling his severed head in her arms, Margaret is so distraught that we must find her absurd. Not only do her trysts and plots make King Henry appear ludicrous in his own court, they render Margaret and her gallant romantic caricatures. No Tristan and Isolde they. Their imprudent and impetuous affair and overweening ambition drain them of nobility, and render their catastrophe "a most humorous sadness." (*As You Like It*, IV, I, 18-19)

Claudio, too, by turning over to a third person the job of winning Hero, botches everything. Olivia in *Twelfth Night* develops a crush on the messenger and ends with a husband other than the proxy she fell for (Cesario). And as for sweet Julia, consenting to courier love's *billet doux* for Sir Proteus is a well-intentioned misjudgment which will render his disloyalty much more difficult to swallow and forget going forward. Shakespeare's lesson is plainly displayed in *Love's Labour's Lost*, in which the wooers in their cleverness defeat their own purposes. Swearing to have nothing to do with women and then pursuing those girls of France under false colors, the King of Navarre and his royal bookmen behave as shallow adolescents. Biron discovers the value of plain speech and direct confession of love ("Henceforth my wooing mind shall be expressed in russet yeas, and honest kersey noes"), but it's too late. He and his fellow chatterboxes are hoist with their own petards, losing their ladies by the very wit with which they were sought. When the penalty year passes, how likely is it that these savvy gals will have any interest in such a pretentious and deceptive crew?

Only Rosalind and her Orlando triumph in the game of mediated love. "Ganymede" in Greek mythology is no cheap dispenser of drink and sex. Traditionally, the "cup bearer" was the host's officer at a feast, one who examined the food and drink to be sure it was wholesome. He watches over the boisterous crowd and gives warning to his sovereign when anything appears untoward or out of place. Instead of imposing an interloper between herself and Orlando, Rosalind manifests incandescently as Ganymede. But he is a numinous missionary akin to Hermes and Eros. Thus when Rosalind assumes the mien of Ganymede she is nothing less than Love itself. Orlando senses this, but is not equipped to truly understand, any more than the neighbors of Philemon and Baucis could recognize the two strangers in their midst. Orsino exults in *Twelfth Night*, "O, spirit of love, how quick and fresh art thou!" (I, i, 9) It is "Swift as a shadow, short as any dream, brief as the lightning in the collied night." (*A Midsummer Night's Dream*, I, i, 144-145) Rosalind instinctively becomes Eros. She is thus in one magnificent moment (1) the flesh-and-blood girl who finds her hero at the wrestling match, (2) the youth Ganymede, (3) the magus who will "make all these doubts even" and Eros himself (V, iv, 25). It is out of this spiritual whirlwind that Rosalind the hermaphroditic goddess speaks to poor bewitched Orlando. Love by proxy, then, is but a species of flawed human desire compromised by reflection. But after his encounter with his Goddess, his anima, Orlando limps no longer in logic, but soars in spirit: "I can live no longer by thinking," says he. (V, ii, 47) The Shakespearean ideal is not a barrier separating us from one another, but a flood of passion that sweeps everything into itself. "The tide is now." (*The Two Gentlemen of Verona*, II, ii, 14) The hazards we will always have with us. But to prevail we must be swift as love itself; when we feel its promptings, hoist sail.

Long ago the Shakespearean ideal was identified by G. Wilson Knight.

> All normal excellence is surpassed and duality transcended into a higher unity . . . on which the best commentary is Shakespeare's own *Phoenix and the Turtle*. As so often in his later work, we find normal categories exhausted in an attempt to categorize some actualization of the indescribable. The thing is 'beyond thought's compass' . . . . The general conception of a superlative beyond thought excellence within

the natural order is akin to and makes contact with Cleopatra's account of her miraculous dream, while Norfolk's use of 'beggar' [in All Is True] recalls 'it beggar'd all description' in the description of Cleopatra on Cydnus. (Knight, 321)

Love by proxy is for Shakespeare is as far from the ideal as we can possibly imagine. What it is can only be hinted at in words, of which the best are these:

So they lov'd, as love in twain
Had the essence but in one:
Two distincts, division none:
Number there in love was slain.

WORKS CITED:

F. H. Bradley, *Appearance and Reality*, Oxford University Press, Clarendon, 1897.

Marjorie Garber, *Shakespeare After All*, Anchor Books, 2004.

Ted Hughes, *Shakespeare and the Goddess of Complete Being*, Farrar Straus Giroux, 1992.

G. Wilson Knight, *The Crown of Life*, Barnes & Noble, 1964.

William Shakespeare, The Complete Works, 2d ed., S. Wells and G. Taylor, eds., Oxford University Press, Clarendon, 2005, including *Phoenix and the Turtle*.

7
Tragedy and Comedy in *Timon of Athens*

I. Introduction: Tragedy Meets Comedy

*I*n *The Most Lamentable Roman Tragedy of Titus Andronicus*, after enduring a series of unspeakable losses, including the sacrifice of a hand, and the beheading of two sons whom that manual sacrifice was meant to protect and liberate, Titus in his boundless melancholy begins to laugh. As he sees the pair of heads and his detached hand brought in on a platter, he reacts as though he'd heard a clever joke. His brother Marcus objects.

MARCUS

Why dost thou laugh? It fits not with this hour.

But the explanation is plain. The soul of Titus has reached the absolute extremity of grief.

TITUS

Why, I have not another tear to shed. (III, i, 264-265)

As so often happens in Shakespeare, tragedy passes into its opposite. And it is in that moment that authentic action and redemption appear as possibilities. Where this is insufficiently noticed, we miss an important dimension of the action.

A parallel development occurs in that neglected masterpiece, *The*

Life of Timon of Athens. Timon, a Greek plutocrat seeking to curry favor with his fellows by impersonating a universal benefactor, has squandered his estate through improvident—indeed reckless—giving. This practice is supported by serial borrowing, so that as catastrophe nears, Timon's bills far exceed his dwindling assets. Approaching for aid those he has befriended, he is spurned and rebuffed, and so undergoes the bleakest and most humiliating of insolvencies, public loss of everything. His genial and generous personality shrivels and blows away, leaving an unmitigated hatred of mankind, as butterfly might revert to caterpillar. His curses on Athens ringing in the air, Timon retreats to the desolate wooded coastline, where, exposed to the elements, he subsists on water and wild tubers. One day as he pokes at the cruel earth, he finds a huge cache of buried gold coins. It is too late, of course, for these, and so he too laughs at the irony.

> What is here?
> Gold? Yellow, glittering, precious gold?
> No, gods, I am no idle votarist:
> Roots, you clear heavens. Thus much of this will make
> Black white, foul fair, wrong right,
> Base noble, old young, coward valiant.
> Ha, you gods! Why this, what, this, you gods? Why,
> This will lug your priests and servants from your sides,
> Pluck stout men's pillows from below their heads.
> This yellow slave
> Will knit and break religions, bless th' accursed,
> Make the hoar leprosy adored, place thieves,
> And give them title, knee and approbation
> With senators on the bench. This is it
> That makes the wappered widow wed again.
> She whom the spittle house and ulcerous sores
> Would cast the gorge at, this embalms and spices
> To th' April day again. Come, damnèd earth,
> Thou common whore of mankind, that puts odds
> Among the rout of nations; I will make thee
> Do thy right nature.
> (IV, iii, 25-44)

At the tragic perigee we find, like buried gold, the jest, the irony: the coveted riches arrive not in time to rescue Timon from despair. Falling into an excoriating pessimism that makes the philosophical cynicism of his day seem contrived and shallow, Timon perishes, broken and alone, yet as utterly transformed as Lear on the heath. As Oedipus' search for the villain who brought the curse on Thebes ends with the awful revelation of his own fault, a recognition which, though fatal, allows him to achieve a final instant of personal integrity through acceptance of responsibility, so Timon's inextinguishable anguish carries with it the ultimate purgation of his soul. He dies in laughter.

II. Reading Timon

The risk, of course, is that some will not get the joke, in fact, not perceive it at all. When that happens, character and drama are misapprehended and improperly evaluated. Though the humor be embedded in the script and on the very lips of the hero, there is something in the grim puritanical soul which will not allow itself the luxury and insight of amusement. A curiously literal perspective through which tragedy is tragedy and comedy is comedy (and never the twain shall meet) keeps many from appreciating the play (and life itself) in all its depth and tantalizing ambiguity.

An example of the failure to come to terms with the comic dimension of tragedy can be found in the edition of the complete works put out by the Royal Shakespeare Company (Bate, Rasmussen, 2007). In their preface to *Timon* the editors make no secret of their dislike of the play. It is and "will always remain one of Shakespeare's least known, least loved and least performed plays." (B&R, 1746) One can almost hear in this a Parthian shot, and with good reason. The reader will of course ask "why?" What makes this play so bad? After all, "for intellectual muscle, the second half of the play is as powerful as anything in Shakespeare." (B&R, 1746) So puissant, yet so unloved. What makes it so?

Well, we are told, there is no love in it. It is all about avarice and "the desire for money." (B&R, 1744) "No character in the play is struck by the dart of love." Evidently for the editors of the RSC edition to be successful a stage drama must include a romantic story line; without it, there must be reliance on a poor substitute, in this case money. *Timon of Athens* represents nothing but a gritty lesson about the consequences of "worshipping money." Instead of tender exchanges of passion between the sexes, there are nothing but nests of viperous loan sharks and their hapless victims locked in unseemly financial struggles.

Lacking amorous intrigues and titillating dalliances, *Timon of Ath-*

ens features nothing more personal than a focus on "the master-servant relationship, as opposed to parent-child or man-woman." (B&R, 1744) But are these two sets of relationships the only ones that make the theatrical world go round? Parent/child and man/woman? What about woman/woman, as in the relationship between Rosalind and Celia in *As You Like It* or man/man as we see it between Marcus and Aufidius in *Coriolanus*? Does the unacceptable narrowness reside in Shakespeare's *Timon*—or in the shrunken critical taxonomy of Bate and Rasmussen? After all, nearly the entire first half of *The Merchant of Venice* focuses on the tensions of male characters caught in money conflicts. Isn't "money" the heart of the matter there? The love quarrel of Portia and Bassanio tacked on at the end could be excised and still preserve the significance of the play. Yet *Merchant* is hailed as one of the most popular in the canon.

In its rush to put the hatchet to *Timon* the RSC forgets that we are dealing with Shakespeare, after all. The principal responsibility of the editor is to give to audiences and readers the keys that will unlock drama and prompt appreciation. Informing the student that this is his "least known, least loved and least performed" play is hardly an inducement to read. The natural reaction to that news is to go do something else.

III. Exegesis

Very well, let's think. Is the play about "money" or the "master-servant relationship"? The short answer is, neither. The principal theme of *Timon of Athens* is friendship—and its foibles. The Greek term is *philia*, a species of love, though the RCS editors can discover love in none of the scenes. Friendship is set in the commercial intercourse of ancient Athens, in which the affective associations of businessmen blossomed in the course of trade. So important were those friendships that they were taken up and transmogrified by the Athenian philosophers, including Socrates, Plato, Aristotle, and later by the Stoics and the Cynics. The ideal love in that cultural milieu was not the "man-woman" relationship at all, but the love of friends of the same sex for one another, whether of a sensual or a "platonic" nature. And though the RSC editors don't mention it, Shakespeare's *Timon of Athens* is one of the two greatest modern reprises of Plato's *Symposium*, the other being the *In Vino Veritas* of the Danish philosopher Soren Kierkegaard. It's that sort of background which is essential to supply if anyone is going to have an incentive to jump in and grapple with the text.

While Socrates, Plato and Aristotle praised *philia* as the royal road to virtue (*arete*) and sought to express its essence in words, in the later stages of Greek thought the noble friendships so admired by these three (and made a cardinal value by Epicurus), were condemned by the Stoics and the Cynics as sources of unhappiness. For like any other worldly good, friendship is fragile and easily lost. Stoicism and Cynicism were attempts to jettison friendship as an ethical ideal and replace it with either a purification of the spirit (Stoicism) or a principled return to nature (Cynicism), more durable modes of tranquility and fulfillment. Doing so would shield the soul from the trauma which must accompany the loss of any important friendship.

The most apparent problem with Lord Timon is not his alleged "love of money" but his failure to have any real friends. Those he believes to be his friends are merely hangers-on whose attentions are functions of his bounty. The protagonist fancies that just as he comes to the rescue of the impecunious citizens of his social class, so would they, in his time of need, step in to save him. This form of amatory insurance is perhaps the single biggest reason for Timon's exuberance in the first half of the play. The cynical philosopher Apemantus attempts in his gruff way to alert Timon to the reality of his situation, that he is being exploited by his cohorts who attend his lavish dinner parties, and that these fellows are in fact really dining on Timon himself, devouring his substance without the slightest thought of reciprocity. It is this fatal blindness to the actual selfishness of men which is the flaw which brings about his undoing. To claim, then, that the play is repugnant in its emphasis on "money" is to err on the most significant point. As in *The Merchant of Venice* with its Duke and ducats, the true issue is the skewed relations of men with one another (*e.g.*, the troubled friendship of Antonio and Bassanio), so in *Timon of Athens* its hero is not undone by the love of money, but by his failure to find and cultivate genuine bonds with others. When the day of reckoning is at hand, Timon is shocked to learn that his "friends" will not lift a finger to help him. Instead of cultivating a guarded realpolitik about human nature, Timon gives himself over to an almost hysterical prodigality, and when he collapses his mood becomes so embittered that it is akin to madness.

As for love, it is most exemplified in this unique play not in heterosexual liaisons, but in the sensibility and loyalty of the steward Flavius, who keeps Timon's accounts and strives (like Apemantus) to warn him of the dangers he is entering into by habitual borrowing to keep his philanthropic ship afloat. Though the bond is not romantic, it is heartfelt and authentic. We see it plainly in the first act ("I bleed inwardly for my lord," I, ii, 204), and again in the play's terrible final moments when Flavius visits Timon in his cave in the wilderness. Here is Flavius' mid-play profession of loyalty.

> Good fellows all,
> The latest of my wealth I'll share amongst you.
> Wherever we shall meet, for Timon's sake
> Let's yet be fellows. Let's shake our heads and say,
> As 'twere a knell unto our master's fortunes,
> 'We have seen better days'.
> Let us take some.
> Nay, put out all your hands. Not one word more.
> Thus part we rich in sorrow, parting poor.
> O, the fierce wretchedness that glory brings us!
> Who would not wish to be from wealth exempt,
> Since riches point to misery and contempt?
> Who would be so mocked with glory, or to live
> But in a dream of friendship,
> To have his pomp and all what state compounds
> But only painted like his varnished friends?
> Poor honest lord, brought low by his own heart,
> Undone by goodness! Strange, unusual blood
> When man's worst sin is he does too much good!
> Who then dares to be half so kind again?
> For bounty, that makes gods, does still mar men.
> My dearest lord, blessed to be most accursed,
> Rich only to be wretched, thy great fortunes
> Are made thy chief afflictions. Alas, kind lord!
> He's flung in rage from this ingrateful seat
> Of monstrous friends;
> Nor has he with him to supply his life,
> Or that which can command it.
> I'll follow and enquire him out.
> I'll ever serve his mind with my best will.
> Whilst I have gold I'll be his steward still.
> (IV, ii, 23-51)

These intentions of love and devotion bring Flavius in the second half of the play to Timon's hovel, where members of his former entou-

rage come, either to exploit him, or lure him back to civilization. Flavius
enters in Act IV, Sc. iii, and descries his poor master:

> O you gods!
> Is yon despised and ruinous man my lord,
> Full of decay and failing? O monument
> And wonder of good deeds evilly bestowed!
> What an alteration of honour has desp'rate want made!
> What viler thing upon the earth than friends,
> Who can bring the noblest minds to basest ends!
> How rarely does it meet with this time's guise,
> When man was wished to love his enemies!
> Grant I may ever love and rather woo
> Those that would mischief me than those that do!
> He's caught me in his eye. I will present
> My honest grief unto him, and as my lord
> Still serve him with my life. — My dearest master.
> (IV, iii, 460-473)

Timon, now a confirmed Über-cynic, distrusts. Isn't Flavius after
something?

> But tell me true —
> For I must ever doubt, though ne'er so sure —
> Is not thy kindness subtle, covetous,
> A usuring kindness, and, as rich men deal gifts,
> Expecting in return twenty to one?
> (IV, iii, 507-511)

The answer is loyalty itself.

> No, my most worthy master, in whose breast
> Doubt and suspect, alas, are placed too late.
> You should have feared false times when you did feast.
> Suspect still comes where an estate is least.
> That which I show, heaven knows, is merely love,
> Duty and zeal to your unmatchèd mind,
> Care of your food and living; and, believe it,
> My most honored lord,
> For any benefit that points to me,

Either in hope or present, I'd exchange
For this one wish: that you had power and wealth
To requite me by making rich yourself."
(IV, iii, 512-523)

So much for the love deemed missing in the play by Bate and Rasmussen.

IV. Philosophical and Religious Meaning

Their failure to observe the Platonic background of the play is compounded by their bizarre neglect of the Biblical theme, for *Timon of Athens* is equally and obviously a restatement of the *Book of Job*. It will be recalled that the latter opens with a comical conceit: a wager between God and Satan—who seem to be on remarkably chummy terms—as to whether the man Job is really pious and virtuous, or a sanctimonious fraud. God permits Satan to go forth and inflict on unsuspecting Job a series of ever-increasing depredations and calamities to test his faith. If Job curses his Maker, the Devil wins, if not, score one for the good guys. Suffering unprecedented catastrophes, and reduced to dust and ashes, Job maintains his spiritual integrity, though his ever-solicitous spouse urges him to "curse God and die." (Job, 2:9) He is then visited by successive acquaintances who reason with him and debate the meaning of his fall. In much the same way, after his absenting from social and political felicity, Timon, no-longer-of-Athens, is forced in the midst of his travail to entertain a series of Athenian intruders who seem to do everything in their power to rankle him still further. Shakespeare's genius, then, in this "unloved" play, is to knit together Plato's Hellenic masterpiece, *Symposium*, and the pinnacle of Hebrew insight, the *Book of Job*, into one single drama. At the conclusion of the *Book of Job*, God loses his patience with Job's kvetching, and decides to pull rank. To the long-suffering man of sorrows, God appears as from "a whirlwind" to challenge the right of a mere mortal to question his treatment at the hands of the Most High. (Job, 38:1 et seq.) "Where wast thou when I laid the foundations of the earth?" And it seems more than a mere coincidence, does it not, that in the midst of Timon's travails, as he bickers with his tormentor Apemantus, he expressly alludes to the "whirlwind" he prays would waft the latter back to Athens? (IV, iii, 290) Shakespeare's *Timon of Athens* is thus not an inconsequential work, but rather an astonishing template of western civilization, one which looks beyond classical literature and scripture to a troubling and prophetic vision of ages to come. In the *Book of Job,* a still caring if befuddled and casuistic deity restores to the mortal He created and permitted to be tortured by his partner the devil nearly all that had been destroyed, so that, as the curtain falls, Job is in possession once again of fields and fortune. Except for his slaughtered sons and daughters, all losses are restored and sorrows end. But Shakespeare, writing on the cusp of the modern age and in the harsh light of cynical philosophy, can extend to Timon no cheap hope or fairy-tale replenishment, and "Misanthropus" perishes with cries of execration on his lips. Thus Shakespeare is our contemporary, our spiritual pioneer, always one step beyond. As Walter Kaufmann observed, he is the precursor of Nietzsche, Camus and Sartre, one who leaps out of the bosom of the middle ages into the wasteland of the future, the modern age of doubt and causeless suffering. *Timon of Athens* should be properly situated as the forerunner of theatre of the absurd, of Samuel Beckett and those who wait in comic fretfulness for a "Godot" who never arrives. It sounds unflinchingly the note of meaninglessness from which we flee in all our bourgeois nostrums and media-driven fantasies. And in that respect it is not surprising that we find Mssrs. Bate and Rasmussen leaving Timon in the gutter. The vision of human existence in *Timon of Athens* and *Waiting for Godot* is not one of human power, nobility and resilience, but despair, impotence—and, in the end, self recognition, and laughter. Hyperbolical Timon even prays that the gods "quell the source of all erection," (IV, iii, 163-164) while in Beckett's masterpiece Gogo and Didi look enviously at the prospect of hanging themselves as it will give them one final erection. With the denial of that biological function would come the cessation of specious happiness and the extinction of a bastard race.

V. An Economic Interlude

Adopting an economic standpoint reinforces our comprehension of Timon's temperament and outlook. In terms of wealth management, the *modus operandi* of Timon is the direct opposite of Shylock's. The latter makes a living lending money at usurious interest; we may infer that to his kinsmen far less or none is charged, thus prospering the Jewish community in Venice. While we are given no information as to how Timon amassed his original fortune, if it was not inherited it probably arose through borrowing funds to buy lands which resulted in increased crops and yields. The mention of Athenian senators letting out coin "upon large interest" (III, vi, 106; see also, III, iv, 53) implies that to build that estate he had to accept soaring measures of debt. Timon far outstrips in *naïveté* the Venetian merchant Antonio, who merely lends monies *gratis*. Not only does Timon not charge for a loan, in the final stages of his enterprise he is just as likely to give cash away as he is to lend it. At times he refuses re-payment. (I, ii, 8-12) Further, he has acquired luxurious tastes, and cultivates the habit of showering his friends with choice gifts. Contrary to the maxim of Polonius, this is all fueled, of course, by ever extended borrowing, borrowing which is needed not only to maintain his lavish lifestyle, give presents to his companions and operate his businesses, but also to make payments on prior loans and interest. Thus the first half of the play, which reflects the ethos of Plato's *Symposium*, also registers the New Testament's *Parable of the Prodigal Son* (Luke 15: 11-32) (the clue word "prodigal" occurring at II, ii, 162).

VI. Philosophical Premises

What is Timon's problem? The keyword "root" running throughout the text implies obliquely that we may "delve [him] to the root," or in colloquial terms, find out what makes him tick. (See, *Cymbeline*, I, i, 28) Can we identify his "tragic flaw"? The RSC editors contend that what ails Timon and his fellows is coarse possessive acquisitiveness, the "love of money." But this is not supported in the script. If Timon treasured money above all he would have kept it, not thrown it away. In the first half of the play he either behaves like Aristotle's "great-souled man," the public benefactor who lavishes his substance on others, or he just spends imprudently on himself. If there had been a Las Vegas in ancient Greece, Shakespeare's Timon would have been one of the "whales," for money for him is a game, not the *ens realissimum*. In the second half, he chooses to live in a desert, and when he finds buried gold, he treats it like trash. We never see him actually working, producing wealth by the sweat of his brow and application of business acumen. Nor are intelligent investments a part of his enterprise. Wealth for Timon arises magically, *ex nihilo*. There is no reason, then, to place a premium on it (*i.e.*, love money) because the arrival of wealth in his hands is just part of the nature of things.

Drawing on principles of economics and philosophy, we can set forth the unspoken tenets and characteristics which lead Timon to his doom.

(1) His implicit credo is incautiously optimistic: human beings are

good-natured, as concerned with one another as they are with themselves.

(2) In the context of "*philia*," (the love of friends), he assumes that those who are treated most extravagantly will be the closest and most reliable, almost as though love and loyalty could be purchased. He is a rationalist who believes in a law of reciprocity as unshakable as the axioms of Newtonian physics: for each favor there is an equal and opposite favor. Prior to his fall, he could never see that his friends were actually parasites.

(3) In Shakespearean language, Timon is an "unthrift," one who spends freely and impulsively.

(4) That prodigality is in turn based on a deeper conception as to the nature of life and reality. So long has Timon enjoys prosperity, he presumes the ground and substance of human society is abundance. The *oikos* is like a wellspring of plenty bubbling up into our coffers.

Plato, to the nayward, taught that the fundamental economic actuality is not wealth but want, scarcity, need and poverty. These negatives goad humankind on to work, to war, and, in some cases, to prosperity. But even if fortunes accumulate, this alters not the nature of things, the negativity of which we ignore at our peril. It is true that Timon lives in an affluent city replete with mansions and temples of gleaming marble. But Athens did not become rich until it defeated its enemies (particularly the Persians) in war. Once its enemies were vanquished, left with no serious impediments in international trade, Athens quickly found itself with a far-flung hegemony and fabled assets. But Timon childishly assumes that wealth is the natural and automatic concomitant of civilized life. In this respect, his underlying metaphysics is a vestigial ontologism which can be traced all the way back to the pre-Socratic philosopher Parmenides, who viewed the world as a plenum and any form of non-being or difference as an illusion. By the time of Timon's Athens philosophers such as Democritus had broken with Parmenides' absolutism by introducing negativities into their thinking (such as the "void" of Democritus in which the "atoms" move). And it is curious in that respect that Karl Marx, who wrote his doctoral dissertation on Democritus, devised a doctrine he could call "dialectical materialism," forgetting that the void can hardly be termed a material substance. Looking at Shakespeare's own metaphysics implicit in *Timon of Athens* and many other works, a more apt term to characterize it would be "dialectical nihilism." Indeed, viewed in philosophical terms, we could express the whole tragedy of Timon as the story of a man who lives as a materialist and dies as a nihilist. (As to Shakespeare's nihilism, a curious reader might commence investigation by reading "The Tragedy of Existence: Shakespeare's *Troilus and Cressida*," by Joyce Carol Oates, which is reproduced on her homepage, and was published originally as two separate essays in *Philological Quarterly*, Spring, 1967, and *Shakespeare Quarterly*, Spring, 1966.)

VII. Cynicism v. Nihilism

We come now to the final charge made against *Timon of Athens* as a work of dramatic art by the RSC editors: the play is a failure because it has no "heroic counter-voice" to lend dramatic tension and interest. (Bate & Rasmussen, 1746) If only the character of Alcibiades had been "more fully developed," they lament, we might have had a real play here. But without such an adversarial colloquy no play can rise to the level of satisfactory stagecraft. This aesthetic theory may well have merit, but in the case of *Timon of Athens* Shakespeare certainly does provide an heroic counter-voice: the cynical philosopher Apemantus. He has an important role to play at the beginning of the action and at the end, when, like Job's so-called "friends," he shows up at Timon's barren bivouac to chide him for appropriating his own philosophy and character. This leads to one of literature's most caustic altercations. As in Plato's *Symposium*, the celebratory feast of playwright Agathon is crashed by both Alcibiades and his teacher Socrates, so in Shakespeare's *Timon of Athens*, the feast of Lord Timon is invaded by the Cynic Apemantus, who refuses meat and wine and spends the whole dinner chewing on a carrot (or some such "root") and mocking the extravagant folly of both his host and the other guests. As the theme of the *Symposium* is eros, so in *Timon of Athens* entertainment is provided by a masked Cupid who sings to the company. The outlook of Apemantus is neatly captured in his prayer before the meal:

> Immortal gods, I crave no pelf.
> I pray for no man but myself.
> Grant I may never prove so fond
> To trust man on his oath and bond,
> Or a harlot for her weeping,
> Or a dog that seems a-sleeping,
> Or a keeper with my freedom,
> Or my friends if I should need 'em.

Amen. So fall to't.
Rich men sin, and I eat root.
(I, ii, 61-70)

The philosophy of Apemantus is a synthesis of several disparate themes: a simple naturalism is wedded to a frank but temperate egoism and a mild asceticism. Whether philosophy affords an example of precisely such a potpourri of principles is a good question for antiquarians to puzzle over. But as a foil to set off the profligacy of Timon it is quite perfect. Apemantus functions like a chorus chiming at regular intervals, registering the excesses and follies of Timon and his companions. He makes himself unwelcome but is tolerated and departs intact, no poison hemlock for him. Thus, in the first half of the play, he is already an effective counter-voice, but not yet one of "heroic" proportions. It is only when he arrives at Timon's crude shelter in the wilderness that he becomes at once the classical antagonist and stand-in for the fans of Job. He has heard by the grapevine that Timon has adopted a personam that can only have been pilfered from himself. "I was directed hither. Men report thou dost affect my manners, and dost use them." (IV, iii, 199-200) It is a transgression of ancient principles of intellectual property and an affront to his dignity. Further, Timon's crash-and-burn fall from grace is an illustration and confirmation of everything he has tried to teach people in general and Timon in particular. In other words, though he claims to be a wise man, he can't resist the temptation to show up and say, "I told you so." Though he rationalizes his appearance at Timon's threshold as a campaign to "vex" Timon (IV, iii, 238) we know better. These two have been at each other's throats for a long time, and in their verbal jousting we hear the echos of *philia* gone awry. Their dialogue is reminiscent of the love/hate relationship of Marcus and Aufidius in Shakespeare's masterpiece *Coriolanus*.

Apemantus' diagnosis of Timon's condition is appropriate cynical: you've fallen from wealth and power and now all the good things you enjoyed are sour grapes.

This is in thee a nature but infected,
A poor unmanly melancholy, sprung
From change of fortune. Why this spade, this place,
This slave-like habit, and these looks of care?
Thy flatterers yet wear silk, drink wine, lie soft,
Hug their diseased perfumes, and have forgot

That Timon ever was. Shame not these woods
By putting on the cunning of a carper.
Be thou a flatterer now, and seek to thrive
By that which has undone thee. Hinge thy knee,
And let his very breath whom thou'lt observe
Blow off thy cap. Praise his most vicious strain,
And call it excellent. Thou wast told thus.
Thou gav'st thine ears like tapsters that bade welcome
To knaves and all approachers. 'Tis most just
That thou turn rascal. Hadst thou thy wealth again,
Rascals should have it. Do not assume my likeness.
(IV, iii, 203-219)

This is the most excellent counter-voice, in spite of the fact that—
or perhaps because—it so closely mirrors Timon's own discourse. Yet
we can see that Apemantus is in error. He has not the intellectual equipment to take the measure of his adversary. He says if Timon were rich
once more he'd revert to his old conduct, not knowing that Timon with
his cache of gold is more affluent than ever. In the words and behavior
of Timon, Apemantus can recognize only reflections of his own philosophy, not ever comprehending the radical nihilism which Timon has
embraced. And it is this incommensurability of Timon's speech on the
one hand and that of Apemantus on the other that gives their bickering
such a comic ambience. Speaking different languages, they are at cross
purposes and yet cannot fathom how and why. Apemantus can only offer pop psychology to account for Timon's beastly transformation.

If thou didst put this sour cold habit on
To castigate thy pride. 'twere well; but thou
Dost it enforcedly. Thou'dst courtier be again
Wert thou not beggar. Willing misery
Outlives incertain pomp, is crowned before.
The one is filling still, never complete;
The other at high wish. Best state, contentless,
Hath a distracted and most wretched being,
Worse than the worst, content.
Thou shouldst desire to die, being miserable.
(IV, iii, 240-249)

That is a speech straight from the *Book of Job*, yet it fails utterly to touch the problematic that gnaws at the innards of Timon, who has "seen the spider" and is changed in the kernal of his very being. (See, *The Winter's Tale*, II, i, 40-47)

Apemantus can see in Timon only a poor and benighted reflection of himself; Timon is a mere student who failed to learn and apply the doctor's teachings. But though he styles himself a misanthrope, there is a vast difference between their respective positions. Apemantus is in fact little more than a temperamental curmudgeon, a cranky grand-dad and professional party pooper, who decks his attitude out in the trappings of philosophy. His asceticism is a comfy minimalism which serves as a warning to his countrymen to avoid various forms of vanity, as we find in the Biblical book of Solomon, *Ecclesiastes*. Cleave to the least, prepare for the worst, and you will be the happiest of men. As a pragmatic nostrum, this kind of sermonizing may have value, but as a proffered insight into life and the nature of things, it is hollow. Timon, on the other hand, despite his rantings, displays the courage of his convictions. If his hate grows "to the whole race of mankind" (IV, i, 39-40), it should logically extend to himself. Timon takes this step; Apemantus does not.

TIMON

All's obliquy;
There's nothing level in our cursèd natures
But direct villainy. Therefore be abhorred
All feasts, societies, and throngs of men.
His semblable, yea, *himself*, Timon disdains.
Destruction fang mankind.
(IV, iii, 18-23)

When Alcibiades encounters Timon in the wasteland, he fails to recognize him at first. "What art thou there? Speak," he demands. The reply is stark: "A beast, as thou art. The canker gnaw thy heart for showing me again the eyes of man." (IV, iii, 49-50) But a man which is a beast is worse than any beast, it's plain to see, and "*tat tvam asi*." The real tragedy is the moment of dramatic discovery: self-accusation. It is this moment, and not Harold Bloom's mere "self-overhearing," which renders us genuinely human. All of Shakespeare's tragic heroes come to terms with their quintessential unworthiness, and were there space herein we could easily make a complete catalogue. All come in one form or another to Hamlet's admission: "O, what a rogue and peasant slave am I." (II, ii,

552) To look honestly at ourselves means to look at our faults as well as our virtues, and acknowledge how much damage those faults occasion in a world in which all misbehave in the same manner. The cynicism of Apemantus contains no such insight. For cynicism, there is a remedy: live like a dog and be a good man. For Timon and Shakespeare's other tragic heroes, the seeming good man turns out to be a cur.

And yet a paradox lies just here. For if one truly hates oneself, one is perforce divided into the hating self and the hated. But to be consistent, the hating self must hate not only the hated self but the hating as well. This obviously creates an infinite regress which may be understood as a "*mise en abyme*" much discussed in critical theory. And what is immediately striking here is that the tragedy of self hatred, drawn to its logical, regressive conclusion, is funny. To hate myself I must have two aspects, the detestably ignoble and the noble which does the hating. But hatred is not a virtue, and if the hate is consistent the hater must be hated as well, by a hater sub-2, etc., etc., *ad infinitum*. And this is absurd, and comical. As Woody Allen once said, "I have only one regret, that I was not born someone else." Here we find the "root" of Shakespeare's tragi-comical vision of "Homo sapiens." We come to recognize that while Apemantus accuses Timon of filching his intellectual identity, Timon is as much like Apemantus as Prince Hamlet is like Polonius.

VIII. Conclusion: Comedy and Tragedy at the Barricades

Before bringing this discussion to an end, it should be pointed out that *Timon of Athens* includes low comedy as well as high. Prostitutes Phrynia and Timandra, who alternate between cursing Timon and groveling before him to obtain gold, are picaresque characters who serve the same comic functions as so many of Shakespeare's lesser personages, including Dogberry, Doll Tearsheet, Mistress Quickly, Saunder Simpcox, Pistol, the bawd and pander in *Pericles*, and many, many more. In what is arguably the most dramatic scene of personal misery in all of Shakespeare, clowns Phrynia and Timandra serve as low foils to set off the existential malaise of Lord Timon. The middle ground is briefly occupied by the satirical portrait of the oligarch Sempronius, whom we see maligning Timon and his request for help, first on the grounds that he should have approached others before him, such as Lords Lucius and Lucullus. When he learns that in fact all the others have already been tapped, he feigns resentment that he was not thought of until last! (III, iii, 1-26) Peremptorily dismissing Timon's importunate manservant,

Sempronius concludes with bit of mock rhetoric, "Who bates mine honour shall not know my coin." (III, iii, 26) In the hands of the right director, this may be expected to amuse.

It is quite possible to dismiss the lesser known works of Shakespeare as undeserving of attention. As they are "substandard," there is no real reason to perform or study them with the care and assiduousness conferred on our favorites. Giving these orphaned plays and poems a condescending nod merely exacerbates our dilemma. Given the poverty of today's theatre and monitory literature, even a minor Shakespearean work such as *Timon* towers above its Lilliputian critics. Shakespeare is the worthy successor to Plato, whose *Symposium* first disclosed the dialectical relationship between tragedy and comedy. By restating that theme in the early modern era, Shakespeare transmits the ancient wisdom to us. The irony is that we should turn our backs on the artist and thinker from whom we might derive the critical insights and learning we need so very badly. In our daily "tragedies" we lose touch with the comic perspective, and fall into maudlin self-pity. The fault is never ours. There is always someone else to blame—and haul into court. Our lives become indistinguishable from the media melodramas in which we wallow. The floodgates of mediocrity are wide open now, and sweep the past away. There is no need of art when the psychiatrist's pharmakon is eager to step into the breach.

It is interesting to listen to the Royal Shakespeare Company sniffing that Shakespeare's *Timon of Athens* has an "incomplete" feel about it, insinuating that it is little more than glorified scrimshaw having no business in the First Folio. Yet, at the same time, like so many traditionalists, the RSC editors are convinced that it is the work of not one but two dramatists, Shakespeare and Thomas Middleton. Yes, it seems the material was so intractable that even with the help of another famous author, the world's supreme literary artist couldn't connect the dots. It's as if one argued that we should scrap the Venus de Milo and other classic sculptures on grounds of amputation. Then there are the canvases of Vincent van Gogh that suffer from a lack of pigment on account of the poverty of the genius who struggled to eat and buy paint. Inferior? Not worth a glance? Hardly. The BBC film production that brought *Timon of Athens* to life testifies to the enduring power of even the least of Shakespeare's works.

In a discussion such as this, appropriate contextualization becomes key. Instead of contrasting *Timon of Athens* with perfectly rounded plays such as *Othello* or *King Richard III*, it might be more illuminating to see in *Timon* a fountainhead of modernism, the source for so much in Joyce, Sartre, Brecht, Beckett, Ionesco, Pinter and the entire theatre of the absurd that moved audiences in the twentieth century. In that setting, Shakespeare's play reemerges as a Himalayan peak whose very austerity and unsparing vision reflects timeless verities.

Of those truths, for us today at least the economic lesson should be considered. Lord Timon is a symbol of what befalls a nation which chooses the path of debt to reach the summit of prosperity, rather like digging oneself a deep hole to scale Olympus. Heedless of the teaching of Shakespeare in this "inferior" work, the United Kingdom and its offspring, the United States of America, having raised themselves up on clouds of exponentially multiplying obligations, are now busy reaping the whirlwind. Just as it was too late for Timon to spend his discovered gold, it may be too late for the English speaking peoples to recover the wisdom of Shakespeare. And that, as Corporal Nym would say, "is the humor of it." The joke's on us.

WORKS CITED:

Joyce Carol Oates, "The Tragedy of Existence: Shakespeare's Troilus and Cressida," accessible on webpage of Prof. Joyce Carol Oates.

William Shakespeare, Complete Works, Jonathan Bate, Eric Rasmussen, eds. The Royal Shakespeare Company, Random House, 2007. Reprinted by Foreign Language Teaching and Research Press, Beijing, 2008.

William Shakespeare, The Complete Works, 2d Edition, Stanley Wells, Gary Taylor, eds. Clarendon Press, Oxford, 2005.

8

Much is False in *All Is True*

I. Remembering *All Is True*

At the beginning of Act 3 of Shakespeare's *All Is True* (popularly referenced as *The Life of King Henry VIII*), Queen Katherine has retreated from the humiliating proceedings at Blackfriars to her rooms at Bridewell. Having denounced Cardinal Wolsey and challenged his authority to sit as her judge, and having departed peremptorily from the consistory, Katherine is profoundly shaken. She has had to respond to allegations that her long marriage to the English king is, and has always been, invalid on grounds of incest, implying the illegitimacy of her daughter Mary. It has taken all her strength to stand up to the pressure placed on her to accede to these charges. Exhausted in her chamber, she knows it's only a matter of time before her relentless husband and his attendant lords will seek her out for further harassment. At this point she is wholly isolated. God is her only refuge. We thus expect to find her kneeling devoutly at her prie-dieu, hands clasped before images of Christ and the Blessed Virgin, imploring Heaven for protection.

Instead we are surprised to witness her calling to her maidservants for a ditty.

QUEEN

Take thy lute, wench; my soul grows sad with troubles;
Sing and disperse 'em, if thou canst. Leave working.

Song

Orpheus with his lute made trees,
And the mountain tops that freeze,
  Bow themselves, when he did sing:
To his music plants and flowers
Ever sprung, as sun and showers
  There had made a lasting spring.

Every thing that heard him play,
Even the billows of the sea,
  Hung their heads, and then lay by.
In sweet music is such art,
Killing care and grief of heart
  Fall asleep or, hearing, die.
(III, i, 1-16)

These charming stanzas are consistent with the pastoral and romantic ballads abounding in Elizabethan literature. Yet in this particular setting they jar. Orpheus is not a Christian saint but a poet, a figure of Greek myth and legend who descends to Hades to rescue Eurydice. From this and other ancient narratives emerged the Hellenistic religion known as "Orphism," a pious hodge-podge which endured for centuries and which centered on the destruction and rebirth of "Orpheus," whose tunes transfixed all who heard them. Suffice it to say there is no evidence that Katherine of Aragon ever took a serious interest in Greek or Roman mythology, or that at such a sensitive moment in her life she would have relished or even tolerated secular diversions. It might be suggested that the death and reconstitution of such a fabled hero as Orpheus resembles in some ways the death and resurrection of Christ. But while an intellectual comparison might be pondered by a professor of comparative religion, it would be wholly incommensurate with the mindset of Katherine of Aragon, especially in the predicament in which she now found herself. She was combating desperately, gallantly, to defend her marriage and queenly throne. In that all-consuming legal contest she had no time for vain displays or entertainments.

G. Wilson Knight in his classic essay, "Henry VIII and the Poetry of Conversion" notes that the Orpheus song is reminiscent of the plights of Marianna in *Measure for Measure* and Desdemona in *Othello* (Knight, 290-291) He writes, "The synchronization of plaintive song with an especial domesticity has closely resembled Desdemona's willow song and her talk with Emilia . . . . In mood and purpose the two songs are analogous." (Knight, 291) Katherine is a "tired, almost broken woman" who reminds us of other Shakespearean females oppressed by overbearing lords.

Portrait of Katherine of Aragon, circa 1502, by Michael Sittow

By showing Queen Katherine entertaining herself with pagan lyrics in her hour of crisis, Shakespeare nudges us away from viewing her in terms of Catholicism. When Cardinals Wolsey and Campeius [Campeggio] arrive and address her in Latin, the language of the Church, Katherine objects: "O, good my lord, no Latin!" (III, I, 46-47) But Latin is the language of the Mass. The fact is that the historical Katherine of Aragon was a staunch Catholic who inherited her faith from militant parents who fought against Moslem incursions in Spain, and who passed that vigorous Romanism on to her; she, in turn, shared it with her daughter Mary.

One historian comments of Katherine's devotion:

She often got up at midnight to say matins, and then again at five for mass, dressing hurriedly and telling her maids that any time spent adorning herself was time wasted. On Fridays and Saturdays she fasted all day; she read the Office of the Blessed Virgin daily and, after dinner, read a saint's life to her women. It was said that when she knelt to pray, she denied herself the comfort of a cushion. (Erickson, 66)

Yet Shakespeare gives in *All Is True* not a single instance in which Katherine exhibits that strident Catholic regimen. Indeed, the words "Catholic" and "Catholicism" do not occur in the script. Though Katherine appeals to the Pope, (II, iv, 128-130), that is preceded by a colorless wish to be advised "by my friends in Spain." (IV, i, 56) Entirely missing is any depiction of her voluntarily engaged in recognizably Catholic activity. No "Hail Marys" for this good lady. Not once is she seen taking Holy Communion, being shriven by a confessor, praying the Rosary (Cp. Part Two, *King Henry VI*, I, iii, 52-61), invoking the Blessed Virgin, fasting, venerating the saints, making a pilgrimage, or performing any action whatsoever identifying her as Roman Catholic. Even at her death, there appears no priest, no administration of Extreme Unction. This is a non-sacramental, non-liturgical dramatic character. Katherine in *All Is True* is shorn of every trace of Roman rites. Yet it is well known historically that she was a conscientious member of the Third Order of St. Francis.

In Act 4, Sc. 2, immediately before her death, she receives a mystical vision in the form of "spirits of peace" who dance and grace her with garlands and palm. This apparition is staged before the audience, which must find in it nothing particularly Catholic. The palm has been employed as a symbol of sanctity or blessing since antiquity, long before Christ. One might go so far as to say the vision she experiences is merely aesthetic in its cavorting of anonymous "spirits." In content it vaguely resembles the mythic ceremony in *The Tempest* involving Iris, Ceres, Juno and their "spirits." (IV, i, 65-156; cp. Bate, Rasmussen, 1384) Let us be clear about this. Had Shakespeare wanted cherubim he would have called for them, as, *e.g.*, he summons "Cupid" and "Amazons" in the masque in Act I of *Timon of Athens*. But the stage instructions in *All Is True* call blankly for "Personages," to whom Katherine refers as "Spirits of peace" and a "blessed troop." (IV, ii, 90, 96) One can certainly reinterpret these figures as "angels," but only by importing such an idea into the text from external sources. It should be remembered that Katherine's Vision recapitulates the earlier masque in the Presence-chamber in York-Place, in which disguised "shepherds" promenade before the Cardinal and his guests. (Act I, Sc. 4) It is soon revealed that these "shepherds" are in fact King Henry and his lords. The second masque of the "Vision" lies in the secular shadow of the first.

Of course, Shakespeare is not averse to depictions of Catholicism. Priests, monks and nuns are positive forces in many plays, including, *inter alia*, *Romeo and Juliet*, *Much Ado About Nothing* and *Measure for Measure*. Isabella in *Measure for Measure* is a novice in the Order of St. Clare who bears the name of Katherine of Aragon's mother. It would have been easy and natural to show Katherine in *All Is True* surrounded or accompanied by members of religious or monastic orders, as we find, for example, in *Richard III*. (III, vii, 95) Her lack of attending clergymen has the inevitable effect of diluting her Catholic identity. It is up to the reader or viewer to furnish what is pretermitted by the playwright. As far as this character's appearance in *All Is True* is concerned, she is oddly nondenominational. Had she not appealed to the Pope we might take her for a Unitarian.

This emerges with some clarity if we attend carefully to the language of the play. Compare the 1554 George Cavendish text of Katherine's Blackfriar's speech with Shakespeare's redaction thereof in *All Is True*. Cavendish was employed by Thomas Wolsey until Wolsey's death in 1530. It is believed he took notes of Wolsey's doings and conversations, and that these notes in manuscript form, including the Blackfriar's speech of Katherine, fell into the hands of Shakespeare. (George Cavendish, *Encyclopedia Britannica* (1911, 11th Edition, Vol. 5, pp. 579-80) The Cavendish text is as complete an historical report of the speech as we are likely to get. Though Shakespeare's rendition tracks Cavendish closely, there are significant changes and omissions. And it is noteworthy that several of these omissions are instances in which Katherine makes reference to the Deity.

Cavendish

"I beseche you for all the loves that hath byn bytwen vs And for the love of god lett me Haue Iustice & right and take of me some some pitie & compassion for I am a poore woman and a Straynger . . . ."

Shakespeare

Sir, I desire you do me right and justice;
And to bestow your pity on me; for
I am a most poor woman, and a stranger . . . .
(II, iv, 14-16)

Cavendish

"I take god & all the world to wytnes that I haue byn to you a trewe humble and obedient wyfe / euer Confirmable to yor wyll and pleasure . . . ."

Shakespeare

Heaven witness,
I have been to you a true and humble wife . . . .
(II, iv, 24)

Cavendish

"this xx yeres I haue byn yor true wife (or more) and by me ye haue had dyuers childerne. Allthough it hathe pleased god to call theme owt of this world wche byn no default in me. And whan ye had me at the first (I take god to be my Iuge) I was a true mayed w'owt touche of man . . . ."

Shakespeare

Sir, call to mind
That I have been your wife, in this obedience

Upward of twenty years, and have been blest
With many children by you. If, in the course
And process of this time, you can report,
And prove it too, against mine honour aught,
My bond to wedlock, or my love and duty,
Against your sacred person, in God's name
Turn me away . . . .
(II, iv, 35-43)

Cavendish

"There for I most humbly requyer you in the way of charitie and for the love of god (who Is the Iust Iuge) spare th' extremytye of thys newe Court vntill I may be aduersied what way & order my frendes is Spayn woll advyse me to take."

Shakespeare

Wherefore I humbly
Beseech you, sir, to spare me, til I may
Be by my friends in Spain advis'd, whose counsel
I will implore.
(II, iv, 54-57)

Five times is God invoked by Katherine in this justly famous exemplar of female integrity, and all five of these references vanish in the First Folio. The euphemistic substitution of 'heaven' for 'god' is particularly glaring. It can hardly be doubted that the practical effect of siphoning off the Christian ejaculations of Katherine of Aragon is to diminish her beatific aura. And with her Christianity goes her Catholicism.

In the minds of traditional English people faithful to the Holy Church of Rome the Blessed Virgin was central. During the period of Katherine's ascendancy and marriage to Henry, she became for those pious souls the living symbol of that veneration. Bate and Rasmussen in their edition of the *Complete Works* note that the architects of the English Reformation who created the myth of Elizabeth as the "Virgin Queen" derived substantial power by "rework[ing] the Roman Catholic cult of the Virgin Mary." (Bate, Rasmussen, 1382) *All Is True*, concluding with the celebrated birth of Elizabeth, destined for spiritual greatness, tracks the subtle transition from the Virgin Mary via Anne Boleyn to the reign of her daughter, the Virgin Queen. To have openly portrayed Katherine of Aragon in *All Is True* as a traduced Catholic saint would have risked inflaming Catholic sensibilities. Katherine of Aragon thus was a problem in public relations, and had to be presented through a glass darkly in a political drama whose *telos* was Elizabeth I and the magnificent Protestant Reformation. *All Is True* is nothing less than a paean to that Reformation and the Tudor myth.

Shakespeare's fondness for monks, nuns and priests is not reflected in ecclesiastics more highly placed. Instead he is resolutely critical. We find in his plays disparaging references to "Popish" and "Papist" doings. (*Titus Andronicus*, V, i, 78; *All's Well that Ends Well*, I, ii, 47) Cardinal Pandulph in *King John* is a scheming rascal. So is Cardinal Beaufort in *King Henry VI*. His revolting death by self-ingested poison with its incriminating raving is a significant indicator of Shakespeare's low estimation of Catholic statesmen. We come then to Cardinal Wolsey in *All Is True*, yet another malevolent prince of the Church and, arguably, the play's tragic soul. We meet this "holy fox" in the opening scene as he busies himself engineering the downfall of the sympathetically drawn Duke of Buckingham. It is Wolsey who seeks to oppose his will to that of King Henry VIII by undermining the approaching marriage to Anne Boleyn. As Henry's Lord Chancellor, he has amassed a huge private fortune at the expense of the state and its people, and as the action commences has imposed on them a burdensome tax of which Henry appears unaware. (I, ii, 40) When Henry orders the tax abolished, Wolsey secretly instructs his secretary to see that he receives credit for this relief. (I, ii, 115-120) Wolsey serves as the King's right hand man in the campaign to dissolve Katherine's marriage to him. At the inquest at Blackfriars, she lashes out before the entire court at Wolsey, publicly denouncing him as an enemy not only to her but to the common weal.

QUEEN

My lord, my lord,
I am a simple woman, much too weak
To oppose your cunning. You're meek and humble-mouth'd;
You sign your place and calling, in full seeming,
With meekness and humility; but your heart
Is cramm'd with arrogancy, spleen, and pride.
You have, by fortune and his highness' favours,
Gone slightly o'er low steps, and now are mounted

Where powers are your retainers, and your words
Domestics to you, serve your will as't please
Yourself pronounce their office. I must tell you,
You tender more your person's honour than
Your high profession spiritual; that again
I do refuse you for my judge, and here,
Before you all, appeal unto the pope,
To bring my whole cause 'fore his holiness,
And to be judg'd by him.
(II, iv, 114-130, following *The Yale Shakespeare* & hereafter)

When King Henry's agents intercept Wolsey's traitorous correspondence, Wolsey is disgraced and cashiered by the King, losing the
totality of his wealth and possessions. He is given a tragic hero's soliloquy as though he were a pedestrian version of Lear or Macbeth.

CARDINAL

So farewell to the little good you bear me.
Farewell! A long farewell to all my greatness!
This is the state of man: to-day he puts forth
The tender leaves of hope; to-morrow blossoms,
And bears his blushing honours thick upon him;
The third day comes a frost, a killing frost,
And when he thinks, good easy man, full surely
His greatness is a-ripening, nips his root,
And then he falls, as I do. I have ventur'd,
Like little wanton boys that swim on bladders,
This many summers in a sea of glory,
But far beyond my depth: my high-blown pride
At length broke under me, and now has left me,
Weary and old with service, to the mercy
Of a rude stream, that must for ever hide me.
Vain pomp and glory of this world, I hate ye.
I feel my heart now open'd. O how wretched
Is that poor man that hangs on princes favours!
There is, betwixt that smile we would aspire to,
That sweet aspect of princes, and their ruin,
More pangs and fears than wars or women have;
And when he falls, he falls like Lucifer,

Never to hope again.
(III, ii, 413-435)

The closing comparison of himself with Lucifer is revealing. The Cardinal is the play's Satanic focus. With 14% of the lines, equal to Henry's own share (Bate, Rasmussen, 1386), he is in a sense *All Is True's* promethean anti-hero, and reminds us of Richard II and Richard III, two other tragic figures in Shakespeare's historical landscape. It is only the general *de casibus* theme of the work and its conclusion in the birth of the salvific Elizabeth that prevent literary critics from classifying this play as a tragedy. Indeed, the words of the Prologue prepare us for tragedy, and the mischievous Cardinal's come-uppance arrives as no surprise.

In his exposition of *All Is True* under the later title *King Henry VIII*, Harold Bloom confesses he "cannot solve the puzzle" of this play. He does find that the "Catholic-Protestant confrontation is . . . muted," so much so that "Shakespeare hardly appears to take sides" (Bloom, 685), but he cannot apprehend the reason therefor. It is not far to seek. *All Is True* is political theatre, the purpose of which is to rationalize a transition from a dim Catholic past to a new England, a sovereign and autonomous nation, independent of Rome and its dark hegemony. To rake over the coals and foreground Queen Katherine as a Catholic "martyr" would be self-defeating in a play whose manifest purpose is to celebrate England's Protestant enfranchisement. The ecclesiastical putsch, which placed the King atop the Church of England, and which would later trigger the brutal reprisals under Queen Mary (1553-1558), could hardly be depicted in gruesome detail, and so takes the symbolic form of the "christening" (not Baptism) of the infant Elizabeth, over whom Archbishop Cranmer (to be burnt alive by Mary) makes his oneiric prognostications.

Everything is done by the author to make that christening the emblematic crucible in which are resolved the social and political contradictions of England. As Anne Boleyn was still controversial and would be brutally destroyed by Henry, she is absent from the christening scene, in which the vicious court infighting and theological squabbles are decorously buried. Instead we behold the proud father beaming as he looks on to see his daughter "made a Christian." (V, iii, 209) The last words are Henry's:

KING

O, lord Archbishop!
Thou hast made me now a man: never, before
This happy child did I get anything.
This oracle of comfort has so pleas'd me
That when I am in heaven, I shall desire
To see what this child does, and praise my Maker.
(V, v, 70-75)

Unfortunately, the facts are otherwise. Henry moved heaven and earth to dump his wife of two decades to marry a young lady (possibly consanguineous with himself) whose sacred mission was to give him a son. When she failed to do so, he was apoplectic with rage. History records:

> The following Wednesday the Lord Mayor and Aldermen in their robes, chains and and ermine came down the river to see the new baby christened by the Bishop of London in the Church of the Franciscans at Greenwich. It was an impressive little ceremony — but *Henry was not there*. Nor were there any bonfires in the streets that night. Anne Boleyn's baby girl did not harmonize with King Henry's grand design. Indeed, she came dangerously close to making a mockery of it. And there were other real life complications which detracted from the glory of the great constitutional edifice Cromwell was constructing to elevate the King's power. It was one thing to pass laws as to what men should believe. It was another to get men to alter their beliefs, or, in some cases, to contradict principles they had always held dear. (Lacey, 137, emphasis added)

In political theater liberty must be taken with certain embarrassing realities. In the case of *All Is True*, the greatest adjustments were made at the beginning and the end. At the outset, the downfall of Katherine is shown as the sad undoing of a noble lady and wife who is discarded to soothe the delicate King's "conscience" about the theological validity of his marriage. (II, vi, 180-222) Hardly a word is breathed about Henry's campaign to generate a viable male heir and Katherine's inability to so provide. The intensity of his hopes in Anne Boleyn in that regard is concealed. Henry's break with the Church of Rome and establishment of the "Church of England" of which he will be the head receive not so much as a nod. The play is concluded with the "christening" of a future monarch who will make of English life a virtual paradise, which her successor will gild with his wisdom and "honour."

CRANMER

This royal infant, — heaven still move about her! —
Though in her cradle, yet now promises
Upon this land a thousand thousand blessings,
Which time shall bring to ripeness. She shall be —
But few now living can behold that goodness —
A pattern to all princes living with her,
And all that shall succeed: Saba was never
More covetous of wisdom and fair virtue
Than this pure soul shall be: all princely graces,
That mould up such a mighty piece as this is,
With all the virtues that attend the good,
Shall still be doubled on her; truth shall nurse her;
Holy and heavenly thoughts still counsel her;
She shall be lov'd and fear'd. Her own shall bless her;
Her foes shake like a field of beaten corn,
And hang their heads with sorrow. Good grows with her.
In her days every man shall eat in safety
Under his own vine what he plants; and sing
The merry songs of peace to all his neighbors.
God shall be truly known; and those about her
From her shall read the perfect ways of honour,
And from those claim their greatness, not by blood.
Nor shall this peace sleep with her; but as when
The bird of wonder dies, the maiden phoenix,
Her ashes new-create another heir
As great in admiration as herself,
So shall she leave her blessedness to one, —
When heaven shall call her from this cloud of darkness, —
Who, from the sacred ashes of her honour,
Shall star-like rise, as great in fame as she was,
And so stand fix'd. Peace, plenty, love, truth, terror,
That were servants to this chosen infant,

Shall then be his, and like a vine grow to him:
Wherever the bright sun of heaven shall shine,
His honour and the greatness of his name
Shall be, and make new nations. He shall flourish,
And like a mountain cedar, reach his branches
To all the plains about him. Our children's children
Shall see this, and bless heaven.

* * * *

She shall be, to the happiness of England,
An aged princess; many days shall see her,
And yet no day without a deed to crown it.
Would I had known no more! But she must die,
She must, the saints must have her; yet a virgin,
A most unspotted lily shall she pass
To the ground, and all the world shall mourn for her.
(V, iv, 23-69)

The idea that King Henry VIII, still fuming over the failure of Anne Boleyn to present him with a male heir, would stand by grinning as such pseudo-biblical palaver is recited is preposterous. Not only is Elizabeth praised before her deeds, but her reign, according to Cranmer, will permanently deprive Henry of male succession, his worst nightmare. Cranmer seems heedless of consequences as he warbles over Elizabeth, a female, not only succeeding Henry but, as a virgin, being unable by issue of her body to place a Tudor on the throne of England. Elizabeth's reign entails that not only will Henry not be directly succeeded by a male, neither will his daughter produce a male heir, thus effectively extinguishing Henry's fondest wish. Cranmer prophesies the end of the Tudors. The real Henry would more likely have taken Cranmer's head than praised him for such thoughtlessness. Yet in the play, Henry is content. In fact, he is inexplicably delighted.

It cannot be overlooked that the monarch we are given in the play is not the redoubtable head of the Church of England but a Catholic King whose minions are princes of the Church of Rome. The hearing at Blackfriar's (June 18, 1529) was commissioned by the Pope in response to Henry' petition. There is thus no textual conflict of doctrine between Henry and his wife Katherine, and her death is not a martyrdom. Of course, in historical actuality, Katherine was resolutely opposed to Henry's command of his new "Church of England," by which he annulled his marriage and filled his depleted coffers, confiscating Church lands. Underneath the political/theological clap-trap is an embarrassingly elementary issue: Katherine had worn herself out in the service (*Measure for Measure*, I, ii, 103) and not produced a viable male heir. Henry's eyes fall on a young lady who promises to simultaneously gratify him romantically and, as a bonus, yield a replica of himself to install on the English throne. Katherine is therefore not an English martyr who embraces death rather than conform to a new religious institution, but a faithful wife who refuses to be scrapped by her philandering husband who blames her for a genetic phenomenon of which he knows nothing. This brute issue is not allowed to surface in a nationalistic fable in which a long-deceased megalomaniac is rehabilitated to rationalize the political status quo. The business of such a tendentious work of art, then, is not to "hold a mirror up to life," but rather to paint a genteel English tableau, in which Albion enjoys a smooth and largely painless transition from Roman subjugation to conjectured Protestant liberty and virtue. If Katherine is the sacrificial lamb in *All Is True*, it is not because she is presented as a Catholic but because she isn't. The faith which gave her the last shred of dignity is taken from her.

II. Katherine As Recusant Martyr

In a recent article, Professor Amy Appleford argues that it is reasonable to view Shakespeare's Katherine of Aragon as a "Recusant Martyr." ["Shakespeare's Katherine of Aragon: Last Medieval Queen, First Recusant Martyr," *Journal of Medieval and Early Modern Studies*, 40:1, Winter, 2010] Though few are unimpressed with the historical Katherine's faith and the suffering she endured at the hands of her esteemed spouse, Henry Tudor, it is unnecessary and inappropriate to seek to elevate Shakespeare's character in this manner. Prof. Appleford's general thesis is that "Shakespeare's presentation of Katherine is part of a conscious Catholization of the history of the English Reformation," (152) a remarkable claim in light of the fact that *All Is True* is a play which goes out of its way to efface the last vestiges of Katherine's Catholicism.

1. Martrydom

In discussing Prof. Appleford's contentions we must bear in mind that she is specifically referring to the character Katherine in *All Is True*, not the historical personage. Her thesis must be evaluated strictly in terms of this drama, not what may be known of Katherine from other sources. "THE VISION" she experiences near the end of the play in Act 4 is taken as evidence of her "martyrdom." But we have already seen that the Vision is ambiguous at best, and that the palm branches held by the "spirits" are consistent with sacred traditions long antedating Christianity. When Katherine has this Vision she is dying. But her mortality is not featured in the Vision itself. The fact is that Katherine of Aragon was neither deliberately tormented nor executed, neither in life nor in literature. Shamefully, disgracefully mistreated, yes; but not subjected to torture and death, and not threatened with either. She was the victim of domestic harassment during the time Henry was having an affair with another woman. She was resented for not bearing a surviving son, setting the lecherous Henry on his philoprogenitive warpath. The word "martyr" in this context is a theological term of art and deserves to be properly employed. Unfortunately, Professor Appleford cites no official Catholic authorities to justify her word choice in this regard.

The *New Advent Catholic Encyclopedia* online defines "martyr" this way:

> [A] martyr, or witness of Christ, is a person who, though he has never seen or heard The Divine Founder of the Church, is yet so firmly convinced of the truths of the Christian religion that he gladly suffers death rather than deny [them].

But unless the rumors of her having been poisoned can be substantiated, Queen Katherine was not executed, nor was she given an ultimatum, that is: deny an article of faith or accept death. Indeed, her principal adversary was Thomas Cardinal Wolsey, a Catholic. Therefore, although exemplary in her devotion, Katherine did not die a martyr nor is she so regarded by her Church. Martyrdom is a personal sacrifice of one's life for the integrity of the faith. It is the deliberate choice of death rather than blasphemy, apostasy or heresy. Katherine did not face such a dilemma, as, for example, Archbishop Cranmer later did during the reign of Mary. In the inquest at Blackfriars, Katherine is not accused of any crime or wrongdoing, including violation of Church doctrine. Henry and Wolsey may have wanted her to voluntarily consent to the abrogation of her marriage by admitting that she had consummated her first marriage with Henry's elder brother, Prince Arthur. That consummation could presumably have been used by the King to extract a judgment from the Church that the subsequent marriage to Henry was incestuous and thus a legal and religious nullity. But on her arrival in England, she and Arthur had quickly succumbed to a serious illness from which Arthur died. When Henry came of age it was decided that he should marry Katherine to recover the full dowry from Spain. At that time, and for the remainder of her life, she steadfastly denied that there had been any physical intimacy between herself and the ailing Prince. As a result, the Church sanctioned the marital union of Henry and Katherine. Henry now was petitioning the Church to reach a judgment directly contrary to its original approval of his marriage to Katherine, without any change in either the underlying facts or canon law. This it properly declined to do. Hence, the frantic campaign of intimidation against Katherine was launched. She was not being asked to renounce her religion or any part of it, but to (1) make a recantation of a matter of fact, that is, that her denial of alleged consummation of the marriage with Arthur was false, or (2) voluntarily enter a convent. (Lacey, 84) In effect, she was being asked to unqueen herself. It is reported that when she was asked to become a nun, she replied that she would do so if Henry became a monk. Under extreme duress, and exhausted from innumerable births and miscarriages, she sickened and died. But matters of fact are not articles of faith, nor is one's last illness to be construed as an execution. Katherine was not a "martyr."

None of this appears in Shakespeare's play, and the reader well may wonder the meaning of these strange proceedings. Their very vagueness seems to afford Professor Appleford the opportunity to suggest that Katherine was "martyred." The burden of proof is substantial. But what we are given is equivocation on the term "martyr" This can be seen plainly if we consult the dictionary. The *Oxford American College Dictionary* (2002) gives several senses of "martyr":

1. A person who is killed because of their religious or other beliefs;
2. A constant sufferer from an ailment [pain or distress]
(Oxford, 829)

Queen Katherine is acknowledged to be a martyr in sense two, not in sense one. Here is the argument verbatim.

Not only must [Henry] submit to a resolution of the play by the birth of a girl, not the boy he wanted; but in her dying vision, Katherine is given a noble send off by powers that lie outside and beyond those of her former husband, receiving tokens not of disgrace and defeat, but of *victory through martyrdom*: the palm of the martyr, such as the palm associated with her namesake, Katherine of Alexandria, and the garland crown associated both with worldly fame and the crown of righteousness of 2 Timothy 4:28. (Appleford, 151, emphasis added)

Here we find a departure from the text. In Shakespeare's *All Is True*, unlike actual history, King Henry VIII makes no big issue of the sex of his child by Anne Boleyn. He would prefer—and expects—a son, but when he learns it is a girl, he has no complaint whatsoever. In fact he gives a gratuity to the bearer of the news and dashes off without another word to felicitate the mother. (V, ii, 192-204) Then, as we have noted, he is ecstatically happy with his infant daughter and the glorious future forecast by Cranmer. Though Professor Appleford's subjects are the characters in Shakespeare's play, the reference to Henry's acute displeasure is derived from the external historical record. When Katherine has her Vision, its solemnities transcend the powers not of Katherine's "former husband," but of her current one. Her former husband was Prince Arthur. Finally, the dramatic victory in the text of *All Is True* belongs to King Henry VIII, who is blessed with a daughter destined to be England's female messiah, a prospect which has Henry fairly gasping with joy. That is the moment the curtain descends. There is no "victory" for Katherine whatsoever. The imaginary and highly ambiguous "Vision" she enjoys is a mere consolation prize, a sop thrown to a wife whose only fault was her fidelity to a tyrannical husband. If she was a "martyr" to anything, it was to childbirth, which utterly depleted her physical resources. Once she is out of the way, the attention of the audience can be directed to the "christening" of the newborn Elizabeth. This is insulting. Let it be remembered that on June 11, 1513 Henry, absent from the realm, appointed Katherine Regent of England. There were many seasoned peers he might have chosen. But he selected his wife, a person of no political or military experience. Though they corresponded frequently, it was Katherine who ruled England during this period. On September 3rd of that year the Scots invaded. Katherine, who was in advanced pregnancy at the time, rode forth in front of her army in full armor to engage them at the Battle of Flodden. As a result she suffered one of many stillborn deliveries. Katherine of Aragon was more, then, than the "housewife" she is depicted as being in *All Is True*.

She was an able administrator and leader, a Spanish woman who, while pregnant, led English troops against the Scots in war. The difficulty of taking *All Is True* seriously is that it scants rather than features a great woman and her achievements. Elizabeth may have rallied the English militia at Tilbury, but she didn't ride pregnant to engage the foe. The play dispenses expeditiously with an accomplished and noble queen to break into dithyrambic ecstasy over the merely hoped-for deeds of a babe in arms. It thus turns reality on its head. The best we can say for its title is that it is a bitter irony.

2. Katherine as Recusant

In addition to the claim of Professor Appleford that the text of *All Is True* shows Queen Katherine as a martyr, it is also maintained that the text supports a conception of her as a forerunner of English recusants associated with the reign of Elizabeth I. By definition, a recusant is one who avoided participation in the services of the Church of England and secretly practiced the rituals of Roman Catholicism. An inspection of the evidence reveals that Katherine of Aragon fails to meet either of these criteria. First, despite the "christening" of Elizabeth there is in *All Is True* no perceptible Church of England or references to same, nor is Katherine shown avoiding attendance at its gatherings. The Archbishop of Canterbury in *King Henry VIII* is thus ecclesiastically indistinguishable from the Archbishop of Canterbury in *King Henry V*. (I, i, 1ff.) Second, although Katherine's Catholicism is downplayed in *All Is True*, neither is it denied or concealed. Her appeal to the Pope (II, iv, 128) is sufficient to establish that as a character she is Catholic, though, as far as the play is concerned, not especially so. In what sense, then, can it be claimed she is a "recusant"? The term has connotations of enthusiasm and dedication to the faith not manifest in Shakespeare's Katherine. The historical Katherine did indeed refuse to recognize Henry as the legitimate head of the Church in England, and as such might appear to be proto-recusant. But as can be seen by the title and argument of Professor Appleford's essay, it is Shakespeare's character who is being examined and about whom the claims are made. And in Shakespeare's *All Is True* there is no Church of England to resist nor any reason for Katherine to conceal her ancestral faith. The nominal Catholicism Shakespeare's Katherine actually exhibits in the context of Henry's own Catholic regime in the play never attains the status of "recusancy," nor is there any apparent attempt by Shakespeare's Katherine to introduce reforms into the Church. We would certainly not wish to urge that somehow

a. The Orpheus song

b. The Vision and

c. Her struggle to remain Henry's spouse, the mother of a legitimate child (Mary), and England's Queen add up to an attempt on her part to demonstrate the "possibility of reform" in English Catholicism. Even in the case of the historical Katherine's resistance to her husband's apostasy, as it was open and notorious, and opposed Henry's absurd willingness to do absolutely anything to be rid of her, the label is inapposite.

Appleford argues that Katherine's attempt to persuade Henry to oppose Wolsey's tax on the commons depicts Katherine as a reformer. It does nothing of the kind. Katherine knows Wolsey is scheming against her and tries to take advantage of his avaricious tax to cast doubt on the Cardinal's probity in Henry's eyes. This is court infighting, not reform. It has naught to do with religion, and everything to do with her marriage and survival as England's Queen.

We then read:

> At key moments in the play, she appears in the character of a critic of the church to which she belongs.

> She repeatedly attacks [Wolsey] for his luxurious lifestyle . . .

How is this a critique of the church? Is Wolsey the church? The issue was one of court corruption in the person of the Lord Chancellor, the man in charge of the day-to-day running of England's affairs. (Lacey, 43) When Lord Buckingham refers to Wolsey as one for whom "no man's pie is freed from his ambitious finger," (I, i, 60-61) does that mean he is functioning as a religious reformer? Katherine was simply one of a number of nobles who knew of and often drew attention to Wolsey's abuses. The theme of personal luxury purchased at the commonwealth's expense was a matter of general notoriety, one to which Henry was particularly sensitive as he was himself a chief offender. Even minor characters pointed to the needed correction of "our travell'd gallants, that fill the court with quarrels, talk [*i.e.*, gossip] and tailors [*i.e.*, extravagant dress]. (I, ii, 26) It should be remembered that in 16th century England, it was customary for well-born or unusually talented and aggressive individuals to seek positions in the church, not because they had religious vocations, but because the church was one of the major estates of English society, and prelates often wore two hats, serving as secular ad-ministrators. Wolsey was a butcher's son. All he ever wanted was power and wealth and everyone knew it. His overreaching must be set in that context. If we go back to Shakespeare's *King Henry VI*, Part One, we see that good Duke Humphrey, the Lord Protector, is at odds with Cardinal Winchester, whom he accuses of "[lov]ing the flesh." (I, i, 41) Does this make Humphrey a religious reformer? Is his death at Suffolk's hands a martyrdom? No. Winchester is merely one of the court's wolfish lords, striving for advantages along with all the rest. So is it with Wolsey.

> In reflecting anxiously on the arrival of Wolsey and Cardinal Campeius to speak with her, Katherine criticizes not the par-ticular ecclesiastics office they hold but rather their failure to conform to the moral standards their church demanded of them. "They should be good men, their affairs as righteous." (Appleford, 60)

This is revealing and only slightly wide of the mark. Katherine's attack is indeed not directed to the church through the bishops' offices, but to the individuals, their intrigues and defalcations. Would she have been as vocal as she appears had they not conspired against her to placate a petulant and wayward monarch? Certainly not. Katherine acts in self-defense. She is neither a martyr, nor reformer nor recusant, but a good woman wronged and a Queen maligned. Rising to turn back those who would slander her is her womanly and royal prerogative and in no way casts her in any of the extraneous roles which would be assigned to her by Professor Appleford.

What basis, then, is there to advance the rubric of recusancy? The answer lies in Professor Appleford's theory of authorship. Instead of ad-dressing the standard question of whether Fletcher or Shakespeare was the author of *All Is True*, or what was the measure of their respective contributions, Professor Appleford takes a different tack, asserting *ex cathedra* that "William Shakespeare" is the author, and that he himself was a Catholic recusant, certainly a novel hypothesis. It flies in the face of the received view that the play is the product of collaboration. No persua-sive evidence is adduced to prove that the writer was indeed a recusant Catholic, nor is there any effort made to discount the countervailing data, including the disparaging references cited above to villainous Car-dinals, popery, etc. Professor Appleford merely adopts the rumor of the author's recusant Catholicism to lend support to the strained thesis that the character Katherine should be viewed as a proto-reforming recusant, neatly begging both questions at a single stroke. Bear in mind that Appleford's main thesis is that "Shakespeare's presentation of Katherine is part of a Catholization of the history of the English Reformation." (Appleford, 152) But how does a Katherine with scarcely a flicker of Catholic activity about her contribute to "Catholization"? The play proceeds in precisely the contrary direction, away from an etiolated Katherine whose vital Catholicism has been sucked out of her, to a vague future in which a Protestant Elizabeth will be the savior of her people.

But let's have Professor Appleford speak for herself.

> The claim that Katherine is Shakespeare's recusant heroine, a Catholic sympathetically portrayed as such in a play that deals, literally, with the cradle of English Protestantism, should seem less surprising than it would have seemed even a few years ago. The rebirth of interest in Shakespeare's own Catholic ties and the possibility of his personal Catholicism is obliging scholars to reconsider a good deal: the famous "lost years" of the playwright's youth between leaving Stratford and appearing in London . . . .

> For after spending two years in his home town – long a center of English Catholic recusancy—Shakespeare returned to London to write the "medieval" *Two Noble Kinsmen* [sic] and . . . the . . . pro-Catholic historiography of this late play [*All Is True*]. (163)

The most that can be said for this is that at least "Shakespeare's Catholicism" is described as a mere "possibility."

Here are some of the problems:

1. The attempt to base an interpretation of the Shakespearean text on a biography of the supposed writer has been repudiated as an exegetical technique for many years. This is of course especially true where, as here, the biographical narrative is merely conjectural;

2. As shown above, Catholic prelates in Shakespeare are always disgraceful rogues;

3. Imagining that Shakespeare spent the "lost years" in the company of recusant Catholics begs the question and is grossly speculative;

4. Even if it were somehow shown that Shakespeare was a recusant Catholic, such a fact would be inconsistent with the watered down reli-

giosity we witness in Shakespeare's Katherine;

5. Professor Appleford completely ignores the most significant aspect of contemporary Shakespearean scholarship: the raging debate about whether William of Stratford or someone else was the author of the plays and poems. To write about such matters, seeking to ground a controversial reading of a play on authorial biography without ever mentioning the authorship controversy is, to say the least, disingenuous;

6. No documentation is provided for the preposterous claim that the author of the Shakespearean corpus retired from London theatre life, sojourned in Stratford for two years, and then returned to London to compose *All Is True* and *The Two Noble Kinsmen*;

7. Current theory attributes a good deal of *All Is True* to Fletcher. How can this attribution, which is the majority view today, not even be mentioned?

8. The man considered by many to have been Shakespeare's collaborator on *All Is True*, was the son of Richard Fletcher, Chaplain to Her Majesty, Queen Elizabeth I. He was a radical Protestant;

9. In fact, John Fletcher's family religious affiliations were of the most radical Protestant variety;

10. It may then be wondered how Shakespeare, according to Appleford, a recusant Catholic, collaborated with John Fletcher, an extreme Protestant, to demonstrate in *All Is True* the"Catholization of the history of the English Reformation."

[See, "John Fletcher as Spenserian Playwright: The Faithful Shepherdess and The Island Princess," by Phillip J. Finkelpearl, *Studies in English Literature 1500-1900*, Vol. 27 No. 2, Spring 1987 pp. 285-302.]

As for recusant Catholicism and its tribulations, the reader is respectfully referred to the contrasting case of poet John Donne, a Shakespeare contemporary, whose well-documented recusant origins bequeathed to him a world of problems. No need for conjecture there.

It is true that there are scraps of documents showing that a William Shaksper inhabited the Warwickshire village of Stratford-upon-Avon. And it is also true that there are documents showing that "William Shakespeare" lived in other counties in Elizabethan and Jacobean England. But it is a stupendous leap to conclude that all these fellows were identical with the genius who authored the works contained in the First Folio of 1623.

Perhaps the most thoroughgoing investigator of William Shakespeare who ever lived is the now-forgotten Mrs. C. C. Stopes, an indefatigable genealogist who traced the Shakespeare family across England going back many generations. Her magnum opus, *Shakespeare's Family*, (London: Elliot Stock, 62, Paternoster E.C.; New York: James Pott & Co.) was published in 1901. Fortunately her book is preserved online at Project Gutenberg, and is available free of charge for reading. To put the matter briefly, Mrs. Stopes searched all birth, death and tax records in the pertinent periods and showed that "Shakespeare" was a common English surname. More to the point, there was a "William Shakespeare" under nearly every rock. England was fairly crawling with them. There can be no caviling on this point, but let the reader see for himself. The plethora of William Shakespeares in various places, *e.g.*, Warwickshire and London, creates problems unconsidered by contemporary writers who blithely suppose that the occurrence of this moniker here and there amongst the documents means that the husband of Anne Hathaway and sometime English poet occupied each place where his name is found. Thus, for example, it is assumed that the William Shakespeare married to Anne Hathaway in Stratford-upon-Avon is none other than the actor and theatre shareholder of London. The greedy grain merchant and loan shark is identical with the refined author of *The Rape of Lucrece*. Of course, had there been only a single man bearing the name William Shakespeare in the 16th and 17th centuries one would need to conclude that this individual traveled from one place to another, carrying his singular identity with him. That easy and reassuring inference is snatched away by the revelation that there was not one person but many of that name. Thus, when a scholar like Professor Amy Appleford informs us that Shakespeare abandoned London after a satisfying career in the theater, returned to Stratford in Warwickshire ("Stratford" was also the name of a borough in London), only to dash back to London two years later to pen *All Is True* and *The Two Noble Kinsmen*, one wonders whether she has consulted stagecoach records, or gratuitously assumed that there was one and only one "William Shakespeare" at all times appertaining thereto.

Take an example.

There was a "William Shakespeare" residing in St. Helens Parish, Bishopsgate in London in 1597, when the poet/dramatist was surely busy with his art. Was this Bishopsgate bloke that poet/dramatist?

The entry is "Affid. William Shakespeare on v. goods, Assessed xiii iii. The "affid" affixed to it shows that this Shakespeare tried to avoid payment on some grounds. It has surprised many and satisfied others as suitable, that the poet should have lived in this neighborhood, near so many of his theatrical friends. But I do not think it is certainly proved that it was our Shakespeare. (Stopes, 143)

The idea is unloosed here that it is perfectly possible, indeed, in the mind of this expert, quite likely, that there were in merrie olde England in 1597 at least two individuals in London both having the name "William Shakespeare." Presumably others frolicked in the hinterlands. Were either of these a recusant Catholic? Was either the author of the works in the 1623 First Folio? Did both of them collaborate with Fletcher? The plot thickens to the point of intellectual turbidity.

Professor Amy Appleford is able to view *All Is True* as an attempt at the Catholization of the English Reformation because it fits with the alluring hypothesis that "William Shakespeare" hailed from Stratford-upon-Avon, a hotbed of recusant activity. Further, she knows that nearing the end of his career, this recusant Catholic poet rushed back to London to pen the "medieval" play *The Two Noble Kinsmen* and the crypto-Catholic *All Is True*. Unfortunately, there is no documentation of any such thing. The mere name "William Shakespeare" in London does not entail that the person associated therewith once resided in Warwickshire. That would require additional information, as would the "possible" claim that the plays were written by a recusant Catholic. Even before we attempt to review Mrs. Stopes' research as no doubt many will, we already have before us a growing number of William Shakespeares:

1. William the husband of Anne Hathaway
2. William the canny grain merchant and food hoarder
3. William the famous poet/dramatist
4. William of St. Helens, Bishopsgate, London

Under the circumstances, we might ask how well founded are the claims made by Professor Appleford about the Catholic design of "All Is True."

III. Conclusion

The best summation of Katherine of Aragon is still G. Wilson Knight's.

Queen Katharine is one of Shakespeare's most striking and feminine creations. She is not a 'character' study like the Nurse in *Romeo and Juliet*, nor, to take another extreme, a great emotional force as is Constance in *King John*; nor a sublime hypothesis, like Lady Macbeth; nor just a creature of dignity and virtue, and not much else, like Hermione. She has the power of forceful heroines woven with the warm, domestic, virtues of a Desdemona, the integrity of Cordelia, and the spiritual worth of Imogen. Katherine is made of all the better qualities—not just the best moments, as is Imogen—of earlier women. They present aspects of womanhood; she seems, more than anyone but Cleopatra. . . a real woman. Her every phrase comes direct from her woman's soul, her typical woman's plight. She is universalized, not by abstraction, but rather by an exact realization of a particular person only lately dead. As with Cleopatra and Imogen, Shakespeare knows precisely what he is doing and gives us his own definition, as when Wolsey describes her 'charity' and 'disposition gentle' together with a 'wisdom o'ertopping woman's power'; and Henry himself characterizes her even more perfectly as a blend of sovereignty, wifehood and saintliness; one 'obeying in commanding' and thus 'the queen of earthly queens'. [T]he Queen sums all Shakespeare's feminine sympathies. (Knight, 296)

Not once does Knight mention the Catholic religion in connection with Katherine of Aragon.

Although *All Is True*, like many 16th and 17th century English plays, subserves a political agenda, that ulterior purpose leaves intact a number of important, well-drawn characters, including Queen Katherine. Her appeal at Blackfriars alone is sufficiently compelling to occasion the play's too rare performances. Her womanly integrity, queenly bearing and sense of self-worth shine through in every line. She represents Shakespeare's perception of the enduring strength that underlies woman's assumed frailty. And though there may be much of the historical Katherine in her speeches, this can hardly detract from Shakespeare's dramatic presentation. The greatness of Katherine as a dramatic personage, however, is not enhanced by a sectarian reading which seeks to focus on her Catholicism to the neglect of her humanity. This is particularly unsatisfying when that sectarian reading fails to disclose the Catholic identity it proclaims and would have us celebrate. Katherine was valued as a model wife and queen, and as a theatrical protagonist, long before scholars began to cast Shakespeare as a religious partisan.

In such a context it is edifying to turn back to earlier generations and apprehend how they took note of her. The key is Henry's encomiastic locution, "the queen of earthly queens." (II, iv, 152) Though she was certainly a paragon of theistic fidelity, Shakespeare gives us a Katherine whose glory is not a gift of God so much as a virtue born of intrinsic nobility and honed to perfection by a lifetime of unremitting effort. She exemplifies the grace that comes from the pure will to goodness, a will independent of Christian theology, and which we see plainly exemplified in Brutus' wife Portia in *The Tragedy of Julius Caesar*. Think of Katherine in late pregnancy clad in full battle armor riding out to confront the Scots at Flodden. This is the same spirit which reverberates in the exhausted and harried figure we see rising to face her foes at Blackfriars. Like Portia, Katherine of Aragon is animated by a legacy imparted to her by proud ancestors who scorned Christian values such as chastity and pacifism. She was a fighter. Her earthly virtue rises to such a pitch that it is all too easy to see in it the handiwork of angels. The credit we would give heaven in such a case must inevitably be subtracted from her.

WORKS CITED:

Amy Appleford, "Shakespeare's Katherine of Aragon: Last Medieval Queen, First Recusant Martyr," *Journal of Medieval and Early Modern Studies*, 40:1, Winter, 2010.

Harold Bloom, *Shakespeare and the Invention of the Human*, Riverhead Books, 1998.

George Cavendish, *The Life and Death of Cardinal Wolsey*, Richard S. Sylvester, ed., Oxford University Press, 1959.

Carolly Erickson, *Great Harry*, St. Martin's Press, 1980.

Phillip J. Finkelpearl, "John Fletcher as Spenserian Playwright: The Faithful Shepherdess and The Island Princess," *Studies in English Literature 1500-1900*, Vol.27, No. 2, Spring 1987, pp. 285-302.

G. Wilson Knight, *The Crown of Life*, Oxford University Press, 1948; Barnes and Noble, 1966.

Robert Lacey, *The Life and Times of King Henry VIII*, Weidenfeld & Nicolson, 1972; Welcome Rain, 1998.

William Shakespeare, Complete Works, J. Bate, E. Rasmussen, Royal Shakespeare Company, 2007; Random House, 2007.

The Yale Shakespeare: The Complete Works, Wilbur Cross, Tucker

Brooke, eds., Barnes and Noble, 2006. [all quotations taken from this treatise]

C.C. Stopes, *Shakespeare's Family*, James Pott & Co., 1901 (available online).

9

Painting the Green World Red: The Brothel in Shakespeare's Plays

$\mathcal{N}$orthrop Frye is remembered for the wondrous notion of the Green World, that rustic site outside the royal court where Shakespearean protagonists are free to undergo growth, resolution and integration. The Forest of Arden in *As You Like It*, the Athenian wood in *A Midsummer Night's Dream*, even that humble graveyard in Act Four of *Hamlet*, among others, all function as places beyond the stresses of palace imbroglios, where the psyche can blossom, find refreshment in nature and reconstitute itself. Less frequently noticed, perhaps, is another kind of space, located within or tangent to the city which affords retreat. That is the brothel. We see this far-less-favored venue featured in *King Henry IV, Pericles* and *Measure for Measure*. Unlike Shakespeare's pastoral scenes, those set in brothels are not intersections for the meeting of courtiers and gentle shepherds, but places where troubled protagonists rub shoulders with a rowdier social element and find themselves invigorated by a common and fundamental humanity. In long-faced dramas such interludes afford comic relief. It should be kept in mind that even in the Green World we encounter disfranchised urbanites, such as the bandits in *The Two Gentlemen of Verona*, the genteel savages Guiderius and Arviragus in *Cymbeline, King of Britain*, the noble woodmen in *As You Like It*, and that begrimed and lunatic saint on the heath in *Lear*. The brothel in Shakespeare is a miniature urban wilderness, a place less insistent on formalities, social distinctions and decorum, allowing for a more direct encounter with the rudiments of life, providing scope for characters to slough off expectations. Neither the Green World nor its ruddy cousin guarantee anything. What they offer is alterity, a shift in identity. How this is fashioned defines the character. Prince Hamlet seems to learn something from his encounter with pirates at sea and comes back to Elsinore rejuvenated. (IV, v, 16-21) Suffolk does not. (*King Henry VI*, Part Two, IV, i) The readiness is all, after all.

Let us take a moment to reconnoiter with Hal and Pointz in the Boar's-head Tavern, Marina and Lysimachus in Mytilene, and Isabella and hoi polloi in the stews of Vienna.

I. The Boar's-head Tavern

Though Falstaff is not on stage in *The Life of King Henry the Fifth*, we know Shakespeare wants us to view it with him in mind. There he sets two scenes in the Boar's-head Tavern, including the off-camera death of Falstaff. (I, i, I, iii) We also know that while on military expedition in France, the past weighs heavily on Harry's mind. (V, i, 286-302) His burden of guilt cannot be gainsaid. Though he betrays Falstaff, banishing him from his court and life, it seems he cannot quite expel him from his thoughts. After all, he is fighting alongside the same boon companions as before: Nym, Bardolph, Pistol and the serving boy, Falstaffians loyal and true. Shakespeare doesn't want us to forget the rollicking Boar's-head days as we plough through Harfleur and Agincourt. Though his ghost does not appear onstage, Harry is haunted by Falstaff.

The Boar's-head "Tavern" is, of course, one of the thinly disguised brothels in Eastcheap, London's red light district.

PRINCE HARRY
(to Falstaff)

What a devil hast thou to do with the time of the day?
Unless hours were cups of sack, and minutes capons,
and clocks the tongues of bawds, and dials the signs
of leaping houses, and the blessed sun himself a fair
hot wench in flame-coloured taffeta, I see no reason
why thou shouldst be so superfluous to demand the
time of the day.
(*King Henry IV*, Part One, I, ii, 5-12)

In other words, Eastcheap is the devil's bailiwick. Burning in the sky above is a gaudy wench presiding over endless debauch, a territory in which deadlines and appointments don't count. Law is mocked. Crimes are hatched here, not boring plans. Time itself has been exiled. Prince Hal projects this debased ambience on his host and mentor, Falstaff, but Hal is living here too, though his own doings are discreetly veiled. It is plain from the beginning that the Hostess, the proprietress, is actually a bawd, "Doll Tearsheet" a streetwalker. If we conceive of Bolingbroke's court as the locus of dull labor, then the Boar's-head is a ludic realm, a Carnival. With Bacchic liberty and easy toleration come song, bombast—even impromptu theatrical performances: Hal and Falstaff take turns impersonating the King interrogating his wayward son. Of course, all of this is well-known.

What is not quite clear is the impact all this has on Hal. Is he daubed within by his scarlet exterior? The issue is underscored by the famous "I know you all" soliloquy (I, ii, 192-214) in which we are taken aback to hear that he is only pretending to be a part of the gaiety and merriment of the Boar's-head, that his friendships with these colorful figures are as false as a Mardi Gras mask. All this sound and fury is but a foil, a stratagem to make his stern reformation and putting on of royal power seem more impressive. But the interaction of prince and paupers is so vivid and compelling that it is nearly impossible to believe that Hal has no feeling, no love for his comrades. Could it all be a cheap charade?

The Green World is a place where characters have adventures and develop in ways they might not have, had they remained at home. Demetrius, in *A Midsummer Night's Dream*, for example, abandons his unsuitable crush on Hermia, betrothed to Lysander, and returns to his affection for Helena. When he speaks of this at the play's end, we hear and believe:

DEMETRIUS (to Theseus)

My lord, fair Helen told me of their stealth,
Of this their purpose hither to this wood,
And I in fury hither followed them,
Fair Helena in fancy following me.
But, my good lord, I wot not by what power —
But by some power it is — my love to Hermia,
Melted as the snow, seems to me now
As the remembrance of an idle gaud
Which in my childhood I did dote upon,
And all the faith, the virtue of my heart,

The object and the pleasure of mine eye,
Is only Helena. To her, my lord,
Was I betrothed ere I see Hermia.
But like in sickness did I loathe this food;
But, as in health come to my natural taste,
Now do I wish for it, love it, long for it,
And will evermore be true to it.
(IV, i, 159-175)

Demetrius is transported by his experience in the Green World and returns to his original love object. What if Oberon's love juice had been smeared on the slumbering eyelids of Prince Harry, who on waking had first seen Doll Tearsheet—or Falstaff himself? What then? There appear huge differences in the Prince—so long as he abides in Eastcheap—but on reversion to the privy chamber and his actual father, he chooses the grey field of work, not play. In so doing, he pays a heavy price. For one can only excise Jack Falstaff from one's heart by sacrificing a piece of oneself. Like Odysseus, tied to the ship's mast, auditing the song of the Sirens, Hal holds himself aloof. He loves Falstaff. He must. And yet . . . it is as if his inner core is frigid and untouched, so that, unlike the case with Demetrius, what melts away at last is not the painted pomp of the court and idle ceremony, (IV, i, 237) but rather Falstaff, the very spirit of revelry.

One disadvantage Hal faces is Pointz, a low-life fellow with an upper-crust bearing consistent with courtly indiscretion. It has been suggested with good reason that Pointz may well be Hal's elder brother, and that it was Pointz who was responsible for conducting Hal to the Boar's-head Tavern originally. (Gontar, 64ff.) Because Pointz is forever at his elbow, Hal's immersion in the Red World is checked, never complete. Pointz is always drawing him aside, reminding him teasingly of his uptown pedigree. A careful reading of Part Two, Act II, scene ii, displays their casual intimacy, as though they had some hidden bond with one another. After chatting tongue-in-cheek about marrying Pointz's sister (that is, half-sister), Hal comments ironically: "Well, thus we play the fools with the time, and the spirits of the wise sit in the clouds and mock us," (II, ii, 133-135), not exactly the sort of bonhomie to be appreciated by Bardolph, Nym or Peto. Hal and Pointz share the same patronizing view of their seedy surroundings.

PRINCE HARRY

This Doll Tearsheet should be some road

POINTZ

I warrant you, as common as the way between
St. Albans and London.
(II, ii, 158-160)

In plain demonstration of their shared condescension, Hal and Pointz once again plot to embarrass Falstaff.

PRINCE HARRY

How might we see Falstaff bestow himself
tonight in his true colours, and not ourselves be seen?

POINTZ

Put on two leathern jerkins and aprons, and wait
upon him at his table like drawers.

PRINCE HARRY

From a god to a bull — a heavy declension —
It was Jove's case. From a prince to a prentice — a low
transformation — that shall be mine; for in everything
the purpose must weigh with the folly. Follow me, Ned.
(II, ii, 161-168)

That evening while Falstaff is disporting himself with Doll, cradling her on his knee, his supposed friends the Prince of Wales and co-conspirator Ned Pointz spy on him. They hear him declaim disparagingly about them both. Shakespeare's meaning is evident: despite the roistering and skylarking, the boozing and camaraderie, the Prince and Pointz don't belong. Their mocking behavior dovetails perfectly with Hal's aforementioned "I know you all" speech. Just as he acts the part of his father in the Boar's-head Tavern spectacle, so are all his doings parts he puts on. Hard as it is to believe in light of the sheer joviality of the vivid scenes Shakespeare conjures, we must conclude that Hal never gives himself to his new home with sincerity and depth. The risk is one he could never tolerate.

Of course, if we stop and think about it, how likely is it that the future King of England would allow himself to become a bohemian, when at any moment he might be summoned to lead his nation? Falstaff was not totally naïve. At times he foresaw the truth with perfect accuracy, as when he pleaded with Hal not to banish him after assuming the throne. (II, v, 471-485) Hal would not take purses from the travelers at Gadshill. "Who, I rob? I a thief? Not I, by my faith." (I, iii, 136) And though the Boar's-head Tavern is transparently a bordello, will the Prince permit himself to have relations with a Doll Tearsheet and risk the creation of another royal bastard? Absolutely not. At every step of the way it is evident that Hal is false. And "False"-staff knows it. Yet, in his love of Hal and in his self-aggrandizing fantasies, he indulges in the silly notion that he would one day sit beside the King of England. The irony is that, truth be told, Hal needs Falstaff just as much if not more than Falstaff needs him. His guilt and loneliness on the eve of Agincourt tell the story. When Hal decides to morph into Bolingbroke, something goes out of him, something precious he possessed only in relation to that old fat knight. The enlargement offered by the Red World was genuine. Hal was not.

II. The Brothel at Mytilene

One of the funniest episodes in the comedy *Pericles, Prince of Tyre* involves a girl without a funny bone in her body. Marina, born in a storm at sea, is the beautiful product of Prince Pericles' priceless *Wanderjahre*. Kidnapped by pirates, and sold into white slavery, she winds up in a trade withering from lack of business. Suffering congenital virtue, she cannot comprehend what she is asked to do, and takes every opportunity to put lusty patrons on the straight and narrow. This causes a fiscal crisis calling for emergency action.

FIRST GENTLEMAN

Did you ever hear the like?

SECOND GENTLEMAN

No, nor never shall do in such a place
as this, she being gone.

FIRST GENTLEMAN

But to have divinity preached there —
did you ever dream of such a thing?

SECOND GENTLEMAN

No, no. Come, I am for no more
bawdy houses. Shall's go hear the vestals sing?

FIRST GENTLEMAN

I'll do anything now that is virtuous,
but I am out of the road of rutting for ever. (Exeunt)

Enter Pander, Bawd, and Boult

PANDER

Well, I had rather than twice the worth of her
she had ne'er come here.

BAWD

Fie, fie upon her, she's able to freeze the god
Priapus and undo the whole of generation. We must
either get her ravished or be rid of her. When she
should do for clients her fitment and do me the kindness
of our profession, she has me her quirks, her reasons,
her master reasons, her prayers, her knees, that she
would make a puritan of the devil if he should cheapen
a kiss of her.

BOULT

Faith, I must ravish her, or she'll disfurnish us of
all our cavalleria and make our swearers priests.

PANDER

Now, the pox upon her green-sickness for me.

BAWD

Faith, there's no way to be rid on't but by the way
to the pox.
(Scene 19, 1-24)

At this point in the action, Marina's father, presuming her mother
to be dead, is drifting over the seas in a cataleptic state. He still flees the
specter of incest he first encountered when he sought to take possession
of the daughter of King Antiochus, who was having an affair with her
own father. Lingering in the background is the implicit possibility that
Pericles might recover and unwittingly patronize the brothel where his
now-grown daughter is employed. Instead, the Governor of the city of
Mytilene, Lysimachus, steps across the brothel threshold incognito. As
she did with the other gentlemen, Marina persuades Lysimachus to find
something better to do than exercise wanton lust. Unbeknownst to anyone, Marina's mother is alive, and a votary of Diana, Goddess of chastity.
Her genial piety reigns invisibly over all.

MARINA

Let not authority, which teaches you
To govern others, be the means to make you
Misgovern much yourself.
If you were born to honor, show it now;
If put upon you, make the judgement good
That thought you worthy of it. What reason's in
Your justice, who hath power over all,
To undo any? If you take from me
Mine honour, you're like him that makes a gap
Into forbidden ground, whom after

Too many enter, and of all their evils
Yourself are guilty. My life is yet unspotted;
My chastity unstainèd ev'n in thought.
Then if your violence deface this building,
The workmanship of heav'n, you do kill your honour,
Abuse your justice, and impoverish me.
My yet good lord, if there be fire before me,
Must I straight fly and burn myself?
(Scene 19, 98-113)

A bit more of this and Lysimachus departs in haste, but with the memory of Marina etched in his brain.

LYSIMACHUS (moved)

I did not think
Thou couldst have spoke so well, ne'er dreamt thou couldst.

(He lifts her up with his hands)

Though I brought hither a corrupted mind,
Thy speech hath altered it,

(He wipes the wet from her eyes)

and my foul thoughts
Thy tears so well hath laved that they're now white.
I came here meaning but to pay the price,
A piece of gold for thy virginity;
Here's twenty to relieve thine honesty.
Persever still in that clear way thou goest,
And may the gods strengthen thee.
(Scene 19, 127-135)

Like Prince Hal, Marina resists the blandishments of the Red World, and teaches Lysimachus and others the same lesson. At this moment, like Lord Angelo in *Measure for Measure*, he falls instantly in love with his young teacher of sanctity. Outraged beyond all consolation, the Bawd and Pander relent when they discover that Marina can make money tutoring the youth of Mytilene in the liberal arts, all of which she has mastered. Soon thereafter, the barnacled vessel of old Pericles moors in the harbor. Marina is summoned thence to see if she can cure him of his depression. As Lysimachus watches from the sidelines, father and daughter realize their filial relationship, causing much relief and celebration. The couple plans to wed. Diana appears to Pericles with news that his beloved wife Thaisa is living still, serving her in Ephesus, to which everyone repairs in joy and happy reunion.

All seems well. But as is the case so often in Shakespeare, a subtle dilemma brews unnoticed. Marina, daughter of a votary of Diana and champion of chastity is marrying an habitual brothel patron. Is there a problem? Transfer this scenario to the real world, our world, and the question answers itself. Will they be content? Is Marina going to be the kind of wife her husband desires? When she is peevish, won't his former unbridled behavior rankle in her heart, rendering both partners miserable? This is the crux of the comedy. Incest has been avoided largely by Accident, which seems the ruling principle of the plot. But it's a narrow miss. Marina has taken a husband much older than herself, a father figure, accustomed to sexual license. Domestic tension is inescapable.

On the surface, Lysimachus, native of the Red World, has been transformed. He loves the thing he would have used or abused. His dignity is restored. In that respect he recapitulates the conversion of Demetrius, who made his recovery in the World of Green. But even Helena might at some point wake up and recollect that her husband actually did woo the beauteous Hermia, a vexing thought. As for Marina, she has not dreamt but known first hand her husband's proclivities, and must face the prospect of backsliding at some point in the future. In a sense, it's up to her. It is Marina who has entered the Red World and encountered beings of a coarser kind, a kind she never knew before. Though she has avoided degradation, her shady surroundings have taught her the ways of the world. "I am a part of all that I have met," says Tennyson's Ulysses. In spite of her non-cooperation, the mere exposure to such raw elements on a daily basis brings her a maturity more stable than adolescent optimism. She has seen more of life. If she can take these gleanings of the Red World and use them in charting a safe marital voyage with her good husband, the prognosis may yet be positive.

III. Gates of Vienna, Gates of Hell

In *The Anatomy of Criticism*, Northrop Frye, in introducing the Green World principle, remarks that "this second world concept is absent from the more ironic comedies *All's Well* and *Measure for Measure*." (Frye, 182) And certainly, to the extent that "second world" is identified with the Green World, that observation is quite correct. With particular reference to *Measure for Measure*, however, there do appear to be signs of what could be termed a "second world," though one not so verdant as those of *A Midsummer Night's Dream* or *The Two Gentlemen of Verona*. Most readers today would probably agree that *Measure for Measure* represents the intersection of two distinct moral and social spheres, one ordered by the state, taken as the normal world, the other that of disorder, *i.e.*, the brothel, which we have denominated a 'Red' zone. For in the Vienna of this play are many taverns in which pleasure may be purchased, while beyond the city gates lie innumerable "houses of resort" which openly do business without apprehension. The culture of indulgence and *sans souci* which prevails in these saloons and parlors is incommensurate with the rule-bound proprieties and gravities of conventional Vienna. That is the reason for their sequestration. The action of Shakespeare's "problem play" or "romance" is triggered by a municipal decision to shutter and destroy all brothels in the outlying districts. As an apparently large segment of the population has recreation and employment there, this action comes as a blow.

MISTRESS OVERDONE

Thus, what with the war, what with the sweat [disease],
what with the gallows, and what with poverty, I am custom-
shrunk.

(Enter Pompey, a tapster)

How now, what's the news with you?

POMPEY

You have not heard of the proclamation, have
you?

MISTRESS OVERDONE

What proclamation, man?

POMPEY

All houses in the suburbs of Vienna must be
plucked down.

MISTRESS OVERDONE

And what shall become of those in the city?

POMPEY

They shall stand for seed. They had gone down
too, but that a wise burgher put in for them.

MISTRESS OVERDONE

But shall all our houses of resort in
the suburbs be pulled down?

POMPEY

To the ground, mistress.

MISTRESS OVERDONE

Why, here is a change in the commonwealth.
What shall become of me?

POMPEY

Come, fear not you. Good counsellors lack no
clients. Though you change your place, you need not
change your trade. I'll be your tapster still. Courage,
there will be pity taken on you. You that have worn
your eyes almost out in the service, you will be
considered.
(I, ii, 80-103)

What is not anticipated by the authorities is that closing the broth-els turns over a wasps' nest of unsavory characters who roam the streets in search of former occupations and diversions. Activities which had been confined to private residences now spill out into plain view. This requires an expanded system of watches, constabularies, prisons, and jurists, a burden on the public treasury. Meanwhile the administration has been turned over to Lord Angelo, a junior magistrate, as Duke Vincentio goes on a mysterious sabbatical. Angelo responds to the crisis by conducting mass arrests and meting out Draconian penalties. The consequence is a sort of civil war, in which those in the demimonde square off against the establishment. Thus, while there are no distinctive brothel scenes in a Vienna which has forbidden the institution, the city has become a sudden confrontation of red and grey factions. While ordinarily, as Prof. Frye taught, heroes in the quotidian sphere enter the Green World to be transformed, in *Measure for Measure* the tides of the Red World engulf its counterpart like a bloom of algae.

Something is bound to ensue, and does.

In the convent of the Sisters of Saint Clare is Isabella, a postulant. She is called by Lucio, a picaresque rogue, to come to the city to plead on behalf of her brother, Claudio, facing execution for fornication. Not delaying to even change her apparel, Isabella rushes to Lord Angelo to beg a reduction in the sentence. During her impassioned and provocative discourse, Angelo, rather like Lysimachus heeding Marina, finds himself overpowered by desire for this maid-in-nun's-attire, and tries to rationalize it as love. (II, iv, 141) Isabella thus functions in *Measure for Measure* as an unwitting emissary of the Red World, inflaming the heart of Angelo with an ardent emotion he can scarcely grasp. Her desperate oration is unconsciously filled with erotic tropes as she, the chaste novice of a convent, pleads that the law excuse her brother's laxity. Faced with temptation, Angelo yields to it, and proposes a shameful *quid pro quo*: he will spare brother Claudio's life if Isabella will give him her body for his pleasure. At first, innocent Isabella fails to get the message.

ANGELO

Admit no other way to save his life —
As I subscribe not that nor any other —
But, in the loss of question, that you his sister,
Finding yourself desired of such a person
Whose credit with the judge, or own great place,
Could fetch your brother from the manacles
Of the all-binding law, and that there were

No earthly mean to save him, but that either
You must lay down the treasures of your body
To this supposed, or else to let him suffer —
What would you do?

ISABELLA

As much for my poor brother as myself.
That is, were I under the terms of death,
Th' impression of keen whips I'd wear as rubies,
And strip myself to death as to a bed
That longing have been sick for, ere I'd yield
My body up to shame.

ANGELO

Then must your brother die.

ISABELLA

And 'twere the cheaper way.
Better it were a brother died at once
Than a sister, by redeeming him,
Should die forever.
(II, iv, 88-109)

As we read passages such as this in *Measure for Measure* it is natural to think again about the fate of Marina in *Pericles*. As was suggested above, stationed where she is in Mytilene, she could not shield herself from contact with the ruder elements of society, and though she never submits to libidinous propositions, she cannot stop her ears or don a blindfold. Perforce she learns much about men and what makes the world go round. She keeps her virginity but must be understood as suffering an internal sea change of which she has only the faintest awareness.

Isabella never occupies a house of ill-repute. She is spared that. And yet, the Red World reaches out to her through Angelo and her brother, and holds her in its grip long enough for her to be affected. Unlike Marina, who is pictured as a bluestocking or bonneted temperance worker, Isabella manifests an erotic energy which crackles just beneath the surface. Indeed, her request to the Order of St. Clare that there be greater restraints and strictures on its sisters (I, iv, 1-5) is suggestive of a person in flight from impulses she can barely contain on her own. Words and phrases in her plea to Angelo by which she means to convey her purity have an altogether opposed resonance in his ear, such as: "the impression of keen whips I'd wear as rubies," "strip myself," "a bed that longing have been sick for," and "yield my body up." These locutions sound with an almost sadomasochistic appeal, of which poor Isabella has no ken. Placed side by side, then, these two young ladies, Marina and Isabella, both of whom pray constantly for renunciation and purity, are subjected to the power of the Red World, with the result that neither of them continues with a life of dedicated abstinence. Rather, both marry and will submit to the embraces of a man.

Further, as indicated above, whether these marriages will be successful is the challenge each couple will face. Marina will need to exercise caution in monitoring her recollections and reactions to the importunities of Lysimachus. As for Isabella, the conclusion of *Measure for Measure* places her under a distinct question mark. She has eluded Angelo's ugly demand for sex by use of the "bed trick," in which, in a dark room, Angelo's former fiancée Mariana, jilted by him, is substituted for Isabella. After hearing Isabella's surprising plea that Angelo be spared the ultimate punishment, the Duke enjoins that Mariana and Angelo be married. It must be recalled that throughout the entire play, Duke Vincentio has been in disguise as Friar Lodowick. In the judgment scene by which the play concludes, the Duke unmasks himself for the first time, revealing that the fellow who helped Isabella save her virtue was not, as she had supposed, a religious monk, but the Duke himself, whom all supposed was absent from Vienna.

Now, standing in front of her, he has the provost reveal that brother Claudio, whom Isabella believed was executed by Angelo in violation of the *quid pro quo*, is still alive.

PROVOST

This is another prisoner that I saved,
Who should have died when Claudio lost his head,
As like almost to Claudio as himself.
(He unmuffles Claudio)
(V, i, 486-488)

Then, just as Isabella is trying to adjust to this momentous and sudden revelation, Friar Lodowick, now the Duke once more, speaks to Isabella.

DUKE

If he be like your brother, for his sake
Is he pardoned; and for your lovely sake
Give me your hand, and say you will be mine.
He is my brother too. But fitter time for that.
By this Lord Angelo perceives he's safe.
Methinks I see a quick'ning in his eye.
Well, Angelo, your evil quits you well.
Look that you love your wife, her worth worth yours.
I find an apt remission in myself . . . .
(V, i, 489-497)

And there it is. No stage directions dictate that Isabella reciprocate and place her hand in his, though it would be hard to find a production in which the director did not call for that response. Just about every critic who writes about this play observes that the loquacious Isabella is stonily silent for its remainder. We never hear her accept the Duke's proposal. Admittedly, many proposals are not given immediate answers but are taken under advisement. But having witnessed the Duke reaching for her hand, who in the audience would not anticipate a gesture or some words from Isabella?

Our prognosis must be guarded. Isabella is being called on to make an eventful decision on the spot after so many disturbing experiences it is doubtful she'll be able to digest her dinner. She is at this moment still a novice in the Order of St. Clare, clad in its habit, and must shortly return to confer with the prioress. Her brother Claudio has been revealed as a "fornicator," one thought dead, and now unveiled as hale and hearty. His fiancée, Juliet, Isabella's good childhood friend, is visibly pregnant. The magistrate before whom she pleaded with artless seductiveness, has been forgiven, largely at her own behest. What could be her feelings for him at his juncture? Few ask. And on top of all this, the man she trusted as Friar Lodowick turns out to be the canny Duke himself, who, in the presence of everyone in Vienna, proposes marriage! Is it any wonder she is mute? Is not Isabella similar to the fair Ophelia, brought down by her Prince and her flowers and water-laden garments? Isabella has wandered from the cloistered security of the nunnery into the confusion of the Red World, and is at least for the instant drowned by a mass of bewilderment. It will be a long while before she can think of herself as she had before. No match made in heaven this, it's not surprising this is termed a "problem play."

One might remark *en passant* the *mélange* of disguises, mistaken identities, flirtations, sensual experiments and dubious marriages we find in Shakespeare turns up later in the operas of Mozart, *e.g.*, *Così fan tutte*, which can hardly be discussed historically without considering their Shakespearean ethos. See, for example, online, "Così fan tutte," by Chia Han-Leon, and the searching review of "The Librettist of Venice," (Rodney Bolt), by Susan W. Bolt, The Schiller Institute, n.d. Opera fans will recall that the ploy of Guglielmo and Ferrando to test their fiancées' fidelity backfires with each disguised Lothario seducing the fiancée of the other. Though there is song and celebration at the finale, with an air of general forgiveness for a clumsy escapade, a shadow of doubt and perplexity falls over the two couples, who no longer seem to know who they are.

IV. Conclusion

It is to Northrop Frye's imperishable credit that we have the Green World to aid us in appreciating Shakespearean transformation. But as we all know, there are many ways in which change may occur, many catalysts in maturation and growth. A boy goes to war and returns a man. Trauma may rob us of our amiability. Some grow old and bitter, others serene. Or, the unrelenting accretion of fortune's slings and arrows may usher in despair. Frye was especially intrigued by the operation of the Green World on account of its associations with myth and nature. But Shakespeare employed a palette of varied hues, and used many tinctures besides chlorophyll. Even within the urban ethos, a schism may occur, as when, in the 1960's, a counterculture of pacifism and free love arose fueled by uncontrolled substances. Those who entered in, were they not changed? Yes, Demetrius and Nick Bottom emerge from the Athenian wood richer and more insightful than when they strayed thence, but so, to a degree, do Hal and Marina. The proletarian dimension into which they were thrust is, of course, merely the necessary, not the sufficient, condition of evolution; had their resistance been less, their souls might have become more ample. Learning is not always in the classroom. As we all know, there may be insight in a chance encounter. Angelo and Isabella are caught in a social upheaval; ultimately they may be all the better for it. Having found unruliness within himself, Angelo might be a more compassionate magistrate. Having seen how the other half lives, Isabella may anchor those high-flown words that come to her so readily.

The moral for the audience is that Hal, Marina, Isabella, Nick Bottom and the rest are only fictions, in the final analysis no more than spots of ink on the page. Of themselves, they'll leave not a wrack behind. It is we who have journeyed, not they. The "second world"—of any color—is the transformative power of the poet's art. The real changes occur in us, not in those beguiling creatures by whom we were so entranced.

WORKS CITED:

Northrop Frye, *The Anatomy of Criticism*, Princeton University Press, 2000.

David P. Gontar, *Hamlet Made Simple and Other Essays*, New English Review Press, 2013.

William Shakespeare, The Complete Works, 2d ed., S. Wells and G. Taylor, eds., Clarendon Press, 2005.

10
Shakespeare's Compassion

Give sorrow words. — Shakespeare

I. Introduction

*I*n approaching anything as vital and significant as Shakespeare's principle of Compassion, a clear grasp of meaning is essential. One finds in his texts such disparate terms as Compassion, sympathy, mercy, pity, heart, charity, pardon, forgiveness, conscience and lenity, all of which carry slightly different connotations. Sorting these out can help in coming to terms with Shakespeare's key principle.

The most ample source of insight into Compassion is Buddhist teaching. Shakespeare's natural proximity to Buddhism has been wonderfully shown in James Howe's *A Buddhist's Shakespeare: Affirming Self- Deconstructions*. But unlike Richard Wagner, the composer whose familiarity with Compassion derives from Buddhism via the writings of philosopher Arthur Schopenhauer, Shakespeare, writing circa 1600, had no access to the wisdom of the far east. It is likely, however, that he did have a copy of the Geneva Bible, which was assiduously studied. This is detailed in the magisterial analysis of Prof. Roger Stritmatter. As dramatist, Shakespeare employed the idea of Compassion in many characters and settings, and with each particular instance its form varied. As a prism breaks pure light into many hues, so the radiance of Compassion is refracted as many subsidiary aspects, depending on the resources and maturity of the individual personality. So is it in the world of our supreme artist, Shakespeare.

What is startling about him is his taxonomic understanding of

Compassion in relation to its lesser forms. For an explanation of the distinction between Compassion and other expressions of solicitude, we turn to the writings of Cynthia Wall, an experienced social worker and psychotherapist who has worked extensively with dying patients, their families and friends. Her careful distinction between Compassion and sympathy has implications for both philosophy and psychological counseling.

> There is nothing anyone can say to take away pain and fear. There is no magic incantation that reduces suffering. What you can do is listen without judging, and offer your time with no expectation it will make a difference. Your willingness to be genuine and kind is all you have to offer. This is the starting point for acting from Compassion. Although sympathy is a form of caring, it implies pity. We express concern and ask what we can do, yet are grateful their problems are not ours. This perpetuates the fear that we couldn't bear the same situation, and keeps us wanting to avoid the truth of their experience. Compassion is a hard-won state of being. Much more than a feeling, compassion is a choice to view suffering as a universal experience. This means viewing illness, loss, and even death as human experiences that are bearable with support. This helps us remain calm and keeps our hearts open, and we become able to sit with someone in great physical or emotional pain. Compassion bridges the distance between people often created by suffering. This is not comfortable to do, as we must acknowledge their problems might reflect our own future.
>
> Separating from someone's pain protects against feeling overwhelmed and helpless. We are born tenderhearted. The presence of pain or problems engenders the impulse to make things better. This is a child's view of how to be helpful. Our job is to make suffering into an enemy and rail against it. The adult perspective embraces the truth that the best gift we have is a willingness to share in their experience without the defense of sympathy. (Wall, online, no pagination)

II. *As You Like It*

In a remarkable passage, Shakespeare comments on the problem of suffering and our attitudes towards it. It occurs in *As You Like It*, when we are introduced to the Old Duke and his compeers in the Forest of Arden, living in the barren woods in inclement circumstances. Rather than being downcast, the Old Duke's mood is grateful, even celebratory.

> Now, my co-mates and brothers in exile,
> Hath not old custom made this life more sweet
> Than that of painted pomp? Are not these woods
> More free from peril than the envious court?
> Here feel we not the penalty of Adam,
> The seasons' difference, as the icy fang
> And churlish chiding of the winter's wind,
> Which when it bites and blows upon my body
> Even till I shrink with cold, I smile, and say
> 'This is no flattery. These are counsellors
> That feelingly persuade me what I am.'
> Sweet are the uses of adversity
> Which, like the toad, ugly and venemous,
> Wears yet a precious jewel in his head;
> And this our life, exempt from public haunt,
> Finds tongues in trees, books in the running brooks,
> Sermons in stones, and good in everything.
> (II, i, 1-17)

In this play of Shakespeare's middle period, perhaps more than any other, the stream of Compassion flows in vigorous purity. Suffering is acknowledged by the Old Duke collectively, not papered over, fled or denied. As shared it is endurable. As a sign of our common mortality it is an important lesson.

When young Orlando, bearing the elderly serving man Adam, arrives exhausted in the forest, he goes immediately in search of food for his loyal companion. His first impulse is Compassion; his hunger is significant in representing the hunger of his old friend. Breaking into the place where the Old Duke and his men are gathering for their meal, Orlando, with drawn sword, attempts to extort food.

DUKE SENIOR

Art thou thus boldened man, by thy distress?
Or else a rude despiser of good manners,
That in civility thou seem'st so empty?

ORLANDO

You touched my vein at first. The thorny point
Of bare distress hath ta'en from me the show
Of smooth civility. Yet am I inland bred,
And know some nurture. But forebear, I say.
He dies that touches any of this fruit
Till I and my affairs are answerèd.

JAQUES

An you will not be answered with reason, I must
die.

DUKE SENIOR

What would you have? Your gentleness shall force
More than your force move us to gentleness.

ORLANDO

I almost die for food; and let me have it.

DUKE SENIOR

Sit down and feed, and welcome to our table.

ORLANDO

Speak you so gently? Pardon me, I pray you.
I thought that all things had been savage here,
And therefore put I on the countenance
Of stern commandment. But whate'er you are
That in this desert inaccessible,

Under the shade of melancholy boughs,
Lose and neglect the creeping hours of time,
If ever you have looked on better days,
If ever been where bells have knolled to church,
If ever sat at any good man's feast,
If ever from your eyelids wiped a tear,
And know what 'tis to pity, and be pitied,
Let gentleness my strong enforcement be.
In the which hope I blush, and hide my sword.

DUKE SENIOR

True is it that we have seen better days,
And have with holy bell been knolled to church,
And sat at good men's feasts, and wiped our eyes
Of drops that sacred pity hath engendered.
And therefore sit you down in gentleness,
And take upon command what help we have
That to your wanting may be ministered.

ORLANDO

Then but forebear your food a little while
Whiles, like a doe, I go to find my fawn
And give it food. There is an old poor man
Who after me hath many a weary step
Limped in pure love. Till he be first sufficed,
Oppressed with two weak evils, age and hunger,
I will not touch a bit.

DUKE SENIOR

Go find him out,
And we will nothing waste till you return.

ORLANDO

I thank ye; and be blessed for your good comfort! (Exit)

DUKE SENIOR

Thou seest we are not all alone unhappy.
The wide and universal theatre
Presents more woeful pageants than the scene
Wherein we play in.
(II, vii, 91-138)

Adam, the aged and faithful servant of Orlando, has given his entire life's savings to the young man to allow him to flee from his abusive elder brother. His kindness to Orlando in his desperate circumstances awakens a corresponding feeling of care in Orlando. When they arrive in the forest, Adam is depleted and famished, and Orlando's first impulse is to find him something to eat. In his conversation with Duke Senior he uses the term "pity," but what moves all three of these characters, Adam, Orlando and the Duke is not "pity" but pure Compassion. According to one teacher:

> The Buddhist compassion has nothing to do with sentimentality or mere pity. Compassion is often thought of as akin to pity, but whereas pity may be condescending, compassion springs from a sense of equality and interconnectedness of life. Genuine compassion is about empowering others, helping them unlock strength and courage from within their lives in order to overcome their problems. The essence of compassion is empowerment. (Soka Gakkai International, no pagination)

Adam's free gift of money to Orlando, then, is not an act of pity, as it is done out of an unadulterated concern for Orlando's plight, and it enables him to flee. Adam's Compassion empowers the young man. So anxious is Orlando for this old fellow's welfare that if necessary he is willing to steal to alleviate Adam's suffering. As Adam's Compassion for Orlando prompts Compassion in the latter, so does Orlando's Compassion invite the Compassion of Duke Senior for him. One Compassionate deed becomes the first link in a chain of goodness, a circle of merit rippling outward in the ocean of life. The "wide and universal theatre" of which the Duke speaks (II, vii, 136) is the world as it is filled with such suffering as is manifest in Orlando, Adam, as well as in the Duke himself and his woodmen. In fact, it is plain that for both Buddhism and

Shakespeare, the field of delusion and suffering ("*dukkha*") is cotermi-nous with that of Compassion. The Duke's response to Orlando's sword and threatening demeanor is neither panic nor condescension, but a calm and deliberate Compassion which grants permission to Orlando to succor Adam, empowering Orlando's own sense of moral initiative. In this the Duke is neither emotional nor distancing himself from Or-lando's plight.

In later scenes of devolution, involving lesser characters, where nobility and wisdom are conspicuous by their absence, genuine Com-passion is supplanted by mere pity—or less. Touchstone's mock sympa-thy with Corin's ignorance of courtly experience and sophistication is a supercilious and disdainful demeanor. (Act III, sc. ii) Corin's reaction to the hunger of Celia (Aliena) is quite different from the feelings of Or-lando and the Old Duke for the want they confront in others; Orlando and the Duke have an immediate and felt insight into what the victim is undergoing. When Corin says, "Faith sir, I pity her" (II, iv, 74) speaking of Celia, though pity is mentioned, the statement is one of mere fact, not sentiment. The heart is untouched. However, when his own interests are involved, as when he is begging shepherdess Phoebe for her favors, his importunacy ("Sweet Phoebe, pity me") (III, v, 85) is truly pitiful. Indeed, his fawning over Phoebe, the very abjection of his condition, renders him in Rosalind's eyes undeserving of pity. (IV, iii, 66) Con-cerned with no one but themselves, Corin and Phoebe appear made for one another. Even the Compassion of Jaques for the deer hunted in the Forest of Arden sets him far above pastoral figures who see in such ani-mals merely a source of venison. (II, i, 21-70) Reading such passages in Shakespeare, then, we learn not to take words at face value. Characters may speak of "Compassion" or "pity," yet intend something quite differ-ent. Nobility of spirit, as exhibited by Orlando, Jaques or Duke Senior, is the *sine qua non* of Compassion. It is generosity of the soul, a magna-nimity which the small of heart cannot afford.

And what of Rosalind? As so many have observed, she transcends all boundaries. Her love of Orlando is like that of Venus for Adonis, a ce-lestial ardor for what is essentially human. Rosalind functions in *As You Like It* not as a mere mortal, but as a magus, an hermaphroditic heroine, an alchemical chameleon in whom heaven is artlessly camouflaged. She has charged herself with the solving of everyone's problems: she would "make these doubts all even." (V, iv, 25) She does not attain Compassion so much as manifest it, and in this respect is an image of a playful or wanton Goddess, one who cannot succeed in her terrestrial aims without bearing everyone else along in the process. In that respect, what seems to be mortal Compassion in Rosalind turns out to be the universal Compassion itself, the pulse that throbs in the very depth of things. In describing the *Dharma*, one scholar observes: "Through meditation we can extend and deepen our own compassion until it transforms into the mind of great compassion—the wish to protect all living beings without exception from their suffering." (*About Dharma*—International Kadampa Buddhist Festival) Rosalind is the great Compassion—traveling incognito.

III. *King John*

Alongside *As You Like It* as an exemplar of true Compassion must be placed *King John*, with its poignant pleading of young Arthur. Struggling King John, anxious to cut off all possible rivals for the crown, wants the boy Arthur, Duke of Bretagne, eliminated. For reasons never stated, John commissions Hubert to not only assassinate him but put out his eyes as well, a shocking and gratuitous cruelty. To show his loyalty Hubert seals to this monstrous bargain.

Fate, however, has other things in store. For Arthur accounts Hubert a friend and guardian. When he learns what Hubert is about, his protest rises to the very peak of eloquence and catches Hubert unprepared. Further, as we will see, Arthur himself embodies the very Compassion he would have bestowed on him by Hubert, and in the face of Arthur's own loving kindness Hubert's resolve melts like the flesh he would have liquidated. As the scene opens, Hubert has stationed the assassins behind the arras.

ARTHUR

Good morrow, Hubert.

HUBERT

Good morrow, little Prince.

ARTHUR

As little prince, having so great a title
To be more prince, as may be. You are sad.

HUBERT

Indeed I have been merrier.
(IV, i, 9-12)

Arthur's recognition of Hubert's distress has immediate impact. It is not a mere perception, but a reaching out, a sign of concern for one with homicide gnawing in a corner of his brain. Hubert concedes he is distressed. The Duke observes that John means him no good, and fancies that he would be safer if he were Hubert's own son, "so you would love me, Hubert." (IV, i, 24) These guileless words sting, making Hubert question whether he can do what he has pledged to do.

HUBERT (aside)

If I talk to him, with his innocent prate
He will awake my mercy, which lies dead;
Therefore I will be sudden, and dispatch.
(IV, 25-27)

This micro-soliloquy reveals the mind of the wrong-doer, who has managed to squelch his better self, only to find it re-awakened as he becomes the object of love. The sheep looks to the wolf for protection. But inside the wolf-in-sheep's-clothing is . . . the heart of a sheep. Hubert must proceed or lose the name of action.

ARTHUR

Are you sick, Hubert? You look pale today.
In sooth, I would you were a little sick,
That I might sit all night and watch with you.
I warrant I love you more than you do me.

HUBERT (aside)

His words do take possession of my bosom.
(IV, i, 28-32)

Here the spark of Compassion is ignited and flies across the gulf, awakening the sleeping love in Hubert, who would quash it before it takes effect. Notice that what is instrumental is the Compassion of the victim.

> He shows Arthur a paper
>
> Read here, young Arthur. (Aside) How now: foolish rheum,
> Turning dispiteous torture out of doors?
> I must be brief, lest resolution drop
> Out at mine eyes in tender womanish tears.
> (To Arthur) Can you not read it? Is it not fair writ?
> (IV, i, 33-37)

Manly Hubert is on the verge of tears. His dastardly courage ebbs, and he hasn't got sufficient conviction to so much as utter his awful intentions. The words would stick in his throat. He shows Arthur the commission instead.

> ARTHUR
>
> Too fairly, Hubert, for so foul effect.
> Must you with hot irons burn out both mine eyes?
>
> HUBERT
>
> Young boy, I must.
>
> ARTHUR
>
> And will you?
>
> HUBERT
>
> And I will.
>
> ARTHUR
>
> Have you the heart? When your head did but ache
> I knit my handkerchief about your brows,
> The best I had — a princess wrought it me,
> And I did never ask it you again —

And with my hand at midnight held your head,
And like the watchful minutes to the hour
Still and anon cheered up the heavy time,
Saying 'What lack you?' and 'Where lies your grief?'
Or 'What good love may I perform for you?'
Many a poor man's son would have lain still
And ne'er have spoke a loving word to you,
But you at your sick service had a prince.
Nay, you may think my love was crafty love,
And call it cunning. Do, an if you will.
If heaven be pleased that you must use me ill,
Why then you must. Will you put out mine eyes,
These eyes that never did, nor never shall,
So much as frown on you?

HUBERT

I have sworn to do it,
And with hot irons must I burn them out.

ARTHUR

Ah, none but in this iron age would do it.
The iron of itself, though red hot,
Approaching near these eyes would drink my tears,
And quench his fiery indignation
Even in the matter of mine innocence;
Nay, after that, consume away in rust,
But for containing fire to harm mine eye.
Are you more stubborn-hard than hammered iron?
An if an angel should have come to me
And told me Hubert should put out mine eyes,
I would not have believed him; no tongue but Hubert's.
(Hubert stamps his foot)

HUBERT

Come forth!
(The Executioners come forth)
Do as I bid you do.

ARTHUR

O, save me, Hubert, save me! My eyes are out
Even with the fierce looks of these bloody men.

HUBERT (To the Executioners)

Give me the iron, I say, and bind him here.
(He takes the iron)

ARTHUR

Alas, what need you be so boisterous rough?
I will not struggle; I will stand stone-still.
For God's sake, Hubert, let me not be bound.
Nay, hear me, Hubert! Drive these men away,
And I will sit as quiet as a lamb;
I will not stir, nor wince, nor speak a word,
Nor look upon the iron angerly.
Thrust but these men away, and I'll forgive you,
Whatever torment you do put me to.
(IV, i, 38-83)

Here Arthur adds to his love and Compassion a token of forgiveness, causing Hubert to hesitate and send the executioners out. Thus far
not one word of panic, rage or hostility has crossed Arthur's lips.

HUBERT (To the Executioners)

Go stand within. Let me alone with him.
(IV, i, 84)

It is at this point that the principle of Compassion breaks into view.

EXECUTIONER

I am best pleased to be from such a deed. (Exeunt Executioners)

ARTHUR

Alas, I then have chid away my friend!
He hath a stern look, but a gentle heart.
Let him come back, that his compassion may
Give life to yours.
(IV, i, 85-89)

Arthur, hearing the executioner's revulsion at their assignment, refers to him as his friend, and in a masterstroke of forensic rhetoric, urges Hubert to call the man back to awaken the embers of Compassion which we have already heard Hubert admit are glowing inside him. If Hubert hears this plea, it is only as sounds in air, for he appears deaf to the language of mercy at this point.

HUBERT

Come, boy, prepare yourself.

ARTHUR

Is there no remedy?

HUBERT

None but to lose your eyes.

ARTHUR

O God, that there were but a mote in yours,
A grain, a dust, a gnat, a wandering hair,
Any annoyance in that precious sense,
Then, feeling what small things are boisterous there,
Your vile intent must needs seem horrible.

HUBERT

Is this your promise? Go to, hold your tongue!

ARTHUR

Hubert, the utterance of a brace of tongues
Must needs want pleading for a pair of eyes.
Let me not hold my tongue, let me not, Hubert;
Or, Hubert, if you will, cut out my tongue,
So I may keep mine eyes. O, spare mine eyes,
Though to no use but still to look on you.
Lo, by my troth, the instrument is cold
And would not harm me.
(I, i, 90-104)

Arthur has bought a minute's respite in this, and raises in subtle form the question of who will be blind, Arthur for the loss of his eyes or Hubert, for being blinded to his essential humanity and love. Though he gives no outward indication, Hubert's defenses are crumbling as he recovers his inner vision.

HUBERT

I can heat it, boy.

ARTHUR

No, in good sooth: the fire is dead with grief,
Being create for comfort, [not] to be used
In undeserved extremes. See else yourself.
There is no malice in this burning coal;
The breath of heaven hath blown his spirit out,
And strewed repentant ashes on his head.

HUBERT

But with my breath I can revive it, boy.
(IV, i, 104-111)

The argument at this point is not about reviving the iron's heat, but about whether Hubert can jump-start his flagging determination to blind and murder Arthur. Hubert's insistence that he can proceed stands in for actually going forward, signaling the defeat of his misbegotten purpose.

ARTHUR

An if you do, you will but make it blush
And glow with shame of your proceedings, Hubert.
Nay, it perchance will sparkle in your eyes,
And like a dog that is compelled to fight,
Snatch at his master that doth tarre him on.
All things that you should use to do me wrong
Deny their office; only you do lack
That mercy which fierce fire and iron extends,
Creatures of note for mercy-lacking uses.

And with this Hubert's valiant campaign to betray his better nature collapses.

HUBERT

Well, see to live. I will not touch thine eye
For all the treasure that thine uncle owes.
Yet am I sworn, and I did purpose, boy,
With this same very iron to burn them out.

ARTHUR

O, now you look like Hubert. All this while
You were disguised.
(IV, i, 112-126)

Arthur uses his eyes, preserved by the recovered Compassion of Hubert, to recognize the recovery of Hubert's true self. The part of sadistic brute and servant of dread authority which Hubert tried to play, proves in the end infeasible. In response to the warmth of Arthur, Hubert's inner frigidity melts, as he becomes capable of love once more. His appearance as bloody executioner was just a mask. Sparing Arthur is not without consequences, of course, since he disobeys the dictates of his sovereign. But, ironically, two scenes later, Arthur, weary of his imprisonment at the hands of John, in the garb of a ship boy, leaps from the high walls to hoped-for freedom—and dies. (IV, iii, 1-10)

IV. Studies in Contrast: *King Lear, King Henry VI, King Richard III*

The lesson of Compassion in Shakespeare is taught in both a positive and negative manner. In the comedy *As You Like It* and in the historically-based *King John*, Compassion is triumphant—however briefly. But often Shakespeare's realism prevails, as we apprehend the bitter consequences of turning one's back on our natural fellow feeling.

1. *King Lear*

Thus, for example, in *King Lear*, in a jolting scene (III, vii) that eclipses in emotional impact the mass entertainments of Hollywood horror, Regan, Lear's second daughter and her vicious husband Cornwall, capture the faithful Gloucester, and subject him to interrogation and punishment. One of Cornwall's servants rises in defense of the innocent Gloucester and challenges Cornwall with sword. He is stabbed in the back by Regan. It is interesting to note that Edmond the bastard son of Gloucester is in the company of Cornwall, and abandons his natural and loving father to the extremities which Cornwall declares he will inflict on this man. "The revenges we are bound to take upon your traitorous father are not fit for your beholding." (III, vii, 6-7) Cornwall tears out one of Gloucester's eyes and stamps on it, then, after killing the brave servant, attacks Gloucester's remaining eye.

CORNWALL

Lest it see more, prevent it. Out, vile jelly!
(He pulls out Gloucester's other eye)
Where is thy lustre now?

GLOUCESTER

All dark and comfortless. Where's my son Edmond?
Edmond, enkindle all the sparks of nature
To quite this horrid act.

REGAN

Out, treacherous villain!

Thou call'st on him that hates thee. It was he
That made the overture of thy treasons to us,
Who is too good to pity thee.

GLOUCESTER

O, my follies! Then Edgar was abused.
Kind gods, forgive me that, and prosper him!

REGAN (to Servants)

Go thrust him out at gates, and let him smell
His way to Dover.
(III, vii, 81-92)

In this nightmare scenario there are no sprouts of kindness anywhere to take root and give benefit of shelter. No form of pity can survive this desert of hate and malice. Regan and Cornwall, being morally
sightless, put out the eyes of poor deluded Gloucester, who could not see
the resentment burning in the eyes of his illegitimate son. And yet, even
in this hell of darkness, Gloucester now sees for the first time the harm
he has done, and begs the gods for forgiveness, which is, after all, the
Compassion which the victim may bestow on the aggressor. The gods in
this tragedy are resolutely silent. Like Hubert in *King John*, Gloucester in
Lear finds again his moral vision. Later, in scene five, Edgar in disguise
as a peasant, leads Gloucester to what he supposes is the cliff at Dover
where the blind man plans to commit suicide. Edgar allows his father to
leap on level ground, believing erroneously that he is throwing himself
off the steep cliff to his death. Blind father and son driven into fits of
madness enter a space of ironic amity, as Gloucester picks himself up
after his attempted suicide. "Henceforth," says the blind and exhausted
father to the son he has yet to recognize, "I'll bear affliction till it do cry
out itself 'Enough, enough,' and die." (IV, v, 75-77) As Edgar privately
forgives his beloved father, Gloucester finds a way to live—and forgive
himself.

2. *King Henry VI*

Unlike young Arthur in *King John*, young Rutland in *King Henry
VI* Part Three (Act I, sc. iii) fails to obtain clemency from an enraged

Clifford on the field of battle. Why? Because in the previous segment of the trilogy, Clifford's father is killed by the Duke of York. His lifeless body is then discovered by Young Clifford.

YOUNG CLIFFORD

Shame and confusion, all is on the rout!
Fear frames disorder, and disorder wounds
Where it should guard. O, war, thou son off hell,
Whom angry heavens do make their minister,
Throw in the frozen bosoms of our part
Hot coals of vengeance! Let no soldier fly!
He that is truly dedicate to war
Hath no self-love; nor he that loves himself
Hath not essentially, but by circumstance,
The name of valour.
        (He sees his father's body)
O, let the vile world end,
And the premisèd flames of the last day
Knit earth and heaven together.
Now let the general trumpet blow his blast,
Particularities and petty sounds
To cease! Wast thou ordainèd, dear father,
To lose thy youth in peace, and to achieve
The silver livery of advisèd age,
And in thy reverence and thy chair-days, thus
To die in ruffian battle? Even at this sight
My heart is turned to stone, and while 'tis mine
It shall be stony. York not our old men spares;
No more will I their babes. Tears virginal
Shall be to me even as the dew to fire,
And beauty that the tyrant oft reclaims
Shall to my flaming wrath be oil and flax.
Henceforth I will not have to do with pity.
Meet I an infant of the house of York,
Into as many gobbets will I cut it
As wild Medea young Absyrtus did.
In cruelty will I seek out my fame.
    (He takes his father's body up on his back)
As did Aeneas old Anchises bear,

So bear I thee upon my manly shoulders.
But then Aeneas bare a living load,
Nothing so heavy as these woes of mine
(Part Two, V, iii, 31-65)

Young Clifford is perhaps the most aggressive of the Lancastrian warriors. He must actually be restrained by Queen Margaret when he would take on the wounded York. (*King Henry VI*, Part Three, I, iv, 52-54) Whether Henry's claim to the throne be strong or weak means nothing to Clifford; once the clarion call to war has been sounded, it is for Clifford a fight to the death. (Part Three, I, i, 160-163) He is used to upbraiding the King himself for lack of forwardness:

My gracious liege, this is too much lenity
And harmful pity must be laid aside.
To whom do lions cast their gentle looks?
Not to the beast that would usurp their den.
(II, ii, 9-12)

Indeed, one may grasp Clifford by setting him beside that earlier Shakespearean warrior, Hotspur. Hotspur fights for honor and glory, Clifford for vengeance and victory. Hotspur is married, and enjoys tender moments with his wife. Clifford seems without a tender bone in his body. We may suppose, then, that even if York had not slain his father, and even if Clifford had not sworn a solemn oath to give no quarter on the field of battle, confronted by the spectacle of helpless Rutland, Clifford would have killed him. But the Clifford who meets young Rutland is in the grip of a hellish rage, and set on the unchecked slaughter of all who oppose him. Any last possibility of relenting has been wiped away by York's slaying of his father. And that is why, though Arthur's words captivate Hubert, to relentless Clifford the pleadings of young Rutland only send the flames of hate higher and hotter.

CLIFFORD

How now — is he dead already?
Or is it fear that makes him close his eyes?
I'll open them.

RUTLAND (reviving)

So looks the pent-up lion o'er the wretch
That trembles under his devouring paws,
And so he walks, insulting o'er his prey,
And so he comes to rend his limbs asunder.
Ah, gentle Clifford, kill me with thy sword
And not with such a cruel threat'ning look.
Sweet Clifford, hear me speak before I die.
I am too mean a subject for thy wrath.
Be thou revenged on men, and let me live.

CLIFFORD

In vain thou speak'st, poor boy. My father's blood
Hath stopped the passage where thy words should enter.

RUTLAND

Then let my father's blood open it again.
He is a man, and, Clifford, cope with him.

CLIFFORD

Had I brethren here, their lives and thine
Were not revenge sufficient for me.
No — if I digged up thy forefathers' graves,
And hung their rotten coffins up in chains,
It could not slake mine ire nor ease my heart.
The sight of any of the house of York
Is as a fury to torment my soul.
And till I root out their accursèd line,
And leave not one alive, I live in Hell.
Therefore —

RUTLAND

O. let me pray before I take my death.
[Kneeling] To thee I pray; sweet Clifford, pity me.

CLIFFORD

Such pity as my rapier's point affords.

RUTLAND

I never did thee harm — why wilt thou slay me?

CLIFFORD

Thy father hath.

RUTLAND

But 'twas ere I was born.
Thou hast one son — for his sake pity me,
Lest in revenge thereof, sith God is just,
He be as miserably slain as I.
Ah, let me live in prison all my days,
And when I give occasion of offence,
Then let me die, for now thou hast no cause.

CLIFFORD

No cause? Thy father slew my father, therefore die.
    (He stabs him)

RUTLAND

Dii faciant laudis summa sit ista tuae. (He dies)

CLIFFORD

Plantagenet — I come, Plantagenet!
And this thy son's blood cleaving to my blade
Shall rust upon my weapon till thy blood,
Congealed with this, do make me wipe off both.
(Part Three, I, iii, 10-52)

Further difficulties are created here for the victim, young Rutland, which were not present in Hubert's case. Hubert and Arthur had been friends, and Arthur had cared for him during an illness. But Clifford and Rutland stand on either side of an abyss in the War of the Roses, and the only thing their families have in common is hate for one another. The entire history sequence beginning with the *Woodstock* manuscript and *King Richard II* and running through *King Richard III* is designed to show how the injustices of one generation are passed down successively in a spiral of social disintegration that leads logically to chaos and anarchy. Such deterioration makes less possible the development and expression of any charitable impulse, and history spins out of control as Yeats attempted to illustrate in his poem *The Second Coming*. The sort of Compassion we see still at work in *King John* is a far scarcer commodity by the time we reach the end of the War of the Roses and the onset of Tudor England. Though the claim to the throne of Henry Tudor was negligible, England seized on him in the hope that he might put an end to the confusion that was bringing England low.

3. *King Richard III*

Despite being dubbed a "tragedy," and for all its sanguinary mayhem, *King Richard III* is a dark comedy. Its larger-than-life protagonist is so deliciously awful, so willing to make of us his accomplices in crime, that we go along for the laughs, just to thrill in the Joker's shadow. Yet, in the midst of all the horror-flick humor, we can detect, if we are attentive, the ever-beating heart of Compassion. It is always present. On reflection we discover that despite the brutality and bombast, Shakespeare manages to instill in us, almost in spite of ourselves, the lesson of what we are to one another and what we might be.

Can a man dedicate himself to wholesale evil and feel no guilt, no remorse? Only if he has no conception of what guilt and evil are, certainly not a fair description of premeditated Gloucester. He may keep the wretchedness of his deeds five fathoms deep, but they linger within, as morally radioactive as Chernobyl. Brilliant self-deception is an essential part of Richard's shtick. It is demonstrated on a cruder level by the goons he sends to the Tower to murder his brother Clarence. Amusingly enough, one of them turns out to be a hit man with a heart. By putting Richard's subtle bad faith in the mouths of less devious and sophisticated knaves, Shakespeare illuminates with uncanny insight Richard's own impossible duplicity.

SECOND MURDERER

What, shall I stab him as he sleeps?

FIRST MURDERER

No, he'll say 'twas done cowardly, when he wakes.

SECOND MURDERER

Why, he shall never wake until the great judgment day.

FIRST MURDERER

Why, then he'll say we stabbed him sleeping.

SECOND MURDERER

The urging of that word 'judgment' hath bred a kind of remorse in me.

FIRST MURDERER

What, art thou afraid?

SECOND MURDERER

Not to kill him, having a warrant, but to be damned for killing him, from the which no warrant can defend me.

FIRST MURDERER

I thought thou hadst been resolute.

SECOND MURDERER

So I am — to let him live.

FIRST MURDERER

I'll back to the Duke of Gloucester [Richard] and tell him so.

SECOND MURDERER

Nay, I pray thee. Stay a little. I hope this passionate humour of mine will change. It was wont to hold me but while one tells twenty.
[He counts to twenty]

FIRST MURDERER

How dost thou feel thyself now?

SECOND MURDERER

Some certain dregs of conscience are yet within me.

FIRST MURDERER

Remember our reward, when the deed's done.

SECOND MURDERER

'Swounds, he dies. I had forgot the reward.

FIRST MURDERER

Where's thy conscience now?

SECOND MURDERER

O, in the Duke of Gloucester's purse.

FIRST MURDERER

When he opens his purse to give us our reward, thy conscience flies out.

SECOND MURDERER

'Tis no matter. Let it go. There's few or none will entertain it.

FIRST MURDERER

What if it come to thee again?

SECOND MURDERER

I'll not meddle with it. It makes a man
a coward. A man cannot steal but it accuseth him. A
man cannot swear but it checks him. A man cannot
lie with his neighbor's wife but it detects him. 'Tis a
blushing, shamefaced spirit, that mutinies in a man's
bosom. It fills a man with obstacles. It made me once
restore a purse of gold that by chance I found. It
beggars any man that keeps it. It is turned out of towns
and cities for a dangerous thing, and every man that
means to live well endeavors to trust to himself and
live without it.

FIRST MURDERER

'Swounds, 'tis even now at my elbow,
persuading me not to kill the duke.

SECOND MURDERER

Take the devil in thy mind, and believe
him not: he would insinuate with thee but to make
thee sigh.

FIRST MURDERER

I am strong framed; he cannot prevail with me.

SECOND MURDERER

Spoke like a tall man that respects thy

reputation. Come, shall we fall to work?
(I, iv, 95-150)

After Clarence is killed by these desperadoes, the Second Murderer's qualms return, and he openly repents what he has done, rejecting the fee to be paid by Richard. (I, iv, 271-273) Even amongst hard-bitten felons, then, the natural feelings for our fellow human beings arise, as Shakespeare shows us here. But their sense of deep wrong is externalized by them as an independent and inexpedient force requiring courage to overcome, an irony depicted with magnificent realism and pathos. These bungling assassins have no conception of Compassion, and seem not particularly acquainted with related ideas such as mercy or pity. They do understand that human beings are afflicted with a psychic appendage called "conscience," which is forever interfering in the natural and convenient course of life. For a man to allow such an ethical animus to get the better of him and so deprive him of the fruits of living is proof of folly and failure. Shakespeare's point is more subtle than this, however, as these grooms are symbols of Richard's own dissembling mind. Like them, Richard thinks of virtue as a tap he can turn off and on at will.

It is in *King Henry VI*, Part Three that we are introduced to the mature Richard of Gloucester and his manner of thinking. Descanting on his own deformity he draws a strange inference: he will be a bad person.

And am I then a man to be beloved?
O, monstrous fault, to harbour such a thought!
Then, since this earth affords no joy to me
But to command, to check, to o'erbear such
As are of better person than myself,
I'll make my heaven to dream upon the crown,
And whiles I live, t'account this world but hell,
Until my misshaped trunk that bears this head
Be round impalèd with a glorious crown.
(*King Henry VI*, Part Three, III, ii, 165-171)

Why, I can smile, and murder whiles I smile,
And cry 'Content!' to that which grieves my heart,
And wet my cheeks with artificial tears,
And frame my face to all occasions.
I'll drown more sailors than the mermaid shall;
I'll slay more gazers than the basilisk;

I'll play the orator as well as Nestor,
Deceive more slyly than Ulysses could,
And, like a Sinon, take another Troy.
I can add colours to the chameleon,
Change shapes with Proteus for advantages,
And set the murderous Machiavel to school.
Can I do this, and cannot get a crown?
Tut, were it farther off, I'll pluck it down.
(III, ii, 182-195)

In other words, he will so manipulate his own feelings, so deceive himself, that he will become absurd, a caricature of a human being, one who can smother his actual feelings to be a monster of malice, an imp of ill intention. But this is impossible. The ghosts which visit him on the eve of Bosworth Field, observes Marjorie Garber, are Richard's "embodied guilt." (Garber, 156) They presage the breakdown of the man who thought he could play not upon others, but upon himself, like a pipe, to achieve his desires. In the end the giddy laughter evaporates. And his last thought, so revealingly, is of the Compassion he had banished from his heart. "Conscience," the very bugbear that so vexed Richard's hirelings, returns at last, but now so toxic that it singes the apprehensive mind.

What do I fear? Myself? There's none else by.
Richard loves Richard; that is, I am I.
Is there a murderer here? No. Yes, I am.
Then fly! What, from myself? Great reason. Why?
Lest I revenge. Myself upon myself?
Alack, I love myself. Wherefore? For any good
That I myself have done unto myself?
O, no, alas, I rather hate myself
For hateful deeds committed by myself.
I am a villain. Yet I lie: I am not.
Fool, of thyself speak well. — Fool, do not flatter.
My conscience hath a thousand several tongues,
And every tongue brings in a several tale,
And every tale condemns me for a villain.
Perjury, perjury in the high'st degree!
Murder, stern murder, in the dir'st degree!
All several sins, all used in each degree,

Throng to the bar, crying all, 'Guilty, guilty!'
I shall despair. There is no creature loves me,
And if I die no soul will pity me.
Nay, wherefore should they? — Since that I myself
Find in myself no pity to myself.
(*King Richard III*, V, v, 134-157)

V. Compassion in *The Tempest*

At the beginning of *The Tempest* we witness a shipwreck, just as though we clung to the deck of the foundering barque, overhearing the cries and prayers of passengers and crew. The scene then shifts to shore, where Miranda pleads with her magician father Prospero to spare these poor voyagers.

MIRANDA

If by your art, my dearest father, you have
Put the wild waters in this roar, allay them.
The sky, it seems, would pour down stinking pitch,
But that the sea, mounting to th' welkin's cheek,
Dashes the fire out. O, I have suffered
With those that I saw suffer! A brave vessel,
Who had, no doubt, some noble creature in her,
Dashed all to pieces! O, the cry did knock
Against my very heart! Poor souls, they perished.
Had I been any god of power, I would
Have sunk the sea within the earth, or ere
It should the good ship so have swallowed and
The fraughting souls within her.
(I, ii, 1-13)

Prospero answers.

PROSPERO

Wipe thou thine eyes; have comfort.
The direful spectacle of the wreck, which touched
The very virtue of compassion in thee,
I have with such provision in mine art

248

So safely ordered that there is no soul —
No, not so much perdition as an hair
Betid to any creature in the vessel,
Which thou heards't cry, which thou saw'st sink.
(I, ii, 25-32)

Shakespeare is deliberate in his craft. He illustrates vividly the principle, defines it, and gives us its name, a term appearing fourteen times in his oeuvre. It is the very fulcrum of his thinking and his teaching. To take on the suffering of others as one's own is goodness itself, running like a golden thread through Shakespeare's poetry.

His choice of trope is also deliberate, for he thereby means to distinguish his teaching from the philosophies of Stoicism and Epicureanism, both of which condemn sympathy and compassion.

Compare Lucretius, in his famous classic, *De Rerum Natura*.

Suave magni maro turbantibus aequora ventis
e terra magnum alteris spectare laborum;
non quia vexari quemquast jucunda voluptas,
sed quibus ipse malis careas quia cemere suave est.
(Book II, line 1)

Rendered in English by Mr. William Ellery Leonard, this is:

'Tis sweet, when, down the mighty main,
The winds from the land
Roll up its waste of waters,
To watch another's labouring anguish far,
Not that we joyously delight that man
Should be thus smitten, but because 'tis sweet
To mark what evils we ourselves be spared.
(*De Rerum Natura*, Project Gutenberg, Book II)

Here is the identical metaphor, but employed by Shakespeare to an opposed purpose and effect. When Lucretius stands on the cliff and descries the storm-tossed ship splitting on the reefs, the victims crying for their lives, he takes delight that he is spared, experiencing the calm of *ataraxia*. To cultivate pity or sympathy in the soul, as does Miranda, would be irrational and contrary to plain sense, as it would cause us suffering to no good effect. The position of Stoicism was much the same, captured in the word "Stoa," which referred to those porches on which the philosophers gathered in Athens to converse and gaze at the cavalcade of untutored misery in the streets, a misery which could not touch their refined spirits. Christianity, with its more humane concept of the universality of suffering, taken on by God himself, prevailed historically, and reached Shakespeare in the form of the Geneva Bible. (Stritmatter, 101)

Although Prospero shows Miranda what emotion she experiences, he himself at the outset of the play is not wholly given over to compassion, as he still smarts from the ill done him by his brother and collaborators, who robbed him of his Dukedom and abandoned him and his infant girl to the hazards of the deep. Yet he is keenly aware of the ideal—and in the end he achieves it, forgiving those who had caused him so much hurt. Prospero is fortunate that he has so pure and genial a spirit from whom he can gain wisdom.

ARIEL

Your charm so strongly works 'em
That if you now beheld them your affections
Would become tender.

PROSPERO

Dost thou think so, spirit?

ARIEL

Mine would, sir, were I human.

PROSPERO

And mine shall.
Hast thou, which art but air, a touch, a feeling
Of their afflictions, and shall not myself,
One of their kind, that relish all as sharply
Passion as they, be kindlier moved than thou art?
Though with their wrongs I am struck to th' quick,
Yet with my nobler reason 'gainst my fury
Do I take part. The rarer action is

In virtue than in vengeance. They being penitent,
The sole drift of my purpose doth extend
Not a frown further. Go release them, Ariel.
My charms I'll break, their senses I'll restore,
And they shall be themselves.
(V, i, 17-32)

The difference between Shakespeare and the ancients, then, is not merely emotional. It has to do with reason itself. The context of reason for Epicurus and Epictetus is self and self alone. How can we carve out for ourselves a life of peace and contentment? Placing aesthetic distance between us and the unruly passions of the world, we come to know the serenity of the gods, models of what we wish to be. That seems the very pith of reason. And yet, do not those others suffer as I do? Am I more important than my neighbor? What species of rationality would answer in the affirmative? Man outside of society is either a beast or a god, said Aristotle, knowing we are certainly not gods. Shakespeare clearly saw that Epicureanism/Stoicism fails not through inefficacious methodology, but for being unable to resolve the tension arising when others are recognized only in terms of their insignificance. *Julius Caesar* represents, among other things, Shakespeare's critique of Roman philosophy, an intellectual creed not well suited for persons thrust into a world of inner and outer embroilments. Those we would spurn turn out to be parts of ourselves, as Caesar's ghost turns out to be the worser aspect of Brutus. (IV, ii, 333) *Dasein ist Mitsein*, says Heidegger. After their quarrel on the eve of battle, Cassius and Brutus make amends—or try to. Their wobbling friendship reflects the utterly ambiguous status of friendship itself in Stoicism, a sterner and more austere philosophy of consolation than its predecessor, Epicureanism. Consider Brutus. As Stoic he is *solus ipse*. Yet he professes the "general good." In fact, he is a feather blown by the breezes of his own ambition. The Stoic thinkers rejected friendship as a virtue, and much of his unhappiness can be traced to his games of one-upmanship with colleagues Cassius, Casca, Caesar, Antony, et al. Exhausted from squabbling with Cassius, Brutus hides his face in his hands:

BRUTUS

O, Cassius, I am sick of many griefs.

To which his partner responds:

CASSIUS

Of your philosophy you make no use,
If you give place to accidental evils.
(IV, ii, 196-198)

Of course, it was never possible for Brutus to have been a thoroughgoing Stoic, enmeshed as he was in skullduggery and infighting. As a human being with barely grasped feelings, he could not insulate himself with "reason." Shakespeare shows us in this play the dark side of Stoicism: callous indifference to the plights of others. After all, Rome was the city that entertained itself by watching people slaughtered in novel ways in the Coliseum. No wonder it was supplanted by Christianity, with its emphasis on *caritas*. Epicureanism and Stoicism were indeed "noble vices."

At the conclusion of *The Tempest*, god-like Prospero is still learning humility. Though he does forgive those who trespassed against him, there is still a burr in his soul. Something eats away at him, as Brutus was kept awake at night by his intrigues. As we are applauding and gathering our things to leave the theatre, we look up and see the weary magus himself step from behind the curtain as the Epilogue. What could he want? Everyone falls silent to listen.

PROSPERO

Now my charms are all o'erthrown,
And what strength I have's mine own,
Which is most faint. Now 'tis true
I must be here confined by you
Or sent to Naples. Let me not,
Since I have my dukedom got,
And pardoned the deceiver, dwell
In this bare island by your spell;
But release me from my bands
With the help of your good hands.
Gentle breath of yours my sails
Must fill, or else my project fails,
Which was to please. Now I want

Spirits to enforce, art to enchant;
And my ending is despair
Unless I be relieved by prayer,
Which pierces so, that it assaults
Mercy itself, and frees all faults.
As you from crimes would pardoned be,
Let your indulgence set me free.
(Epilogue, 1-20)

Though he has forgiven, Prospero still wants forgiveness for himself. He has terrorized the sea travelers. Though he has manumitted them, Prospero originally enslaved Ariel and Caliban, aspects of himself, perhaps, and was an overbearing and manipulative father, afraid to allow Miranda to chart her own course in life. His great powers are buried, not bequeathed to her. What passed between him and Sycorax we shall never know. The genius of the play is that it offers us, the audience, the opportunity to enter the action, to practice the compassion to which we were introduced at the beginning. Do we not see something of ourselves in this still befuddled egotist, stripped of his gear before us? Letting him hear the sound of our Compassion is the least we can do.

Finally, it may be observed that what Prospero calls "compassion" in the response of Miranda to the shipwreck would probably be better denominated "pity." As the victims are beyond succor or communication and their particular harms and feelings unknown, she cannot embrace them in any meaningful way. Further, she has a sense of guilt which arises from (1) the contrast between her safety and their harrowing condition, and (2) her suspicion that the ship was capsized on account of her own father's actions. Her identification with the suffering she saw is therefore incomplete and strained, and her exclamations overly demonstrative. There is just a touch of condescension and theatricality in her expression more typical of pity than pure compassion. Yet the scene is a most eloquent one which leaves an indelible mark on the audience, and serves as an implicit critique of Roman indifference.

VI. *Titus Andronicus*

That very Roman indifference and its consequences is explored at length in *Titus Andronicus*. When victorious Titus returns to Rome with soldier sons and barbarian captives in tow he is given the hero's welcome to which he has become accustomed. After opening the family crypt to receive more of his soldier sons slain in his service, Titus listens to Lucius' request that he be permitted to make a sacrifice to the gods of one of the defeated Goths, Alarbus.

LUCIUS

Give us the proudest prisoner of the Goths,
That we may hew his limbs and on a pile
Ad manes fratrum sacrifice his flesh
Before this earthly prison of their bones,
That so the shadows be not unappeased,
Nor we disturbed with prodigies on earth.
(I, i, 96-101)

To Titus' approval of this cruelty, Tamora, Queen of the Goths, protests.

TAMORA (kneeling)

Stay, Roman brethren! Gracious conquerer,
Victorious Titus, rue the tears I shed —
A mother's tears in passion for her son —
And if thy sons were ever dear to thee,
O, think my son to be as dear to me!
Sufficeth not that we are brought to Rome
To beautify thy triumphs, and return
Captive to thee and to thy Roman yoke;
But must my sons be slaughtered in the streets
For valiant doings in their country's cause?
O, if to fight for king and commonweal
Were piety in thine, it is in these.
Andronicus, stain not thy tomb with blood.
Wilt thou draw near the nature of the gods?
Draw near them then in being merciful
Sweet mercy is nobility's true badge.
Thrice-noble Titus, spare my first-born son.
(I, i, 104-120)

Request denied.

LUCIUS

See, lord and father, how we have performed
Our Roman rites. Alarbus' limbs are lopped
And entrails feed the sacrificing fire,
Whose smoke like incense doth perfume the sky.
Remaineth naught but to inter our brethren
And with loud 'larums welcome them to Rome.
(I, i, 142-147)

During the course of this long and violent play so many calamities fall on Titus' head it is easy to see him as a figure of suffering Job, forgetting that his willingness to make a spectacle of Alarbus' dismemberment is the very summoning of Nemesis. To adopt a better biblical metaphor, Titus is the Samson who pulls the roof down on himself as well as his enemies. Think of Odysseus, who after he has put out the eye of the Cyclops, in response to that Titan's cry to know the perpetrator of this deed, shouts from the safety of his ship that it was he who did it. This boast leads swiftly to the revenge of Neptune and a host of troubles. Odysseus had his victory; he didn't need to sing advertisements for himself at just that moment. In the case of Titus Andronicus, his cruelty to Alarbus is his act of hubris. He already had his northern triumph. Why should more blood be shed, more agony endured? As King Richard III observes above, our viciousness is ultimately viciousness against ourselves. Outrage begets outrage. Soon enough Tamora has become the wife of Roman Emperor Saturninus, and is plotting with her surviving sons for revenge on Titus. Prompted by Goth ally Aaron the moor, Chiron and Demetrius lay a trap for Bassianus and his betrothed, Lavinia, only daughter of Titus. After Bassanius is stabbed to death by them, his body thrown into an ugly forest pit, they turn their attention to Lavinia, for rape and an unspeakable dismemberment which echoes the brutish hacking of Alabus' limbs. Now it is the Andronicus clan's turn to bid for Compassion.

LAVINIA

O, Tamora, thou bearest a woman's face —

TAMORA

I will not hear her speak. Away with her!

LAVINIA

Sweet lords, entreat her hear me but a word.

DEMETRIUS   (To Tamora)

Listen, fair madam, let it be your glory
To see her tears, but be your heart to them
As unrelenting flint to drops of rain.

LAVINIA

When did the tiger's young ones teach the dam?
O, do not learn her wrath! She taught it thee.
The milk thou sucked'st from her did turn to marble,
Even at thy teat thou hadst thy tyranny.
Yet every mother breeds not sons alike.
(To Chiron) Do thou entreat her show a woman's pity.

CHIRON

What, wouldst thou have me prove myself a bastard?

LAVINIA

'Tis true. the raven doth not hatch a lark.
Yet I have heard — O, could I find it now —
The lion, moved to pity, did endure
To have his princely paws pared all away.
Some say that ravens foster forlorn children
The whilst their own birds famish in their nests.
O, be to me, though thy hard heart say no,
Nothing so kind, but something pitiful.

TAMORA

I know not what she means. Away with her!

LAVINIA

O, let me teach thee for my father's sake,
That gave thee life when well he might have slain
Thee.
Be not obdurate, open thy deaf ears.

TAMORA

Hadst thou in person ne'er offended me
Even for his sake am I pitiless.
Remember, boys, I poured forth tears in vain
To save your brother from the sacrifice,
But fierce Andronicus would not relent.
Therefore away with her, and use her as you will —
The worse to her, the better loved of me.
(II, iii, 136-167)

Lavinia forgets not only her father's savagery in allowing Tamora's son to be hideously sacrificed, but also the words of derision and contempt she directed to Tamora when, a few minutes earlier, she and Bassianus discovered Tamora's tryst with Aaron the Moor. How could she be so obtuse? She knew quite well on entering the forest that Tamora was now a queen of power in Rome and still fuming over her eldest son's public slaughter in the streets. What could have possessed her as she hurled insults at Tamora? (II, iii, 66-71; 80-84; 86-87) Her thoughtlessness mimicked that of her father, Titus. Seeing her in her ravished and amputated condition, Titus goes entirely berserk, yet still projects responsibility for all his family's suffering on Tamora and sons, Saturninus, and Aaron. Of course these people are themselves a clan of sadistic felons, but the wrong Titus imposes on them is a red flag in front of the wrong bull. And, by the way, might we dare to ask what the armies of Rome were doing in the land of the Goths in the first place? Was not Rome an ever-expanding behemoth entrenching on the lands of simpler peoples? Had they no right to defend themselves in their own home?
    The madness of Titus is provoked in part by the presence within

him of loving impulses which are suppressed by his outward aggression. He has spent a lifetime as a killing machine, but has not yet quite killed the spirit of Compassion in himself. How does such a one love and receive love? That is his dilemma. And so one day it all tumbles out in the open. The Andronicus family is at their table having dinner when his brother Marcus strikes at a fly with his knife.

TITUS

What dost thou strike at, Marcus, with thy knife?

MARCUS

At that I have killed, my lord — a fly.

TITUS

Out on thee, murderer! Thou kill'st my heart.
Mine eyes are cloyed with view of tyranny.
A deed of death done on the innocent
Becomes not Titus' brother. Get thee gone.
I see thou art not for my company.

MARCUS

Alas, my lord, I have but killed a fly.

TITUS

'But'? How if that fly had a father, brother?
How would he hang his slender gilded wings
And buss lamenting dirges in the air!
Poor harmless fly,
That with his pretty buzzing melody
Came here to make us merry — and thou hast killed him!

MARCUS

Pardon me, sir, it was a black ill-favoured fly,
Like to the Empress' Moor. Therefore I killed him.

TITUS

O, O, O!
Then pardon me for reprehending thee,
For thou hast done a charitable deed.
Give me thy knife. I will insult on him,
Flattering myself as if it were the Moor
Come hither purposely to poison me.
            (He takes a knife and strikes)
There's for thyself, and that's for Tamora. Ah, sirrah!
Yet I think we are not brought so low
But that between us we can kill a fly
That comes in likeness of a coal-black Moor.
(III, ii, 52-77)

Out of hearing, Marcus laments:

MARCUS

Alas, poor man! Grief has so wrought on him
He takes false shadows for true substances.
(III, ii, 78-79)

What is learned in this remarkable passage? Compassion for Shakespeare lies close to the *ens realissimum*. It is not something on which we turn our backs without consequences. Titus, a career homicide and now victim of a vendetta managed by Aaron, has gone so far as to slay one of his own sons, Mutius, who had the audacity to oppose him. (I, i, 285-290) The negative energy exuded by Rome and channeled by Titus circulates throughout the city and returns to Titus as Nemesis. This is figured in the mangled body of Lavinia which awakens Titus' sleeping sympathy and draws from him streams of tears. That sympathy aroused and active within him is unfamiliar and uncontrolled, and as such is part of the nervous breakdown he is suffering. He is sick of the sea of bloody violence and, alas, more awaits him. In this distraught condition he reacts to the killing of a fly by Marcus. Regarded by his brother as a symptom of lunacy, Titus' response to the fly's death may be understood as the awakening of Compassion within him, akin, for example, to the lamentations of Jaques in *As You Like It* for the deer hunted in the Forest of Arden. The life of Titus functions as the *reductio ad ab-*

surdum of universal carnage and destruction. That is why Titus laughs earlier when he is confronted with his severed hand and the heads of his two sons brought by messenger from Aaron and Saturninus. And yet he is still resisting Compassion, as a sworn enemy.

MARCUS

Why dost thou laugh? It fits not with this hour.

TITUS

Why, I have not another tear to shed.
Besides, this sorrow is an enemy,
And would usurp upon my wat'ry eyes
And make them blind with tributary tears.
Then which way shall I find Revenge's cave?
(III, i, 264-269)

When Marcus suggests he killed the fly because it was an image of the dark-hued Aaron, the unsteady mind of Titus swings in the other direction and he stabs at the dead insect and curses it. Compassion is within him, but in a bleeding form, seeping through his soul like a lymph or rheum, a rising flood which cannot be usefully applied. By chance it alights on a fly. But it does so in a man who will shortly slit the throats of Demetrius and Chiron and grind their bones, using their bodily substances as ingredients in a pie to be consumed by their unknowing mother. Following that act of insanity, the hero of this tragedy will snuff out the life of his own poor daughter as havoc ensues and death embraces all. Through the mayhem we can still discern Shakespeare's philosophy of Compassion, owed by us to all sentient creatures. As we turn against this, we turn against ourselves, the very pith of tragedy. Madness is the last refuge in our hopeless attempt to hide from what we have made of ourselves.

VII. A Theological Medley

The universality and ideality of Compassion naturally raises a theological question in Shakespeare: it is a form of what is called today the "problem of evil," a toy of professional philosophers. For Shakespeare it was a burning coal in the human heart. If the gods are the citadel of all that is holy and good, how is it that they permit us to suffer? When this is taken up it is always as a cry of anguish, not as an abstract puzzle. A few examples will illustrate.

1. *Titus Andronicus*

Recall that as she pleads with Titus to show mercy to her first-born son, Alarbus, Tamora cites the model of the gods, who embody goodness and restraint.

TAMORA

Andronicus, stain not thy tomb with blood.
Wilt thou draw near the nature of the gods?
Draw near them then in being merciful.
Sweet mercy is nobility's true badge.
(I, i, 116-119)

The source and validity of this idea may be questioned. Was the Roman pantheon a wellspring of Compassion? The mythic content implies otherwise. Is the Thunderbolt merciful? Are there not passion, jealousy and vengeance on Mt. Olympus? Were the Goths known for their gentility? Setting aside this caveat, and accepting for the sake of discussion that it has always been plausible to identify the gods with goodness (as mere etymology will always imply), the problem is obvious. Why is suffering permitted? Do the gods draw near themselves, learn their own lesson? It would seem not. Death is the most reliable form of mercy we can expect from those quarters, and delivery is often delayed.

Shakespeare is an artist, not a discursive philosopher. The issue comes to the fore not in dispassionate argument, but in the cry of helplessness at moments of loss and nearly unbearable sorrow, the sort of harrowing experiences counselors like Cynthia Wall must confront in the course of their business. (See, Introduction, *supra*) Thus, later in the play, we hear the question of divinity sounded again, as Titus meets his pillaged daughter, arms hacked off and tongue cut out to silence her.

MARCUS

O, why should nature build so foul a den,
Unless the gods delight in tragedies?

(IV, i, 58-59)

Here the awful logic is traced to its apparent conclusion. If the gods might shield us but decline, is that mere indifference ... or sadistic entertainment? Do the gods have their own amphitheatre and recline as did the Romans in their Coliseum, thrilling at sanguinary spectacles to keep away ennui? Then the gods are monsters, not the noble benefactors we had so delusively imagined. We live in hell. That intellectual option has always been open. On the other hand, a common Tribune like Marcus is hardly going to explore the question in detail. His utterance is a mere ejaculation, a verbal extremity, a Job-like lamentation, not the preface to a discourse. It might be observed in that context that it is difficult to imagine the function of Compassion in the abstract. How would the gods exercise their bountiful mercy in the absence of suffering creatures upon whom to bestow it? In other words, though the possibility can be raised (and always will be raised) that divinity is wickedness itself, the delight in the agonies of sentient creatures, the conclusion is not compelling. If we follow Stoicism and siphon off the anthropomorphic dimension of the divine, and then swerve by substituting undiluted Compassion for apatheia, we arrive at a position that may have been occupied by Shakespeare, one close to the animating spirit of Buddhism.

Also not to be ignored is Shakespeare's jab at his own profession. What are we who "delight in tragedies"? Is the poet's art humanity's opportunity to "purge" (that is, burn away) pity and fear, or indulge in lurid fantasies of inner and outward torments?

What resolution does Marcus find in his dilemma?

MARCUS

O heavens, can you hear a good man groan
And not relent, or not compassion him?
Marcus, attend him in his ecstasy,
That hath more scars of sorrow in his heart,
Than foemen's marks upon his battered shield,
But yet so just that he will not revenge.
Revenge the heavens for old Andronicus!
(IV, i, 122-128)

We cannot "trouble deaf heaven with [our] bootless cries." (Sonnet 29, l. 3) Our voices will not be heeded or even heard. The part of Compassion, neglected by the immortals, must be taken up by ourselves, and this good Tribune and brother resolve to do. Unfortunately, the Compassion of Marcus extends only to Titus, not to his enemies, and so falls short of that precept that enjoins us to love our enemies and pray for those who persecute us. After all, these are the folks that gave the world the gift of crucifixion. So Marcus will "compassion" his brother while the Andronicii pursue their enemies with no less a fury than theirs. The only difference between the homicides of Titus and Aaron is that Aaron boasts openly of his wickedness, while Titus decorously camouflages his with the Roman flag. One man forthrightly professes evil, while his opposite number adds hypocrisy to his repertoire by speaking of ideals while slitting throats and taking the lives of his own children. In that regard, compare the murder of Mutius by his father Titus with the tender solicitude of Aaron for his newborn son. Aaron yearns for outrages, but, unlike Titus, he has the decency to spare his own. Shall we call this Aaron's tragic flaw?

2. *Pericles, Prince of Tyre*

Picture a storm-tossed ship at sea. As the ship lurches from watery peaks to valleys of doom, the wife of a weary king is giving birth. In the end of her agony, she perishes, but the infant is preserved, and given on the howling deck to her father, whose plight reminds us of Lear on the heath.

PERICLES

The god of this great vast rebuke these surges
Which wash both heav'n and hell; and thou that hast
Upon the winds command, bind them in brass,
Having called them from the deep. O still
Thy deaf'ning dreadful thunders, gently quench
Thy nimble sulph'rous flashes. — O, ho, Lychordia!
How does my queen? — Thou stormest venemously.
Wilt thou spit all thyself? The seaman's whistle
Is as a whisper in the ears of death,
Unheard. — Lychordia! — Lucina, O!
Divinest patroness, and midwife gentle
To those that cry by night, convey thy deity
Aboard our dancing boat, make swift the pangs

Of my queen's travails! — Now, Lychordia.

(Enter Lychordia with an infant)

LYCHORDIA

Here is a thing too young for such a place,
Who, if it had conceit, would die, as I
Am like to do. Take in your arms this piece
Of your dead queen.

PERICLES

How, how, Lychordia?

LYCHORDIA

Patience, good sir, do not assist the storm.
Here's all that is left living of your queen,
A little daughter. For sake of it
Be manly, and take comfort.

PERICLES

O you gods!
Why do you make us love your goodly gifts,
And snatch them straight away? We here below
Recall not what we give, and therein may
Vie honour with you.
(Scene 11, 1-26, following not Taylor & Wells, but the Strat-
ford Town Edition, 1904)

This kind of protest is always a possibility for distraught mortals.
The Los Angeles Times, September 29, 2009 reported the murder of a
young Hispanic boy. The boy's mother was quoted as having cried out:
"Why did God bring him to me if he was going to take him away so
quickly?" Had Marlene Ramirez read *Pericles*?

Here the paradox of evil is resolved in a slightly different way. The
gods are not portrayed as torturers wielding whips and thumbscrews,
but as insincere donors who give us just enough time with our bless-

ings to cherish them and then rudely take them back. Like an angry Odysseus, Pericles raises his fist to the sky and rebukes the gods, reminding them the gifts we mortals confer on one another are genuine, not yanked back after the recipients have come to love them. Pericles spits in the faces of the Olympians and dares them to do their worst. What saves him and his newborn daughter from annihilation? It is beyond question the invocation of Diana, referred to here as "Lucina," the patroness of childbirth. It is her beneficent spirit that presides over the entire play and leads critics to term it a "romance" rather than comedy. Not happenstance but providence rules these actors. It is Diana who brings the still-respiring Queen Thaisa in her richly appointed casket to the studio of magus Cerimon, who will blow upon the glowing embers of life and restore Pericles' queen. Her first words on awakening are: "O dear Diana, Where am I? Where's my lord? What world is this?" (Scene 12, l. 3-4) Believing her husband and daughter drowned, Thaisa announces her intention to take "a vestal liv'ry" and "never more have joy," whereupon Cerimon recommends she seek refuge in Diana's Temple at Ephesus. Much later, after Pericles is re-united with his grown daughter Marina, the Goddess Diana appears to him to inform him that his long-lost wife survives, a votary in her Order. What we witness in this tale is the evolution of the Goddess herself, whose origins are as austere and forbidding as any of the gods, as we can see by considering the myth of Artemis and Actaeon. But by the time Shakespeare begins to focus on her as the principal deity of his own pantheon, Diana has grown to become the very embodiment of Compassion, the western equivalent of Chinese Kuan Yin, she who hears the cries of the world.

3. *Macbeth*

To make "the very firstlings of [his] heart" the firstlings of [his] hand," Macbeth sends murderers to slaughter Macduff's wife and children, acting quickly before he is reproached by pangs of doubt. "No boasting like a fool, This deed I'll do before the purpose cool." (IV, i, 69-70) When this awful deed becomes known, it is the sad duty of the Thane of Ross to acquaint Macduff with what has happened.

ROSS

Your castle is surprised, your wife and babes
Savagely slaughtered. To relate the manner

Were on the quarry of these murdered deer
To add the death of you.

MALCOLM

Merciful heaven!
(To Macduff)
What, man, ne'er pull your hat upon your brows.
Give sorrow words. The grief that does not speak
Whispers the o'erfraught heart and bids it break.

MACDUFF

My children too?

ROSS

Wife, children, servants, all
That could be found.

MACDUFF

And I must be from thence!
My wife killed too?

ROSS

I have said.

MALCOLM

Be comforted.
Let's make medicines of our great revenge
To cure this deadly grief.

MACDUFF

He has no children. All my pretty ones?
Did you say all? O hell-kite! All?
What, all my pretty chickens and their dam

At one fell swoop?

MALCOLM

Dispute it like a man.

MACDUFF

I shall do so,
But I must also feel it as a man.
I cannot but remember such things were
That were most precious to me. Did heaven look on
And would not take their part?
(IV, iii, 205-226)

Such is the language of shock and heart rending grief. Could the gods have presided over such an unspeakable loss? It is interesting to note that though many take such incidents to disprove the existence of God, it is precisely to religion that people repair in times of insupportable sorrows. Thus Malcolm exclaims "Merciful heaven!" meaning, "Merciful heaven protect us from such harms!" We want to blame the gods and wind up calling on their mercy instead. What does this imply, except the dumb but stubborn faith we have as human beings that in some way we cannot quite articulate we are loved and cared for not just by each other but by That which brought us to this place of woes? As we are flesh and blood, there is a limit to our tolerance and ability to absorb, and so we lash out in vengeful reprisals. But, contradictory creatures that we are, we sense at the same time that we are not alone, and that the Compassion we share with others is Something larger than ourselves. Notice the supporting roles played in this scene by Macduff's friends Ross and Malcom. Whether a sage might not grant Malcolm's words of consolation and encouragement the highest marks, who could read them and not feel the tenderness and sharing of pain?

4. *King Henry V*

King Harry is the great pragmatist in Shakespeare, full of high sentence and a bit of a knave. He will play dice with the Deity and try to rig the game. Speech is a sharp tool he uses to attain his objectives, and if necessary he will clip the coin of truth for an advantage in bargaining.

One of his favorite guises is paragon of mercy. As we are struggling to maintain our love for him we must swallow down his banishment of his friend and mentor, Falstaff. It turns out that he was just using Sir John and the Boar's head group to make a bigger impression on his accession to the throne. He tells us this in a notorious soliloquy. (Part One, I, ii, 192-214) Henceforward we tend to take his words with a grain of salt. Had Harry been merciful, Falstaff would never have been publicly humiliated and rudely banished. What about the faction of traitors who plot against him and are apprehended at Southampton on the eve of the invasion of France? Harry tricks them into denying themselves mercy by pretending to suspend the sentence on a soldier who got drunk and railed against the King. Cambridge, Masham and Northumberland, the faction, protest that this soldier (a fiction devised by Harry as bait) should be severely punished for his insolence. When their treason is revealed, all three instinctively beg for mercy, which is denied on the grounds that this was waived by pleading for a heavier punishment for the aforementioned soldier. Harry is then in a position to execute them summarily, as a warning to others. Of course, his clemency toward the drunken soldier was nothing more than a charade. What Harry really wanted was the heads of Cambridge, Masham and Northumberland set up on pikes. Further, Harry represents that these traitors acted against his regime and planned to assassinate him merely because of bribes from the French. Yet we learn later that Harry has only a doubtful claim to the throne, and was keeping Edmund Mortimer, the true heir, locked up in a dismal prison, no mercy there. Mortimer had done no wrong to spend all his adult years in a stone-cold cell. (*King Henry VI*, Part One, II, v, 1-129) It was not French bribes that led these lords to rebel against Harry, but rather the illegitimacy of his title, inherited from his usurping father, Bolingbroke. This is all admitted by Harry on his knees in prayer on the eve of Agincourt. When Harry speaks of "mercy" it is either to dissimulate or to threaten, as he does before the gates of Harfleur.

> How yet resolves the Governor of the town?
> This is the latest parle we will admit.
> Therefore to our best mercy give yourselves,
> Or like to men proud of destruction
> Defy us to our worst. For as I am a soldier,
> A name that in my thoughts becomes me best,
> If I begin the batt'ry once again
> I will not leave the half-achievèd Harfleur

Til in her ashes she lie burièd.
The gates of mercy shall be all shut up,
And the fleshed soldier, rough and hard of heart,
In liberty of bloody hand shall range
With conscience wide as hell, mowing like grass
Your fresh fair virgins and your flow'ring infants.
(*King Henry V*, III, iii, 84-97)

What kind of person confines his use of "mercy" to threats? An even more graphic illustration of Harry's curious version of clemency can be found in Act III, sc. vi, when it is explained to him that Bardolph, the aide-de-camp of Falstaff, now dead of a broken heart following his banishment by Harry, is awaiting hanging for pilfering from a French church. Without so much as a blink of the eye, the merciful King Harry, a/k/a Hal-of-the-Boarshead Tavern, approves the execution of his erstwhile chum and drinking buddy. His words are a small miracle of deceit.

We would have all such offenders so cut off, and we
here give express charge that in our marches through
the country there be nothing compelled from the
villages, nothing taken but paid for, none of the French
upbraided or abused in disdainful language. For when
lenity and cruelty play for a kingdom, the gentler gamester
is the soonest winner.
(III, vi, 108-114)

Harry's idea of lenity is to hang his own friend from a tree for pilferage rather than return the stolen items or compensate the church for the loss. Ironically, in the conversation between Gower and Fluellen in Act IV, sc. vi, in extenuation of Harry's harshness, and in distinguishing Harry from Alexander the Great who killed his best friend Cleitus, Gower protests: "Our King is not like him in that. He never killed any of his friends." (IV, vii, 38-39) Well, that's a strange thing to say, since we have just confirmed Harry's killing of his friend Bardolph. And what about his betrayal of Falstaff? Is that forgotten by the troops? Not quite

FLUELLEN

As Alexander killed his friend Cleitus, being in his ales and his cups, so also Harry Monmouth, being in his right wits and his good judgments, turned away the fat knight with the great belly-doublet — he was full of jests and gipes and knaveries and mocks — I have forgot his name.

GOWER

Sir John Falstaff.

FLUELLEN

That is he. I'll tell you, there is good men porn at Monmouth. (IV, vii, 43-50)

Fluellen's sarcasm is almost palpable. First the good King Harry casts out his mentor, protector and friend, Falstaff, causing him to die of a broken heart. This is followed up by hanging their mutual friend Bardolph, as faithful a companion as ever drew breath, for the snatching of a few unconsidered trifles.

Scholars have also noted that at the conclusion of Act IV, sc. vi, the "merciful" King Harry orders the slaughter of all the French prisoners, a heinous act and contravention of the rules of war to which Fluellen refers extensively in Act III, sc. iii. (See also, IV, i, 66-75) These scenes are regularly scanted by jingoistic directors in Hollywood bent on using *King Henry V* for hero worship and the rationalization of international aggression. A close reading of the text will show that Harry orders the destruction of the French prisoners of war not because the French attack the English boys and carriers but rather because they have the temerity to continue to defend their homeland, and send in reinforcements. What a guy! (See, IV, vi, 35-37)

On the eve of Agincourt we are graced with "a little touch of Harry in the night." (IV, 0, 47) The King lurks about the camp in disguise to spy on his own men. What he hears is disturbing. There is full realization amongst the ranks that they are being used as cannon fodder to promote a dubious enterprise. (IV, i, 133-45) Maintaining his disguise, Harry indulges in gross sophisms to put a smiley face on grim visaged war. (IV, i, 146-184) The result is an unseemly quarrel between the Monarch/General and one of his miserable footmen. (IV, i, 190-216) Though he later pardons this aggrieved soldier after the battle, that pardon comes only after the soldier points out that he was entrapped by the King who incited him to reveal his fears and resentment and then bickered with him.

WILLIAMS

All offences, my lord, come from the heart.
Never came any from mine that might offend your
majesty.

KING HARRY

It was ourself thou didst abuse.

WILLIAMS

Your majesty came not like yourself. You
appeared to me but as a common man. Witness the
night, your garments, your lowliness. And what your
highness suffered under that shape, I beseech you take
it for your own fault, and not mine, for had you been
as I took you for, I made no offence. Therefore I beseech
your highness pardon me.
(VI, viii, 47-57)

The pardon we see granted is the only act of clemency we see of
King Harry. It is granted to a poor common soldier tricked by the King-
in-disguise into revealing his real fears of death before a battle in which
most of the English fully expected to perish. This is not a feather in Harry's cap but a nail in his moral coffin.

In a stroke of genius, Shakespeare gives a better peek at the noc-
turnal Harry by letting us overhear his soliloquy and prayer before the
dawn of armed combat. It turns out that Harry lives in disgraceful envy
of the common men who serve him and feels sorry for himself for having a monarch's responsibilities. (IV, i, 227-281)

The prayer is revealing and worth looking at.

O God of battles, steel my soldiers' hearts.
Possess them not with fear. Take from them now
The sense of reck'ning, ere th' opposed numbers
Pluck their hearts from them. Not today, O Lord,
O, not today, think not upon the fault
My father made in compassing the crown.
I Richard's body have interrèd new new,

And on it have bestowed more contrite tears
Than from it issued forcèd drops of blood.
Five hundred poor have I in yearly pay
Who twice a day their withered hands hold up
Toward heaven to pardon blood. And I have built
Two chantries, where the sad and solemn priests
Still sing for Richard's soul. More will I do,
Though all that I can do is nothing worth,
Since that my penitence comes after all,
Imploring pardon.
(IV, i, 286-301, but following Stratford Town edition)

Here the truth — or most of it — emerges. Harry is guilty. And yet, even before the King of Heaven, Harry plays the dissembler. Shakespeare could hardly paint a more shameful picture of the human soul. Hours before one of the bloodiest sieges in history, the leader of the English forces confesses he has no actual right to the English throne, which by law belongs to the imprisoned Edmund Mortimer. But if Harry is not rightful King, how does he behead Scroop, Masham and Northumberland? What is he doing making war abroad but following his crafty father's counsel to "busy giddy mind with foreign quarrels"? (*King Henry IV*, Part Two, IV, iii, 342-343) If no King of England, none of France. (II, ii, 189-190) The man who hangs his friend Bardolph for pilfering a paten in a church is willing to spend the lives of thousands to rob a whole nation. At the end he entreats God Almighty to show him Compassion and forgiveness, after cataloguing most of the reasons he is undeserving. But still he wants to fight, and asks the Maker of Heaven and Earth to be his accomplice by sending his hapless soldiers into battle with "hearts of controversy." (*Julius Caesar*, I, ii, 111) In the character King Harry of England, Shakespeare gives us a handsome rogue whose self-knowledge is limited to the burnished reflection of himself he sees in his armor. Whatever his swashbuckling bravado, he is a sweet-faced villain who can only talk about charity, not do it. What Compassion preserved his person and career we shall never know.

5. *Measure for Measure*: A Psychiatric Case History

Patient's name: Isabella
Gender: Female

Age:	23
Parents:	Deceased
Siblings:	One brother
Education:	BA , Rhetoric Major, Minor in Theology
Vocation:	Postulant, Order of St. Clare, Vienna, Austria

THERAPIST

Isabella, are you aware we're recording today's session?

ISABELLA

Yes.

THERAPIST

And you understand we're doing this to train counselors?

ISABELLA

Yes.

THERAPIST

And we have your permission to do this, correct?

ISABELLA

Yes.

THERAPIST

Now, I understand you've returned here to the Convent, is that right?

ISABELLA

Yes. Well, not exactly. You see, the prioress granted me a short leave to take care of some urgent family business and I did that, but now I'm not really sure I want to remain with the Sisters. I may just pack my things and confer with the prioress.

THERAPIST

Hmmm. Sounds complicated. I imagine something happened during your stay in town.

ISABELLA

Uh, yeah, you could say that.

THERAPIST

You weren't injured?

ISABELLA

No, but a lot happened. I met a man I like. But not right away, I mean, I met him but I didn't know who he was, and, uh, you see, my brother was in jail, and they were trying to execute him for having sex with my cousin, and she was pregnant and so I tried to talk to the Magistrate to get him released.

THERAPIST

Sounds like you had a big adventure.

ISABELLA

Yeah, it was crazy there for a while.

THERAPIST

And I take it that your brother's OK now?

ISABELLA

Yes. But even at the last hearing I thought he was dead.

THERAPIST

And what about the man you met? Who is he?

ISABELLA

It's the Duke. He asked me to marry him.

THERAPIST

Duke Vincentio?

ISABELLA

Yes.

THERAPIST

Did he know you were a postulant?

ISABELLA

Well, at first he was a friar, and then I was trying to help my brother and the Magistrate, he tried to . . .

THERAPIST

Tried to what?

ISABELLA

It's rather hard to say.

THERAPIST

Go ahead.

ISABELLA

Well, OK, see, he said he wouldn't commute the sentence, my brother had to die, and I tried to get him to be merciful. And he wouldn't do it.

THERAPIST

So what happened?

ISABELLA

Uh, so he did a really bad thing. He said if I would sleep with him, he'd let Claudio go free.

THERAPIST

Really? And did you do it?

ISABELLA

No, of course not.

THERAPIST

Where was the Duke all this time?

ISABELLA

Oh, he was around, I would talk to him, but I thought he was Friar Lodowick.

THERAPIST

Isabella, let's talk for a moment about what happened with the Magistrate, OK?

ISABELLA

OK

THERAPIST

What's his name?

ISABELLA

His name is Lord Angelo.

THERAPIST

Had you ever met him before?

ISABELLA

No.

THERAPIST

So why do you think he made an indecent proposal to you? Did you behave seductively in any way?

ISABELLA

How can you ask such a question? I was pleading for Claudio's life! I'm just a novice in this Order. How could I be seductive?

THERAPIST

I don't know. I am just trying to understand what happened. Do you remember?

ISABELLA

Well, I was trying to tell him he should be merciful and he kept saying that he'd show more mercy to others by punishing the offender than letting him go. (II, ii, 102-103)

THERAPIST

OK, then what happened?

ISABELLA

Well, he kept, like, insinuating things, I don't know. He talked in riddles and asked me what I would do if my brother was going to die and the only way to save him was to "lay down the treasures of my body," what would I do?

THERAPIST

What did you say? Do you recall?

ISABELLA

Yes, I do, exactly. I'll never forget.

THERAPIST

Tell me.

ISABELLA

I said:

As much for my poor brother as myself.
That is, were I under the terms of death,
Th' impression of keen whips I'd wear as rubies,
And strip myself to death as to a bed
That longing have been sick for, ere I'd yield
My body up to shame.
(II, iv, 99-104)

THERAPIST

What happened then?

ISABELLA

He asked me to take off my clothes (II, iv, 138) and asked me to give him love.

THERAPIST

And you refused?

ISABELLA

Naturally.

THERAPIST

Then what?

ISABELLA

He got very angry and said Claudio was going to be executed, and that if I told anyone about what he proposed, it would be my word against his and no one would believe me. (III, iv, 154-170)

THERAPIST

And do you have any idea why he behaved as he did?

ISABELLA

Honestly, no.

THERAPIST

None at all?

ISABELLA

No. No, I don't. Do you know why?

THERAPIST

Do you think of yourself as attractive, Isabella?

ISABELLA

Well, uh, yeah, I mean, reasonably. I'm not ugly if that's what you mean, but . . .

THERAPIST

How did you feel when I asked you if you were attractive?

ISABELLA

I got annoyed. I thought you were implying I came on to the Magistrate.

THERAPIST

But just setting that aside, would you agree you aren't ugly?

ISABELLA (laughing)

Well, if you put it that way. . .

THERAPIST

Yes?

ISABELLA

OK, you win. I know I'm not bad looking.

THERAPIST

Right. And you were discussing a sex act with the judge, correct?

ISABELLA

What are you implying?

THERAPIST

Claudio and Juliet had sex, correct?

ISABELLA

Right.

THERAPIST

And you were there to tell him that that wasn't something so bad, correct?

ISABELLA

Yes.

THERAPIST

And then he asked you to have sex with him, I take it?

ISABELLA

Right.

THERAPIST

So what do you think?

ISABELLA

I don't know.

THERAPIST

What about those words you used?

ISABELLA

What words?

THERAPIST

"Impression of keen whips"

"Wear as rubies"
"Strip myself"
"bed"

ISABELLA

Were those bad words?

THERAPIST

May be something there to think about . . .

ISABELLA

OK.

THERAPIST

Tell me about your mother and father.

ISABELLA

OK, my mom died when I was nine.

THERAPIST

And you had a younger brother.

ISABELLA

Yeah.

THERAPIST

And after your mom died, did your father remarry?

ISABELLA

No, he didn't.

THERAPIST

So, who took care of the household after your mom passed away?

ISABELLA

I did.

THERAPIST

You took care of your Dad?

ISABELLA

Yes.

THERAPIST

You cooked?

ISABELLA

Yes, and did the laundry and I also had my studies to keep up with.

THERAPIST

Right. You were still in school.

ISABELLA

Right.

THERAPIST

And then your Dad died too.

ISABELLA

Yeah, after three years.

THERAPIST

I see. And during those three years were you pretty close to him?

ISABELLA

What do you mean by that? What are you suggesting?

THERAPIST

Isabella, you know I'm trying to find out what happened to you.

ISABELLA

Yes.

THERAPIST

So what happened with you and your Dad?

ISABELLA

Nothing. Everything was normal. He loved me. I respected him. That's all.

THERAPIST

Is that what you told the intake nurse?

ISABELLA

I think so.

THERAPIST

You didn't mention one night your Dad came into your room?

ISABELLA

Oh. Yeah, one time he came in to check on me.

THERAPIST

What happened?

ISABELLA

I asked him to leave.

THERAPIST

And after that?

ISABELLA

I don't remember.

THERAPIST

Do you remember coming to see the prioress? You wanted to move out of your house?

ISABELLA

Yes.

THERAPIST

And what happened?

ISABELLA

Dad died.

THERAPIST

And then you were living alone with your brother, weren't you?

ISABELLA

Yes.

THERAPIST

And he was starting to see your friend, Juliet, right?

ISABELLA

Yes, that's when I decided to try living in the Convent.

THERAPIST

Yes, seven months ago. Now we're almost out of time, I want to ask you one more thing.

ISABELLA

OK.

THERAPIST

I understand that at the last hearing the Duke asked you to marry him.

ISABELLA

Yes, that's right.

THERAPIST

And you wouldn't say yes or no.

ISABELLA

Correct.

THERAPIST

And the Duke sentenced Angelo to death.

ISABELLA

He did.

THERAPIST

And what did you do?

ISABELLA

I begged the Duke for mercy.

THERAPIST

Mercy on the man who tried to coerce you into sex, right?

ISABELLA

Yes.

THERAPIST

Do you recall the words you said on that occasion?

ISABELLA

Yes, shall I repeat them?

THERAPIST

Please.

ISABELLA

Most bounteous sir,
Look, if it please you, on this man condemned
As if my brother lived. I partly think
A due sincerity governed his deeds,
Til he did look on me. Since it is so,
Let him not die. My brother had but justice,
In that he did the thing for which he died.
For Angelo,
His act did not o'ertake his bad intent
That perished by the way. Thoughts are no subjects,

Intents but merely thoughts.

THERAPIST

So you pleaded for mercy on behalf of the man who would not show mercy to your brother unless you gave him sex. Is that right?

ISABELLA

Yes, I guess so.

THERAPIST

So, what will you do now, Isabella? Remain in the convent or return to Vienna and be the Duke's wife?

ISABELLA

I don't know.

THERAPIST

That's right, you don't. But our hour is up, isn't it?

ISABELLA

Yes.

THERAPIST

See you next time.

ISABELLA

Thanks. Good-bye.

6. *Hamlet*: The Petition of Claudius

We close with a recollection of Compassion in *Hamlet, Prince of Denmark*. Illumination may be gained by glancing at Claudius' prayerful soliloquy in Act III. This presents again the question of absolution for misdeeds, and how that is to be achieved by those who have committed substantial offenses, crimes so significant that they imply irremediable faults of character. This is surely the case with Claudius. As he rounds out the speech, Hamlet approaches from behind, and for a moment each of them is in a state of suspended animation.

O, my offense is rank! It smells to heaven.
It hath the primal eldest curse upon't,
A brother's murder. Pray can I not.
Though inclination be as sharp as will,
My stronger guilt defeats my strong intent,
And like a man to double business bound
I stand in pause where I shall first begin,
And both neglect. What if this cursèd hand
Were thicker than itself with brother's blood,
Is there not rain enough in the sweet heavens
To wash it white as snow? Whereto serves mercy
But to confront the visage of offence?
And what's in prayer but this twofold force,
To be forestallèd ere we come to fall,
Or pardoned being down? Then I'll look up.
My fault is past — but O, what form of prayer
Can serve my turn? 'Forgive me my foul murder'?
That cannot be, since I am still possessed
Of those effects for which I did the murder —
My crown, mine own ambition, and my queen.
May one be pardoned and retain th'offence?
In the corrupted currents of this world
Offence's gilded hand may shove by justice,
And oft 'tis seen the wicked prize itself
Buys out the law. But 'tis not so above.
There is no shuffling, there the action lies
In his true nature, and we ourselves compelled
Even to the teeth and forehead of our faults
To give in evidence. What then? What rests?

Try what repentance can. What can it not?
Yet what can it when one cannot repent?
O wretched state, O bosom black as death,
O limèd soul that, struggling to be free,
Art more engaged! Help, angels! Make assay.
Bow, stubborn knees; and heart with strings of steel,
Be soft as sinews of the new-born babe.
All may be well.
(III, iii, 36-72)

Well, all here is ill, not well. Claudius has a heart so "brassed" that it is "proof and bulwark against sense;" it will not soften and yield. (III, vi, 36-37) What he seeks from angels is the mercy he cannot grant himself. And though it be true that he stands still possessed of the things for which he did the crime, that is not the full extent of his plight. Nowhere in this speech does he actually say he's sorry for what he's done, nor does he decide to reform. He will apologize to none, not even to God, though he begs forgiveness on his knees. He is indeed "a man to double business bound," and poorly served by deep duplicity. Will he go to Gertrude and ask her to pardon him for the mess he's made of everything? No. His wife stands but in the suburbs of his affection, and at his core is naught but cold and darkness. He has not learned that forgiveness is not a gift that falls from heaven like a roof tile on our heads, but a reflection of our own genuine resolve. Because he has no Compassion for others he has none for himself, and is his own worst enemy.

But to take the full measure of Claudius' corruption, we need to go a back a few lines, to the opening of this scene, when Claudius strides onstage with Rosenkrantz and Guildenstern. Hamlet is being sent to England where by letters and commission it has been arranged that Hamlet will be killed. (IV, iii, 66-70) These instructions are found by Hamlet, and re-written to entail the deaths of these two toadying courtiers. (V, ii, 1-63) What is significant is that in Act III, sc. iii, Claudius has already signed Hamlet's death warrant. The planned assassination is no mere postscript. Claudius refers directly to their "commission." (III, iii, 3) Having then decided to have his nephew (who is most likely his own bastard son) exterminated in England, he proceeds to fall on his knees in prayer, petitioning God for mercy and complaining that he cannot do so with unction and authenticity. "My words fly up, my thoughts remain below. Words without thoughts never to heaven go." (III, iii, 97-98)

If Claudius were truly desirous of reconciliation, he would summon Rosenkrantz and Guildenstern and cancel the order to have Hamlet slain in England. Instead, with this murder pending, he pounds like a peddler on heaven's gate.

Meanwhile, something is happening to our beloved Prince. In his adventures at sea, in the outwitting of the King's emissaries, in crossing swords with pirates, some switch is thrown in Hamlet's brain. For the first time since childhood he manages to get his head screwed on straight. Whether he be the child of Hamlet the Dane or Claudius is irrelevant to his own worth as a person. In this mood of renewal he encounters the skull of Yorick, the kind and witty jester who gave the boy Hamlet unconditional love. For one instant the whole dusty course of life rests in Hamlet's hands. Then follows the discovery of Ophelia's death. Thus is Hamlet's action now charted: he will do what needs to be done.

> We defy augury. There is a special
> providence in the fall of a sparrow. If it be now, 'tis
> not to come. If it be not to come, it will be now. If it
> be not now, yet it will come. The readiness is all. Since
> no man has aught of what he leaves, what is it to leave
> betimes?
> (V, ii, 165-170)

Some attentive readers will notice that in saying "We defy augury," Hamlet employs the royal "we." By contrast, in *Twelfth Night* Sir Toby Belch exclaims, "Lechery? I defy lechery." (I, v, 121) In his readiness to encounter his fate, Hamlet has mastered himself. He is promoted, now the captain of his soul.

VIII. Conclusion

The conclusion is that there is no conclusion of Compassion. Like the bounteous love of which Juliet boasts, Compassion is as "boundless as the sea." (II, i, 175) And on that sea are we now afloat, propelled by our own capacities for fellow feeling. When his characters suffer pain or trauma, Shakespeare shows us how their hearts contract, grow smaller, diminishing humanity. The flood of Compassion seems to narrow, and in its stead we find emotions like sympathy and pity, or penance and forgiveness. As the soul shrinks in fear, it lacks not only a full compassion to bestow on others, but just as much a kindly regard for the self in all its tenderness and fragility. In cases of dim wittedness Compassion is regarded as an external agency we confront as "conscience." (*King Richard III*)

As life draws to a close we find to our dismay the tensions which have crept into all our relations. Too late we try to restore amity, make amends. But late is better than never. In *King Richard III*, Act II, sc. i, the dying King Edward IV suddenly is struck by all the grim infighting in his court, and takes desperate steps to bring the squabbling to an end. Rivers, Hastings, the Queen, and Buckingham, even Richard himself, all set aside their quarrels and profess their love for one another. (II, i, 1-73) That is, like ourselves, they suffer correction. But each vessel can hold only according to its volume. The pledges of love, peace and cooperation are uttered not *sua sponte* but at the behest of a dying monarch, to please him. And when Richard announces the death of Clarence, all these vows are blown out the window. There is always the risk in reading Shakespeare that we will recognize in this character or that something of ourselves and our own half-realized foibles. But that risk is offset by Shakespeare's clear presentation of Compassion in its purity. In his imperishable dramas we learn that when realism is allowed to complete its mission it becomes the most edifying idealism.

WORKS CITED:

Marjorie Garber, *Shakespeare After All*, Anchor Books, 2004.

James Howe, *A Buddhist's Shakespeare: Affirming Self-Deconstructions*, Associated University Press, 1994.

"About Dharma," International Kadampa Buddhist Festival

Soka Gakkhai International (Online).

The Los Angeles Times, September 29, 2009.

William Shakespeare: The Complete Works, Second ed., S. Wells, G. Taylor, eds., Clarendon Press, Oxford, 2005.

Roger Stritmatter, *The Marginalia of Edward de Vere's Geneva Bible: Providential Discovery, Literary Reasoning, and Historical Consequence*, Oxenford Press, 2003.

Cynthia Wall, "Compassion and Sympathy" (Online).

11
Royal Envy

I. Introduction: Situating Royal Envy

*S*uccessive soliloquies of Kings Henry the Fourth, Fifth and Sixth reflecting desperate envy of peasantry and proletarians are challenging for readers of Shakespeare. What do these discourses signify, and what are we to make of an apparent transmission of heterodox desire across three generations? While there may be no satisfactory answers, recent scholarship at least offers a context in which these déclassé iterations can be situated. In *King-Commoner Encounters in the Popular Ballad, Elizabethan Drama, and Shakespeare*, Rochelle Smith draws attention to the traditions of the English pastoral on the one hand and the King-Commoner Ballad on the other. Though the passages of regental envy cited below are not expressly addressed, her treatment of ballad and pastoral conventions allows us to trace a movement from fanciful rustication to a more sober-minded realism climaxing in late scenes of the *King Henry VI* trilogy. Following King Henry's encounter with the gamekeepers in Act 3, sc. 2, the glorification of the lesser ranks which had preoccupied three royal Lancastrian characters ends. As the red rose bleeds to ghastly white, such romantic conceits vanish from England, never to return.

II. Speeches of Royal Envy

1. Introit: The Anxiety of King Richard II

As Richard Plantagenet huddles in his bare cold cell awaiting fate, his mind turns to ordinary mortals not plagued by sovereign miseries. Their very lowliness has spared them.

> Thoughts tending to content flatter themselves
> That they are not the first of fortune's slaves,
> Nor shall not be the last — like seely beggars,
> Who, sitting in the stocks, refuge their shame
> That many have, and others must, set there;
> And in this thought they find a kind of ease,
> Bearing their own misfortunes on the back
> Of such as have before endured the like.
> Thus play I in one person many people,
> And none contented. Sometimes am I king;
> Then treason makes me wish myself a beggar,
> And so I am.
> (V, v, 23-34)

This early evocation of pedestrian security arises in the context of Bolingbroke's confiscation of the throne. Given the hazards facing a king, is not a peasant's bovine condition to be preferred? Of course, the pendulum also swings the other way.

> Then crushing penury
> Persuades me I was better when a king.
> Then am I kinged again, and by and by
> Think that I am unkinged by Bolingbroke,
> And straight am nothing.
> (V, v, 34-38)

Then comes a prophecy.

> But whate'er I be,
> Nor I, nor any man that but man is,
> With nothing shall be pleased till he be eased
> With being nothing.
> (V, v, 38-41)

The mention of Bolingbroke at this poignant juncture seems to imply that if Richard, the deposed King, is put in the awkward position of glancing wistfully at the peasant's hut, so one day may the usurping

Henry. As we will see, that is what comes to pass in the next installment, when it becomes Bolingbroke's turn to feel reduced to nonentity.

2. *King Henry IV*

Haunted by memories of the rebellion which catapulted him to supremacy, and hedged about by truculent lords who would pull him down, Henry IV has fallen ill. Beside his sick bed, he muses on the loneliness of life at the pinnacle of puissance.

> How many thousand of my poorest subjects
> Are at this hour asleep? O sleep, O gentle sleep,
> Nature's soft nurse, how have I frighted thee,
> That thou no more wilt weigh my eyelids down
> And steep my senses in forgetfulness?
> Why, rather, sleep, liest thou in smoky cribs,
> Upon uneasy pallets stretching thee,
> And hushed with buzzing night-flies to thy slumber,
> Than in the perfumed chambers of the great,
> Under the canopies of costly state,
> And lulled with sound of sweetest melody?
> O thou dull god, why li'st thou with the vile,
> In loathsome beds, and leav'st the kingly couch
> A watch-case, or a common 'larum bell?
> Wilt thou upon the high and giddy mast
> Seal up the ship-boy's eyes, and rock his brains
> In cradle of the rude imperious surge,
> And in the visitation of the winds,
> Who take the ruffian billows by the top,
> Curling their monstrous heads, and hanging them
> With deafing clamour in the slippery clouds,
> That, with the hurly, death itself awakes?
> Canst thou, O partial sleep, give thy repose
> To the wet sea-boy in an hour so rude,
> And in the calmest and most stillest night,
> With all appliances and means to boot,
> Deny it to a king? Then happy low, lie down.
> Uneasy lies the head that wears a crown.
> (*King Henry IV*, Part Two, III, i, 1-31)

He seems not to think here of Richard, whom he cast down as others now seek his destruction, and yet, how can he not? For even in the midst of overturning him, Bolingbroke remained Richard's subject, and never asserted any colorable claim to divest him *de jure* of the diadem. Rather, coerced abdication was his *modus operandi*. Richard's eloquence throughout his deposition in *King Richard II* is that of a poet King whose muse is catastrophe. Henry's muse is mere actuality. He lets harsh facts speak for him. But all the while that stolid circumstances were serving as Bolingbroke's heralds, his pleading attorneys, he was in thrall to Richard's soaring rhetoric, in which it seemed that nobility itself was on the rack. Having assimilated Richard's verbal pyrotechnics (as in, *e.g.*, the well-known "mirror scene," in which he inspects the image of his face in shattered glass) it is as though Richard's articulation of loss has infiltrated Henry's very soul and festered there, gnawing at him like a succubus, filling him with guilt if not remorse. Then, faced with his own political demise, Henry can conveniently re-enact Richard; his ventilations are echoes of poor Richard's painful descants on dissolution.

Later, as the death of his father, Henry IV, approaches, Prince Harry slips into the bedchamber and, believing his father to be deceased, notices the crown and addresses it with these words.

Why doth the crown lie there upon his pillow,
Being so troublesome a bedfellow?
O polished perturbation, golden care,
That keeps't the ports of slumber open wide
To many a watchful night! — Sleep with it now;
Yet not so sound, and half so deeply sweet,
As he whose brow with homely biggen bound
Snores out the watch of night. O majesty,
When thou dost pinch thy bearer, thou dost sit
Like a rich armour worn in heat of day,
That scalds't with safety. — By his gates of breath
There lies a downy feather which stirs not.
Did he suspire, that light and weightless down
Perforce must move. — My gracious lord, my father! —
This sleep is sound indeed. This is a sleep
That from this golden rigol hath divorced
So many English kings. — Thy due from me
Is tears and heavy sorrows of the blood,
Which nature, love, and filial tenderness

Shall, O dear father, pay thee plenteously.
My due from thee is this imperial crown,
Which, as immediate from thy place and blood,
Derives itself to me.
(IV, iii, 152-174)

And so Prince Harry sets himself on the path of becoming his father. The most excellent and model sleeper is not, again, the royal personage swaddled in comforts, but the lowly swain "whose brow with homely biggen bound snores out the watch of night." That is a brow most common.

Yet this identification of father and son has its roots in much earlier scenes. Hal's notorious "I know you all" soliloquy in *King Henry IV*, Part One, is plainly nothing more than a restatement of Bolingbroke's firmly held philosophy and apparently oft given counsel to his eldest son. Both discuss the desired relationship of monarch and his people. Pay particular attention to the use of the term "seldom" in both discourses.

PRINCE HARRY

I know you all, and will a while uphold
The unyoked humour of your idleness.
Yet herein will I imitate the sun,
Who doth permit the base contagious clouds
To smother up his beauty from the world,
That when he please again to be himself,
Being wanted he may be more wondered at
By breaking through the foul and ugly mists
Of vapours that did seem to strangle him.
If all the year were playing holidays,
To sport would be as tedious as to work;
But when they seldom come, they wished-for come,
And nothing pleaseth but rare accidents.
So when this loose behavior I throw off,
And pay the debt I never promisèd,
By how much better than my word I am,
By so much shall I falsify men's hopes;
And like bright metal on a sullen ground,
My reformation, glitt'ring o'er my fault,
Shall show more goodly and attract more eyes

Than that which hath no foil to set it off.
I'll so offend to make offence a skill,
Redeeming time when men think least I will.
(I, ii, 192-214)

From whence might such a manipulative policy be had? Like father, like son. And yet the King can hardly see it.

KING HENRY [to Prince Harry]

God pardon thee! Yet let me wonder, Harry,
At thy affections, which do hold a wing
Quite from the flight of all thy ancestors.
Thy place in Council thou hast rudely lost —
Which by thy younger brother is supplied —
And art almost an alien to the hearts
Of all the court and princes of my blood.
The hope and expectation of thy time
Is ruined, and the soul of every man
Prophetically do forethink thy fall.
Had I so lavish of my presence been,
So common-hackneyed in the eyes of men,
So stale and cheap to vulgar company,
Opinion, that did help me to the crown,
Had still kept loyal to possession,
And left me in reputeless banishment,
A fellow of no mark nor likelihood.
By being seldom seen, I could not stir
But, like a comet, I was wondered at,
That men would tell their children, 'This is he.'
Others would say, 'Where, which is Bolingbroke?'
And then I stole all courtesy from heaven,
And dressed myself in such humility
That I did pluck allegiance from men's hearts,
Loud shouts and salutations from their mouths,
Even in the presence of the crownèd King.
Thus did I keep my person fresh and new,
My presence like a robe pontifical —
Ne'er seen but wondered at — and so my state,
Seldom but sumptuous, showed like a feast,

And won by rareness such solemnity.
The skipping King, he ambled up and down
With shallow jesters and rash bavin wits,
Soon kindled and soon burnt, carded his state,
Mingled his royalty with cap'ring fools,
Had his great name profanèd with their scorns,
And gave his countenance, against his name,
To laugh at gibing boys, and stand the push
Of every beardless vain comparative;
Grew a companion to the common streets,
Enfeoffed himself to popularity,
That, being daily swallowed by men's eyes,
They surfeited with honey, and began
To loathe the taste of sweetness, whereof a little
More than a little is by much too much.
So when he had occasion to be seen,
He was but as the cuckoo is in June,
Heard, not regarded, seen but with such eyes
As, sick and blunted with community,
Afford no extraordinary gaze
Such as is bent on sun-like majesty
When it shines seldom in admiring eyes,
But rather drowsed and hung their eyelids down,
Slept in his face, and rendered such aspect
As cloudy men use to their adversaries,
Being with his presence glutted, gorged, and full.
And in that very line, Harry, standest thou;
For thou hast lost thy princely privilege
With vile participation. Not an eye
But is a-weary of thy common sight,
Save mine, which hath desired to see thee more,
Which now doth that I would not have it do —
Make blind itself with foolish tenderness.
(He weeps)
(*King Henry IV*, Part One, III, ii, 29-91)

King Henry incoherently complains about Hal's failure to maintain his place in Council while boasting of his own royal hide-and-seek.
Yet, whether from example, tutelage or instinct, Hal practices the same
guileful tactics his father employed. As an usurper, Bolingbroke had to

pay special attention to the masses. He could not rely on descent of the crown. In his fawning over the commons he is ridiculed by King Richard.

KING RICHARD

> He is our cousin, cousin; but 'tis doubt,
> When time shall call him home from banishment,
> Whether our kinsmen come to see his friends.
> Ourself and Bushy, Bagot here, and Green
> Observed his courtship to the common people,
> How he did seem to dive into their hearts
> With humble and familiar courtesy,
> What reverence he did throw away on slaves,
> Wooing poor craftsmen with the craft of smiles
> And patient underbearing of his fortune,
> As 'twere to banish their affects with him.
> Off goes his bonnet to an oysterwench.
> A brace of draymen bid God speed him well,
> And had the tribute of his supple knee
> With 'Thanks, my countrymen, my loving friends',
> As were our England in reversion his,
> And he our subjects' next degree in hope.
> (*King Richard II*, I, iv, 19-35)

And while it is true that much of Bolingbroke's demonstrative populism can be chalked up to rallying public support, we can also detect in Richard's contemptuous anecdotes the not far-fetched idea that Bolingbroke's affinity for the common herd runs with an embarrassing depth. In his chastising of his own son and heir, then, for his carousing in Eastcheap, he forgets his own unusual affiliations with the commons. It is only at the end, however, that we discover his actual distaste for the rough reins of power, and his envy of those not so burdened. Like his predecessor Richard, King Henry IV is revealed as one unhappy as a subject and equally miserable as a monarch. Thus it is that when in *King Henry IV*, Part Two, Henry receives good news about the discomfiture of the rebels, he reacts with a sudden nausea:

> Will fortune never come with both hands full,
> But write her fair words still in foulest letters?

She either gives a stomach, and no food —
Such are the poor, in health — or else a feast,
And takes away the stomach — such are the rich,
That have abundance and enjoy it not.
I should rejoice now at this happy news,
And now my sight fails, and my brain is giddy.
(IV, iii, 103-110)

What is left such a one but perpetual envy?

3. *King Henry V*

Let us stride once more unto the breach, and listen with new ears to the oft-quoted soliloquy of King Harry on the dark morn of Agincourt.

KING HARRY

'Let us our lives, our souls, our debts, our care-full wives,
Our children, and our sins, lay on the King.'
We must bear all. O hard condition,
Twin-born with greatness: subject to the breath
Of every fool, whose sense no more can feel
But his own wringing. What infinite heartsease
Must kings neglect that private men enjoy?
And what have kings that privates have not too,
Save ceremony, save general ceremony?
And what art thou, thou idol ceremony?
What kind of god art thou, that suffer'st more
Of mortal griefs than do thy worshippers?
What are thy rents? What are thy comings-in?
O, ceremony, show me but thy worth.
What is thy soul of adoration?
Art thou aught else but place, degree, and form,
Creating awe and fear in other men?
Wherein thou art less happy, being feared,
Than they in fearing,
What drink'st thou oft, instead of homage sweet,
But poisoned flattery? O be sick, great greatness,
And bid thy ceremony give thee cure.

Think'st thou the fiery fever will go out
With titles blown from adulation?
Will it give place to flexure and low bending?
Canst thou, when thou command'st the beggar's knee,
Command the health of it? No, thou proud dream
That play'st so subtly with a king's repose;
I am a king that find thee, and I know
'Tis not the balm, the sceptre, and the ball,
The sword, the mace, the crown imperial,
The intertissued robe of gold and pearl,
The farcèd title running fore the king,
The throne he sits on, nor the tide of pomp
That beats upon the high shore of this world —
No, not all these, thrice-gorgeous ceremony,
Not all these, laid in bed majestical,
Can sleep so soundly as the wretched slave
Who with a body filled and vacant mind
Gets him to rest, crammed with distressful bread;
Never sees horrid night, the child of hell,
But like a lackey from the rise to set
Sweats in the eye of Phoebus, and all night
Sleeps in Elysium; next day, after dawn
Doth rise and help Hyperion to his horse,
And follows so the ever-running year
With profitable labour to his grave.
And but for ceremony such a wretch,
Winding up days with toil and nights with sleep,
Had the forehand and vantage of a king.
The slave, a member of the country's peace,
Enjoys it, but in gross brain little wots
What watch the King keeps to maintain the peace,
Whose hours the peasant best advantages.
(IV, i, 228-281)

Is this not remarkable consistency—and bad faith? In the battles
for the throne there are no spoils, save ceremony, a mere empty show. A
Richard of Gloucester may decapitate dozens as he carves out a bloody
path to the crown, but, when he gets it, he finds it an empty prize. It
imposes the most unsettling of duties and cares, yet affords no corresponding rewards. Duke Humphrey's ambitious wife Eleanor urges her

husband to put forth his hand, "reach at the glorious gold" which is the crown of England (*King Henry VI*, Part Two, I, ii, 11), but, as we will confirm again below, it turns out to be only a burden and mirage of happiness. Genuine fulfillment, ironically, is available not to distressed sovereigns but to the huddled masses yearning to breathe the salubrious atmosphere of court. Both sides dwell in interminable envy.

4. *King Henry VI*

We come at last to that most unlikely and tormented English King of all, Henry VI. He is portrayed by Shakespeare as a congenital pacifist and amateur theologian, precisely the opposite of his warlike father and grandfather. Never one to willingly take up arms against a sea of troubles ("frowns, words, and threats shall be the war that Henry means to use," Part Three, I, i, 3-4) Henry VI is outmatched by the aggressive House of York, which presses on the illegitimacy of Lancastrian claims to vigorously and successfully prosecute the Wars of the Roses. Yet despite vast differences in temperament and policy, Shakespeare's Henry VI recapitulates the inverted class envy of his royal predecessors.

Reduced to the status of a mere spectator in his own fractured realm, Henry sits on a molehill and contemplates the civil clash of arms in eerily familiar terms.

> This battle fares like to the morning's war
> When dying clouds contend with growing light,
> What time the shepherd, blowing of his nails,
> Can neither call it perfect day nor night.
> Now sways it this way like a mighty sea
> Forced by the tide to combat with the wind,
> Now sways it that way like the selfsame sea
> Forced to retire by fury of the wind.
> Sometime the flood prevails, and then the wind;
> Now one the better, then another best —
> Both tugging to be victors, breast to breast,
> Yet neither conqueror nor conquerèd.
> So is the equal poise of this fell war.
> Here on this molehill will I sit me down.
> To whom God will, there be the victory.
> For Margaret my queen, and Clifford, too,
> Have chid me from the battle, swearing both

They prosper best of all when I am thence.
Would I were dead, if God's will were so —
For what is in this world but grief and woe?
O God! Methinks it were a happy life
To be no better than a homely swain.
To sit upon a hill, as I do now;
To carve out dials quaintly, point by point,
Thereby to see the minutes how they run:
How many makes the hour full complete,
How many hours brings about the day,
How many days will finish up the year,
How many years a mortal man may live.
When this is known, then to divide the times:
So many hours must I tend my flock,
So many hours must I take my rest,
So many hours must I contemplate,
So many hours must I sport myself,
So many days my ewes have been with young,
So many weeks ere the poor fools will ean,
So many years ere I shall shear the fleece.
So minutes, hours, days, weeks, months, and years,
Passed over to the end they were created,
Would bring white hairs unto a quiet grave.
Ah, what a life were this! How sweet! How lovely!
Gives not the hawthorn bush a sweeter shade
To shepherds looking on their seely sheep
Than doth a rich embroidered canopy
To kings that fear their subjects' treachery?
O yes, it doth — a thousandfold it doth.
And to conclude, the shepherd's homely curds,
His cold thin drink out of his leather bottle,
His wonted sleep under a fresh tree's shade,
All which secure and sweetly he enjoys,
Is far beyond a prince's delicates,
His viands sparkling in a golden cup,
His body couchèd in a curious bed,
When care, mistrust, and treason waits on him.
(II, v, 1-54)

This is the most emphatic and unequivocal paean to simplicity in all the soliloquies we have examined. Henry's profound dejection and undisguised envy are palpable. Like his forebears, Henry VI has shouldered the cares of state with sincerity, but the weakness of his title (I, i, 135), the ruthlessness of his adversaries, and his monkish personality all conspire to bring his reign to a bad end. Though his envy is ironically incongruent with the Tenth Commandment, as Henry might admit, his childlike admiration for the shepherd's way of life, seems over-determined. In the back of his mind are all those biblical tropes involving shepherds and lost sheep, and, in Henry's case, it seems he might have better taken on the role of sheep than shepherd. For after all, what protection had he to offer anyone?

In Act III, sc. 1 Henry, now a refugee, appears disguised as the commoner he has always wanted to be. He thus encounters two conniving gamekeepers who overhear his complaint.

SECOND GAMEKEEPER

Say, what art thou that talk'st of kings and queens?

KING HENRY

More than I seem, and less than I was born to:
A man at least, for less I should not be;
And men may talk of kings, and why not I?

SECOND GAMEKEEPER

Ay, but thou talk'st as if thou wert a king.

KING HENRY

Why, so I am, in mind — and that's enough.

SECOND GAMEKEEPER

But if thou be a king, where is thy crown?

KING HENRY

My crown is in my heart, not on my head;

Not decked with diamonds and Indian stones,
Nor to be seen. My crown is called content —
A crown it is that seldom kings enjoy.
(*King Henry VI*, Part Three, III, i, 55-65)

For a brief moment, garbed as an ordinary man, Henry feels he has sloughed off the cares of state. In that moment he relishes what he supposes is the peace of mind enjoyed by quotidian mortals. Yet the commoners he meets are not bucolic shepherds, but a pair of canny hirelings, who drag poor Henry back into the royal nightmare.

III. Pastoral versus Ballad

The remarkable sequence of soliloquies we have canvassed may be aptly characterized as proto- or quasi-pastoral. Though in none of these plays does the lamenting monarch actually retire to woodland or meadow to frolic with sheepherders, the contrastive discourse that sets the life of the care-worn ruler against the *sans souci* world of flocks and verdant valleys is implicitly pastoral. These are conceits of royal imagination. While King Henry IV tosses and turns in insomniac frustration, he conjures in his jealous mind images of the "smoky cribs" of his meanest subjects, who sleep their blessed nights away untroubled by the strife of nations. The days of a king distill the substance of urban existence into a toxic essence that renders them intolerable. Nature is seen not as ravenous, but as a bucolic sanctuary, nurturing and thereby ultimately liberating. A tempestuous ocean is not a maw of death but a hand that rocks the cradle in which the ship boy snores. The rest that nature denies to the great king she bestows on a meager lad in the crow's nest. Counting sheep in these circumstances is the last thing one would try. Bolingbroke's envy is obvious.

The "peasant" who "sweats all day in the eye of Phoebus" gets to close his eyes at night, observes the rueful King Harry on the eve of Agincourt. The dread responsibilities of a sovereign which must compel him to engage in wars in which thousands of innocent subjects are slaughtered are sources of guilt and angst. It is no wonder the invading English commander stalks his camp the whole night before the battle.

It is when we reach *King Henry VI*, however, that the implicit pastoralism which animated the ruminations of Bolingbroke and Hal finally breaks into the open. Seated on his molehill, right from the very start Henry identifies as a shepherd. (II, iv, 3) Sidelined in a war for which he has no stomach, he sings the praises of the "homely swain" whose life is a well-regulated chronicle of satisfaction. How much better are the ordinary shepherds gazing "on their seely sheep," than is the king living in shadow of wolfish lords. Everything about the retired life is better: not just the joy of sleep, but the 'homely curds," the pure drink from a leather bottle, and peaceful solitude. It is an enchanting vision of vigorous, healthful years designed by nature herself, in which everything has its season in just proportion. "Ah, What a life were this!" he exults. "How sweet! How lovely!" Using the first person singular ("So many hours must I tend my flock") Henry shows he is no mere spectator; he has a rustic heart himself. Thus he finds refuge from the chaos erupting all about him. Disguised as a humble fellow of low estate, he wanders about, prayer book in hand. For perhaps the first time in his earthly career, Henry is happy, happy, that is, until the bubble bursts and he is accosted by two gamekeepers. Overhearing his talk about the war, they perceive a prize. What is a king doing in such a place? Where is his crown? And as if in a beautiful dream, Henry answers:

> My crown is in my heart, not on my head;
> Not decked with diamonds and Indian stones,
> Nor to be seen. My crown is called content —
> A crown it is that seldom kings enjoy.
> (III, i, 62-65)

In the space of a few days, Henry has been pacified, the anguish in his heart bated. This contentment is depicted as expressly pastoral, borrowed from the romantic conceptions of the day. Unfortunately, the characters he meets are not jolly men of hill and dale, but rascals scavenging for opportunity. Henry is taken prisoner, and away contentment flies, like a bird which merely perched an hour on his shoulder. The kindly, sporting natives Henry probably expected to find never materialize.

Rochelle Smith properly identifies a body of king-commoner encounters in English literature as pastoral. In Shakespeare, such interludes may be found *inter alia* in *Henry IV*, *Henry V* and *As You Like It*. Focusing largely on Prince Hal and his interactions with the denizens of the Boars-head Tavern, she points out that he is well received by the associates of Poins and Falstaff, with whom he can drink and revel. Once Hal assumes his father's position, however, these patrician/plebeian exercises end. As Bolingbroke remains in the royal sphere, entering into no similar overt dealings with *hoi polloi*, the king-commoner leitmotif applies not to him.

Opposed to the pastoral theme, Ms. Smith helpfully suggests, are the conventions of the English ballad, which frequently feature king-commoner encounters. But while such gatherings in the green-wood are in the pastoral convention idyllic and charming, the ballad tradition strikes a different chord. Ms. Smith writes:

> The ballad king, who crosses class lines and enters the green-wood in search of pastoral retreat is hoping for fair weather, good hunting and simple loyal subjects. More often he en-counters a harsh reality that teaches not the pastoral virtue of contented innocence but rather the political virtue of humil-ity gained from a broader experience of the world.

In copious examples drawn from extant ballads, Ms. Smith shows that rude indifference—or worse—greets the straying monarch. Instead of fair weather, uncomfortable storms dampen his spirits. The forest cottages are poor, and cruel hunger drives their occupants to poach the sovereign's deer, an enterprise fraught with risk. In the pastoral theme the king is frequently recognized as royal or at least suspected of being some sort of VIP. But in the ballad, the king travels incognito, and is frequently not trusted. Trying to accommodate himself to a strange and harsh environment, the king, though at times guided by his hosts, proves himself an inept learner, and is chastened for his lack of skill. "The king-commoner ballad," notes Ms. Smith, "refuses to idealize ei-ther king or subject, instead presenting in comic form the conviction that those in the highest seats of power have much to learn from a rough encounter with common life." Most importantly, what the king discov-ers amongst the wood-notes wild is not contentment, but envy of aris-tocratic advantages and luxuries. Most of the hard-scrabble peasantry, it turns out, would gladly exchange their subsistence lifestyles for the feasts and pastimes of the court.

And this is what makes these plays so fascinating. For while in the ballad tradition the serfs envy the nobility, in Shakespeare's pastoralism there is a marked tendency for the nobles, including the king, to envy the serfs. In *As You Like It*, though the jester Touchstone upbraids the rustic Corin for never having been educated in the ways of the court, a close reading will show that it is Corin who has the better part. Touch-stone's comic condescension is understood to be largely facetious, while the words of the countryman ring true.

CORIN

Sir, I am a true labourer. I earn that I eat, get that I wear; owe no man hate, envy no man's happiness; glad of other men's good, content with my harm; and the greatest of my pride is to see my ewes graze and my lambs suck.
(III, ii, 69-75)

The truth is that Touchstone does well in the greensward, taking as his bride no courtly maid, but Audrey, a buxom goatherd. She will be his precious memento of a better life when they return to the Duke's court.

IV. Conclusion

Applying the categories of pastoral and ballad as presented by Ms. Smith to the family of kings in the Henry plays, we can at once diagnose all three Lancastrian rulers as suffering from a pastoral syndrome. The sleeplessness which afflicts them is a symptom of urban malaise magnified by the tribulations of leadership. This was an historical reality, and surely resonated with Queen Elizabeth I herself, who wrote:

To be a king and wear a crown is a thing more glorious to them that see it than it is pleasant to that bear it. The cares and troubles of a crown I cannot more fitly resemble than to the drugs of a learned physician, perfumed with some aromatic savor, or to bitter pills gilded over, by which they are made acceptable or less offensive, which indeed are bitter and unpleasant to take. And for my own part, were it not for conscience' sake to discharge the duty that God hath laid upon me, and to maintain His glory, and keep you in safety, in mine own disposition I should be willing to resign the place I hold to any other, and glad to be freed of the glory with the labours; for it is not my desire to live or reign longer than my life and reign shall be for your good. (Strachey, 280)

We can see in these words precisely the sort of personage to whom the pastoral drama would have had such an appeal.

What sets the pastoralism of the three 'Henry' kings apart from the normal variety is that it is not so much a function of actual encounters as it is of royal fantasy. We see it primarily in the day dreams of distressed monarchs who give expression to a fantasy of genteel rustication. Its manifestation in four successive Plantagenet monarchs (Richard II, King Henry IV, King Henry V and King Henry VI) makes it seem a sort of genetic disposition (though Bolingbroke is not Richard's son).

The idealization of country life (or its remnants) endured well after the English renaissance. It was still thriving in late 18th century in France, where its votaries ventured well beyond the confines of mere conjecture. Parisian aristocrats would physically troop out to the villages to observe the happy peasant festivals and dances. Marie Antoinette, having even greater resources at her disposal, constructed at Versailles an entire farm, Le Petit Hameau, complete with residence, dairy and poultry yard. Attendant ladies clad themselves in simple gauze dress tied at the waist with ribbons and played at being shepherdesses. Of course, inside the mock farmhouse were sufficient goodies to keep Marie safely within the standard of indulgence to which she had become so richly accustomed. One commentator remarks dryly, "And even more than the money spent on the Petit Hameau, the many hours spent there in the company of other women, outside the sight and supervision of her husband, gave rise to rumors that were not innocent at all." ("Marie Antoinette and the French Revolution," online) In the following century, American intellectuals still cultivated the ideal of woodland innocence and peace. Thus, Harvard graduate Henry David Thoreau built with his own two hands a cabin at Walden Pond out of used boards obtained from a neighbor's torn down homes and barns. There in prosperous Concord he sought to pursue the life of a noble savage, and when he was in need of foodstuffs or other amenities of a corrupt and decadent civilization, he would clamber up onto the railroad tracks beside the pond and march over to his mother's house, whose ample cupboards contained whatever he might desire. For what is pastoralism, after all, but the perfection of the urbane?

In the *Henriad*, then, Shakespeare illustrates the conceptual pastoralism of three generations of English kings. Under the weight of their transgressions, overreaching, war-making and incessant undermining by belligerent lords, it was evidently hard for monarchs to get a decent night's sleep. It was easy, however, to suppose that yokels starving in the forest were dozing soundly. Pastoralism was therefore largely a creature of the aristocratic fancy. Hence, its purveyors, *e.g.*, Spenser, Sidney, were typically court personalities. Things were otherwise with the ballad, which bubbled up from the recesses of the autochthonous population. The ballad was perhaps the principal exemplar of the English oral traditions, and the "bard" was he who collected and polished the ballad and carried it forward. For the balladeers, the kingly visitor was the outsider, a suspect vagabond who shows up one day looking for a free lunch. It is a wonder kings were tolerated at all. As for Shakespeare, his case is more complex, but as a pastoral poet we must place him squarely in court. It is the content of his writings, not any "snobbery," that compels us to do so. We may therefore say that the difference between the pastoral and ballad conventions is that the pastorals idealized the rural commons, while the ballads treated royal interlopers in a spirit of realism, resentment and smoldering envy.

Taken together, Shakespeare's envious soliloquies in the *Henriad* form a spiritual interregnum within a series of bloody wars and insurrections, and show a succession of kings seeking intellectual solace from the trials of monarchy and its attendant struggles. It is not surprising that the peasants should have been so marveled at, so coveted. But the pacific trajectory which culminated in the shepherd worship of Henry VI, comes to grief the moment that king steps outside his palatial cocoon and encounters those ruffian gamekeepers. At that moment, the pastoral ceases as a valid literary form, and Shakespeare's voice becomes ever more resolutely realistic.

WORKS CITED:

"Marie Antoinette and the French Revolution," online.
Rochelle Smith, "King-Commoner Encounters in the Popular Ballad, Elizabethan Drama and Shakespeare," *Studies in English Literature, 1500-1900*, Vol. 50, Number 2, Spring 2010, pp. 301-336.
William Shakespeare, The Complete Works, 2d ed., S. Wells, & G. Taylor, eds., Clarendon Press, Oxford, 2005.
Lytton Strachey, *Elizabeth and Essex: A Tragic History*, 1928; Mariner Books, 1969.

12

"Dost Know This Water-fly?" - Effeminacy in Shakespeare

I. Introduction

*U*nlike his predecessor, Christopher Marlowe (1564-1593), many of whose works reflect preoccupation with male sexual irregularity, the writings attributed to William Shakespeare are consistently orthosexual, treating deviations as unsalutary and symptomatic of social necrosis. In an age in which sexual "ambiguity" is celebrated and promoted by a veritable orgy of sensationalist journalists, psycho-babbling critics, and "queer theorists," it's not surprising that many are anxious to enlist the prestigious "William Shakespeare" in the cause. Unfortunately, such efforts are vain and doomed to failure, for they must always be conducted at the expense of content. In what follows we examine several Shakespeare plays to reveal his negative assessment of effeminacy and male intimacy.[1] We will find that readings of Shakespeare which allege same-sex promotion are doctrinaire and intellectually transgressive.

II. A Sparrow Falls, Look Out Below!

A few notes snatched from the rising chorus should suffice. In a recent essay, "A Sparrow Falls: Olivier's Feminine Hamlet," Prof. Sky Gilbert announces that Prince Hamlet is an "effeminate" character: "A close reading of the text of *Hamlet*, and also an examination of the text in

---

1 We need not take up the Sonnets. See, Hank Whittemore, *The Monument*, Meadow Geese Press, 2005, which explains their personal and historical significance.

performance, reveals [sic] that . . . issues of effeminacy and sexuality are and have always been central to our perception of one of Shakespeare's most famous plays." (240) Critics "often discuss his effeminacy." (241) "I would suggest that Hamlet is effeminate—by both early modern and contemporary standards—and that the transhistorical link between homosexuality and effeminacy makes any discussion of Hamlet's characteristics necessarily a discussion of his sexuality." (241)

"O this learning, what a thing it is!" (*The Taming of the Shrew*, I, ii, 157)

> Hamlet criticizes himself for being more womanly than manly, and is clearly not secure in his identity as an adult male. Indeed there are moments in the play where Hamlet points to his own effeminacy, characterizing himself as more like a boy or a woman than a man. One of the essential distinctions made between men and boys in Shakespeare's day was facial hair, and when Hamlet discourses on his own cowardice in his second soliloquy, he imagines himself beardless: 'Am I a coward? Who calls me villain? Breaks my pate across? Plucks off my beard and blows it in my face?' (Gilbert, 242)

How might this show or tend to show him to be "effeminate"? Keep in mind that one advancing the novel and significant thesis bears the burdens of proof and persuasion. These are forensic obligations of the affirmative position occupied by Dr. Gilbert. Let the standard be a mere preponderance of the evidence. Are those burdens successfully discharged? Unfortunately not. We are reminded that Hamlet, a university student at Wittenberg, sports a beard, certainly not the rule for male undergrads. According to Dr. Gilbert, a beard is—none too surprisingly—a token of masculinity. Hence, the evidence adduced supports the contrary proposition. Hamlet is manly, not feminine.

What actions or features of Prince Hamlet are consistent with "effeminacy"? Does he lisp? Exhibit a mincing gait? A limp wrist? No? There must be something else, then—but what?

Yes, he is certainly beset by self-doubt. This may be the result of his inability to fulfill his pledge to the ghost in Act 1, scene 5 to avenge the King's death by slaying Claudius. But is murder a stroll in the park? How many young men among us could plunge a deadly blade into the bowels of the reigning monarch? If a scholar is reluctant to return his books to the library and rush out to publicly butcher a family member and sovereign on the asseverations of a "ghost," does that suggest he is "effeminate"? *Non sequitur.* Or, looked at subjectively, if he laments privately the fact of his inability to become a bloody regicide, and frets about his puissance in the process, do those perfectly understandable doubts entail "effeminacy"? Not at all. To think that way is to give the word a new wrinkle indeed. But the plain fact is that Hamlet's malaise commences not in the second soliloquy (II, ii, 551-607) but the first (I, ii, 129-159), at which point he has not yet been apprised of the late King's assassination. Yet here he already contemplates suicide ("self-slaughter") (II, ii, 132) That's pretty serious. What's ailing him? Many wish they knew. Though T.S. Eliot is correct to have observed that a mere hasty remarriage on the part of his mother is insufficient to account for the Prince's anguish, he is wrong to contend that there is no reasonable explanation. First of all, it is plain that Hamlet expected to inherit the throne from his father, but arrives in Elsinore to discover his amiable uncle's *derrière* resting on it. (Gontar, 399-401) Second, there is a not-so-subtle implication in those hasty nuptials, namely, that they may be a mere rubber-stamp placed on a pre-existing misalliance of some vintage. And that in turn raises the uncomfortable question of Hamlet's own provenance and legitimacy. These issues are never squarely faced, however, either by Hamlet himself or by our incisive pundits. As a result, he has continued to be an enigma. Psychologically speaking, it is easier for him to seek refuge in doubts about his resolve to commit murder (colorfully repackaged by Dr. Gilbert as "effeminacy") than it is to face the deeper and more imposing issues of lost crown and illegitimacy, which would undermine his very identity, and suggest the loathsome "uncle" is none other than his biological father.

Utterly insensible of these considerations, then, textual tourists must either throw up their hands in blank despair with Eliot, and set down the world's greatest tragedy as an artistic "failure," or, with A.C. Bradley, seek out a psychological syndrome to account for Hamlet's self-hatred. When that is done, tragedy shrivels to melodrama. It is not difficult for a critic as fixated as Dr. Gilbert with same-sex relations to attribute to Prince Hamlet an uninviting quality such as "effeminacy." It's a cinch to throw mud, especially if you think your target looks better wearing it. But such an offhand rubric constitutes nothing less than a disinclination to think, an abdication of critical responsibility. If one wanted to contend that Hamlet is "effeminate," the most forthright way to do it would be to cite with particularity aspects of his activity, deportment and demeanor which have been acknowledged by critical consensus to be so. There is no such consensus. Above all, one would want to be quite sure one possessed the most cogent and up-to-date exegesis of the material. Do we?

Alas, at this point, Dr. Gilbert's golden words are spent. The argument begins to circle the drain.

> A few lines later, Hamlet criticizes himself for his lack of action and obsession with talk by comparing himself to a female prostitute: 'Must I like a whore unpack my heart with words, And fall a-cursing like a drab, a stallion?' Shakespeare could not be clearer that Hamlet is emasculated by his own lack of action. (242)

Not at all.

To doubt one's solvency is not necessarily bankruptcy. To play the valetudinarian is not to be ill, nor is stewing about one's measure of manhood the same thing as effeminacy. More plausibly, what is at stake in this context is Hamlet's personal identity and unwillingness to face the possibility that he might be a court bastard who never had a chance to take the throne.

> Near the end of the play, Hamlet again compares his misgivings about the upcoming duel with Laertes as womanish: 'It is but foolery, but it is such a kind of gainsgiving as would perhaps trouble a woman.' (242)

Hamlet has an eerie premonition he may not survive a sporting match with blunted weapons. And he does not. When the shadow of death gives a man concern, shall we say his apprehensions of mortality are symptoms of "effeminacy"? To pose such a question is to have our answer: no.

Dr. Gilbert tries to argue that Laertes exceeds Hamlet in masculinity, but is brought up short by the fact that Laertes sheds tears while "effeminate" Hamlet does not. (242-243) He then falls back into the worst position of all, clinging desperately to Eliot's strained contention that there is no "objective correlative" and that Hamlet is deeply yet gratuitously neurotic in relation to his mother. (245) This ground has been trodden to death and has rarely if ever been thought to yield "effeminacy." That was certainly not Eliot's conclusion.

In short, Dr. Gilbert doesn't even come close to demonstrating an effeminate protagonist in Hamlet; on the contrary, the only fact adduced is his beard, a masculine property. His putative argument begs the question.

Other points may be examined.

i. While crossing the ocean Hamlet's vessel is attacked by pirates. (IV, vi, 15) In the ensuing fracas, the Danish prince leaps boisterously onto the pirate deck to give armed resistance. (IV, vi, 17) Typically effeminate behavior? One might expect a truly girlish passenger to expose an alluring ankle or daring dècolletage, not to confront the adversary with drawn sword. Hamlet's conduct at sea is super-masculine, the sort of swashbuckling derring-do that might set feminine hearts a-flutter.

ii. When the ghost beckons, Hamlet is determined to follow, heedless of the danger. His companions try to restrain him. There follows this exchange:

HAMLET

It wafts me still. (to the Ghost) Go on, I'll follow thee.

MARCELLUS

You shall not go, my lord.

HAMLET

Hold off your hand.

HORATIO

Be ruled. You shall not go.

HAMLET

My fate cries out,
And makes each petty artere in this body
As hardy as the Nemean lion's nerve

(The Ghost beckons Hamlet)

Still am I called. Unhand me, gentlemen.

By heav'n, I'll make a ghost of him that lets me.
I say, away! (to the Ghost) I'll follow thee.

    (Exeunt the Ghost and Hamlet)
(I, iv, 57-63)

Effeminacy should be made of softer stuff. Hamlet struggles hardily with his comrades, threatening to destroy them unless they let him sojourn with an ominous and unknown spirit. Is this guy a sissy? Dr. Gilbert thinks so.

    iii. The people would prefer to be ruled by Hamlet, not Claudius.

        The other motive
Why to a public count I might not go
Is the great love the general gender bear him,
Who, dipping all his faults in their affection,
Would, like the spring that turneth wood to stone,
Convert his guilts to graces; so that my arrows,
Too slightly timbered for so loud a wind,
Would have reverted to my bow again,
And not where I had aimed them.
(IV, vii, 16-24)

Why do the people want Prince Hamlet as their King, to succeed the redoubtable King Hamlet the Dane? Because they perceive him as "effeminate"? That strikes us as a tad counterintuitive. To the contrary, Claudius finds him politically invulnerable, an Über-candidate against whose flinty figure slanderous arrows bounce back to their sender.

    iv. Hamlet leaps into Ophelia's grave and grapples with Laertes. When the duel is proposed, though his adversary is a consummate swordsman, Hamlet accepts the challenge with alacrity.

HORATIO

You will lose this wager, my lord.

HAMLET

I do not think so. Since he [Laertes] went into France, I have been in continual practice. I shall win at the odds.

(V, ii, 155-157)

Words spoken by an effeminate fellow? We may want to recall Viola as Cesario in *Twelfth Night* for contrast. She shivers when tricked by Sir Toby Belch into a duel with Sir Andrew Aguecheek, who also quakes in his boots. Cesario is seen as "effeminate" because he is actually a woman in disguise.

VIOLA

I will return again into the house and desire some
conduct of the lady. I am no fighter.
(III, iv, 235-236)

Pray God defend me. A little thing would make
make me tell them how much I lack of a man.
(III, iv, 293-294)

Here Viola's mock effeminacy (*i.e.*, femininity) is apt and used to marvelous comic effect. Prince Hamlet on the other hand possesses an intact manhood, battling with pirates and enraged siblings, with his life in jeopardy on both occasions.

v. In the not-too-distant past, Ophelia was courted by the young prince with poetry, gifts and true affection. At that time, were there noted in him any defects of masculine character that might support the claims of Dr. Gilbert? No, there weren't. Courtiers and ladies in the circle of King Claudius do not comment that in his moodiness, sulking and petulant manner, Hamlet is just continuing to act as he always did. Instead, surprise and disappointment show in their reaction to his scandalous words and sullen countenance. So as the curtain rises and Hamlet unpacks his heart, it must be that he has almost overnight and without cause become "effeminate," as preposterous a notion as any one might devise. The so-called "effeminate" Hamlet speaks of his alleged father thus:

[He] was a man. Take him for all in all,
I shall not look upon his like again.
(I, ii, 186-187)

Hamlet, too, is a man among men. He knows the value of manhood and that is one of the reasons we value him.

    vi. Interestingly, Shakespeare underscores Hamlet's virile temperament by introducing near the climax a manifestly effeminate character. Claudius selects the fop Osric to deliver Laertes' challenge and terms of wager. Though Dr. Gilbert can find in Osric nothing more than a "flatterer" (247), his language is not gross fawning. The effeminate lord was a stock character on the London stage in Elizabethan England, instantly recognized by the audience. Thus, when he greets the Prince, welcoming him back to Denmark, Hamlet nudges Horatio and whispers, "Dost know this water-fly?" (V, ii, 83-84) What does this import? No words of flattery have yet passed Osric's lips, yet Hamlet instantly sets him down in disparaging locution. Osric is a flamboyant fussbudget with a mincing gait, or, to use Dr. Gilbert's enchanting lexicon, a "queer." Viewers will automatically recall Hotspur's conversation with Bolingbroke in *King Henry IV*, Part One, in which a Hotspur seeks to rationalize his failure to surrender his prisoners to the King.

HOTSPUR

My liege, I did deny no prisoners;
But I remember, when the fight was done,
When I was dry with rage and extreme toil,
Breathless and faint, leaning upon my sword,
Came a certain lord, neat and trimly dressed,
Fresh as a bridegroom, and his chin, new-reaped,
Showed like a stubble-land at harvest-home.
He was perfumèd like a milliner,
And 'twixt his finger and his thumb he held
A pouncet-box, which ever and anon
He gave his nose and took't away again —
Who therewith angry, when it next came there,
Took it in snuff — and he smiled and talked;
And as the soldiers bore dead bodies by,
He called them untaught knaves, unmannerly
To bring a slovenly unhandsome corpse
Betwixt the wind and his nobility.
With many holiday and lady terms
He questioned me; amongst the rest demanded
My prisoners in your majesty's behalf.
I then, all smarting with my wounds being cold —

To be so pestered with a popinjay! —
Out of my grief and my impatience
Answered neglectingly, I know not what —
He should, or should not — for he made me mad
To see him shine so brisk, and smell so sweet,
And talk so like a waiting gentlewoman
Of guns, and drums, and wounds, God save the mark!
And telling me the sovereign'st thing on earth
Was parmacity for an inward bruise,
And that it was a great pity, so it was,
This villainous saltpetre should be digged
Out of the bowels of the harmless earth,
Which many a good tall fellow had destroyed
So cowardly, and but for these vile guns
He would have himself been a soldier.
(I, iii, 28-63)

Reading this account by Hotspur in *Henry IV* helps us to situate Hamlet's Osric, a later specimen of the same stamp. It is plain that not only are Hotspur's feelings about this namby-pamby more than a little condemnatory, so too are the playwright's. Hotspur and Prince Hamlet are both touched with nobility of spirit, though of course in different ways, and both spurn open and notorious effeminacy. The reader may also examine the features of "Monsieur Le Beau" in *As You Like It*, yet another instance of a visibly non-masculine male having no respect in court society. (I, ii, 87ff.) And what of poor "Sir Eglamour" in *The Two Gentlemen of Verona*? We admire his kindness, but in relation to the favors of the beauteous Silvia, he is plainly not a competitor for obvious reasons.

vii. What Hamlet prizes above all is friendship. And by this he does not intend the baser variety of Platonic eros. (See, *e.g.*, *Phaedrus* 253d, and following) Despite being emotionally distraught, in a moment of dramatic lucidity and frank self-revelation, Hamlet details his ideal relations with members of his own sex. It is as far from effeminacy as one might get.

HAMLET

Horatio, thou art e'en as just a man
As e'er my conversation coped withal.

HORATIO

O my dear lord —

HAMLET

           Nay, do not think I flatter;
For what advancement may I hope from thee,
That no revenue hast but thy good spirits
To feed and clothe thee? Why should the poor be flattered?
No, let candied tongue lick absurd pomp,
And crook the pregnant hinges of the knee
Where thrift may follow feigning. Dost thou hear? —
Since my dear soul was mistress of her choice
And could of men distinguish, her election
Hath sealed thee for herself; for thou hast been
As one in suff'ring all that suffers nothing,
A man that Fortune's buffets and rewards
Hath ta'en with equal thanks; and blest are those
Whose blood and judgement are so well commingled
That they are not a pipe for Fortune's finger
To sound what stop she please. Give me that man
That is not passion's slave, and I will wear him
In my heart's core, ay, in my heart of heart,
As I do thee.
(III, ii, 52-72)

Here is a frank statement of Shakespeare's ethical ideal. It is derived from such thinkers as Epicurus, Lucretius and Castiglione. The classic ethos looks to friendship amongst noble men as the very pinnacle of virtue. Precisely repudiated here are the mutability and instability which render men mere feathers of passion, swept up by every passing impulse, fickle and capricious. Horatio is the prototype of manliness, thoughtful, faithful and autonomous, one who could never be "a pipe for Fortune's finger, to sound what stop she please." By contrast, Rosenkrantz and Guildenstern, dwelling in the "privates" of Fortune (II, ii, 235), in their deviousness and lack of integrity, are incapable of such proud friendship. Has anyone asked what their relationship is? Returning to the same trope he employed in his encomium to Horatio, Hamlet accuses R&G of treating him like a pipe made to sound what notes others may please to produce in him.

HAMLET

Why, look you now, how unworthy a thing you
make of me! You would play upon me, you would
seem to know my stops, you would pluck out the heart
of my mystery, you would sound me from my lowest
note to the top of my compass; and there is much
music, excellent voice in this little organ, yet cannot
you make it speak. 'Sblood, do you think I am easier
To be played on than a pipe? Call me what instrument
you will, though you can fret me, you cannot play
upon me.
(III, ii, 351-360)

But Hamlet is not a pipe for others to blow on. There isn't a shred of evidence that he is—or should be considered to be—effeminate. Quite the contrary.

If we now ask how it is that someone might wish to persuade us that Hamlet is a girly man, a glance in Dr. Gilbert's direction will do. Information available online informs us he is a professor of theater and drama at the University of Guelph in Canada, and also a "drag performer" whose alter ego is "Jane." This transvestite gentleman has devoted considerable energies to staging and promoting "LGBT drama." He is a practitioner of something called "queer theory." On his website one finds an ode written to former President Bill Clinton praising him (tongue-in-cheek?) for his effeminate proclivities. It is one of the more discouraging aspects of "Homo" sapiens that we often tend to project our own profile onto others. Long ago this was observed by the pre-Socratic philosopher Xenophanes (c. 570 — c. 480 BC) who quipped, "If animals worshiped the gods, horses would portray them as horses, oxen as oxen." And so it is in literary studies.

Having examined *Hamlet* and *King Henry IV*, Part One, it may be well to turn to other moments in Shakespeare in which there are instances of effeminacy and its concomitants. We continue with *Antony and Cleopatra*.

III. My Man of Men

In his histories, Shakespeare often drops us into the midst of the broil, the thickest part of the tumult. We are there at Agincourt, hearing the cries of the soldiers, we are blood bedecked in the clashes of Shrewsbury, at Bosworth Field we witness Richard's desperate predicament. We behold Talbot's incomparable bravery, see Margaret place the paper crown on York's still unbowed head. But in the tragedies, it seems the dramatis personae have often beheld the best of their time. When we meet him, Othello has put up his bright sword, and recollects his victories as the old warrior, famousèd for worth. His glories are burnished by a setting sun. The triumphs of Titus Andronicus lie behind him, as do those of the distinguished Thane of Cawdor. So is it, too, for Marcus Antonius. What has happened to him? Where is he when he's needed?

> From Alexandria this is the news: he fishes, drinks, and wastes
> The lamps of night in revel; is not more manlike
> Than Cleopatra, nor the Queen of Ptolemy
> More womanly than he . . . .
> (I, iv, 1-7)

He is now "a man who is the abstract of all faults / That all men follow." (I, iv, 8-9) This is especially painful for those can remember the deeds that made magical the very name Antony, the Triple pillar of the world. Caesar in particular looks back in anger.

> Antony,
> Leave thy lascivious wassails. When thou once
> Was beaten from Modena, where thou slew'st
> Hirtius and Pansa, consuls, at thy heel
> Did famine follow, whom thou fought'st against —
> Though daintily brought up — with patience more
> Than savages could suffer. Thou dids't drink
> The stale of horses, and the gilded puddle
> Which beasts would cough at. Thy palate then did deign
> The roughest berry on the rudest hedge.
> Yea, like the stag when snow the pasture sheets,
> The barks of trees thou browsed. On the Alps
> It is reported thou didst eat strange flesh,
> Which some did die to look on; and all this —

It wounds thine honour that I speak it now —
Was borne so like a soldier that thy cheek
So much as lanked not.
(I, iv, 55-71)

And that is not the worst of it. Anyone who reads in succession the tragedies of *Julius Caesar* and *Antony and Cleopatra* must be struck by the fact that, in phenomenological terms, the "Mark Antony" of the latter is a completely different person from the Mark Antony of the first. As we saw in the relationship of Prince Hamlet and Horatio, what defines the Mark Antony in *Julius Caesar* is his unshakable bond of friendship with Caesar. It is this which gives the character of Antony its gravitas, its credibility. In his great encomium after the faction has done its awful deed, Antony installs that friendship with Caesar as the keystone in his arch of virtue: "He was my friend, faithful and just to me." (III, ii, 86) That friendship is central to the earlier soliloquy, in which we can almost hear the beating of Antony's heart; in fact, it's hard to think of any dramatic performance which can rival Marlon Brando's (1956) rendition of these astonishing lines:

O pardon me, thou bleeding piece of earth,
That I am meek and gentle with these butchers.
Thou art the ruins of the noblest man
That ever livèd in the tide of times.
Woe to the hand that shed this costly blood!
Over thy wounds now do I prophesy —
Which like dumb mouths do ope their ruby lips
To beg the voice and utterance of my tongue —
A curse shall light upon the limbs of men;
Domestic fury and fierce civil strife
Shall cumber all the parts of Italy;
Blood and destruction shall be so in use,
And dreadful objects so familiar,
That mothers shall but smile when they behold
Their infants quartered with the hands of war,
All pity choked with custom of fell deeds;
And Caesar's spirit, ranging for revenge,
With Ate by his side come hot from hell,
Shall in these confines with a monarch's voice,
Cry 'havoc!' and let slip the dogs of war,

That this foul deed shall smell above the earth
With carrion men, groaning for burial.
(III, i, 257-278)

For Shakespeare, then, virtue is not an abstraction, but has its roots in noble comradeship, as we see exemplified in the relations of Hamlet and Horatio, Antony and Caesar, Theseus and Pirithous, Pericles and Helicanus and other male pairs. What so bitterly disappoints Octavius in *Antony and Cleopatra*, then, is not the general's debauchery and revels as much as his unwillingness or inability to honor his friendship with Octavius, as he had with Julius Caesar. The American philosopher Josiah Royce in his ethical writings and lectures used to urge the maxim of being "loyal to loyalty." And it is the failure to live up to such a maxim which lies at the root of Antony's fall from grace. He has so lost his way that he is no longer capable of *philia*; not only does he betray worthy individuals, he besmirches the very idea of fidelity. In playing the game of romance to the hilt, Antony turns his back on friendship, forgets it ever existed. Though he dotes, devoutly dotes, upon Cleopatra, she is not his friend. And that non-friendly idolatry is going to have big consequences for Antony as the action unfolds.

Though Cleopatra is Antony's obsession, he is constantly beset by the feeling of drowning emotionally; he must flee before he is altogether sucked in and consumed. As he is being absorbed by his arachnoid love object, he is progressively unmanned. It's as though he were a swishy fan of a "gay icon" like Judy Garland or Bette Midler who finally gets to meet the queen—and become her roommate. It's all too much. Antony refuses to attend to business; instead he wants to plot each evening's concupiscent diversion: "Tonight we'll wander through the streets and note / The qualities of people. Come, my queen. Last night you did desire it." (I, i, 55-57) Cleopatra, for her part, sensing his frantic wish to break free, redoubles her efforts to hold him fast by any means possible. When he finally escapes her clutches and wafts back to Rome, she amuses herself by teasing the "unseminar'd eunuch" Mardian, an emblem of Antony's own evaporating masculinity. "Hast thou affections?" she challenges.

MARDIAN

Yes, gracious madam.

CLEOPATRA

Indeed?

MARDIAN

Not in deed, madam, for I can do nothing
But what is honest to be done.
Yet I have fierce affections, and think
What Venus did with Mars.
(I, v, 12-18)

Cleopatra may salivate over the brute but always seems to prepare the *castrato* for her entrée. She could no more accept a non-emasculated lover than she could dine on an uncooked fish. And Antony is the poor fish for which she is forever angling. (II, v, 10-18) Who knows? There might be a spark of life in him she's overlooked and needs to snuff out.

What Venus did with her bellicose god, of course, is conquer him, as Cleopatra is intent on conquering her man of war. This is boldly illustrated by Sandro Botticelli in his 1483 canvas, *Venus and Mars*, in which the hero is depicted *post coitum*, sufficiently sated to have lost consciousness, appearing nothing short of dead, as mock cherubs try in vain to revive him. Botticelli's Mars is a soft, beardless youth, not the tough veteran stained with blood and sweat. Venus gazes at her captive in satisfaction and triumph. (It is more than likely that Oxford, the actual author, was familiar with the painting as a result of his 1575 tour of Italy.) Shakespeare's Cleopatra is a tragic figure because the greater her efforts to squeeze the last drop of titillation from Antony, the smaller, weaker and less appetizing he becomes. Psychologically castrating this aging soldier is the only way she knows to keep him. She is an emotional vampire, a cousin of the serpents she so lovingly employs to extinguish herself when what is left of Antony expires in her arms.

> O, see, my women,
> The crown o'th' earth doth melt. My lord!
> O, withered is the garland of the war.
> The soldier's pole is fall'n. Young boys and girls
> Are level now with men. The odds is gone,
> And there is nothing left remarkable
> Beneath the visiting moon.
> (V, 16, 64-70)

Thus croweth the femme fatale of Egypt over her prize. As she dons her finest robes and tiara to keep her long awaited date with death (V, ii, 223-275) it isn't likely that Cleopatra will recall the night

> I drunk him to his bed,
> Then put my tires and mantles on him whilst
> I wore his sword Philippan.
> (II, v, 21-23)

Indeed, in one early scene, when Cleopatra rushes onstage clad in Antony's helmet and breastplate, Enobarbus thinks she is Antony, and has to be corrected by handmaid Charmian. (I, ii, 70-71)

Cleopatra's fetid penumbra of luxury, ennui and erotic whimsy at last takes its toll on Antony, whose last vestiges of drive and determination fade just as the advancing shadow of Roman legions brings him to his senses. Too late. With testosterone tank on "empty," and still under his unfair lady's spell, Antony is a mere caricature of his former self. Rome declares war on Cleopatra, and responsibility for Egypt's defense falls on his now slumping shoulders. To make matters worse, Cleopatra insists on participating in the war personally.

ENOBARBUS

> Your presence needs must puzzle Antony,
> Take from his heart, take from his brain, from's time
> What should not then be spared. He is already
> Traduced for levity; and 'tis said in Rome

That Photinus, an eunuch, and your maids
Manage this war.

CLEOPATRA

       Sink Rome, and their tongues rot
That speak against us! A charge we bear i' th' war,
And as the president of my kingdom will
Appear there for a man. Speak not against it.
I will not stay behind.
(III, vii, 10-19)

The problem is, Cleopatra is not a martial woman, on a par with real fighters like Joan of Arc and Queen Margaret. She knows combat only as a game played with the now enervated Antony. Enobarbus is therefore correct: her presence in the fray can serve as a distraction only. More gravely, "Cleopatra [is] unintentionally fighting on Octavius Caesar's side . . . . As a foreign queen, she [is] no more popular with Antony's soldiers than with the enemy." (Asimov, 367) Her admiralty is therefore little better than an illusion; her legions will change sides at the slightest provocation. Undeterred, she bungles her way into strategy, where her bad ideas impose themselves on her man of wax. As a general, he always excelled in land engagements. But Cleopatra has her own fleet, including the flagship Antoniad, from whose incensed pavilions she plans to observe Antony confound the Roman navy as though a naval engagement were a child's cartoon. And as Asimov observes, "a sea victory . . . would include the Egyptian fleet and entitle her to a share in the glory and the profits." (Asimov, 369) She insists he fight on sea, not land. "I have sixty sails, Caesar none better." (III, vii, 49) That settles it.

The Battle of Actium is launched, with predictable results. Confronted directly by Caesar's squadrons, Cleopatra turns and flees, as though she'd left a cake in the oven. She is followed by most of her sixty sail, with the dazed Mark Antony bringing up the rear.

SCARUS

      She once being luffed,
The noble ruin of her magic, Antony,
Claps on his sea-wing and, like a doting mallard,
Leaving the fight in height, flies after her.

I never saw an action of such shame.
Experience, manhood, honour, ne'er before
Did violate so itself.
(III, 10, 18-23)

Antony's leave-taking from Actium is not a retreat; it is the desertion by a leader of his own forces. History provides no other instance of such betrayal. Would the Antony of Philippi have ever dreamed of such disgrace? This has happened because that Antony is no more. He has been replaced by a neutered pod stripped to the root. Though Plato argues theoretically in the *Politeia* for the inclusion of women in the guardian class of citizens (that is, the army), the lesson of history is plain. Shakespeare follows Plutarch on this point. The fag hag has no business in battle.

One must go beyond the quadrangle to obtain a sensible view of this. Even Camille Paglia in *Sexual Personae* celebrates the "sexual ambiguity" which generates what is arguably the most unseemly moment in western civilization. That genocidal maniac Captain George Custer appears more admirable at Little Big Horn than Antony at Actium. Let us listen to Mr. Asimov's brief for common sense.

> This is the point at which the world is lost and Antony is forever disgraced. There might be reasons for Cleopatra running away; the only reason for Antony is an impulse of love. This impulse might be understandable, even admirable, to romantics, and surely there is nothing so worth a sigh as to witness some great game tossed away for love.

> Yet we must admit that however admirable it may be to ruin oneself for love, however noble to go down to personal death for love, it is not noble to cast away the lives and fortunes of thousands of others for love. Antony abandoned a fleet that was fighting bravely on his behalf, and in the confusion and disheartenment that followed his flight, many men died who might have lived had he remained. What's more, he abandoned thousands of officers and men on the nearby mainland, who had been prepared to die for him, leaving them only the alternative of useless resistance or ignoble surrender. We may understand Antony, but we cannot excuse him.
> (Asimov 1, 371)

But it may be doubted whether Mr. Asimov, for all his historical erudition, actually does understand Antony. He thinks that Antony runs from Actium on account of "love." But the affective state in which Antony subsists is uncertain at the outset and poorly characterized by a generic term such as "love." Go back to the first words spoken by Cleopatra in the play: "If it be love indeed, tell me how much." (I, i, 14) IF it be love. Why does Shakespeare write "if"? That has clearly been a sticking point between these two in their mad affair. And nothing in the text convinces us in the end, not even Cleopatra's fantasy of meeting Antony in the world-to-come, that Antony was motivated by what is commonly called "love." In his response to Schleiermacher's hypothesis that religion is best defined as the "feeling of dependence," Hegel is said to have caustically remarked that if religion is the feeling of dependence then a dog is the best Christian. To push the metaphor, Antony in Shakespeare's play is not a man but a mere cur. And can a dog really love a cat? We find the same model in Tennessee Williams' *Cat on a Hot Tin Roof*, in which emasculated alcoholic Brick, recovering from his idealization of his chum Skipper, conceives of himself as in love with "Maggie the cat." Limping on crutches and obviously impotent, there is no foundation for the view that Brick has ever actually loved Maggie. And it should not be overlooked that Hollywood chose actress Elizabeth Taylor (the raptor who seized the feckless Eddie Fisher in her talons) to play both Cleopatra and Maggie the cat.

It is naïve in the extreme, then, to suggest that Antony deserts his troops on account of anything as sane as love. Hotspur loves his wife Kate. Does he take her to Shrewsbury? (See, *King Henry IV* Part One, II, iv, 1-115) Does Brutus on the Ides of March take Portia to the Senate house? If a man loves his wife he would certainly not expose her to the hazards of armed combat. Antony should never have permitted Cleopatra to intrude into the battle, and seeing her depart to presumed safety should have uplifted his spirits. Instead of relief at her withdrawal, Antony does the absurdly unaccountable thing and follows her.

CLEOPATRA

> O my lord, my lord,
> Forgive my fearful sails! I little thought
> You would have followed.

ANTONY

> Egypt, thou knew'st too well
> My heart was to thy rudder tied by th' strings,
> And thou shouldst tow me after. O'er my spirit
> Thy full supremacy thou knew'st, and that
> Thy beck might from the bidding of the gods
> Command me.
> (III, xi, 54-61)

But this is most inadequate, for even if it is true that Antony was under her thumb (and it is), there was no call, no beck from her. This is no soldier obedient to command. We thought to find:

> . . . some Hercules,
> A second Hector, for his grim aspect
> And large proportion of his strong-knit limbs.
> Alas, this is a child, a seely dwarf.
> It cannot be this weak and writheled shrimp
> Should strike such terror to his enemies.
> (*King Henry VI*, II, iii, 18-23)

The words are apt. Antony is not "a lover, that kills himself most gallant for love," (*A Midsummer Night's Dream*, I, ii, 20) but by his own admission a child tied to his mother's apron's strings, and is nothing more than a miniaturized version of her, an extension of herself. That is ultimately the problem with "sexual ambiguity." Antony even botches his own suicide (IV, xv, 95-106) and must be salvaged by Cleopatra and the girls. (IV, xvi, 10-40) By whittling down the full dimensions of the masculine we lose those greater aspects of manhood which we admired and which promised our comfort and protection in the first place. In *Antony and Cleopatra*, Shakespeare returns to the image of the dominant female which was strongly adumbrated in *Romeo and Juliet*. (Gontar, 51-63) Antony does not "love" Cleopatra, he is engulfed by her, swallowed whole and spat out. And Shakespeare is at pains to show that the loss of Antony's "inches" is nothing to celebrate.

IV. The Men Who Love to Hate and the Woman Who Hates to Love

Roman general Caius Martius Coriolanus is up to the gills with plebians and tribunes. But the Volsces are in arms under their hero Tullus Aufidius, and plan to strike at Rome. It is left to Coriolanus to mount a defense, and skirmishes ensue. (I, iv, 20-29) Tullus and Caius are old adversaries: "If we and Caius Martius chance to meet, / 'Tis sworn between us we shall ever strike / Till one can do no more." (I, ii, 34-36) Martius is enthusiastic.

MARTIUS

           They have a leader,
Tullus Aufidius, that will put you to't.
I sin in envying his nobility,
And were I anything but what I am,
I would wish me only he.

COMINIUS

You have fought together!

MARTIUS

Were half to half the world by th' ears and he
Upon my party, I'd revolt to make
only my wars upon him. He is a lion
I am proud to hunt.
(I, i, 228-236)

What have we here? At the furthest verge of manhood and combat a different scent is in the air. The feelings of Martius for the enemy of Rome are curiously enticing. Aufidius' nobility is of such a degree that it is envied, a sin against hate. The truth is that Martius is so drawn to Tullus Aufidius that he would have no metaphysical objection to being that very person! He is "a lion" that Martius is "proud" to hunt. With a slight adjustment, could we say that Martius loves to hunt this beast? Yet, Aufidius remains "the man of my soul's hate." (I, vi, 10) How does love square with hate?

At the gates of the city of Corioles, the Romans make a humiliating retreat and are excoriated by Martius. Under his stern command, the Volces are beaten back to the city gates and collapse within. With the gates still ajar, Martius gives the order to enter the city for the *coup de grâce*. He strides forward, heedless of the fact that no one in his legions is following him. The gates slam shut behind him. Hours pass. Finally Martius emerges, blood stained but alive, a champion unexcelled. But where is Tullus Aufidius? Lo, the twain doth meet.

MARTIUS

I'll fight with none but thee, for I do hate thee
Worse than any promise-breaker.

AUFIDIUS

          We hate alike.
Not Afric owns a serpent I abhor
More than thy fame and envy. Fix thy foot.

MARTIUS

Let the first budger die the other's slave,
And the gods doom him after.

AUFIDIUS

If I fly, Martius,
Holla me like a hare.

MARTIUS

Within these three hours, Tullus,
Alone I fought in your Coriole's walls,
And made what work I pleased. 'Tis not my blood
Wherein thou seest me masked. For thy revenge,
Wrench up thy power to th' highest.

AUFIDIUS

Wert thou the Hector
That was the whip of your bragged progeny,
Thou shouldst not scape me here.

(Here they fight, and certain Volsces come
in the aid of Aufudius. Martius fights till
the Volsces be driven in breathless, Martius
following)
(I, ix, 1-13)

In the case of Cleopatra's Antony we encountered an emasculated warrior who has seen his manhood consumed by a virago of the Nile. But with Coriolanus and Aufidius, while there is no diminution in manly bravura and chest beating, we have a sense that, like Magellan reaching the east by sailing west, in Martius we have gone so far in the direction of masculinity that we have attained the South Sea of Effeminacy, where narcissistic beefcake heroes make oeillades at each other as they cavort in the fray. For in the dialectic of sex, masculinity turns into its contrary. Unbeknownst to these two big sissies, each has a crush on the other. That is why women are so frequently repelled by body builders and steroid pill-poppers. When a man's real love is found in the mirror what appears as masculine has undergone a sad mutation. As we will see below, this syndrome may be traced to Ancient Greece and is most clearly exemplified in the lollygagging of Achilles and his Ganymede, Patroclus.

Take a close look at Coriolanus. The big figure in his life is not his retiring wife, Virgilia, whose business appears to be to occupy the position of spouse as a faithful lieutenant might hold a strategic hillside. She is a cipher. It is Coriolanus' mommy, Volumnia, who holds sway over him. It is she who has reared him in bravery and the martial arts, and has taught him that the only truly honorable life for a man of Rome is to suffer injuries and die for one's country.

MENENIUS

Is he not wounded? He was wont to come home wounded.

VIRGILIA

O, no, no, no!

VOLUMNIA

O, he's wounded, I thank the gods for't!

In considering her son's honour and bravery, Volumnia is not shy to claim these manly virtues for herself and tell her son he derived them from her (surely a slap in the face to his father's memory):

VOLUMNIA

        Do as thou list.
Thy valiantness was mine, thou sucked'st it from me,
But owe thy pride thyself.
(III, ii, 127-129)

VOLUMNIA

I pray you, daughter, sing, or express yourself
in a more comfortable sort. If my son were my husband,
I should freelier rejoice in that absence wherein he won
honour than in the embracements of his bed where he
would show most love. When yet he was but tender-
bodied and the only son of my womb, when youth
with comeliness plucked all gaze his way, when for a
day of kings' entreaties a mother should not sell him
an hour from her beholding, I, considering how honour
would become such a person — that it was no better
than, picture-like, to hang by th' wall if renown made
it not stir — was pleased to let him seek danger where
he was like to find fame. To a cruel war I sent him,
from whence he returned his brows bound in oak. I
tell thee, daughter, I sprang not more in joy at first hearing
he was a man-child than now in first seeing
he had proved himself a man.
(I, iii, 1-17)

VIRGILIA (to Volumnia)

Beseech you give me leave to retire myself.

VOLUMNIA

Indeed you shall not.
Methinks I hear hither your husband's drum,
See him pluck Aufidius down by th' hair;
As children from a bear, the Volsces shunning him.
Methinks I see him stamp thus, and call thus:
'Come on, you cowards, you were got in fear
Though you were born in Rome!' His bloody brow
With his mailed hand then wiping, forth he goes,
Like to a harvest-man that's tasked to mow
Or all or lose his hire.

VIRGILIA

His bloody brow? O Jupiter, no blood!

VOLUMNIA

Away, you fool! It more becomes a man
Than gilt his trophy. The breasts of Hecuba
When she did suckle Hector looked not lovelier
Than Hector's forehead when it spit forth blood
At Grecian sword, contemning.
(I, iii, 29-48)

Shakespeare shows us, then, several ways to ruin a man. Too soft
or too hard, both spell masculine disaster. A siren like Cleopatra can so
capture a man's fancy that he becomes a trifle for her amusement, letting
him sink deeper and deeper in a vortex of lubricity until he's snuffed
out altogether like a wasp in honey. The pretext there is "love." Or, in
the names of "manhood" and "honor" a mother may raise a young man
to scorn any end that falls short of total martyrdom. Once a popular
ideal in the west, we tend to see this perverse syndrome nowadays only
in the lunatic idolatries of the middle east. Volumnia thinks of herself
as a noble Roman matron who has discharged her duty to Rome and

its tutelary deities by raising a man of steely patriotism. But what she bequeaths to the world is a killing machine which but slenderly knows itself. (*Lear*, Quarto, I, i, 283-284) In seeking at his mother's instigation to extrude from himself the last vestiges of sympathy, Coriolanus completely loses touch with the feminine, and so can take as a love object only what is like himself, male. Effeminacy of this type is no less real for being concealed. As the soul vaporizes and the external body becomes armored in sinews and musculature, the vacuity of the inner digestive and excretory tracts is inevitably highlighted and eroticized, signaling availability for penetrative possession. This is the nightmare that haunts Volumnia's distraught son.

Because of his emotional immaturity, Coriolanus cannot master the art of politics, which must be done if his career is to continue. His pride and contempt for ordinary people alienates the commons and the tribunes have no difficulty turning the masses against him. Though a hero of Rome, he is banished. While a Bolingbroke might gather his friends to form an army to conquer despised Rome (we see this also in Alcibiades' plot to invade Athens in *Timon of Athens*), Coriolanus proceeds incognito to the city of the Volsces where he seeks out—of all people—his sworn foe Tullus Aufidius, proposing an alliance! Their interaction at this point is instructive. For what we find is that the mutual "hate" which animated them turns inside out. As Caius Martius unmasks in front of his most despised enemy, and proposes that they unite against the loathed city of Rome, he offers Tullus his throat to cut (IV, v, 97) if he should choose to reject the venture of an alliance. Why that particular organ? He might have offered his head, after all. His adversary is stunned, and responds in a rather revealing manner.

AUFIDIUS

O Martius, Martius!
Each word thou hast spoke hath weeded from my heart
A root of ancient envy. If Jupiter
Should from yon cloud speak divine things
And say "Tis true', I'd not believe them more
Than thee, all-noble Martius. Let me twine
Mine arms about that body whereagainst
My grainèd ash an hundred times hath broke,
And scarred the moon with splinters.
      (He embraces Coriolanus)

> Here I clip
> The anvil of my sword, and do contest
> As hotly and as nobly with thy love
> As ever in ambitious strength I did
> Contend against thy valour. Know thou first,
> I loved the maid I married; never man
> Sighed truer breath. But that I see thee here,
> Thou noble thing, more dances my rapt heart
> Than when I first my wedded mistress saw
> Beside my threshold. Why, thou Mars, I tell thee
> We have a power on foot, and I had purpose
> Once more to hew thy target from thy brawn,
> Or lose my arm for't. Thou hast beat me out
> Twelve several times, and I have nightly since
> Dreamt of encounters 'twixt thyself and me —
> We have been down together in my sleep,
> Unbuckling helms, fisting each other's throat —
> And waked half dead with nothing. Worthy Martius,
> Had we no other quarrel else to Rome but that
> Thou art thence banished, we would muster all
> From twelve to seventy, and, pouring war
> Into the bowels of ungrateful Rome,
> Like a bold flood o'erbear't. O, come, go in,
> And take our friendly senators by th' hands
> Who now are here taking their leaves of me,
> Who am prepared against your territories,
> Though not for Rome itself.
> (IV, v, 102-136)

In the classic BBC video production, Aufidius embraces his beloved foe, cradling Martius' head against his own torso. The astounding speech he delivers is one, not of mere reconciliation, but of *philia* and *eros*. Martius, for his part, accepts these affections as though natural and sought after. It turns out that this great antagonist of Coriolanus, the one who hates his guts with a febrile passion, in fact cultivates an ardent love for him surpassing the desire he felt for his young bride on their wedding night! Though he had longed to "hew thy target from thy brawn" (that is, cut out your heart—or—unman you), Aufidius' actual feeling is quite to the contrary. Long before this sudden rapprochement Aufidius has been dreaming every night of a curious intercourse with

Coriol"anus" (whose very name suggests a target organ). In Aufidius' repetitive dream, these two haters descend ("we have been down together"), undress one another ('unbuckling'), and exhaust themselves in violent intercourse or fellatio ("fisting each other's throats"). Here is the fantasized (and therefore actual) meaning of their hostile relationship. As Patroclus is to Achilles, so is Aufidius to Coriolanus, the latter's male varlet. Long before Freud, Shakespeare had charted the labyrinth of dreams, and Freud, the assiduous student of Shakespeare from childhood, learned much from the unrivalled master of the human mind. (See, Harold Bloom, *The Anxiety of Influence*, 1997)

Is the unconscious amour of Aufidius and Coriolanus an affair which exemplifies Shakespeare's ideals? Does he admire these two thoughtless adversaries? No. Their masculinity is not genuine but symptomatic of unresolved issues. It is crypto-effeminacy. Its conclusion is tragedy and death. Aufidius chafes under the sway of Coriolanus' autonomy, and soon enough the emotion which had switched from hate to love, flips back again to hate. The fate of Caius Martius is thus sealed.

Let us note in passing that much contemporary scholarship fails to come to terms with *Coriolanus*. Typical is the "cultural materialism" of Prof. Jonathan Dollimore, so preoccupied with political ideology that it is blinded to the most obvious and significant components of the text.

Quite gratuitously, Dollimore denies that Volumnia delights in her son's wounds, suggesting that her real object of excitement is the "political capital" that accrues thereby. (Dollimore, 219) He then proceeds to deny that Aufidius loves Caius Martius, but merely "the power he signifies." (Dollimore, 221) But how could Aufidius rejoice at the "signified power" of his enemy? Is he the manager of Caius Martius' campaign for the consulship? Only a critic preoccupied with politics could twist the text to make its sense political rather than personal. What "political capital" accrued when Hector's forehead "spit forth blood" at Grecian sword? There is none. Watch Dollimore's brand of thinking in action:

> It is ironically significant that when they meet, Aufidius repeatedly fails to recognize Coriolanus even though they have many times fought each other:

> Thou hast beat me out
> Twelve several times, and I have nightly since
> Dreamt of encounters 'twixt thyself and me —
> We have been down together in my sleep,

Unbuckling helms, fisting each other's throat —
And wak'd half dead with nothing.

Despite this, Aufidius only recognises Coriolanus when he is
told his name. The implication is clear: Aufidius loves not the
man but the power he signifies; he puts a face to the name,
not vice-versa. (Dollimore, 220-221)

The willful poverty of this argument is embarrassing. Coriolanus
is absolutely the last person on earth Aufidius expects to stride uninvited into his vestibule. He enters muffled and disguised, and appears in
a night where a few late candles burn. Though he "unmuffles," his face
is begrimed by hard travel. His disguise remains on. Is it any surprise
that Aufidius doesn't know this stranger? Does that perceptual problem
in any way imply that Aufidius' speech of extreme love (inverted hate)
for Martius was a sham? Here is an inference hanging in thin air. Dollimore prefers to accord more weight to his own political agenda than to
the mere text, the helpless victim of his tortuous deconstructions. Most
shocking of all is the scanting of the passage partially quoted, which we
would expect a phalanx of psychoanalysts to recognize as a symphony of
veiled sexual desire. Unfortunately, Dollimore's botching of *Coriolanus*
is not atypical of contemporary criticism, which, with its camps of new
historicism, cultural materialism, feminism and the like, is as stridently
ideological and incoherent as any philosophy it chooses to vet.

V. Confederacy of Varlets

Shakespeare's most extensive portrayal of same-sex eroticism is
Troilus and Cressida. It is a side show of degeneracy pendant to the Tro-
jan War, in which many are speared and none is spared. Young Troilus,
apprehending that his capacity to give delight and satisfaction to his
lascivious lady is faltering, adopts the stratagem of cuckoldry. (Gontar,
100-107) He might have considered other options. While a complete
literary treatment of alternatives to normalcy has yet to be written (De
Sade and Jean-Paul Sartre are the best attempts), Shakespeare's play is a
fairly thorough exploration of two: cuckoldry and same-sex eroticism.
That is a logical pairing, for if delved to the root one would discover that
the latter is the *telos* of the former. That is, cuckoldry is a half-way house
on the dialectical path to pederasty. One of Shakespeare's main purposes in this perplexing play is to expose the rottenness that lies beneath

advanced civilizations, and there can be little doubt as to the immediate locus of the action: London circa 1600. (Think of the Weimar Republic, 1919-1933, a later European side show of decadence lodged between two phases of global conflagration.) Priam's Troy is crawling with discreditable and—dare we use the word?—disgusting people.

For example, Cressida's uncle, given the opprobrious moniker "Pandarus" [= pander] is an effeminate matchmaker trying to seductively interest his alluring but cynical niece in Troilus. While Helen in *All's Well That Ends Well* merrily defends virginity in the face of Parole's critique thereof (I, i, 9-161), Cressida's smutty banter with Pandarus is replete with brown and copper noses. Though the meaning is childishly apparent, Bate and Rasmussen crawl out on a hermeneutical limb by suggesting that "brown" refers to "someone with a dark complexion," and that "copper" is "red (from drinking; conceivably suggests the metal noses occasionally worn by those who had lost their real noses to syphillis.)" (Bate, 1486) When schoolboys teasingly accuse one another of being "brown nosers" in relation to the teacher, is that a reference to people with "dark complexions"?

The scene shifts to the Greek camp, where some are emboldened to take Achilles' name in vain.

ULYSSES

The great Achilles, whom opinion crowns
The sinew and the forehand of our host,
Having his ear full of his airy fame,
Grows dainty of his worth, and in his tent
Lies mocking our designs. With him Patroclus
Upon a lazy bed the livelong day
Breaks scurrile jests
And, with ridiculous and awkward action,
Which, slanderer, he 'imitation' calls,
He pageants us. Sometime, great Agamemnon,
Thy topless deputation he puts on,
And like a strutting player, whose conceit
Lies in his hamstring and doth think it rich
To hear the wooden dialogue and sound
'Twixt his stretched footing and the scaffoldage,
Such to-be-pitied and o'er-wrested seeming
He acts thy greatness in. And when he speaks

'Tis like a chime a-mending, with terms unsquared
Which from the tongue of roaring Typhon dropped
Would seem hyperboles. At this fusty stuff
The large Achilles on his pressed bed lolling
From his deep chest laughs out a loud applause,
Cries 'Excellent! 'Tis Agamemnon just.'
Now play me Nestor, hem and stroke thy beard,
As he being dressed to some oration'.
That's done as near as the extremist ends
Of parallels, as like Vulcan and his wife.
Yet god Achilles still cries, 'Excellent!
'Tis Nestor right. Now play him me, Patroclus,
Arming to answer in a night alarm'.
And then forsooth the faint defects of age
Must be the scene of mirth: to cough and spit,
And with a palsy, fumbling on his gorget,
Shake in and out the rivet. And at this sport
Sir Valour dies, cries, 'O enough, Patroclus!
Or give me ribs of steel. I shall split all
In pleasure of my spleen'. And in this fashion
All our abilities, gifts, natures, shapes,
Severals and generals of grace exact,
Achievements, plots, orders, preventions,
Excitements to the field or speech for truce,
Success or loss, what is or is not, serves
As stuff for these two to make paradoxes.
(I, iii, 142-184)

What may be gleaned from this passage? Though the war began
with an effort by the Greeks to recover the wife of Menelaüs, Helen of
Troy, protection of the integrity of the biological family was not of paramount importance to many if not most members of the Greek troops.
Indeed, as the siege of Troy is said to have spanned an entire decade, and
wives did not accompany the Greek warriors, it may be wondered what
sort of conjugal fulfillment might have been accorded the invaders over
such a long period of time. The most outstanding example of ingenuity
in the ranks is certainly the hero Achilles, who seems for whatever reason to have had no respect for the mission of recovering a leader's wife.
Shakespeare shows him doting on and cohabiting with a young man,
Patroclus, with whom he was obviously intimately involved. These two

pass the time either in copulation or by putting on loud satirical performances which mock the leadership of the Hellenes, making laughing stocks of Agamemnon and his brother. Why should a self-willed man like Achilles, physically and emotionally bonded with Patroclus, have any concern about foolish old Menelaüs and his trophy bride? The behavior of Achilles reported to the general staff by Ulysses is conduct unbecoming to an officer and would certainly lead today to investigation, a court martial and dishonorable discharge, punishment, or both. One would want to eliminate such behavior as soon as possible, as it would be imitated by others and could soon undermine morale. And this is precisely what Shakespeare depicts.

NESTOR

And in imitation of these twain
Who, as Ulysses says, opinion crowns
With an imperial voice, many are infect.
Ajax is grown self-willed and bears his head
In such a rein, in full as proud a place
As broad Achilles, and keeps his tent like him
Makes factious feasts, rails on our state of war
Bold as an oracle, and sets Thersites,
A slave whose gall coins slanders like a mint,
To match us in comparisons with dirt,
To weaken and discredit our exposure,
How rank so ever rounded in with danger.
(I, iii, 185-196)

What is the attitude of the author towards Achilles and Patroclus? One hundred percent negative. Choice of private indulgence over family, hearth and the protection of the nation is as bad a decision in Shakespeare's eyes as one could possibly imagine. The standpoint of Achilles is a particularly foul and unseemly brand of hubris which reflects nothing but his own personal glory and fulfillment. Instead of viewing same-sex intimacy as a legitimate exercise of individual freedom and right, without any negative consequences for others or for the body politic, Shakespeare demonstrates the invidious consequences which follow such a line of conduct: the undoing of society and state. Such is the impact of effeminacy according to Shakespeare.

The character of Thersites, a misanthrope distally related to Timon and Apemantus in *Timon of Athens*, is the nemesis elicited by the hubris of Achilles. The initial confrontation occurs when Achilles and Patroclus come upon Thersites harassing the helpless clod Ajax. It soon turns out that the sharp tongued Thersites has nothing but contempt for Achilles and his boyfriend. (II, ii, 100-128) Thersites is not a philosopher, however, but a self-taught observer and social critic who speaks his mind, come what may. He suspects that as a result of sexual promiscuity in the Greek camp, disease ("the Neapolitan bone-ache") will spread. (II, iii, 17-20) Achilles, whom the Greeks hold in such awe, he terms a fool. (II, iii, 60-64) And for self-serving arguments designed to rationalize repugnant activities Thersites has no patience.

THERSITES

Here is such patchery, such juggling and such knavery. All the argument is a whore and a cuckold. A good quarrel to draw emulous factions and bleed to death upon. Now the dry serpigo on the subject, and war and lechery confound all.
(II, iii, 70-74)

This line of bombast continues in Act 4.

PATROCLUS

Here comes Thersites.

ACHILLES

How, now, thou core of envy,
Thou crusty botch of nature, what's the news?

THERSITES

Why, thou picture of what thou seemest, and
idol of idiot-worshippers, here's a letter for thee.

ACHILLES

From whence, fragment?

THERSITES

Why, thou full dish of fool, from Troy.

PATROCLUS

Who keeps the tent now?

THERSITES

The surgeon's box or the patient's wound.

PATROCLUS

Well said, adversity. And what need these tricks?

THERSITES

Prithee be silent boy. I profit not by thy talk.
Thou art thought to be Achilles' male varlet.

PATROCLUS

'Male varlet', you rogue? What's that?

THERSITES

Why, his masculine whore. Now the rotten
diseases of the south, guts-griping, ruptures, catarrhs,
loads o' gravel i'th' back, lethargies, cold palsies, and
the like, take and take again such preposterous
discoveries!

Taylor and Wells provide a longer rant of Thersites from the Quarto:

Why, his masculine whore. Now the rotten
diseases of the south, the guts-griping, ruptures, loads
o' gravel in the back, lethargies, cold palsies, raw
eyes, dirt-rotten livers, wheezing lungs, bladders full of
impostume, sciaticas, lime-kilns i' th' palm, incurable

bone-ache, and the rivelled fee-simple of the tetter [skin dis-
ease],
take and take again such preposterous discoveries.
(Taylor & Wells, 776)

PATROCLUS

Why, thou damnable box of envy thou, what
mean'st thou to curse thus?

THERSITES

Do I curse thee?

PATROCLUS

Why, no, you ruinous butt, you whoreson
indistinguishable cur, no.

THERSITES

No? Why art thou then exasperate? Thou idle
immaterial skein of sleave-silk, thou green sarsenet flap
for a sore eye, thou tassel of a prodigal's purse, thou!
Ah, how the poor world is pestered with such waterflies!
Diminutives of nature.
(V, i, 3-31)

Here, of course, the argument comes full circle. We saw in *Hamlet*
that "water-fly" is a Shakespearean code word for an effeminate man. Yet
few note that in *Troilus and Cressida* in castigating Patroclus as Achilles' "male varlet," Thersites numbers him among the world's "waterflies,"
meaning, of course, the set of effeminate men. This proves conclusively
that in *Hamlet* the Prince's *sub rosa* question to Horatio intends to draw
attention to Osric's effeminacy. And given the author's close identification with the playwriting Prince Hamlet, it is beyond denial that male
same-sex intimacies are an abomination to Shakespeare.

VI. Conclusion

The foregoing discussion has not addressed same-sex relations in general, but only the male variety. Shakespeare's handling of female same-sex relations is taken up elsewhere.

Effeminacy is not a virtue. In his *Funeral Oration*, that fountainhead of pride and probity from which our western world in part derives, Pericles of Athens said, "We cultivate refinement without extravagance, knowledge without effeminacy." He was boasting. Our hardy ancestors, now lost in the mists of millennia, struggling in fields of corn and battle for their existence, had no use for weakness—or its simulacra. Before the advent of civilization, masculine strength and forwardness were universally admired. They were the very instruments of human survival. Male aggression meant safety and the ability to expand and prosper. Men could be proud of themselves as men. They had a purpose based on life itself. But, as Aristotle observes, a necessary concomitant of civilization is leisure, and with leisure come peace and softness, as days are spent less frequently in contention with the raw elements. We dwell indoors today, where women rule the roost. The appreciated man, the welcome and attractive fellow, perforce must be gentle. Today in the United States, we have seen the flight of male employees from the moribund factories to the construction industry, which itself suffered a seemingly mortal blow in 2008. Millions of carpenters, riveters and joiners lost their jobs. Can these decent outdoorsmen now squeeze into flimsy cubicles to support their families with finicky keyboards and monitors? Their masculine spirits are dashed, and their view of life has become an anti-value, an anachronism in the eyes of geeky bloggers and website designers. In the hot-house environment we have created, a real man is a stranger, clumsy and ridiculous, an unsophisticated brute, a bull in our urbane china shop. What is relentlessly advertised as progress is, in actual terms, social decay, in which the unreduced man has no function but to serve as cannon fodder in our exciting military excursions, or to mount quixotic political campaigns for handguns and automatic weapons. Televised football is a Neanderthal fantasy, a souvenir of the prehistoric past when Goths were Goths and Tamora was queen. (*Titus Andronicus*, I, i, 140) In such an artificial, fragile, micro-sized environment, natural male aggression must either be channeled outward, as leaders scheme to "busy giddy minds with foreign quarrels," (*King Henry IV*, Part Two, IV, iii, 342-343), or explode in the increasingly frequent domestic tragedies that baffle our *soi disant* experts.

Thus it is that we set a premium on effeminacy, whose arch so-phistication is so splendidly congruent with the inanities of television and the "entertainment" industry. You see, dearie, we're all "metrosex-uals" now. Haven't you heard? What could be more amusing than see-ing body-builder / action hero Arnold Schwarzenegger in a Hollywood movie playing the part of a nanny? Don't you get it? "There's the respect that makes calamity of so long life." (*Hamlet*, III, i, 70-71) When those reared in such an effete era turn to cast a wan and Lilliputian eye in the direction of Shakespeare's Rorschachian pages, what must they see if not images of themselves? That is all they know on earth, and all they need to know.

WORKS CITED:

Isaac Asimov, *Asimov's Guide to Shakespeare*, Wings Books, 1970.

Jonathan Dollimore, *Radical Tragedy,* Duke University Press, 1993.

Sky Gilbert, "A Sparrow Falls: Olivier's Feminine Hamlet," *Brief Chronicles*, Vol. I, 2009, 237.

David P. Gontar, *Hamlet Made Simple and Other Essays*, New English Review Press, 2013.

Camille Paglia, *Sexual Personae*, Vintage Books, 1991.

William Shakespeare, Complete Works, J. Bate, E. Rasmussen, The Royal Shakespeare Company, 2007.

William Shakespeare, The Complete Works, 2d Edition, G. Taylor & S. Wells, eds., Clarendon Press, Oxford, 2005. (all quotations from this text unless otherwise indicated)

Hank Whittemore, *The Monument*, Meadow Geese Press, 2005.

13

The Heart's Abundance: Seduction and Bad Faith in *The Reign of King Edward III*

"From the heart's abundance speaks the tongue"—King Edward III

*A*rguably the first literary employment of a "Freudian slip" occurs in Shakespeare's *The Reign of King Edward III*. The early part of this largely unrecognized play is concerned with protagonist Edward's love of another man's wife, the Countess Salisbury. Though he is supposed to be readying an invasion of France, he becomes so distracted by her that he has trouble concentrating on business. When the Earl of Derby attempts to report the cooperation of the Holy Roman Emperor, he is only half heard by an addled Edward.

KING EDWARD

What news with you?

AUDLEY

I have, my liege, levied those horse and foot,
According as your charge, and brought them hither.

KING EDWARD

Then let those foot trudge hence upon those horse,
According to our discharge, and be gone.

Derby, I'll look upon the Countess' mind anon.

EARL OF DERBY

The Countess' mind, my liege?

KING EDWARD

I mean the Emperor. Leave me alone.

AUDLEY (to Derby)

What is his mind?

EARL OF DERBY

Let's leave him to his humour.

KING EDWARD

Thus from the heart's abundance speaks the tongue:
'Countess' for 'Emperor' — and indeed why not?
She is as imperator over me, and I to her
Am as a kneeling vassal that observes
The pleasure or displeasure of her eye.
(Sc. 3, 29-42)

But the lapse of focus is revealing.

Like a practiced analysand, Edward understands its meaning: the Countess rules over him as might a monarch. By use of this device, Shakespeare is showing us how to read his dramatic poetry, not by taking things at face value, but by treating even minor inadvertences as symptoms of unacknowledged feelings. This principle applies across the board, not just to Edward alone. As we learn about him by hearkening to his use and misuse of language, so we can and should approach other characters in this manner, including Countess Salisbury.

King David II of Scotland has made incursions on the marches, holding Countess Salisbury hostage at Roxsburgh Castle. Both he and Sir William Douglas harbor designs on her, (Sc. 2, 42-47) but are interrupted by the approaching English army. The Countess is making use of her status and charm as a means of shielding herself from the more hasty ravishments of the foe. As the Scots flee, Edward and his peers occupy the stage, where the King is instantly smitten by her. In interpreting their dialogue the reader will understand that she is a mature and savvy woman unaware of neither her beauty nor the impact she has had on King David, Lord Douglas, and now on England's sovereign. As the Chorus in *Henry V* bids us exercise our imagination in approaching the history plays (*King Henry V*, I, i, 23-31), let us discreetly observe the Countess. As she kneels and bows before Edward, does she not reveal a calculated décolletage? (Sc. 2, 107) Again, she can hardly ignore his reaction: he is stunned. (Sc. 2, 128-136) Repeatedly she begs him to stay, which under the circumstances means to spend at least several days and nights under her roof. She makes the obligatory reference to her husband, realizing that this will have a stimulating rather than a dampening effect on the royal ardor. (Sc. 2, 121) Then follows her full invitation. Each segment should be parsed with care. Notice in particular that Edward's encomium is cast in rhyme. (Sc. 2, 128-136) Though she may not overhear what he says, her own words continue the fulsome rhyming, most unusual in this play.

COUNTESS SALISBURY

1. Let not thy presence, like the April sun,
Flatter our earth, and suddenly be done.

King Edward is compared to the sun which might warm the earth but soon vanish. If the sun is male, then must the earth in this setting be a woman. A real man does not shine on his world and vanish the next moment; for he has the power to endure, to prove himself. Use of the verb 'flatter' shows Edward that the Countess is pleased with his manner and ministrations.

2. More happy do not make our outward wall
Than thou wilt grace our inner house withal.

Readers of Shakespeare will know that he commonly treats the human body as an enclosing wall. (See, *e.g.*, *Twelfth Night*, I, i, 44-45) This concept emerges naturally from courtly speech which customarily veiled amorous references in decorous but easily deciphered terms.

"Our outward wall" would thus allude to the Countess' body. In that context, "inner house" refers to what might be termed her corporeal "privy" chamber. On the surface she says, "Don't just make the outer walls of this castle glad with your presence; enter, come inside, and grace our warm rooms with your strength and becoming appearance." A coarser but quite reasonable acceptation would be: "Don't just feast your eyes on my face and figure; come make love to me."

It should be noted too that the Countess' discourse is prefaced with the fact that she is married. So, for that matter, is Edward. The King and his court know full well that the Earl of Salisbury is off in the defense of his country, which creates a "David and Bathsheba" atmosphere. Indeed, the Countess has just fended off a "King David" (of Scotland). And isn't Bathsheba the gal who chose to take a bath on her rooftop in full view of the King? What was she thinking? The Countess is her descendant. Rather than putting on modesty and simplicity, Countess Salisbury goes out of her way to play the vamp, or, in Elizabethan language, the wanton.

> 3. Our house, my liege, is like a country swain,
> Whose habit rude, and manners blunt and plain,
> Presageth naught, yet inly beautified
> With bounty's riches and fair hidden pride.

Here there is an apparent gender switch. The Countess' house, which had been a feminine object suitable to enter and possess, now with the presence of the King of England becomes a "country swain." Is there any reader of Shakespeare who doesn't know that in Elizabethan English "country" was on occasion used as an oblique reference to the pudenda? (See, *The Tragedy of Hamlet, Prince of Denmark*, III, ii, 111-115; A similarly notorious play on words is found in *King Henry V*, III, iv, 1-55.) In fact, even "countess" can be used with the same off-color connotation. Husband Salisbury is not a "count" but an earl, while his wife is a "Countess." "Country swain" may therefore be glossed as "a virile commoner engaged in sexual intercourse." This is supported by "habit rude" and the phallic "blunt and plain." "Naught" is but a short step to "naughty" and also points to vaginal vacancy. Recall King Richard's upbraiding of Sir Robert Brackenbury in *King Richard III*:

> Naught to do with Mrs Shore? I tell thee, fellow:
> He that doth naught with her — excepting one —
> Were best to do it secretly alone.

BRACKENBURY

What one, my lord?

RICHARD GLOUCESTER

Her husband, knave. Wouldst thou betray me?
(I, i, 99-103)

"Bounty's riches" is polymorphously perverse. "Fair hidden pride" is robustly phallic.

> 4. For where the golden ore doth buried lie,
> The ground, undecked with nature's tapestry,
> Seems barren, sere, unfertile, fruitless, dry;
> And where the upper turf of earth doth boast
> His pride, perfumes and parti-coloured cost,
> Delve there and find this issue and their pride
> To spring from ordure and corruptions stied.

What's this? It seems an almost metaphysical disquisition on nature. The trope setting forth a contrast between barren surface and rich, pungent depth is extended. Though the exterior may appear dry and "unfertile," the act of "delving" will find "issue" (that is, generation) and a foundation of lush decadence. That is to say, "I appear to be plain and lacking in sensuality, but if you plumb me to my depths you will find me moist and yielding." Keep in mind that the Countess' ostensible purpose is nothing more than a perfunctory proposal that the King of England take rest in her castle. How the above words might be construed and confined to that end is hard to see. Bear in mind that within this castle is the Countess' bedroom, just as within the body of this allegedly austere woman is her sex.

> 5. But, to make up my all-too-long compare,
> These ragged walls no testimony are
> What is within, but like a cloak doth hide
> From weather's waste the under garnished pride.
> More gracious than my terms can, let thee be:
> Entreat thyself to stay a while with me.
> (Sc. 2, 149-161)

The exterior/interior theme is reiterated. The outside may be plain, but wonders within await. What could they be? Edward is solicited to tarry, not in the Salisbury manse, but "with me." A concealing "cloak" beckons for removal. This lady does everything but wink. Words and metaphors exuding a frank sexuality are put in play, a veritable orgy of sensual signifiers. And at whom is this "perfumed" stream of discourse aimed? At the man standing before her, whom she must know by his every expression and gesture is utterly dazzled by her. The Countess could hardly be more seductive without disrobing in front of him. We have here not a mere Freudian slip but a veritable down-hill slalom of innuendo. Or to shift the metaphor, she is not making a Freudian "slip" but wearing one. Her sibilant discourse makes her appear "slippery." (*The Winter's Tale*, I, ii, 275)

The interesting question—the question of the ages—is whether the Countess is speaking deliberately and is conscious of the unavoidable construction that vulnerable Edward would put on her words, or whether, as in the case of the Freudian slip, the use of these terms is somehow not actually so construed by her. Could she have missed her own meaning?

The following encounters of King Edward and this seductress have, however, a sharply contrasting tone: when approached by him for intimacy, she is shocked. One passage suffices.

KING EDWARD

I wish no more of thee than thou mayest give,
Nor beg I do not, but I rather buy —
That is, thy love; and for that love of thine
In rich exchange I tender to thee mine.

COUNTESS SALISBURY

But that your lips were sacred, good my lord,
You would profane the holy name of love.
The love you offer me you cannot give,
For Caesar owes that tribute to his queen.
That love you beg of me I cannot give,
For Sarah owes that duty to her lord.
He that doth clip or counterfeit your stamp
Shall die, my lord: and will your sacred self

Commit high treason 'gainst the king of heaven
To stamp his image in forbidden metal,
Forgetting your allegiance and your oath?
In violating marriage' sacred law
You break a greater honour then yourself:
To be a king is of a younger house
Than to be married. Your progenitor,
Sole reigning Adam o'er the universe,
By God was honoured for a married man,
But not by him anointed for a king.
It is a penalty to break your statutes,
Though not enacted with your highness' hand;
How much more to infringe the holy act
Made by the mouth of God, sealed with his hand!
I know my sovereign — in my husband's love,
Who now doth loyal service in his wars —
Doth but so try the wife of Salisbury,
Whether she will hear a wanton's tale or no.
Lest being therein guilty by my stay,
From that, not from my leige, I turn away.
(Sc. 2, 417-444)

This lecture would be all well and good had it not been preceded by effusive flirtation. The gentleman has been led on. Where are the lovely rhymes we heard before? Except in the emphatic couplet ("stay," "away") they are gone. Later, to prevent Edward's intrusions, Countess Salisbury goes so far as to threaten suicide. (Sc. 3, 165-183) Why, then, in the absence of her esteemed husband, was the lady so intent on taking into her house the ardent King of England? Why seek to draw him in with silver tones laden with erotic imagery? If courtly etiquette required a conventional gesture of hospitality, it could have been kept straightforward and to the point: "If my leige be weary of broils, he can rest himself here in our home." Period. Nothing more would have been required. While in objective terms we think her attractive, how much more fetching would Countess Salisbury would have been for us had she been blessed with the gift of artless speech, of "russet yeas and honest kersey noes"! (*Love's Labours' Lost*, V, ii, 413) Alas, she is forthright only in conflict and chastisement. Remember that King Edward at first declines the invitation to spend the night. (Sc. 2, 126-126) There was no wooing then. Considering her concern with propriety and her professed horror of infidelity, how can we account for her persistence once her offer is refused by Edward? How explain the coquettishness of her invitation?

We witness this sort of behavior in other Shakespearean heroines. For example, Isabella, the beautiful religious postulant in *Measure for Measure*, in seeking to persuade Lord Angelo to spare her brother's life, defends her chastity in language so graphic that Angelo becomes increasingly libidinous.

ANGELO

Admit no other way to save his life —
As I subscribe not that nor any other —
But, in the loss of question, that you his sister,
Finding yourself desired of such a person
Whose credit with the judge, or own great place,
Could fetch your brother from the manacles
Of the all-binding law, and that there were
No earthly mean to save him, but that either
You must lay down the treasures of your body
To this supposed, or else to let him suffer —
What would you do?

ISABELLA

As much for my poor brother as myself.
That is, were I under the terms of death,
Th' impression of keen whips I'd wear as rubies,
And strip myself to death as to a bed
That longing have been sick for, ere I'd yield
My body up to shame.
(II, iv, 88-104)

Is this, perhaps, a tad more than called for? Why not just decline? Again, the woman here is speaking to her would-be seducer, to the one professing love and need for her. (II, iv, 141) Is this the ideal moment to chat about being stripped naked, adorned with bleeding wounds resembling rubies, as one trundles off to a "bed" of death? Prominent critic Jonathan Dollimore has gone so far as to call this language pornographic. The fact is that no woman is going to use such words to preserve chastity—unless her mental condition is disintegrating.

Think of Lucrece, the victim of rape at the hands of Prince Tarquin in Shakespeare's long poem. Why in the absence of her husband does she invite the Prince into her home and share a long intimate meal with him late at night? Why, in a house heavily guarded, does she not struggle or scream? (Gontar, 206ff.)

The answer to these questions is that the human mind is complex, and what emerges superficially may not convey all that lies within, in our "heart's abundance." King Edward is asked about the Emperor, but accidentally answers referring to the Countess. The Countess Salisbury may be chaste, but speaks far too enticingly to a man she knows is lusting after her. So does Isabella in *Measure for Measure*. The behavior of Collatine's wife is congruent.

What these passages demonstrate is that powerful impulses can't easily be papered over. When we tell a simple untruth, we deceive someone. But when we try to smother our own deepest urges, we must deceive ourselves. There lies bad faith. Countess Salisbury, Isabella, and Lucrece blind themselves not merely to their own sexuality, but to the significance of their ribald utterances and conduct for men who pursue them.

The most thorough attempt in modern thought to address this syndrome is that of Jean-Paul Sartre in *Being and Nothingness*. Sartre is unique in being both a playwright and trained philosopher. His treatment of bad faith is part of a complete metaphysical system too complex to be presented here. But it may be useful to give an indication of how one of the few thinkers to tackle this sort of bad faith proceeds. It isn't suggested that Sartre answers all questions, but rather that Shakespeare and Sartre explore a little understood aspect of human life. Here is a representative section from "Patterns of Bad Faith" in *Being and Nothingness*.

Take the example of a woman who has consented to go out with a particular man for the first time. She knows very well the intentions which the man who is speaking to her cherishes regarding her. She knows also that it will be necessary sooner or later for her to make a decision. But she does not want to realize the urgency; she concerns herself only with what is respectful and discreet in the attitude of her companion. She does not apprehend this conduct as an attempt to achieve what we call 'the first approach'; that is, she does not want to see possibilities of temporal development which his conduct presents. She restricts this behavior to what is in the present; she does not wish to read in the phrases which he addresses to her anything other than their explicit meaning. If he says to her, 'I find you so attractive!' she disarms this phrase of its sexual background; she attaches to the conversation and to the behavior of the speaker, the immediate meanings, which she imagines as objective qualities. The man who is speaking to her appears to her sincere and respectful as the table is round or square, as the wall coloring is blue or gray. The qualities thus attached to the person she is listening to are in this way fixed in a permanence like that of things, which is no other than the projection of the strict present of the qualities into the temporal flux. This is because she does not quite know what she wants. She is profoundly aware of the desire which she inspires, but the desire cruel and naked would humiliate and horrify her. Yet she would find no charm in a respect which would be only respect. In order to satisfy her, there must be a feeling which is addressed wholly to her *personality* — *i.e.*, to her full freedom — and would be a recognition of her freedom. But at the same time this feeling must be wholly desire, that is, it must address her body as object. This time then she refuses to apprehend the desire for what it is; she does not even give it a name; she recognizes it only to the extent that it transcends itself toward admiration, esteem, respect and that it is wholly absorbed in the more refined forms which it produces, to the extent of no longer figuring anymore as a sort of warmth and density. But then suppose he takes her hand. This act of her companion risks changing the situation by calling for an immediate decision. To leave the hand there is to consent in herself to flirt, to engage herself. To withdraw it is to break the troubled and unstable harmony which gives the hour its charm. The aim is to postpone the moment of decision as long as possible. We know what happens next; the young woman leaves her hand there, but she *does not notice* that she is leaving it. She does not notice because it happens by chance that she is at this moment all intellect. She draws her companion up to the most lofty regions of sentimental speculation; she speaks of Life, of her life, she shows herself in her essential aspect — a personality, a consciousness. And during this time the divorce of the body from the soul is accomplished; the hand rests inert between the warm hands of her companion — neither consenting nor resisting — a thing.

We shall say that this woman is in bad faith. But we see immediately that she uses various procedures in order to maintain herself in this bad faith. She has disarmed the actions of her companion by reducing them to being only what they are; that is, existing in the mode of the in-itself. *But she permits herself to enjoy his desire*, to the extent that she will apprehend it as not being what it is, [not recognizing] its transcendence. Finally while sensing profoundly the presence of her own body, to the point of being aroused, perhaps — she realizes herself as not being her own body, and she contemplates it as though from above as a passive object to which events can happen but which can neither provoke them nor avoid them because all its possibilities are outside of it.
(Sartre, 96-98, emphasis added by Sartre, except in line starting "But she . . .")

It is clear that Shakespeare is giving dramatic form to the same phenomenon Sartre approaches in an expository manner. Countess Salisbury savors the attentions of the King of England. It would be a feather in her cap to have him stay the night and be entertained in her home. Further, it is inconceivable that she is unaware of the inclinations and passions of the men around her (Sc. 2, 1-14); she can surely see the effect she has on Edward well before he announces his desires. She is not satisfied to accept the King's refusal to spend an unspecified time as her houseguest, and reacts by using all her feminine wiles to get him to remain with her. She enjoys his enthusiasm and his flattery, yet obviously doesn't admit to herself what she is doing when she cajoles him with florid and insinuating rhetoric. The Countess Salisbury is no dull housewife. She is thrilled by her exchanges with the King of England. In Sartrean terms, "she permits herself to enjoy his desire," stokes the fire and is astonished by the heat.

The reader will also recall that in *The Winter's Tale* King Leontes could not succeed in persuading his friend Polixenes to remain with him and his wife Hermione as their guest. He agrees that she should try herself to persuade Polixenes to stay, but when she prevails and he consents to remain, Leontes is consumed with jealousy, imagining that they are having a tryst. In *King Edward III*, the Countess, like Queen Hermione, succeeds in persuading a King to sojourn a while in her home. Like Hermione, Countess Salisbury is enchanting and flirtatious, and like Polixenes, Edward consents. But Polixenes is not in love with Hermione as Edward is with the Countess. In *The Winter's Tale* the bad faith lies in Leontes and his boundless and groundless jealousy. He cannot admit that Polixenes runs away not because of alleged guilt but because Leontes commissioned Camillo his steward to murder Polixenes. Camillo discloses this to the targeted houseguest, after which they both flee. Their escape fails to prove anyone's guilt except Leontes'. Because of his gross self-deception, we can say that Leontes is up to his eyeballs in bad faith. In the case of *King Edward III*, on the other hand, the Countess plays a game of faux seduction, as though she really intended to allow Edward the intimacies for which he "delves." The truth is she relishes being the object of his intense masculine interest, and cannot admit to herself that her behavior is actually inflammatory and misleading. When, quite predictably, he presses his case, the Countess rises into the stratosphere of remonstration, hardly believing that Edward would dare be so forward, overlooking the not-so-subtle role she herself played in encouraging his advances. The plays of Shakespeare are home to many deceivers. As Catherine says in *King Henry V*, "*O bon Dieu! Les langues des hommes sont pleines de tromperies.*" (V, ii, 116-117) But equally—if not more—vexatious in Shakespeare are the self-deceivers, those who can do anything so long as they know nothing about it.

WORKS CITED:

David P. Gontar, *Hamlet Made Simple and Other Essays*, New English Review Press, 2013.

Jean-Paul Sartre, *Being and Nothingness*, Hazel Barnes, trans., Philosophical Library, 1956.

William Shakespeare, The Complete Works, 2d Ed., S. Wells, G. Taylor, eds., Oxford University Press, Clarendon, 2005.

14

On the Frontiers of Psychiatry: Ophelia and the Jailer's Daughter

Abstract

*T*his article examines common themes in a pair of Shakespeare's works, one famous (*Hamlet*), the other (*The Two Noble Kinsmen*) still largely unknown. As each features a female character who experiences a mental or emotional breakdown, they have attracted the attention of scholars and health care professionals concerned with what in the 16th and 17th centuries was called "madness." Beyond cognitive dysfunction, Ophelia and the Jailer's Daughter share other significant markers and characteristics, including imagination, youth, romantic interests, dominating fathers and absence of a female parent. Ophelia, it will be recalled, loves Prince Hamlet, and the "Jailer's Daughter" (she has no other name in the play) adores a Theban soldier named Palamon. As each of these relationships comes undone, the female partners are incapable of restoring their equanimity, descending instead into chaotic behavior and unintelligibility. Some writers have proposed that, despite their raving, both Ophelia and the Jailer's Daughter seek to somehow criticize or amend oppressive social institutions and customs which may have prompted or exacerbated their misery. To this counterintuitive reading objections are raised. Close inspection shows such psychic symptoms are not well explained as oblique messages about social and political problems, but rather represent efforts by traumatized women to shield themselves from facts too painful to be assimilated.

Familiarity with these plays is presumed. *The Two Noble Kinsmen* is derived from the *The Knight's Tale* in Chaucer, who reworked the story told by Giovanni Boccaccio in his Italian epic *Teseida delle Nozze d'Emilia.*

Exposition

1. Ophelia

What makes Ophelia lose her bearings? It is surprising how little insight is displayed in modern criticism on this point. The child of an overbearing court sycophant, she has fallen under the spell of Prince Hamlet, the supposed son of the late King. Though we are given no information, there is no hint of divorce; we must infer that Polonius is a widower. How has Ophelia been affected by this implied privation? Polonius stands resolutely opposed to her relationship with Hamlet, who is beginning to show signs of imbalance. He has stressed that her social station is far beneath Hamlet's—("Lord Hamlet is a Prince out of thy star" — II, ii, 142)—as she is a commoner, while he is a noble, and a distraught one at that. Yet Hamlet has favored her—and the match could in theory succeed. In a dramatic confrontation, Hamlet seems to fall apart right before her eyes, and he speaks to her in a grossly abusive manner. (III, i, 93-164) Yet in the very next scene, at the presentation of The Mousetrap, he can flirt with her so flagrantly in front of the entire court audience that she must find herself utterly humiliated. (III, ii, 106-122) A bit later in the same scene, Hamlet proceeds to make a fool out of her father (III, ii, 364-370) and, shortly after that, dispatches him by stabbing through the arras where Polonius is hiding in Gertrude's chamber. No sooner has Hamlet disclosed to Claudius the location of her father's remains in the most demeaning of terms (IV, iii, 19-37) than Ophelia's disintegration commences. The next time we see her, she is wandering in a dither. (IV, v) After this, she drowns, joining her unmentioned mother in death, a possible suicide. (IV, vii, 135-156)

Shakespeare gives us more than enough to grasp the meaning and causes of her madness and untimely death. For what do we expect when one's daffy boyfriend kills one's remaining parent, the man who warned us to stay away from him? Isn't this enough to send a girl over the edge?

How does the absence of a mother fit this scenario? Would she not have offered solace, counsel and reassurance to Ophelia? Might not a genuine maternal embrace have acted as a buffer between slings and arrows of outrageous fortune and her child? Even more than most of us,

Ophelia suffers a deficit of love and affection. At no time does anyone seem to embrace her and assure her that she is ok and that all will be well.

A father is not a substitute for a mother. Without the female spouse, the father-daughter relationship can assume an undesirable propinquity and intimacy, issuing in compulsive control by the isolated male parent. Love that should be directed to a wife gets deflected to the child, who is not in a position to deal with it. In the case of Polonius we find a meddling and overly directive father.

> And then I precepts gave her,
> That she should lock herself from his resort,
> Admit no messengers, receive no tokens . . . .
> (II, ii, 143-145)

It is well known that fathers who seek to govern a daughter's choice of mate are often acting out proscribed consanguineous impulses. In place of possessing the daughter, a paternally chosen surrogate may suffice. Shakespeare alludes to this, *e.g.*, when in *A Midsummer Night's Dream*, Lysander upbraids Demetrius about the interference of Hermia's father Egeus, saying: "You have her father's love, Demetrius; Let me have Hermia's. Do you marry him." (I, i, 93-94) The point is clear: the personal involvement of Egeus is felt as hyperbolical and inappropriate, signifying a paternal figure too invested in his daughter's love life. As Egeus identifies with Demetrius he can approve a match for Hermia with him. But the implications are pathological. By removing the imago of Ophelia's mother from Hamlet, Shakespeare underscores such excessive paternal inclinations. She is situated in a zone of tyranny—and danger.

At the end of the play, when Hamlet leaps after Laertes into Ophelia's grave, he wildly shouts his feelings for her:

HAMLET

> I loved Ophelia. Forty thousand brothers
> Could not, with all their quantity of love,
> Make up my sum.
> (V, i, 266-268)

But can this young genius be so obtuse as to fail to understand what's happened to her? Is it possible he's forgotten how shamefully he treated her, how he snarled and showed contempt? Doesn't he know he just ran through her father with a "bare bodkin" and left the corpse slumped in gore in Elsinore? Does he consider that she is now parentless? After hacking down Polonius, does he ever reflect how it might affect this woman for whom he professes such tender regard? Evidently not. Wouldn't our hero want to approach her and beg forgiveness? Thus the original parapraxis of the overlooked and absent mother metastasizes into the forgetting of her daughter, the woman Hamlet fancies he loved more than could forty thousand brothers. Mother, father—and then Ophelia herself—slip away, as if all had never been, sucked down in the "weeping brook" of unconsciousness. (IV, vii, 147)

Act IV, scene 5 is revealing. Ophelia's madness is first confirmed by Gertrude. Horatio informs her that Ophelia is murmuring about her father. (IV, v, 4) Ophelia sings demented ditties about a dead man and desertion by a lover. Claudius enters and comments that in her desultory utterances Ophelia is bewailing her father's death, (IV, v, 44) yet in his mindlessness asks Gertrude "How long hath she been thus?" (IV, v, 66) "O, this is the poison of deep grief!" he exclaims. "It springs all from her father's death." (IV, v, 74-75) With everyone aware that Ophelia is beside herself at the loss of her father at the hands of the young man whom Claudius calls "my son," no one can muster a syllable of sympathy for her. No one speaks to her of her trauma. This conspiracy of silence is as damaging as the injuries she has undergone. But the mouths of Gertrude and Claudius are sealed by guilt. Were they to say anything, too much of the truth would come tumbling out.

Here is Gertrude's revealing soliloquy as she awaits the appearance of Ophelia.

GERTRUDE

To my sick soul, as sin's true nature is,
Each toy seems prologue to some great amiss.
So full of artless jealousy is guilt,
It spills itself in fearing to be spilt.
(IV, v. 17-20)

Fully half the riches of Shakespeare lie in nuggets like this.

Madness in his plays is often represented as the horrified soul's flight from realities too painful to be acknowledged. Putting aside arid, hair-splitting debates about whether Ophelia is "insane" or not (which mimic the equally vacuous arguments about Hamlet's own insanity), we can acknowledge that the freight of agonies weighing down on Ophelia is crushing. Can the man who loved her more than forty thousand brothers and wooed her with affection, gifts and poetry be the same chap who curses her to her face ("Get thee to a nunnery") and then butchers her father? The court is indeed a wilderness of tigers, and not a single individual comes forward to commiserate with her, perhaps the unkindest cut of all. It would be surprising under such circumstances if she did not become unmoored.

2. The Jailer's Daughter

It is now generally conceded that it is the picaresque subplot of the Jailer's Daughter that carries the action of *The Two Noble Kinsmen* forward. The love-hate relationship of Palamon and Arcite is a stiff tableau which requires the raw energy of subalterns to attain its ironical end. In the main plot, two curiously fey Theban warriors (forerunners of the Sacred Band of Thebes) are captured in battle by Duke Theseus. Lodged in a cell in Athens they spy from their window the young and dazzling Amazon Emilia and are inexplicably smitten by her, leading to armed struggle for her favors. Each has his own tutelary deity. The patron of the chaste Emilia is, of course, Diana (the principal deity of the Shakespearean pantheon). Arcite prays to Mars for victory, while Palamon is protected by Venus. In the final battle, personally choreographed by Theseus, Arcite defeats Palamon. But as each god has its prerogatives, the ultimate triumph is a compromise or mixed blessing. Thrown from his prancing steed, Arcite is wounded and dies. Thus Emilia, who had prayed to Diana to continue in her chaste band, is awarded to Palamon as his shaken bride. Venus prevails.

In the midst of these preposterous goings-on we meet the Jailer's Daughter, who tends the prisoners in their confinement. Like Ophelia, this nameless teenager has no mother, and, like Ophelia, she goes berserk. The proximate cause is her gratuitous desire for Palamon, whom she worships as god on earth—though he is barely distinguishable from his cousin-in-arms. And, like warriors bleeding in armed combat, modern critics have in argument over this child's amour spilled their precious ink, largely in vain.

In the iconography of *The Two Noble Kinsmen*, two goddesses contend, Venus and Diana. Emilia represents Diana; the Daughter's passionate craving for Palamon recalls the boundless desire of Venus for Adonis as set forth at length by Shakespeare in his best-selling poem of 1593. And as Venus' ardor for the narcissistic lad is not gratified, neither is the Jailer's Daughter's love for Palamon returned. The difference is that mortal Adonis is beneath Venus (in every sense), while noble Palamon towers above the plebian Daughter.

In this narrative, we have the Jailer taking the part of the manipulative Polonius. He has arranged for yet another nameless character, the Wooer, to marry his daughter. In flight from destiny, the Jailer's Daughter latches on to the resplendent Palamon. Unfortunately, she is barred from her hope, not, as in the case of Ophelia, by her beloved's growing dementia, but by the fact that Palamon is wholly infatuated with another woman, the demigoddess Emilia. His commitment to winning her is the absolute which the passion of the Jailer's Daughter reprises. And the crux of the matter is that Palamon's ardor for that other woman is at no time acknowledged, discussed or considered by the Jailer's Daughter. As a submerged taboo, the realization that Palamon is entirely and forever unavailable cannot be digested. The rival woman, a necessary blank, recapitulates that other *tabula rasa* in her mind, her seemingly forgotten mother, whose absence places her squarely in the possession of her father, the appropriately denominated "Jailer."

As one scans the text, it is hard to see how the Daughter cannot perceive that Palamon is preoccupied with Emilia. As long as they are in their cell together, Arcite and Palamon are feuding over her, threatening one another, and waiting for the opportunity to engage in armed combat for her, never once considering whether their claims over her would be welcomed. Does the Daughter not attend on them and learn what's going on?

Let us listen to the silly colloquy and subsequent falling out of these sententious soldiers, and then reflect on the significance of the Daughter's characterization of their plight.

ARCITE

Yet, cousin,
Even from the bottom of these miseries,
From all that fortune can inflict upon us,
I see two comforts rising — two mere blessings,
If the gods please, to hold here a brave patience
And the enjoying of our griefs together.

Whilst Palamon is with me, let me perish
If I think this our prison.

PALAMON

Certainly, 'tis a main goodness, cousin, that our fortunes
Were twined together. 'Tis most true, two souls
Put in two noble bodies, let 'em suffer
The gall of hazard, so they grow together,
Will never sink; they must not, say they could.
A willing man dies sleeping and all's done.

ARCITE

Shall we make worthy uses of this place
That all men hate so much?

PALAMON

How, gentle cousin?

ARCITE

Let's think this prison holy sanctuary,
To keep us from corruption of worse men.
We are young, and yet desire the ways of honour
That liberty and common conversation,
The poison of pure spirits, might, like women,
Woo us to wander from. What worthy blessing
Can be, but our imaginations
May make it ours? And here being thus together,
We are an endless mine to one another:
We are one another's wife, ever begetting
New births of love; we are father, friends, acquaintance;
We are in one another, families —
I am your heir, and you are mine; this place
Is our inheritance: no hard oppressor
Dare take this from us. Here, with a little patience,
We shall live long and loving. No surfeits seek us —
The hand of war hurts none here, nor the seas

Swallow their youth. Were we at liberty
A wife might part us lawfully, or business;
Quarrels consume us; envy of ill men
Crave our acquaintance. I might sicken, cousin,
Where you should never know it, and so perish
Without your noble hand to close mine eyes,
Or prayers to the gods. A thousand chances,
Were we from hence, would sever us.

PALAMON

You have made me —
I thank you, cousin Arcite — almost wanton
With my captivity. What a misery
It is to live abroad, and everywhere!
'Tis like a beast, methinks. I find the court here;
I am sure, a more content; and all those pleasures
That woo the wills of men to vanity
I see through now, and am sufficient
To tell the world 'tis but a gaudy shadow,
That old Time, as he passes by, takes with him.
(II, ii, 55-104)

PALAMON (contd.)

Is there record of any two that loved
Better than we two, Arcite?

ARCITE

Sure there cannot.

PALAMON

I do not think it possible our friendship
Should ever leave us.

ARCITE

Til our deaths it cannot.

(II, ii, 112-115)

And it is at the very apogee of this absurd and delusive rapture that Palamon—and then Arcite—notice Emilia strolling in the garden below with her maid.

Instantly these two male lovers who have just declared their eternal bond with one another are at each other's throats.

PALAMON

What think you of this beauty?

ARCITE

'Tis a rare one.

PALAMON

Is't but a rare one?

ARCITE

Yes, a matchless beauty.

PALAMON

Might not a man well lose himself and love her?

ARCITE

I cannot tell what you have done; I have,
Beshrew my eyes for't. Now I feel my shackles.

PALAMON

You love her then?

ARCITE

Who would not?

PALAMON

And desire her?

ARCITE

Before my liberty.

PALAMON

I saw her first.

ARCITE

That's nothing.

PALAMON

But it shall be.

ARCITE

I saw her too.

PALAMON

Yes, but you must not love her.

ARCITE

I will not, as you do, to worship her
As she is heavenly and a blessed goddess!
I love her as a woman, to enjoy her —
So both may love.

PALAMON

You shall not love at all.

ARCITE

Not love at all — who shall deny me?

PALAMON

I that first saw her, I that took possession
First with mine eye of all those beauties
In her revealed to all mankind. If thou lov'st her,
Or entertain'st a hope to blast my wishes,
Thou art a traitor, Arcite, and a fellow
False as thy title to her. Friendship, blood,
And all the ties between us I disclaim,
If thou once think upon her.

ARCITE

Yes, I love her —
And if the lives of all my name lay on it,
I must do so. I love her with all my soul —
If that will lose ye, farewell, Palamon!
(II, ii, 153-180)

Now it is precisely this situation which confronts the Jailer's Daughter hour by tedious hour as she tends this pair in her housekeeping rounds. Of this she gives ample testimony.

JAILER'S DAUGHTER

These strewings are for their chamber.
'Tis a pity they are in prison, and 'twere a pity they should
be out. I do think they have the patience to make any
adversity ashamed; the prison itself is proud of 'em,
and they have all the world in their chamber.

JAILER

They are famed to be a pair of absolute men.

JAILER'S DAUGHTER

By my troth, I think fame but stammers
'em — they stand a grece above the reach of report.

JAILER

I have heard them reported in the battle to be the only doers.

JAILER'S DAUGHTER

Nay, most likely, for they are noble
sufferers. I marvel how they would have looked had
they been victors, that with such a constant nobility
enforce a freedom out of bondage, making misery their
mirth, and affliction a toy to jest at.

JAILER

Do they so?

JAILER'S DAUGHTER

It seems to me they have no more
sense of their captivity than I of ruling Athens. They
eat well, look merrily, discourse of many things, but
nothing of their own restraint and disasters. Yet
sometime a divided sigh — martyred as 'twere i'th'
deliverance — will break from one of them, when the
other presently gives it so sweet a rebuke that I could
wish myself a sigh to be so chid, or at least a sigher
to be comforted.
(I, iv, 21-45)

In other words, the Jailer's Daughter is well acquainted with these
fellows. The very ambience of their relationship, the surreal strategy
they concoct, are as familiar to her as her own garter. What is that "divided sigh" that breaks forth from these jealous souls if not the emblem
of their enmity? And yet, she seems entirely unaware that both these
dreamers are completely captivated by Emilia. Is that plausible? How

could she know so much, yet so little about the man at the very center of her universe?

JAILER'S DAUGHTER

Why should I love this gentleman? 'Tis odds
He will never affect me. I am base,
My father the mean keeper of his prison,
And he a prince.
(II, iv, 1-4)

He has as much to please a woman in him —
If he please to bestow it so — as ever
These eyes yet looked on. Next, I pitied him,
And so would any young wench, o'my conscience,
That ever dreamed or vowed her maidenhead
To a young handsome man. Then I loved him,
Extremely loved him, infinitely loved him . . . .
(II, iii, iv, 9-15)

And so it is that this eros-obsessed young lady uses her access to the prison to help Palamon escape, only to find that, once freed, he shows no interest in her. Though she has told him to meet her behind a sedge, he fails to appear. For this she has not a glimmer of an explanation.

JAILER'S DAUGHTER

He has mistook the brake I meant, is gone
After his fancy. 'Tis now well nigh morning.
No matter — would it were perpetual night,
And darkness lord o'th' world. Hark, 'tis a wolf!
In me hath grief slain fear, and, but for one thing,
I care for nothing — and that's Palamon.
I reck not if the wolves would jaw me, so
He had this file. What if I hollered for him?
If he not answered, I should call a wolf
And do him but that service. I have heard
Strange howls this livelong night — why may't not be
They have made a prey of him? He has no weapons;
He cannot run; the jangling of his gyves

Might call fell things to listen, who have in them
A sense to know a man unarmed, and can
Smell where resistance is. I'll set it down
He's torn to pieces: they howled many together
And then they fed on him. So much for that.
Be bold to ring the bell. How stand I then?
All's chared when he is gone. No, no, I lie:
My father's to be hanged for his escape,
Myself to beg, if I prized life so much
As to deny my act — but that I would not,
Should I try death by dozens. I am moped —
Food took I none these two days,
Sipped some water. I have not closed mine eyes
Save when my lids scoured off their brine. Alas,
Dissolve, my life; let not my sense unsettle,
Lest I should drown or stab or hang myself.
O state of nature, fail together in me,
Since thy best props are warped. So which way now?
The best way is the next way to a grave,
Each errant step beside is torment. Lo,
The moon is down, the crickets chirp, the screech-owl
Calls in the dawn. All offices are done
Save what I fail in: but the point is this,
An end, and that is all.
(III, ii, 1-38)

This way madness lies, of course. But what set us on this track towards ultima Thule? Willful ignorance, apparently. What woman, intrigued by a man, fails to inquire about his marital or relational status? Is Palamon married? The Jailer's Daughter never wonders. Is he betrothed? Involved? A committed bachelor? Pining after someone else? Uninterested in the opposite sex? Questions unasked cannot be answered. Yet we must inquire: Why would a woman switch off her radar and sail into a cliff of indifference—or repugnance—unless there were something she dimly suspected but didn't want to confront? The Jailer's Daughter has already revealed to us in her conversation with her father that when it comes to Palamon and Arcite she has a fearful intuition; she has divined the very essence of their life and relationship. She has heard their "divided sighs." What makes them divided, these two who are so unprecedentedly close to one another? What might the Jailer's Daughter see in that dark abysm of a man's brain from which she would perforce avert her gaze? What else, if not a Woman? Let it be thought I am too low in social station. Let that be the explanation for why he could never be mine. At least with matters of rank exceptions and alterations might be made. After all, did not "the Lady of the Strachey marr[y] the yeoman of the wardrobe"? (*Twelfth Night*, II, v, 37-38) Aboard the *H.M.S. Pinafore*, love can level ranks, and therefore, one has a fighting chance. But if the obstacle should turn out to be a heart brimming with love of another, a competitor whose beauty and demeanor threaten to eclipse the sun, the predicament is hopeless and the entire fantasy comes crashing down around a maiden's ears. This must not be seen, not admitted. And in fact, as a worker in the municipal administration of Athens, the Jailer's Daughter is well aware of Emilia, and in her interminable blabber as the play winds down actually mentions her. (IV, iii, 12) What to do, then, with this toxic specter of that other woman, as unsettling as Sylvia's portrait was to Julia? (*The Two Gentlemen of Verona*, V, ii, 195-202) As with Ophelia, there is a convenient site, which is the place where that absent and unmentionable woman dwells who is the Daughter's Mother. Conceal the "other woman" there and she is just a blank. But, of course, once she is effectively repressed, there is no longer any reasonable or rational explanation why such a man, given the signal, would not at least play the rogue. For despite their pious rhetoric, both Palamon and Arcite are experienced womanizers. They are accustomed to boasting of their conquests. (See, III, iii, 28-38) In that case, madness and suicidal ideation were merely postponed, not avoided. When self-deception fizzles, we have only lunacy to protect us from the less flattering aspects of life. Tennessee Williams' Blanche DuBois is fashioned of the same fraying cloth.

However, unlike Ophelia, who does perish as a passive suicide, the Jailer's Daughter survives. In her distraction it becomes possible for her to accept the Wooer as "Palamon." As her condition is utterly broken otherwise, this ruse is acceptable to her father, who promoted the Wooer all along. So far as the audience can tell, this Wooer and the Jailer's Daughter become a couple, under the pretence that the man is Palamon. It is interesting to note that *The Two Noble Kinsmen* contains Shakespeare's most detailed presentation of the treatment of mental illness. Unlike Ophelia, the Jailer's Daughter has a physician (though she seems unaware of him—he advises the Jailer and the Wooer). The reader will recall there was a doctor in *Macbeth* too. He admits that Lady Macbeth exhibits a strange somnambulism, but confesses: "This disease is beyond my practice." (V, i, 56) King Macbeth challenges him.

> Canst thou not minister to a mind diseased,
> Pluck from the memory a rooted sorrow,
> Raze out the written troubles of the brain,
> And with some sweet oblivious antidote
> Cleanse the fraught bosom of that perilous stuff
> Which weighs upon her heart?

To which the physician replies,

> Therein the patient must minister to himself.
> (V, iii, 42-48)

The doctor in *The Two Noble Kinsmen*, however, is made of sterner stuff, though at the outset he echoes his colleague in *Macbeth*: "I think she has a perturbed mind, which I cannot minister to." (IV, iii, 56) Shortly thereafter, however, we hear one of the most extraordinary prescriptions in annals of psychiatry. Informed that prior to her obsession with Palamon, the Daughter was engaged to the Wooer, who still cares and yearns for her, and is willing to do anything to help and possess her, the doctor gives this advice.

DOCTOR

> That intemperate surfeit of her eye hath
> distempered the other senses. They may return and settle
> again to execute their preordained faculties, but they
> are now in a most extravagant vagary. This you must
> do: confine her to a place where the light may rather
> seem to steal in than be permitted; take upon you,
> young sir her friend, the name of Palamon; say you
> come to eat with her and to commune of love. This
> will catch her attention, for this her mind beats upon —
> other objects that are inserted 'tween her mind and
> eye become the pranks and friskins of her madness.
> Sing to her such green songs of love as she says
> Palamon hath sung in prison; come to her stuck in as
> sweet flowers as the season is mistress of, and thereto
> make an addition of some other compounded odours

which are grateful to the sense. All this shall become
Palamon, for Palamon can sing, and Palamon is sweet
and every good thing. Desire to eat with her, carve
her, drink to her, and still intermingle your
petition of grace and acceptance into her favour. Learn
what maids have been her companions and playfreres,
and let them repair to her, with Palamon in their
mouths, and appear with tokens as if they suggested
for him. It is a falsehood she is in, which is with
falsehoods to be combated. This may bring her to eat,
to sleep, and reduce what's now out of square in her
into their former law and regiment. I have seen it
approved, how many times I know not, but to make
the number more I have great hope in this. I will
between the passages of this project come in with my
appliance. Let us put it in execution, and hasten the
success, which doubt not will bring forth comfort.
(IV, iii, 67-98)

In other Shakespeare plays such a device would be termed a "bed-trick." But the doctor's objective is different, as it is therapeutic and aims at a change in the patient. Here the person duped is the woman, not the man, as we find in *All's Well That Ends Well* (Bertram) and *Measure for Measure* (Angelo). More importantly, the purpose in the instant case is not to gain advantage over someone by deceit but to actually minister to a mind diseased and restore as much functioning as possible, in the hope of establishing a viable relationship.

Although it is plain that this treatment has a sexual dimension, it is equally evident that it is not a coarse regimen of sex, or a crude attempt to cure hysteria or psychosis through lubricity. What is sought, rather, is the fostering of an atmosphere of emotional intimacy which may or may not issue in sexual activity. In other words, though the doctor's treatment plan contemplates the prospect of a physical consummation, to describe the remedy as "sex" is no more accurate than thinking reductively of marriage as intercourse. What the doctor recommends is the creation of a relationship of trust, security and love, not mere copulation. In that respect, it bears resemblance to the psychotherapeutic environment. If she wants to hear you sing, advises the doctor, sing for her. (V, iii, 13-14) "You should observe her every way," he counsels. (V, iii, 14) And so the Wooer, disguised as Palamon, and the Jailer's Daughter, prepare to spend the night together. As Act V, scene 4 unfolds, the Jailer's Daughter, reassured by the Wooer's gentle demeanor and obvious love for her, finds the courage to express her wish for physical gratification. (V, v, 88; V, v, 110) This is then immediately connected by her to marriage and raising a family. "We shall have many children," she declares with evident satisfaction. (V, v, 94)

The final dialogue is poignant and positive.

WOOER (to the Jailer's Daughter)

Come, sweet, we'll go to dinner,
And then we'll play at cards.

JAILER'S DAUGHTER

And shall we kiss too?

WOOER

A hundred times.

JAILER'S DAUGHTER

And twenty.

WOOER

Ay, and twenty.

JAILER'S DAUGHTER

And then we'll sleep together.

DOCTOR (to the Wooer)

Take her offer.

WOOER (to the Jailer's Daughter)

Yes, marry, will we.

JAILER'S DAUGHTER

But you shall not hurt me.

WOOER

I will not, sweet.

JAILER'S DAUGHTER

If you do, love, I'll cry.

The reader may compare the treatment regimen in *The Two Noble Kinsmen* with the medical counsel in *The History of King Lear* (Quarto edition), Sc. 21, 13-80. The Jailer's Daughter, then, is more fortunate than sad Ophelia, who finds herself totally isolated in the cruel court of King Claudius. She has no loving suitor and no social safety net, complete with medical staff, to rescue her, as does the Jailer's Daughter. As such, she is lost. Considering the tenderness of the Wooer, coupled with the support of the Jailer and the family physician, even though it seems at the conclusion of many Shakespearean comedies that the festive unions cannot endure in light of past trauma, in this case we can offer a cautiously favorable prognosis. Of course we do not know exactly whom the Daughter thinks she is marrying. To assert that it is "Palamon" may be a tad naïve. But it is plainly the doctor's reasonable hope that as the visage of the Wooer gradually replaces that of Palamon, the Daughter may learn that genuine love carries with it a greater chance of happiness than the fantasy of stealing a foolish god from his elusive goddess.

Argument

3. The Voice of Literary Criticism

It is instructive to examine the way in which these two characters are approached by the academic literary establishment. We will entertain views which emanate from the University of Chicago, and also from a workshop "Reading Women and Madness in Medical, Dramatic and Visual Texts" sponsored by the symposium "Attending to Women in Early Modern England," held at the Center for Renaissance and Baroque Studies at the University of Maryland, College Park, 8-9 November, 1990.

The writer is Michelle Erica Green, M.A. Her article cited above, "Mythogyny: Madness and Medicine in Hamlet and The Two Noble-Kinsmen" appears online. Ms. Green's Notes and Works Cited provide a comprehensive and thorough overview of the scholarly literature on the subject.

After providing some historical background on women's emotional illnesses in the 16th and 17th centuries, as well as taking account of certain theological and political writings, Green turns to our most renowned literary treasure, *The Tragedy of Hamlet, Prince of Denmark*. As Laertes and Hamlet leap into Ophelia's grave, let us leap in *medias res* into Green's discussion.

What we find is an interpretation of Ophelia as a socially oppressed young Elizabethan female who feigns madness in order to deliver subtle comments on court intrigue and politics in Denmark. She is not concerned with her never-mentioned mother or murdered father, but with the transmission of encrypted editorials. In the scene in question, Ophelia makes her first appearance since seeing the production of "The Mousetrap" which dramatized the killing of Gonzago. It was then that Hamlet had treated her so disrespectfully in front of the royal family. Ophelia then disappears momentarily. The next significant event is the Closet Scene, in which Hamlet excoriates his mother and in the process kills Polonius in her room, Act III, scene 4. Claudius in Act IV, scene 3, extracts from Hamlet the location of Polonius' body. But there is no funeral or ceremony, no formal burial or anything of that nature. There is thus no reliable way in which grieving can occur. The chief advisor to the King departs without mourners or remembrances. Claudius seizes on the violent death of Polonius to order Hamlet to his pre-arranged doom in England. (IV, iii, 39-45) And in the very next substantial scene Ophelia returns, having just learned of her father's untimely demise. She is in shock.

What say the scholars?

The Gentleman, Horatio, and the Queen fear Ophelia's sanity more than her madness. The Gentleman prefers his belief that her words make no sense to the alternative conclusion, that she intends the interpretations her listeners draw. Her inchoate speech makes it difficult for him to tell. That her free-wheeling signifiers could lead to damage to the rulers' reputations is made clear through Horatio's suggestion that

'Twere good she were spoken with, for she may strew / Dangerous conjectures in ill-breeding minds. The queen [now lower case 'q'] seems certain that Ophelia wants something of her, at first refusing to admit her [!], then asking what Ophelia would "have." Ophelia's wanton sexual displays may recall the queen to her own lusts and guilt, but the girl's symbolic potential alone cannot account for the queen's nervousness. Rather, Gertrude seems to dread another verbal attack on her character like Hamlet's at III, iv.

It is thus stated as a plain fact by Ms. Green that Horatio is afraid that Ophelia is sane. But that bizarre statement is not supported by the text, nor by what he says. What he says is that she is "importunate" and "distraught," and "will needs be pitied." He then declares that Ophelia speaks much of her father. (IV, v, 4). Not surprising, is it? But what *is* surprising is that Michelle Green would attribute Gertrude's words to Horatio. For it is not Horatio but Gertrude who utters: 'Twere good she were spoken with, for she may strew / Dangerous conjectures in ill-breeding minds." (IV, v, 14-15) It is true that in some nineteenth century editions of the play this line was attributed to Horatio, but for him it makes no sense, and in both the standard RSC edition and in Taylor and Wells, the line clearly belongs to Gertrude. Worse, Green introduces a new character, the "Gentleman," to whom she attributes the entirety of Horatio's eleven line speech. (IV, iii, 4-15) Yet no "gentleman" appears until the messenger arrives with news of Laertes' arrival and fomented rebellion. (IV, v, 97-106) If a scholar wanted to lay emphasis on a certain line which most authoritative editions give to Gertrude, it is her fundamental responsibility to discuss the situation and explain to the reader why she attributes the line to Horatio. But there is no clue in the subject article that the author is aware of any textual discrepancy at all.

Gertrude fears Ophelia in her madness, not her supposed "sanity." Recall that it was in her son's rage in her bedroom, remonstrating with her, that he slew Ophelia's father. That is the guilt Gertrude feels. Psychotics are frequently glib and loquacious and liable to say anything. Gertrude's fear, then, is that a babbling Ophelia may possibly go about Denmark blurting out that her son Hamlet is behaving crazily in Elsinore and has just assassinated the avuncular figure of Polonius. In fact, the people, with Laertes, are already up in arms about this and supporting Laertes as their new leader. This is why Claudius has just commanded Hamlet to depart for England, the rationale being that it is for his own safety. Gertrude does not know that her husband has arranged for her son's death in England. Furthermore, Ophelia has no information about any murder of old King Hamlet the Dane, and can hardly be understood to be sending camouflaged messages in a false madness to comment on Claudius' crime. And as most commentators do not associate Gertrude with the poisoning of her spouse, what guilt over that deed might Gertrude have? For Michelle Green, Ophelia is not a wretched young lady who has lost a father through a bloody crime perpetrated by her own lover, but rather a befuddled automaton spitting out "free-wheeling signifiers" related to questions no one raises about the royal succession, primogeniture, paternal authority and other aspects of Elizabethan culture.

> Claudius wants to pass off Ophelia's behavior as brooding about her father's death — thus displacing *his own guilt* onto Hamlet, Polonius' killer — but she refuses to have her distress attributed to this cause, demanding, "Pray let's have no more of this." (4. 5. 46, emphasis added).

First of all, Claudius' words, "Conceit upon her father," which appear to draw forth Ophelia's objection, are an aside to Gertrude. (IV, v, 44) Ophelia cannot be presumed to have heard them.

Horatio tells us before Ophelia enters that she is wailing about her father. She is not "brooding" about her father's death, but is in the throes of grief so severe it is trenching on hysteria. "Brooding" is a word better applied to Hamlet in Act I, whose rumination over his own father's death is tied in with his uneasy sense that something is amiss in Denmark. But there is a new King on the throne treating him with kindness, and he has no idea his supposed father has been murdered. There is no evidence that Claudius is trying to "pass off his guilt" to Hamlet since no one except Hamlet and Horatio know what Claudius has done, and Ophelia is well aware of Hamlet's responsibility for her father's death.

> Claudius then tries to press Ophelia to become her former self, but she refuses to become the "pretty lady" he wishes to see, bursting instead into an uncourtly song about a maid losing her virginity. As David Leverenz argues, her bawdy song may criticize the mixed messages Ophelia has been receiving from Claudius, Polonius, and Hamlet about what kind of woman she ought to be; her words offer implicit crit-

icism of all the love relationships she has witnessed, which label women either bawds or passive models of chastity.

The problem with feminist criticism is that it becomes a kind of literary cosmetics, far more interested in its own tropes and strained ideological agenda than the texts it takes up to exploit. If Ophelia had any knowledge of Claudius' murder of his brother the King, and sought to convey coded commentary on that, why would she sing an "uncourtly" song about a maid losing her virginity? Is Ophelia in a state of grief over a slaughtered father or is she engaged in the "criticism" of social mores in Denmark's upper social echelons? She is not a doctoral candidate at an Ivy League academy penning a thesis on the treatment of women in Scandinavian countries. A few hours ago her only parent was hacked down by the man who was wooing her so ardently before he returned to Wittenberg. The King has recovered the body and hastily cast it in the earth (IV, v, 82). Are there not reasons for her tears and despair? They are plainly reiterated in the anger displayed by Laertes when he comes home from France. As for sex, we must ask again, are Ophelia's songs theoretical indictments of male hegemony—or expressions of personal distress? The note of bawdry was struck by Prince Hamlet personally the last time we saw Ophelia, at the performance of "The Mousetrap." What did he say?

QUEEN GERTRUDE

Come hither, my good Hamlet. Sit by me.

HAMLET

No, good-mother, here's mettle more attractive.
(He sits by Ophelia)

Polonius (aside)

O ho, do you mark that?

HAMLET (to Ophelia)

Lady, shall I lie in your lap?

OPHELIA

No, my lord.

HAMLET

I mean my head upon your lap.

OPHELIA

Ay, my lord.

HAMLET

Do you think I meant country matters?

OPHELIA

I think nothing, my lord.

HAMLET

That's a fair thought to lie between a maid's legs.

OPHELIA

What is, my lord?

HAMLET

Nothing.

OPHELIA

You are merry, my lord.
(III, ii, 104-116, following the RSC edition)

Now we hear Ophelia in extremis descanting on the theme of a lass betrayed by a man who has taken her virginity. Is this dispassionate social criticism or an outpouring of feelings about herself? Can we not detect Prince Hamlet humming in the background? At "The Mouse-trap" Hamlet drew unseemly and unexpected attention to his affair with Ophelia, the girl who angered him so recently by trying to break up with him. (III, i, 95-97) Now their liaison, lying in uneasy suspension, is suddenly ruptured by his killing of Polonius. What must her feelings be now? No attention to any of this is paid by Michelle Green. But the issue is significant. What evidence is there that Ophelia has not already yielded herself to the Prince of Denmark? None. If that was not a re-alistic prospect, why did she receive admonitions from her father and brother to resist his advances? If she and Hamlet engaged in sexual rela-tions, would she advertise this to her father? No, he would have no way of knowing. Thus the songs Ophelia sings in her delusive state about a maid being wronged point squarely at herself and the betrayal she has experienced at Hamlet's hands, a betrayal we can see emerging in his disgraceful behavior towards her at "The Mousetrap." For the frankness of his sexual mockery implies intimate contact between them, and he is in subtle form humiliating her on account of her attempted abandon-ment of him.

Green then states that Hamlet has "fled the court, much to his mother's chagrin." What could this mean? Everyone knows he's being shipped to England on the rationale that his homicide might trigger a reaction amongst the people. His nonchalance when interrogated by an angry monarch about the whereabouts of the body reflects a complete lack of interest in "fleeing" anything.

> Ophelia's parting speech to Claudius sounds quite sane —
> dangerously sane. She worries about a 'him' whom 'they
> would lay . . . i' th' cold ground.' Even if she refers to the
> dead 'true love' of the first song and not an actual person, her
> words recall the murdered king and the conspiracy against
> Hamlet's life engineered by Claudius. She warns that her
> brother will be told 'of it' — though whether the 'it' refers
> to an actual plot or an imagined one is unclear — and exits
> thanking them for their counsel.

The magnitude of such misunderstanding suggests the delusion lies in the critical exegesis, not the character being scrutinized. Clau-dius has rushed "hugger-mugger" to unceremoniously dump the body of Polonius in a nameless pit, (IV, v, 82) something of which Ophelia is painfully aware. "I cannot choose but to weep to think they should lay him in' th' cold ground" means, "I weep to think you bury my father bereft of any fitting rites." Can anything be more purblind than the failure to apprehend this? The "it" which Green finds so mystifying is the death of Polonius, an inference any fourth grader could accomplish. And her brother is indeed told of "it" and reacts as one might expect.

LAERTES

O thou vile king,
Give me my father.

QUEEN GERTRUDE

Calmly, good Laertes.

LAERTES

That drop of blood that's calm proclaims me bastard,
Cries cuckold to my father, brands the harlot
Even here between the chaste unsmirched brow
Of my true mother.
(IV, v, 114-118)

[Here is the one oblique reference to the presumed mother of Ophelia.]

CLAUDUIS

What is the cause, Laertes,
That thy rebellion looks so giant-like? —
Let him go, Gertrude. Do not fear our person.
There's such divinity doth hedge a king
That treason can but peep to what it would,
Acts little of his will. — Tell me, Laertes,
Why thou art thus incensed. — Let him go, Gertrude. —
Speak, man.

LAERTES

Where is my father?

CLAUDIUS

Dead.
(IV, v, 119-126)

What is true of Laetres is true of his sister. Their principal and shared concern is their father's fate. Ophelia's situation only differs in its complexity, for she has been affianced to the man who killed their father, and thus her lamentations are filled with anguish over her treatment at the hands of his slayer, Hamlet.

Green's conclusion sounds as though it was composed by a politically-minded space alien unacquainted with literature and life on Planet Earth.

> Ophelia is the only character who directly challenges the gender system, both through her words and through the transgressive act of theatrical madness. Her demise, more than any other event, indicates that something is rotten in the state of Denmark beyond the regal crises of the moment. Something is rotten in the body of Denmark, where sexuality and corruption cannot be separated.

To this we might reply, Ophelia is a major character in Shakespeare who undergoes most egregious losses and injuries. She is not well understood as a crypto-suffragette, or undergraduate victim of date rape at Harvard, but as a vulnerable girl destroyed by a court bastard (Hamlet) and his lethal adversaries. Her madness is the consequence of having been compelled to reject the most dazzling courtier of Europe, who wooed her with all his eloquence, and then most likely seduced her, and embarrassed her publicly at the court theater. This he followed by murdering her father. As there is no reconciling the love and hate in her heart, Ophelia's inner equilibrium, her very sense of self, is destroyed. Thus she perishes.

We can now turn briefly to Ms. Green's exposition of *The Two Noble Kinsmen*. She contends unpersuasively that while Ophelia's madness is a mere mask, the Jailer's Daughter is indeed crazy. The challenge is to find the cause, and thus the meaning. As there are many species of mental illness it isn't easy to base a diagnosis on a mere reading of a work of fiction. Ms. Green, however, is undaunted. She earnestly assures us on the basis of literary commentaries she has perused that the Jailer's

Daughter has lost her mind. The reason is in plain sight: she wants to be more highly placed in society and fails. Why isn't this category in Psychiatry's DSM-5? We could call it "Social Status Adjustment Disorder," and make the appropriate psycho-pharmacological recommendations. The problem is, there isn't any such thing, and if there are any other cases of psychosis induced by a lack of social standing or prestige, Ms. Green isn't telling us about them. What then is the evidence for her claim?

Here's what we're given.

1. Paul Bertram recognizes that her will to rise above her station, rather than an inexplicable lust for Palamon, is the real source of her madness.

2. She rejects not love but the social frame which constrains it. This behavior takes her outside not only society but also the self-structure around her gender, class and familial role — which interacts with that society.

3. As Richard Abrams describes her decision, 'Craving the glamour of association with a gentleman too dear for her possession, the Daughter, fallen from both sexual and social innocence, hopes to raise her status by venturing boldly.'

Here are the problems.

1. First there is zero evidence that the Jailer's Daughter wishes to marry Palamon to enhance her social standing. In her doubts about why he does not return her affections, she suspects it may be on account of their discrepant positions in the social hierarchy. In that she is totally wrong. We know from the text Palamon wants Emilia and only Emilia. There is all the difference in the world between suspecting that the reason one is rejected is because of inadequate social position and attempting to marry someone because doing so will enhance that standing.

2. There is no competent psychiatric diagnosis of the Jailer's Daughter offered by Green.

3. There is no demonstrated connection between an inability to advance socially on the basis of marriage and any established psychiatric malady.

4. Citing second-hand opinions of English teachers speculating about the causes of a fictional character's mental disorder is no substitute for textual evidence and proof. Who cares about the mere assertions

of "Paul Bertram," "Richard Abrams" or anyone else, for that matter?

5. There is no evidence that there is any serious reflection in the mind of the Jailer's Daughter on "gender, class and familial role." This is not a social scientist, but a jilted adolescent.

6. Green brings forward in support of her thesis the Jailer's Daughter's participation in the May Festival and the Morris Dance. But rustic exuberance tends to show willingness to abide within the scope of one's social class. Had she been alienated from her cohorts she would never have engaged in those flamboyant gesticulations.

7. Occam's principle of economy of explanation militates against a remote theory which portrays the Jailer's Daughter as social critic. More accessible by far is the fact we know beyond any doubt: Palamon is in love with another woman. As that is sufficient to account for the phenomenon we need look no further.

4. Conclusion

It is odd that teachers of English persist in using antiquated terms like "madness" in light of the sophistication of contemporary psychiatry and the DSM-5. "Madness" was clearly an earlier age's undiscriminating catch-all for a wide spectrum of emotional and mental dysfunctions. To engage in conjectural exercises, then, concerning the "causes" of a particular "madness" is to raise clouds of intellectual debris. Shakespeare, who mocks mechanical and amateurish accounts of madness in *Hamlet* (II, ii, 146-152), is at pains in all his works to exhibit the inner workings of the human mind in relation to character and external events, and after 400 years we continue to find him second to none in his dramatic psychology. There has been and will continue to be useless chatter about whether Hamlet and Ophelia were "mad" or not. Both characters exhibit behaviors and use language suggestive of mental acuity as well as disorder. But in the final analysis such academic exercises are sterile. We want to understand what has happened to Ophelia, and Shakespeare harnesses his extraordinary art to show how trauma and irremediable inner conflict can interfere with or destroy normal cognitive and affective processes. There is abundant textual evidence that in the not-too-distant past Hamlet and Ophelia were a couple. Hamlet anticipated with some reason that he would succeed his father as King of Denmark, but inside there were always doubts about his identity, doubts raised to the boiling point on his return to Elsinore to find Claudius atop the Danish Throne. He then becomes convinced that Claudius murdered Hamlet,

Sr. and seeks a condign revenge—without results—knocking his life in the hazard. It is in this context that his relationship with Ophelia becomes insupportable. This would of course make any prior sexual activity between them a source of much discomfort for Ophelia, whose virginity is questionable. Hamlet upbraids and disgraces her and then kills her father, leaving her without parents at a young age. No one comes to her aid or offers her genuine comfort. She is not afforded any reasonable grieving process for her dad, which recapitulates a maternal loss not disclosed. Her emotional state leaves no way to reconcile her inner turbulence, as figures of respect and love are shown to be indifferent or hostile. There is thus no *modus vivendi*. For Shakespeare, madness is the failure of self-deception. As long as Ophelia can persuade herself that Hamlet loved her or at least cared for her, she can endure. But his abuse, coupled with his destruction of her father, leaves no way to jumpstart her world. Only a censoring of reality can cushion the blow. But even in "madness" the truth seeps out, to the consternation of Gertrude and Claudius. Indeed, the last vestige of Ophelia's humanity is that very madness. Efforts to rob her of that thin shroud of dignity, accusing her of dissembling to advance an anachronistic political agenda, is to make light of her wounds, forming an alliance with the wolfish forces which devour her soul. This is the ultimate and intolerable betrayal, ironically brought about by something calling itself "feminism."

The situation is much the same with the Jailer's Daughter. When she first encountered Palamon, there was no aim at marriage, something she regarded at the outset as "hopeless." (II, iv, 4) Rather, she wanted to "enjoy" him. (See, *e.g.*, II, iv, 30) That is, her first instincts were largely sensual. "What pushes are we wenches driven to, / When fifteen once has found us?" (II, iv, 6-7) The Jailer's Daughter quite naturally feels the need for physical affection, that is, love. Yet in the way stands doubt. Palamon behaves with great kindness to her in his cell, even kissing her. (II, iv, 20-26) So terrified is she of discovering he is unavailable that she skirts the issue altogether, as though he were invisible—and blind. Rationally, she knows quite well how attractive he is. "He has as much to please a woman in him—/ If he please to bestow it so / as ever / These eyes yet looked on." (II, iv, 9-11) But the logical question, whether he is taken or not, is not addressed. The fact that the question doesn't surface in explicit form doesn't mean the possibility is not felt. We can only seek to avoid that of which we are in some sense aware. And the Jailer's Daughter is keenly aware of Palamon's allure for women in general. She tells us so.

Hence, as argued above, when she releases Palamon from bondage only to be deserted by him, the Jailer's Daughter faces a dilemma. The answer is staring her in the face but it is absolutely intolerable. Ophelia's predicament is that Hamlet has behaved seductively with her, and may have obtained what he wanted. In the case of the Jailer's Daughter, who would be only too happy to have a fling with Palamon, there is no masculine seduction, not even a hint of it. Instead, he flees. The only escape from a harsh and unacceptable reality is madness, in which the forbidden thought is suppressed at the cost of one's reason.

What she has never understood is that the Wooer is not merely a candidate promoted by her father, but a chap who genuinely desires and cares for her, even in her disabled condition. Once she loses a grip on reality, however, it would appear to be doubly difficult to win her. It is precisely here that the doctor's remedy commends itself. As she is "mad," that is, less able to distinguish real from unreal, and still fixated on the idea of "Palamon," the doctor finds an opportunity for the Wooer to "become" the desired love object. Repeated doses of love, security, warmth and affection allow treatment to gain traction. And because the patient's fancy for Palamon began with a pronounced eroticism, it is appropriate that genital congress be the *terminus ad quem*. Marriage may yet occur. All this is elementary and easy enough to apprehend for eyes not glazed over by intellectual fads. But just as the Jailer's Daughter could not look at Palamon directly and see in him his emotional entanglements, so many contemporary critics cannot view *The Two Noble Kinsmen* in its concreteness and depth of insight. Since it fails to contain what they wish, they must insinuate the missing elements themselves.

WORKS CITED:

"Mythogyny: Madness and Medicine in Hamlet and The Two Noble Kinsmen," Michelle Erica Green, online, and works cited therein.

William Shakespeare, The Complete Works, 2d edition, G. Taylor and S. Wells, eds., Clarendon Press, Oxford, 2005.

William Shakespeare, Complete Works, Jonathan Bate, Eric Rasmussen, eds., The Royal Shakespeare Company, Random House, 2007.

For a more complete account of *Hamlet*, the reader is respectfully referred to *Hamlet Made Simple and Other Essays*, New English Review Press, 2013.

15

"Shylock Wrote Shakespeare"

How courtesy would seem to cover sin
When what is done is like an hypocrite,
The which is good in nothing but in sight.

— Pericles

I. Introduction: Shakespeare's Moral Philosophy

*I*n *As You Like It*, when young Orlando is about to flee from the homicidal rage of his brother Oliver and usurping Duke Frederick, he realizes that to escape requires financial reserves he doesn't possess. Told of Orlando's plight, and the possibility that he will have to turn to robbery just to survive, the elderly family servant Adam offers to put his entire life savings of five hundred crowns at Orlando's disposal.

ADAM

But do not so. I have five hundred crowns,
The thrifty hire I saved under your father,
Which I did store to be foster-nurse
When service should in my old limbs lie lame,
And unregarded age in corners thrown.
Take that, and he that doth the ravens feed,
Yea providently caters for the sparrow,
Be comfort to my age. Here is gold,

All this I give you. Let me be your servant.
(II, iv, 39-47)

Passages such as this catch the distilled essence of Shakespeare. And it should go without saying that words such as these are not known to those unsteeped in his art. Wealth is an instrument allowing us to live, but for Shakespeare, poet and dramatist, the meaning of life lies elsewhere, in our wavering devotion to nobility, grace, beauty, and to those who embody those ideals. The frequent error of taking the means for the end, existing for the sake of gain, is for Shakespeare the perennial perversion of mankind.

In Act II, Sc. iv, as Rosalind and Celia enter disguised into the forest of Arden, Celia (now Aliena) is exhausted and fainting with hunger. (II, iv, 60-62) Rosalind immediately stops Corin the shepherd and requests food for her.

ROSALIND

I prithee, shepherd, if that love or gold
Can in this desert place buy entertainment,
Bring us where we may rest ourselves, and feed.
Here's a young maid with travel much oppressed,
And faints for succor.
(II, iv, 70-74)

Pitying Aliena, Corin pledges: "I will your very faithful feeder be." (II, iv, 98)

Further on, in another part of the forest, Orlando must halt because Adam is too weary and famished to take another step. ("O, I die for food.") With no thought of himself, the youth promises to bring relief.

ORLANDO

Why, how now, Adam? No greater heart in
thee? Live a little, comfort a little, cheer thyself a little.
If this uncouth forest yield anything savage I will either
be food for it or bring it for food to thee. Thy conceit
is nearer death than thy powers. For my sake be
comfortable. Hold death awhile at the arm's end. I will

here be with thee presently, and if I bring thee not
something to eat, I will give thee leave to die. But if
thou diest before I come, thou art a mocker of my
labour. Well said. Thou lookest cheerly, and I'll be with
thee quickly. Yet thou liest in the bleak air. Come, I
will bear thee to some shelter, and thou shalt not die
for lack of a dinner if there live anything in this desert.
Cheerly, good Adam!
(II, vi, 4-15)

Suffering from hunger himself, Orlando's only thought is of his old
and loyal companion.

In the next scene we witness Orlando's encounter with Duke Senior and his band of men of the forest sitting at their table to feast. Orlando, near crazed with desperation, bursts in, sword drawn.

Once more the magnanimous spirit of Shakespeare unfolds before
us.

ORLANDO

Forbear, and eat no more!

JAQUES

Why, I have eat none yet.

ORLANDO

Nor shalt not till necessity be served.

JAQUES

Of what kind should this cock come of?

DUKE SENIOR

Art thou thus boldened, man, by thy distress?
Or else a rude despiser of good manners,
That in civility thou seem'st so empty?

ORLANDO

You touched my vein at first. The thorny point
Of bare distress hath ta'en me from the show
Of smooth civility. Yet am I inland bred,
And know some nurture. But forbear, I say.
He dies that touches any of this fruit
Till I and my affairs are answered.

JAQUES

An you will not be answered with reason, I must die.

DUKE SENIOR

What would you have? Your gentleness shall force
More than your force move us to gentleness.

ORLANDO

I almost die for food; and let me have it.

DUKE SENIOR

Sit down and feed, and welcome to our table.

ORLANDO

Speak you so gently? Pardon me, I pray you.
I thought that all things had been savage here,
And therefore put I on the countenance
Of stern commandment. But whate'er you are
That in this desert inaccessible,
Under the shade of melancholy boughs,
Lose and neglect the creeping hours of time,
If ever you have looked on better days,
If ever been where bells have knolled to church,
If ever sat at any good man's feast,
If ever from your eyelids wiped a tear,
And know what 'tis to pity, and be pitied,

Let gentleness my strong enforcement be.
In the which hope I blush and hide my sword.

DUKE SENIOR

True it is that we have seen better days,
And have with holy bell been knolled to church,
And sat at good men's feasts, and wiped our eyes
Of drops that sacred pity hath engendered.
And therefore sit you down in gentleness,
And take upon command what help we have
That to your wanting may be ministered.

ORLANDO

Then but forebear your food a little while
While's, like a doe, I go to find my fawn
And give it food. There is an old poor man
Who after me hath many a weary step
Limped in pure love. Till he be first sufficed,
Oppressed with two weak evils, age and hunger,
I will not touch a bit.

DUKE SENIOR

Go find him out,
And we will nothing waste till you return.

ORLANDO

I thank ye; and be blessed for your good comfort! [exit]

DUKE SENIOR

Thou seest we are not all alone unhappy.
This wide and universal theatre
Presents more woeful pageants than the scene
Wherein we play in.
(II, vii, 88-138)

Throughout these sublime exchanges we cannot avoid being impressed with Shakespeare's desire to illustrate profound compassion and appreciation of the agonies of human want and deprivation. Indeed, in this last stanza cited above, his view of the entire terrestrial realm as one "map of woe" comes into focus. (*Titus Andronicus*, III, ii, 12) It is in that killing field of universal sorrow that the deed of sympathy takes on the greatest meaning. In such utterances, reiterated throughout his works, we hear above the chatter the authentic voice of Shakespeare, teaching mercy to an inhumane humanity.

It resonates again in *Cymbeline*. Imogen, disguised as Fidele, arrives at the cave of Belarius, alone, frightened, and empty of sustenance. Drawing her sword, she enters to forage for food. As she emerges, she walks directly into the presence of Belarius and the two grown sons of Cymbeline, Guiderius and Arviragus.

IMOGEN

Good masters, harm me not.
Before I entered here I called, and thought
To have begged or bought what I took. Good truth,
I have stol'n naught, nor would not, though I had found
Gold strewd i'th'floor. Here's money for my meat.
I would have left it on the board so soon
As I made my meal, and parted
With prayers for the provider.

GUIDERIUS

Money, youth?

ARVIRAGUS

All gold and silver rather turn to dirt,
As 'tis no better reckoned but of those
Who worship dirty gods.
(*Cymbeline*, III, vi, 44-55)

Once more, the primacy of need and our duty to alleviate the pain of want is contrasted with base coin, and those who worship that "dirty god." Could anything show more clearly where Shakespeare's emphatic sentiments lie? The same theme, over and over, is etched in stone.

II. A Biographical Variance

It is therefore surprising to learn that not only did Shakespeare not possess the qualities and virtues he extolled in these selections from his works, he was, in fact, at the very antipodes in relation thereto. Contemporary research by certified scholars has reinforced the traditional view of William Shakespeare as a miser of the most egregious sort, a greedy and sadistic brute who took pleasure in the financial exploitation of helpless individuals. This unsettling story was unveiled April 1, 2013 by no less an authority than the *BBC New Mid-Wales* in a report entitled "William Shakespeare: Study Sheds Light on the Bard as Food Hoarder." This was evidently replicated by Ms. Marah Eakin, using a caption so distasteful it is not suitable for scholarly citation. The following quote will do:

> Researchers from the Potterian-sounding [the reference is to the authoritative *Harry Potter* series] Aberstwyth University have discovered that William Shakespeare was a tax-evading grain hoarder. According to Dr. Jayne Archer and Professors Margaret Turley and Howard Thomas, Shakespeare made a lot of his money by buying up large amounts of grain, malt, and barley to store, later selling it for inflated prices when his fellow countrymen were struggling.
>
> They believe the *playwright* did this for 15 years and faced fines for illegal hoarding, as well as being threatened with jail time for failing to pay his taxes. (Eakin, no page available, emphasis added)

It turns out that, contrary to the ideals for which he is acclaimed, Shakespeare was a loan shark, a manipulator of monies who never hesitated to charge usurious interest and then bring suit to collect against his impecunious victims. He was, to put it bluntly, a financial vampire.

To the list of his unseemly features, including loan shark, usurer, habitual grain hoarder, tax-dodger, law breaker, and exploiter of the downtrodden, we would also add that he was surely the biggest hypocrite that ever lived. The cognitive dissonance created by the discrepancy between what he taught in imperishable verse and the life he actually led is like a knife thrust into the brain of any caring and discerning reader. For Shakespeare the mega-hypocrite was well aware of the vice of hypocrisy and treated it in his plays, in fact, returning to it ten times. Shakespeare excoriates "hypocrites" in *Pericles, Much Ado About Nothing, Measure for Measure, King Henry VI* Parts One and Two, and *Hamlet*. He scorns "hypocrisy" in *Henry VIII, Love's Labour's Lost, Othello* and *King Richard II*. Condemning the ugliness of hypocrisy in his works, Shakespeare scores a literary first by being the only known writer to be a hypocrite about hypocrisy!

In assessing his fault, he must be set down as far worse than Shylock in *The Merchant of Venice*. Shylock's conduct reflects custom and the social constraints in the city of St. Mark, and at no time does he condemn the lending of money at interest. In fact, he defends it. Shakespeare, on the other hand, composes a play in which the usurer is the villain, when in fact he himself is a super-usurer who puts down usury and hypocrisy as mischief. Is it plausible to imagine that Shylock could write a play in which the loan shark is the villain?

Let us dwell on the pedagogical implications of this "discovery." So far as can be ascertained from news accounts, these scholars are arguing that the author of the plays was a financial bloodsucker and grotesque hypocrite. It is thus the author's reputation which is being blackened here. And blackened for whom? Shakespeare is being ruined principally for young people, most sensitive to those who preach high doctrine while indulging in the very things of which they publicly disapprove. In an age of multiculturalism, shrinking attention spans and text messaging addiction, Shakespeare, the quintessential "dead white male" is hardly a rising star. Quite the contrary. As of this writing, he is rapidly disappearing as required reading for university English majors across the United States. Learners are already disdainful of him, and eager for any excuse to scrap him. Hearing of the poet's unsavory character and behavior can only make this situation worse. Not only was Shakespeare of lowly origins, it turns out he was a crook. Could anything be more discouraging? When a nobody like Marah Eakin can hurl mud at Shakespeare, what does the future hold for young readers today? Have we not indeed seen the best of our time?

III. A Modest Proposal

It is well known to every scholar in Renaissance studies that there has been for at least a century a furious debate about Shakespeare's identity. Thousands of books and articles have taken up the question of whether the *bricoleur* from Stratford-Upon-Avon could actually have penned the world-famous material attributed to him. There is no dodging that. How is it, then, that news reports about the findings of Archer, Turley and Thomas never once broach the alternative that, since William of Stratford was an unprincipled hooligan, we might do better by attributing the plays, as has been long proposed, to someone else?

Of course hypocrisy is common. Many a rabble-rousing preacher has fallen into the sins he railed against. But what is apparently alleged now is that the world's most refined artist and eminent educator was in fact a zealous barbarian, the very prototype of Shakespearean monstrosity. It's like finding out that Blaise Pascal was all along the Marquis de Sade. If journalistic accounts are credited, one must wonder what could be in the minds of people like Archer, Turley and Thomas. Have they read Shakespeare—or just confined themselves to relics of the courts? In personal correspondence with Dr. Jayne Archer, April 4 2013, she declined to indicate whether in her forthcoming lecture she intends to distinguish the nefarious activities of William Shakspere from the views of the author of the poems and plays. But as things stand, the tale being set before us of Homo stratfordianus is about as congruent with the plays of Shakespeare as two autos in a head-on collision.

WORKS CITED:

William Shakespeare, The Complete Works, 2d edition, G. Taylor and S. Wells, eds., Clarendon, 2005.

"William Shakespeare: Study Sheds Light on the Bard as Food Hoarder," *BBC New Mid-Wales,* 1 April 2013, online.

"New Study Finds That Shakespeare Was a Tax-Evading Grain Hoarding [-------]," Marah Eakin, *A. V. Club,* 1 April 2013, online.

16
Shakespeare's Sweet Poison

I am a soldier and now bound to France. — Queen Eleanor

Stay, stay thy hands! Thou art an Amazon, and fightest with the sword of Deborah.
— Charles, Dauphin of France to Joan of Arc

*I*n an article in *The Shakespeare Institute Review*, Vol. 1, June, 2012, titled "Murther Most Foul: poison as a gendered weapon in Shakespeare," Dara Kaye's lead sentence is this:

"Shakespeare's characters use poisons or potions in six plays, but in only one, *Hamlet*, is poison wielded by a man." (Kaye, 18) A few sentences later that individual is identified as King Claudius ("the outlier"). (Kaye, 18)

No others are mentioned in that categorical introit.

Yet in Act Four, sc. 7, it is Claudius and Laertes who conspire to kill the Prince in a fencing match. Claudius' idea is that one of the swords should be not blunt (as for play) but razor sharp. Poison is not mentioned by him.

CLAUDIUS

He, being remiss,
Most generous, and free from all contriving,
Will not peruse the foils; so that with ease,
Or with a little shuffling, you may choose

A sword unbated [=unblunted, see, Bate, 1985, n. 119], and in a
pass of practice,
Requite him of your father.
(IV, vii, 107-112)

There is nothing of poison in this scheme.

Laertes immediately responds that he has already bought a potent
poison to use on Hamlet. That is, poisoning Hamlet is proposed not by
Claudius but by Laertes.

LAERTES

I will do't,
And for that purpose I'll anoint my sword.
I bought an unction of a mountebank
So mortal that, but dip a knife in it,
Where it draws blood no cataplasm so rare,
Collected from all simples that have virtue
Under the moon, can save the thing from death
That is but scratched withal. I'll touch my point
With this contagion, that if I gall him slightly,
It may be death.
(IV, vii, 112-121)

It is as clear as crystal, then, that Laertes is a principal in the murder of Hamlet by poison. He buys the deadly substance and identifies
himself as the one who will coat his sword with it. Yet Ms. Kaye insists
that Claudius is the sole poisoner: "*Hamlet*'s Claudius is the only man in
Shakespeare who uses poison for violent ends." (Kaye, 24)

What could be more obvious than that—and more patently erroneous?

After Hamlet and Laertes are mortally wounded with the poisoned
foil, Laertes declares his responsibility: "I am justly killed with mine
own treachery." (V, ii, 260) That is, he has with premeditation tainted
his sword and fought a sportive bout with the Prince in which both are
lacerated by the envenomed blade. He is a self-confessed poisoner. In
a moment of mortal desperation he then tries to shift responsibility to
Claudius ("The King, the King's to blame," V, ii, 274), but the admission
against interest (V, ii, 260) is already on record: Laertes' excited utterances confessing homicide by poison create an irrebuttable presump-

tion of his guilt.

Ms. Kaye adds:

> While preparing poison for Laertes' sword and for the cup of
> wine intended for Hamlet, Claudius leaves the actual sword-
> play to Laertes and Hamlet. Hamlet knows which end of a
> sword to hold, as demonstrated against Laertes, and could
> be too threatening to Claudius in direct combat. (Kaye, 25)

Why would a middle-aged gourmand contemplate crossing swords
with youthful, athletic Hamlet? This is an idea from outer space. There
is nothing to suggest that the alcoholic and sybaritic King is expert or
even competent in the martial arts. Further, he has no reason to grapple
with Hamlet. It is Laertes who is incensed against Hamlet, the killer of
his father Polonius. He returns from Paris enraged at the King for presiding over his father's demise and his sister's madness. When Claudius
sputters that he could not proceed directly against Hamlet on account of
the immense affection Gertrude feels for her son, and "the great love the
general gender bear him," (IV, vii, 5-25) Laertes consents to satisfy his
need for revenge by doing away with Hamlet in a rigged fencing match.
Claudius' wrong is not that he eschews a duel with Hamlet on account
of physical cowardice, but that he takes advantage of Laertes' anger to
continue the career of skullduggery by poison he began with the murder
of his brother, King Hamlet the Dane.

The texts of this play in Taylor and Wells and Bate and Rasmussen
offer no evidence that Claudius prepared poison for Laertes' sword, a
strange thing to do as Laertes has told him that he has his own poison
and plans to tip his sword with it. Has there been a change of plans?
What Claudius does say is that in addition to the toxic foil to be provided by Laertes, he (Claudius) will arrange for a cup of poisoned wine to
slake Hamlet's thirst at half-time.

> I ha't! When in your motion you are hot and dry —
> As make your bouts more violent to that end —
> And that he calls for drink, I'll have prepared him
> A chalice for the nonce, whereon but sipping,
> If he by chance escape your venomed stuck,
> Our purpose may hold there.
> (IV, vii, 128-134)

What these passages show us is that the factual claim made by Ms. Kaye is false. Claudius is not the only male poisoner in Shakespeare. He is not the only male poisoner in *Hamlet*. What is she trying to accomplish with this misleading information?

> Honorable conflict in Shakespeare typically involves physical challenge. Romeo faces Tybalt avenging Mercutio. Prince Hal defeats Hotspur in battle. In *Richard II* Mowbray and Bolingbroke bring their dispute before the their king, who sanctions a duel.

> Duels, then, test and prove hierarchical order, affording opportunity for providence to aid the righteous.

> Women, however, generally have neither access to such dueling rituals nor the strength and training to defeat male opponents. (Kaye, 18)

The difference between armed combat and poisoning is that the latter is sneaky, a subterfuge that renders its victim unaware and incapable of self defense. It is a contemptible form of struggle. When Shakespeare allegedly shows five female poisoners and only a single male poisoner, he is representing women in an unbalanced way, as inherently duplicitous. Of course, the trope of poison as a "gendered weapon" is silly on its face, since poison is essentially neutral. It has no sex. Only poisoners are "gendered." What is meant is that in Shakespeare women are not depicted with as much integrity as men. In conflicts men show themselves aboveboard and decent. They challenge each other and allow for ordered, regulated combat. (See, especially, *The Two Noble Kinsmen*, III, i, 73-93) Women, however, take advantage, conceal differences and act surreptitiously, that is, criminally, against their perceived enemies.

Yet this simplistic distinction is immediately upended in the very example offered from *Hamlet*. The "either-or" choice is shown to be a false abstraction. Laertes does challenge Hamlet to a fencing match in the usual way of medieval and Renaissance men, but he combines that honorable outward aspect with deceit, adding an undisclosed, sharpened and poisoned sword and Claudius' fatal cup to the program. According to the Jiminy Cricket dualism proffered by Ms. Kaye, this should not be possible. Yet there is no comment in her essay about this anomaly. The truth is that there are two male poisoners in *Hamlet*, not one, as claimed by her.

Could there be others?

Naturally, we all recall that poison is featured in *King Henry VI, Part Two*. Where is the lone female hand there? Suffolk, York, Cardinal Beaufort and Queen Margaret conspire together to rid the court of good Duke Humphrey. This cabal is comprised of three men and one woman. Do these grand personages throw down the gauntlet to Gloucester, inviting him to show his mettle in a Field of Cloth of Gold tourney? No. They put their heads together for the purpose of getting rid of him as soon as possible, by stealth. The means don't matter.

SUFFOLK

And do not stand on quillets how to slay him;
Be it by gins, by snares, by subtlety,
Sleeping or waking, 'tis no matter how,
So he be dead; for that is good conceit
Which mates him first that first intends deceit.
(III, i, 261-265)

Which individual will take actual responsibility for putting Humphrey out of commission is not clarified. But one thing is clear: it will not be the lady, Margaret. At the conclusion of the conspiratorial colloquy, Beaufort signals his active involvement. "No more of [Humphrey]," he tells Suffolk, "for I will deal with him that henceforth he shall trouble us no more." (III, i, 323-324) This makes sense since from the beginning of the trilogy Humphrey and Cardinal Beaufort (Winchester) have been at each other's throats, even agreeing to have at each other with swords. (II, i, 35-53) In the very next scene, however, we see hired murderers snuffing out the life of Humphrey and reporting back to Suffolk. Wasn't Cardinal Beaufort in charge of the dirty work?

FIRST MURDERER

Run to my lord of Suffolk — let him know
We have dispatched the Duke as he commanded.

SECOND MURDERER

O that it were to do! What have we done?

Didst ever hear a man so penitent?

FIRST MURDERER

Here comes my lord.   ʌ

SUFFOLK

Now, sirs, have you dispatched this thing?

FIRST MURDERER

Ay, good my lord, he's dead.

SUFFOLK

Why, that's well said. Go, get you to my house.
I will reward you for this venturous deed.
The King and all the peers are here at hand.
Have you laid fair the bed? Is all things well,
According as I gave directions?
(III, ii, 1-12)

Here is a mode of homicide not mentioned by Kaye: death by hired assassin, a frequent male device in Shakespeare. Should this not have been included as a third type of fighting, along with poison and open armed combat? Plots, schemes and traps are devices common to both genders in Shakespeare, an inconvenient truth for doctrinaire feminists. When Shakespearean male characters engage in such murderous plots and schemes are they behaving nobly—or as no better than poisoners? Let us bear in mind that Shakespeare's King Richard III, as he claws his way to the English throne, accomplishes his nefarious aims not by combat but largely by stealth and subterfuge. Hiring two goons who drown George, Duke of Clarence in the malmsey butt (I, iv, 265) is a symbolic poisoning. History records that Richard was actually a good king, but he must be vilified by Shakespeare as a schemer so as to make Henry Tudor, the usurper at Bosworth Field, a noble hero. Such is the force of the Tudor Myth. For were Richard not smeared with perfidy, the crown of Elizabeth I would have been a far more uneasy burden.

But wait, there's more.

In Act Three, sc. 3, we are confronted with the surprise death of one of our four conspirators, Cardinal Beaufort. The poor fellow is visited on his death bed by King Henry, Warwick and Salisbury.

Enter King Henry and the Earls of Salisbury and Warwick. Then the curtains be drawn revealing Cardinal Beaufort in his bed raving and staring as if mad.

KING HENRY

How fares my lord? Speak, Beaufort, to thy sovereign.

CARDINAL BEAUFORT

If thou beest death, I'll give thee England's treasure
Enough to purchase such another island,
So thou wilt let me live and feel no pain.

KING HENRY

Ah, what a sign it is of evil life
Where death's approach is seen so terrible.

WARWICK

Beaufort, it is thy sovereign speaks to thee.

CARDINAL BEAUFORT

Bring me unto my trial when you will.
Died he not in his bed? Where should he die?
Can I make men live whe'er they will or no?
O, torture me no more — I will confess.
Alive again? Then show me where he is.
I'll give a thousand pound to look upon him.
He hath no eyes! The dust hath blinded them.
Comb down his hair — look, look: it stands upright,
Like lime twigs set to catch my wingèd soul.
Give me some drink, and bid the apothecary

Bring the strong poison I bought of him.

KING HENRY

O Thou eternal mover of the heavens,
Look with a gentle eye upon this wretch.
O, beat away the busy meddling fiend
That lays strong siege unto this wretch's soul,
And from his bosom purge this black despair.
WARWICK

See how the pangs of death do make him grin.

SALISBURY

Disturb him not; let him pass peaceably.

KING HENRY

Peace to his soul, if God's good pleasure be.
Lord Card'nal, if thou think'st on heaven's bliss,
Hold up thy hand, make signal of thy hope.

Cardinal Beaufort dies

He dies and makes no sign. O, God, forgive him.

WARWICK

So bad a death argues a monstrous life.
(III, iii, 1-30)

Though there are unanswered questions here, the scene bears directly on the contention of Ms. Kaye that the only male poisoner in Shakespeare is Claudius. We have seen this claim disconfirmed by the actions of Laertes. It is also refuted by the instance of Cardinal Beaufort, who confesses deliriously on his deathbed that he made preparations to kill Gloucester by means of a substance purchased from an apothecary. (III, ii, 18-19) Beaufort is therefore another Shakespearean male poisoner. Though the text makes plain that his death was really brought about by agents of the Duke of Suffolk, Beaufort's intention was to use the poison to murder the Duke. For though he is raving, it appears the subject of Beaufort's hysteria is Humphrey, whose appearance to Beaufort ("Comb down his hair, — look, look: it stands upright") tallies with the actual physical condition of the dead Duke Humphrey when viewed by Warwick and Henry: "His hair, you see, is sticking; His well-proportioned beard made rough and rugged, Like to the summer's corn by tempest lodged." (III, ii, 174-176) The most natural inference is that shortly after the assassins did their mortal deed, Beaufort entered Humphrey's chamber and was shocked to behold the hideous visage of the man he'd been planning to poison. The impact of this spectacle on Beaufort resembles the effect on Macbeth of Banquo's ghost. The corpse has all the indicia of murder. As Warwick declares, "It cannot be but he was murdered here." (III, ii, 177) In a flash, the Cardinal realizes that as he is part of Suffolk's faction, and assumed responsibility to take off the Duke himself, he will most likely be identified as Humphrey's killer. This sends him over the edge—into madness. The most likely account of his condition in this scene, then, is that in a state of mortal sin related to his attempted homicide, and the condition of his dead victim, Cardinal Beaufort hastily consumes the poison he had intended for Humphrey, and so perishes in agony, unshriven.

That means there are at least three male poisoners in Shakespeare, not one.

What about *The Tragedy of Richard II*? Picture yourself in the Tower of London, a fly on the wall of deposed King Richard's cold, barren cell. What do we behold? A keeper enters bearing food, and dismisses the attending groom. Has the King a hearty appetite—or does he view that prospective meal as his last?

Listen.

KEEPER (to groom)

Fellow, give place. Here is no longer stay.

RICHARD (to groom)

If thou love me, 'tis time thou wert away.

GROOM

What my tongue dares not, that my heart shall say.

KEEPER

My lord, will't please you to fall to? [That is, will you eat this food?]

RICHARD

Taste of it first, as thou art wont to do.

KEEPER

My lord, I dare not. Sir Piers of Exton,
Who lately came from the King, commands the contrary.

RICHARD (striking the Keeper)

The devil take Henry of Lancaster and thee!
Patience is stale, and I am weary of it.
(V, v, 95-104)

Here Sir Piers of Exton and his goons, huddled behind the door, rush in and slaughter their sovereign. Though their hope that Richard would consume the tainted meat and perish of poison is frustrated, they have a Plan "B": attack him *en masse* with pikes and blades and stab him to death.

These results are then duly reported to Bolingbroke, now minding his royal business on the throne as King Henry IV. His reaction is instructive.

EXTON

Great King, within this coffin I present
Thy buried fear. Herein all breathless lies
The mightiest of thy greatest enemies,
Richard of Bordeaux, by me hither brought.

KING HENRY

Exton, I thank thee not, for thou hast wrought
A deed of slander with thy fatal hand
Upon my head and all this famous land.

EXTON

From your own mouth, my lord, did I this deed.

KING HENRY

They love not poison that do poison need;
Nor do I thee. Though I did wish him dead,
I hate the murderer, love him murderèd.
The guilt of conscience take thou for thy labour,
But neither my good word nor princely favour.
With Cain go wander through the shades of night,
And never show thy head by day or night.

* * *

Lords, I protest my soul is full of woe
That blood should sprinkle me to make me grow.
Come mourn with me for what I do lament,
And put on sullen black incontinent.
I'll make a voyage to the Holy Land
To wash this blood from off my guilty hand.
(V, vi, 30-50)

Based on this text, Exton does not disclose to King Henry the actual mode of murder. Henry doesn't realize that Richard is slain by steel.
That is why his mind reverts to "poison." (V, vi, 38) Shakespeare is telling
us that it was Henry who ordered the elimination of the imprisoned
Richard by poison. He also shows us Henry's feelings of guilt, which
parallel those of Cardinal Beaufort in *King Henry VI*. Unlike the situation in *King Richard III*, in which King Edward IV sought to reverse the
order of execution of his brother Clarence (killed in the Tower by Richard), only to discover that his commutation of sentence had not been
heeded (II, i, 86-95), here hand-wringing Bolingbroke never rescinds

the order to assassinate Richard. Hence his load of guilt. He is a *de facto* poisoner.

How many Shakespearean poisoners have we then? In *Richard II*, three males collaborate to knowingly and deliberately poison King Richard II. They are Bolingbroke, Exton and the keeper, who delivers the lethal supper and knows full-well what menace it contains. These three added to the three Shakespearean poisoners previously identified above give us a total of six male poisoners.

It would be jolly to continue in this vein. What would we say of the macabre Titus Andronicus, for example, who slaughters Chiron and Demetrius and grinds their bones to make the pie he serves as a "dainty" dish to their mother, Tamora Queen of the Goths? When she learns what was actually on the menu, is the result ptomaine, or mere upset stomach? As Titus stabs her before dessert, we'll never know for sure. (*Titus Andronicus*, V, iii, 53-63) As the *modus operandi* is identical to that of the classic poisoner, we must include Titus, making at the very least seven male Shakespearean poisoners.

Before turning to potions, we should pause to reflect on women and force of arms. It is a notable irony that, in its haste to portray women as perennial victims, feminism offers demeaning caricatures of female literary characters. A good example of this tendency is provided by Ms. Kaye, when she says "A wronged woman's only honorable options are to prevail upon a male intermediary or die." (22) That is fortunately true neither in life nor in Shakespeare. In *King John*, for example, Queen Eleanor is a martial figure who commands an army, as the epigraph of this essay attests. (*King John*, I, i, 150) As far back as Plato, the fountainhead of Shakespeare's intellectual art, able women were to be included in the warrior/guardian class, as was made clear in *Politeia* 455d. Though Ms. Kaye states unequivocally that early modern England women had neither the training nor the ability to wield a sword, Shakespeare knew better than that. Has Ms. Kaye forgotten Joan of Arc in *King Henry VI*, who defeats Charles, Dauphin of France, in hand-to-hand combat? (*King Henry VI*, Part One, 70-84) What about Queen Margaret in the same play, who responds to Henry's shameful concessions to the York faction by assembling her own army, hunting down Richard and killing him on the reeking field of battle? Why didn't she just use poison instead? We should also not forget that Hippolyta, of *A Midsummer Night's Dream* and *The Two Noble Kinsmen*, is a professional warrior who fought with her sword gallantly against the uninvited Theseus.

Since Ms. Kaye's contention includes "potions" as well as poisons, we need to consider whether male figures in the plays use non-lethal substances to achieve their ends as well. One of the six plays listed by Ms. Kaye is *A Midsummer Night's Dream*. Not much is said about it, however. We must be edified by this: "*A Midsummer Night's Dream* has been similarly treated, as Puck is non-human and uses potion as a toy for play, not as a substitute for violence." (21) Well, the potioner is not Puck, a mere agent of the royal will, but Oberon, King of the Fairies. And his use thereof is not as a game, jest or toy, but to restore the proper order of love amongst four misguided and stumbling mortals.

OBERON

> I know a bank where the wild thyme blows,
> Where oxlips and the nodding violet grows,
> Quite overcanopied with luscious woodbine,
> With sweet musk-roses, and with eglantine.
> There sleeps Titania sometime of the night,
> Lulled in these flowers with dances and delight;
> And there the snake throws her enamelled skin,
> Weed wide enough to wrap a fairy in;
> And with the juice of this I'll streak her eyes,
> And make her full of hateful fantasies.
> Take thou some of it, and seek through this grove.
> A sweet Athenian lady is in love
> With a disdainful youth. Annoint his eyes;
> But do it when the next thing he espies
> May be the lady. Thou shalt know the man
> By the Athenian garments he has on.
> Effect it with some care, that he may prove
> More fond on her than she upon her love;
> And look thou meet me ere the first cock crow.
> (II, i, 248-267)

To the list of seven male poisoners in Shakespeare, we must add the employer of potions, Oberon, bringing the total number of males to eight. When Oberon proceeds to strive against his marital adversary Titania in a child custody dispute, he personally dopes her with an hallucinogen, the juice of that "little western flower," causing her to have a love affair with a talking animal. While she is distracted in the coils of fantastic bestiality, Oberon kidnaps her adopted child. What is this if not substituting stealth for violence to commit a patent wrong?

It is hardly possible to object that Oberon is "non-human," as we do not judge him by the artifice of ontological taxonomy, but always as a human exemplar. His purposes are not ludic but in deadly earnest, carried out with all the tenacity and zeal of parties litigant in a contested domestic action in Los Angeles County. Ms. Kaye is willing to set Cleopatra down as a user of poisons and potions though she imposes on no one. "Antony and Cleopatra is suffused with language about potions and drugs. Cleopatra is repeatedly compared with serpents and venom. She is a drug user . . . ." (Kaye, 21) So what? Cleopatra inflicts potions and poisons on no one. With Anthony dead, and trapped by the forces of Rome, she commits suicide the most painless way available, the bite of the asp. Her serving maids voluntarily do likewise. How logical is it to say Cleopatra is a user of potions and poisons and Oberon is not? A better argument would be that Oberon, who takes advantage of Titania by smearing a love potion on her sleeping face, making her lose control of her sexuality, is the genuine potioner, not Cleopatra, whose final actions are confined to herself, as were, say, the suicides of Brutus and Antony.

Take *Romeo and Juliet*, mentioned by Ms. Kaye but omitted from her list of six relevant plays. Romeo Montague commits suicide by poison purchased by him in an apothecary's shop. He is a male. Juliet (female) has no contact with poison. She is important for our purposes, however, as her death-like slumber in the tomb of her ancestors is engineered by Friar Laurence, a fellow with some knowledge of potent substances. It was he who gave her the herbal potion which so closely mimics death. His is a mind worth inspecting.

FRIAR LAURENCE

The grey-eyed morn smiles on the frowning night,
Chequ'ring the eastern clouds with streaks of light
And fleckled darkness like a drunkard reels
From forth day's path and Titan's fiery wheels.
Now, ere the sun advance his burning eye
The day to cheer and night's dank dew to dry,
I must up-fill this osier cage of ours
With baleful weeds and precious-juicèd flowers.
The earth, that is nature's mother, is her tomb.
What is her burying grave, that is her womb,
And from her womb children of divers kind

We sucking on her natural bosom find,
Many for many virtues excellent,
None but for some, and yet all different.
O mickle is the powerful grace that lies
In plants, herbs, stones and their true qualities,
For naught so vile that on earth doth live,
But to the earth some special good doth give;
Nor aught so good but, strained from that fair use,
Revolts from true birth, stumbling on abuse.
Virtue itself turns vice being misapplied,
And vice sometime's by action dignified.
Within the infant rind of this weak flower
Poison hath residence, and medicine power,
For this, being smelt, with that part cheers each part;
Being tasted, slays all senses with the heart.
Two such opposèd kings encamp them still
In man as well as herbs — grace and rude will;
And where the worser is predominant,
Full soon the canker death eats up that plant.
(II, ii, 1-30)

In Friar Laurence we have a philosophical botanist whose knowledge of nature spans good and evil properties. He may be viewed as our ninth Shakespearean male potioner/poisoner. Though essentially an amateur healer, he has sufficient knowledge of toxic substances to be able to concoct efficacious poisons. We do not know if he has done so. He can also tap into the healthful and curative resources of his herbal environment. Most importantly, he has acquired insight into the relationship between these positive and negative dimensions, perceiving, for example, that nothing is either purely good or bad in itself. "For naught so vile that on the earth doth live, but to the earth some special good doth give." (II, ii, 17-18) This is a theme that runs like an underground current through Shakespeare, turning up at unexpected moments. Thus we find King Harry in *The Life of King Henry the Fifth*, when faced with the perils of battle, musing this way:

There is some soul of goodness in things evil,
Would men observingly distill it out —
For our bad neighbor makes us early stirrers,
Which is both healthful and good husbandry.

Besides, they are our outward consciences,
And preachers to us all, admonishing
That we should dress us fairly for our end.
Thus we may gather honey from the weed,
And make a moral of the devil himself.
(IV, i, 4-12)

Another example of the same insight can be found in *As You Like It*, when Duke Senior praises his harsh outdoor environment:

Now, my co-mates and brothers in exile,
Hath not old custom made this life more sweet
Than that of painted pomp? Are not these woods
More free from peril than the envious court?
Here feel we not the penalty of Adam,
The seasons' difference, as the icy fang
And churlish chiding of the winter's wind,
Which when it bites and blows upon my body
Even til I shrink with cold, I smile, and say
'This is no flattery. These are counsellors
That feelingly persuade me what I am'.
Sweet are the uses of adversity
Which, like the toad, ugly and venomous,
Wears yet a precious jewel in his head;
And this our life, exempt from public haunt,
Finds tongues in trees, books in the running brooks,
Sermons in stones, and good in everything.
(II, i, 1-17)

That is to say, there is a distinctly toxic element to life, which, while it is a difficulty, is not absolutely so. It may be compared to a poisonous toad, which yet carries within itself a precious jewel of wisdom and of healing. Meeting the stressful and painful aspects of life affirmatively and with judgment, Shakespeare teaches, may make us better, more durable, more patient persons, giving us cause to be thankful not only for life's blessings but equally for its hurdles and impediments. Even poison has its uses. Radiation, for example, which can cause cancer, may also be employed to destroy malignant lesions. Anger, a fault, may rescue us in emergencies. Homeopathic medicine is based on the principle that small doses of a known toxin may either render us immune to certain illnesses or help us to regain health. Foreshadowing this dialectical philosophy of Friar Laurence earlier in the play, Romeo's friend, Benvolio, advises:

> Tut, man, one fire burns out another's burning,
>   One pain is lessened by another's anguish.
> Turn giddy, and be holp by backward turning.
>   One desperate grief cures with another's languish.
> Take thou some new infection to thy eye,
> And the rank poison of the old will die.
> (I, ii, 44-49)

Here Shakespeare characterizes romantic love, with all its pain, not as a virtue, but as a spiritual infection. Romeo's desire for Rosaline can be cured homeopathically by accepting the more severe disease of a prettier girl. Here, in the tradition of Socratic philosophy, we witness the intersection of wisdom and ironic humor.

In Act IV, sc. i, we see the practical implementation of Friar Laurence's metaphysic. The prescription for Juliet is a small dose of death.

> Take thou this vial, being then in bed,
> And this distilling liquor drink thou off,
> When presently through all thy veins shall run
> A cold and drowsy humor; for no pulse
> Shall keep his native progress, but surcease.
> No warmth, no breath shall testify thou livest.
> The roses in thy lips and cheeks shall fade
> To wanny ashes, thy eyes' windows fall
> Like death when he shuts up the day of life.
> Each part, deprived of supple government
> Shall, stiff and stark and cold, appear like death;
> And in this borrowed likeness of shrunk death
> Thou shalt continue two-and-forty hours,
> And then awake as from a pleasant sleep.
> (IV, i, 93-106)

We know the rest. Unbeknownst to the well-intentioned Friar, his messages explaining the plan to Romeo will never get delivered, and Juliet's affair with death is fated to be consummated. Yet even here, in the face of tragedy, all is not lost. Our principal consolation is not the mere end of the feud between the houses of Capulet (one almost writes "Copulate") and Montague, but, far more profoundly, the illustration of the ideal moment of absolute love and unqualified devotion. Our lesser world of checks, contingencies and compromises is in one instant lit up by this dramatic skyrocket of the Unconditioned. Who would have it otherwise? Mr. and Mrs. Montague paying monthly bills in their Verona flat while the baby screams? No, thanks.

From Friar Laurence's alchemy we may advance to others who look even more searchingly and creatively at life. For example, poison takes on fresh meaning in the tropes of Shakespearean characters who stand more distally from habit and convention and act as critics to oppose them. A newcomer like the Bastard in *King John* thinks outside the box, and can use his insights constructively, both for his own progress and the betterment of the world. If complacency and self-interest tend to social decay, then we exist already in a state of toxic decomposition. Paradoxically, the antidote is the "poison" of criticism, that is, ideas which must sound painfully in the ears of social parasites and reactionaries. Recall Socrates' comparison of himself to a stinging fly that bites the nag of state. (*Apology* 30d) They poisoned him in requital of that. (*Phaedo*) Think of the Fool in *Lear,* with his stinging barbs. Do they not fester? One could even argue that it is with such "poisonous" outsiders that Shakespeare identifies most closely.

> But this is worshipful society,
> And fits the mounting spirit like myself;
> For he is but a bastard to the time
> That doth not smack of observation;
> And so am I — whether I smack or no,
> And not alone in habit and device,
> Exterior form, outward accoutrement,
> But from the inward motion — to deliver
> Sweet, sweet, sweet poison for the age's tooth;
> Which, though I will not practise to deceive,
> Yet to avoid deceit I mean to learn;
> For it shall strew the footsteps of my rising.
> (*King John*, II, i, 205-216)

Jaques in *As You Like It* sings the same tune, but in a minor key.

> I must have liberty

Withal, as large a charter as the wind,
To blow on whom I please, for so fools have;
And they that are most gallèd with my folly,
They most must laugh. And why, sir, must they so?
The way is plain as way to parish church:
He that a fool doth very wisely hit
Doth very foolishly, although he smart,
Seem aught but senseless of the bob. If not,
The wise man's folly is anatomized
Even by the squandering glances of the fool.
Invest me in my motley. Give me leave
To speak my mind, and I will through and through
Cleanse the foul body of th'infected world,
If they will patiently receive my medicine.
(II, vii, 47-61)

Conclusion

The physician and the poisoner share a knowledge of deadly substances, but with important differences. The poisoner acts covertly, with malice, and has a narrow understanding of his art and its substances. The true physician, on the other hand, familiar though he is with toxic elements, is apprised of their benefits and antidotes as well, how they can heal as well as hurt. Moreover, he has taken a Hippocratic Oath to "do no harm." The liar, the slanderer and the propagandist are masters of deception, and the rumors they scatter in today's electronic winds go quickly "viral" and pandemic. Once in place, ideologies, dogmas and prejudices are almost impossible to root out. Civil society sickens and falls into decay. Many a necropolis slouching its way to extinction has been proclaimed a utopia by cheering voices. At that point rational philosophy is useless. Only the ironic artist, the satirist wielding caustic pen or tongue, has any chance of cleansing the foul body of our infected world. But the prophet's message is painful; no one but an oracular spirit of the most transcendent genius can hope to deliver it and be heeded. That is Shakespeare. In the words of Northumberland, grieving over the loss of his only son:

For this I shall have time enough to mourn.
In poison there is physic; and these news,
Having been well, that would have made me sick,

Being sick, have in some measure made me well;
And, as the wretch whose fever-weakened joints,
Like strengthless hinges, buckle under life,
Impatient of his fit, breaks like a fire
Out of his keeper's arms, even so my limbs,
Weakened with grief, being now enraged with grief,
Are thrice themselves.
(*King Henry IV*, Part Two, I, i, 136-145)

Plato and Shakespeare sought to demonstrate that a malefactor is his own first victim. I must believe the lie myself to spread it abroad. To make others ill I must first have the contagion myself. In his vivid portrait of the death of Cardinal Beaufort in *King Henry VI*, Shakespeare shows us how the putrefaction of the soul is madness and the bad death of the body as well. On the other hand, a true physician, like Cerimon of Ephesus in *Pericles* (Sc. 12) can bring the seeming dead back to life. And Cerimon is Shakespeare's puppet.

In a rotten society thought falls ill, and bears the form of ideology, a disorder which may be regarded as the influenza of the intellect. It is prejudice writ large. The ideological bacillus hijacks the cerebral cortex and rapidly multiplies arguments designed to bolster some preconceived and expedient idea. As this happens, objectivity shuts down, and the ability to perceive competing facts which might conduce to different conclusions evaporates.

That which calls itself "feminism" today is an anti-wisdom, dogma masquerading as thought. One of its most common symptoms is blindness to more holistic outlooks and the evidences that support those outlooks. Feminism is a species of faddism, the assumption that what is new and popular is better than anything in the past. As "ye olde Shakespeare," the "dead white male," is blithely tossed in with the dinosaurs (he didn't have Twitter or an iPhone, did he?), he is the bogeyman, the perfect target. You see, Shakespeare had one boot in the Middle Ages, and believed with everyone else that men are noble and women aren't. Just look at the plays. When the men have spats they march out into the field like mountain goats in rut and start butting each other's heads. Women just get bitchy. See the difference? When a brain infected with the germ of feminism attempts to perform literary exegesis, it is pre-programmed to select and process only data favorable to its "women-as-victim, man-as-oppressor" narrative.

Ms. Dara Kaye sets out six plays in which poisons or potions are used, and blandly announces that in only one of them is the user male. Patient study will reveal that of the alleged instances of aggressive female use of such substances, only Goneril in *Lear* is valid. (V, iii, 89-100) The other cases are all so equivocal as to be without probative value. In the arguments made above we have seen not one but nine male characters who make significant use of potions and poisons. In fact, for good measure we should probably add as male poisoner the physician Cornelius in *Cymbeline*, who teaches the Queen the malicious use of toxic substances as number ten. How many has he bumped off? This is the kind of blunder that happens when texts are reflected in the Fun House mirrors of feminist ideology: up becomes down, black becomes white, and poison acquires "gender." Such is the singular advantage of knowing everything in advance; it spares us the trouble of actually reading. We can finish typing early and have lunch with the girls up in Westport.

The mature response, of course, is not to demonize feminism. Like the winter weather Duke Senior exults in, the lessons we learn from the "politically correct" have a special savor, the sweetness of adversity. These are the venomous toads of our time. When their minds are carefully dissected, we can still find that precious jewel of truth within.

WORKS CITED:

Dara Kaye, "Murther Most Foul: poison as a gendered weapon in Shakespeare," *The Shakespeare Institute Review*, Vol. 1, June, 2012.

Plato: The Collected Dialogues, Edith Hamilton, Huntington Cairns, eds., Princeton University Press, Bollingen Series LXXI, 1989.

William Shakespeare, Complete Works, J. Bate & E. Rasmussen, eds., Royal Shakespeare Company, 1985.

William Shakespeare, The Complete Works, 2d edition, S. Wells, & G. Taylor, eds., Clarendon Press, Oxford, 2005.

17
Shakespeare Versus Montaigne

There is something unknown in knowing. — Richard Eberhart

I. Introduction

*R*ecent Shakespeare criticism has suggested a substantial influence on the English dramatist by the 16th century French essayist. Though the point has been reiterated until well-nigh taken for granted, its accuracy and scope may be questioned. For it is hard to imagine two more different authorial voices. Shakespeare created a vast dramatic realm, including larger-than-life heroes embroiled in *Sturm und Drang*. We thrive in the passions of these promethean characters. High tension and radical transformation are his meat. Whether one considers the bathetic escapades of the comedies, the unrelenting confrontations of his histories or the explosive self-revelations of the tragedies, all set forth in the most compelling language ever to emerge from the human soul, Shakespeare is the master of life's affective dimension, the Michelangelo of the mind. His characters' emotional contortions enlarge and illuminate our own follies and triumphs. We participate in their lives vicariously, learning their lessons without undergoing their trials. Their catharsis is ours too.

Montaigne, on the other hand, is not a thespian but a thinker. His sere sensibility, forged over a lifetime of study and contemplation, is cool, unruffled and deliberate. His anecdotes are emblematic rather than engrossing. His personal heroes are not wounded giants but rather reserved and resourceful geniuses, sages who sift the sands of human experience to bring forth kernels of wit and wisdom. Epicurus, Lucretius and Pyrrho, philosophers whose teachings aim at the overcoming of passion and tempestuous struggles in favor of meditation, insight and inner peace, are his models. While it may be that Shakespeare perused these *Essays*, allowing us to recognize in his oeuvre what seem to be borrowed phrases or themes, such instances are not what most of us mean by "influence." For over the course of living, everything leaves its mark in one way or another. As Tennyson's Ulysses famously says, "I am a part of all that I have met." But most of the traces within us are mere shades which color but do not constitute what we are. Had Montaigne exercised a detectable influence on Shakespeare, we'd have a different corpus today. In addition to such tormented figures as Lear, Coriolanus, Troilus and King Richard II, we would find other, more restrained and refined protagonists, seeking to hold themselves aloof, above the fray, beyond the rough and tumble of the quotidian round. Of course, Shakespeare knew philosophy and made use of it. But his characters simply do not manifest the serene and steady aim of a Montaigne. Cicero has a cameo appearance in *Julius Caesar*, but Brutus, trained as a Stoic, fails conspicuously to make use of the doctrines in which he was schooled. Cassius tells him so. (IV, ii, 197-198) Apemantus' bickering with Timon in Act Four of *Timon of Athens* is a harsh and discordant departure from the wry ripostes he delivers earlier. The fact is that Shakespeare's restless spirit dwells not at the "still center of the turning world," but at the margins, the extremities of life, whose roaring tides we must navigate or perish. Shakespearean humanity becomes what it is, and reveals itself as such, through opposition and stress. Over and over, he teaches that we must strive, use our talents, make ourselves reflected in the world and leave a legacy, or we are nothing. (See, *e.g., Troilus and Cressida*, III, iii, 90-114) Martius strides into the city of the Corioles alone. (*Coriolanus*, I, v, 16) Banished from Rome, he embraces his enemies and wars upon his erstwhile countrymen. Yet it is his indomitable ego which more undoes him than the tribunes, the commons and Aufidius. For Shakespeare the dramatist, dull peace is rarely an option; it is barren, idle, of no more significance than "the lascivious pleasing of a lute." (*King Richard III*, I, i, 13) On the other hand, unchecked war is a curse. The Stoic philosophers who clustered on their high porches to poke fun at the foibles of mankind would not be in his terms fully present. They are mere observers, not participants. Though arguably proof against despair and anxiety, they could not achieve the pinnacle of human glory or purchase the profound and searching self-knowledge they sought. With the possible exception of Marcus Aurelius, they were unwilling to pay the price of action. Remember that Christianity triumphed over Stoicism precisely because of the passion of Christ. The god of Stoicism has no preferences, no cares. If Montaigne were advising Tennyson's Ulysses, then, his counsel would be to build a stony tower in Ithaka and stay put. Why tempt fate again, putting oneself in harm's way? In brief, then, those who would contend that Shakespeare's art betrays the imprint of Montaigne, though they advance an intriguing hypothesis, bear a heavy burden of persuasion. In the following pages we will inspect their argument and find it wanting.

II. Skepticism

As the principal link between Montaigne and Shakespeare is alleged to be the philosophy of skepticism, and as that descended from the ancient Greeks, we should first seek to grasp what it portended for those in whom it had its inception and roots, the philosophers of Athens and their progeny. The Socratic turn brought philosophy down "from heaven to earth," making the axiological concerns of human life, rather than physical and cosmological speculations, the center of investigation. Not "What is Nature?" but "What are We?" becomes the issue for Socrates and his students. Out of his dialectical colloquies emerge the great academic philosophies of Plato and Aristotle, which concentrate increasingly on the acquisition and elaboration of knowledge understood as a comprehensive system resting on metaphysical principles. Of at least equal importance, however, is another strain of thought which would eventually send philosophy in a different direction, one consonant with the primary Socratic concern with human affairs. As the hegemonic control of Athens, Sparta and their associated city states began to unravel, many sought to employ philosophy to cope with gathering uncertainties. The nature of happiness (*eudaemonia*) was an urgent personal agenda before it became a conceptual puzzle. In this connection, a number of thinkers and schools arose offering, in the face of historical setbacks and disasters, philosophies of consolation, including hedonism, Epicureanism, cynicism, stoicism and skepticism. Those outlooks were variations on the theme of civilized life, a cognitively based enterprise which conceived of its proper end as a wisdom which might afford its possessors not merely theoretical insight but, more importantly, those accessible fulfillments and gratifications suitable for giddy creatures such as ourselves. One of these, stoicism, rose to become the dominant standpoint of the ancient world, its name synonymous with philosophy itself.

In the case of skepticism, however, on account of the contemporary application of the term, it is difficult for moderns and "post-moderns" (whatever they may be) to comprehend what it meant to our ancestors. Modern "skepticism" arose in the context of the physical and cosmological ideas and revelations of Copernicus and Galileo, who urged among other things the superiority of the heliocentric hypothesis. After 1609-1610, when the telescope began to be used to survey the heavens, it became apparent that geocentricity could no longer be maintained. This astounding discovery, celebrated as a breakthrough which finally set forth the nature of the cosmos for "Homo sapiens," carried darker and more ominous implications. Soon Blaise Pascal was complaining that "the eternal silence of these infinite spaces terrifies me." Implicit was the stark fact that our race had been utterly deluded about the nature of things from the beginning of recorded time. To put it bluntly, we were wrong, very wrong. To wake up after a gross delusion of 10-20,000 years and embrace a new and incongruous vision of the world may have been momentarily exhilarating, but on reflection must also have been a humbling and even unsettling turn of events. What were regarded as fundamental and self-evident truths had to be jettisoned. And it is likely that the full consequences of this sea-change have yet to be assessed. To make matters worse, modern learning could set in place of the traditional *Weltanschauung* no definite image, no fixed concept or idea, but rather an interminable succession of hypotheses and theories. Indeed, the very word "modern" implies a mere "mode" or form of comprehension, to be replaced sooner or later by another. The citadel of truth had been razed by error, and in its place loomed a yawning abyss.

The philosophical response to this predicament was swift and dramatic. In 1641, René Descartes, a close student of Galileo's physics and astronomy, published in Latin his *Meditations on First Philosophy*, which lamented the state of human ignorance and sought to employ doubt, not self-evident principles, as the ground of any future knowing. A first-hand witness to the overthrow of ancient cosmology and its bi-polar physics, Descartes wrote that our condition was like that of someone thrown into deep water, who had no way of telling what was up and what was down. A sense of intellectual vertigo became prevalent. All so-called "knowledge" was suspect. Hence, although he is remembered primarily as a "rationalist," Descartes was in method and heuristic attitude a skeptic who so impugned the adequacy of extant knowledge that none of it survived as such. This was nothing short of a spiritual putsch.

And though he attempted to restore the *status quo ante* on the basis of unimpeachable rational deductions, what emerged from his pen was quickly seized on by other skeptics who demolished Cartesian rationalism's house of cards. Modern skepticism exudes, then, an atmosphere of incalculable devastation. Its mood is *au fond* one of defeat and resignation, the waiving and surrendering of any claim to durable and reliable knowledge. This is the central theme in modern philosophy, exhibited by such devices as British empiricism on the one hand and Jacques Derrida's deconstruction on the other. It is the intellectual catastrophe of modern skepticism, then, which leads institutions and journalists to batten a perplexed people on electronic gizmos and vapid images of "exploration" and "conquest" of a "universe" hazily understood at best. "Progress" is the chief dogma of modernity, our sacred cow, a way of keeping doubt at bay. Yet sooner or later the dark must dawn.

When students of literature look back at classical skepticism without sufficient care, they may tend to suppose that the limitations and frustrations of our generation were also felt by the ancients. But as suggested above, this view is largely a coarse anachronism. For the original skepticism was not a crisis but a program of edification designed, like its allies, hedonism, cynicism, Epicureanism and stoicism, as a roadmap to contentment. Its ambience was not despair but genial delight. And as we are about to see, much the same misunderstanding occurs when literary critics and philosophers seek to argue that a supposedly subversive skepticism of Michel de Montaigne exercised an unnerving influence on the art of William Shakespeare. That claim can only be held in ignorance of Montaigne's skeptical stance and the nature of his philosophical enterprise in general. We will find at all times that Shakespeare and Montaigne stand at the metaphysical antipodes.

III. Pyrrhonian Skepticism

Classical skepticism is a philosophy of consolation. It was formulated not as a "theory of knowledge" in our sense of the term, but as a cognitive recipe for detachment and inner peace. Contemporary skepticism, on the other hand, is symptomatic of a dilemma. What is termed "epistemology" by writers of the 20th and 21st centuries is a concoction of those who call themselves "professional philosophers," academics whose business it is to tussle with problems of perception and truth which are the detritus of such sciences as physics and physiology. Hence classical and modern skepticism are not merely different, they are wholly inimical to one another in feeling-tone and meaning. Contemporary philosophers would find absurd the idea of any connection between the "theory" of skepticism and personal satisfaction. On the contrary, the whole thrust of modern philosophy is the refutation of skepticism's challenge and its supplanting by a robust, if superficial, common sense. Modern skepticism is a Problem; ancient skepticism was a Solution. Unless this contrast is kept firmly in mind, any discussion of "the influence of Montaigne on Shakespeare" can only confound and mislead.

It was dissatisfaction with Cyrenaic Hedonism's identification of happiness with pleasure which led to the development of Epicureanism, which measured satisfaction not by intensity of sensual gratification but by the absence of pain and woe. In fact, for Lucretius, the foremost exponent of Epicureanism, high voltage pleasure is a derangement of the soul akin to torture. The pacification of consciousness yields a state known as "*ataraxia*." The Stoics, by a different and more theistic route, denominated the goal as the similar "*apatheia*." The teachings of the Epicureans and the Stoics were designed to wean people away from crude notions of happiness to something more accurate, practical and productive. And this was the aim also of Pyrrho of Elis (360 BC - 270 BC), the first known Skeptic, who adapted the concept of "*ataraxia*" to signify the equilibrium of beliefs and opinions achieved by declining to embrace any of them. Much as Socrates said that the fear of death is a pretended knowledge, so Pyrrho taught that our anxiety in the face of any unknowing is basically delusive and grounded in needless and inappropriate pretensions. To the welter of opinions which compose our discourse the ancient skeptics steadfastly demurred, refusing to choose. If you argued for "A," the skeptic would defend "not A," and vice versa. Seeing the impossibility of any single ideology or argument vanquishing its rivals, the classical skeptic disavowed all positions, withholding assent at every moment. The "cash value" (William James) of this strategy is not the shallow smugness of agnosticism, but a spiritual liberty which attends the recognition that theory always elicits its nemesis. Thus it was that Pyrrho of Elis achieved the same "*ataraxia*" which Epicurus and Lucretius accomplished with their rejection of unrestricted pleasure. Not libertinism but intellectual fraternity affords true happiness. Instead of the clash of ideas which divides us from one another, Pyrrhonian skepticism is consistent with an amity in which colleagues shrug off the burdens of contentious knowledge, and return to the modesties of common sense, not because it is established as veridical, but rather because at the end of the day, none of the fractious ideologies is left standing. As G.E. Moore was to say in defense of our common world: "here is one hand, here is the other." No rarefied epistemic doubt has the compelling vigor of the simplest article of habitual belief, and when we finally step off the carousel of assertion we find ourselves content. Thus to the catalepsia of the Stoics, a binding principle in which intellectual insight coheres with the data of sense, the Pyrrhonian skeptics opposed their "acatalepsia," in which more joy is found in normal human ignorance than in partisan claims which all hound one another.

Pyrrho of Elis appears in a well-known picture by Petrarca-Meister (aka Hans Weiditz), "The Philosopher Pyrrho in Stormy Seas." In the middle of a foundering ship he is seated calmly, his back to the mast, his head shrouded in a blue wide-brimmed hat. One leg rests calmly athwart a rolling canon. Sailors and passengers are in pandemonium. Pyrrho points to a pig mindlessly grubbing about the rolling deck. We know this tale: he admonishes the frightened crew that a mere pig, a most ignorant brute, has no fear of pelting rain and churning sea. Why should those denominated "Homo sapiens" exhibit less self-possession than a lowly beast? Do we know that this storm is a manifest evil for us? No. That would be presumptuous. Suppose we go to watery graves. Might we not thereby be spared far greater horrors? Pyrrho teaches by the example of his own insularity. Of course *das Narrenschiff* is a metaphor for the clash of opinions, including the debate about the fate of the soul after death. The Pyrrhonian view is that there is more to fear in that interminable disputation than in death itself.

It is interesting to note, by the way, that a philosophy identical to Pyrrho's arose in ancient China. Its originator and foremost exponent was Chuangtse. Pyrrho and Chuangtse both died c. 270 BC. How these two creative thinkers could have developed identical metaphysical views at the same historical moment in different languages on opposite sides of the planet is an intriguing puzzle. [To sample Chuangtse's presentation of Pyrrhonian skepticism, See *The Wisdom of Laotse*, by Lin Yutang, Foreign Language Teaching and Research Press, Beijing, 2009, Book one, pp. 013ff.]

IV. Montaigne's Skepticism

It is thus fairly clear that it is not enough to speak casually of Montaigne's skepticism in general. Just what sort of skepticism did this 16th century thinker advance? As he died prior to (1) the use of the telescope in astronomy (1609-1610), (2) the physics and astronomy of Galileo, (3) Descartes' *Meditations on First Philosophy*, and (4) the appropriation of Cartesian principles by the English-speaking empiricists beginning with John Locke (1632-1704), we can say with confidence that the *Essays* of Michel de Montaigne preceded the epistemological problematic by at least half a century. As a writer of the later Renaissance, his philosophizing emerged out of a broadly based humanistic ethos which can be traced back to 15th century Italian thought which itself derived from the Socratic turn in ancient Greece. As might be expected, then, in an author as well versed as he was in the literature of antiquity, Montaigne's skepticism owed much to the philosophies of consolation mentioned above, most particularly to the original skepticism of Pyrrho of Elis.

We'll first consult the authoritative Introduction to *The Complete Essays of Montaigne*, by editor M.A. Screech.

> i. By any standards the publication in 1562 by Henri-Estienne of the first edition of the original Greek text of Sextus' account of Pyrrho's scepticism was a major event. Montaigne probably relied chiefly on his Latin translation — also found in the second edition of 1567, but engraved quotations from the original Greek enlivened his tower library. (xxxiv)

ii. Opinion is not knowledge. Pyrrhonist sceptics reveled in that fact. Sextus Empiricus systematized that contention into a powerful engine of doubt *which helped a wise man to suspend his judgement and so to attain tranquility of mind.* (xxxiv, emphasis added)

Where is the tranquility of mind in Cartesian skepticism? There is none. In fact, in a moment of literary paranoia, Descartes in his *Meditations* conjures up the prospect of a malignant genie who might exercise his powers to instill in the poor philosopher's mind ideas, apprehensions and notions all misleading and delusive. This leads Descartes to consternation and dejection. Certainly the revelation that the human understanding of heaven and earth is, as perceived, scarcely better than a mirage is a thorn in his side until he has set up a proof that our perceptions of the world are reliable and indicative of the nature of things. The skeptical moment for Descartes or any other modern epistemologist is one of concern and dismay.

For Pyrrho and his disciple, Montaigne, on the other hand, doubt itself is the desideratum, for intellectual equilibrium yields equanimity, the solace of incredulity.

Montaigne writes:

[T]he professed aim of Pyrrhonians is to shake all convictions, to hold nothing as certain, to vouch for nothing. Of the three functions attributed to the soul (cogitation, appetite and assent) the Sceptics admit the first two but keep their assent in a state of ambiguity, inclining neither way, giving not even the slightest approbation to one side or the other. (Montaigne, 560)

Now the Pyrrhonians make their faculty of judgment so unbending and upright that it registers everything but bestows its assent on nothing. This leads to their well-known *ataraxia*: that is a calm, stable rule of life, free from disturbances (caused by the impress of opinions, or of such knowledge of reality as we think we have) which give birth to fear, acquisitiveness, envy, immoderate desires, ambition, pride, superstition, love of novelty, rebellion, disobedience, obstinacy and the greater part of our bodily ills. In this way, they even free themselves from passionate sectarianism, for their disputes are mild affairs and they are never afraid of the other side. (Montaigne, 560)

If it is a child who makes the judgment, he does not know enough about the subject: if it is a learned man, then he has made up his mind already! — Pyrrhonians have given themselves a wonderful strategic advantage by shrugging off the burden of self defence. It does not matter who attacks them as long as somebody does. Anything serves their purpose: if they win, your argument is defective; if you do, theirs is. If they lose, they show the truth of Ignorance; if you lose, you do. If they can prove that nothing is known: fine.

They make it their pride to be far more ready to find everything false than anything true and to show that things are not, rather than that they are. They prefer to proclaim what they do not believe, rather than what they do. Their typical phrases include: 'I have settled nothing'; 'It is no more this than that'; 'Not one rather than the other'; 'I do not understand'; 'Both sides seem likely'; 'It is equally right to speak for and against either side'. To them, nothing seems true which cannot also seems false. They have sworn loyalty to the word *epokhé* [transliterated from Greek]: 'I am in suspense'; I will not budge. (Montaigne, 562-563)

After a deep and extensive analysis and considering all objections, Montaigne accepts Pyrronistic skepticism. The key is the secure foundation it provides for human satisfaction and security.

We would be better off if we dropped our inquiries and let ourselves be moulded by the natural order of the world. A soul safe from prejudice has made a wondrous advance towards peace of mind.

* * *

No system discovered by Man has greater usefulness nor a greater appearance of truth [than Pyrrhonism] which shows us Man naked, empty, aware of his natural weakness, fit to accept outside help from on high: Man, stripped of all human learning, and so all the more able to lodge the divine within him, annihilating his intellect to make room for faith; he is no scoffer, he holds no doctrine contrary to established custom; he is humble, obedient, teachable, keen to learn — and as a sworn enemy of heresy he is freed from the vain and irreligious opinions introduced by erroneous sects. (Montaigne, 564)

The stamp of Pyrrhonism on Montaigne can be found throughout the *Essays*. In the midst of the strife of systems, he remains free, yet judicious. The carnage of intellectual battle confirms his faith. He is "cool," like the cynics and their modern descendants, the beatniks. "We do not go; we are borne along like things afloat, now bobbing now lashing about us as the waters are angry or serene." (Montaigne, 375) "We float about among diverse counsels; our willing of anything is never free, final or constant." (Montaigne, 375) In passage after passage, he raises polite and sober criticisms of mental turmoil and agitation as root causes of sadness and folly, illustrating the point with apt and ironical tales. He is content to let the technical and speculative arguments of philosophy fall by their own weight, leaving the mind free to embrace a natural life of moderate pleasures, marriage and friendship, supported by a time-tested religious faith which had proved itself to be one of civilization's most successful institutions, a bulwark against nihilism. In that he differs from Lucretius, who excoriated religion as a source of fear. For Montaigne, however, the Christian faith was apprehended not as disease but as supererogatory remedy, one that was congruent with or extensive of—rather than contrary to—the deliverances of Pyrrhonism.

Such is Montaigne, philosopher and human being. In studying him, we are reminded of Hume's admonition, "Be a philosopher; but amidst all your philosophy, be still a man."

The question we pose at this point is about Shakespeare. Is there anything in the philosophy we have been expositing which finds its echo in him? Are there characters in his drama who evince the *epokhé*—or a reasonable facsimile? No. And yet the acceptation of Shakespeare as a disciple of the French sage will not down.

We turn now to its evaluation.

V. Tragic Skepticism

In a recent book, Professor Millicent Bell seeks to make a case for something called Shakespeare's "tragic skepticism." It is suggested that in staging "tragic skepticism," Shakespeare expresses the spirit of Michel de Montaigne. In that context, however, something is amiss. For if the foregoing analysis is correct, "tragic skepticism" is an oxymoron at best, and possibly a contradiction in terms. We have noted that for Pyrrho of Elis, the founder of the skeptical movement in philosophy, far from being tragic, skepticism is the antidote to tragedy, the anodyne that relieves us of all suffering related to our ideas. When every diagnosis is differential, none is lethal. In strictly philosophical terms, the telos of Pyrrhonian skepticism is the *epokhé* and *ataraxia*, or inner peace and tranquility. By the time of Sextus Empiricus (c. 200 AD), who inherited and gave systematic expression to the skeptical philosophy in the generation following Pyrrho, skepticism's connection to human fulfillment was still of cardinal importance. "By scepticism," he wrote, "we arrive first at suspension of judgment, and second at freedom from disturbance." (Magee, 43) Skepticism emanating from the classic line of Greek antiquity would be wholly adverse to any form of reversal or misery, including tragedy.

Bell first brings forward the notion "tragic skepticism" in her Introduction. It is: "the way tragedy results from skeptic disillusion." (Bell, 4) What could these words portend? The pairing of "skeptic" and "disillusion" would be unintelligible to the founders of skepticism, Pyrrho and Sextus Empircus. They would find it quite impossible to understand what connection there is between tragedy and education in skepticism. In fact, we just learned a moment ago that skepticism for Sextus leads us not to disillusion or tragedy but to "freedom from disturbance." What is Bell talking about?

The answer, it seems, lies in Shakespeare.

[H]amlet feels *at one and the same time* the wonder of the human creature and the beauty of the world which has become a "sterile promontory" to him. His mood is one of tragic loss from which there seems no recovery." (Bell, 4, emphasis in original)

What shall we make of this? There is no question that at the opening of *The Tragedy of Hamlet, Prince of Denmark*, Prince Hamlet is dejected. It would be appropriate to say he is in a despondent mood, one which occurs well before his encounter with the ghost who gives news of the murder of King Hamlet by Prince Claudius, the king's brother.

In Act I, Sc. 2, he is contemplating suicide. (I, ii, 129-132) The manifest reason for his malaise is the accelerated remarriage of his mother to Claudius, but we all know that that is not an adequate explanation. No one suffers self-destructive ideation over breaches in etiquette or epistemological puzzles. But Prince Hamlet has been passed over for the Danish throne. That telling fact, coupled with the hasty remarriage of his mother implies he may be a court bastard and thus barred from the succession. This unsettling possibility has nothing to do with the skepticism of Pyrrho and Sextus Empiricus. Those philosophers would advise Hamlet to cultivate a judiciously skeptical point of view to allay the worries that nag at him. As we can never know exactly who we are, why not just relax and take each moment as it comes? Classic skepticism yields peace, not anxiety or "disillusion."

Prof. Bell then follows up with this:

> That ideas contend with one another in Shakespeare's writings is a quality he shares with the skeptic near-contemporary with whom I find him comparable, Michel de Montaigne. Montaigne's curiously moving, often evasive, often self-revelatory confessions of alternating belief and unbelief are not merely a feature of his response to the dogmas of his religion. They are duplicated in his attitudes toward numerous other generally accepted assumptions about mankind and the world. Taken as a whole, Montaigne's essays dramatize the unreadiness of his belief to come down on any conclusion without allowing for the possibility of its opposite. It is that representative skeptic method [sic] of balancing opposing views which was to be inherited from Montaigne by Pierre Bayle, who, at the end of the seventeenth century, made his famous encyclopedic dictionary a dramatization of the "method of doubt," in which one opinion was posed against [sic] another. I am suggesting that Shakespeare's thought . . . is, like Montaigne's or Bayle's, dialectic or dialogic. It pits an idea against its opposite. It looks to me as though Shakespeare — writing as he did at a time of cultural crisis when old convictions and new doubts were contending in men's minds — put contrary views into combat to test their strength. His plays are never allegorical — they never dramatize directly the contest of ideas — yet in them ideas contend from line to line in the richest language the stage has

ever known. Through the action and language of the plays he invites his audiences to question from moment to moment, the inherited, standard truths of his time. He allows his audience to view fearfully the results of abandoning the prop of such beliefs. This is the hidden structure of argument in Shakespeare's plays. (Bell, 4-5)

This rambling is not easily followed. Let's look closely. Bell asserts no influence of Montaigne on Shakespeare, but merely finds them "comparable." Yet the contours of this similarity remain veiled. Montaigne is here not afforded so much as a single quotation. Instead, a series of pejorative epithets is sprinkled on the page: "curiously moving," "often evasive," "self-revelatory," and "dogm[atic]." Montaigne is accused of having cultivated "attitudes" toward "generally accepted assumptions about mankind." And then we have reference to his "unreadiness" of belief to "come down on" any conclusion without allowing for the possibility of its opposite. Yes, Montaigne embraced classical skepticism, but hardly because of a lack of preparation. Instead of demonstrating the connection of his "attitudes" to Shakespeare with particularity, we find an irrelevant allusion to Montaigne's supposed influence on Pierre Bayle (1647-1706), a relatively obscure figure in late seventeenth century thought, who is said to have practiced a "method of doubt." What is the point of this detour? How would Pierre Bayle, who post-dates Montaigne and Shakespeare, shed light on their similitude? Notice that by the time she returns to Shakespeare, we are told that he seeks to use skepticism to induce "fear" in his audiences, a dubious proposition and entirely unsupported. Any fear-inducing attitude in Shakespeare is certainly not inherited from Montaigne, a figure of calm and equanimity. On the contrary, one of the principal sources of fear for Shakespeare's characters is awe at the indifference or malevolence of the gods. That is the product not of doubt but of belief.

Such divagations do nothing to assist the reader to come to terms with the vague claims being asserted about Shakespeare. There is no recognition anywhere in the discussion that there are a variety of skepticisms, and that in discussing the subject it is necessary to distinguish them to avoid mix-ups. We have already seen above that the originator of modern epistemological skepticism was not Pierre Bayle in the late seventeenth century, but René Descartes earlier that century. It was Descartes, not Bayle, who famously practiced the "method of doubt," as Prof. Bell herself later admits. (Bell, 14)

As for the actual relationship of Montaigne and Bayle, attending to the scholars who have devoted themselves to that subject is well advised. Here are the important comments of Karl C. Sandberg in the *Journal of History of Philosophy* (Vol. 8, No. 1, January, 1978, pp. 103-104), reviewing the analysis of Prof. Craig B. Brush in his book, *Montaigne and Bayle: Variations on the Theme of Skepticism* (The Hague: Martinus Nijhoff, 1966).

> The conclusion of this study establishes similarities and dissimilarities between Bayle and Montaigne, who have often been carelessly lumped together under the catch-all word of "skeptics." Noting that both of them endorsed a form of religious fideism and argued that skepticism prepared the mind to receive Grace, Professor Brush touches upon the very thorny problem of defining Bayle's religious belief, which he characterizes semi-fideism. He notes by way of contrast that Montaigne, by not sharing the Calvinist austerity of Bayle's character, came at the end of his life to a particular brand of gay wisdom that Bayle never knew. Where Montaigne attained to the prize of self-knowledge at the end of his life of inquiry, Bayle found only an unmitigated pessimism, producing in his *Dictionnaire* a documented indictment of the human race.

Prof. Brush's point is well taken. Montaigne's Pyrrhonism cannot be conflated with other less sunny forms of skepticism, a tendency we see in Prof. Bell.

Later in the Introduction she criticizes Montaigne for assembling a suspect mélange of doubt and belief in his fideistic Catholic faith. In this she detects a fundamental "ambivalence" in Montaigne's thinking. (Bell, 13) But that so-called "ambivalence" is a function of Bell's unwillingness to find in his Pyrrhonism a philosophy of consolation, and acknowledge that it culminates in the same *ataraxia* we see in Lucretius. It is also akin to the *apatheia* of Stoicism. When once we apprehend the natural *telos* of Montaigne's classical skepticism, we can set aside such charges as syncretism and ambivalence. Professor Brush's point is well taken: skepticism prepares the mind for Grace, and this in a double sense: first by sweeping aside the chaff of seeming knowledge, and more importantly, by giving to the human soul a foretaste of Grace in *ataraxia*. Thus, for Montaigne, reason plays a somewhat larger role in our religious sensibility than is allowed in the Aristotelian system of St. Thomas Aquinas, where strictly rational arguments can show the existence of God but not what He actually is, an understanding that can be received through divine self-disclosure or revelation only. As in the Augustinian tradition in which the soul is restless 'til it rests in the Rock of Ages, we may think of the skeptical *ataraxia* as the cooling shadow cast by that sturdy Rock. There is no "ambivalence." After all, why would the Divine leave mankind in absolute darkness for untold millennia, deferring any sense of salvation until the Prophets? One might think, then, of Montaigne's philosophy as a negative theology which clears a path not only to the idea of God but also to a sense of His nature.

Even when she touches on Pyrrhonism by name, Bell fails to say what it signifies. She writes, "Both Shakespeare and Montaigne exhibit, I believe, the effects of the current inclination of thought called "Pyrrhonism, after Pyrrho, the third-century B.C. Greek who taught that nothing can be known." (Bell, 14) After fourteen pages of exposition during which there is a failure to identify the nature of Montaigne's philosophy, we finally witness a half-hearted attempt to approach it, only to find ourselves short-changed. The abstract dogma that "nothing can be known" is not Pyrrhonism. This was already explained above. And if Shakespeare is best understood as a follower of "Pyrrhonism," it's rather strange that it took four centuries to come to such a realization. Like so many would-be philosophers, Prof. Bell writes sentences about high-sounding topics which turn out to be mere subjectivities ("I believe").

Another swipe at Montaigne is taken on the subject of the supernatural. As her quotation from him employs archaic form, we will use a modern translation (M.A. Screech) from Chapter 27 of the *Essays* for better understanding.

> It is not perhaps without good reason that we attribute to simple-mindedness a readiness to believe anything and to ignorance the readiness to be convinced, for I think I was once taught that a belief is like an impression stamped on our soul: the softer and less resisting the soul, the easier it is to print anything on it .... The more empty a soul is and the less furnished with counterweights, the more easily its balance will be swayed under the force of its first convictions. That is why children, the common people, women and the sick are more readily led by the nose. On the other hand there is a silly arrogance in continuing to disdain something and to

condemn it as false just because it seems unlikely to us. That is a common vice among those who think their capacities are above the ordinary.

I used to do that once: if I heard tell of ghosts walking or of prophecies, enchantments, sorcery, or some other tale which I could not get my teeth into . . . I used to feel sorry for the wretched folk who were taken in by such madness. Now I find that I was at least as much to be pitied as they were. It is not that experience has subsequently shown me anything going beyond my original beliefs (nor is it from nay lack of curiosity on my part), but reason has taught me that, if you condemn in this way anything whatever as definitely false and quite impossible, you are claiming to know the frontiers and bounds of the will of God and the power of nature our Mother; it taught me also that there is nothing in the whole world madder than bringing matters down to the measure of our own capacities and potentialities. (Montaigne, 200-201; cp. Bell, 16-17)

In all wisdom literature it would be hard to find more incisive judgment and adroitness of expression than this. But for Prof. Bell it is just a symptom of Montaigne's addle-headedness.

The passage is as good an illustration as one can find in Montaigne's Essayes of the character of his skepticism, which regards all things doubtfully, and even applies doubt to the act of doubting, because so many things cannot be known. (Bell, 17)

Well, that's just not what Montaigne says. What he does is admit to a modest credulity when it comes to paranormal phenomena.

Earlier, Prof. Bell mocks Montaigne's skepticism in comparison with "modern disbelief" which is "a kind of certainty in itself." (Bell, 13) Montaigne's skepticism, on the other hand, robs us of modern disbelief by its "readiness not so much to deny what had always been believed as to say that one could not really know one way or the other." (Bell, 13) In this respect, not only does Montaigne show greater depth and intelligence than his critics, but so also does Shakespeare, whose plays are filled with instances of fate, prophecy and the proximity of the gods.

We recall Shakespeare writing in *All's Well That Ends Well*: "They say that miracles are past, and we have our philosophical persons to make modern and familiar things supernatural and causeless. Hence it is that we make trifles of terrors, ensconcing ourselves into seeming knowledge when we should submit ourselves to an unknown fear." (II, iii, 1-6) And given such sentiments and the prominence of supernatural elements in Shakespeare, does this lead to the conclusion that Shakespeare was under the spell of Montaigne and Pyrrho? Not at all. For any fair reading of Shakespeare will show that he inclined not to Pyrrhonism, an abstract doctrine, but rather to the presence and efficacy of a supervenient agency in human affairs. (Gontar, 161ff.) The philosophy of Montaigne is a blueprint for human fulfillment and satisfaction, seeing through the pretensions of "knowledge." Shakespeare, on the other hand, operates in an entirely different intellectual laboratory, focusing on the Laocoön-like travails of larger-than-life individuals who are liable to various forms of self-deception. Had Shakespeare been preoccupied with "knowledge" he would have given us Faust, not Othello.

Returning once again to the singularity of Montaigne's skepticism, we should not overlook the penetrating and even-handed treatment provided by the *Stanford Encyclopedia of Philosophy*, which exposes with great care the two moments of Montaigne's skepticism, allowing us to see the reason why his position is so often misunderstood by contemporary thinkers. The key passages are these.

> We find two readings of Montaigne as a Sceptic. The first one concentrates on the polemical, negative arguments drawn from Sextus Empiricus, at the end of the "Apology" [for Raymond Sebond]. This hard-line scepticism draws the picture of man as 'humiliated.' Its aim is essentially to fight the pretensions of reason and to annihilate human knowledge. 'Truth,' 'being' and 'justice' are equally dismissed as unattainable. Doubt foreshadows Descartes' *Meditations*, on the problem of the reality of the outside world. Dismissing the objective value of one's representations, Montaigne would have created the long-lasting problem of 'solipsism'. We notice, nevertheless, that he does not question the reality of things — except occasionally at the very end of the "Apology" — but the value of opinions and men. The second reading of his scepticism puts forth that Cicero's probabilism is of far greater significance in shaping the sceptical content of the *Essays*. After the

1570's, Montaigne no longer reads Sextus; additions show, however, that he took up a more and more extensive reading of Cicero's philosophical writings. We assume that, in his search for polemical arguments against rationalism during the 1570's, Montaigne borrowed much from Sextus, but as he got tired of the sceptical machinery, and understood scepticism rather as an ethics of judgment, he went back to Cicero. The paramount importance of the Academica for XVIth century thought has been underlined by Charles B. Schmitt. In the free enquiry, which Cicero engaged throughout the varied doctrines, the humanists found an ideal mirror of their own relationship with the Classics. 'The Academy, of which I am a follower, gives me an opportunity to hold an opinion as if it were ours, as soon as it shows itself highly probable,' wrote Cicero in *De Officiis*. Reading Seneca, Montaigne will think as if he were a member of the Stoa; then changing for Lucretius, he will think as if he had become an Epicurean, and so on. Doctrines or opinions, beside historical stuff and personal experiences, make up the nourishment of judgment. Montaigne assimilates opinions, according to what appears to him as true, without taking it to be absolutely true. He insists on the dialogical nature of thought, referring to Socrates' way of keeping the discussion going: 'The leaders of Plato's dialogues, Socrates, is always asking questions and stirring up discussion, never concluding, never satisfying...' Judgment has to determine the most convincing position, or at least to determine the strengths and weaknesses of each position; but if absolute truth is lacking, we still have the possibility to balance opinions [*i.e., isothenia*]. We have resources enough, to evaluate the various authorities that we have to deal with in ordinary life.

The original failure of commentators was perhaps in labelling Montaigne's thought as 'sceptic' without reflecting on the original meaning of the essay. Montaigne's exercise of judgment is an exercise of 'natural judgment', which means that judgment does not need any principle or any rule as a presupposition. In this way, many aspects of Montaigne's thinking can be considered as sceptical, although they were not used for the sake of scepticism. For example, when Mon-

taigne sets down the exercise of doubt as a good start in education, he understands doubt as part of the process of the
formation of judgment. This process should lead to wisdom,
characterized as '*always joyful.*' Montaigne's skepticism is not
a desperate one. On the contrary, it *offers the reader a sort of
jubilation* which relies on the modest but effective pleasure
in dismissing knowledge, thus making room for the exercise
of one's natural faculties. (Stanford, n.p.n., emphases added)

The meaning is clear. So-called "hard-line" skepticism is employed
by Montaigne to achieve a fair and accurate assessment of the state of
human knowledge, that is, it is to put us in our proper place as the only
species which seeks to compensate for its inevitable ignorance by making
vain and inflated claims to "knowledge," or, in some cases, omniscience.
To employ a humble metaphor, such negative skepticism may be compared to the rough kneading of dough before the baking of bread. It is
not the food itself but a part of its manufacture. Once the human mind
is jolted out of its gnostic fetish, Montaigne can proceed homeopathically to show how the relaxation of intellectual pretensions serves as a
restorative yielding natural felicity. As Socrates taught long ago, as long
as we think we know, we cannot learn. Only when we are shorn of our
intellectual pretensions can we proceed on the path of education. When
it finally dawns on us how steep that path is, we shrug off the burden of
Gnosis and content ourselves with the modest blessings of life.

It is therefore inexcusable to attribute to Montaigne the sort of ago-
nized modernity which bemoans the strictures of the anthropoid mind,
and then—worse—attributes the tragic confusions of Shakespeare's major characters, Lear, Hamlet, Macbeth, Othello, Coriolanus, *et al.*, to the
negative influence of Montaigne upon the English poet. Not a single one
of these characters exhibits the critically important *epokhé* and *ataraxia*
which are the signs of intellectual maturity and wisdom as outlined by
Montaigne. His bright and balanced outlook is altogether missing in
them and in their creator. Nor, as we will see, is it clear that the principal
dilemma of these characters arises out of a mere failure of comprehension or cognition. And it is not without significance that it was not until
the twentieth century that anyone dreamed of arguing that epistemological issues lay at the core of Shakespeare. Four hundred years of criticism
passed without anyone seeking to read him that way. Should all those
earlier readings now be swept into the dustbin? Limitations of space
prevent a complete analysis of Professor Bell's interpretations of Shake-

speare's tragedies. But there is no need to multiply examples which rest on premises demonstrated to be faulty. Instead, we will attend to Professor Colin McGinn and the meaning of "Shakespeare's philosophy."

VI. Shakespeare's Philosophy

Colin McGinn is not a literary critic or Shakespeare scholar, but a professor of philosophy who managed to compose a steady stream of academic and quasi-academic works at Rutgers University and the University of Miami. Aiming at the mass market, he accomplished the seemingly impossible, getting his volumes placed on the bookshelves of the nation's largest bookstore chains, where they might easily fall into the hands of an unsuspecting public. Professor Stanley H. Nemeth comments:

> Though occasionally insightful in its readings of specific passages, McGinn's book suffers from a questionable approach, the effort to discover the meaning behind Shakespeare's plays by dressing the author in borrowed clothes, the too tight doublet and hose of the smaller Montaigne and the completely inappropriate straightjackets of Hume or Wittgenstein. Thus for McGinn Shakespeare emerges as a sort of skeptical naturalist, a thesis difficult to maintain if one examines the plays in their entirety, neither neglecting nor distorting passages that undermine such a narrow view. (Nemeth, Amazon Book Review, January 7, 2007)

> According to McGinn, Shakespeare lived in an age before 'science.' Between the dogmas of the medieval worldview on the one hand and claims of the modern period on the other, Shakespeare inhabited a no man's land of 'doubt and uncertainty.' (McGinn, 3)

> [T]he most relevant fact about this period is that it preceded the Scientific Revolution, so that science was in its infancy in Shakespeare's day. Very little that we now take for granted was understood — in astronomy, physics, chemistry, and biology. The achievements of Descartes, Leibniz, Galileo, Newton, Boyle and other heroes of the Renaissance were still in the future. (McGinn, 2)

Ironically, a passage such as this is itself just as dubious and uncertain as anything in the time of Shakespeare. McGinn refers to something called the "Scientific Revolution" without any citations or references. What is the purpose and meaning of the capital letters? Sir Isaac Newton was largely a theologian, and his best known "scientific" work, *Principia Mathematica*, was published in 1687. In what way could he have been a "hero of the Renaissance"?

> The laws of mechanics were unknown; disease was a mystery; genetics was unheard of. Intelligent people believed in witchcraft, ghosts, fairies, astrology, and all the rest. Eclipses were greeted with alarmed superstition. Scientific method was struggling to gain a foothold. The conception of the world as a set of intelligible law-governed causes was at most a distant dream. (McGinn, 2)

One would infer that "the laws of mechanics" are universally known and understood in our own enlightened era. Yet how many of us are acquainted with these "laws"? The fact is that "laws of mechanics" is a metaphor, and not a very good one. Laws are properly creatures of legislation, and unless Mr. McGinn would like to argue that some divinity drafted the "laws" of nature, we would have no way to account for them. People obey laws because they are promulgated, and, conscious of their meaning, we strive to heed and follow them. How would this apply in the field of "mechanics"? Do billiard balls colliding on a table recognize and obey "laws"? If not, what is the meaning of referring to them as such? What ontological status would such "laws" have, and how would they impinge on and influence the objects and events described by "mechanics"? If one retreated into positivism and said that the locution was not to be taken literally, and that "laws of mechanics" is meant only as a way of referring to measurable regularities and patterns of material behavior, in the absence of actual "laws" how would we account for those regularities? To deal with these simple threshold issues is already to be thrust into the midst of the "philosophy of science," where all those nasty "doubts and uncertainties" we had banished from our "science" still lie in wait for us, belligerent and unresolved.

"Witchcraft, ghosts, fairies and astrology" are all spiritual phenomena. Has everything spiritual been exorcised from our lives, as Mr. McGinn implies? Not really. What is consciousness? No one knows. Why am I born this person rather than that? No one knows. What happens after death? Our modern geniuses are still scratching their heads over that one. Can "science" account for itself strictly on the basis of the "laws of mechanics" or any other "scientific laws"? Who has accomplished such a thing? Not only are spiritual, mental and psychic events common features of everyday life (including the hypotheses and theories of "science") the very concept of matter has been so conceptually pulverized that, compared with the atoms of Democritus or the "substance" of Locke, in the 21st century it is completely unrecognizable.

Apparently, Philosopher McGinn imagines it is self-evident that "the conception of the world" (whatever that means) is to be understood as a "set" of "intelligible law-governed causes." How do the ibis and mongoose fit in here? "O, this learning, what a thing it is!" (*The Taming of the Shrew*, I, ii, 157) Try as we might to barricade the doors and keep out haunting questions, they are importunate and thrust themselves upon us. What is denoted by the phrase "the world"? Would all agree about this? What is the relation between "the world" and our "conception of the world"? Is it our conception which is a "set," or is it the world itself? How can a "world" consist of "sets"? Is there anything else in our world of sets besides "causes"? If so, why not say so? What is space? What is time? Are they parts of "the world"? Are all "law-governed causes" intelligible? How would that be demonstrated? Again, how do "laws" "govern" "causes"? Is it all so clear? Is "the world" wholly translucent and comprehended exhaustively? Do we know everything? Why not?

The difference between Shakespeare's view of the world and ours today is like the difference between darkness and light, says McGinn. He didn't know, we do. Simple, isn't it?

> When Shakespeare looked up into the night sky, he had very little idea of what he was seeing, and the earth was still generally considered the center of the universe. (McGinn, 2)

How is it, then, that Prince Hamlet is able to so easily make reference to "infinite space"? (II, ii, 257) Is that the locution of a neanderthal geocentrist? Shakespeare lived in a world of astronomical ferment, whose superstars included Giordano Bruno (1548 - 1600), Tycho Brahe (1546 - 1601) and John Dee (1527 - 1608). Hamlet's castle at Elsinore was the Kronborg castle, completed in 1585, and this was a stone's throw away from the observatory of Tycho Brahe. Bruno publicized the infinity of space in London and was rewarded by being burned at the stake in 1600. May there not still be a few things in heaven and earth unknown in our modern philosophy?

Contrast that Stygian darkness with contemporary cosmology, in which all is as plain as the nose on your face. Hear, for example, breaking news from *Nature: International Weekly Journal of Science*, December 10, 2013, courtesy of Mr. Ron Cowen.

SIMULATIONS BACK UP THEORY THAT UNIVERSE IS A HOLOGRAM

A Ten Dimensional Theory of Gravity Makes the Same Predictions As Standard Quantum Physics in Fewer Dimensions

A team of physicists has provided some of the clearest evidence yet that our universe *could be* one big projection.

In 1997, theoretical physicist Juan Maldacena proposed that an audacious model of the universe in which gravity arises from infinitesimally thin, vibrating strings could be reinterpreted in terms of well established physics. The mathematically intricate world of strings, which exist in nine dimensions of space, plus one of time, would be merely a hologram: the real action would play out in a simpler, flatter cosmos, where there is no gravity. Maldacena's idea thrilled physicists because it offered a way to put the popular but *still unproven theory* of strings on solid footing — and because it solved apparent inconsistencies between quantum physics and Einstein's theory of gravity. It provided physicists with a mathematical Rosetta stone, a duality that allowed them to translate back and forth between two the languages, and solve problems in one model that seemed intractable in the other and vice versa. But although the validity of Malcadena's idea has pretty much been taken for granted ever since, *a rigorous proof has been elusive.* In two papers posted on the arXiv repository, Yoshifumi Hyakutake of Ibaraki University in Japan and his colleagues now provide, if not an actual proof, at least compelling evidence that Malcadena's conjecture is true. (Cowen, n.p.n., emphases added)

Is this knowledge—or a frank advertisement of nescience? Almost wholly unintelligible to the non-mathematical layperson, this assessment of our "universe" is not reassuring. The language is confusing and tentative. There are no unqualified claims of "knowledge," nor, based on what is read here, are there ever likely to be any, as one mathematical model after another unfolds before us, including the inconceivably fecund "strings" of which everything is supposed (by some) to be made. Read carefully. The "universe" (whatever that is) "could be" one big projection, that is, an illusion. Is this knowledge? The line between "science" and "science fiction" is wafer thin. So, although when Shakespeare looked up at the night sky, he was unaware of exactly what he saw, we with our super-charged "knowledge" stand in much the same position: we don't know either. And if this "projection" theory were adopted (for none of these ideas can ever be proven), with what would we be left but an unfathomable illusion? *Que sait-on*? Consider that on March 27, 2015 astronomers boldly declared in the news media that our "universe" would collapse in on itself in only "a few billion years." But for nearly a quarter of a century these same geniuses had assured a befuddled humanity that the "universe" would expand indefinitely. Woops, back to the drawing board!

The project of "science" initiated in the late Renaissance has not been completed. There is no "GUT" or unified field theory. There is no generally received image of what "the universe" is. And the mathematical games played by theoretical physicists and cosmologists are utterly foreign to ordinary human beings seeking to grasp who and where we are. The most fundamental concepts of space, time, matter and energy are thrown about like playthings of the imagination. "Theories" consisting primarily of mathematical formulae are presented to a bewildered public as though they represented a revelation of the very nature of things. And yet there is no common understanding, no imaginable "cosmos." Though Shakespeare may have had no "knowledge" when he gazed at the starry firmament, he at least had the advantage of not being totally alienated and lost, the immediate effect of what is reported in the journal *Nature* above.

Were Montaigne alive today, his assessment of this situation would remain unaltered. How, he would ask, can the geocentric worldview be discarded when the theory of relativity holds sway? If motion is not absolute, what basis is there for stating that the apparent revolution of the heavens is the exclusive product of the earth's rotation on its axis? In all of this well-funded speculation we see once again why Socrates abandoned cosmology: it was and remains a matter of surmise and speculation. Immanuel Kant, F. H. Bradley and other great philosophers showed repeatedly that the very categories of modern science are basically incoherent, and as such cannot yield univocal knowledge. Thomas Kuhn has shown that so-called "science" is a cavalcade of replaceable "paradigms" (that is metaphors) which are subject to periodic supplanting. What Professor McGinn offers, then, is a huge oversimplification.

(The reader wishing to pursue such issues pertaining to the adequacy of scientific knowledge may wish to read: "Ruminating on the Stephen Hawking Phenomenon," by Colin Bower, *New English Review*, August 26, 2006.)

Things go from bad to worse, as Prof. McGinn identifies "knowledge and skepticism" as the first of three themes promoted by "Shakespeare's philosophy." (McGinn, 3) As human existence has always been viewed as the vessel of "knowledge," Shakespeare must be understood as at least a maverick and, depending on the degree of one's principles, possibly a modern heretic. For the great thinkers of western civilization according to McGinn defined human nature in terms of its capacity for knowledge. (McGinn, 4) The lone dissenting voice was that of Socrates, who advised caution, the testing of our ambitious ideas, and who counseled "epistemological modesty." (McGinn, 5)

> It was left to the Greek skeptics, notably Sextus Empiricus, to push the Socratic lesson to its conclusion: that knowledge, however desirable, is simply not within our grasp. Plato's entire philosophy therefore founders, since it is just not possible to know anything worthwhile . . . Man does not have the capacity to satisfy his epistemological desires — he is too prone to illusion, error, and uncertainty. We cannot be sure that our senses are not deceiving us, or that our reasoning faculties yield sound inferences, even whether we are dreaming. Man is a small and feeble creature, epistemologically blighted, and not able to comprehend the universe. At its extreme, such skepticism claims that no belief has any greater justification than any other, so that belief itself is an irrational act (this is the school known as Pyrrhonism). The skeptics accepted Aristotle's dictum [that the purpose of human being is to achieve knowledge] but argued that it is man's nature also to be thwarted in his desire for knowledge. (McGinn, 5)

These claims are false. As stated by McGinn, human existence, defined by the desire for a knowledge which is incessantly being "thwarted," would be doomed to frustration and despair. But, quite to the contrary, Pyrrhonistic skepticism, as we have seen, was a practical path leading not to hopelessness but to unshakeable reserve.

In his taxonomy of skepticism, Montaigne put his finger on the confusion.

> Whoever sets out to find something eventually reaches the point where he can say that he has found it, or that it cannot be found, or that he is still looking for it. The whole of Philosophy can be divided into these three categories; her aim is to seek true, certain knowledge.
>
> 1. Peripatetics, Epicureans, Stoics and others think they have discovered it. They founded the accepted disciplines and expounded their knowledge as certainties.
> 2. Clitomachus, Carneades and the Academics *despaired of their quest*; they conclude that Truth cannot be grasped by human means. Their conclusion is one of weakness, of human ignorance. This school has had the greatest number of adherents and some of the noblest.
>
> 3. As for Pyrrho and the other Sceptics or Ephetics, whose teachings many of the Ancients derived from Homer, the Seven Sages, Archilochus and Euripides, and associated with Zeno, Democritus, and Xenophanes), they say they are still looking for Truth. They hold that the philosophers who think they have found it are infinitely wrong. They go on to add that the second category — those who are quite sure that human strength is incapable of reaching truth — are overbold and vain. To determine the limits of our powers and to know and judge the difficulty of anything whatsoever constitutes great, even the highest, knowledge. They doubt whether Man is capable of it. (Montaigne, 560, emphases added)

McGinn manifestly errs in consigning Pyrrhonism to Montaigne's second category, those who claim knowledge is impossible. This is the view against which Socrates campaigned his whole life. Bradley and other philosophers have acknowledged its contradictoriness. Pyrrhonistic skepticism, on the other hand, is not a knowledge claim, and on that basis it avoids the inherent contradiction of skeptical absolutists who maintain that knowledge is impossible. McGinn is thus seen making the same mistake we have witnessed repeatedly in the course of our examination of this subject. Pyrrho and his friends never "despaired" over the paucity of human knowledge. On the contrary, they rejoiced that the entire enterprise could be avoided altogether, preserving our essential sanity and equanimity.

Not content with misrepresenting skepticism and its varieties in the history of philosophy, McGinn goes on to make an extraordinarily equivocal general claim:

> I shall be arguing ... that Montaigne had a profound influence on Shakespeare's works — or, to be more cautious, that many passages in Shakespeare echo passages from Montaigne. [!] In particular, a skeptical thread can be seen running through the plays, which draws upon the kind of skeptical thinking Montaigne revived from the Greeks. (McGinn, 6-7,)

Well, which is it, a "profound influence," or textual echoes? Shall be we cautious — or not? Almost as if he wanted to advance a claim in which he had no confidence, McGinn no sooner avers a "profound influence" of Montaigne on Shakespeare than he retracts it. One thing is plain: he has no hesitation in identifying Montaigne's skepticism as the doctrinaire variety which has caused so many to despair over the possibility of knowledge. After demonstrating to his own satisfaction that Shakespeare studied Montaigne with all the assiduity with which he labored over the *Holy Bible*, McGinn provides a vivid description of the sort of skepticism Montaigne bequeathed to English drama.

> Montaigne was especially noted for his eloquent revival of Greek skepticism, particularly in his long essay "An Apology for Raymond Sebond." Here he dwells with some relish on the limitations on man, his feeble senses, his preposterous overconfidence, his desire not just to obey God, but to imitate Him. In Montaigne's view, man is but a paltry animal, inferior to many animals in his acuity and good sense, far too fond of his Reason .... So Shakespeare would be exposed to full-blown philosophical skepticism in Montaigne's writings, and in a form I suspect he would have found especially appealing — since Montaigne is a dramatic, anecdotal, poetic, and powerful writer. Not for Montaigne the dry tomes of the

traditional philosopher; his essays are personal, lively, and pungent. I myself, some five hundred years later, find them unusually persuasive and affecting, full of rugged wisdom and brutal honesty — the very characteristics, indeed, which leap from the page of Shakespeare. The word "unflinching" aptly describes the style of both authors — yet with a wry humanity. The great subject of death is never far from either writer, with a steady-eyed contemplation of its terrors and mysteries. But most of all it is Montaigne's contrarian skepticism that seems to have impressed Shakespeare — as it did many of his contemporaries. (McGinn, 6)

No attempt is made to parse the philosophy of skepticism to identify exactly what type was practiced by Montaigne and his alleged student, Shakespeare. As only destructive and frustrating skeptical theories are treated, there is no alternative but to conclude that Montaigne's principled jubilation remains unknown to McGinn, despite references to the "Apology for Raymond Sebond" and other essays. By "full-blown skepticism" it is fairly plain that he intends the setting up of aggravating doubts hostile to happiness. It is, then, not the consolamentum of skepticism but its "problems" which McGinn says are inherited by Shakespeare. There isn't a hint anywhere in the plays (except for Cassius' allusion to Stoicism in *Julius Caesar*) of authentic Pyrrhonian thought. Of course, Montaigne's thinking was hardly confined to skepticism. His essays teem with thousands of citations to Latin and Greek authors of every persuasion, including Plato, Aristotle, Plutarch, Cicero, St. Augustine, *et al*. He chatted amiably on a dizzying variety of subjects. In philosophical terms, he borrowed as he felt like it, yet on the whole his oeuvre gives an impression of homogeneity and coherence. For example, while Epicurus and Lucretius praise friendship, the main line of Stoicism dismisses it as a source of disquietude. Though he might have remained on the sidelines of this debate, by recounting the joys of his own friendship with Etienne de la Boëtie, he added an element not inconsistent with the teachings of Pyrrho. For after all, why should we not enjoy the fruits of philosophy together? This is what Plato was after all along.

In 1912, Bertrand Russell published a small book which exercised an impact out of all proportion to its diminutive size: *The Problems of Philosophy*. There he departed from the traditional view of philosophy as either a vehicle of wisdom or a presentation of reality as a systematic whole, casting it instead as the puzzling over certain issues which are largely the dregs of modern science. Up until that point, the fore-most philosopher in the English-speaking world had been F. H. Brad-ley, whose major work, *Appearance and Reality* (1893), argued along neo-Hegelian lines that our lived world of relational experience is inco-herent and non-veridical, and contained and resolved in a supra-rela-tional Absolute. Against this metaphysical system, Russell proposed that the business of philosophy is to confirm the content of quotidian expe-rience by disposing of the challenges of epistemology in such a way that we can be confident that the real world corresponds closely to the world of human apperception. Against the idealism of Bradley, then, Russell erected an epistemological realism. Ever since that time, Anglophone philosophers have sought to practice philosophy not in the context of wisdom seeking, nor in systematic manner, but as an attempt to put to rest the particular intellectual riddles of their day. Perennial visions of Truth and Transcendence have been off limits in academic philosophy for more than a century.

Colin McGinn is a bird of that feather. He accepts Russell's at-omistic conception of philosophy as an assortment of disassociated "problems," and approaches Shakespeare in this vein, as though he had been not a sixteenth century poet but a twentieth century Oxford don. The result is a travesty which manages to make a hodge-podge of both philosophy and Shakespeare simultaneously, no mean feat. Under the heading of "knowledge and skepticism," a topic, as we have seen, en-tirely misconceived as a transmission of Montaigne, McGinn proposes that "what Shakespeare added to this ancient skepticism was a special form of skeptical concern—the problem of *other minds.*" (McGinn, 7, emphasis in original) Though actually an aspect of the problem of the existence of the so-called "external world," the issue of solipsism centers on our seeming inability to prove the reality of other people conceived as foci of mental activity. Needless to say, of this far-fetched quandary William Shakespeare had not an inkling. It is therefore entirely false and misleading to attribute such a concern to him. Unfazed, McGinn alters the meaning of the "problem of other minds" from the philosophical issue of solipsism to the everyday challenge of understanding other peo-ple. The result is a dismaying caricature of philosophy.

> The problem arises from a basic duality in human nature —
> the split between interior and exterior. It seems undeniable
> that all we observe of another person is his or her body —
> that is all that we can see and touch and smell. But another

person's mind belongs to the interior aspect of the person — which we cannot see, touch, or smell There is something hidden about other people's minds, which we can only infer from what is publicly available. People can keep their thoughts and motives to themselves, simply by not expressing them, and this puts us in a position of not knowing. (McGinn, 7)

Presented as philosophy, this is embarrassing. To paraphrase Oscar Levant on Leonard Bernstein, Mr. McGinn is busy disclosing secrets which have been well-known for the last 100,000 years. At best, these "truths" are trivial, as evident to children as to those calling themselves philosophers. Yet McGinn goes on and on, as though he'd unearthed the Ark of the Covenant.

I may know that I have dubious motives in regard to someone else, but I also know that you do not know this — and I know that I can easily prevent you from knowing it. This is what makes deception possible — the asymmetry between my knowledge of my mind and your knowledge of my mind. There is a sense, then, in which my mind is private, and known to be so, while my body is public property. (McGinn, 7)

Ironically, Shakespeare himself repudiated the "split between interior and exterior" in *Julius Caesar*, a play never mentioned in *Shakespeare's Philosophy*. In discussing the incendiary political situation in Rome, Cassius asks Brutus rhetorically if he can see his own face. Brutus replies he cannot, for "the eye sees not itself but by reflection, by some other things." (I, ii, 54-55) Cassius answers:

'Tis just;
And it is very much lamented, Brutus,
That you have no such mirrors as will turn
Your hidden worthiness into your eye,
That you might see your shadow.
(I, ii, 56-60)

Therefor, good Brutus, be prepared to hear.
And since you cannot see yourself

452

So well as by reflection, I, your glass,
Will modestly discover to yourself
That of yourself which you yet know not of.
(I, ii, 68-72)

In other words, though according to Professor Colin McGinn, Brutus should know far more about himself than any other man, the fact is that Cassius knows important things about Brutus to which Brutus himself is blind. Here the mind of Shakespeare soars above the "problem of other minds" to teach us a far more searching lesson: we are often open books to others, who can read our souls more easily and thoroughly than can we ourselves. Brutus is ambitious. But he cannot admit that ambition. He fears that Caesar will not allow him to succeed him as the leader of Rome, but of that fear he sees almost nothing, preferring to represent himself to himself as a champion of "honor" and the general welfare only. His "mind" (to use McGinn's term) knows not itself. Brutus is a self-deceiver. Of such complexities McGinn seems entirely innocent.

Other minds actually are, in a quite everyday sense, extremely hard to know about, and radical mistakes are not only possible but also common. The philosopher's skeptical problem is thus rooted in mundane realities. I think Shakespeare was acutely conscious of this problem, and that it powers and structures many of his plays, notably *Othello*. He is working out the dramatic consequences of a philosophical problem, as this problem affects people locked into very real and intimate relationships. All our social relationships, from the most casual to the most intimate, as in marriage and family connections, are conditioned by the fundamental inaccessibility of other minds. Everything becomes a matter of interpretation, of competing hypotheses, with the perpetual possibility of massive error. Overconfidence is the besetting sin here, as people leap to unwarranted conclusions about the motives and thoughts of others. Tragedy can result. (McGinn, 7-8)

The skeptic, we might say, is a kind of tragedian about knowledge: he admits Aristotle's dictum [All human beings desire knowledge] is correct — people do desire to know; they are not indifferent to knowledge — but he claims that this desire is necessarily thwarted. Thus a basic value in human life is declared unrealizable, and this is our tragedy.

> I shall suggest that Shakespeare's tragedies often revolve around the tragedy of knowledge itself. It is a tragic fact that one of our deepest desires must go unfulfilled, and from this tragedy other tragedies ensue. (McGinn, 8)

Reading such palaver one is reminded of Hippolyta's comments on *Pyramus and Thisbe*: "This is the silliest stuff that ever I heard." (*A Midsummer Night's Dream*, V, i, 209)

Let's clarify.

First, secrets are kept not by "minds" but by people, you, me and others. That there are misunderstandings between and amongst people is not exactly a revelation. The addition of the term "minds" adds nothing whatsoever to our understanding of the foibles of human communication. Second, that we frequently misunderstand one another is in no way, shape or form a philosophical issue, and McGinn cites not a single authority in support of that jarring proposition. Third, the notion that we as human beings have privileged access to our thoughts and feeling has often been challenged by critical philosophers, a fact that McGinn is chary of mentioning. The passage cited above from *Julius Caesar* remains to be reckoned with by students of the "problem of other minds." In the case of *Othello*, while it's pretty obvious its hero is clueless about Iago's true nature and intentions, Iago understands Othello better than the dark general comprehends his inner darkness. Fourth, making mistaken judgments about the thoughts and feelings of others can result in tragedy only when "tragedy" is used in the popular sense of a serious event resulting in grief or anguish. But McGinn is writing about Shakespeare, a classical tragedian, and there the word has a specialized meaning not reducible to everyday setbacks reported by sensationalistic journalists for whom every traffic fatality is "tragic." McGinn equivocates on the term in order to make good his claim that mere social blunders based on misunderstandings can be the stuff of "tragedy." But the fact that human beings are largely ignorant and err thereby is merely unfortunate, not "tragic."

Classical tragedy issues not from mere blunders caused by the "inaccessibility of other minds," but from self-deception. And strangely enough, McGinn almost recognizes this. "The self," he says,

> is not always a harmonious whole, running on rational prin-

ciples, but often a mélange of conflicting forces, the source of which is unclear. We are as much victims of ourselves as we are of the world around us . . . Accordingly, we can be mysteries to ourselves, bewildered by our feelings and actions; the conscious rational will has limited sway.

Self-knowledge, therefore, like knowledge of other selves, is not always reliable; a person can be quite wrong about his character, and the way his mind operates. Self- knowledge, when possessed, is a hard-won achievement, not a given; it tends to come to Shakespeare's characters only toward the end of their ordeals. (McGinn, 12-13)

This, of course, is an improvement, but still wide of the mark, missing the essential insight, for as expressed by McGinn it still boils down to mere mistake, a dearth of data, this time not about others but about ourselves. Brutus' problem is not that he lacks adequate information but that he deceives himself about who and what he is. Put directly, he lies to himself. Once we do that, we are alienated; we remain in flight from reality, and it is that flight from ourselves and life itself that issues in tragedy. We allow ourselves to act monstrously and rationalize such actions by our neurotic self-narrations, those private press releases we rehearse over and over to avoid confronting what we have made of ourselves and others. For what could possibly be tragic about mere error? We miscalculate, forget, overlook, sometimes with dreadful consequences. And some of these blunders may be morally significant. But even these fail to rise to the level of true tragedy. Do Romeo and Juliet perish because of a mere breakdown in communications? No. That there is a failure to send and obtain facts accurately is undeniable, yet those mechanical snafus are not the source of tragedy. This can be traced, rather, to the troubled heart of Juliet, a young but genuinely tragic heroine whose obsession with death is willfully misunderstood and misapprehended as love. (Gontar, 51ff.) King Lear tyrannizes over others, including his own children, but portrays himself to himself and others as a victim. Within Macbeth's heroism lies a will so malignant that it can be admitted only in witches, hit men, his spouse and Banquo's ghost. We take our demons and project them outwards onto others. The bad guys surround me. Oedipus is himself the villain he has been seeking. Othello's anxiety about his own potency is translated into a bizarre conviction that his wife has been unfaithful. He is socially and sexually compromised in

Venice and hurls himself into cuckoldry as Empedocles hurled himself into Aetna. (Gontar, 114ff.) The suggestion that his troubles are somehow attributable to his failures as an "epistemologist" is ludicrous. Epistemology is an arid game played primarily by white, upper middle class, male professors of philosophy in English speaking nations, not negro generals languishing in quattrocento Europe. Tragedy, then, has little to do with empirical error and nothing to do with theory. Were the tragic protagonist merely mistaken he would be far less culpable, and, perhaps, deserving of forgiveness or exoneration. As Jean-Paul Sartre explained it in *Being and Nothingness* and illustrated it in his own left-bank dramas, tragedy is "*mauvais fois,*" that is, bad faith. The characters in the bourgeois hell of "No Exit" are condemned to spend eternity peeling back the layers of self-deception with which they camouflaged the meaning of their actions in life. We find the same motif in the "pipedreams" cultivated by the bar room habitués in Eugene O'Neill's *The Iceman Cometh*. And it is manifest in the delusions of Blanche Dubois in Tennessee Williams' *A Streetcar Named Desire*. These are all in one way or another descendants of Shakespeare's tragic psychology.

One more point. Colin McGinn puts forward a text bearing the title "Shakespeare's Philosophy: Discovering the Meaning Behind the Plays," as though we were going to have a look at least at a decent cross section of the corpus. In this natural expectation we are defeated. There are chapters on only six plays, four tragedies and two comedies. The histories are entirely omitted, as are the long poems and sonnets. How on the basis of so little one could presume to extract anything resembling Shakespeare's "philosophy" is not easy to see. It is normal and appropriate for philosophy to be drawn to art, as it is to religion and history. And philosophers who immerse themselves in Shakespeare can learn much that is helpful. F. H. Bradley cited Shakespeare many times. Hegel wrote extensively on him, as have many other thinkers. But art is not thought, and poetry is not philosophy. The essence of the latter is reason expressed in argument, something we don't find in Shakespeare and frankly don't want. Those most familiar with his writings marvel at their many-faceted aspects, perspectives and dimensions, placing any conclusory maxim or metaphysical summation beyond reach. But at the very least one would anticipate that a would-be critic would take the time to immerse himself in such panoramic material before hurling his tiny thunderbolts. In Mr. McGinn's case, he began to make a "detailed study of Shakespeare" in 2004-5 (McGinn, vii), delivering the benefit of his revelations in 2006. It is therefore hard to avoid the impression that we have here not a fellow with something to say, but one who has to say something. Not only is this shallow writer unqualified to do a book about Shakespeare, there is even less warrant for him to be commenting on Michel de Montaigne, a philosopher who was apparently faintly scanned, and whose teaching is not once adequately or correctly formulated. One shudders to think how many minutes were invested in studying him. Out of his depth in Shakespeare, one would expect that a professional philosopher would at least be able to fairly present the views of as famous a forebear as Montaigne. All in all, it is a discreditable performance, a marginal yet well-promoted manuscript, glossy but ghastly, which has managed to become a staple of popular Shakespeare exegesis, as a visit to any large bookstore will confirm.

VII. Shakespeare Versus Montaigne on War

Let's expand the scope of the conversation by considering a representative event in Shakespeare not taken up by Professors Bell and McGinn. In The Second Part of *King Henry the Fourth*, Act 4, Sc. 1 there is a parley between Prince John, representing his father Bolingbroke, now King Henry IV, and the leaders of the rebellion, the Archbishop of York, Lord Bardolph, Thomas, Lord Mowbray and Lord Hastings. On the brink of a momentous battle the rebel forces are ill prepared to undertake, the issues are discussed with John on the plain where the fight must unfold. John surprises the enemy princes with an acceptance of all their grievances and promise of redress, provided they dismiss their armies and retire.

WESTMORELAND

Pleaseth your grace to answer them directly
How far forth you like their articles.

PRINCE JOHN

I like them all, and do allow them well,
And swear here, by the honour of my blood,
My father's purposes have been mistook,
And some about him have too lavishly
Wrested his meaning and authority.

(to the Archbishop)

My lord, these griefs shall be with speed redressed;
Upon my soul they shall. If this please you,
Discharge your powers unto their several counties,
As we will ours; and here between the armies
Let's drink together friendly and embrace,
That all their eyes may bear those tokens home
Of our restorèd love and amity.

ARCHBISHOP OF YORK

I take your princely word for these redresses.
PRINCE JOHN

I give it you, and will maintain my word;
And thereupon I drink unto your grace.
(He drinks)
(IV, i, 278-294)

Upon this solemn pledge of the Prince, the rebel lords dismiss their squadrons, only to find too late that the King's forces have not been released, and that they are prisoners of the stealthy Prince.

HASTINGS

Our army is dispersed.
Like youthful steers unyoked, they take their courses,
East, west, north, south; or, like a school broke up,
Each hurries toward his home and sporting place.

WESTMORELAND

Good tidings, my lord Hastings, for the which
I do arrest thee, traitor, of high treason;
And you, Lord Archbishop, and you, Lord Mowbray,
Of capital treason I attach you both.

MOWBRAY

Is this proceeding just and honourable?

WESTMORLAND

Is your assembly so?

ARCHBISHOP OF YORK

Will you thus break your faith?

PRINCE JOHN

I pawned thee none.
I promised you redress of these same grievances
Whereof you did complain; which, by mine honour,
I will perform with a most Christian care.
But for you rebels, look to taste the due
Meet for rebellion and such acts of yours.
Most shallowly did you these arms commence,
Fondly brought here, and foolishly sent hence. —
Strike up our drums, pursue the scattered stray.
God, and not we, hath safely fought today.
Some guard these traitors to the block of death,
Treason's true bed and yielder up of breath.
(IV, i, 328-349)

Prince John is a perfidious liar. Using phrases like "by the honour of my blood," he declared that upon agreement of the rebels to dismiss their forces he would do the same, but instead he maintained his army and arrested the King's adversaries. Furthermore, the Prince has limited authority and rectitude, as he himself, emissary of his father Bolingbroke, is a rebel against King Richard II who was deposed by Bolingbroke. If anyone deserves death in this scene it is John.

Is there philosophy here? Not in form, perhaps, but in principle. Is it grasped by Professors Bell and McGinn. Not at all. Does it reflect the "influence of Montaigne"? Absolutely not.

The rebels have been misled. Does this show an interest in Shakespeare in skeptical philosophy and the watery academic "problem of other minds"? Hardly. What it shows is that war is a scourge of mankind, and that as it ravages the human race we become increasingly savage and degenerate. These northern lords were allies with Bolingbroke in overthrowing King Richard II. Now, resentful of his heavy-handed rule, they would rise up and eject the man they installed on the English throne. Injustice begets injustice, and ahead lie the Wars of the Roses, the undoing of countless "nobles" grasping for power and wealth.

Montaigne had a tolerant attitude towards war, somewhat as we find it represented in *Much Ado About Nothing* or *All's Well That Ends Well*, where a young man with no occupation might "go to the wars" as an adventure or to promote himself, a plateau on life's way as presented by Jaques in his famous "All the world's a stage" speech in *As You Like It* (II, Sc. 7, 149-153).

The difference between Montaigne and Shakespeare, however, is that when Shakespeare looked closely at war he found an unspeakable horror beyond any rationalization or justification. War was in his considered judgment a penalty imposed on an unruly and improvident human race, an inferno of suffering indicative of the rupture of justice and order. Think of Queen Margaret taunting Richard with the blood of young Rutland in *King Henry VI*, Part Three, (I, iv, 68-180) or the scene of fathers and sons who unwittingly slay one another and then discover whom they have killed. (II, v, 55-93) Will the word "honour" adequately compensate the conscript for his amputations? (*King Henry IV*, First Part, V, ii, 131-141) Falstaff's question still resonates today. In the *Henriad* Shakespeare's disgust with violence in battle rises to a pitch not to be seen again until Pablo Picasso's *Guernica* stunned the world with the debacle of modern combat in 1937.

For all his wisdom, Montaigne never occupied this point of view.

A recent study of Montaigne's notion of war in the *Essays* has reached the conclusion that, while the French gentleman does not explicitly praise war, neither does he condemn it. (See, "Montaigne on War" by Alfredo Bonadeo, *Journal of the History of Ideas*, Vol. 46, No. 3, July - Sept 1985, pp. 417-426)

As Lucretius, the Epicurean poet, beholds a ship foundering at sea, its crew and passengers drowning in cold water, he experiences the sublime indifference of *ataraxia*. There is something in the classical wisdom of Montaigne, too, that fairly insulates him from the harrowing agonies of life. Indeed, that was for him the very *raison d'être* of philosophy. Quite different is Shakespeare, bound as he is by compassion for suffering humanity. Look at Miranda in *The Tempest*. No remote contemplative she.

When she witnesses the storm-tossed ship, her emotional reaction is a contravention of Montaigne's repudiation of emotion. (Montaigne, 7, 11ff.)

MIRANDA

If by your art, my dearest father, you have
Put the wild waters in this roar, allay them.
The sky, it seems, would pour down stinking pitch,
But that the sea, mounting to the welkin's cheek,
Dashes the fire out. O, I have sufferèd
With those I saw suffer! A brave vessel,
Who had, no doubt, some noble creature in her,
Dashed all to pieces! O, the cry did knock
Against my very heart! Poor souls, they perished.
Had I been any god of Power, I would
Have sunk the sea within the earth, or ere
It should the good ship so have swallowed and
The fraughting souls within her.
(I, ii, 1-13)

In war or peace, Shakespeare is the poet of the passions.

VIII. Conclusion

Many have tried to capture Shakespeare, but few, if any, have succeeded. Of himself he writes not a word. Montaigne, to the contrary, even when he seems to be occupied with a host of external topics, is always in one way or another talking about himself. Is it plausible that two such totally divergent figures had common purposes and procedures? Did the world's most garrulous yet modest egoist mold the most private and invisible of poets? The burden of proof will always rest on those promoting the novel affirmative. While we cannot go to Shakespeare for information about himself and his sources of inspiration, Montaigne, like the later philosophical autobiographer, Rousseau, is only too glad to exhibit himself to us. Montaigne spreads himself throughout the *Essays*. He disseminates. Take his squib on Democritus and Heraclitus. As Montaigne's focus on them has more to do with temperament than doctrine, his analysis may prove more revealing of his own personal mindset than his comments on dogmatists and skeptics.

Let us attend to this passage carefully, listening with what Theodore Reik called the "third ear."

Democritus and Heraclitus were both philosophers, the former, finding our human circumstances so vain and ridiculous, never went out without a laughing and mocking look on his face: Heraclitus, feeling pity and compassion for these same circumstances of ours, wore an expression which was always sad, his eyes full of tears.

I prefer the former temperament, not because it is more agreeable to laugh than to weep but because it is more disdainful and condemns us men more than the other — and it seems to me that, according to our deserts, we can never be despised enough. Lamentation and compassion are mingled with some respect for the things we are lamenting: the things which we mock at are judged to be worthless. I do not think that there is so much wretchedness in us as vanity; we are not so much wicked as daft; we are not so much full of evil as of inanity; we are not so much pitiful as despicable. Thus Diogenes who frittered about all on his own trundling his barrel and cocking a snook at Alexander, accounting us as no more than flies or bags of wind, was a sharper and harsher judge (and consequently, for my temperament, a juster one) than Timon who was surnamed the misanthropist. For what we hate we take to heart. Timon wished us harm; passionately desired our downfall; fled our company as dangerous, as that of evil men whose nature was depraved. Diogenes thought us worth so little that contact with us could neither trouble him nor corrupt him: he avoided our company not from fear of associating with us but from contempt. He thought us incapable of doing good and evil.

Statilius' reply was of a similar character when Brutus spoke to him about joining in their plot against Caesar: he thought the enterprise to be just but did not find that men were worth taking any trouble over; which is in conformity with the teaching of Hegesias (who said the wise man should do nothing except for himself, since he alone is worth doing anything for) and the teaching of Theodorus, that it is unjust that the

wise man should hazard his life for the good of his country,
so risking his wisdom for fools.

Our own specific property is to be equally laughable and able
to laugh. (Montaigne, 339-340)

It is no surprise to find that Montaigne is allied with Democritus
against Heraclitus (though it is wondered if he studied the paradoxical
epigrams of the latter as carefully as they deserve). After all, Democritus' philosophy descended to Epicurus and thence to Lucretius, a major
thinker in Montaigne's conceptual pantheon. What is life, Democritus
seems to ask, if not a show put on by an infinite concatenation of in-
finitesimals, a vain display not to be taken seriously? From Heraclitus,
child of *phusis*, an urgent and importunate message emerges with which
each man must wrestle in the depths of his soul. Democritus is more
accommodating, inviting us to skate over the glittering surface of things
and laugh at those who ardently crash. Quite obviously, Montaigne sides
with comedy against the tragic sense of things. Is this a thinker whom
Shakespeare could wholly embrace? There is a one-sidedness here from
which thinkers such as Shakespeare and Hegel must inevitably recoil, no
matter its scope and magnanimity.

Yet, the passage is astonishing in that it anticipates ironically two
of Shakespeare's tragedies, *Julius Caesar* and *Timon of Athens*. Timon's
misanthropy cuts directly against the grain of Montaigne's restrained
but lively bonhomie. We may be quite sure that if Shakespeare did read
him he crafted Timon not in emulation but in spite of Montaigne. Classical cynicism is pushed to its existential limits in Shakespeare's unsparing crucible and crumbles. Had Montaigne ever attended a performance
of *Timon of Athens* he would have been utterly revolted and demoralized by the foregrounding of everything he condemned. Worse, had he
been counseling the young Shakespeare, he would have advised that *The
Tragedy of Julius Caesar* never be written, for its topic (the very deeds
of men) is unworthy, not "worth taking any trouble over." (Montaigne,
340) Yet this is the writer of whom it is claimed with all the insistence of
a mantra that he was a major influence on Shakespeare.

Shakespeare, like life, is too protean and encompassing to be
shrunken to doctrine, maxim or formula. Such a colossus cannot be
glossed in any system or *summa*; he is better approached in essay form.
In that respect, it is unfortunate that he was not read by Montaigne, who
surely would have had a piquant *bon mot* to offer. But we have thus far

not been vexed by anyone claiming that Shakespeare had an impact on Montaigne.

In youth melancholy and brooding, Montaigne rose through study and reflection to the peaks of genius, and attained happiness in the company of bygone sages who showed the way to human fulfillment. He learned that our emotions and impulses are often the engines of our undoing, and he developed a profound antipathy to the passions. Shakespeare took a more Olympian route to enlightenment. Montaigne was, after all, a magistrate, a judge, a hearer of gritty disputes, and the essays in many ways resemble reports of appellate decisions. Such a figure was familiar to Shakespeare, who, if the Oxfordians are correct, was a member of the bar himself. Brutus (*Praetor Urbanus*), Shallow, Angelo and Escalus are all judges. That is to say, the mind of Montaigne already appears inscribed in Shakespeare as

> the justice,
> In fair round belly with good capon lined,
> With eyes severe and beard of formal cut,
> Full of wise saws and modern instances
> (*As You Like It*, II, Sc. 7, 153-156)

Hence, as prodigious an intellect and personality as Montaigne is, an imperishable legacy to the humanity he teased and cajoled, in comparison to Shakespeare there is no comparison. Montaigne is a compendium of opinions, Shakespeare a fashioner of souls. Montaigne is a philosopher, one who seeks to persuade through arguments, anecdotes and authorities. Shakespeare is a poet who, like Prospero, tosses us on the billows of language and brings us safely home. Montaigne is aloof and in his best moments impervious to the sensational. Only for his friend did he remove the mask of indifference. Shakespeare takes another tack, releasing at every turn the power of our hearts to make us new, more fully engaged and animated, compassionately attuned to ourselves and others.

When Leontes enters the hidden chamber and stands in front of the statue of Hermione, the departed wife he wronged sixteen years earlier, he is struck by its uncanny verisimilitude and vivacity. How could it be so real? In truth, it has taken her so many years to recover from the losses of her children, her family. She was stone for so long. But now she is ready to forgive. Let's join them for a moment.

PAULINA

No longer shall you gaze on't, lest your fancy
May think anon it moves.

LEONTES

Let be, let be!
Would I were dead but that methinks already.
What was he that did make it? See, my lord,
Would you not deem it breathed, and that those veins
Did verily bear blood?

POLIXENES

Masterly done.
The very life seems warm upon her lip.

LEONTES

The fixture of her eye has motion in't,
As we are mocked with art.

PAULINA

I'll draw the curtain.
My lord's almost so far transported that
He'll think anon it lives.

LEONTES

O sweet Paulina,
Make me to think so twenty years together.
No settled senses of the world can match
The pleasure of that madness. Let't alone.

PAULINA

I am sorry, sir, I have thus far stirred you; but
I could afflict you farther.

LEONTES

Do, Paulina,
For this affliction has a taste as sweet
As any cordial comfort. Still methinks
There is an air comes from her. What fine chisel
Could ever yet cut breath? Let no man mock me,
For I will kiss her.

PAULINA

Good my lord, forbear.
The ruddiness upon her lip is wet.
You'll mar it if you kiss it, stain your own
With oily painting. Shall I draw the curtain?

LEONTES

No, not these twenty years.
(V, iii, 60-84)

And so the statue of Leontes' beloved wife comes alive before his eyes, descends to him, and they embrace. Here is a piece of pathos indeed.

What fine chisel could ever cut this breath? None but the pen of Shakespeare, the chisel of blood and tears, laughter and despair, anguish and exaltation. Red was the color of his ink.

For Montaigne life is but froth, and he would have delighted hugely in the fanciful moments of Shakespeare (*e.g.*, *The Merry Wives of Windsor*) But Shakespeare himself was not partial; he was "the complete consort, dancing together." He took the road more traveled, the one which leads straight through the heart. That lesson is best exemplified in *King Lear*, a tragedy. Two fractured souls, father and daughter, are torn apart by a father's demented love and foolish pride. Even Cordelia's name refers to that great organ, and throughout the play Lear's own heart, metaphorical and organic, beats at the center of the action, his rage, his terrible fall, purgation in the elements, and deliverance. In the end, though shattered, he is reborn, not so much as Cordelia's father as her child. In the last moment, that noble heart breaks, and Lear asks that the button on his garment be undone to help him breathe his last.

(V, iii, 285) Each time we enter this tragedy we too are remade. That is the miracle of Shakespeare, one which Michel de Montaigne, for all his Solomon-like sagacity, could never have imagined. Shakespeare dwells in the ultima Thule of the human spirit, where tragedy and comedy coalesce. Such glorious works as *The Winter's Tale* are not "problem plays"; they are responses to the human condition. Man's sentences are his answer to the sentence on him.

Prophecy was a craft denied to Montaigne. But it was granted by the gods to Socrates and his student Plato. A playwright himself, Plato understood that comedy and tragedy are ultimately two sides of a single coin, and that the day would come when one individual artist would so master both that he would redeem the human race in art, "cleans[ing] the foul body of the infected world." (*As You Like It*, II, vii, 60) In his masterpiece, *Symposium*, Plato shows us the morning after the drinking party, when only a few of the revelers are still upright. Aristodemus is one of those dozing.

> He slept on for some time, for this was in the winter and the nights were long, and when at last he woke it was near daybreak and the cocks were crowing. He noticed that all the others had either gone home or fallen asleep, except Agathon and Aristophanes and Socrates, who were still awake and drinking out of an enormous bowl which they kept passing round left to right. Socrates was arguing with the others — not that Aristodemus could remember very much of what was said, for, besides having missed the beginning, he was still more than half-asleep. But the gist of it was that Socrates was forcing them to admit that the same man might be capable of writing both comedy and tragedy — that the tragic poet might be a comedian as well.

> But as he clinched the argument, which the other two were scarcely in a state to follow, they began to nod, and first Aristophanes fell off to sleep and then Agathon, as day was breaking. Whereupon Socrates tucked them up comfortably and went away, followed of course, by Aristodemus. And after calling at the Lyceum for a bath, he spent the rest of the day as usual, and then, toward evening made his way home to rest. (223c-d)

Shakespeare is the supreme dramatist heralded by Socrates. It is he who spans the gap between mirth and misery, adopting us as his lesser characters. Under his tutelage we struggle, grow and prosper, and our little lives are rounded still with sleep. We shall not see his like again.

WORKS CITED:

Millicent Bell, *Shakespeare's Tragic Skepticism*, Yale University Press, 2002.

Colin Bower, "Ruminating on the Stephen Hawking Phenomenon," *New English Review*, August, 2006.

Alfredo Bonadeo, "Montaigne on War," *Journal of the History of Ideas*, Vol. 46, No. 3, Jul-Sept, 1985, pp. 417-426.

Ron Cowen, "Simulations Back Up Theory That Universe is a Hologram," *Nature: International Weekly Journal of Science*, December 10, 2013.

David P. Gontar, *Hamlet Made Simple and Other Essays*, New English Review Press, 2013.

Bryan Magee, *The Story of Thought*, DK Publishing Company, 1998.

Colin McGinn, *Shakespeare's Philosophy*, Harper Collins, 2006.

Michel de Montaigne, *The Complete Essays*, M.A. Screech, trans., Penguin Books, 1991.

Stanley H. Nemeth, *Review of Shakespeare's Philosophy*, Amazon Books, January 7, 2007.

Plato, *The Collected Dialogues*, Edith Hamilton, Huntington Cairns, eds., Bollingen Series, Princeton University Press, 1961.

Karl C. Sandberg, *Review of Montaigne and Bayle: Variations on the Theme of Skepticism* (The Hague: Martinus Nijhoff, 1966) in *Journal of the History of Philosophy*, Vol. 8, No. 1, Jan. 1978, pp. 103-104.

William Shakespeare, *The Complete Works*, 2d edition, S. Wells, G. Taylor, eds., Oxford University Press, Clarendon, 2005.

Stanford Encyclopedia of Philosophy, "Montaigne"

Lin Yutang, *The Wisdom of Laotse*, Foreign Language and Research Press, Beijing, 2009.

18
A Raid on the Articulate: G. Wilson Knight and the Battle of Elsinore

And so each venture / Is a new beginning, a raid on the inar-
ticulate / With shabby equipment always deteriorating / In the
general mess of imprecision of feeling, / Undisciplined squads
of emotion.

— T. S. Eliot

I. Introduction

*W*hat Eliot says so well about the fashioning of poetry applies also to its reception by readers and audiences. Where the richest tropes are concerned, rarely are we equal to the task. Outnumbered by words, we leap from book-strewn trenches when exegetical duty calls to try to gain a few hundred yards of insight before we are tossed aside by winds of doctrine. Indeed, the bones of many a once-renowned *littérateur* lie bleaching in the sun. Among those forgotten heroes is G. Wilson Knight (1897-1985), in his day the prolific doyen of *belles-lettres* and Shakespearean exposition. Knight rests now, buried in footnotes and interminable bibliography. It will be argued here that what led to his discomfiture was not inadequacy of principle, but rather a seeming inability to cleave to the very concepts and distinctions which made him a unique and powerful voice in twentieth century commentary. For Knight and his critical heirs, the "raid" was not upon elusive moods and sentiments but on poetical and dramatic texts, each possessing at their

469

core a "hard gem-like flame" making of disparate elements a living unity. Regrettably, in his treatment of particular plays he seemed to descend into precisely the sort of carping criticism he discommended in more general discussions. Yet, despite departures from his own protocols, Knight's legacy is significant. His idea of a literary work as an aesthetic gestalt or organic mystery which naturally resolves seeming difficulties has had a salutary influence on the art of reading and deserves reconsideration today.

II. The Critique of Criticism

In the first chapter of *The Wheel of Fire* (1930), "On the Principles of Shakespearean Interpretation," Wilson Knight defends his key distinction between popular criticism, which aims at the detection of narrative imperfections, and interpretation, which seeks the "root metaphor" (See, Stephen C. Pepper, *World Hypotheses*) out of which the work arises and whose apprehension tends to put everything in proper order. As the title (drawn from *King Lear*) implies, each Shakespearean drama may be conceived as a wheel from whose hub the disparate elements of the play emerge. There burns that "right Promethean fire" in and through which all is vital and integrated. As the generative moment is essentially insusceptible of reproduction, we can never sound a Shakespearean play to its very depths, for it "hath no bottom." (*A Midsummer Night's Dream*, IV, i, 214) Nevertheless, we are naturally capable of achieving a resonant *Verstehen* of each work, if only we can preserve "something of that child-like faith which we possess, or should possess, in the theatre." (Knight, 3) Our readings and viewings thus remain fresh and engaging, undiminished by ivory tower niggling. That, at least, is the hope.

For instance, Shakespeare's early comedy, *The Two Gentlemen of Verona*, lacks top marks for some scholars in large part because of Valentine's inopportune surrender to the cad Sir Proteus of his rights in Silvia (V, iv, 83), a gesture hard to square with his betrayal of Valentine and attempted ravishment of his lady at the play's close. (V, iv, 83) After "much throwing about of brains" amongst contemporary analysts, this minor wrinkle is still presented as a text-marring blunder. But though a minor issue might ruin the play as far as conventional literary experts are concerned, Knight would observe that such caviling needn't spoil the fun for audiences. The paradoxical theme of youth's coupling of fickleness and fidelity, from which the action emerges, provides sufficient context in which Valentine's blunder is rendered aesthetically harmless, as is cross-dressed Julia's incongruous willingness to woo Silvia on behalf of Proteus. In *All's Well That Ends Well*, Helen continues her dogged pursuit of Bertram even after she learns of his plan to seduce Diana of Florence. (III, v, 65-75) As this brand of devotion is inconsistent with actual life and sentiment, modern criticism would tend to set such a "flawed" play down as unrealistic and thereby substandard. Wilson Knight dissents. Though "criticism" might hold its nose, an interpretation which hearkens back to the original vision underlying the play would affirm the comedy's symbolic integrity: Helen is not a weakling who would be Bertram's absurd "spaniel," (See, *A Midsummer Night's Dream*, II, i, 203); she is rather an icon of devotion who "looks on tempests and is never shaken." (See, Sonnet 116) This view tends to reinforce the dictum of Harold Bloom and others that the plays of Shakespeare are not "stories" so much as poetry, the complete consort of images dancing together.

The initial distinction between criticism and interpretation is stated this way:

> Criticism to me suggests a certain process of deliberately objectifying the work under consideration; the comparison of it with other similar works in order especially to show in what respects it surpasses, or falls short of, those works; the dividing its 'good' from its 'bad'; and, finally, a formal judgement as to its lasting validity. 'Interpretation', on the contrary, tends to merge into the work it analyses; it attempts, as far as possible, to understand its subject in the light of its own nature, employing external reference, if at all, only as a preliminary to understanding; it avoids discussion of merits, and, since its existence depends entirely on its original acceptance of the validity of the poetic unit which it claims, in some measure, to translate into discursive reasoning, it can recognize no division of 'good' from 'bad'. Thus criticism is active and looks ahead, often treating past work as material on which to base future standards and canons of art; interpretation is passive, and looks back, regarding only the imperative challenge of a poetic vision. Criticism is a judgement of vision; interpretation a reconstruction of vision. In practice, it is probable that that neither can exist . . . quite divorced from the other. The greater part of poetic commentary pursues a middle course between criticism and interpretation. But sometimes work is created of so resplendent a quality, so massive a solidity of

imagination, that adverse criticism beats against it idly as the wind that flings its ineffectual force against a mountain-rock. Any profitable commentary on such a work must necessarily tend towards a pure interpretation. The work of Shakespeare is of this transcendent order. (Knight, 1-2)

There follows a rich and evocative discussion of the critical/interpretive duality, attempting its elucidation on the basis of a number of interrelated tropes. An abstract of these categories is provided below.

III. Criticism focuses on temporal sequence, interpretation on "spatial" configuration

To receive this whole Shakespearean vision within the intellectual consciousness demands a certain and very definite act of mind. One must be prepared to see the whole play in space as well as in time. (Knight, 3)

This presentation of poetic drama in spatial terms runs throughout Knight's exposition, and gives the impression that each Shakespearean drama may be regarded as a kind of symbolic tableau in which deeds are generated as a display of more primal meaning. That meaning is best quarried not by making of chronicity the play's substance, but by looking to the creative fount out of which its atmosphere arises and in which its sequencing is situated. (Knight, 3) Taking *Hamlet* as an illustration, Knight urges that while criticism dithers fruitlessly over the puzzle of why the hero cannot dispatch his homicidal uncle (Knight, 2), a recognition of the underlying "death-theme" in that play draws us closer to its molten center, resolving a number of apparent aporia with a single insight or feeling tone. (Knight, 3) "The spatial, that is, the spiritual, quality uses the temporal, that is, the story, lending it dominance in order to express itself more clearly." (Knight, 4)

Knight's theory of "interpretation" will naturally remind some of F. S. C. Northrop's later principle of the "undifferentiated aesthetic continuum" which he opposed to the western "theoretical component" (science, causality, and technology) in his classic study of culture, *The Meeting of East and West*. Northrop utilized the spatial dimension in Chinese landscapes to represent what is most singular in eastern civilization. Corresponding to Northrop's "theoretical component" is Knight's concept of "criticism" which tends to focus on such secondary factors as intentions and sources, rather than submit ourselves to "the original poetic experience." (Knight, 6-7) We might also bear in mind that Hesiod's initial cosmological category was not a *logos* but rather "Chaos," a pre-rational feminine substratum which gives birth to the differentiated cosmos. And it is worth noting the role that "feeling" plays as a metaphysical foundation in F. H. Bradley's *Appearance and Reality* and also in *The Principles of Psychology* of William James. That impression of the primacy of feeling probably descends to Knight via the influence of A. C. Bradley, the philosopher's brother. The reader will note in T. S. Eliot's Introduction to *The Wheel of Fire* his mention of F. H. Bradley's comment on "instinct." (Knight, xix, xxii) It is well known that Eliot did his doctoral dissertation at Harvard on F. H. Bradley's theory of knowledge. And instinct itself receives interesting comment in *King Henry IV*, Part One, II, v, 275, where we learn from an unimpeachable authority that "instinct is a great matter." The entire complex of interpretation, feeling, poetic experience, and instinct stands at odds with the spirit of criticism as understood by Knight.

IV. Interpretation Entails Mystery

This suggests that more is involved here than methodology. The reversionary exercise of interpretation may be seen for G. Wilson Knight as return to the sense of mystery. (Knight, 6, 8, 10, 13, 15, 32, 44, 45, 53, *et al.*) This is unsurprising, as we can no more fathom the nature of poetic creation than we can know the nature of things generally. As Montaigne says, *"Que sais-je?"* That is why the ancients turned to divine muses and inspiration to account for poetry. The conflagration at the center of the "wheel of fire" may be tended by the human spirit but surely is not kindled by it. That is plainly the view of Shakespeare, who credits heaven for his art. (*A Midsummer Night's Dream*, V, i, 1-17) Poetry is ultimately a gift of the gods. And that means each great poem bears within a spark of the primal mystery. Again, we find that sense of mystery expressly acknowledged by Shakespeare himself in various contexts. (*Measure for Measure*, IV, ii, 26-45; *The Tragedy of King Lear*, V, iii, 16; *Hamlet*, III, ii, 364; *Timon of Athens*, IV, iii, 455; and see Knight, 7-8) Thus it is that Wilson Knight encourages a due respect for the art of reading, of which interpretation is the main component. Viewed in terms of literature, each play, says Knight, is "an expanded metaphor." (Knight, 14) In spiritual terms, the same works can be understood "as mystical representations of a mystic vision." (Knight, 15) By contrast, the critic starts from "a point on the circumference," and "instead of working into the heart of the play, pursues a tangential course, riding, as it were, on his own life experiences farther and farther from his proper goal." (Knight, 11)

V. Interpretation and Criticism Remain Complementary Terms

It is quite apparent, then, that Knight's initial sympathies lie wholly with the interpretive approach to the text. Indeed, he goes so far as to urge that "we should not . . . think critically at all," an extraordinary injunction. (Knight, 3) We should saturate ourselves rather with the "atmosphere" of each work, allowing that "omnipresent and mysterious reality brooding motionless over and within the play's movement" (Knight, 5) to leaven our diagnostic impulses with heavy doses of the play's symbolic vision. So far as possible we should refrain from problematizing the text at the expense of its integrity, always remembering "the quality of the original poetic experience, and . . . translating this into whatever concepts appear suitable. . . ." (Knight, 7) Indeed, to the extent we criticize we "falsify [our] own experience." (Knight, 12) There is something idealistic and yet natural in this outlook. After all, who has not noticed that each of Shakespeare's plays possesses its own unique style? Could a stanza from *Twelfth Night* ever occupy a place in *The Merry Wives*? It would never mesh with its surroundings. In terms of Knight's thesis, a molecule of one would generally import the wrong "atmosphere" into the other.

Yet at just this point, we are bought up short by Knight's realism: interpretation and criticism turn out to be two aspects of reading which are indispensable and mutually implicative.

[I] would emphasize that I here lay down certain principles and make certain objections for my immediate purpose only. I would not be thought to level complaint against the value of 'criticism' in general. My private and personal distinction between 'criticism' and 'interpretation' aims at no universal validity. It can hardly be absolute. No doubt I have narrowed the term 'criticism' unjustly. *Much of the critical work of today is, according to my distinction, work of a high interpretive order.* Nor do I suggest that true 'criticism' in the narrow sense I apply to it is of any lesser order than true interpretation: it may well be a higher pursuit, since it is, in a sense, the more creative and endures a greater burden of responsibility. The relative value of the two modes must vary in exact proportion to the greatness of the literature they analyse: that is why I believe the most profitable approach to Shakespeare to be interpretation rather than criticism. (Knight, 15-16, emphasis added)

Perhaps what is meant here is that in the early twentieth century such philosophies as positivism pushed literary thought in the direction of criticism (as was the case with T. S. Eliot himself), and that under the circumstances the only legitimate corrective was a strengthening of the importance of interpretation. Unfortunately, that is not what Knight writes. What he bestows in one moment on interpretation he seems to snatch away with the next. Nevertheless, this much may be granted: Wilson Knight's critique of criticism is a brilliant and revealing illustration of the non-rationalistic foundations of literature, and remains a permanent contribution to the theory and art of reading. It is congruent with a sense of the openness of the human mind, and our conviction that in absorbing the best of poetry we transcend the banausic forces of life that conduce to our diminution. As F. H. Bradley once wrote:

All of us, I presume, more or less, are led beyond the region of ordinary facts. Some in one way and some in others, we seem to touch and have communion with what is beyond the visible world. In various manners we find something higher, which both supports and humbles, both chastens and transports us. (Bradley, 5)

Knight's principal contribution to literary theory may well be the finding of that "something higher" in Shakespeare's poetry. Of course, he was not the first to do so, but he did it at a time when it was becoming badly needed, and that remains his merit as a thinker.

VI. The Stumbling Block of *Hamlet*

Curiously, in his very first words Knight gives us a candid disclaimer:

My remarks are . . . to be read as a counsel of perfection. Yet, though I cannot claim to follow them throughout in practice, this preliminary discussion, in showing what I have been at pains to do and to avoid, will serve to indicate the direction of my attempt. (Knight, 1)

The simplified order of discourse in "On the Principles of Shakespeare Interpretation" is therefore as follows:

1. I am going to present in this essay my key principles of reading;

2. However, these principles are not consistently heeded, *even by myself*;

3. There are two approaches to exegesis: criticism and interpretation;

4. Criticism is an impoverished mode of coming to terms with the text that focuses on abstraction, and fault finding. It should be avoided;

5. Interpretation, our sense of poetic vision, is by far superior;

6. However, in the final analysis both methods are valid aspects of reading.

It is respectfully submitted that, as revealing and influential as Knight's argument is, it is so qualified and conditioned as to border on incoherence. While interpretation is shown to be the only respectable route to the mysterious middle of the wheel of fire which is the Shakespearean text, Knight confesses that he cannot always take that route "in practice," and there may be good reasons to remain at the level of shallow or tangential exegesis. And when we turn to the first case, we are astonished to find that instead of approaching *Hamlet* via interpretation, Wilson Knight unleashes a barrage of criticism of the very variety he condemned in his opening chapter. In particular, though he rejects at the outset an "unduly ethical criticism," we will see that this is exactly what he gives us in his exposition of Shakespeare's most renowned play. (Knight 8) In the notorious "The Embassy of Death: An Essay on Hamlet," Knight offers a sustained *ad hominem* assault on the character of its protagonist.

He begins with this young man's condition before encountering the Ghost of Hamlet, Sr. He is the picture of frantic misery, and busies himself with self-destructive ideation.

> O, that this too too solid flesh would melt,
> Thaw and resolve itself into a dew!
> Or that the Everlasting had not fix'd
> His canon 'gainst self slaughter! O God! O God!
> How weary, stale, flat and unprofitable
> Seem to me all the uses of this world!
> Fie on't! ah fie! 'tis an unweeded garden,
> That grows to seed; things rank and gross in nature
> Possess it merely.
> (I, ii, 129-137)

Knight's explanation?

> He suffers from misery at his father's death and agony at his mother's quick forgetfulness: Such callousness is infidelity, and so impurity, and, since Claudius is the brother of the dead king, incest. It is reasonable to suppose that Hamlet's state of mind, if not wholly caused by these events, is at least definitely related to them. Of his two loved parents, one has been taken for ever by death, the other dishonoured for ever by her act of marriage. To Hamlet the world is now an 'unweeded garden'. (Knight, 18-19)

Though this issue was treated extensively in *Hamlet Made Simple*, let's have one more look.

Is there a single scrap of evidence in *The Tragedy of Hamlet, Prince of Denmark*, that its protagonist and the late King enjoyed a close emotional bond? Not one anecdote or recollection from any source connects the Prince with his supposed father by anything more than their names. The life expectancy in those days was what?—forty or fifty years? And so the old man dies. Must his brilliant son now exhibit self-destructive urges? Recall that: "Moderate lamentation is the right of the dead; excessive grief the enemy of the living." (*All's Well that Ends Well*, I, i, 52) There is nothing in the text to suggest that Hamlet was this way before.

He wooed and courted Ophelia, studied philosophy and enjoyed the life of an accomplished courtier. What has happened? His father has expired of apparently natural or accidental causes, lamentable to be sure, but, as Claudius would observe, no cause for hysteria.

What about Gertrude? True, she loses no time in wedding and bedding Claudius, but in those days it was customary for the man to propose marriage to the lady, an honorable gesture. It implies, "You were Denmark's magnificent Queen. Now, I am its new monarch, and as I love you, you shall be my wife and continue as our esteemed Queen." Gertrude presumably does nothing more than accept the King's proposal (though many, including the present writer, see her as a passive accomplice in regicide). One might think it tacky not to wait a longer interval, but Claudius, as the new sovereign, is in a celebratory mood and wants to enjoy his good fortune to the hilt, so to speak. You might not like it, but there it is. Now what's all this about misery and suicide? What indeed.

Let's back up.

Hamlet has no siblings. All his life has been spent as heir apparent to the Danish throne. This is his destiny and his identity. While at school in Wittenberg he receives word his father has passed away, and hastens back to Elsinore, fully expecting to receive the crown, only to be jolted by the discovery that his uncle reigns already. Claudius, not Prince Hamlet, is King. Then he is forced to sit through the smarmy wedding ceremony. Could it possibly be that Prince Hamlet is a bit put off to learn that Uncle Claudius has made a peremptory strike and stolen his birthright as Denmark's rightful successor and king? It is, to say the least, embarrassing that so few make any connection between Hamlet's loss of a kingdom and his unquiet mood. Since when are kingdoms pushpins? Recall how upset was Prince Edward when he found himself disinherited by his timorous father, *King Henry VI*: "Father, you cannot disinherit me. If you be king, why should not I succeed?" (*King Henry VI*, Part Three, I, I, 227-228) Such actions lead to war. That this personal catastrophe should not even be mentioned by those seeking to account for the Prince's malaise is shocking. When Rosenkrantz questions him about his melancholia, Hamlet gives the straightforward answer: "Sir, I lack advancement." (III, ii, 327) That is, when my father died, I wasn't promoted. Hamlet tells us point blank the cause of his distemper. (III, ii, 324-327) Even if that were not in itself sufficient, it should at least be taken into account.

The problem grows. For if the assembled nobles pass over Prince

Hamlet in their "election," there must be a very good reason: a legal impediment. The Prince has every qualification and is beloved of the people. That points in only one direction: ineligibility. "Hamlet Junior" doesn't inherit the kingdom from Hamlet the Dane because, as nearly everyone knows, he isn't the King's son.

And there we have the worm gnawing at Hamlet's cerebrum when he arrives at Elsinore for the funeral and marriage ceremonies. His failure to accede to the throne implies his bastardy. Hamlet "eat[s] the air, promise-crammed." (III, ii, 90-91) That is the whispered insinuation which, of course, cannot be openly acknowledged. The subject of Hamlet's personhood, his being, has been taboo all his life, and now is certainly not the moment to broadcast it. So he is just left to drift.

It gets worse. For suppose he is a bastard. Who is his biological father? The field of paternal candidates is limited.

Now let your imaginary forces fix for one moment upon a nuptial ceremony. We are in the royal chapel. The cold stone walls are draped with faded tapestries. Standing just behind his mother is a glum Prince clad in black. A psalter is clutched in his sweaty hands. As he listens absently to the droning priest and unctuous exchange of vows, a sickening idea flickers at the margins of his mind. The celerity of this union suggests its stars may not be exactly strangers to one another. In fact, it looks as though they have been an item for some while, perhaps a long time, and that it has always been understood that if the king were, say, slain in battle, Claudius would rouse himself, assume the helm, and take Gertrude as his trophy bride. It is therefore just as likely—if not more likely—that the "Prince of Denmark" is the actual offspring of King Claudius.

That is the reason why Hamlet is so upset by the "hasty" marriage, not because it might be viewed as untimely by a Danish Emily Post, but because, coupled with his failure to take the throne, it signals his bastardy. Yet no sooner does this specter of an idea arise than it is smothered. It remains in his mental cellarage, haunting him. *This* is the real ghost in the play, not the bellowing shadow of his putative "father."

One more thing. In the closet scene we see with a noonday clarity that Prince Hamlet loathes and detests his supposed Uncle. To acknowledge that this complacent mediocrity, this bale of corpulence, could be his own father is a conclusion so repugnant that it cannot be consciously admitted. The result is cataclysmic depression and possible madness.

Return to the first soliloquy, the one which takes place before Hamlet meets "the Ghost." Wringing his hands in despair, he cries out in anguish that his "too too solid flesh" keeps him like a prisoner in life's unweeded garden. Better to be dead than lose the crown to such a miscreant, a varlet who turns out to be one's own progenitor! What could be more supremely disgusting? Imagine then his feelings when he learns that this human canker, this Claudius, has slain the universally admired King Hamlet the Dane. Yet taking vengeance upon one's own biological sire may not be as easy as it sounds. Might there not be a moment of hesitation?

It is with all of this in mind that we repair to our critic, G. Wilson Knight. Naturally he has no trouble putting his finger on the causes of Hamlet's dysthymic mood: his "father's" death and his mother's insouciant "forgetfulness." Claudius and Gertrude have much to forget, apparently. But Knight's failure to reflect on the implicit dynamics of the play leads him badly astray. Instead of making sense of the action, Knight, along with just about everyone else, contents himself with a hero for whom paternal expiration is a howling nightmare and a widow's impulse to drown her sorrow in the arms of a second husband is the end of the universe. And as this makes no sense, there is no alternative but to pin the blame on Hamlet. He is the "ambassador of death." His father's passing away and his mother's remarriage trigger the implosion of Hamlet's very soul, turning him from man to Hollywood vampire in the blink of an "I." And all this transpires well before he even hears of a Ghost stalking the crenelated towers of Elsinore. Is this a reasonable rendering of the play?

It should be mentioned in all candor that Knight's essay is notorious in academic circles, and at least one critic (David Auerbach) has gone so far as to suggest that Knight was well aware of its hyperbolical manner and outrageous claims, *e.g.*, that Hamlet is a rogue on a par with Iago. (Knight, 29) Perhaps, as Auerbach proposes, he was merely being provocative. But the deeper problem is theoretical. Having advanced the distinction between (1) criticism which seizes on and magnifies dramatic flaws (bad) and (2) interpretation which sets dramatic action in the context of an underlying metaphor (good), to then immediately trash that important polarity and excoriate the leading character in western literature as a menace to society risks being perceived as a reader grossly confused or (rather like Hamlet) conflicted. On page 3 of *The Wheel of Fire*, for example, we learn that *Hamlet*, like the other "final plays" of Shakespeare's career, is best conceived as based on a "death theme" which lends it "atmosphere." (Knight, 3) It is that pervasive "atmosphere" which allows us to digest the turbulent conduct and many-faceted moods of its tormented Prince. But by the time we reach page 47, we learn that Hamlet "has *no* dominating atmosphere, no clear purposive technique to focus our vision." (Knight, 47, emphasis added) Well, is there or is there not a dramatic atmosphere in *Hamlet*? If there is, all may be well. If not, what alternative will we have but to set Hamlet down as malicious and perverse? Sadly, the latter end of Knight's argument forgets its beginning, and he opts to contradict himself and deny atmosphere in *Hamlet*. He thus condemns our finest example of early modern literature as the celebration of an inexplicable rogue and psychopath. In so doing he follows in the footsteps of T. S. Eliot, who, as mentioned above, contributed the Introduction to Knight's book. Eliot's 1919 screed *Hamlet and His Problems*, composed under the baleful influence of logical positivism, contended that, as there was no "objective correlative" to warrant Hamlet's shameful treatment of his mother in the closet scene, this character's entire story is little better than nonsense. *The Tragedy of Hamlet*, Eliot famously concluded, is an "artistic failure." Wielding his profound distinction between criticism and interpretation in the first chapter of *The Wheel of Fire*, Wilson Knight might have responded so as to rescue the Prince and his play from such sophomoric criticism. Knight was in an ideal position to show the significance of the play's atmosphere and perhaps even read it closely enough to exhume Hamlet's real problem discussed above: illegitimacy. Alas, such was not to be. Instead of correcting Eliot, Knight evidently sought to outdo him in derogation, engaging in one of literature's most flagrant hatchet jobs. So egregious was Knight's performance that he later sought to modify or retract it, enlisting the intellectual services of Friedrich Nietzsche (Knight, 338-366), all to no avail.

Failing to read closely, neither Eliot nor Knight comes to terms with Shakespeare's *Hamlet*. Neither had the perspicacity to return to the text with fresh eyes and consider that its patent aporia entail that critical premises could and should be revised. Wilson Knight praises Claudius and condemns Prince Hamlet, never noticing their similarities, similarities thoroughly discussed in *Hamlet Made Simple*. Neither of these eminent critics takes the measure of Hamlet's psyche prior to the advent of the ghost, nor do they ever stop to consider the impact that Hamlet's loss of the crown has on him. It is inexcusable. Generations of readers have paid a high price for the myopia of such blundering scholars. They could have done so much better. Eliot deserted the wisdom of the Bradley brothers (F. H. and A. C.) for the siren call of logical positivism and thus disqualified himself as an interpreter of Shakespeare, as did Wilson

Knight by throwing in his lot with William James, whose *Varieties of Religious Experience* is used as a club to cudgel Prince Hamlet into deformity as "the sick soul." (Knight, 20, 31)

Very well, but exactly how does Knight hate Hamlet? Let us count the ways.

1. The sickness of Hamlet's soul "only further infects the state – his disintegration spreads out, disintegrating." (Knight, 21)

2. Hamlet suffers from "the abnormality of extreme melancholia and cynicism." (Knight, 23)

3. He "dwells on the thought of foulness as the basis of life." (Knight, 24)

4. "Hamlet's soul is sick. The symptoms are, horror at the fact of death and equal detestation of life, a sense of uncleanness and evil in the things of nature; a disgust at the physical body of man; bitterness, cynicism, hate. It tends to insanity. All these elements are insistent in Hamlet." (Knight, 24)

5. "Hamlet looks inward and curses and hates himself for his lack of passion, and then again hates himself the more for his futile self-hatred." (Knight, 25)

6. He speaks with the "voice of cynicism." (Knight, 26)

7. He "denies the existence of romantic values." (Knight, 27)

8. He "denies the significance of humanity." (Knight, 27)

9. His "cynicism borders on madness." (Knight, 28)

10. He "tortures" Ophelia and Gertrude. (Knight, 28)

11. He is "like Iago." (Knight, 29)

12. He "takes a devilish joy in cruelty." (Knight, 29) This of course is the very pith of wickedness.

13. He is guility of "callous cruelty." (Knight, 29)

14. He is "brutal" and "sarcastic." (Knight, 30)

15. His words are "horrible" and "disgusting." (Knight, 30)

16. "Hamlet's disease is mental and spiritual death." (Knight, 31)

17. He speaks with "the grating voice of cynicism." (Knight, 32)

18. He is "morbid," "cynical," "disgusting,""cruel" and "evil." (Knight, 32)

19. He exhibits the "cancer of cynicism in his mind." (Knight, 33)

20. "He is the ambassador of death walking amid life." (Knight, 35)

21. " . . . the consciousness of death and consequent bitterness, cruelty, and inaction . . . not only grows in his own mind but disintegrating it as we watch, but also spreads its effects outward among the other

persons like a blighting disease, and, as the play progresses, by its very passivity and negation of purpose, insidiously undermines the health of the state, and adds victim to victim until at the end the stage is filled with corpses. It is, as it were, a nihilistic birth in the consciousness of Hamlet that spreads its deadly venom around." (Knight, 35)

22. "Hamlet is inhuman." (Knight, 37)

23. Hamlet's philosophy is the negation of life. (Knight, 37)

24. He is a "danger to the state." (Knight, 38)

25. "Inhuman, cynical, not of flesh and blood." (Knight, 41)

26. "Hamlet is an element of evil in the state of Denmark." (Knight, 42)

27. "The poison of his mental existence spreads outwards among things of flesh and blood, like acid eating into metal." (Knight, 43)

28. "Hamlet is a living death in the midst of life." (Knight, 45)

29. "Pity enlists Hamlet not in the cause not of life but of death." (Knight, 48)

30. "We properly know Hamlet himself only when he is alone with death." (Knight, 49)

In the midst of this bizarre defamation of one of literature's most treasured characters, Wilson Knight turns his attention to Hamlet's supposed "uncle" with equal errancy. Several pages are devoted to eulogizing an outright rogue, one of the "eminently likable people" who surround our hero. (Knight, 41) For you see, while Hamlet's very breath infects the air at Elsinore, everyone else is agreeable and charming, including "considerate Claudius, the affectionate mother, Gertrude, the eminently lovable old Polonius, and the pathetic Ophelia." (Knight, 47) Hamlet "is the *only discordant element*." (Knight, 43, emphasis added) Why, even the Ghost fits right in with "the healthy bustle of the court"! (Knight, 42) When we see Claudius fall to his knees and confess to God his bloody crime of murdering his own brother and stealing his wife and crown, we must appreciate "this lovely prayer" (Knight, 39) in which any sense of grace or absolution eludes the penitent yet winsome homicide.

What has gone wrong here? In abandoning his own principle of interpretation, Wilson Knight loses his way, and falls into the tempting trap of painting Hamlet in lurid colors. There could be no more impressive illustration of the mistake of pseudo-empirical criticism than the one that Knight himself provides. A noble mind, "the glass of fashion and the mould of form," (III, I, 156) is here o'erthrown personally by G. Wilson Knight. No consideration is given to what Hamlet was, as against what he has become, nor has this critic any way to account for this ugly transformation other than looking to his father's death and his mother's early remarriage.

If we glance back at Knight's first chapter on the principles of Shakespearian interpretation we recall that setting the apparent faults of Shakespearian personae in the context of the "original poetic experience" of the play was fairly guaranteed to resolve such faults automatically. And since all Mr. Knight can behold are faults piled one on top of the other in Prince Hamlet, he knows not what to do with that theory when applied to this tragedy. There must be a "burning central core" in *Hamlet* where seeming abrasive elements are reduced and absorbed, but since all we can see are Hamlet's sins (and not those of eminently likable Claudius) we seem driven to conclude that there is no atmosphere in this our greatest tragedy. Or, if there is an atmosphere, it is the death theme compounded of the hostile thoughts and conduct of this hateful protagonist.

The fundamental problem is that when second-rate minds seek to sit in judgment on Shakespeare the result will rarely be commendable.

Coleridge, repelled by the horrors in *King Lear*, admitted that the author's judgement, being so consistently faultless, was probably superior to his own: and he was right. (Knight, 2)

Wilson Knight teaches the lesson but has much trouble learning it. It is not we who sit in judgment on *Hamlet*, but just the other way round: *Hamlet* takes the measure of us, its readers, viewers . . . and critics.

Let us follow Mr. Knight when his better angel is perched on his shoulder. What is the underlying theme of *Hamlet*? Is it death? No, for that is merely a symptom of the deeper issue. Every other moment in *Romeo and Juliet* touches death, but its theme is love. The redoubtable Thane of Cawdor wades in a river of blood, but it springs from sources in his soul of which he knows nothing. What then of Prince Hamlet? What makes him tick . . . and makes him sick? Don't we know by now? *Pace* Horatio, it was Ophelia who knew him best. What does she say? Her beloved prince was "Th' expectancy and rose of the fair state." (III, i, 155) That is, Hamlet lived in the expectation of the crown, as his people expected to see him crowned—or so he thought. Equally important is that this is how early modern English audiences would have seen him, understanding Prince Hamlet as a figure cut from the same cloth as, say, Prince Hal, heir to King Henry IV. For who should succeed the father if not the son? Hamlet was denied advancement. He tells us so.

It is therefore difficult to overestimate the magnitude of the trauma he suffers when he returns to Elsinore to discover that he has been passed over for the diadem of Denmark in favor of Claudius. That's bad enough, but his loss is quickly compounded when he half-realizes that the reason Claudius could so easily become king is because he, the "prince," is inel-igible. And the only ineligibility there could be is bastardy. This means that Hamlet discovers (if "conscience" will permit it) at the beginning of the play that he is not what he seems to be or, more strongly, that he is not what he is (a standard theme in Shakespeare). Consider what that would be like. You spend your entire youth as a royal prince, blessed with all the graces of a splendid courtier and look forward to reigning as Denmark's King. You are admired, envied, and celebrated, and live at the pinnacle of noble society. And yet, there is something else, some subtle "atmosphere" in the court that sends a different message. There is a kind of strange condescension in the manner of the people, as patronizing smirks rise to their lips which they haven't the craft to conceal. What could this portend? There IS an atmosphere, but what is it?

Then one day you wake up and realize you aren't the Prince at all, but a mere court bastard, not the son of the Hyperion King but spawned by the repulsive Claudius with the cooperation of your own mother! This is news so profoundly unsettling that it cannot be quite swallowed down. And the oscillation of this thought in the brain is the very germ of madness.

Finally, as if in a dream, you discover in conversation with a ghost that your biological father is a ghoulish murderer who, with your moth-er's apparent cooperation, has destroyed the great man you thought was your father! Might not these revelations send you headlong into the abyss? Might not your consciousness be darkened, and Denmark now appear to be the prison from which you cannot escape? Suppose you kill Claudius (your own father) in "revenge." It is useless, unless you kill yourself too, for as his son, you too are Claudius.

It is this unappetizing scenario which is the "objective correlative" for which Eliot (and Knight) searched in vain. And it is this scenar-io which explains as no other reading does why Hamlet falls into the madness that consumes him. His mind is henceforth wrapped in a *nueé ardente* which he can neither grasp nor escape.

If we now revert to the question of the original poetic experience, the "burning core" at the heart of the wheel of fire, we can see that it is not death. The idea of death is a mere side effect, an escape valve that could perhaps relieve the tormented mind of a heroic young man who has been cast down from clouds to clods. He languishes in the pit of despair until the very end when he encounters the laughter of Yorick, the companion and muse of his youthful innocence. There is a theme, then, in *Hamlet*, one which is fully capable of resolving his enigma and explaining why it is that 99.999 percent of viewers and readers do not come to the negative conclusions of G. Wilson Knight about this character. That theme is: ALIENATION. Hamlet is not only altogether alienated, his predicament is far worse. Edmond and Don John, for example, are bastards and know it. Their knowing resentments spill over into schemes, plots and devices borne of disaffection. And Wilson Knight has no trouble likening Prince Hamlet to such villains. The difference is Hamlet cannot thrust his illegitimacy into center stage in his mind. Edmond suffers simple alienation, and so chooses the path of vengeful self-advancement. But Hamlet is cursed with a genuine nobility of spirit with roots unwittingly embedded in ordure. He cannot view himself squarely and deliberately, any more that Brutus could. Though circumstances strongly suggest that he is not who he thinks he is, he flees in the opposite direction, and his noble mind falls into delirium.

If we look at the roster of epithets used by Wilson Knight to castigate Hamlet, we notice that some of them are drawn from the vocabulary of ethics and morality, and others are medical terms. Hamlet is "evil" and "cynical" but he is also "diseased" and "poisoned." These two sets of predicates clash with one another, and allow us to observe the confusion in the mind of the Prince of Denmark and also in his critic. There isn't a scintilla of evidence that prior to learning that he was being rejected as heir to the Danish throne and witness to the union of Gertrude and Claudius that he suffered the harrowing self-doubts he exhibits as the curtain rises. His psyche has suffered a tremendous blow and is plainly traumatized. This is the root of his partial paralysis. But human beings are not usually condemned for the injuries they have suffered, unless they have through negligence or intentional misdeeds brought those injuries on themselves. We do not blame King Hamlet for having been poisoned by his malignant brother. How then shall we blame Lord Hamlet for the poisoning of his mind? Suppose for the sake of argument that Hamlet is the biological son of Claudius but has always been treated as the son of King Hamlet. On the basis of the impediment of illegitimacy he is suddenly rejected as a candidate for Kingship, though Claudius assures him he will accede to the throne after the death of the new king. Somewhere in the deeper regions of his mind he senses that he is not the son of the man he loved and admired but rather the offspring of the smiling villain he despises and is commanded to murder. These facts are too ugly and destructive of his identity to be consciously acknowledged. He collapses mentally, the victim of psychological trauma, and consequently loses his fiancée on whom he depended for emotional support. Will it then be appropriate to employ the language of judgment and condemn such a one as "evil," "cruel" and "cynical"? Other than G. Wilson Knight, it is hard to think of any other serious reader of Shakespeare who treats Hamlet in this demeaning manner. His "child-like faith in the theatre" somehow deserted him when it was most needed. In fact, Knight himself was sufficiently troubled by his handling of "the embassy of death" that years later he penned another long piece in 1947 to modify his argument, assimilating Hamlet to Nietzsche, much as Jonathan Dollimore would do later. (Knight, 338-366) But he never recanted his arguments and remained firmly committed to his moral opposition to Prince Hamlet.

VII. Conclusion

In so doing, this critic failed, and failed tragically. Having elaborated a method of literary interpretation which was available to put Hamlet's antic disposition in proper context, Wilson Knight might have found his way out of his overreaction to Hamlet's "unhappy consciousness" (to borrow a phrase from Hegel's *Phenomenology*). He might have read the play closely enough to see that once Hamlet returns home and finds his legitimate expectations defeated, he is driven to the brink of acknowledging that it is his illegitimacy which is the impediment, and that it was Gertrude's indiscretion which gave rise to her son's existential dilemma. Knight betrays the very insight that could have conveyed him to the heart of the wheel of fire, where he would have encountered Hamlet's burning soul. Instead, he stumbled, and his raid on Elsinore went down in flames.

WORKS CITED:

F. H. Bradley, *Appearance and Reality*, Oxford University Press, 1893, 1930.

G. Wilson Knight, *The Wheel of Fire*, Routledge, 1989.

F. S. C. Northrop, *The Meeting of East and West*, Ox Bow Press, 1979.

Stephen C. Pepper, *World Hypotheses*, University of California Press, 1961.

William Shakespeare, The Complete Works, 2d ed., G. Taylor and S. Wells, eds., Oxford, 2005.

19

Shakespeare's Double Play

In which we hoist a dram of eale with Messrs. Frank Kermode and Ted Hughes

This heavy-headed revel east and west
Makes us traduced and taxed of other nations.
They clepe us drunkards, and with swinish phrase
Soil our addition; and indeed it takes
From our achievements, though performed at height,
The pith and marrow of our attribute.
So, oft it chances in particular men
That, for some vicious mole of nature in them —
As in their birth, wherein they are not guilty,
Since nature cannot choose his origin,
By the o'ergrowth of some complexion,
Oft breaking down the pales and forts of reason,
Or by some habit that too much o'erleavens
The form of plausive manners — that these men,
Carrying, I say, the stamp of one defect,
Being nature's livery or fortune's star,
His virtues else be they as pure as grace,
As infinite as man may undergo,
Shall in the general censure take corruption
From that particular fault. The dram of eale
Doth all the noble substance over-daub
To his own scandal.
(Q2, I.4 (I. 18. I))

I. Hamlet's Secret Identity

*I*n his recent *Shakespeare's Language*, Frank Kermode draws attention to Prince Hamlet's blog on the "dram of eale," claiming it's a sort of personal confession rather than abstract disquisition.

> [Hamlet] may be thought to have *himself* in mind, not as a drunkard, of course, but perhaps as a melancholic. He is saying something obliquely *about himself* in the context of a generalization about human character. . . . (Kermode, 107, emphases added)

This is plausible. But in employing the "dram of eale" trope does Hamlet intend his sadness, or that which yields it? A "vicious mole of nature" planted in the human breast bears toxic fruit, *n'est-ce pas*? This "dram," then, is a conceit used to characterize not melancholy but rather that from which it stems. Shakespeare seems to imply that there is a dose of toxin in our constitution which often undermines the strengths of individuals and conduces to their own "scandal." We may view this as a secular reprise of an old religious idea. (See, *e.g.*, Genesis, 3:1-24) We are invited to consider that in the dram of eale oration Prince Hamlet is pondering the root of his private disconsolation.

What makes him so ill-sorted, so cranky? In Act One, he actually muses about doing away with himself on account of nothing more than the insouciant coupling of Gertrude and Claudius. ("O, that this too too solid flesh," I, ii, 129-159) Grant that sprinting to the altar after the loss of a husband may not be in the best of taste, it will yet be readily agreed that no one in the "real world" becomes self-destructive on that account alone. And childish pouting at those nuptials is conspicuously poor deportment indeed. Certainly this hysterical behavior is a clue to the original condition of Hamlet's psyche. Ignoring it might allow the meaning of the tragedy to slip away.

Horatio and Marcellus lead their grumbling friend to the ramparts at Elsinore where a peregrine spirit resembling his father has been seen in the wee hours taking a turn amongst the crenellations. As festive cannons blast the frigid air, Hamlet delivers this jeremiad on the "dram of eale." As he hasn't yet come across the ghost, he knows nothing of his putative father's murder. The "dram of eale" refers not to that. It may be associated with his queasy sense that something is amiss in Denmark, but, whate'er it be, it is squarely lodged within himself, as coterminous with his "birth." And yet there is nothing palpable. What bothers him is a mere quiddity, its features not yet come to light. It must be something "scandalous" in him—but what? This is the cryptogram we are charged with deciphering on pain of misconceiving the entire drama. When he sets out on the path of revenge, we tend to forget that Hamlet's malaise precedes that mission. The only thing we know at first is that he professes to be in protracted mourning over father's death, and seems to come all unglued over the union of his mother with the late king's brother. Yet a similar deed ruffled no feathers when young Henry Tudor took to wife Katherine of Aragon, the widow of his deceased brother Arthur. And the Gertrude/Claudius match is easily accommodated at the amiable court of Claudius. Only the dark Prince is distressed, a solitary party pooper. Why should this "common"conjugal union (I, ii, 72-72) trouble him so? Even as an affront to public decency, it's trivial, a mere social wrinkle. The atmosphere at court is that of a jazz funeral. Aren't Claudius and Gertrude right to chide him for his surly manner? What's he to Gertrude or she to him that he should weep over her, especially during her honeymoon?

We must either lay hold of the secret or give up on these maddening scenes. But to prevail we need to recognize that the most searching question is not, "Why does Hamlet delay in taking revenge for his father's murder?" but rather: What is the basis for the state of profound dejection in which we find him as the curtain rises? Unless these early doings are pure chaff, they serve a vital purpose. Perhaps if we focus on what the "dram of eale" represents we will be in a better position to understand Hamlet's temporizing. But the more closely we examine Kermode's exegesis the less it appears to teach us about the nature and significance of this lethal brew.

It is more than a little curious that not only does Hamlet not explain his moroseness, he rejects out of hand the crowd of eager do-gooders who would assist him in learning what ails him. The ministrations of Claudius, Gertrude, Ophelia, Polonius, Rosenkrantz and Guildenstern are sharply resented by him. Recall his shrill accusation that R&G would presume to "pluck out the heart of my mystery." (III, ii, 353-354) Aren't they at least in part acting in his own behalf? Would he prefer to suffer hidden grief in isolation? His intolerance of their curative interventions appears as an extension of his unwillingness to look with sufficient intensity into himself to detect the cause of his unhappiness. What on earth is so disturbing that it cannot even be glimpsed?

Most striking is that Hamlet's willful myopia about himself is shared not only with his compatriots but with the audience as well. The "inexpressibly horrible thing" which T. S. Eliot complains Hamlet cannot "heave up" into his consciousness remains lodged within his soul and ours, no more to be exhumed by us than it could be by the anguished hero himself. And whatever is afflicting him behaves like a contagion. René Girard's thesis that love in Shakespeare is transmitted mimetically seems to apply, then, to other phenomena as well. Hamlet's nescience is mesmerizing.

What is this play into which we march so boldly but a hall of mirrors, a respiring dream with which we so merge with the protagonist that we become afflicted by his complexes and limitations? After all, you can't have it both ways. Fail to identify with the protagonist and it's impossible to appreciate and understand him. But just to the extent I do identify with him, his symptoms become mine, and the objectivity necessary to know him dispassionately or scientifically evaporates. We are stunned. We cannot perceive his blindness because we ourselves have a blind spot as voracious as any black hole in space. In attending to this play, then, we do not read "about" Hamlet, but enter body and soul into his dream of life with him. There is thus no way to make our entrance into Hamlet's cosmos without becoming entranced. Can we awaken in the midst of his reverie without bursting its seams?

The proof of our utter somnolence and oneiric delusion is the astounding fact that, although all the information we require is in plain sight, after 400 toilsome years, what lies at the root of Hamlet's psyche remains clouded. So tainted are we by Hamlet's pathology that we cannot connect the dots.

Take Frank Kermode as an example. What's on his radar?

1. The dram of eale speech is Hamlet's personal confession. (Kermode, 107)

2. It is about Hamlet himself. (Kermode, 107)

3. The dram of eale is a fundamental defect, the moral correlative of "birth." (line 9)

4. It so undermines the virtues of its host that it causes a "scandal." (line 22)

5. The drinking analogy is suggestive of a seminal substance

taken within the body so as to cause corruption. (line 19)

6. It is "obvious" that at work in the language of Hamlet are the topics of adultery and incest.(Kermode, 101)

7. These ideas are related to questions of personal or dual identity. (Kermode, 101)

8. When we are introduced to Prince Hamlet, his mood is strongly dysthymic. Particularly disturbing to him is the habit of Claudius of referring to him as "my cousin . . . and my son." (Kermode, 103)

9. The first words Hamlet speaks, "A little more than kin, and less than kind," are a bitter retort to Claudius' reference to Hamlet as "my son." (Kermode, 103)

10. Whatever is ailing the Prince is internal. ("I have that within which passeth show;" Kermode, 104)

11. Hamlet refers to Claudius as "my uncle-father." (Kermode, 112)

12. Hamlet is revolted and disgusted with incest. (Kermode, 112)

13. As everyone knows, Gertrude and Claudius marry soon after the coronation.

14. Hamlet is passed over for the Danish throne.

15. Prince Hamlet seems to have a great fear of women because of the risk of being cuckolded by them. (Kermode, 115-116)

Can these jig saw fragments be assembled in such a way that we begin to discern at least in outline what Hamlet's problem is? Can we detect the elephant which is not only in the room but treading on our toes? Let's see.

Hasty marriage implies prior acquaintance. We have no way of knowing how long Gertrude and Claudius have known one another, and there is certainly a dramatic insinuation that King Hamlet has been cuckolded. As the dram of eale is potable, it connotes sexual deliquescence. Exchanging and internalizing of bodily fluids would have been involved in any such amatory enterprise and could easily have led to pregnancy and birth. These were the days before birth control and abortion. Any child born of such an extramarital affair would be the product of adultery and incest. Under those circumstances the reference of Claudius to Hamlet as "my son" would gain in sense, as would Hamlet's reference to Claudius as my "uncle-father." Conceiving of Hamlet as an incestuous bastard would entail an "unkindness" on his parents' parts. Were he the son of Claudius, Hamlet would be the object of a great scandal, explaining why his actual identity is never vouchsafed to him by his mother or anyone else. In practical terms, Hamlet would be left with a dual identity, at once the son of King Hamlet the Dane and simultaneously the son of Claudius! There would then be excellent reason for him to be disgusted with his mother, not, weakly, on account of free-floating misogyny, but directly, because her infidelity brought him into this condition of low repute. And Hamlet's genealogical corruption would render him ineligible to succeed King Hamlet the Dane, hence explaining why he is passed over for the Danish throne at the outset of the play. These interlocking implications achieve an extraordinarily high degree of coherence and explanatory value. It is that coherence and heuristic potency which have yet to be addressed by conventionally minded readers.

No doubt all of this can be discussed and even challenged, but the fact that these implications are never confronted so as to bring the issue up for examination strongly suggests that the brains of generations of readers have been short-circuited. Myopic literary criticism recapitulates the neurotic rationalizations and prevarications of the lead character. As good exegetes, we would certainly need to rule out the possibility that Hamlet is an incestuous bastard. But unless those terms were included in a differential diagnosis they could not be rationally set aside. The condition precedent to insight is raising the right question. To do so we must emerge from our mental fog. What we are constrained to acknowledge at last, therefore, is the existence of a mass parapraxis whose astonishing longevity implies that this play has never been read objectively but always in a state akin to hypnotic trance. Like his predecessors, Frank Kermode had in his possession every scrap of data needed to grasp the crux of Prince Hamlet's malaise. He knows quite well that

Hamlet's emotional breakdown commences prior to the encounter with the ghost. Yet this crucial fact is glossed as complacently as if we were all high school sophomores.

> We . . . hear Hamlet's first soliloquy well before Hamlet has understood that he is to be forced into the role of avenger, although he already hates his life because of his mother's too hasty marriage to a man he despises, his false father. (Kermode, 104)

Really?

Notice that in this characterization the aspects of (1) mourning and (2) incest are omitted, allowing full responsibility for Hamlet's suicidal despair to be chalked up to Gertrude's zestful remarriage to her brother-in-law. But, after all, how old is this guy, now an advanced philosophy major at the university? Is he a helpless child confined in a flat and forced to put up with an abusive step-father? On the contrary, he is a dazzling courtier, a brilliant young grad student trained in the arts, residing independently at Wittenberg. Can such a royal superstar, "th' observed of all observers," having noted his mother's rush to conjugate the verb "to be" with a loutish lord, suddenly "hate his life" and toy with self-annihilation? Impossible. As Eliot in his positivist mood pointed out, an objective correlative is wanting. Kermode does nothing more than repeat the same canard he heard in prep school, never considering its incongruity and insufficiency. Yet ironically, it is just here that we totter on the brink of revelation: of course Hamlet hates his life, but not because Gertrude marries Hamlet's "false father" but rather because she weds his true one. The drummer to which Mr. Kermode marches detours in the absolutely wrong direction, and his followers are either blind or sleepwalking.

It is thus crucially important to assess Hamlet's cognitive state at this juncture. Though he is introspective, spectacularly intelligent and aware of everything, he is unable to fathom what is happening to him. He is running away from something but afraid to turn round to see what it is. For it's not the fear of mere illegitimacy, but the hideous prospect that he may be the son of the man he hates above all others, his *bête noir* "Uncle" Claudius, which leads to Hamlet's disintegration. Descent from Claudius spells his ruin. Intense dread thus smolders throughout the action, belching forth in the Closet Scene like ash and smoke in a seismic eruption. Think of it: like father, like son; were Hamlet the offspring of Claudius it would be all too likely that those wretched qualities for which Hamlet despises him are, if truth be known, part and parcel of the prince. In a very real sense, "Hamlet" is Claudius, Jr. That is a revelation so repugnant that the slightest color thereof would hurl him into madness. It cannot be. But how to ward off an idea without some sense of what it is and what it portends? Under such circumstances, consciousness oscillates, swings from vague apprehension of the very worst to panic, flight and forgetfulness. Madness, then, is not mere deviance or delusion, but the desperate attempt on the part of human beings to escape from a painful reality which is already in some sense intuited. During his entire life, Hamlet has been uneasy. Rumors about him have long circulated at court. He is different. He scents an atmosphere of derision, and naturally attempts to clear the air with bonhomie, jests and diversions. He plays the fool. All to no avail. His stubbornly keen perceptions of those around him convey the unwanted tale, for "there is a kind of confession in [their] looks which [their] modesties have not craft enough to colour." (II, ii, 281-282) Over and over he tells himself their smirks are cordial smiles, and at times almost believes it. Thus it stands when he receives word at Wittenberg that his father has died. He hies him home to find his uncle-father on the throne. His uncle? Prince Hamlet, the only son of King Hamlet the Dane, beloved scion of the Danish people, superlatively educated and groomed for rule, is thrust aside in favor of the late king's smarmy, complacent, mediocre brother. Why? Why elect the "incestuous" brother instead of the royal son and heir apparent? Is not the most refulgent character in all literature bright enough to tie his own shoelaces? Put two and two together? Can he not see that the reason he is not chosen as Denmark's sovereign is because those rumors slithering through the drafty halls of Elsinore are true? "Daylight and champaign discovers not more." (TN, II, v, 154) There is an absolute bar. He is not the late king's son. Of course he can figure this out, but it's too repulsive. He must therefore exercise all his ingenuity not to make the inevitable inference—but to avoid it. And that is what this awesome play is all about.

Hence with his return to Elsinore, Hamlet's existence becomes a prison. (II, ii, 246) It is a nightmare, a condition too awful to be true. It is a "bad dream." (II, ii, 256-267) And it is that bad dream into which we are flung, like the discombobulated visitors to Prospero's magic isle.

Not to worry. After a few hours we settle everything. We become scholars. Not only do we understand the play in its totality, we are lords of the text. We can evaluate it, detect its flaws, nod sagely with T. S. Eliot when he pronounces it an aesthetic "failure," or take refuge in the inertia of literary history. We are sophisticated, transcendent, above the clouds, gazing down in benign condescension on poor William of Stratford and his quixotic efforts at stagecraft. And yet, strangely, we omniscient ones are no more successful than the play's demented hero, who cannot bring himself to see the painfully obvious. What has become of our vaunted insight? Our hermeneutical passion? Our relentless objectivity? They are as useless here as the weapons raised against Prospero by his unruly guests. We parrot what we learned in high school, and *voila!*—The problem vanishes. We are indeed such stuff as dreams are made on (*The Tempest*, IV, i, 156-157), and when we step inside Hamlet's world we drain the cup of eale with him. Naturally our hasty textual renderings and conjectures, all clashing with each other and ushering in interminable disputes and ivory tower dust ups, soon collapse, persuading many cynical minds that the text is really nothing in itself, void of meaning, and will be, like an overly cooperative wench, whatever we wish it to be. We can trample it at will. Thus we pass in an instant from knowing everything to knowing nothing about *Hamlet*. We are then even less able to discern the truth of his being. Whether we play the role of theatrical conquistador, or clueless library visitor, in the end we crash and burn, and do so because we have not once taken the script for what it is. We have not the perspicacity of modest Bottom, who exults that he has dreamed a dream "past the wit of man to say what dream it was." (*MND*, IV, i, 203)

We are blinded by hubris. Paul de Man points out that each critic is afflicted by his own blind spot. The greater our insight, the more we inevitably overlook. It seems too that there is something infectious about this blindness, because there is an "aspect of literary language [which] causes blindness in those who come into close contact with it." (de Man, 106)

> The insight exists only for a reader in the privileged position of being able to observe blindness as a phenomenon in its own right—the question of his own blindness being one which he is by definition incompetent to ask . . . He has to undo the explicit results of a vision that is able to move toward the light only because, being already blind, it does not have to fear the power of this light. But the vision is unable to report correctly what it has perceived in the course of its journey. To write critically about critics thus becomes a way

to reflect on the paradoxical effectiveness of a blinded vision that has to be rectified by means of insights that it unwittingly provides. (de Man, 106) [*Blindness and Insight: Essays in the Rhetoric of Contemporary Criticism*, by Paul de Man, University of Minnesota Press, 2d ed., 1983]

Reading and criticism have been dim for the past four centuries as a consequence of Hamlet's own inability to see himself. As he fears unconsciously to see himself as a possible son of his supposed uncle, and remains in flight therefrom, so it falls out that everyone who follows his footsteps, entering into his language and spirit, embraces to an indeterminate extent the prince's neurosis. Everything is taken at face value. Hamlet is Hamlet. Who would quibble over that? But if, as Harold Bloom contends, *The Tragedy of Hamlet, Prince of Denmark,* is actually an extended poem, that is, a constellation of shifting metaphors afloat on the tides of language, it can never be explicated in literal terms. The son of the late King Hamlet the Dane casts a long shadow as the son of the King's brother. Modern criticism, for all its vaunted sophistication, misses that shadow.

But while we can acknowledge esoterically that Hamlet is none other than the son of Claudius (thus neatly accounting for why he cannot rush to his revenge), at the same time we cannot just dismiss the exoteric reading which, with some warrant, treats Hamlet as the son of King Hamlet the Dane. (Gontar, 406) Hamlet is the literary character par excellence, pointing like the Cheshire cat in opposed directions. He will not be reduced to a monocular apparition, a one-dimensional man.

Let's dwell on this for a moment. *The Tragedy of Hamlet* is a work of fiction. Prince Hamlet as we know him in this play never existed. As such, it would be a piece of arrant nonsense to contend either that this non-entity was the actual "son" of the late king or his brother. The question is not, Who is Hamlet's father?—but: What is the most satisfactory reading we can have of this play? Had these strange events actually occurred, what sense could we make of them? And it should be obvious that there is more than one way of accomplishing that. At first blush the Prince is generally received as the son of Hamlet the Dane. It is only after sustained reflection that we eventually find (with critics such as T. S. Eliot) that taken superficially the play presents so many baffling questions as to be nearly indigestible. As we gasp and grapple with this dilemma, it gradually dawns on us that some of these nagging questions and dilemmas might be eased if we perceive Hamlet's origins differently.

Though he misses the content of Hamlet's secret identity, Mr. Kermode makes a substantial contribution to the subject by underscoring Hamlet's doubling technique as an external representation of the protagonist's personal dualism. Thus, over and against Prince Hamlet we have the pedestrian Laertes, a natural foil. (Kermode, 105) We note Shakespeare's use of gratuitously paired persons, including minor figures Cornelius and Voltemand, and Rosenkrantz and Guildenstern. (Kermode, 102) Why are we given a couple of Tweedle Dee and Tweedle Dum courtiers? Why should two ambassadors have been sent to Norway? (I, ii, 26-41; II, ii, 59-85) Couldn't one have done the job? After all, Mountjoy the herald of France who visits King Harry in *King Henry V,* is *solus.* As for Hamlet, sooner or later we find that he has not one self but two, at once the son of King Hamlet the Dane and, as doppelgänger, the bastard son of Prince Claudius. There is not one ghost in Hamlet but two: (1) the ghost of the late king, and (2) the ghost-like Prince Hamlet, son of Claudius. Haunted by his secret identity, Hamlet cannot fend off mental dissociation. The doubled figures in the play reflect and underscore Hamlet's schizoid identity.

This pregnant line of inquiry is extended and reinforced if we recall Hans Holbein the Younger's renowned 1533 English portrait *The Ambassadors* (below) fashioned during the later reign of King Henry VIII. The reader will recall this painting, featuring an anamorphic skull visible only at an awkward angle. Though it's hard to imagine how a country bumpkin such as William of Stratford might ever have seen such a masterpiece, Edward de Vere, the 17th Earl of Oxford, Great Lord Chamberlain, and most likely a grandson of Henry VIII through Henry's daughter Elizabeth, would have long been familiar with this remarkable *tour-de-force* depicting George de Selve, Bishop of Lauvar (1508-1541) and the esteemed French envoy Jean de Dinteville (1504-1555). The hypothesis that Shakespeare's Cornelius and Voltemand are patterned after Holbein's Dinteville and Selve should not be peremptorily dismissed. For it may well be that Holbein's ghostly skull is the forebear of Hamlet's spectral self and graveyard skull. The analogy is plain: as Holbein situates the spectral skull between the pillar-like figures of two French nobles, so Shakespeare gives us a divided Prince Hamlet suggestive of being simultaneously the son of Hamlet, Sr. on the one hand and Prince Claudius on the other. Lodged between these two father figures is the ghostly Prince Hamlet, exhibiting Janus-faced features which may not be resolved. Just as we cannot see Holbein's anamorphic skull unless we view the painting at an odd angle, so we cannot see Hamlet's ghost-like second self unless we step back from the action and observe the play from a different perspective, one in which we refrain from taking the narrative as it appears in plot summaries. When we begin to interrogate the play as it interrogates itself, Hamlet's second self suddenly materializes before us. Negative capability is all.

It should be mentioned in passing that this is not the first time that Hans Holbein the Younger enters Shakespeare commentary. In the analysis of the character Pointz in *King Henry IV*, we noted that in 1533, the same year *The Ambassadors* was painted, this artist made a well-known sketch of an English noble, "N. Poines, Knight." This startling fact adds weight to the view that the author of the Shakespearean corpus was familiar with Holbein and influenced by him. (See, Gontar, 77-78) If we then repeat the exegetical exercise by considering the author himself, we see that Edward de Vere, the 17th Earl of Oxford suffers the same psychological ambiguity: on the surface he is of course properly remembered as the son of John de Vere, the 16th Earl of Oxford. But a more thorough probing reveals compelling evidence that in reality he was—and remains—the biological son of Thomas Seymour and Princess Elizabeth. Oxford, the secret son of Seymour, writes his major play about Prince Hamlet, the secret son of Claudius. It is these shadows, these ghosts, which haunt the popular Shakespeare industry today.

It bears repeating, then, that the thesis advanced in *Hamlet Made Simple* and in the present essay is emphatically not the wooly-headed notion that the literary character Prince Hamlet "is" the son of literary character "Claudius." That sort of naïve literalism is ruled out *ab initio*. What we have done is trace the deconstructive action of the play in which an exoteric Prince Hamlet is shown to collapse into his opposite, as we apprehend the filial relationship of this Prince to "uncle" Claudius. Significantly, the dialectical transition from the fatherhood of the late king to that of his brother depends on the affirmation of the former. What makes the melancholy Prince so fascinating is precisely the way in which the shadow cast by the son of King Hamlet the Dane morphs into the "Mr. Hyde" figure of the bastard son of Claudius. Thinking through Hamlet's initial identity forces us to a more thorough understanding. What we are brought to see is that, from a phenomenological point of view, Hamlet is double. Seeing him that way gives him three dimensionality and meaning.

What role does the dram of eale play in all this? It is nothing less than a symptom of a "mind diseased." (*Macbeth*, V, iv, 42) The dram of eale soliloquy dramatically demonstrates that, prior to visiting his supposed father's spirit and learning of the murder, Hamlet is not only suffering depression but has reflected on his dysthymic mood, and located its source in a kind of physical and metaphysical poison which taints him at the heart's core. Though his severe father complex prevents him from a clear idea of his origins, like a good shaman, Prince Hamlet uses figurative language whose particular terms, when extracted and set in order, point unmistakably in the direction of his mother's extramarital affair and pregnancy at the hands of Claudius. Hamlet is thus despoiled *ab ovum*. He has two fathers. He knows and knows not. That is his tragedy and his glory.

We turn now to Shakespeare's use of language to see how that reinforces Hamlet's dual identity.

II. Shakespeare's Double Play

1. Frank Kermode

Looking back once more at the dram of eale speech, we notice it features a number of conjunctive locutions. "East and west," "pith and marrow of our attribute," "pales and forts of reason," and "nature's livery or fortune's star," constitute a set of paired phrases typical of Shakespeare's style, especially, claims Kermode, in *Hamlet*. This recourse to phrasal coupling has been taken up by Ted Hughes in *Shakespeare and the Goddess of Complete Being* (1992), and more recently by Frank Kermode in *Shakespeare's Language* (2000). Both focus on the way in which conjunctive language is related to and expressive of theme and action in the plays and poems. As we began with Kermode's analysis of the text, we will continue with that, and then have a look at Ted Hughes.

Early on, Kermode is struck by the prominence of duality in the play's verbiage.

> Meanwhile, the doubling and antithetical phrases continue as an undertone: "This spirit, *dumb* to us, will *speak* to him"; "As *needful* in our loves, *fitting* our duty." (Kermode, 100, emphases in original)

> The language of *Hamlet* continually varies in this and similar ways. It is dominated to an extent without parallel in the canon by one particular rhetorical device: it is obsessed with doubles of all kinds, and notably by its use of the figure known as *hendiadys* [hen.dī.e.dïs]. This means, literally, one-through-two, and can be illustrated by some common expressions such as "law and order" or "house and home." (Kermode, 100-101, emphasis and pronunciation added)

> The play has many doublings, but those which exhibit hendiadys are marked by identifiable *tension or strain*, as if the parts were related in some not perfectly evident way. (Kermode, 101, emphasis added)

The Fifth Edition of *The American Heritage Dictionary of the English Language* puts the meaning of "hendiadys" this way: "A figure of speech in which two words connected by a conjunction are used to express a single notion that would normally be expressed by an adjective and a substantive, such as grace and favor instead of gracious favor." (*American Heritage*, 819)

Kermode continues as follows.

> It would be perhaps too much to claim that a study of this device can take us to the heart of the play . . . My purpose in drawing attention to hendiadys is largely to show that in the rhetoric of Hamlet there may be a strain, virtually unnoticed, of a kind of compulsion that reflects the great and obvious topics, adultery and incest, deep preoccupations given external representation. These preoccupations seem to be related to a concern with questions of identity, sameness, and the union of separate selves — joined opposites . . . as in marriage and, in a pathologised form, incest. (Kermode, 101, emphasis added)

This exposition relating the congruent structures of Shakespeare's dramatic language and the major themes of the play is nothing short of an epiphany. The conjunctive phrases mirror Hamlet's divided being, mired in incest and adultery. The "tension and strain" of hendiadys come to embody the tension and strain in Hamlet's splintered psyche. The problem is that the oppositional elements noted by Kermode's analysis (adultery, incest, identity, union of separate selves, *et al.*) only come cleanly into focus when we perceive Hamlet's shadow self as son of Claudius. Note that the adultery and incest Kermode has in mind are exclusively functions of marriage to a deceased brother's wife. That is "adultery" in a weak sense of the term, based on the inference that, having become one flesh with her husband, mating with his surviving brother is consanguineous *de jure* and so proscribed. What are these two selves? Kermode isn't very helpful on that one. But think about it. The Ghost calls his brother an "incestuous [and] adulterate beast." (I, v, 42) As we have nothing in the text to demonstrate that Claudius engages in sexual relations with anyone other than Gertrude, the implication in accusing him of adultery is that Claudius' affair with her began during her marriage to King Hamlet. Nothing rules that out, while cohesion with much in the play rules it in. Hamlet thus unconsciously fears that his mother had an adulterous, extra-marital liaison with Claudius, of which he, Hamlet, is the product. He is a legitimate son because he is born within the bounds of marriage, but illegitimate insofar as he is not his lawful father's issue. As Hamlet the Dane's child, he is putative heir to the throne of Denmark, but as the son of Claudius he cannot become king on the death of the reigning sovereign. Ironically, the "strain, virtually unnoticed," is unnoticed by Kermode himself, that is, the tension between Hamlet's two different progenitors and the Prince's two selves that eventuate and square off against one another in the darkest recesses of his soul. This is Shakespeare's double play.

A particularly illustrative linguistic doubling is observed by Kermode in the exchanges with Rosenkrantz and Guildenstern.

> Hamlet ends his interview with the spy-courtiers by mentioning that radical doublet "my uncle-father and aunt-mother," which contains in little the whole charge of incest. Later (IV, iii, 49-52) he will call Claudius "mother," disgusted at the idea that Claudius is of one flesh with Gertrude, as in a different sense he himself is. Here is an exquisitely horrible case of there being "division none," [referring to *The Phoenix and Turtle*] now characterized not by happiness of true love but by its opposite, the disgustingness of incest. (Kermode, 112)

It is ironic that this analysis does not foreground Hamlet's doubleness but actually conceals it. On the conscious level, operative in a surface reading of the text, it is the union of Claudius and Gertrude in matrimony and intimacy ("one flesh") which makes of Claudius Hamlet's "mother." But unconsciously, however, there is a stronger and more turbid current of meaning: Hamlet as the issue of Claudius and Gertrude is the product of the incest he abominates. This situates the "disgustingness of incest" in Hamlet himself and raises its significance exponentially. The dram of eale lies within him, working to his scandal. Thus, it is not correct to say that the locution "my uncle-father and aunt-mother" "contains in little the whole charge of incest," as that charge must perforce include Hamlet himself, who is much more than innocent bystander. If husband and wife are "one flesh," then when the marital union of King Hamlet and Gertrude is followed by the union of Claudius and Gertrude, Prince Hamlet has three mothers and three fathers, and he is of "one flesh" with all these. That is, in ultimate terms, Prince Hamlet cannot be distinguished from the substance of the man who made him an incestuous bastard. Further, in Gertrude's incestuous and adulterous conduct Hamlet must find himself. It is the sheer magnitude and force of this egoistic vortex which so dominates the text of this play that it pervades its very language. Mr. Kermode notes the linguistic symptomatology but neglects its ground.

Consider "To be or not to be." A fair interpretation of that most famous discourse is the acid test of any reading of *Hamlet*. What Kermode proffers on this score is wide of the mark. Remember that this critic begins by observing that in the dram of eale speech Hamlet isn't talking about humanity but about himself. (Kermode, 107) But by the time we reach the soliloquy to end all soliloquies eight pages later, we learn just the opposite.

> [O]ne thing is surely obvious: Hamlet is referring his own to a more *general view of the human condition*. . . . (Kermode, 115)

The soliloquy is "a way of considering the *human condition more largely*." (Kermode, 115, emphases added). Would it not make more sense instead of creating a glaring contradiction to just admit that both speeches have general and personal meaning and application?

Though some scholars have stood on their heads to deny that the "to be or not to be" speech in Act III is about suicide, when it is read in the context of "O, that this too too solid flesh would melt" speech in Act I, the conclusion that both speeches center on self-destruction is unavoidable. Hamlet has not in Act III forgotten the suicidal impulse which plagued him in Act I. Should I live (and act) or should I cash in my chips and depart?—is the question. But why is Hamlet wrestling again with the same suicidal ideation? He doesn't tell us immediately, though we learn more in the ensuing dialogue with Ophelia. Again he gives no express explanation for his impulse to do away with himself in "to be or not to be." Has anything changed? Well, Hamlet now knows that his Uncle Claudius is a murderer who poisoned the King and appropriated the Queen his mother. If, then, he is nauseated by the prospect of being the natural son of this reprobate, this adulterous villain, he must be now even more offended, considering the likely prospect that his actual father is a murderer and now his step-father.

Hamlet tells us that he is in dread. (III, i, 80) But in the compression of the soliloquy that term "dread" is not completely unpacked. Yes, we dread the "something" after death, but part of that dread (*pace* Socrates) is precisely our ignorance of what that something is. We fear the unknown. But there is implicitly more. The dread of death is counterpoised to the dread of life. As living, I must accept my dram of eale, *i.e.*, my origins in the loins of some unknown progenitor who has passed his concupiscence and other peccancies on to me. On a symmetrical reading, if I choose to embrace death and emigrate to that "undiscovered country from whose bourne no traveler returns," might I not discover that in fact the traveler does return, to be reborn as yet another link in the chain of bastardy? For in essence, none of us knowing our paternity, we are one and all *de facto* bastards, as we learn from Posthumus Leonatus (*Cymbeline*, II, v, 2) and Thersites (*Troilus and Cressida*, V, viii, 5-14) Hamlet's dilemma in the "to be or not to be" soliloquy is thus consonant with the theme of doubled existence. As living self, I dread the discovery of adulterous, incestuous origins; as self-destroying self, I dread the eternal return which will send me back into this world of bastards.

Sequent to this great soliloquy is the cruel encounter with Ophelia, in which Hamlet challenges her "honesty," that is, her chastity. "Why," he asks her, "woulds't thou be a breeder of sinners?" (III, i, 123-124) Mr. Kermode notes properly that in the Nunnery scene, Hamlet dwells in horror on women's capacity to cuckold their husbands. (Kermode, 115-116) But on the standard model of the plot which Kermode follows, in which Gertrude and Claudius do nothing worse than marry without extensive delay, there is no cuckoldry. That syndrome involves a woman who betrays her husband during marriage. The scenario adopted by Kermode contains no cuckoldry. Why, then, would this allegation be uppermost in Hamlet's mind at this particular moment? The "Hamlet" who speaks these lines is he who fears that Gertrude did cuckold her first husband. Hamlet's anxiety reflects the unease and profound pessimism of an incestuous bastard. As such, he feels that, were he to marry Ophelia, she would likely cuckold him and possibly humiliate him by bearing some other man's child. But Mr. Kermode doesn't pick up Shakespeare's cues and has no way to account for the reference to cuckoldry. He notes that Hamlet accuses his mother of quickly marrying Claudius because of "inordinate sexual appetite," (Kermode, 122) never considering that the pall cast over Hamlet with respect to that concupiscence reflects his fear that he is not the son of the man whose name he bears.

2. Ted Hughes

Though unmentioned by Frank Kermode, perhaps the earliest scholar to seriously explore Shakespeare's linguistic doubling was the Poet Laureate of England (1984-98), Ted Hughes (1930-1998). His *Shakespeare and the Goddess of Complete Being* performs *en passant* a searching analysis of this trope, its structure and meaning. Like Kermode, Hughes is a traditionalist who attempts to press the juggernaut of Shakespearean poesy into the shallow and incommensurable straits of Stratfordian biography. (See, *e.g.,* Hughes, 127, 134) But where Kermode identifies *The Tragedy of Hamlet, Prince of Denmark* as the *summa* of double epithet and hendiadys, Ted Hughes offers a developmental account of these devices whose apotheosis is not *Hamlet* but *All's Well That Ends Well*. Where Kermode helpfully explains such replications as the "external representation" of Prince Hamlet's two divergent personae, for Ted Hughes the purpose and significance of such poetic conjunctions are far broader and more polyvalent. He approaches Shakespeare as a systematic mythographer whose poems and plays are (excepting the histories) one and all celebratory variations on the bipartite divinity standing as the fountainhead of western culture. (Gontar, 161ff.) Of course it isn't possible to cover Hughes' vast and intricate metaphysics and literary theology in a few pages. In what follows we will focus attention on the functional role played by the double epithet in Shakespeare, tracing Hughes' exposition from *Titus Andronicus* through the history plays (which employ the locution in question absent the mythology), to the crescendo in *All's Well*, and then on to *Hamlet*. We will find that although neither Kermode nor Hughes ever grasped the author's (or Hamlet's) actual or full identity, and could not make valid textual or historical correlation with the polarities of the double epithet, both these thinkers shed light on Shakespeare's utilization of this conceit, and, ironically, they form a brace of analysts whose work recapitulates the double epithet they took up individually.

Although he concedes that Shakespeare had some recourse to paired epithets prior to *Hamlet*, Frank Kermode sees that tragedy as the grand finale of doubling. (Kermode, 100) In this it is "without parallel in the canon." (Kermode, 100) Yet no effort is made in *Shakespeare's Language* to demonstrate the truth of this claim or assess the role of dual phrasing in the works which precede (or follow) *Hamlet*.

Ted Hughes, on the other hand, tells us that "something like [the doubling in *Hamlet*] occurs from quite early on." (Hughes, 132) He begins with a citation from the early *Titus Andronicus*.

TAMORA

They told me, here, at the dead time of night,
A thousand fiends, a thousand hissing snakes,

Ten thousand swelling toads, as many urchins,
Would make such *fearful and confused cries*,
As any mortal body hearing it
Should straight fall mad, or else die suddenly.
(II, iii, 99-104, emphasis added)

Though this seems innocent and straightforward enough, the conjunct in the fourth line is full of strain and tension, strain and tension presaging the scene in which Bassanius is slain and Lavinia raped and disfigured. Under Ted Hughes' microscope a seemingly inert conjunct is revealed in startling motion.

> The 'and', it seems, is not only filler but a symbol . . . of impassioned headlong flight. . . . At the same time, the two adjectives begin to look less perfunctory. 'Fearful' bears the two opposite meanings of 'full of fear' and 'causing fear'; 'confused means only suffering from confusion'. When the two words are combined in this way — that is, separated for distinction and comparison to be made by that 'and' — while the context evokes the active sense of 'fearful', the participle 'confused' activates its passive sense. The line then creates a dramatic scene, in which fiends, snakes, toads and urchins are making noises so frightful that they themselves are terrified by them and so crying worse — in a howl-back amplification of their own cries, an especially diabolical idea of infinite terror in a dark wood: existence terrified by its own existence. (Hughes, 133)

Hughes might easily have gone into greater detail to expose the power of Shakespeare's conceit here. For example, this speech of Tamora stands diametrically opposed to her seductive invitation to Aaron given moments before in which this very part of the forest is described as though it were an earthly paradise where snakes make no frightful noises in a dank pit of doom but "[lie] rollèd in the cheerful sun." (II, iii, 13) Tamora's contradictory characterization of this glade is therefore itself "fearful and confused." Because of the ambiguity in this locution, it suggests in miniature the disposition of the parties, Tamora and her sons "fearful" and Lavinia "confused." On the other hand, insofar as the two descriptive terms amount to the same thing, they reflect the villainous siblings, Chiron and Demetrius, who murder Bassanius and pillage

Lavinia. When these two barbarians are in turn executed by Titus, they also utter their own fearful and confused cries.

Hughes moves now to the more mature Shakespeare of the history plays. Four illustrations are given.

1. "A beauty-waning and distressed widow" (R3, III, vii, 184)

2. "Seduc'd the pitch and height of his degree" (R3, III, vii, 187)

3. "Be judg'd by subject and inferior breath" (R2, iv, 128)

4. "The tediousness and process of my travel" (R2, II, iii, 12)

The "double epithet" as used by Shakespeare runs the gamut from tautology (*i.e.*, mere filler or rhythmic marker) to contradiction. As we continue to examine various specimens throughout the corpus, we find greater subtlety and variety of sense and significance. "In each case," says Hughes, "it seems clear enough that the two qualifiers are being weighed against each other — across the fulcrum of that 'and' — and with conscious deliberation. In general, each word supplies a different point of view . . . ." (Hughes, 134)

However, we have to do here with no literary quirk. In order to help us to grasp the rich and full meaning of what is unfolding, Hughes interrupts his technical treatment of double epithet to set this locution in social and political context. It is nothing less, he says, than "a sort of regal gesture" or a "small grand moment." (Hughes, 134) That is, as we have long suspected, the language of Shakespeare is the idealized language of the court, the monarch being always the prototypical speaker. So far, so good. But at this point Hughes descends into Stratfordian bathos, which we reproduce here for the reader's edification.

There is little doubt that Shakespeare delighted in 'stateliness' — to the point of infatuation. The huge proportion of his work devoted to kings and their courts being 'stately' and 'ceremonious' was satisfying a powerful hunger. It touched those 'strong shudders' and 'heavenly agues' that stirred in the base of his spine. His addiction to the 'grand' was like a permanent psychological pressure. It is one aspect of his sheer sense of theatre, of what suddenly hushes the groundlings and makes the gods listen, but was no small part of the tremendous sense of 'things high and working, full of state and woe' for which he was able eventually to create a whole new kind of drama. These lines [*e.g.*, 1-4 above] speak directly for that ear. (Hughes, 134)

There is nothing objectionable in placing the Shakespearean conceit in its early modern social setting. The foregoing is admirable. But Hughes' Stratfordian presuppositions make of our poet a grotesque snob, toadying up to elites whose ranks he would give his own mellifluous tongue to invade. Is Shakespeare to be viewed as Malvolio? (See, Gontar, 121ff.) There is no evidence that the author of the plays was "addicted" to sycophancy, or given to "low-crooked curtsies and base spaniel fawning." (*Julius Caesar*, III, i, 43) On the contrary. The author of these poems and plays was opposed to snobbery with every fiber of his being. Rather than portray such a genius and teacher of humanity as a hopeless lick-spittle and hypocrite, it would obviously be more congenial and economical to view the proclivity to stately and grand language not as an affectation of a bizarrely gifted groundling but as the natural self-expression of an artistic lord. Wouldn't that be William of Ockham's (1285-1349) view of the dispute?

At any rate, as we study Hughes' painstaking analysis we do begin to see that the conjoined antecedent and consequent nouns and adjectives differ in connotation and linguistic origin and point of view. Usually it is the antecedent which carries the loftier tone. Thus:

In the second example, the two qualifiers seem tautologous enough to resemble a cut and a slash, or the right barrel then the left for good measure (and for filler). Yet 'pitch' carries the idea of the height from which a falcon might dangerously stoop [sic, as 'swoop' was plainly intended] — might pitch, in fact. In other words it brings 'height' as a threat into hovering balance with 'height' as a dignity — a fateful uncertainty everywhere in these plays about pathological kings. (Hughes, 135)

The reader will of course be reminded of King Richard II's mock on Sir Thomas Mowbray, "How high a pitch his resolution soars." (*The Tragedy of King Richard II*, I, i, 109) This neatly illustrates Hughes' lesson, combining "height" and "pitch" with a plain allusion to Richard's superiority over Mowbray symbolized by the royal sport of hawking.

The quivering epithets signal how uneasy lies the head that wears King Richard's crown. The third illustration, "be judg'd by subject and inferior breath" recreates "the essential Shakespearean scene, the king's confrontation with the victorious rebel." (Hughes, 135) As for the fourth, "The tediousness and process of my travel," we easily apprehend two "contrasting points of view": "tediousness takes care of the inside point of view, the subjective impression of what had to be undergone, while 'process' accounts for the external record, the actual onerous sequence of obstacles, logistical problems, inconvenience, and so on." (Hughes, 136) Supporting Hughes' argument is the fact that for Shakespeare the antecedent term "tediousness" is a Latinate term bound to be unfamiliar to the commons, who might be expected to know "process."

LEONATO

Neighbors, you are tedious.

DOGBERRY

It pleases your worship to say so, but we are
the poor Duke's officers. But truly, for mine own part,
if I were as tedious as a king I could find it in my heart
to bestow it all on your worship.

LEONATO

All your tediousness on me, ah?
(*Much Ado About Nothing*, III, v, 17-22)

Hughes' third stage of epithetical pairing is consistent with the earlier ones, but takes an additional step to reach what he dubs "translation." This occurs when Shakespeare confronts the challenge of communicating dramatically with both the noble theatre patrons, eager for every new and recondite word or phrase, and the groundlings, who also covet such fancies, yet hardly know what to make of them (as the Dogberry incident above shows). Shakespeare's stage gambit is to toss to the lords and educated patrons the unusual vocabulary term as the antecedent, to be followed consequently by the prosaic 'translation' or rough synonym for the thrill of the commons. Once more, Hughes portrays Shakespeare as a learned fool such as the Pedant in *Love's Labour's Lost,* that is, a semi-educated and pompous word addict who stumbles into literary greatness in the manner of Christopher Sly. (*The Taming of the Shrew*, Induction 1) "One supposes," speculates Hughes glibly, "words simply stuck to him, like tunes to an Irish piper." (Hughes, 138) "Supposes," indeed. Why suppose any such thing? Just as there is no reason to "suppose" that Shakespeare was a snob obsessed with mimicking the English nobility, by the same token there is no reason to "suppose" that Shakespeare's massive vocabulary was anything other than what large vocabularies usually are, the natural product of wide reading, excellent breeding, and good taste. Whatever else he may have been, the author of the quartos, sonnets, long poems and *First Folio* was a supremely educated polymath of the highest order. He was able to give the nobility the words after which they hankered not because he was an idiot savant (as Hughes "supposes") but because he was a lord par excellence, a teacher's teacher.

Hughes misses the obvious. Though it's possible to characterize Shakespeare's technique of doubling epithets as a pandering to the patricians and a patronizing of the poor, in the end such a description lacks concreteness. History tells a story of more illuminating and efficacious events. After the battle of Hastings in 1066 A.D., William the Bastard and his Norman compeers had a stranglehold on England, evicting the English nobility who were supplanted by Norman French aristocrats. By edict of William, the official language of Britain now became French. Old English went underground along with pagan customs, culture and religion. For many years there were then two languages in England, and the rustic simplicities of Anglo-Saxon were the object of Norman apprehension, scorn and derision. This linguistic alienation then began to slowly ebb in scope and force, as a close reading of Chaucer will show. Once again English kings took up the native tongue, though it was heavily Gallicized. The "small grand moment" mentioned by Ted Hughes was the Shakespearean heyday during the reign of Elizabeth Tudor. All looked back proudly to the English wars against the French during the reigns of Kings Henry V, VI and VIII. Meanwhile it often seemed to the French that in combating the English they were in fact seeking to destroy their cousins.

DAUPHIN

O Dieu vivant! Shall a few sprays of us
The emptying of our father's luxury,

Our scions, put in wild and savage stock,
Spirit up so suddenly into the clouds
And over-look their grafters?

BOURBON

Normans, but bastard Normans, Norman bastards!
Mort de ma vie, if they march along
Unfought withal, but I will sell my dukedom
To buy a slobb'ry and a dirty farm,
In that nook-shotten isle of Albion.
(*King Henry V*, III, iii, 5-14)

Hughes' "small grand moment" was therefore a political and cultural triumph in which England affirmed its independence of Continental forces, particularly Spain and France. It was not, as is sometimes thought, the adoption or assertion of "pure" Anglo-Saxon, but rather the fructifying collision of Latin, French and English which exploded in the national consciousness in the works of William Shakespeare. It was this which created that national language and crystallized England's collective consciousness. As the linguistic templates surged against one another the result was not polyglot or pidgin but poetry. The rich and evocative cadences of Shakespeare were the crucible in which modern English—and modern England itself—were born.

Ted Hughes deserves credit for drawing our attention to a commonly overlooked detail in this vast panorama: the employment of the double epithet in Shakespeare's plays. Across the conjunctive plain two mighty hosts confront one another and clash, as do subject and predicate via the copula. The result is a chain of metaphor strong enough to bind a nation together at the very instant of its ascendancy. Thenceforward what was to lie at the heart of the English people was poetry, a poetry capable of ratifying and sustaining heroism in a manner not seen since Homer and Vergil. Though he doesn't quite rise to the occasion, we can detect Hughes' awareness that more was going on in the double epithet than the elaboration of poetic technique.

With a mediumistic author such as Shakespeare, whose compelling theme happened to be an extreme case of the common psychic conflict, the commercial dilemma became a national opportunity. A true 'language of the common bond'

in drama, at every level of theme, action and speech, became
essential. And, in finding it, Shakespeare invented, as if inci-
dentally and inadvertently, a new kind of drama and a new
poetic vernacular. (Hughes, 140)

That, "new poetic vernacular" is, of course, the English language.
What occurred in Shakespeare was indeed "the intermarriage of two
different linguistic stocks," as Hughes says. (Hughes, 149) But his characterization of those opposing partners as merely "high" and "low" is
too abstract, and ignores the relations of language to nationality and
culture. Hughes' demonstration of Shakespeare's employment of double
epithet in *All's Well That Ends Well* is masterful, however, and were there
sufficient time and patience we might relish his illuminating exposition
of "on the catastrophe and heel of pastime," (142) and "this captious and
intenible sieve," (149).

Those pleasant tasks are left for the reader. For we must turn to
Hughes' reading of *Hamlet*. Curiously, while Frank Kermode discovers
the most consistent usage of doubling language in *Hamlet*, Ted Hughes
finds almost nothing of that. The slings and arrows of outrageous fortune
sail into the sea of troubles with hardly a bubble of concern. (Hughes,
145) Hughes' merit in explicating *Hamlet* is that he recognizes the essentially problematic character of the play. He is thus keenly aware of
Eliot's critique, and takes his objections seriously.

Eliot pointed out that *Hamlet*, as a work of art, seems to
struggle with a mass of highly pressurized, obscure material
that cannot be dragged into the light, as if plot and characters
were somehow inadequate to express what Hamlet, and behind Hamlet, Shakespeare, seem to be aware of and involved
with. (Hughes, 235)

This highly significant comment means that for Ted Hughes, as
for T. S. Eliot, the standard model of Hamlet is unsatisfactory. We cannot take the play as first given, as little minds would have us do. Prince
Hamlet, says Hughes, suffers a "doubled vision," seeing "his mother
from both the loving son's and the loving husband's [Claudius'] point
of view, and thereafter he carries the reaction of his father as well as
his own." (Hughes, 233-234) "[H]e cannot separate the mother he loves
from the mother he hates." (Hughes, 234) Of course, we have already
seen why this is so. Hamlet's perceptions are double because his inner

state is schizoid: As Gertrude's "loving son" Hamlet sees himself as the son of the late king. But as the despiser of this woman he feels himself to be at one with Claudius. And as we have seen, the steady drum beat of double epithets which stand in opposition to one another mirrors the adverse identity of Hamlet in relation to his supposed uncle. Let Ted Hughes expound on the Prince's conflicted psyche:

> The Prince's murder of Claudius becomes a replay of Claudius' Murder of King Hamlet, but a more complicated example of the Type. In this action one catches sight of the weird perpetuum mobile that spins the whole drama into a vertiginous other dimension. When King Hamlet's ghost rises out of Purgatory . . . Hamlet sees, as in a mirror, an image of his own mythic self. He sees himself, that is, as his mother's consort, punished for that incestuous crime by death and now by Purgatory. In the same way he sees Claudius as another image of his own mythic self. In this case he is again his mother's consort, not yet punished, but definitely, inevitably to be punished, and to be punished by him, Prince Hamlet. But this punishment, of himself as Claudius, by himself, will make his mythic life a reality. (Hughes, 237)

There follow three mentions by Hughes of the "something tortuously inexpressible" (238-239), the phrase first used by Eliot to identify and explain the hero's darkness and ultimate failure as a literary character for us. We just don't understand him. That is, we don't understand him so long as we do not recognize that he is just as much the son of Claudius as he is of Hamlet the Dane. Hughes embraces Eliot's thesis that the play is a failure on account of its lacking an objective correlative, that is, a rationale for Hamlet's hyperbolic rage at his mother. But *a posteriori* we know the play is anything but a failure, and that the adequate emotional correlative exists. Hughes tries to get around the dilemma by suggesting that Hamlet's hidden self is merely symbolic or mythical, but that would not be sufficient to account for the self-loathing that runs through the action like a radioactive current. The play quite obviously is not about Hamlet's hate for Claudius but about the hate he cultivates for himself. Remember that Claudius, too, hates himself. (III, iii, 36-72) The idea that Hamlet hates himself because he can't kill Claudius founders on the plain fact that Hamlet hates himself before he knows anything of the murder and before he swears to take revenge. In fact, Hamlet is so busy hating himself that he is incapacitated and cannot perform the deed he is sworn to do. Killing Claudius will in fact be a useless act for it will not kill off the Claudius inside of Hamlet. These tragic twins must die together.

III. Conclusion

Inner conflict is the hallmark of dramatic art. And while Prince Hamlet's inner conflict has been endlessly debated, those squabbles have done little but disseminate that dilemma among ourselves. Only when we descend to the level of flesh and blood does his predicament become real. Along with the "O that this too too solid flesh would melt" soliloquy, Shakespeare doubles down on the theme by giving us the dram of eale speech of Q2, later cut from the *First Folio* for unknown reasons. It is a great loss. Together, these two orations establish that Hamlet's malaise is not a function of ghostly deliverances, but emerges from (1) his lifelong suspicions of illegitimacy and (2) the confirmation of that illegitimacy when bypassed for the Danish throne. All of this was thoroughly canvassed in *Hamlet Made Simple*. What has been accomplished in the present paper is to show how the dram of eale speech and the first soliloquy both reflect Hamlet's pre-Ghost anxiety and, by use of the double epithet, give symbolic expression to Hamlet's complex self. We owe a great deal to Ted Hughes and Frank Kermode for their pioneering work in exposing the significance of the doubling theme in the play which reinforces our sense of Hamlet's divided self. Mr. Kermode noted that Hamlet is all about "the union of separate selves." We know now what selves these were. Already in the first soliloquy we encountered: "things rank and gross in nature." And it was pointed out in *Hamlet Made Simple*, that one of the chief points of resemblance between Hamlet and Claudius is their use of the term "rank" as denoting something viscerally offensive. At the same time, the term "rank" also refers to the topmost station in society from which Hamlet is barred.

In the dram of eale speech, in which Hamlet dwells on his own corruption, we find a veritable eruption of doubles, including "east and west," "traduced and taxed of other nations," "pith and marrow of our attribute," "the pales and forts of reason," and "nature's livery or fortune's star." In light of all that has been found in this study, we should now be in a position to roughly "translate" the dram of eale speech.

There is something in our natures (especially my own nature) which saps the pith and marrow of my achievements, (that is, the substance of what I am). When I was born there was already something inside me that ruined me and my virtues, even though I did not choose to be born as this person. This "vicious mole of nature" has destroyed my reason, and reduces me from a free and self-determining man to a plaything of fate. Whatever spawned me was a dab of evil that will eventually make me an object of scandal and derision.

What distinguishes this taint from the doctrine of original sin is that the latter is a spiritual legacy of Adam's fall, whereas what Hamlet is talking about is an errant insemination which has left him as a clone of a venal and callow rogue of the type which has always triggered his disgust and revulsion. The corruption then is not cosmetic or symbolic, but resident in the "pith and marrow" of this sad Prince's very bones. Can there be a valid reading of this central document of western culture which ignores these factors? Consider that 99% of the time, *Hamlet* is mechanically trotted out as a humdrum tale of an overly sensitive youth so lost in internal debate that he cannot fulfill his promise to his father's tormented spirit to avenge his murder at the hands of his brother. What is there about human beings that allows them to prefer blindness to insight and cleave to truism instead of truth, unless some vicious mole of nature hath all their noble substance over-daubed to their own scandal? Is being English an intellectual liability? Falstaff seems to hint at that when he observes that "it was alway[s] yet the trick of our English nation, if they have a good thing, to make it too common." (*King Henry IV*, Part Two, I, ii, 15-17) Isn't that what they have done to their black prince? "Ay, it is common," we hear a ghostly voice respond. (I, ii, 74)

WORKS CITED:

Paul de Man, *Blindness and Insight*, University of Minnesota Press, 1983.

T. S. Eliot, *The Sacred Wood*, Alfred A. Knopf, 1921.

David P. Gontar, *Hamlet Made Simple and Other Essays*, New English Review Press, 2013.

Ted Hughes, *Shakespeare and the Goddess of Complete Being*, Farrar, Straus, Geroux, 1992.

Frank Kermode, *Shakespeare's Language*, Farrar, Straus, Geroux, 2000.

G. Wilson Knight, *The Crown of Life,* Barnes & Noble, 1948, 1964.

William Shakespeare, The Complete Works, Second ed., S. Wells, G. Taylor, eds., Oxford University Press, Clarendon, 2005.

20

Remembering Falstaff

To the vulgar, Falstaff will be forever just vulgar.
— H. C. Goddard

Wisdom and goodness to the vile seem vile.
— Duke of Albany

I. Falstaff Dismembered

*I*n *The Life of King Henry the Fifth* there is no appearance by
Falstaff. After all, he's been irrevocably barred from the royal
presence. Yet he is expressly remembered. (II, i, 112-122; II, iii, 5-41;
IV, vii, 38-49) Why? He's not a part of the tale of King Henry's invasion of France, which occurs after Sir John has died, the victim of Hal's
egregious betrayal. Yet Shakespeare goes out of his way to see that he's
not forgotten, and that the grim slaughters at Harfleur and Agincourt
take place in Jack Falstaff's ample shadow. Becoming acquainted with
Shakespeare's dedicated memorializing of this plus-sized literary hero
may help us to better understand Sir John's character and meaning in
the canon.

Shortly before the French surrender (IV, vii, 84), Captains Fluellen
and Gower are debating Henry's place in military history. The talk turns
to a comparison with Alexander the Great. Fluellen notes that Alexander "kill[ed] his best friend, Cleitus," leading Gower to distinguish the
two leaders: "Our King is not like him in that. He never killed any of his
friends." (IV, vii, 38-39) Fluellen will not go along with this bit of hero

worship and obfuscation.

FLUELLEN

It is not well done, mark you now, to take the
tales out of my mouth ere it is made an end
and finished. I speak but in the figures and comparisons of
it. As Alexander killed his friend Cleitus, being in his
ales and his cups, so also Harry Monmouth, being in
his right wits and with his good judgments, turned away
the fat knight with the great-belly
doublet — he was full of jests and knaveries and mocks —
I have forgot his name.

GOWER

Sir John Falstaff.

FLUELLEN

That is he. I'll tell you, there is some good men in Monmouth.
(IV, vii, 40-50)

That is, it is not correct to say, as does Gower does, that Henry has never killed any of his friends, because by cruelly banishing his devoted host Jack Falstaff and breaking his heart, Henry is responsible for that death, just as much as Alexander was responsible for the death of Cleitus. Fluellen's closing words are therefore heavy with sarcasm. Good men don't do ill deeds. Henry's lethal rejection of his boon companion and mentor is plainly common knowledge in the ranks.

What, then, are we to make of the fact that Fluellen at this moment fumbles for Falstaff's name? He has forgotten, and as Gower reminds him, so we, the audience, are reminded by Shakespeare. As the ghost of King Hamlet admonishes the prince in the words, "Remember me," (I, v, 91) so "Remember Falstaff," is the message to us. Of course, the fat knight was full of faults, "jests, knaveries and mocks," but those human imperfections in the final analysis cannot for Fluellen justify King Henry's traducing of the man who was his true friend and benefactor. Nor can those faults warrant our dismissal of Falstaff as a character unworthy of our notice or admiration. Whatever he was—and is—it is more than the sum of his misdeeds, and that "more" is what Shakespeare encourages us to preserve.

A contrary view of Falstaff is presented in a recent article, A "Completely Good Man is Hard to Find: Welles' Defective Falstaff" by Carl C. Curtis. (*New English Review,* February, 2015) While Mr. Curtis' ostensible target is film-maker Orson Welles, he has a lot to say about Falstaff along the way. The overriding issue, of course, and the one which concerns us, is not whether any particular artist has given us a full or less-than-full portrait of Falstaff, but whether taken on the whole Falstaff is anything more than a trivial scofflaw. Welles seems to have felt that Falstaff is a "completely good man," whatever that may have meant. Though he never comes to terms with what Welles did mean by that locution, for Curtis the answer is plainly negative: Falstaff is a knave and nothing more. "In my view Shakespeare's Falstaff is not—not even 'almost'—a good man." He possesses not a single redemptive virtue. He is "hardly good for anything except snapping up everything he fancies." Such harsh judgments naturally raise a problem, for they create an uncomfortable discrepancy between a total and irredeemable degenerate and the high esteem and genuine affection with which he has been received by the public for four hundred years. Indeed, if it is so evident that Falstaff is, in his own words, "one of the wicked," (Part One, I, ii, 94) why is it necessary to try to prove it? To argue the point implies that the accepted view of Falstaff is that of a comic hero and icon of humanity. That seems to be the attitude of Shakespeare himself; at least Curtis does nothing to show otherwise. And it would seem difficult to reverse that positive evaluation by simple enumeration of well-known vices which the accused would be the first to admit. At least one might credit him with candor if nothing else. In short, in seeking to defame and dismember Falstaff, Curtis shoulders an enormous burden of proof he cannot and does not carry. It is a dubious mission.

It may be observed in passing that over the past several years Shakespeare's *Henriad* in general and the figures of Hal and Falstaff in particular have been regularly vetted in *NER* on a monthly basis. One would think that before leaping into print to proclaim Falstaff's utter baseness, Mr. Curtis would have perused those many articles, taken their arguments into account, and explained to the readers of *New English Review* why the appreciation of Falstaff set forth therein may have been unsatisfactory. Yet of these discussions dedicated to the identical issue Curtis is mute. Well, either he read that material or he did not. In either case, a grave omission confronts us. The scholar's first responsibility is to study the literature and make the reader understand in what way a new contribution is being made to the ongoing conversation. That duty is violated by Mr. Curtis, with predictable consequences. Ironically, though he accuses Falstaff of being selfish and self-centered, Curtis, in complacently ignoring nearly forty pertinent essays which precede him in this very journal, exhibits an inexplicable intellectual solipsism. Not only are the pages of *New English Review* overlooked, Mr. Curtis somehow manages to overlook the legions of learned defenses of Falstaff, preferring to focus his attack on this sympathetic character in the midst of a film review of Welles' *Chimes at Midnight*. Having created his portly straw man, Curtis proceeds to demolish it, as though by trashing Welles' cinematic encomium he had exorcised the spirit of Jack Falstaff. Following King Harry's vindictive lead, many have banished Falstaff, but luckily for us he is immortal and will not desert us.

Let's indulge in a comparison. In *Twelfth Night*, the steward Malvolio hates Feste the jester. Does that hate have a rational foundation? Feste is a brilliant but melancholy fool who cobbles together an uncertain living by song and riddling wit. The ineffable sadness of life is the foundation of his comic art. He is not a regimented servant, but in all he does, like a naughty child, he colors outside the lines. For example, he outrages Malvolio by loud partying late at night. He goes AWOL and teases the lady of the house. Very well, admit all his faults. Is Malvolio justified in his hatred? It's a rhetorical question. Readers and theatre-goers have always treasured Feste and laughed at Malvolio. Why? Because seeking to make a career of imposing rules on one's fellows is to turn oneself into a rigid and sadistic automaton and others into asses-bearing-burdens. We laugh with Feste and at Malvolio. That is the crucial difference. Suppose Falstaff applied for the job of jester at the home of Olivia in *Twelfth Night*. Though he might alleviate her sorrow by making her laugh, do you think that Malvolio would recommend him for the job? Falstaff? A known thief and drinker? Why, that would be to add another Sir Toby Belch to an already troubled household! Out of the question, m'lady. Such fellows as Feste, Toby and Falstaff are rogues, scoundrels and scalawags, with no redeeming qualities whatsoever. Imagine that. If Malvolio were successful in this hypothetical scenario, he would deprive Falstaff of the position and consign the Lady Olivia to a routine of unrelieved misery. Isn't the guy who makes us laugh of any value? If not, why be grateful to Shakespeare for his comedies? When Biron goes to the hospital to bring a few moments of mirth and joy to the patients with his shtick, is he not performing a service? (See, *Love's Labour's Lost*,

V, ii, 844-857)

In Act Two of *King Henry IV,* Part One, after the Gadshill robbery in which Hal and Pointz in disguise relieve Falstaff of the money he has stolen from the stagecoach passengers, Falstaff is confronted by them with the facts: he was not waylaid by fifty men with whom he did battle, as he boasted, but only two: Ned and Hal. Why did he run away instead of defending his ill-gotten gains?

POINTZ

Come, let's hear, Jack; what trick hast thou now?

SIR JOHN

By the Lord, I knew ye as well as he that made ye.
Why, hear you, my masters: was it for me to kill the
heir-apparent? should I turn upon the true prince?
why, thou knowest I am as valiant as Hercules: but
beware instinct; the lion will not touch the true
prince. Instinct is a great matter; I was now a
coward on instinct. I shall think the better of
myself and thee during my life; I for a valiant
lion, and thou for a true prince. But, by the Lord,
lads, I am glad you have the money. Hostess, clap
to the doors: watch to-night, pray to-morrow.
Gallants, lads, boys, hearts of gold, all the titles
of good fellowship come to you! What, shall we be
merry? shall we have a play extempore?
(II, v, 269-283)

Falstaff has been duped by Pointz and Hal and shown to be not forward but cowardly. How does Falstaff respond? With a lie, but a pleasant and transparent one: as he recognized Hal and Pointz he retreated rather than wound them with his sword. His virtue was instinctive. Is he angry at having been exposed in his greed and cowardice? No. He attempts to place a flattering and noble construction on his flight which is so amiable and generous that it almost might be believed. He is polite, affectionate and respectful of Hal's nobility. Good fellowship is invoked amid general merriment. He then he calls for a play. It will not be one in which the Boar's-head principals will be in the audience; it will be one in which Hal and Sir John impersonate each other and Hal's father the king. What we have in this play is actually a form of amateur psychotherapy in which Jack tries to help Hal to work through some of his problems. Is this villainy? Falstaff has been tricked and humiliated but his response is gentlemanly, witty and entertaining. He's committed a crime in taking purses on the highway, but it was a collective project. After all, the robbery was not his idea but originated with Pointz. The Prince of Wales is apprised of the deed but does nothing to stop it. Why not alert the sheriff or chief justice? In fact, Hal commits armed robbery himself in stealing the money from Falstaff. It's all a pleasant lark, and Hal will eventually return the money to its owners. Notice that Falstaff does not attempt to deny his flight, but to explain it away humorously. And who knows, perhaps unconsciously he did recognize Hal and Pointz in their disguises after all. That remains a tantalizing possibility. This, then, is Shakespeare's Falstaff, a felon, but a good and jovial associate who loves the Prince of Wales and acts at all times in the spirit of bonhomie. There is not a drop of resentment, hostility or antagonism in his capacious body. Yet this is the fellow Curtis belives should be "hanged." Malvolio would agree.

He too was deceived, you see. Maria tricked him into believing that Lady Olivia was in love with him. As a result, he changes his behavior and seeks to romance his employer, the countess, imagining that he (a commoner) will marry her and become "Count Malvolio." Instead, she has him locked up as a lunatic. How does he react when Maria's device is revealed and Malvolio's snobbery and inappropriate ambition are plain for all to see? His anger is boundless. "I'll be revenged on the whole pack of you," says he, not excluding his lady love, Olivia. (V, i, 374) That is the difference between Malvolio and Falstaff. Malvolio is a moral microbe, a nano-ego puffed up by fantasy. At the root of his ambition is his wish to dominate and control those beneath him. Though he is contemptible, Shakespeare allows us to at least render him human by our laughter at his mechanical actions and pretensions. He is ever shrinking in our estimation. Falstaff, on the other hand, is encompassing and grand, a symbol of humanity in its basic needs and wish for gratification. Nothing human is alien to him. His *avoirdupois* then, is a symbol of his spiritual generosity. When he implores Hal, "Banish not him thy Harry's company, Banish plump Jack and banish all the world," (II, v, 484-485), Falstaff is not exhibiting ordinary egotism, as Curtis meanly charges. On the contrary, Falstaff is a comic giant and exemplar of our species, and has the good sense to know it. He is archetypical and universal, and each of us must recognize something of himself in him, his vices and (one hopes) his virtues as well. He teaches us not only to relish life but also to question the status quo and the reigning ideologies of the day. If Curtis were correct and Falstaff were a cheap egotist or megalomaniac, how is it that after four centuries he stands in the literary limelight as precisely the universal man he claims to be? History has spoken: Falstaff is acquitted. Hal ignores Falstaff's plea and as a consequence loses his own soul. For that is what Falstaff is, Hal's very soul, and when it is jettisoned, he becomes a self-important husk, a silhouette of his father Bolingbroke, spouting high-sounding words to cover an inner emptiness.

We see the theme of Falstaff's cowardice again in the battle of Shrewsbury, where he feigns death in order to protect himself. But as we are taking the measure of a man's character it is appropriate to set his actions *in situ*. Has he a compelling reason to sacrifice his life to help resist Hotspur and the northern rebels? Falstaff is characterized as having been in his youth page to Thomas Mowbray, the mortal enemy of Bolingbroke in *Richard II*. He is keenly aware that the claim to the throne made by Hal's father is unsound. Bolingbroke stole the kingdom from Richard, and this is well known. To put it simply, the reigning English monarch is worse than a common thief. Why, then, should Falstaff put himself in mortal jeopardy to quell the northern rebels? These civil broils are not about protecting England from its foes, or even extending the kingdom farther afield. Recall, then, the Gadshill incident once more. When Hal declines to participate in the planned robbery, he is met with Falstaff's sharp admonishment:

FALSTAFF

There's neither honesty, manhood, nor good
fellowship in thee, nor thou camest not of the blood
royal, if thou darest not stand for ten shillings.
(Part One, I, ii, 136-139)

Falstaff's meaning is plain. How can you put on airs, Hal, and refuse to have a bit of fun holding up the stage coach for a few pounds, when your father had the nerve to seize the entire realm from Richard? You couldn't possibly be Bolingbroke's son. If you were really his descendant you'd find it quite easy to engage in a petty theft. The truth must be that you aren't really an ally to us of the Boar's-head Tavern, and are too cowardly to fight a few paunchy burghers for their money.

Consider the larger implications of this comment. Hal is caught uncomfortably between two father figures, Bolingbroke and Falstaff. The latter is not shy about reminding the Prince of Wales that it would be sheer hypocrisy to fight on behalf of his father, a monstrous thief, and turn up his nose when it comes to helping the poor Boar's-head patrons obtain a bit of badly needed cash. In a subtle way, Falstaff is teaching Hal an important lesson: if you are willing to benefit from a major theft, you can hardly scruple to refuse a minor one, or criticize those who must steal to survive. Falstaff here raises a significant ethical question that Hal would rather sidestep: what is acceptable conduct when one is being succored by the biggest crook in Britain? What is nobility after all? In using our vast powers to put down the northern lords, are we righteously resisting evil insurgents, or in fact doing nothing more than cementing our grip on the power of the state? Close reading, then, shows that Falstaff serves as Hal's mentor. This is, of course, no surprise. Even a text as elementary and unsearching as *The Essential Shakespeare Handbook* has no problem stating that "Prince Harry is [Falstaff's] pupil, not only in rabble-rousing, but also in understanding human nature." (*Essential Shakespeare Handbook,* by Leslie-Dunton-Downer and Alan Riding, DK Publishing, Inc., 2004, p. 124) Consider the dictum we heard Falstaff utter in the preceding chapter: "it was alway[s] yet the trick of our English nation, if they have a good thing to make it too common." (Supra, 517) Does a mere criminal express himself in the vein of a philosopher? Doesn't Falstaff anticipate his 21st century critics by noting that all such persons make him "too common"?

As eminent Shakespeare scholar Harold C. Goddard quipped in his magisterial *The Meaning of Shakespeare,* "To the vulgar Falstaff will be forever just vulgar." (Goddard, Vol. 1, 179) We have to look between the lines and beneath the surface to see who and what he actually is. In this respect, as we will see, he resembles his spiritual forebear, the ancient Greek philosopher Socrates. Plato in his *Symposium* has Alcibiades comment on the need to listen closely if we wish to fathom a profound teaching and take the measure of our teacher.

> Well, gentlemen, I propose to begin my eulogy of Socrates with a simile. I expect he'll think I'm making fun of him, but, as it happens, I'm using this particular simile not because it's funny, but because it's true. What he reminds me of more than anything is one of those little sileni that you see on the statuaries' stalls; you know the ones I mean — they're mod-

eled with pipes or flutes in their hands, and when you open them down the middle there are little figures of the gods inside. (*Symposium*, 215b)

Little figures of the gods . . . inside the man who was prosecuted and executed by the Athenians for corrupting the youth. What an irony. The medieval philosophers had an important maxim: When you meet a contradiction, make a distinction. Harold Goddard, faced with a libertine and wastrel who is at the same time one of the most outstanding and memorable sages of literature, resisted the temptation to condemn Falstaff. Instead he made a distinction. "The truth," he wrote, "is that there are two Falstaffs . . . , the Immoral Falstaff and the Immortal Falstaff, and the dissension about the man comes from a failure to recognize that fact. That the two could inhabit one body would not be believed if Shakespeare had not proved they could. That may be one reason he made it so huge." (Goddard, 176)

What, then, is Falstaff the Immortal? He is Life. He is Wit. He is Comradeship. Again we find Goddard echoing Plato. Falstaff is "Imagination conquering matter, spirit subduing the flesh." (Goddard, 178)

What wonder that this contradictory being — as deminatured as a satyr or a mermaid, who is forever repeating within himself the original miracle of creation, has taken on the proportions of a mythological figure. *He seems at times more like a god than a man.* His very solidity is solar, his rotundity cosmic. To estimate the refining power we must know the grossness of what is to be refined. To be astounded by what lifts we must know the weight of what is to be lifted. Falstaff is levitation overcoming gravitation. At his wittiest and most ariel, he is Ariel tossing the terrestrial globe in the air as if it were a ball. And yet — as we must never forget — he is also that fat old sinner fast asleep and snoring behind the arras. The sins, in fact, are the very things that make the miracle astonishing, as the chains and ropes do a Houdini's escape. (Goddard, 178, emphasis added)

What a curious fellow this Falstaff is! One writer finds nothing in him but a cad or cur (Curtis), yet another discovers in his person the apotheosis of mankind. The latter view is alive and well today in those Shakespeareans who detect in Falstaff a representation or appearance of

Bacchus himself, the Lord of Misrule. (See, *e.g., Shakespeare After All,* Marjorie Garber, 317, 325ff.) Can we measure a god by our petty bourgeois standards? Falstaff, like so many other Shakespearean characters, is an inkblot test. What we see in him tells us more about ourselves than it does about Shakespeare and his characters.

Long before Mr. Carl Curtis thought to edify us by showing that there is nothing in Falstaff but a scoundrel, the battle was already fought and lost by Falstaff's detractors. The year was 1951, when these words of Harold Goddard were first published by the University of Chicago Press. As it is better to show the best rather than attempt an imperfect summary we quote at length.

> Dover Wilson (following Professor R. A. Law) would have us take *Henry IV* as a morality play wherein a madcap prince grows up into an ideal king. Falstaff is the devil who tempts the Prince to Riot. Hotspur and especially the Lord Chief Justice are the good angels representing Chivalry and Justice or the Rule of Law. It is a struggle between Vanity and Government for the possession of the Royal Prodigal. [Note: the identical contention was also made by Martin Lings in *Shakespeare's Window Into the Soul,* Inner Traditions, 1984, 2006. See also, David Gontar, "An Islamic Reading of *King Henry IV,*" in *Hamlet Made Simple and Other Essays,* New English Review Press, 2013, pp. 355ff.]

> The scheme is superbly simple and as moral as a Sunday-school lesson. But it calmly leaves the Immortal Falstaff quite out of account! If Falstaff were indeed just the immoral creature that in part he admittedly is, Wilson's parable would be more plausible, though even the words he picks to characterize Falstaff are singularly unfortunate. "Vanity" by derivation means emptiness or absence of substance, and "riot" quarrelsomeness. Imagine calling even the Immoral Falstaff empty or lacking in substance — or quarrelsome! He had his vices but they were not these. For either vanity or riot there is not a single good word to be said. To equate Falstaff with them is to assert that not a single good word can be said of him — a preposterous proposition. Wit, humour, laughter, good-fellowship, insatiable zest for life: are these vanity or does Falstaff not embody them? That is the dilemma in

which Mr. Wilson puts himself. And as for the Lord Chief Justice, he is indeed an admirable man; a more incorruptible one in high position is not to be found in Shakespeare. But if the poet had intended to assign him any such crucial role as Mr. Wilson thinks, he certainly would have presented him more fully and would have hesitated to let Falstaff make him look so foolish. For the Chief Justice's sense of justice was better developed than his sense of humor. And even justice is not all.

Henry IV does have a certain resemblance to a morality play. The two, however, between whom the younger Henry stands and who are in a sense contending for the possession of his soul are not Falstaff and the Chief Justice, but Falstaff and the King. It is between Falstaff and the Father . . . that Henry finds himself.

Now in the abstract this is indeed Youth between Revelry and Responsibility. But the abstract has nothing to do with it. Where Henry really stands is between this particular companion, Falstaff, and this particular father and king, Henry IV. Of these two, which was the better man?

Concede the utmost — that is, take Falstaff at his worst. He was a drunkard, a glutton, a profligate, a thief, even a liar, if you insist, but withal a fundamentally honest man. He had two sides like a coin, but he was not a counterfeit. And Henry? He was a King, a man of 'honour,' of brains and ability, of good intentions, but withal a 'vile politician' and respectable hypocrite. He was a counterfeit. Which, if it comes to the choice, is the better influence on a young man? Shakespeare, for one, gives no evidence of having an iota of doubt.

But even if Falstaff at his worst comes off better than Henry, how about Falstaff at his best? In that case, what we have is Youth standing between Imagination and Authority, between Freedom and Force, between Play and War. My insistence that Falstaff is a double man, and that the abstract has nothing to do with it, will acquit me of implying that this is the whole of the story. But it is a highly suggestive part of it.

The opposite of war is not 'peace' in the debased sense in which we are in the habit of using the latter word. Peace ought to mean far more, but what it has come to mean on our lips is just the absence of war. The opposite of war is creative activity, play in its loftier implications. All through these dramas the finer Falstaff symbolizes the opposite of force. When anything military enters his presence, it instantly looks ridiculous and begins to shrink. Many methods have been proposed for getting rid of war. Falstaff's is one of the simplest: laugh it out of existence. For war is almost as foolish as it is criminal. 'Laugh it out of existence'? If only we could. Which is the equivalent of saying: if only more of us were like Falstaff! These plays should be required reading in all military academies. Even the 'cannon-fodder' scenes of Falstaff with his recruits have their serious implications and anticipate our present convictions on the uneugenic nature of war.

How far did Shakespeare sympathize with Falstaff's attitude in this matter? No one is entitled to say. But much further, I am inclined to think, than he would have had his audience suspect or than the world since his time has been willing to admit. For consider the conditions under which Falstaff finds himself: Henry has dethroned and murdered the rightful king of England. The Percys have helped him to obtain the crown, but a mutual sense of guilt engenders distrust between the two parties, and the Percy's decide to dethrone the dethroner. Falstaff is summoned to take part in his defense. 'Life is given but once.' Why should Falstaff risk his life on earth, which he is enjoying as not one man in a hundred million does, to support or to oppose the cause of either of two equally selfish and equally damnable seekers after power and glory? What good would the sacrifice of his life accomplish comparable to the boon that he confers daily and hourly on the world, to say nothing of himself, by merely being? This is no case of tyranny on one side and democracy on the other, with liberty or slavery of a world at stake. This is strictly dynastic quarrel. When two gangs of gunmen begin shooting it out on the streets of a great city, the discreet citizen will step behind a post or into a doorway. The analogy may not be an exact one, but it enables us to understand Falstaff's point of view. And there is plenty of Shakespearean warrant for it.

'See the coast clear'd, and then we will depart,' says the Mayor of London when caught, in *Henry VI*, between similar warring factions,

'Good God! These nobles should such stomachs bear;
I myself fight not once in forty year.'
(Goddard, 185-187)

The problem with Curtis' polemic, then, is not so much that he offers nothing new, contenting himself with a laundry list of Falstaff's flaws, but that in ignoring the refutation of such simple-mindedness he sets literary history back an entire century. More is required to turn a saint into a fiend than to recite an inventory of his human shortcomings, shortcomings well known to all students of early modern literature. What Goddard is driving at is that through Falstaff Shakespeare makes us reflect. If, as Bolingbroke on his deathbed tells his wayward, vacillating son, the best strategy to pursue when one has no valid right to the crown is to "busy giddy minds with foreign quarrels," (Part Two, IV, iii, 342-343), it is important that those conscripted into those adventitious broils be prompted to reflect on their moral quality. The fact that so few English perished at Agincourt hardly means the invasion of France had any purpose other than making Hal look heroic so he could fend off those who recognized his monarchy was a fraud. For the French that field of blood was a vicious abattoir. And in the midst of that senseless decimation of the French defenders, it is telling, is it not, that while he babbles about the loveliness of "lenity," (*Henry V*, III, vi, 113) Harry approves the hanging for pilferage of Falstaff's aide-de-camp Bardolph, with whom the Prince of Wales partied in Eastcheap? (*Henry V*, III, vi, 99-114) What a sport! He'd have hung Falstaff personally if the poor man had survived his banishment long enough to be drafted. Of course, that would certainly not trouble Mr. Curtis, who assures us that Falstaff is "guilty of crimes for which he justly would have been hanged." Frankly, what is Curtis' essay, after all, but the lynching of Falstaff in effigy? This is precisely the kind of mindset that led to Socrates, that corruptor of the youth, being forced to drink the hemlock. It's not hard to know how Curtis would have voted on that Athenian jury.

It is true, as Prof. Kenji Yoshino notes in his even-handed article, "The Choice of Four Fathers: Henry IV, Falstaff, the Lord Chief Justice and the King of France in the *Henriad*," Yale Journal of Law and the Humanities, Vol. 22, Iss. 2, article 8, that once the war starts, Falstaff accepts money from more affluent conscripts while drafting into his platoon the poor, ragged and impoverished, and that most of these men die at Shrewsbury. One needs to consider, however, that it was common and acceptable in bygone centuries for men to use money to buy out their military obligations. Falstaff had no choice but to participate in Henry's campaign to retain his phony kingship, a campaign that put thousands of lives at risk and caused many deaths and injuries. To his credit, Falstaff does not flee but takes his men into the thick of the battle where most of them perish. Would it have been preferable to sacrifice the lives of those better placed in society, stout yeomen with families and children who depended on them? Our purpose here is not to extenuate Falstaff's misdeeds, but to place them in historical and dramatic context. Falstaff is seen with his troops by the lords in Bolingbroke's service at the commencement of the engagement and allowed to go forward. Such are the chances of war. The fact is that in his opposition to an unjust war Falstaff is placed in a dilemma. Such situations should be carefully analysed, not exploited to demonize the hapless souls on whom those terrible risks and burdens fall.

Our business is to think. And Falstaff makes us think. That's why he's dangerous. He makes us question dominant ideologies and political passions. That makes him inexpedient. Just as Socrates raises questions such as, What is Justice? What is Piety? What is Friendship?, so Falstaff asks "What is Honor"? (*King Henry IV*, V, i, 134) In fact, Plato does explore this very principle in the *Politeia*. We all remember Brutus and his friends in *Julius Caesar*. Were they not "honourable" men? (*Julius Caesar*, III, ii, 13-47; 74-128) Let Falstaff fall with Caesar! When Hal banishes Falstaff in a very real sense he banishes thought itself. When we are treated to that "little touch of Harry in the night," (*King Henry V*, IV, 0, 47) we hear in the anguished doubts and protests of common soldiers Bates and Williams an echo of Falstaff's critique of "honor." Falstaff's question is every man's question.

II. Remembering Falstaff

Another way of assessing Shakespeare's view of Falstaff, the one he would have us absorb, is to approach this character not via the vexing histories but through comedy, particularly, *The Merry Wives of Windsor*. Here Falstaff is portrayed as a dedicated adulterer and seducer of other men's wives. It is an entertaining bedroom farce and wonderfully funny. At the end of the pratfalls, after he is apprehended and punished by pinching for his wanton misbehavior, he finds himself surrounded by those he has wronged. Trapped in his sins, with no way out, Sir John does the decent thing: he confesses his wrongs.

SIR JOHN

Well, I am your theme; you have the start of
me. I am dejected. I am not able to answer the Welsh
flannel. Ignorance itself is a plummet o'er me. Use
me as you will.
(V, v, 59-161)

Page, one of the wronged husbands, responds.

PAGE

Yet be cheerful, knight. Thou shalt eat a posset
tonight at my house, where I will desire thee to
laugh at my wife that now laughs at thee.
(V, v, 168-170)

Mistress Page adds:

Good husband, let us every one go home,
and laugh this sport o'er a country fire,
Sir John and all.
(V, v, 233-235)

To which Page warmly responds,

Let it be so, Sir John.
(V, v, 235)

The rascal is forgiven. It would be much harder, would it not, to forgive a sexual rogue like Tarquin in *The Rape of Lucrece*? Or a sleazy philanderer like King Edward IV in *King Henry VI*, Part Three, Act 3, Sc. ii? What makes the difference? What is it about Sir John that makes us able to forgive him? Whatever that quality may be, it must be an important point in his favor, precisely the redeeming factor Curtis denies is present. Call it innocence. Call it childish insouciance, or a congenital inability to refrain from temptation, what you will. Sir John's trespasses never outrage us but instead amuse. He candidly tells us he would give up his escapades if he could, but like so many of us, he cannot summon the resolve. Shall we join those who were the first to cast stones at him? Shakespeare is not of their party. His Falstaff is like a kid. Look at him in the throng with Bardolph, Shallow, Pistol and the Page, standing on tip-toe to catch a glimpse of his dear pal, newly crowned in London. Falstaff has ridden all night in excitement to see him. How many of us have spent an entire night galloping on horseback? Does he expect to benefit from having the King of England as his personal friend? Of course. But at that moment such thoughts are far away, and what we behold is the thrill and joy he feels to see Hal on his mount riding proudly through the streets of London. How many of us in his position would have similar feelings? But in Falstaff they are unrestrained, exuberant, effervescent, beyond adult control. He waves, he shouts, at Hal's moment of glory. Then the axe falls: From that very man on horseback he hears the dreadful words, "I know thee not, old man." It is a lie. Yet Falstaff is banished. Crestfallen, he tries to regroup, to snatch at the bare possibility that he will be sent for privately. It never happens. What is exhibited by this wonderful man? Vulnerability. Loving as he does, he is exposed to emotional injury, and when it comes Falstaff has no defenses. His heart is cut in twain, and so he dies soon thereafter. Hal, perched atop his white charger, is as callous and cold as Falstaff is open, warm, and enthusiastic. Although he's forgiven by Page in *The Merry Wives* for seducing his wife, Hal in *Henry IV* seems unable to forgive Falstaff—for what: the unspeakable crime of loving him? It is hard to think of a tale so ironically sad.

* * * *

Instead of peering down one's nose at Falstaff for his human frailty and independence, we might wish to gain perspective by appraising his foibles in the light of his dramatic forebears. It is agreed by just about everyone that he is not a wholly unprecedented or novel character but is compounded by Shakespeare of matter quarried from earlier historical and literary individuals. He is complex. It may be illuminating to trace the features of Falstaff back to some of his predecessors. Though there is no firm and universal consensus as to who they are, at least four will be considered here: (1) Sir John Oldcastle, (2) Sir John Fastolfe, (3) Gargantua and (4) Socrates. Professor Harold Bloom would also nominate King David of ancient Israel and Chaucer's Wife of Bath as Falstaffian ancestors. We will leave those tantalizing leads to the industrious reader.

1. Sir John Oldcastle (c. 1370 – 1417)

It cannot be overemphasized that the original name of Shakespeare's character in *King Henry IV* was not "John Falstaff" but "Sir John Oldcastle," a personality drawn from the contemporaneous historical period. This fact is of far more than nominal importance. For the character could hardly have been called "John Oldcastle" unless he bore sufficient resemblances to the historical figure of that name to be credible. Indeed, in their authoritative edition of *William Shakespeare: The Complete Works*, (2005) Gary Taylor and Stanley Wells in their version *King Henry IV* do not use the name "Falstaff" at all but revert to the original moniker, "Sir John Oldcastle" They write:

> The earliest title page [of The First Part of *Henry IV*] advertised the play's portrayal of "the humourous conceits of Sir John Falstaff"; but when it was first acted, probably around 1596 or 1597, the character bore the name of his historical counterpart, the Protestant martyr Sir John Oldcastle. Shakespeare changed his surname as the result of protests from Oldcastles descendants . . . Our edition restores Sir John's original surname for the first time in printed texts . . . A play called *The Famous Victories of Henry V*, entered in the Stationers Register in 1594, was published anonymously . . . in 1598. This text . . . also features Oldcastle as a reprobate. (Taylor & Wells, 481)

No explanation is hazarded by Taylor and Wells as to how and why the character of a Protestant martyr (that is, a dedicated Christian) was willy-nilly (no pun intended) transformed into a wine-bibbing libertine. We can only wonder. Yet one particular scenario commends itself. It is likely that at some time in the late 16th century (probably around 1590) the author of the plays and poems we find today in the quartos and folios was commissioned by the post-Armada Crown to write a comprehensive patriotic history of England, glorifying the reign of Elizabeth, buttressing her right to govern, and rousing the nation in light of continuing Continental threats and uncertainties. When "our bending author" (*King Henry V*, V, 0, 2) came to present the life of England's most puissant champion, King Henry the Fifth, it was useful to portray him as someone not "born great" but to a degree made so by dint of effort, ingenuity and instruction. The commonly understood historical fact was that Hal (Harry, Henry) was good friends at all pertinent times with Sir John Oldcastle, a noted soldier who accompanied him in several campaigns. Oldcastle at some point came under the spell of John Wyclif (c. 1330 – 1384) and became an impassioned Lollard, that is, a member of a group of early Christian enthusiasts who in many ways anticipated later religious reformers. Oldcastle was eventually a leader of this incendiary group. At the same time he maintained his bond with the young King Henry. Oldcastle was investigated and came under suspicion of heresy and possible sedition. He was prosecuted and thrown into the Tower of London, from which he escaped into the London demimonde. Though he appealed to Henry for protection and assistance, as circumstances became more and more serious there was little the King could do. It became apparent that Oldcastle was gathering supporters to revolt against the regime. Henry severed his ties with the man. He was captured, tried and executed by hanging and burning. It is reasonable to suppose that the author of *King Henry V* found it unwise in Elizabethan England to depict an illustrious English monarch as a close friend of a radical heretic who planned rebellion against church and state. The character was therefore altered in name and nature to "Falstaff," a self-indulgent soldier with no real political agenda at all. Profound as those changes may have been, some tincture of Sir John Oldcastle, Christian martyr, remained. Not only is the comradeship and rupture thereof kept in place, but so are the aspects of nonconformity and autonomy. After all, Falstaff is no mere party animal. He has ideas. There is evident in his discourses a preternatural intellect as formidable as his expansive waistline. Despite his carousing, he has thought deeply and abides by his own code of principles. Conventional society he mocks. In Falstaff's rough-and-tumble credo, then, we catch just a glimpse of Oldcastle, and Hal's awful break with the fat knight has a vital precedent. Thus, when we overhear Falstaff dream wistfully on the occasion of Hal's promotion of throwing out the Lord Chief Justice, his constant foe (and Hal's foe), it is all-too-easy to imagine that Falstaff harbors substantial and dangerous political aims or plots of anarchy. That is a confusion which fails to detect the ghost of Oldcastle. Those who accuse Falstaff of such stuff are wide of the mark. Falstaff's muttered imprecations against the Lord Chief Justice are the taunts of a child. He is light years removed from the seriousness of a

Hotspur or Jack Cade. Mr. Curtis, a professor at a Christian university, is surprisingly off the scent when he sees rebellion in Falstaff. As Socrates told Antisthenes that he could see his vanity through the holes in his cloak, we should be able to see Oldcastle's Christian zeal and ambition peeping through the tattered garments of the playful Jack Falstaff.

2. Sir John Fastolfe (1380 – 1459)

It's interesting that sources vary as to whether it was John Oldcastle or John Fastolfe who was page to Thomas Mowbray, Duke of Norfolk, a role assigned by Shakespeare to Falstaff. (*King Henry IV*, Part Two, III, ii, 23-25) This is important because in *Richard II* we see that Thomas Mowbray was the mortal enemy of Bolingbroke, future King and father of Prince Hal. It is natural, then, that on the unruly ascension of Bolingbroke to the throne that former page would tend to view the reign of King Henry IV with skepticism, to say the least. Falstaff therefore stands in opposition to the Machiavellian seizure and exploitation of power represented by Bolingbroke, a Machiavellianism passed on to his sons, Princes Hal and John.

Fastolfe was a knight who fought in King Henry V's army. He took part in the seige of Harfleur in 1415 and was elevated to Knight of the Garter in 1426. He fought against the French who were led by Joan of Arc. Because of incidents at the Battle of Patay Fastole was accused of desertion or cowardice, but his reputation was restored on further hearing. He apparently had a proprietary interest in the Boar's-head Tavern, which identifies that place as a part of actual history. There were rumours he had been sympathetic to the Lollard cause, but these may have been the result of confusion. Because of his supposed cowardice and association with the Boar's-head Tavern, it is believed that Shakespeare adapted his name when dropping Oldcastle's, thus creating our comic hero. Fastolfe is mentioned expressly in negative terms in *King Henry VI* as a coward, but in fact we know almost nothing about what sort of person John Fastolfe was. The substance of Falstaff's personality comes from other sources and from Shakespeare's poetic imagination.

3. Gargantua (appeared as character in the writings of Rabelais in 1532, 1534)

Gargantua was a major literary character created by Francois Rabelais (1494 – 1553) as part of a massive campaign of satire in the first part of the 16th century. Shakespeare was certainly familiar with him, as we can be sure since (1) he was immediately famous in Europe, (2) the resemblances between Gargantua and Falstaff are uncanny and impressive, and (3) Shakespeare refers to Gargantua in *As You Like It* (III, ii, 220). In *Shakespeare – The Invention of the Human*, Prof. Harold Bloom points out that it was Algernon Charles Swinburne who first showed the affinities of Rabelais' Panurge (one of Gargantua's relations) and Falstaff.

Gargantua Being Fed Mustard by Four Men by Gustave Doré

Algernon Charles Swinburne, now mostly forgotten as both poet and critic, yet superb as both, adroitly compared Falstaff to his true companions, the Sancho Panza of Cervantes and the Panurge of Rabelais. He awarded the palm to Falstaff, not just for his massive intellect but for his range of feeling and indeed even for his "possible moral elevation." Swinburne meant a *morality of the heart, and of the imagination,* rather than the social morality that is the permanent curse of Shakespearean scholarship and criticism, afflicting historicists old and new, and Puritans sacred and secular. Here Swinburne anticipated A. C. Bradley, who rightly remarked that all adverse moral judgments upon Falstaff are antithetical to the nature of Shakespearean comedy. (Bloom, 281, emphasis added)

A few illustrative comments from M. Pierre Beaudry may be helpful in giving us a sense of the Gargantuan temperament.

In comparison with the smallness of feudal man's thinking, Rabelais' Rennaissance man is a giant of intellectual and moral standing, who breaks with all of the old rules, all the taboos, all the old habits of a decrepit medieval society, breaking with all types of formalism and hypocrisy, especially religious hypocrisy. While the Sorbonne theologians based their recruitment to the Church on guilt, Rabelais destroyed guilt and replaced it with laughter. His characters Gargantua and his son Pantagruel are therefore quite naturally giants, because they are accomplishing a gigantic task proportional to their size. Both of them are the most outrageously loquacious talkers, great eaters and great pissers, [See, *King Henry IV*, Part Two, I, ii, 1] who will overwhelm any in their path, with the most powerful weapons of war against littleness: metaphors which they spin and weave without end, sparing no one in their masterful irony, from parody to satire to gross exaggeration. Their favorite targets are backward monks, manipulative and hypocritical churchmen, scholastic teachers, Aristotelian sophists, lawyers [and] courtly manners . . . .

Even the names of Rabelais' characters are gigantic. For instance, when Gargantua came into the world he cried out 'Drink, Drink, Drink', whereupon his father . . . decided to name him 'great gullet.'

But laughter is the best thirst quencher of all . . . .

Rabelais, who was a practicing doctor in Lyon, used moderate wine drinking as a curative means of eliminating diseases of tension, and he believed that laughter — here no limits were prescribed — had a similar curative effect on both the soul and the body. Rabelais gave the highest priority to jokes as curative means of solving problems of the mind. That is why, in a warning to the reader, Gargantua emphasizes that *'Laughter is the proper characteristic of man'*. Laughter, wine and dirty jokes become political weapons in the war against the pervasive disease of oligarchism. (Pierre Beaudry, "What Does It Mean To Be Rabelaisian?" The Schiller Institute, *Fidelio*, Vol. IX, No. 4, Winter, 2000, emphasis added, n.p.)

Astute students of cultural history will recognize that Gargantua is a modern version of the Greek god Dionysus, who was worshipped as Bacchus, the god of wine and merriment, by the Romans. Literary presentation of this standpoint begins with *The Bacchae* of Aristophanes. The Bacchic sensibility is today carried forward in Carnival celebrations in Rio de Janeiro, Brazil and New Orleans, Louisiana.

Later figures in the same tradition echo Falstaff. Consider the "Ghost of Christmas Present" in Charles Dickens' *A Christmas Carol*. He appears to Ebenezer Scrooge as a jolly long-haired giant capped with holly wreath and glittering icicles. He bears a cornucopia and sits before a vast feast. His most eloquent accoutrement is a scabbard without a sword, a symbol of peace. From this merry Ghost it is but a small step to that winking old elf, Father Christmas (Saint Nicholas, Santa Claus), with his great sack stuffed with toys for children.

Looked at from the point of view of modern philosophy, all these personages, Dionysus/Bacchus, Gargantua, Falstaff, the Ghost of Christmas Present and Father Christmas are restatements in artistic form of the Life Force identified and articulated in the voluntaristic metaphysics of Arthur Schopenhauer (1788 – 1860), Friedrich Nietzsche (1844 – 1900) and Henri Bergson (1859 – 1941). Significantly, it was Bergson who extrapolated from the *"elan vital"* or life force to the first important theory of comedy and laughter. Whether we approach the matter from the point of view of myth, theology or philosophy, we find ourselves confronted with Something transcending the boundaries of mundane human affairs. Viewed in terms of secular philosophy, Falstaff is the Life Force. In terms of myth, he is Bacchus. This transcendent ethos is the real reason lapses in propriety do not drag him down into disrepute. This is comedy, after all. Puritanical critics of Falstaff seem to forget that. When Punch strikes Judy, do we chuckle —or call the police? A sense of humor is a gift from the gods, but sadly some have been short-changed in that department. These are the Malvolian literalists among us who never get the joke. Amusingly, for them Falstaff must always be a villain. But he remains always above—or below—with the gods. He is a chthonic personage indistinguishable from the life force itself. In that respect, Dionysus should never have been classed with the Olympians. His roots are subterranean. As Apollo is above, Dionysus rules here below. The ambit of our daily round is narrow; we measure out our lives with coffee spoons, as Eliot put it. But in our dreams, in myth and art, we are in contact with the Transcendent (or Immanent), with Something that breaks through the carapace of everydayness and transforms and liberates the human spirit. Once this is grasped we are free to smile, to appreciate a character so much larger than ourselves that we too are enhanced. Where we were grim, we laugh; where we were tedious, we play; where we plodded, now we dance.

4. Socrates (469 – 399 BC)

In Plato's *Phaedo*, after Socrates consumes the poison hemlock, he covers himself with a shroud and quietly passes away. A moment later, his disciples are astonished to see him sit up and address them. "Crito," he says, "we ought to offer a cock to Asclepius [Greek god of healing]. See to it and don't forget." (*Phaedo*, 118)

These are his last words to us: "Don't forget."

The man all thought was dead still lived and had something to impart to his friends: death may be an illusion after all, seems to be the implication.

Now update to the battle of Shrewsbury. Hapless Jack Falstaff is dueling with the fierce and implacable Earl of Douglas, an infinitely more skillful and dangerous adversary than himself. He is on the brink of death, then collapses on the ground as though slain. Hotspur and Prince Hal cross words and swords, and after a terrible struggle Hal destroys Hotspur. Seeing the prostrate remains of Sir John, Hal speaks.

> What, old acquaintance! Could not all this flesh
> Keep in a little life? Poor Jack, farewell.
> I could have spared a better man.
> O, I should have a heavy miss of thee,
> If I were much in love with vanity.
> Death hath not struck so fat a deer today,
> Though many dearer in this bloody fray.
> Embowelled will I see thee by and by.
> 'Till then, in blood by noble Percy lie.
> (*Henry IV*, Part One, V, iv, 101-109)

Strange to hear Hal's poetry in the midst of battle. What elicits it? What sentiment is here expressed? We have not the haughty disdain shown by the newly crowned King in *King Henry IV*, Part Two, (V, iv, 47-69). Not at all. What we hear are almost words of love, restrained and unrecognized as such. Hal can't quite bring himself to mourn, to shed a tear, to use the word "friend" instead of "acquaintance." But the truth was friendship, the animadversions of Hal to the contrary notwithstanding. One can sense it in Hal's voice, finding Falstaff, his companion, supporter and mentor, dead at his feet: "O, I should have a heavy miss of thee, If I were much in love with vanity." What does this couplet mean? What is felt is love and remorse. Hal will keenly miss his just departed friend, and, in fact, misses him "dearly" (note that usage) already. But no sooner felt, the sentiment is squelched by the business-like Prince of Wales, our sometime poet. He chokes off what he feels, letting stern calculation trample it down. "Well," he seems to rationalize, "I won't actually miss you, Jack, because, after all, our pursuits when I frolicked with you in Eastcheap were vain. I'm grown up now, no longer a lover of vanity." Good bye Falstaff. Here a virtue is built out of sheer hypocrisy. Perfect shallowness and self-deception are caught in the very act. The love is there, present inside Hal, but on account of his swelling pride he cannot acknowledge it. The felt bond is sufficiently strong to fuel a paean in iambic pentameter, but too weak to appear to him as what it is. The courage necessary to admit his love of Jack Falstaff is not part of Hal's nature. He has just slain Percy and is well on his way to becoming a clone of his biological father, brave enough to contend with enemies in battle, but not brave enough to confess his love for his friend, even to himself. Who's "cowardice" is greater: that of the fellow who played dead to save his life, or the guy who hasn't the candor and gumption to admit his own feelings of friendship?

Hal departs, and Falstaff, the dead person, like Socrates, arises from sullen earth. Unlike Socrates, who cheered up his disciples and wiped away their tears as he prepared for a death he fully accepted, knowing his soul would outlast his body, Falstaff rises having heard his student (Hal) declare the withholding of his love because of his teacher's "vanity," as he prepares to march to the throne. Can we blame Falstaff? Had he allowed Douglas to actually take his life who would gain from it? Falstaff denies that he "counterfeited" death in that it is death which is the counterfeit of the living person. For Falstaff "the better part of valor is discretion," and many who have benefited from his instruction on this score now wish to turn and snarl at him. The positions of Socrates and

Falstaff are tantalizingly congruent on the issue of life and death. For Socrates the corpse is a counterfeit human because it is the body alone; the real individual is the soul. For Falstaff, in rejecting the accusation that he is counterfeiting, he reasons that pretending to be a counterfeit demonstrates one's reality and authenticity. He appears dead to have life more abundantly. As Harold Goddard said in the passage cited above, it is Prince Hal in his cynical realism who is the counterfeit of humanity. To play at falsity (as an actor does onstage) is to find the truth: all the world's a stage. (*As You Like It,* II, vii, 139) Socrates and Falstaff almost agree: death is a counterfeit. Socrates teaches that the deceased's life is elsewhere, while for Falstaff only the whole man is real. Neither accepts the value of the husk. What is significant here is that behind the roistering clown Falstaff is a world of moral thought, a world unrecognized by his detractors.

Let us bid farewell once more to these two philosophers. Here is the end of Socrates by hemlock.

> Up till this time most of us had been fairly successful in keeping back the tears, but when we saw that he was drinking, that he had actually drunk it, we could do so no longer. In spite of myself the tears came pouring out, so that I covered my face and wept brokenheartedly — not for him, but for our own calamity in losing such a friend. Crito had given up even before me, and had gone out when he could not restrain his tears. But Apollodorus, who had never stopped crying even before, now broke out into such a storm of passionate weeping that he made everyone in the room break down, except Socrates himself, who said, 'Really my friends, what a way to behave! Why this was my main reason for sending away the women, to prevent this sort of disturbance, because I am told that one should make one's end in a tranquil frame of mind. Calm yourselves and try to be brave.' This made us feel ashamed, and we controlled our tears. Socrates walked about, and presently, saying that his legs were heavy, lay down on his back — that was what the man recommended. The man — he was the same one who administered the poison — kept his hand upon Socrates, and after a little while examined his feet and legs, then pinched his foot hard and asked if he felt it. Socrates said 'no'. Then he did the same to his legs, and moving gradually upward in this way let us see that he was

getting cold and numb. Presently he felt him again and said when it reached his heart, Socrates would be gone. The coldness was spreading about as far as his waist . . . .

After a little while he stirred, and when the man uncovered him, his eyes were fixed. When Crito saw this, he closed the mouth and eyes.

(*Phaedo*, 117c – 118)

Again, here is Mistress Quickly talking about Falstaff's final moments.

So a bade me lay
more clothes on his feet. I put my hand into the bed
and felt them, and they were as cold as any stone.
Then I felt to his knees, and so up'ard and up'ard, and
all was as cold as any stone.
(*King Henry V*, II, iii, 21-25)

Such congruences are hardly accidental. They reflect the most profound of influences and conjoint purposes.

This is partially recognized by Prof. Harold Bloom, who observes that "Scholars have recognized that Mistress Quickly's account of Falstaff's death, in *Henry V*, clearly alludes to Plato's story of the death of Socrates, in the *Phaedo*." (Bloom, 292) This parallelism Bloom attributes to Shakespeare having read Montaigne, from whom our author is supposed to have derived the bulk of his knowledge of ancient wisdom, including this account of the demise of Socrates. Bloom deserves much credit for demonstrating that Falstaff is indeed the Socrates of Eastcheap. Unfortunately for Bloom's particular explanation of influence, an examination of Montaigne's writings will reveal that the account of Socrates' death in the *Phaedo* appears nowhere in Montaigne. (See, *The Complete Essays of Michel de Montaigne*, M.A. Screech, ed., Penguin Classics, 1991) That means "Shakespeare" got the narrative of Socrates' death somewhere else. The fine detail suggests nothing so much as "Shakespeare's" reading of Plato, which would of course have been in ancient Greek. There is a point to ponder.

We may round things out with a medley of Socrates/ Falstaff commonalities, understanding that this enumeration should not be taken as final.

1. Socrates and Falstaff are both poor.

2. They are both physically unhandsome.

3. They both enjoy and provoke laughter

4. Falstaff and Socrates are comic characters. (See Aristophanes, *The Clouds*)

5. Falstaff and Socrates are both drawn to *caritas, philia* and *eros*.

6. Each was the most eloquent speaker of his time.

7. Both raised philosophical questions.

8. The manner of their deaths is strikingly similar.

9. Both had powerful enemies who finally succeeded in destroying them.

10. Each of them died because of his dedication to his chosen nonconformist mode of living.

11. Socrates and Falstaff both maintained "thinking shops" in which they took up a wide range of topics with anyone who would listen and participate. Shakespeare's Falstaff holds forth at the Boar's-head, while Socrates maintained a "think shop" where he consorted with disciples and other interlocutors from 431 to 424 BC. (See, R. Hackforth, *The Composition of Plato's Apology*, Cambridge, University Press, 1933, 156-157. See also, David P. Gontar, "The Problem of the Formal Charges in Plato's Apology," *Tulane Studies in Philosophy*, Vol. xxvii, 1978.)

12. Socrates is hen-pecked by his wife, Xanthippe; Falstaff is arrested at the suit of harridan Mistress Quickly.

The challenge in writing about a literary character such as Falstaff is that to do so constructively one must have training and expertise in the history of thought, especially philosophy. Those whose experience is restricted to an isolated discipline such as "literary criticism" or "English literature" are at a disadvantage in taking on texts composed by polymathic geniuses such as "Shakespeare" who tread the wide stage of history and the world's wisdom literature.

III. Conclusion

Reducing the richness and complexity of Falstaff to the one-dimensionality of a Vice figure cannot be viewed as anything but a loss. When one of the most important roles in all literature is trivialized, so are the dramas in which he stars. Such diminution of character implicitly challenges the ability and judgment of Shakespeare, who lavished so much care and learning on Falstaff. Shrink wrapping the sage of Eastcheap is a mode of forgetting him, neglecting to consider Shakespeare's heartfelt injunction to remember this man. It is to attempt to perch in the clouds and look down on Falstaff and his creator. But up so high everything below must seem insignificant. In applying white glove standards to Falstaff one sacrifices greatness on the altar of mediocrity, as though anyone pushing his shopping cart down the aisles of the local discount store could determine the relative merits of Moses, Napoleon, Beethoven and Tolstoy. What was their credit rating? This is to turn the world upside down. The danger of what calls itself literary criticism is that its practitioners sit in judgment on artists whose shoelaces they are unworthy to unlatch. The works of the ages are dismissed with a curt wave of the hand. But we do not sit in judgment on Lear, Hamlet and Falstaff. Their creator, through them, takes our measure, and when we wade into print it is evident to all the limitations we bring to our task. Scorning Falstaff for his irregular deportment is like lashing out at Mt. Everest for its snowy crags and boulders.

There was only one historical Socrates. But three very different writers, Xenophon, Aristophanes, and Plato each gave distinctly different presentations of his life and personality. Xenophon, a military man innocent of irony and the depths of philosophy, saw only what he was equipped to see: a purveyor of prudence and nostrums. Today minds the size of a walnut presume to check the cynosure of the dramatic heavens and pronounce on his worthiness. In so doing they become comic, pygmies who would add to their stature by looking askance at gods, heroes and giants. That is not the path to growth. Shakespeare enlarges us not when we belittle him but when we catch a glimpse of the scope and depth of his world, a world he wishes to share with us. Instead, our contemporaries reduce the great to erase anything beyond their ken. Falstaff is aware of the syndrome. "Men," he says, "take a pride to gird at me. The brain of this foolish-compounded clay, man, is not able to invent anything that tends to laughter more than I invent, or is invented on me. I am not only witty in myself, but the cause that wit is in other men." (*King Henry IV*, Part Two, I, ii, 6-10)

There have been many who can only find in Falstaff a bad man. Socrates might observe that such persons must be experts in the nature of goodness. He might invite them to explain what goodness is that we, too, might be wise. If that feat proves challenging, we might pause and view with more patience the larger-than-life personality of Falstaff. Plato taught that the very essence of learning and education is a recollection of the content of our own souls. He called it "anamnesis." When we learn, we remember. We come to know ourselves. As we absorb the characters of Shakespeare we change, we develop, we grow. And when after many years we look within, we will be most fortunate if we find there something of Falstaff.

WORKS CITED:

BOOKS
Harold Bloom, *Shakespeare - The Invention of the Human*, River Head Books, 1998.

Leslie Dunton-Downer, Alan Riding, *Essential Shakespeare Handbook*, DK Publishing Co., 2004.

Marjorie Garber, *Shakespeare After All*, Anchor Books, 2004

Harold Goddard, *The Meaning of Shakespeare*, 2 Vols., The University of Chicago Press, 1951. (Interested readers will enjoy online "The Spirit of Falstaff," by Joseph Sobran.)

David P. Gontar, *Hamlet Made Simple and Other Essays*, New English Review Press, 2013.

R. Hackforth, T*he Composition of Plato's Apology*, Cambridge University Press, 1933.

Martin Lings, *Shakespeare's Window Into the Soul*, Inner Traditions, 2004.

Michel de Montaigne, Complete Essays, M.A. Screech, ed., Penguin Classics, 1991.

Plato, *The Collected Dialogues*, Edith Hamilton, Huntington Cairns, eds., Bollingen Edition, Princeton University Press, 1996.

William Shakespeare, The Complete Works, G. Taylor and S. Wells, eds., 2d Edition, Oxford, Clarendon Press, 2005.

ARTICLES
Pierre Beaudry, "What Does It Mean To Be Rabelasian?" *Fidelio*, The Schiller Institute, Vol. IX, No. 4, Winter, 2000.

Carl C. Curtis, "A 'Completely Good Man' Is Hard to Find: Welles' Defective Falstaff," *New English Review*, February, 2015.

David P. Gontar, "The Problem of the Formal Charges in Plato's Apology," *Tulane Studies in Philosophy*, Vol. XXVII, 1978.

Kenji Yoshino, "The Choice of Four Fathers: Henry IV, Falstaff, The Lord Chief Justice and the King of France in the Henriad," *Yale Journal of Law and the Humanities*, Vol. 22, Iss. 2, Article 8.

Afterword

*H*aving made their way through a mass of seemingly unrelated essays readers may well ask whether we may draw any general conclusions about the reading of Shakespeare. Obviously there is no formula or prescribed method of exposition one can adopt, and it is a truism that people find in our protean author what their capacities and experiences dispose them to find. We have seen, however, the baleful effects of front-loading our reading with doctrinal agendas and intellectual fads. All too often theory functions not as a speculum in which we can behold pure meaning, but rather as a palimpsest which, applied to passages, obscures them to such a degree that they seem to decompose before our eyes. Worse, we note discrepancies between Shakespeare's content and what theory would have. We cannot hope to anatomize a text draped in dogma, no matter how popular. The task of identifying the contradictions between applied theory and the text before us is the principal task of criticism in the 21st century.

Reading is best done with open hearts and minds. Naturally none of us is free of prejudices, but openness remains the ideal. To submerge the text in the shadow of what "authorities" have made of it is to relinquish our judgment and surrender reading to others. Shakespeare himself cautions against this: "Small have continual plodders ever won, save base authority from others' books." (*Love's Labour's Lost*, I, i, 86-87)

We can all recall the thrill of discovery we felt at our first encounter with Shakespeare. The goal of each reading should be to deepen, enhance and so recapture that moment, not extinguish it. As a beautiful painting tarnished with age can be lovingly restored that we can bask in its original glory, so we can restore and maintain the plays and poems by stripping away the mental accretions which cling to them like so many barnacles marring Shakespeare's authorship.

With respect to the vexed question of Shakespeare's identity, preconceived ideas, no matter how often reiterated, are rarely helpful in coming to terms with dramatic poetry. The imposition of biographical fables on these plays is the most common and insidious way to miss their meaning. Unreading Shakespeare must begin with putting aside childish legends. We do not attempt to grasp American history via Paul Bunyan, nor should we ground our approach to Shakespeare on stories of the deer poaching Stratford youth who hacks down the mulberry tree. Such patent fictions are painfully incommensurate with what we find in Macbeth and Antony and Cleopatra. Better by far is suspended judgment, allowing our idea of the author to emerge from our encounter with the text, rather than seeking to grasp the text based on what we may suppose about life in sixteenth century Stratford-on-Avon. Keats' idea of Negative Capability applies with full force when it comes to the authorship issue. Shakespeare gives himself to us in his art, and it is there we must find him.

In the ancient world, Socrates taught that in order to learn one must rid oneself of the presumption of knowledge. That is the major obstacle to learning. Philosophy is perhaps best understood not as doctrine but as the identification and discarding of nonsense, of creeds outworn. Shakespeare's Prince Hamlet, true to Socratic wisdom, declares that he will "wipe away all trivial fond records, all saws of books, all forms, all pressures past," so that life will burst fresh and pure "within the book and volume of [his] brain." (I, v, 99-103) René Descartes, the father of modern philosophy, began his meditations by subjecting the entirety of knowledge to doubt, building up a novel system from scratch. And Descartes' scholarly heir, Edmund Husserl, bracketed and set aside everything except the phenomena given to consciousness. These thinkers are the world's intellectual heroes. We can follow their lead by prefacing every reading of Shakespeare by an unreading which purges our minds of dross and prepares us for the vivid revelations of poetry. Rinse the mind's palate to relish all the better the piquancy of Shakespeare's language. Let us give ourselves leave to unread first, and we will "through and through cleanse the foul body of th' infected world."